Critical Thinking, Thoughtful Writing

A Rhetoric with Readings

THIRD EDITION

John Chaffee, Ph.D.

Director, NY Center for Critical Thinking and Language Learning
LaGuardia College, City University of New York

Christine McMahon
Barbara Stout

English Department, Montgomery College

Houghton Mifflin Company   Boston   New York

For Jessie and Joshua

Executive Editor, English: Suzanne Phelps Weir
Development Manager: Sarah Helyar Smith
Senior Development Editor: Meg Botteon
Editorial Assistant: Anne Leung
Senior Project Editor: Carol Newman
Senior Manufacturing Coordinator: Priscilla Bailey
Senior Marketing Manager: Cindy Graff Cohen

Cover image: © CNAC/MNAM/Dist. Réunion des Musées Nationaux/Art
     Resource, NY.
Back cover photo: Jerry Bauer.

Text credits begin on page 626.

Library of Congress Catalog Number: 2004108376
ISBN: 0-618-44220-0

23456789-CW-08 07 06 05

Brief Contents

Contents

CHAPTER 6   Revising Thoughtfully, Using Language Ethically 153

Preface

Leo Tolstoy eloquently observed that "the relations of word to thought, and the creation of new concepts, is a complex, delicate, and enigmatic process unfolding in our soul." Writers and teachers of writing have long recognized intricate relationships between the extraordinary human processes of thought and language. In general, textbook writers and publishers have not clearly translated this insight into a comprehensive approach that helps beginning college students become thoughtful writers. Experts in the thinking process (philosophers and psychologists, for example) have not generally concentrated on the complex challenges of teaching writing. Experts in teaching writing have found integrating the critical thinking process into their pedagogy a sometimes problematic endeavor.

Critical Thinking, Thoughtful Writing: A Rhetoric with Readings presents an integrated approach to teaching the thinking, writing, and reading skills that first-year composition students need in order to successfully complete academic work. As students develop higher-order thinking abilities, they learn to articulate their ideas through writing. And as they develop their abilities to navigate the writing process, students learn to think coherently, precisely, and creatively. This approach integrates the development of thinking skills with writing skills so they not only reinforce each other but also become inseparable.

This book stimulates and guides students to think deeply and beyond superficialities, to refuse to be satisfied with the first idea they have, to look objectively at the pros and cons of issues, and to formulate their own informed conclusions. It helps students develop an interest in research and in delving into possibilities rather than into commonplace answers. It encourages students to be independent in their thinking and courageous in their convictions. And it shows them how to organize information, interpret different perspectives, solve challenging problems, analyze complex issues, and communicate their ideas clearly.

Advantages of a Critical Thinking Framework

The critical thinking framework of this text helps instructors and students in the following ways:

- **By providing an intellectual and thematic framework** that helps writing teachers place structural and grammatical concerns in a meaningful context. *Critical Thinking, Thoughtful Writing* challenges and guides students to think and write about important topics that build on their cognitive activities and critical explorations. This process enables students to improve both the technical aspects of their writing (coherence, organization, detail, use of grammatical conventions) and the quality of their writing (depth, insight, sophistication).

- **By leading students to understand the reciprocal relationship** between the process of thinking and the process of writing. The text stimulates students to explore their own composing processes, gradually mastering the forms of thought and critical thinking that are the hallmark of mature and thoughtful writing.

- **By helping students to appreciate that reading is a thinking activity** rather than a series of decoding skills. This understanding accelerates and enhances reading development. Students are better able to understand and develop the interrelated thinking abilities that the reading process comprises, including problem solving, forming and applying concepts, and relating ideas to larger conceptual frameworks.

Content and Organization

MOVEMENT FROM THE PERSONAL TO THE SOCIAL

The book moves logically from introducing creative and critical thinking to explaining how these tools can be used in different kinds of writing. Part One helps students understand themselves as thinkers and writers; the Writing Projects in this section ask them to write from their own experiences and observations. Part Two explores important thinking patterns and language issues; here, the Writing Projects ask them to incorporate some ideas from others into their expository writing. Part Three uses an increasing number of sources as students work with problem solving, argumentation, and research. This logical progression pulls students beyond their personal experiences and pushes them to think and write about challenging issues and concepts, while seeing how social issues are connected with their own lives. The practical strategies will help students address writing assignments in other academic classes and in the workplace.

FOUR INTEGRATED ELEMENTS TO EACH CHAPTER

1. **Critical Thinking Focus** examines the thinking skill central to each chapter. Examples of critical thinking skills are thinking about thinking, creative thinking, decision making, evaluating perspectives, causal reasoning, conceptualizing, constructing knowledge, problem solving, and developing reasoned arguments.

2. **Writing Focus** provides strategies and Thinking-Writing Activities that draw upon the chapter's critical thinking skill.

3. **Reading Focus** comprises 47 professional readings (essays, articles, or book chapters) and 17 student essays, on themes including creativity, decision making, intercultural issues, gender issues, language discovery, ecological relationships, problem solving, and arguments on controversial topics. Each chapter offers three or more pieces of professional writing (such as essays, stories, newspaper articles, and poems) and at least one student essay. The readings reflect the critical thinking focus in each chapter and provide the basis for assignments that initiate students' writing.

4. **Writing Project** builds on the reading themes and skills developed through the chapter's activities. These carefully structured projects move systematically through stages toward a finished project, providing guidance for each stage of the writing process. Each chapter includes at least one student example of the completed Writing Project.

Special Features

Practical Critical Thinking Strategies for Writing   The concept of critical thinking often seems abstract to students, but this book introduces the process of thinking critically as a practical and powerful approach to writing as well as to life in general. For example, in learning a thoughtful approach for making decisions, students apply the decision-making process to revising drafts as well as to making important decisions in other areas of their lives. By developing their problem-solving abilities, students become able both to compose a problem-solving essay and to be more effective in solving problems beyond the classroom.

Comprehensive Thinking-Writing Model   The Thinking-Writing Model introduced in Chapter 1 (page 6) and reinforced throughout the book provides a clear graphic representation of the writing process and of the connections between critical thinking and thoughtful writing, as well as creative thinking and inventive writing.

Creative Thinking to Enrich the Writing Process The book shows that creative thought can and should be an integral part of academic writing. All aspects of the writing process can be approached creatively, including topic selection, generating ideas and drafting, using specific details, and writing introductions and conclusions. In learning to think creatively, students discover strategies to make their writing more inventive, while also infusing creative energy into other areas of their lives.

Emphasis on Collaboration The value of collaboration in thinking and writing is emphasized throughout, with this special icon highlighting Thinking-Writing Activities and other material specifically designed for collaboration and peer review. Critical thinking is emphasized in the active exploration of ideas, listening to others, and carefully evaluating opinions and arguments, and provides a context for collaborative learning. Students learn to examine their own opinions more analytically and relate these opinions to the world at large. They learn to assess alternative points of view in dialogue with others, contributing to their development into a community of concerned thinkers and writers.

Cross-Disciplinary Approach Recognizing that first-year composition courses prepare students to write in all of their courses and after college, this book presents examples, selections, and assignments from sociology, psychology, linguistics, history, cultural studies, economics, and the natural and hard sciences.

Critical Thinking as a Tool for Living The book views learning to think, write, and read as integral dimensions of an individual's personal growth and transformation. It aims to help students grow. While learning how to think and write, students are encouraged to apply these critical and creative thinking skills to all facets of their lives, enabling them to make enlightened decisions, solve challenging problems, analyze complex issues, communicate effectively, nurture creative talents, and become more thoughtful and socially aware citizens.

Changes to the Third Edition

The third edition of *Critical Thinking, Thoughtful Writing* makes even clearer the connections between critical thinking, thoughtful writing, and active reading. New chapters, features, and content include the following:

- **NEW: Four characteristics of a critical thinker.** Adapted from John Chaffee's best-selling text *Thinking Critically*, these four characteristics—open-mindedness, creativity, curiosity, and knowledge—are woven consistently throughout the newly revised writing and reading pedagogy. These four characteristics are both easily recognizable by students and achievable as goals inside and outside the classroom.

- **NEW: Chapter 2, "Reading Actively, Reading Critically."** Moving from active reading strategies (annotation, summary, etc.) to thinking critically about and responding thoughtfully to readings, this new chapter complements the book's existing writing pedagogy while giving students even more opportunity to practice their critical thinking skills as they develop their ability to work with more complex or challenging texts.

- **NEW: Casebook on environmental issues.** Chapter 10, "Exploring Cause and Effect: Writing to Speculate" now includes three compelling perspectives on global climate change. Each essay serves as a model of causal reasoning as well as demonstrating how writers work to avoid causal fallacies.

- **NEW: Casebook on gender and sexuality.** Chapter 8, "Exploring Concepts: Writing to Classify and Define" now includes multiple voices and genres on the timeless topic of gender and difference. From Jamaica Kincaid to Theodore Roethke to Louise Erdrich, from poetry to scholarly commentary, this casebook allows students to experience the many possibilities for defining, exploring, and understanding concepts in their own writing.

- **NEW: Student essays with process models.** New student essays throughout the text serve as models of the Four Characteristics of a Critical Thinker, and all student essays are now supported by process materials (outlines, rough drafts, etc.) that demonstrate how each student worked through different stages of the process.

- **REVISED: Readings and revised and expanded readings apparatus.** Nearly one-third of the professional and student readings in the third edition are new, reflecting a contemporary and diverse array of voices and opinions on topical subjects. Every reading is now prefaced by a brief biographical headnote, often including an observation by the author on the work of writing. Two kinds of post-reading questions now specifically prompt students to focus on matters of rhetoric and style as well as to think more critically and creatively about the ideas presented in the reading.

- **REVISED: Streamlined and updated discussion of the writing process.** Chapters 4, 5, and 6 in Part One now clearly reflect stages of the writing process (idea generation, drafting, and revising) while demonstrating how each reflects the Four Characteristics of a Critical Thinker.

- **REVISED: Enhanced discussion of plagiarism**—what it is and how to avoid it—with critical thinking exercises and specific guidelines for detecting and averting the common errors in research that can lead to plagiarism, now that so much material can be accessed and copied easily.

- **REVISED: Accessible discussion and definition of critical thinking for composition students and instructors**. Critical thinking terms, especially in Chapter 1, are immediately *defined* and *contextualized* within the framework of a composition classroom.

- **REVISED: APA coverage added to the research chapter.** To reinforce the interdisciplinary focus of critical thinking, the research chapter now includes guidelines for APA documentation (as well as updated MLA documentation), with particular attention to citing and documenting online sources.

Supplements

Instructor's Resource Manual   A revised edition of the manual offers thoughtful suggestions for teaching the third edition, including recent scholarship; discussion of collaborative learning and peer review; sample syllabi; teaching suggestions; handouts and transparency masters for key processes and diagrams; as well as a writing inventory and reader response guidelines; and suggestions for additional readings, films, and videos.

Web Site   The accompanying web site includes links to sites on critical thinking, creativity, research, and many of the topics discussed in the readings as well as interactive step-by-step directions for completing each of the Writing Projects. Students will enjoy working with "Tom Randall's Halloween Party," an interactive court case that allows them to analyze evidence, devise cross-examination questions, and serve as judge and jury evaluating the case of a college student charged with serving alcohol to an underage guest.

The Authors

Critical Thinking, Thoughtful Writing is the result of collaboration of three authors. John Chaffee is Director of the New York Center for Critical Thinking and Language Learning, and Professor of Philosophy at The City University of New York. His best-selling textbook *Thinking Critically,* going into its Eighth Edition, presents a comprehensive, language-based approach to learning that helped define the field of critical thinking. His trade book, *The Thinker's Way,* has been translated into six languages. Barbara Stout and Christine McMahon, both former English professors at Montgomery College, used *Thinking Critically* in their composition courses for seven years, which made them ideally suited to adapt its critical thinking approach to the teaching of writing, resulting in this text.

Acknowledgments

The following reviewers offered wise insights to and suggestions for the manuscript over this or earlier editions:

Cathryn Amdahl, Harrisburg Area Community College
Larry Beason, University of South Alabama
Patricia Bizzel, College of the Holy Cross
Paul Bodmer, Bismark State College
Stephanie Byrd, Cleveland State University
Christine Caver, University of Texas, San Antonio
Frankie Chadwick, University of Arkansas at Little Rock
Gina Claywell, Murray State University
Sarah Dangelantonio, Franklin Pierce College
Charlie Davis, Boise State University
Thomas Fink, LaGuardia College
Adam Fischer, Bowie State University
Kim Grewe, Wor-Wic Community College
Judith A. Hinman, College of the Redwoods
Frederick T. Janzow, Southeast Missouri State University
Margaret Johnson, Idaho State University
John H. Jones, Jacksonville State University
Dipo Kalejaiye, Prince George's Community College
John Kinkade, University of Southern Indiana
Anna M. Lang, University of Indianapolis
Shirley Wilson Logan, University of Maryland
Linda McHenry, Fort Hays State University
Paul J. Morris, II, Pittsburgh State University
Joan Mullin, University of Toledo
Elizabeth A. Nist, Anoka-Ramsey Community College
Shirley Roberts, Brookhaven College
Denise Rogers, University of Louisiana at Lafayette
Kenneth Rosenauer, Missouri Western State College
Nicholas Schevera, College of Lake County
Isaiah Smithson, Southern Illinois University
Byrin Stay, Mount St. Mary's College
Kay Stokes, Hanover College
Leslie Stoupas, Colorado Mountain College
Michael Thomas, College of the Redwoods

William Vaughn, Central Missouri State University
Elizabeth Wahlquist, Brigham Young University
Jane Armstrong Woodman, Northern Arizona University.

John Chaffee would also like to thank Christine McMahon and Barbara Stout for the dedication and expertise they brought to the unique project of extending his work in critical thinking to the field of composition. Their approaches to teaching writing and their active involvement in the composition field have contributed significantly to a text that is practical, effective, and adaptable to a variety of instructional contexts.

John has been privileged to work with a stellar team of persons at Houghton Mifflin Company who are all exemplary professionals and also good friends. The incomparable Suzanne Phelps Weir is the soul of this book: she helped conceive of its unique approach to thinking and writing, has guided its evolution with wisdom, and has been its resolute champion. Suzanne is extraordinary in every way. Sarah Helyar Smith orchestrated this revision with the same commitment to excellence that she brings to every project, integrating an incisive intelligence, a conscientious attention to detail, a blessedly succinct use of email, and hilarious commentary at the most unlikely times. The enriched and exemplary quality of this revision is due primarily to the talent and spirit of Meg Botteon. She played a formative role in developing the ambitious revision plan, researched and shaped the book's inventive themes and provocative readings, guided and nurtured the manuscript's progress each step of the way, and brought to the entire process astute insight and genuine creativity. Carol Newman is always a special pleasure to work with: passionately exacting, unwilling to compromise when excellence is involved, and with an authentically matchless perspective on the world that encourages you to always expect the unexpected. The remarkably gifted Cindy Graff Cohen continues to display an uncommon ability in devising innovative marketing strategies and implementing them with aplomb.

A special acknowledgment goes to Joyce Neff at Old Dominion University for her superb work in writing the earlier editions of the Instructor's Resource Manual. John is particularly indebted to the members of the English Department at LaGuardia College for their creative collaboration in linking the writing and critical thinking programs, a process that was initially supported with funding from the National Endowment for the Humanities.

John's children, Jessie and Joshua, and his wife, Heide Lange, have provided ongoing love, support and guidance that have enhanced this book and brought purpose and meaning to his life.

Christine McMahon gratefully acknowledges the W. K. Kellogg Foundation, whose Beacon College Project supported the Critical Literacy Institute at Oakton College, and the faculty at Oakton who invited Montgomery College to be an associate college; she came to know John Chaffee's work through them. She is indebted to the administrators at Montgomery College who chose her as the Project Director for the grant and who continue to provide generous support for

Montgomery's critical literacy program. Barbara and John have been wonderful co-authors. The students Christine has taught, some of whose work appears in this book, helped her learn how to teach and motivated her to share what she knows. Her husband, Michael, helped her in every way, while her grownup children, Gregory and Beth, provided love and support, and her granddaughter, Brooke, kept her spirits up.

Barbara Stout is grateful to countless colleagues from many colleges and universities whose scholarship in composition, rhetoric, and writing across the curriculum is the foundation for informed teaching, programs, and textbooks. She is grateful to the Conference on College Composition and Communication, the Two-Year College English Association, and the national Writing Project for providing opportunities for sharing information and ideas. Her thanks also extend to the faculty and administrators in Montgomery College's Critical Literacy Project, to the English Department's office staff and faculty colleagues, and to her students, from whom she always learns more than she can teach. She greatly appreciates John's and Chris's friendship and sound thinking. Of course, her most heartfelt thanks are to her family: David, Richard, Rebecca, Sally, Lyn, Mitch, Roxanne, Patrick, Kathleen, Sean, and Florence.

Critical Thinking, Thoughtful Writing

A Rhetoric with Readings

Tools of Thinking and Writing

Writing and reading are how our minds explore and explain our world. The use of language is what makes us human; it is how we argue, how we tell stories, how we learn, how we creatively and politically express ourselves. To write is to use language thoughtfully, with a sense of inquiry and audience. When you write, you pay close attention to the words that you choose, the structure of your paragraphs, the images you create. You contemplate your subject, search for exactly the right word to describe an observation, draw together different pieces of evidence to persuade a reader to think as you do. Writing helps you make sense of your self and your world by illuminating your thought processes; writing is your mind in motion, working to clarify and understand. Learning to read critically helps you to become more aware of the strategies available to thoughtful writers. Reading engages your mind with other conversations and opens up additional perspectives.

Thinking clearly and critically about your reading strategies and your writing process will greatly enhance your ability to express yourself in all areas of your life. Part One of this book sharpens your awareness of the relationships between thinking, reading, and writing, and introduces you to ways of becoming a critical thinker and reader and a thoughtful writer.

1

Thinking Through Writing

"I write to understand as much as to be understood." —Elie Wiesel

Critical Thinking Focus: Thinking through writing

Writing Focus: The writing process

Reading Themes: Writing as self-expression

Writing Activity: Reflecting on past critical thinking

Thinking and Writing in College

The writer E. M. Forster once remarked, "How do I know what I think until I see what I say?" What did he mean by this? That you can't write better than you think! In many ways college is a whole new world. Not only are you expected to do more work in your courses, but you also are expected to work at a higher level: to *write more analytically,* to *think more conceptually,* and to *read more critically* than ever before. In your previous education, "good writing" might have meant in large part mastering the basics of organization, grammar, and spelling. Although these are essential, as a college writer, you are expected to do more: to write with depth, insight, and analytical understanding. In order to achieve this level of sophistication in writing, you need to develop comparably advanced thinking abilities.

This book is designed to improve your writing abilities while you develop your critical thinking abilities. For example, instead of simply telling you how to write a paper using a problem-solving format, this course will teach you to *think* like a problem solver and then to write like one. Rather than providing you with guidelines on how to write an analytical or argumentative essay, this book will help you to think through the processes of analyzing complex issues and constructing compelling arguments and then to express your understanding in effective writing.

Becoming an effective writer enables you to represent the rich fabric of your experience with clarity and precision. As you may have learned from your writing experiences thus far, the very process of using language serves to generate ideas. As a vehicle for creating and communicating your ideas, writing can be thought of as a catalyst that stimulates your personal and intellectual development. Since the writing process also enlarges your understanding of the world, becoming an effective writer is at the heart of your college education.

To improve your writing abilities, you need to write on a regular basis, integrating writing into your life as a vital and natural element. Therefore, this book offers you Thinking-Writing Activities. These can be done in various ways: out of class or in, individually or in pairs or groups, and in whatever format your instructor specifies. He or she might ask you to record your responses in a special journal to be reviewed periodically or on separate sheets of paper to be handed in. Your writing may also be shared with classmates or used as a basis for discussion. The thinking you do for the Thinking-Writing Activities will help to prepare you for the Writing Projects that conclude each chapter. These will give you an opportunity to think deeply about important subjects, to express your own distinctive point of view in a thoughtful and organized fashion, and to analyze the ideas of others from a variety of sources.

Thinking and writing are active processes that all of us learn by engaging in them. By participating in the Thinking-Writing Activities, applying ideas presented in this book to your own experiences, and completing the Writing Projects, you will be sharpening your thinking and writing abilities, and by sharing your ideas with other members of the class, you will expand your own thinking and theirs. Each student has a wealth of experiences and insights to offer the class community, so there will be special Collaborative Activities that will provide the opportunity to enrich your writing by working with other students.

Thinking ↔ Writing Activity

Recalling a Learning Experience

Recall a memorable learning experience that you have had, either in school or outside. Describe that experience and explain why it has had a lasting impact on you. Discuss how the experience has contributed to your development as a thinker and writer.

WHO IS A "CRITICAL THINKER"?

Who is a critical thinker, and how do you become one? Traditionally, when people refer to a critical thinker, they mean someone who has developed an understanding of today's complex world, a thoughtful perspective on ideas and issues, the capacity for insight and good judgment, and sophisticated reasoning and language abilities. Critical thinkers are able to

- Articulate their ideas clearly and persuasively in writing
- Understand and evaluate what they read
- Discuss ideas in an informed, productive fashion

These goals of higher education have remained remarkably consistent for several thousand years. In ancient Greece, most advanced students studied rhetoric in order to effect persuasion and studied philosophy in order to achieve wisdom. (The Greek word *philosophos* means "lover of wisdom.") In the modern world, many college students do likewise in order to become informed critical thinkers and capable writers and speakers.

The word *critical* comes from the Greek word *kritikos*, which means "able to perceive, detect, judge, or analyze." By questioning and analyzing, by evaluating and making sense of information, you examine your own thinking and that of others. And by clearly expressing your ideas in writing, you enter a larger community of thinkers and writers who enrich and sharpen your own thoughts through their responses. These thinking and writing activities help us reach the best possible conclusions and decisions.

WRITING THOUGHTFULLY

A thoughtful writer is a person who thinks critically while moving through the process of writing. This writer reflects deeply on the ideas to be expressed and thinks carefully about the language and organization needed to meet the goals of the writing situation. In short, a thoughtful writer is a critical thinker. No collection of writing tips and strategies will ever enable you to write thoughtfully if you're not thinking critically.

Throughout this text, we focus on four qualities that characterize critical thinkers and thoughtful writers, and we will tie these thinking-writing qualities into specific stages of the writing process.

- Open-minded
- Knowledgeable
- Creative
- Curious

Let's explore these qualities in greater depth.

Curious   Thoughtful writers explore situations with probing questions that penetrate beneath the surface of issues, instead of being satisfied with superficial explanations. (They *want* to learn, to discover . . .)

Open-minded   Thoughtful writers explore their subjects from many different perspectives, willing to listen carefully to every viewpoint, and evaluating each perspective carefully and fairly. Rather than being locked in to one point of view or a single limited framework, they strive to understand and communicate the complex dimensions of their themes. For example, if you are writing about a social issue, strive to present different perspectives on the issue as you reason your way to an informed conclusion.

Knowledgeable   Thoughtful writers always work to support their opinions with facts, evidence, and reasons. They recognize that opinions have value only to the extent that they are *informed* opinions. On the other hand, if they lack knowledge of the subject, they acknowledge this and set out to research what they need to know.

Creative   Thoughtful writers strive to develop inventive approaches to subjects; their writing is fresh and imaginative, avoiding clichés and tired conventions. They seek to break out of established patterns of thinking and approach themes and ideas from innovative directions.

Thinking critically by carefully exploring your thinking process is one of the most satisfying aspects of being a mature, educated human being. Analogously, **writing thoughtfully** involves thinking critically as you move through the process of writing so that you can express your ideas effectively.

People are able to think critically and to write thoughtfully because of their natural human ability to *reflect*—to think back on what they are thinking, doing, or feeling. By carefully reflecting on your thinking, you are able to see how that thinking operates, so you learn to think more effectively. In the same way, reflecting on your language use, and particularly on the way you write, enables you to improve and refine your writing abilities. In the following chapters, you will be systematically exploring the many dimensions of how the human mind works.

The Thinking-Writing Model

The paradox of acquiring any complex ability is that in the best of all possible worlds, you would learn all the component parts of the activity at the same time. For example, learning to drive a car requires you to master a variety of component skills that operate simultaneously: watching the road ahead, steering, applying the appropriate pressure on the gas pedal, braking, keeping a proper distance from other vehicles, watching for traffic signs and traffic lights, keeping an eye open for pedestrians, and so on. Yet a book on driving, or a video, focuses on one skill at a time because that is how information is presented most easily. Somehow you have to make the leap from learning all of the skills separately in a linear, step-by-step fashion to using them all at the same time, in complex relationships with one another.

Learning the complex skills of thinking critically and writing thoughtfully poses a similar dilemma. Although it is essential to learn each of the component parts of these processes, what distinguishes critical thinkers and thoughtful writers is that they can use all of these individual skills simultaneously.

The visual Thinking-Writing Model (Figure 1.1) presents each of these processes in relationship to each other. As you work on the various chapters and activities in this book, you will become more familiar with the different dimensions of the thinking-writing process as they function in the model we provide and as they function for you.

As you examine the model, the writing process typically begins with a question. What is the *Purpose* of this communication? What is the *Subject?* Who is the

Figure 1.1 The Complete Thinking ↔ Writing Model

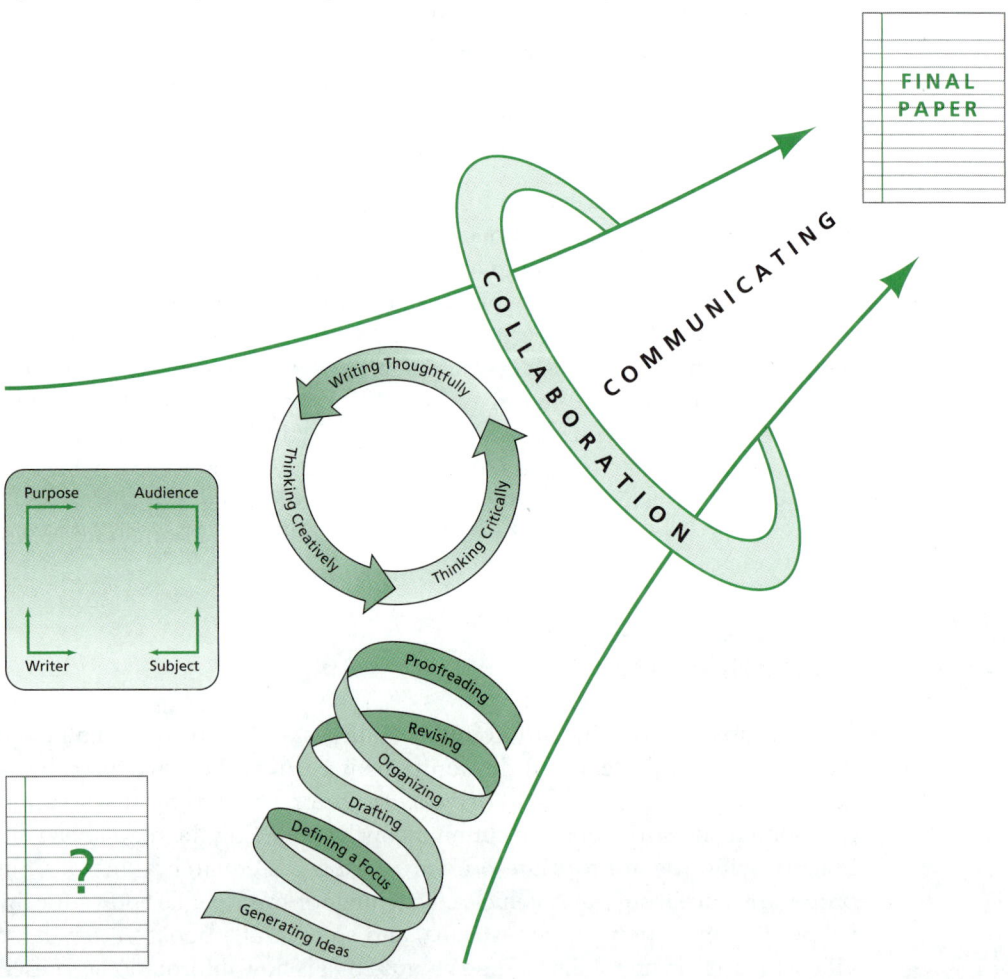

Audience? Who is the *Writer* and what is the writer's perspective? Engaging these questions utilizes our core abilities to *Think Creatively* about ideas we want to communicate, *Think Critically* in order to organize and clarify these ideas, and *Write Thoughtfully* by using the appropriate vocabulary and language forms to communicate our ideas.

The writing process itself is dynamic and holistic. The key elements of the process are: *Generating* ideas, *Defining* a focus, *Drafting, Organizing, Revising,* and *Proofreading.* For most writers, these activities rarely occur in a neat, orderly sequence: the process is much more organic and recursive. Effective writers also *Collaborate* with other people in order to help them produce the highest quality of writing, and their assistance can occur at any stage in the writing process.

At the very center of the model is *Communicating,* the process by which we share our thoughts, feelings, and experiences. Communication creates miraculous moments when our minds touch and engage other minds. The word *communicating* comes from the Latin word *communicare,* which means "to share, to impart, to make common." As members of a social species, we need to share thoughts and feelings with other human beings. As technologies allow speedier and speedier communication throughout the world, critical thinking and thoughtful writing are evermore vital to the survival and progress of humanity.

This book is designed to offer you opportunities to build on the strengths you have and to grow as a critical thinker and thoughtful writer. The following Thinking-Writing Activity asks you to reflect on your own thinking-writing process as a starting point.

Thinking ↔ Writing Activity

Analyzing a Writing Experience

Describe in detail a writing experience that you found particularly satisfying or successful: for example, a paper you wrote for school, a market analysis you created for your company, or a letter in which you expressed important thoughts and feelings. After completing your description, answer the following questions in your journal or notebook.

- What was your goal or purpose in writing?
- What was the reaction of the people who read it—your audience?
- How did you think of the key ideas you included?
- How did you organize your ideas?
- Did you use other sources (such as readings) to provide support and context for your writing?
- In what ways did you revise your writing?
- How did you feel after completing your writing?

Your analysis will probably demonstrate that you already use many of the abilities that are integral to the Thinking-Writing Model. Carefully examine the Thinking-Writing Model in Figure 1.1. Before long, the model will become familiar, and you will be able to use it as a powerful guide to strengthen and clarify your thinking and writing. Let's explore the various dimensions of the Thinking-Writing Model and see how they work together to produce clear thinking and effective writing.

The Writing Situation

Writing always occurs in a **situation** within which the act of writing takes place. Or, to state it another way, no writer works in a vacuum. Writers have reasons to write, someone to whom they wish to write, a subject about which they have something important to say, and a sense of self as a writer that they want to project. Although these ideas are of great importance today, they are not new. They come from the study of *rhetoric,* the principles developed in ancient times for speaking and writing effectively. The word *rhetoric* comes from the Greek word *rhetorike,* the art of oratory. Rhetoric was intended to help speakers invent or discover their ideas, arrange them in the most persuasive way, and then express them in suitable language in order to have the desired effect on their audiences. Today the word *rhetoric* has both a negative and a positive meaning: language that is insincere and not to be taken seriously—"mere rhetoric"—and the positive meaning with which this book is concerned, the study of the principles and rules for effective writing.

We begin our study of rhetoric with the components of the writing situation: **purpose, audience, subject,** and **writer.** In Figure 1.2, these four components appear in the first part of the model because they need to be considered when the writer begins to write, but they also need to be thought about at every stage of writing. To help you develop your rhetorical skills, these components are discussed individually at the beginning of each of the Writing Projects in subsequent chapters.

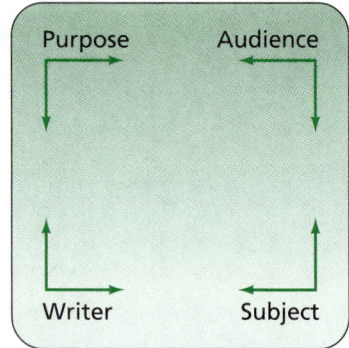

Figure 1.2 The Writing Situation

PURPOSE

Every act of writing has a *purpose.* When you complete a paper for a college course, you hope to show your professor that you can make significant statements about concepts relevant to the class. In a business setting, your aim is to transmit information or requests in a memo or a report; in your social life, you want to communicate with friends through letters or email; in your private life, you write in your journal so that you can later recall your activities and feelings. A crucial part of becoming a thoughtful writer is maintaining a clear sense of the specific goals of whatever piece you are working on.

AUDIENCE

Thoughtful writing is shaped by consideration of its *audience,* the intended reader or readers. Although there are some instances when you write only for yourself (a diary entry, for example), you probably intend most of your writing to be read by someone else: the person receiving your letter, the coworkers reading your memo, the friend enjoying your poem, or the instructor grading your paper. The more you think about your audience, the more concerned you will be about making yourself clear, and the better your writing will become. The real skill lies in writing so clearly and coherently that your audience receives exactly the same message that you intended to send.

Thoughtful writers are able to put themselves in their readers' place and to view their own writing through their readers' eyes. This perspective-taking helps them to craft their writing so that it will best communicate the ideas and emotions they seek to convey. In other words, they think about how much background information their audience will need, or won't need, to understand the intended message. Anticipating possible questions that their audience may have, they try to answer such questions at appropriate places. Understanding that the audience may have strong feelings about the topic, they consider those feelings as they write.

SUBJECT

Writing has to be about someone or something—a *subject.* Sometimes the subject originates in your own experience, but often it comes from ideas and information provided by others. Much of college writing involves responding to ideas presented in textbooks, class lectures, or research sources. Today, much research is done on the Internet, so the ability to find and evaluate online sources is crucial. Your writing task is usually to demonstrate your understanding of the ideas presented and also to apply, analyze, synthesize, or evaluate the ideas being expressed. The quality of your writing depends on the quality of your thinking as you process ideas and present them in order to communicate your own informed perspective on the subject.

WRITER

Of course, any writing situation calls for a *writer,* and the characteristics of the writer affect what is written and how it is produced. A writer's identity as a woman or a man or as a member of an ethnic or other social group often influences approaches and attitudes. The relationship of the writer to the language or dialect being used makes a difference; whether the writer is tired or energetic, happy or sad, and so forth, makes a difference, too.

The relationship of the writer to the intended audience also makes a difference. When writing notes or letters to friends, casual style and the admission of a lack of information on a subject are permissible. But college writers are expected to write with some authority as they join in a larger conversation of educated authors. If a piece of writing is about your own life and experiences, you automatically have that authority since no one knows your life better than you do. But many college assignments call for subjects related to class material, and you are still expected to write with authority. This can be intimidating at first, and the best way to overcome it is to make sure that you have good, solid information on the subject you must write about. That is why the library and the Internet are so important to you; by gathering information you can become knowledgeable on almost any subject. One of the worst ways for a college writer to begin is, "I don't know much about this subject, but here goes."

FROM

My American Journey

BY COLIN POWELL (b.1937)

In the following excerpt from his best-selling autobiography My American Journey, *Secretary of State Colin Powell writes with authority about his life. Secretary of State Colin Powell was born in New York City to immigrant parents from Jamaica. He attended public schools in the city, graduating from the City College of New York with a degree in geology. As a student at CCNY he participated in ROTC, receiving a commission as an Army second lieutenant upon graduation. Powell served for thirty-five years, rising to the rank of four-star General and holding, from 1989 through 1993, the position of Chairman of the Joint Chiefs of Staff, the highest military position in the Department of Defense.*

Powell's name has often been mentioned as a candidate for public office. He has been awarded two Presidential Medals of Freedom and the Congressional Gold Medal, among other military honors and decorations.

I have made clear that I was no great shakes as a scholar. I have joked over the years that the CCNY [City College of New York] faculty handed me a diploma, uttering a sigh of relief, and were happy to pass me along to the military. Yet, even this c-average student emerged from CCNY prepared to write, think, and communicate effectively and equipped to compete against students from colleges that I could never have dreamed of attending. If the Statue of Liberty opened the gateway to this country, public education opened the door to attainment here. Schools like my sister's Buffalo State Teachers College and CCNY have served as the Harvards and Princetons of the poor. And they served us well. I am, consequently, a champion of public secondary and higher education. I will speak out for them and support them for as long as I have the good sense to remember where I came from.

Shortly before the commissioning ceremony in Aronowitz Auditorium, Colonel Brookhart called me into his office in the drill hall. "Sit down, Mr. Powell," he said. I did, sitting at attention. "You've done well here (in ROTC). You'll do well in the Army. You're going to Fort Benning soon."

He warned me that I needed to be careful. Georgia was not New York. The South was another world. I had to learn to compromise, to accept a world I had not made and that was beyond my changing. He mentioned the black general Benjamin O. Davis, who had been with him at West Point, where Davis was shunned the whole four years by his classmates, including, I assumed, Brookhart. Davis had gotten himself into trouble in the South, Brookhart said, because he had tried to buck the system. The colonel was telling me, in effect, not to rock the boat, to be a "good Negro." . . .

The Army was becoming more democratic, but I was plunged back into the Old South every time I left the post. I could go into Woolworth's in Columbus, Georgia, and buy anything I wanted, as long as I did not try to eat there. I could go into a department store and they would take my money, as long as I did not try to use the men's room. I could walk along the street, as long as I did not look at a white woman. . . .

5   One night, exhausted and hungry, I locked up the house and headed back toward the post. As I approached a drive-in hamburger joint on Victory Drive, I thought, okay, I know they won't serve me inside, so I'll just park outside. I pulled in, and after a small eternity, a waitress came to my car window. "A hamburger, please," I said.

She looked at me uneasily. "Are you Puerto Rican?" she asked.

"No," I said.

"Are you an African student?" She seemed genuinely trying to be helpful.

"No," I answered. "I'm a Negro. I'm an American. And I'm an Army officer."

10   "Look, I'm from New Jersey," the waitress said," and I don't understand any of this. But they won't let me serve you. Why don't you go behind the restaurant, and I'll pass you a hamburger out the back window."

Something snapped. "I'm not that hungry," I said, burning rubber as I backed out. As I drove away, I could see the faces of the owner and his customers in the restaurant windows enjoying this little exercise in humiliation. . . .

Racism was still relatively new to me, and I had to find a way to cope psychologically. I began by identifying my priorities. I wanted, above all, to succeed at my Army career. I did not intend to give way to self-destructive rage, no matter how provoked. If people in the South insisted on living by crazy rules, then I would play the hand dealt me for now. If I was to be confined to one end of the playing field, then I was going to be a star on that part of the field. Nothing that happened off-post, none of the indignities, none of the injustices, was going to inhibit my performance. I was not going to let myself become emotionally crippled because I could not play on the whole field. I did not feel inferior, and I was not going to let anybody make me believe I was. I was not going to allow someone else's feelings about me to become my feelings about myself. Racism was not just a black problem. It was America's problem. And until the country solved it, I was not going to let bigotry make me a victim instead of a full human being. I occasionally felt hurt; I felt anger; but most of all I felt challenged. I'll show you!

Questions for Active Reading

1. What purpose or purposes do you think Secretary Powell had in mind while writing? How does he try to achieve his purpose(s)? List two specific examples from the reading to support your answer.

2. What audience do you think Powell had in mind while writing? Identify a specific audience, either one person or a group of persons, to whom you would recommend this reading.

3. Describe the writer as specifically as you can. What is your attitude toward him, now that you have read this? Does this represent any change in your attitude toward Secretary Powell?

Questions for Thinking Critically

1. Describe an experience in which you were the victim of discrimination or prejudice. How did it make you feel? How did you deal with it?

2. Colin Powell was determined to achieve his goals, despite many obstacles. Describe in your own words the thinking approach he used to deal with the pervasive racism that he encountered.

3. Powell concludes his autobiography with an affirmation regarding the United States that seems particularly relevant in these perilous times: "We will come through because our founders bequeathed us a political system of genius, a system flexible enough for all ages and inspiring noble aspirations for all time. We will continue to flourish because our diverse American society has the strength, hardiness, and resilience of the hybrid plant we are."

   Explain whether you agree with Powell that America's ethnic diversity is a source of strength and resilience, and list the reasons why or why not.

WRITING THOUGHTFULLY, THINKING CREATIVELY, THINKING CRITICALLY

The next part of the Thinking-Writing Model, Figure 1.3, indicates the reciprocal relationships among writing thoughtfully, thinking creatively, and thinking critically. When you first decide to write something, you need to come up with some initial ideas to write about. Your ability to *think creatively* makes producing such ideas possible. When you think creatively, you discover ideas—and connections among ideas—that are illuminating, useful, often exciting, sometimes original, and usually worth developing. We can define **thinking creatively** as discovering and developing ideas that are unusual and worthy of further elaboration.

Figure 1.3 Core Abilities

Simultaneously (or *almost* simultaneously), these beginning ideas find form in language expressed in writing. Yet the process of writing thoughtfully elaborates and shapes the ideas that you are trying to express, especially if you are to bring your critical thinking abilities to bear on this evolving process. This extraordinarily complex process typically takes place in a very natural fashion, as creative thinking and critical thinking work together to produce thoughtful writing, which in turn gives form to our ideas and communicates them to others.

Effective writers not only use each of these processes but also are able to integrate them. For example, it is impossible to write thoughtfully without creating ideas that reflect your vision of the world or without using your critical thinking abilities to evaluate the accuracy and intelligibility of your writing. Unfortunately, these essential abilities are not always taught explicitly. Too often, writing is emphasized as a way of putting words together in conventional forms, not as a dynamic means of personal expression that liberates us to articulate our creative perspectives—tempered by critical evaluation.

The Writing Process

THE RECURSIVE NATURE OF THE WRITING PROCESS

Despite the many different writing forms and contexts, the basic elements of the writing process remain constant:

- Generating ideas
- Defining a focus (main idea or *thesis*)

- Organizing ideas into various thinking patterns
- Drafting
- Revising, editing, and proofreading
- Collaborating, which can weave through all these activities

These elements of the writing process occur within the writing situation as a result of creative and critical thinking, and they are depicted in the third part of the Thinking-Writing Model (Figure 1.4). For most writers, these activities rarely occur in a neat, orderly sequence. Instead, writers move in different ways, from generating ideas to drafting to more generating to organizing to revising to generating to editing—around and around—as they develop ideas and clarify them.

You have probably discovered that the process of writing does not merely express your thinking; it also stimulates your

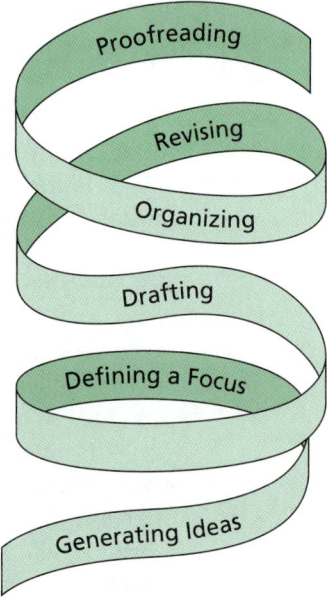

Figure 1.4 The Writing Process

thoughts, bringing to the surface new ideas and ways to explore them. So although you may begin a writing project by generating some ideas, you may find yourself returning to generate more ideas later on as you work to organize and draft your thoughts, developing new or refined concepts to write about. And as you gain more experience with collaboration, you may find yourself turning to others more frequently to benefit from their ideas and perspectives, which may send you back to generating, focusing, drafting, or organizing.

GENERATING IDEAS

Most writing efforts begin with identifying something to write about. Since ideas are not created in isolation but are almost always related to a particular subject, you expand ideas by exploring that subject. Some writing projects have very specific requirements; others may be more open-ended. In most cases, however, you will be expected to come up with your own ideas. Even when you are responding to an assigned topic or a reading selection, you are typically expected to offer an original insight or viewpoint. As a thoughtful writer, you are expected to be open minded, creative, and curious. At this stage of generating ideas, a number of strategies are useful, such as brainstorming, creating mind maps, freewriting, and asking key questions to stimulate your creative thinking. These strategies will be explored in depth in a later chapter.

DEFINING A FOCUS

After generating a number of possible ideas to write about, academic writers need to define a focus. Academic writing is *expected* to have a focus; classmates, professors, and others interested in your subject expect more than a list of facts. Once selected, your main idea—known as a **thesis**—will organize and direct your thinking. Your thesis will also guide your exploration of the subject and suggest new ideas. Of course, a variety of main ideas can develop out of any particular situation, and your initial working thesis will probably need redefining as you draft your paper.

Sometimes you will need to do some drafting and organizing before you are ready to define your focus. And sometimes you will need to refocus your thesis as you do further drafting.

ORGANIZING IDEAS

Once you have a tentative thesis, you may be ready to plan the organization of your paper. But at this point or even earlier, you may realize that you don't have enough information on your subject to fulfill your purpose. Remembering that a thoughtful writer is knowledgeable, you may need to generate more ideas or to consult other sources of information in order to write with authority. When you are ready to begin organizing, ask yourself, "What are my main points, and how should they be presented to my audience?" You can use a variety of thinking patterns as you organize your writing, such as reporting chronologically, comparing and contrasting, or dividing and classifying. Your choice of thinking pattern will depend on the subject you are exploring, your purpose, and your audience.

It usually helps to have a tentative organization to guide your drafting, but often your organization changes as you draft and revise. This is a natural and productive part of most people's writing processes.

DRAFTING

Drafting begins when you actually put words on paper. *What* you write reflects your previous work from the initial stages of the writing process: generating ideas, defining a focus, and thinking about an organizational structure. Your writing expresses how far your thinking on the subject has progressed to that point. It is unlikely that your writing will emerge in finished form. In fact, your initial draft may undergo substantial revision until it finally represents your mind's best work. So don't get obsessed with trying to craft the perfect sentence, fashion the ideal metaphor, or secure the optimal word. You'll have time to do that later on. The most important goal in drafting is to *do it*. Get those vague and evolving ideas onto paper, where they can be examined, reflected upon, and re-fined. If you sit there in front of the blank screen waiting for polished, incisive prose to emerge from your fingertips, you may never get started! The purpose of a draft is to begin the writing process in earnest, with the assumption that you will be returning to rework, refashion, and revise these initial efforts.

Often you will find it useful to draft in sections, according to the plan you established. But be prepared to let the writing process take you to new places that you didn't anticipate. The process of writing is a catalyst for your thinking process, creating new ideas and leading in unexpected directions. Trusting your writing/thinking process leads to creative breakthroughs that will enrich your original plan.

Naturally, what you are drafting—a summary, a news story, an essay—in-fluences the way you express and organize your thinking. Much of your aca-demic writing will be in the form of essays in which you are expected to take a position, analyze a concept, or interpret a subject. The structure normally used to organize ideas in an essay typically reflects the basic questions raised when you discuss ideas with others. As you draft, keep in mind the questions posed by Mina Shaughnessey in her book *Errors and Expectations:*

> *What is your point?* (stating the main idea)
>
> *I don't quite get your meaning.* (explaining the main idea)
>
> *Prove it to me.* (providing examples, evidence, and arguments to support the main idea)
>
> *So what?* (drawing a conclusion)

REVISING, EDITING, AND PROOFREADING

Because thinking and writing are recursive processes, you are continually re-vising your thinking and writing as you work on almost any paper. An early draft is usually just a starting point. Some writers need to produce multiple drafts with—they hope—increasing levels of effectiveness; other writers can get things on paper in relatively good shape quickly. Whatever your work style, though, once you have expressed your thinking in language, you must be able to go back and "re-see" (the origin of the word *revise*) your drafts as clearly as possible.

Most writers have a hard time looking objectively at their own writing. They know what they mean; they sometimes like certain words, sentences, or clever ideas and don't want to change them. But thoughtful writers have ac-quired the ability to be critical readers of their own work and to accept the fact that they may need to make major changes in their drafts.

As they revise, they are aware of a second voice in their heads, their Reader/Editor. This voice asks useful questions, not unlike those listed above under Drafting:

Have you made your main point clear?

Have you proved your point to your audience by giving enough information and examples?

Could you reorganize any of your ideas to help your audience understand more easily?

Many writers wait until they are satisfied with the content and organization before they *edit* smaller components, such as paragraph division, topic sentences, sentence variety, connections, and transitions. Then they *proofread*, checking spelling and punctuation. And sometimes while they are editing or proofreading, they see content and organization problems that require more revision!

FROM *Writing Down the Bones*

Writing Is Not a McDonald's Hamburger
BY NATALIE GOLDBERG

Acclaimed as much for her intuitive, compassionate teaching of writing as she is for her own well-received prose, Natalie Goldberg's 1986 book Writing Down the Bones *(from which "Writing Is Not a McDonald's Hamburger" is excerpted) has become a touchstone not only for aspiring writers but for anyone wishing to live more creatively. Goldberg has continued to mine her personal life, her deeply engaged study of Zen Buddhism, and her painterly observations of the natural world (particularly the landscape around her home in Taos, New Mexico) in such books as* Wild Mind: Living the Writer's Life *(1990),* Long Quiet Highway: Waking up in America *(1993), and* Thunder and Lightning: Cracking Open the Writer's Craft *(2000). Her 1995 novel* Banana Rose *explores the idealism and fallout of the 1960s counterculture. Goldberg lives with her partner in Taos, New Mexico and St. Paul, Minnesota. She gives many creative writing workshops each year and is studying to become a Zen teacher.*

Sometimes I have a student who is really good right from the beginning. I'm thinking of one in particular. The air was electric when he read, and he was often shaking. The writing process split him open; he was able to tell about being fourteen years old in a mental hospital, about walking the streets of Minneapolis tripping on LSD, about sitting next to the dead body of his brother in San Francisco. He said he had wanted to write for years. People told him he should be a writer, but anytime he sat down to write he couldn't connect the words on paper with the event or his feelings.

That is because he had an idea of what he wanted to say before he came to paper. Of course, you can sit down and have something you want to say. But then you must let its expression be born in you and on the paper. Don't hold too tight; allow it to come out how it needs to rather than trying to control it. Yes, those experiences, memories, feelings, are in us, but you can't carry them out on paper whole the way a cook brings out a pizza from the oven.

Let go of everything when you write, and try at a simple beginning with simple words to express what you have inside. It won't begin smoothly. Allow yourself to be awkward. You are stripping yourself. You are exposing your life, not how your ego would like to see you represented, but how you are as a human being. And it is because of this that I think writing is religious. It splits you open and softens your heart toward the homely world.

When I'm cranky now, miserable, dissatisfied, pessimistic, negative, generally rotten, I recognize it as a feeling. I know the feeling can change. I know it is energy that wants to find a place in the world and wants friends.

5   But yes, you can have topics you want to write about—"I want to write about my brother who died in San Francisco"—but come to it not with your mind and ideas, but with your whole body—your heart and gut and arms. Begin to write in the dumb, awkward way an animal cries out in pain, and there you will find your intelligence, your words, your voice.

People often say, "I was walking along [or driving, shopping, jogging] and I had this whole poem go through my mind, but when I sat down to write it, I couldn't get it to come out right." I never can either. Sitting to write is another activity. Let go of walking or jogging and the poem that was born then in your mind. This is another moment. Write another poem. Perhaps secretly hope something of what you thought a while ago might come out, but let it come out however it does. Don't force it.

The same student mentioned above was so excited about writing that he immediately tried to form a book. I told him, "Take it slow. Just let yourself write for a while. Learn what that is about." Writing is a whole lifetime and a lot of practice. I understood his urgency. We want to think we are doing something useful, going someplace, achieving something—"I am writing a book."

Give yourself some space before you decide to write those big volumes. Learn to trust the force of your own voice. Naturally, it will evolve a direction and a need for one, but it will come from a different place than your need to be an achiever. Writing is not a McDonald's hamburger. The cooking is slow, and in the beginning you are not sure whether a roast or a banquet or a lamb chop will be the result.

Questions for Active Reading

1. What purpose or purposes do you think Goldberg had in mind while writing? Specify any one thing in the reading that helps you to identify her purpose.

2. What audience do you think she had in mind while writing? What other audiences might benefit from reading his? What audiences might not benefit?

3. What is her subject? Be as specific as you can in describing it. What is her attitude toward her subject?

Questions for Thinking Critically

1. Goldberg, a Zen Buddhist, claims in paragraph 3 that she believes "writing is religious." How does she define and understand "religious," and what specific qualities of writing make it a "religious" activity or experience? Do you agree with her definition of "religious?" Compare your own definition of a "religious" activity or mindset to Goldberg's.

2. Athletes often describe their feeling at peak performance as being "in the flow." Goldberg describes something similar about the process of inspiration. Describe a time when you felt like you were "in the flow" of an activity (physical, artistic, or intellectual). How did you get "in the flow"? Is there a specific strategy or ritual that you use to help you get "in the flow"?

3. Goldberg uses an amusing metaphor to describe what writing is *not*. Do you agree with her metaphor? Create other metaphors that describe your feeling about writing (especially academic writing).

COLLABORATING

When you work with other people in the writing process, you participate in collaboration. You can collaborate with others at every stage of the writing process. People can help one another generate ideas, identify a main idea to pursue, or suggest possible approaches and ways of organizing. Some entire pieces of writing, especially in business, are produced collaboratively by a team of writers. Since collaborating can occur in all writing process activities, the line representing collaboration circles around them in the model in Figure 1.1.

We often discover new perspectives when others review drafts of our writing. This is the moment when writers get a sense of how effective their efforts at communication are. No matter how clearly you try to keep your audience in mind as you write, you may not succeed at first. There is no substitute for having your audience (or people like your intended audience) let you know what you have and have not communicated. With their suggestions, you can improve and refine your writing so that it will better convey what you intended. As a critical thinker and informed writer, you will learn to work with others in developing your thinking and writing, welcoming their advice when you are the sole author and contributing well when you are part of a writing team. Opportunities for collaborating are marked throughout the book with the symbol.

Of course, in writing any collaboration, you also have a responsibility to respond critically to the writing of others. *Critical* is related to *criticize,* which means "to question and evaluate." Unfortunately, the ability to criticize is often used destructively to tear down someone else's thinking. Criticism, however, should be *constructive*—analyzing for the purpose of developing better

understanding. To develop your abilities to think critically and write thoughtfully, it is important to offer and receive constructive criticism.

Becoming a critical thinker and a thoughtful writer does not simply involve
mastering certain life skills; it affects the entire way that you view the world and
live your life. You already use critical thinking in many aspects of your life: how
you make decisions, how you relate to others, and how you deal with controversial issues. These abilities can be improved with information, strategies, and
practice, and you will continue to develop them as you move forward through
college and your career.

The Marginal World

BY RACHEL CARSON (1907–1964)

*An aquatic biologist by training, and a poet by nature, Rachel Carson is considered a
founder of the twentieth-century movement for environmental justice. The author of
many books, including* The Edge of the Sea, *from which this essay is adapted, Carson
is best known for her 1962 bestseller* Silent Spring. *In that book, Carson's deeply informed research into the effects of widely used pesticides (especially DDT) on the natural
world combines with her moral outrage and unflinching descriptive abilities to build
an eloquent argument for environmental protection.*

The edge of the sea is a strange and beautiful place. All through the long history of Earth it has been an area of unrest where waves have broken heavily
against the land, where the tides have pressed forward over the continents, re-
ceded, and then returned. For no two successive days is the shore line precisely
the same. Not only do the tides advance and retreat in their eternal rhythms, but
the level of the sea itself is never at rest. It rises or falls as the glaciers melt or
grow, as the floor of the deep ocean basins shifts under its increasing load of sed-
iments, or as the earth's crust along the continental margins warps up or down
in adjustment to strain and tension. Today a little more land may belong to the
sea, tomorrow a little less. Always the edge of the sea remains an elusive and in-
definable boundary.

The shore has a dual nature, changing with the swing of the tides, belonging now to the land, now to the sea. On the ebb tide it knows the harsh extremes
of the land world, being exposed to heat and cold, to wind, to rain and drying
sun. On the flood tide it is a water world, returning briefly to the relative stability of the open sea.

Only the most hardy and adaptable can survive in a region so mutable, yet
the area between the tide lines is crowded with plants and animals. In this difficult world of the shore, life displays its enormous toughness and vitality by occupying almost every conceivable niche. Visibly, it carpets the intertidal rocks;
or half hidden, it descends into fissures and crevices, or hides under boulders,
or lurks in the wet gloom of sea caves. Invisibly, where the casual observer

would say there is no life, it lies deep in the sand, in burrows and tubes and passageways. It tunnels into solid rock and bores into peat and clay. It encrusts weeds or drifting spars or the hard, chitinous shell of a lobster. It exists minutely, as the film of bacteria that spreads over a rock surface or a wharf piling; as spheres of protozoa, small as pinpricks, sparkling at the surface of the sea; and as Lilliputian beings swimming through dark pools that lie between the grains of sand.

The shore is an ancient world, for as long as there has been an earth and sea there has been this place of the meeting of land and water. Yet it is a world that keeps alive the sense of continuing creation and of the relentless drive of life. Each time that I enter it, I gain some new awareness of its beauty and its deeper meanings, sensing that intricate fabric of life by which one creature is linked with another, and each with its surroundings.

5   In my thoughts of the shore, one place stands apart for its revelation of exquisite beauty. It is a pool hidden within a cave that one can visit only rarely and briefly when the lowest of the year's low tides fall below it, and perhaps from that very fact it acquires some of its special beauty. Choosing such a tide, I hoped for a glimpse of the pool. The ebb was to fall early in the morning. I knew that if the wind held from the northwest and no interfering swell ran in from a distant storm the level of the sea should drop below the entrance to the pool. There had been sudden ominous showers in the night, with rain like handfuls of gravel flung on the roof. When I looked out into the early morning the sky was full of a gray dawn light but the sun had not yet risen. Water and air were pallid. Across the bay the moon was a luminous disc in the western sky, suspended above the dim line of distant shore—the full August moon, drawing the tide to the low, low levels of the threshold of the alien sea world. As I watched, a gull flew by, above the spruces. Its breast was rosy with the light of the unrisen sun. The day was, after all, to be fair.

Later, as I stood above the tide near the entrance to the pool, the promise of that rosy light was sustained. From the base of the steep wall of rock on which I stood, a moss-covered ledge jutted seaward into deep water. In the surge at the rim of the ledge the dark fronds of oarweeds swayed, smooth and gleaming as leather. The projecting ledge was the path to the small hidden cave and its pool. Occasionally a swell, stronger than the rest, rolled smoothly over the rim and broke in foam against the cliff. But the intervals between such swells were long enough to admit me to the ledge and long enough for a glimpse of that fairy pool, so seldom and so briefly exposed.

And so I knelt on the wet carpet of sea moss and looked back into the dark cavern that held the pool in a shallow basin. The floor of the cave was only a few inches below the roof, and a mirror had been created in which all that grew on the ceiling was reflected in the still water below.

Under water that was clear as glass the pool was carpeted with green sponge. Gray patches of sea squirts glistened on the ceiling and colonies of soft coral were a pale apricot color. In the moment when I looked into the cave a lit-tle elfin starfish hung down, suspended by the merest thread, perhaps by only a single tube foot. It reached down to touch its own reflection, so perfectly de-lineated that there might have been, not one starfish, but two. The beauty of the reflected images and of the limpid pool itself was the poignant beauty of things that are ephemeral, existing only until the sea should return to fill the little cave.

Whenever I go down into this magical zone of the low water of the spring tides, I look for the most delicately beautiful of all the shore's inhabitants—flow-ers that are not plant but animal, blooming on the threshold of the deeper sea. In that fairy cave I was not disappointed. Hanging from its roof were the pendent flowers of the hydroid Tubularia, pale pink, fringed and delicate as the wind flower. Here were creatures so exquisitely fashioned that they seemed unreal, their beauty too fragile to exist in a world of crushing force. Yet every detail was functionally useful, every stalk and hydranth and petal-like tentacle fashioned for dealing with the realities of existence. I knew that they were merely wait-ing, in that moment of the tide's ebbing, for the return of the sea. Then in the rush of water, in the surge of surf and the pressure of the incoming tide, the del-icate flower heads would stir with life. They would sway on their slender stalks, and their long tentacles would sweep the returning water, finding in it all that they needed for life.

10   And so in that enchanted place on the threshold of the sea the realities that possessed my mind were far from those of the land world I had left an hour be-fore. In a different way the same sense of remoteness and of a world apart came to me in a twilight hour on a great beach on the coast of Georgia. I had come down after sunset and walked far out over sands that lay wet and gleaming, to the very edge of the retreating sea. Looking back across that immense flat, crossed by winding, water-filled gullies and here and there holding shallow pools left by the tide, I was filled with awareness that this intertidal area, al-though abandoned briefly and rhythmically by the sea, is always reclaimed by the rising tide. There at the edge of low water the beach with its reminders of the land seemed far away. The only sounds were those of the wind and the sea and the birds. There was one sound of wind moving over water, and another of water sliding over the sand and tumbling down the faces of its own wave forms. The flats were astir with birds, and the voice of the willet rang insistently. One of them stood at the edge of the water and gave its loud, urgent cry; an answer came from far up the beach and the two birds flew to join each other.

The flats took on a mysterious quality as dusk approached and the last evening light was reflected from the scattered pools and creeks. Then birds be-came only dark shadows, with no color discernible. Sanderlings scurried across the beach like little ghosts, and here and there the darker forms of the willets stood out. Often I could come very close to them before they would start up in alarm—the sanderlings running, the willets flying up, crying. Black skimmers flew along the ocean's edge silhouetted against the dull, metallic gleam, or they went flitting above the sand like large, dimly seen moths. Sometimes they "skimmed" the winding creeks of tidal water, where little spreading surface ripples marked the presence of small fish.

The shore at night is a different world, in which the very darkness that hides the distractions of daylight brings into sharper focus the elemental realities. Once, exploring the night beach, I surprised a small ghost crab in the searching beam of my torch. He was lying in a pit he had dug just above the surf, as though watching the sea and waiting. The blackness of the night possessed water, air, and beach. It was the darkness of an older world, before Man. There was no sound but the all-enveloping, primeval sounds of wind blowing over water and sand, and of waves crashing on the beach. There was no other visible life—just one small crab near the sea. I have seen hundreds of ghost crabs in other settings, but suddenly I was filled with the odd sensation that for the first time I knew the creature in its own world—that I understood, as never before, the essence of its being. In that moment time was suspended; the world to which I belonged did not exist and I might have been an onlooker from outer space. The little crab alone with the sea became a symbol that stood for life itself—for the delicate, destructible, yet incredibly vital force that somehow holds its place amid the harsh realities of the inorganic world.

The sense of creation comes with memories of a southern coast, where the sea and the mangroves, working together, are building a wilderness of thousands of small islands off the southwestern coast of Florida, separated from each other by a tortuous pattern of bays, lagoons, and narrow waterways. I remember a winter day when the sky was blue and drenched with sunlight; though there was no wind one was conscious of flowing air like cold clear crystal. I had landed on the surf-washed tip of one of those islands, and then worked my way around to the sheltered bay side. There I found the tide far out, exposing the broad mud flat of a cove bordered by the mangroves with their twisted branches, their glossy leaves, and their long prop roots reaching down, grasping and holding the mud, building the land out a little more, then again a little more.

The mud flats were strewn with the shells of that small, exquisitely colored mollusk, the rose tellin, looking like scattered petals of pink roses. There must have been a colony nearby, living buried just under the surface of the mud. At first the only creature visible was a small heron in gray and rusty plumage—a reddish egret that waded across the flat with the stealthy, hesitant movements of its kind. But other land creatures had been there, for a line of fresh tracks wound in and out among the mangrove roots, marking the path of a raccoon feeding on the oysters that gripped the supporting roots with projections from their shells. Soon I found the tracks of a shore bird, probably a sanderling, and followed them a little; then they turned toward the water and were lost, for the tide had erased them and made them as though they had never been.

15   Looking out over the cove I felt a strong sense of the interchangeability of land and sea in this marginal world of the shore, and of the links between the life of the two. There was also an awareness of the past and of the continuing

flow of time, obliterating much that had gone before, as the sea had that morning washed away the tracks of the bird.

The sequence and meaning of the drift of time were quietly summarized in the existence of hundreds of small snails—the mangrove periwinkles—browsing on the branches and roots of the trees. Once their ancestors had been sea dwellers, bound to the salt waters by every tie of their life processes. Little by little over the thousands and millions of years the ties had been broken, the snails had adjusted themselves to life out of water, and now today they were living many feet above the tide to which they only occasionally returned. And perhaps, who could say how many ages hence, there would be in their descendants not even this gesture of remembrance for the sea.

The spiral shells of other snails—these quite minute—left winding tracks on the mud as they moved about in search of food. They were horn shells, and when I saw them I had a nostalgic moment when I wished I might see what Audubon saw, a century and more ago. For such little horn shells were the food of the flamingo, once so numerous on this coast, and when I half closed my eyes I could almost imagine a flock of these magnificent flame birds feeding in that cove, filling it with their color. It was a mere yesterday in the life of the earth that they were there; in nature, time and space are relative matters, perhaps most truly perceived subjectively in occasional flashes of insight, sparked by such a magical hour and place.

There is a common thread that links these scenes and memories—the spectacle of life in all its varied manifestations as it has appeared, evolved, and sometimes died out. Underlying the beauty of the spectacle there is meaning and significance. It is the elusiveness of that meaning that haunts us, that sends us again and again into the natural world where the key to the riddle is hidden. It sends us back to the edge of the sea, where the drama of life played its first scene on earth and perhaps even its prelude; where the forces of evolution are at work today, as they have been since the appearance of what we know as life; and where the spectacle of living creatures faced by the cosmic realities of their world is crystal clear.

Questions for Active Reading

1. List all the verbs Carson uses in paragraph 3. How does her use of so many verbs convey the idea of "enormous toughness and vitality"?

2. Carson does not, herself, enter the essay until the fourth paragraph. How effective is her use of the first person in this essay? Why does she choose to wait until the fourth paragraph to make her appearance?

3. Carson uses sensory description—what she sees, hears, smells—to vividly evoke this tidal world. Which of her descriptive passages do you find most intriguing, and why? Were there any creatures named, or adjectives used, that sent you to the dictionary? Which words or images were most evocative for you?

Questions for Thinking Critically

1. An epiphany is a sudden realization, like a bolt of lightning. When you have an epiphany about something, you will never see it in the same way again. Carson describes a kind of epiphany in this essay. What provoked her epiphany? Describe that epiphany in your own terms.

2. In the last paragraph of her essay, Carson describes a "meaning and significance" in the beauty of the natural world. What, to your mind, is that "meaning and significance?" Does Carson explicitly describe the "meaning and significance" of what she has described?

Thinking ↔ Writing Activity

Expressing a Deeper Meaning

This Thinking-Writing Activity gives you an opportunity to apply some of the ideas we have been exploring in this chapter. Think of a place—or, if you can, go and visit a place—that has special meaning for you, a place that led you to a realization about life, much like the one that Rachel Carson describes. Write a description that effectively communicates *where* you are as well as expressing a deeper kind of meaning. What kind of meaning, exactly, is up to you, and depends on the feelings that the place evokes. Use Carson as a guide: "In that moment time was suspended; the world to which I belonged did not exist and I might have been an onlooker from outer space. The little crab alone with the sea became a symbol that stood for life itself—for the delicate, destructible, yet incredibly vital force that somehow holds its place amid the harsh realities of the inorganic world." Reach deep within yourself and discover an analogous feeling to articulate in your writing.

- Consider the audience for whom you are writing and the purpose you would like to accomplish.

- After writing your first draft, *rewrite* your paper to more fully express your feelings and ideas.

- Add details that communicate your meaning as specifically as possible.

- Craft your sentences so that they flow together and create a consistent "picture" of the place you are describing.

- Share your paper with your classmates. Ask them what feelings and ideas your description communicated to them.

- As a group, discuss which steps of the writing process for this assignment came easily, and which required more effort.

Keeping a Journal or Notebook

Keeping a journal or notebook is rewarding in several ways. First, as you already know, the process of writing stimulates your mind and helps shape your thinking. Also, writing creates a record of your thoughts and feelings that you can return to and perhaps use as the starting place for a finished piece of writing. Journal entries should be freely written, with no concern for punctuation or polished prose. Nor should you evaluate your ideas. Just let them flow, write them in a notebook or a computer file, and make journal keeping a part of your daily life.

Here are some guidelines for creating and using a journal described by Beth Baruch Joselow from her book *Writing Without the Muse.*

If you have not been keeping a notebook or a journal, it's time for you to get started with one. Find a notebook that is a convenient size for you to carry with you as often as possible. Choose a format that will make it easy for you to take notes, whether it's a small, spiral-bound notepad or a folded sheaf of papers that you put into a ringbinder or file folder at the end of each day. Carry a pen with you at all times, too.

Now, when you are hit with an idea for something you would like to think about, research, or write about, write it down in your notebook immediately. Use your notebook as well for writing down an interesting bit of dialogue you overhear, a musical line for a poem that pops into your head, or for doodling a description when you are waiting for a train, waiting for an appointment, or when you're stuck in traffic. People doodle pictures all the time—try doodling in words. Use your notebook to "talk" to yourself about ideas you are thinking of developing. Thinking changes when we write things down. Ideas develop in ways that don't occur when we keep our ideas silently to ourselves. These notes will remain your private notes, but by opening a kind of dialogue with the pages of your notebook, you will expand your thinking ability and be more productive. You will also be making a habit of writing, and that helps keep the writing engine oiled. Try to develop at least one idea from your notebook each week.

2

Reading Actively, Reading Critically

"Read not to contradict nor to believe, but to weigh and consider"
—Francis Bacon

Critical Thinking Focus: Reflecting on and responding to reading

Writing Focus: Thinking about rhetorical choices and writing in response to reading

Reading Themes: Using reading to create new writing and redefine the familiar

Reading in College

Let's begin this chapter with a question: What does it mean to read? Not so long ago, to "read" meant to turn the pages of a book, a newspaper, or an owner's manual. Reading was a physical activity that required lamplight or daylight, and texts were physical objects that you carried around in a backpack or briefcase. When you went to the library, it was usually to borrow a book that you would read and then return two weeks later. When you woke up in the morning, you read a newspaper as you drank your coffee. And when you got home from classes, you stayed up late into the night with your textbooks and a dictionary.

The physical act of reading—of opening, turning, flipping back and forth, underlining, inserting a bookmark—seems at times to be almost quaint, like rollerskating instead of rollerblading, or using a dial-up modem instead of a high-speed digital connection. And yet reading—the deciphering of, and interacting with, ideas and language—is at the core of a liberal education. You read to be entertained, to be informed, to learn. Even though most of us might do most of our "reading" without ever getting near a book, the fundamental skills of deciphering and interacting are equally applicable to the screen and the page. And whatever, however, or wherever you plan to communicate in your professional life, those fundamental reading skills will make you a better writer in any medium.

The four qualities of a critical thinker also apply to an active and thoughtful critical reader. An active, critical, thoughtful reader is:

Curious   You are motivated to read out of a genuine desire to know more, to learn something different, to expand your worldview. When you read an online article, for example, you may click on suggested links or hypertext connections solely out of a sense of adventure—just to see what else is there, or what connections the author would like you to make.

Open-minded   Whether you're in class, at dinner with a group of friends, or attending a religious service, you don't simply get up and leave when the conversation takes a turn toward the unfamiliar or the unsettling. In the same way, an open-minded reader doesn't simply close the book or click to a different web site when a text becomes difficult or even unpleasant. If there is something to be learned, an alternative point of view to be gained, a thoughtful reader will extend the same courtesy to the author that she would to a guest or a friend.

Knowledgeable   When you come to an unfamiliar phrase, allusion, or word in a reading, what do you do? A thoughtful reader either goes immediately to a dictionary or search engine for clarification, or jots it down to look up later. The knowledge to be gained from reading is not solely on the overall subject matter, but from the writer's use of language and store of general knowledge (historical, cultural, political, etc.).

Creative   When you read creatively, you think about how to incorporate the text's viewpoint or information into your own context (either in your writing, or your life). The text becomes more than a series of interlocking ideas—it stimulates you to do something differently, to take action, to reflect critically, to change your mind.

Thinking ↔ Writing Activity

Taking a Reading Inventory

In your journal, respond to any or all of these questions. Your teacher may ask you to share and discuss your responses with other students.

1. Is there anyone in your life to whom you read—a child, an older person, a friend? (Or perhaps you read aloud as part of a religious service, or a professional presentation.) In what context do you read aloud? How does reading aloud define or contribute to your relationship to your audience?

2. Who taught you to read? Do you remember learning to read? Have you helped anyone else learn to read?

3. What was the last thing you read out of sheer curiosity or pleasure? Were you surprised by your response to that text? Would you recommend it to a friend, or was this purely a "guilty" pleasure?

Reading Actively

To read actively is to work at deciphering the many layers of a text. An active reader has a dictionary (online or print) at hand, along with annotating tools, plenty of time, and the will to jot down questions and comments either on the printed page (or printout), in a reading journal, or in a word processing document. When you read actively, you give your full concentration and attention to the text. (Passive reading, on the other hand, is usually marked by boredom and daydreaming. If you look up from the page or screen and can't remember what you were just "reading," you weren't really reading at all—you were just looking at words.)

Active reading is also productive reading. You have a sense, as you begin to read, of what you might expect to discover. Active—and critical—reading also imply *re*-reading; the following strategies will require you to work through a new text at least twice, becoming familiar with its structure as you delve into its content.

The following strategies for active reading will help to make any reading task—academic, professional, or even leisurely—more productive. They also apply equally to print texts and web sites.

REVIEW THE TABLE OF CONTENTS OR CHAPTER OUTLINES

The table of contents and chapter outlines of a book or web site provide you with the general structure and organization of a text. By beginning with these elements, you can develop an overall understanding of the reading, the organization of its major ideas, and the way specific details fit into this organization. It's as if you are taking an aerial view of the territory you are going to explore, looking for key landmarks, examining the patterns of connecting roads, and developing a sense of the terrain.

Review the table of contents in this book, taking particular note of the topics that are covered and the way these topics are organized. Now look at where this chapter fits in relation to the overall design of the book. How do the topics of this chapter relate to the other topics in the book?

READ THE INTRODUCTORY PARAGRAPHS AND THE CONCLUDING PARAGRAPHS OR SUMMARY

After reviewing the table of contents or chapter outline, review next the opening and closing paragraphs or summary. In academic textbooks, authors generally explain the major goals of the chapter in the introduction and then conclude by reviewing the key topics that have been explored. Reviewing these sections should help you fill in the mental map you are creating of the reading assignment and help you develop a plan for exploring the material.

Other kinds of writing—essays, journalism, web logs—often include a thesis statement in the opening paragraph and summarize the overall argument or problem in the concluding paragraph. Note the topic sentence of each paragraph, which will give you an overall sense of the text's structure and organization.

Review the opening and concluding sections of this chapter. What additional information have you gathered about the chapter?

SCAN THE READING ASSIGNMENT, TAKING PARTICULAR NOTE OF SECTION HEADINGS, ILLUSTRATIONS, AND DIAGRAMS

The next step is to scout the territory by completing a rapid scan of what lies ahead. Move quickly through the material, focusing on the section headings, boxed or shaded areas, illustrations, diagrams, and other defining features. This should help you continue to fill in and elaborate your mental map, noting key points, concepts, definitions, and relationships.

Quickly scan this chapter, noting the features mentioned above. What new information have you gathered as a result of this scouting process?

Thinking ↔ Writing Activity

Previewing a Reading Assignment

Select a reading assignment from one of your courses, and before beginning to read, apply the previewing strategies that we have been considering:

- Examine the table of contents or chapter outline.
- Read the introductory paragraphs and the concluding paragraphs or summary.
- Scan the reading assignment, taking particular note of section headings, illustrations, and diagrams.

Then write a short paragraph, reporting specifically what each of the three strategies showed you about the assignment.

ANNOTATING

Annotation is one of the most productive techniques that you will use in your college reading. It involves writing, or entering, your reactions to a text as you are reading, either with pen or pencil on paper or with your computer's graphic tools to annotate something that you have downloaded. When annotating, you are talking *with* the text, not allowing it to talk *at* you.

Your annotations will reflect your agreement and disagreement with what you read, your questions, what you see as important ideas, where you see relationships among parts of the texts, and where you see connections with additional ideas. Some methods are:

- Underlining and numbering key points
- Circling key words and drawing lines to show relationships—for example, between a main idea and support for it.
- Using question marks to indicate parts that you do not understand.
- Commenting on the author's ideas or language or writing techniques.
- Noting connections with your life or with other texts.

Most word processing programs include annotation features such as highlighting, changing a font color, or inserting comments and questions. To annotate an online source, either save the online text in your word processing file or simply print out the page and highlight it on paper. (Many web sites for periodicals, newspapers, and journals offer a "printer-friendly" option for articles, which allows you to print only the text, on continuous pages, without having to "click" through each separate page or print out banner advertisements.)

SUMMARIZING

When you summarize a text, you use your own language to briefly and succinctly restate the author's main point. A summary follows the structure and organization of the original text, and might directly quote (using quotation marks) particularly interesting or apt words and phrases. When you summarize, you do not comment on or evaluate the text (that comes later); instead, writing the summary is a cognitive tool to ensure that you understand both the content and the structure of the text.

Summarizing is a strategy that is most effective at your second or third reading of a text, after you have annotated the text and looked up any unfamiliar terms or concepts.

Reading Critically

After reading actively in order to understand the content of a text, a thoughtful reader looks at it again, this time to read it critically. As a critical reader, you will analyze the text and evaluate its ideas and methods of presenting them. You will think of other subjects or issues to which the text might be connected.

ASKING QUESTIONS

Asking **questions** will help you read critically. One set of useful questions is based on the components of writing that you learned in Chapter 1: purpose, audience, subject, writer, and context.

Who is the *writer,* and what perspective does she bring to the writing selection?

What is the *subject* of the selection, and how would you evaluate its cogency and reliability?

Who is the intended *audience,* and what assumptions is the writer making about it?

What is the *purpose* of the selection, and how is the author trying to achieve it?

Some questions often used to generate writing also help with critical reading.

Questions of Interpretation   Questions of interpretation probe for relationships among ideas.

> Is a *time sequence* given in this text? If so, what is its importance?
>
> Is a *process of growth or development* explained in this text? If so, what is its importance?
>
> What is *compared or contrasted* in this text? What are the purposes of any comparisons?
>
> What is the *context* of the selection and what contextual components might be significant? (For example, the time of its writing; characteristics of that time; the relationship to other works by the same author; whether or not it is a translation)
>
> Are *causes* discussed in this text? If so, what is suggested about those causes and their effects?

Questions of Analysis   Questions of analysis look at parts of a text and the relationship of those parts to the whole, and at the reasoning being presented.

> Is this text divided into identifiable *sections?* What are they? Are sections arranged logically?
>
> What *evidence* or *examples* support the ideas presented in the text?
>
> Does the text give *alternatives* to the ideas presented?

Questions of Evaluation   Questions of evaluation establish the truth, reliability, applicability—the value of the text. They usually address the effectiveness of the writing as well.

> What is the *significance* of the ideas in this text?
>
> What is the apparent level of *truth* in this text? What criteria for truth does it meet?
>
> What are the sources of information in this text? Are they *reliable?* Why?
>
> Can the ideas in this text be *applied* to other situations?
>
> What is *effective* about the writing in this text? Clarity?
>
> The right tone? Appropriate—or imaginative—word choices? Organization?

Of course, you are not likely to ask all these questions about everything you read, and you will find other questions to ask, as well.

USING A PROBLEM-SOLVING APPROACH

Successful readers often approach difficult reading passages with a problem-solving approach.

Step 1: What is the problem? What don't I understand about this passage? Are there terms or concepts that are unfamiliar? Are the logical connections between the concepts confusing? Do some things just not make sense?

Step 2: What are the alternatives? What are some possible meanings of the terms or concepts? What are some potential interpretations of the central meaning of this passage?

Step 3: What is the evaluation of the possible alternatives? What are the "clues" in the passage, and what alternative meanings do they support? What reasons or evidence support these interpretations?

Step 4: What is the solution? Judging from my evaluation and what I know of this subject, which interpretation is most likely? Why?

Step 5: How well is the solution working? Does my interpretation still make sense as I continue my reading, or do I need to revise my conclusion?

Of course, expert readers go through this process very quickly, much faster than it takes to explain it. Although this approach may seem a little cumbersome at first, the more you use it, the more natural and efficient it will become. Let's begin by applying it to a sample passage. Carefully read the passage that follows; and use the problem-solving approach to determine the correct meanings of the italicized concepts and the overall meaning of the passage.

> *Existentialism,* of which I am a representative, declares with greater consistency that if God does not exist there is at least one being whose existence comes before its essence, a being which exists before it can be defined by any conception of it. That being is man or, as Heidegger has it, the human reality. What do we mean by saying that existence precedes essence? We mean that man first of all exists, encounters himself, surges up in the world—and defines himself afterwards. If man as the existentialist sees himself as not definable, it is because to begin with he is nothing. He will not be anything until later, and then he will be what he makes of himself. Thus, there is no human nature, because there is no God to have a conception of it. Man simply is. Not that he is simply what he conceives himself to be, but he is what he wills, and as he conceives existence. Man is nothing else but that which he makes of himself. This is the first principle of existentialism. . . . If, however, it is true that existence is prior to essence, man is responsible for what he is. Thus, the first effect of existentialism is that it puts every man in possession of himself as he is, and places the entire responsibility for his existence squarely upon his own shoulders. . . . That is what I mean when I say that man is condemned to be *free*. Condemned, because he did not create himself, yet is nevertheless at liberty, and from the moment that he is thrown into this world he is responsible for everything he does. . . . In life, a man commits himself, draws his own portrait and there is nothing but that portrait.

Step 1: What parts (if any) of this passage do you find confusing?

Step 2: What are some possible definitions of the italicized words, and what are some potential interpretations of this passage?

Existentialism: (a) _____

                     (b) _____

Free: (a) _____

                     (b) _____

Overall Meaning: (a) _____

                         _____

Overall Meaning: (b) _____

                         _____

Step 3: What contextual clues can you use to help you define these concepts and determine the overall meaning? What knowledge of this subject do you have, and how can this knowledge help you understand this passage?

Step 4: Judging from your evaluation in Step 3, which of the possible definitions and interpretations do you think are most likely? Why?

Step 5: How do your conclusions compare with those of the other students in the class? Should you revise your definitions or interpretation?

Practicing Active and Critical Reading: One Student's Approach

Here is how one student, Joshua Bartlett, used previewing, problem-solving, annotating, and summarizing with an essay that his philosophy professor assigned to show students how ideas from more than 2,500 years ago can apply to their lives today.

Previewing   Because this was an instructor's handout, Joshua's previewing started with a look at the title, the first two paragraphs, and the concluding paragraph. Because this is a short essay, Joshua moved quickly to scanning, reading through, and annotating. He was a bit confused when he read the first paragraph since the class had not yet begun studying Plato.

Problem-solving   Joshua realized that his major *problem* with this text was his lack of knowledge about Plato and Socrates. He decided that his *alternatives* were (1) to look them up in his philosophy class book or the encyclopedia or (2) to go on reading. He quickly *evaluated* the alternatives. Consulting his book or the encyclopedia would take some time, and he wanted to finish this assignment before he had to go to work. He knew that he would learn about Plato and Socrates next week in his class. His previewing had shown him that these problem paragraphs would be explained later in the essay. He *solved the problem* by deciding to go on reading. He felt that his solution *worked well* when he was able to summarize the essay.

Annotating   Joshua gave Tanner's essay a second and then a third reading, each time using a colored pen to draw his attention to specific points in the text. He underlined important points, placed question marks next to parts he did not understand, and commented on the writer's rhetorical strategies to better help him understand the writer's argument.

Summarizing   Joshua's philosophy professor asked the students to prepare a summary of the essay and be ready to share it with the class. She did this so that class discussion would be focused. Joshua took his annotations to class, too, so he was able to participate effectively. Here is his summary:

"On Plato's Cave" claims that much of what we see, hear, and read may give us inaccurate images and projections of points of view and that we need to try to discover what is really solid, rather than believe what might not be. This essay begins by quoting Plato's description of human beings chained in a cave, seeing only reflections of people, animals, and material items. The essay connects this fantasy situation with our experiences with the media, and even with what parents and teachers tell us. The essay says that Plato tells of a person escaping from the cave and seeing the real world. It says that we, too, can climb out of darkness by understanding how received information and our resulting beliefs need to be examined so that we can have "substantiated knowledge."

On Plato's Cave

BY SONJA TANNER

In the seventh book of Plato's dialogue *The Republic*, he offers an image of education in which humans are likened to prisoners in a cave. To understand this fully, we can attempt to render this image.

?

I guess we'll learn about socrates next week – that I'll get this funny use of word.

"Next, then," (Socrates) said, "make an image of our nature in its education and (want) of education, likening it to a condition of the following kind. See human beings as though they were in an underground cave-like dwelling with its entrance, a long one, open to the light across the whole width of the cave.

They are in it from childhood with their legs and necks in bonds so that they are fixed, seeing only in front of them, unable because of the bond to turn their heads all the way around. Their light is from a fire burning far above and behind them. Between the fire and the prisoners there is a road above, along which we see a wall, built like the partitions puppet-handlers set in front of <u>the human beings</u> and over which they show the puppets."

"I see," (Glaucon) said.

"Then also see along this wall human beings carrying all sorts of artifacts, which project above the wall, and statues of men and other animals wrought from stone, wood, and every kind of material. . . ." (514a1–515a2, Allan Bloom, trans.)

We see persons at the bottom of a cave, <u>chained so as</u> to prevent them from leaving the cave and from turning around to see what is behind them. Positioned in this way, they can only watch the shadows projected onto the back wall of the cave, by the passing of the artifacts in front of the fire. Behind the prisoners is a low wall which obscures the persons carrying these artifacts. This projection is like those we create around campfires, or in front of slide projectors, where a set of hands may look like a barking dog or a flying bird. A similar distortion takes place in the cave. Further up the cave is a fire and beyond that lies the cave's opening to the sunlight.

Having sketched what is happening within the cave literally, we must now try to <u>interpret what this image means figuratively</u>. When Glaucon remarks upon how strange these prisoners are, Socrates tells him <u>that they are like us</u>. How are we like these passive and helpless prisoners? <u>Do we ever receive information or entertainment without thinking about where it actually comes from?</u> Although Plato was writing over two thousand years before the invention of cathode ray tubes, the modern example of television may show us what he meant. If the projected images are analogous to those televised to us, then

Margin annotations:

spooky

? the ones in the cave? - no -

who?

OK - clearer than bonds

-or with a flashlight

aha!
where?

important point

now it's making sense

important point

what might the <u>persons behind the wall represent? Acting as filters of informa-tion, they might be seen as television networks, advertisers, or the media in general</u>. They and their motivations for presenting information about the world to us through their particular perceptual lenses are obscured from view like the persons who pass behind the wall in the cave. As the chains prevent the

This whole paragraph is important

prisoners from turning to see what is causing the images they watch, we are sometimes prevented by ignorance or uncritical thinking from recognizing the

maybe the thesis

interests and persons served by the way in which information is presented to us. When we are unaware as to how perceptual lenses shape what it is we then believe, the information we receive and the beliefs we build upon this information may be distorted, like the shadows projected onto the wall. Many

They sure do!

other persons shape the information we receive and the beliefs we hold. Authorities of all sorts fulfill this function—politicians, journalists, parents, teachers, writers and sometimes even ourselves.

!!

Plato does not think us <u>doomed to</u> this unreflective state, however. Escape from the cave, though mysterious, is possible. Someone is apparently released from their bonds, turns around, and despite the confusion and pain from the dazzling light and arduous ascent, both of which they are unaccus-

good comparison

tomed to, is able to leave the cave. Just as when we leave <u>a matinee movie and enter</u> bright sunlight, we are at first dazzled and our eyes need a few moments to adjust to the light, the ascendant may experience disorientation or confusion upon first turning around. Turning from the shadows, this person discovers the objects causing these projections and the persons carrying them and, once outside the cave, the beings which these artifacts are made

!

to resemble. The <u>journey upwards is one of turning from images to their origi-nals, ending ultimately in one's view of the sun itself,</u> which, as the earth's <u>source of heat and light,</u> is a cause of all of the beings described in this allegory.

5

escape → journey
another explanation

But how is <u>escape</u> from chains which bind at the neck and legs possible? Does someone release the prisoner and force them up into the light, and if so, who is this and why do they do it? Perhaps we are taking this image too literally in seeing this as a physical journey. Taking a cue from the aforementioned example in which the <u>projections represent beliefs and information we take on uncritically,</u> perhaps this journey is not <u>physical</u> but <u>mental</u>. The chains <u>may signify</u> ignorance and the uncritical taking over of second-hand opinions or beliefs and, as such, the chains themselves may even be self-imposed. Such an <u>intellectual journey</u> begins with a recognition that what we see and believe are only images, and by turning away from such appearances towards reality.

repeats

If the ascent <u>is intellectual</u>, rather than <u>physical,</u> a problem presents itself. Although Plato describes the release of a prisoner as though she or he were dragged up and out of the cave by the scruff of their neck, this type of force seems unlikely to guide an intellectual journey. Could one truly be <u>forced or compelled to think independently?</u> What else would motivate the journey? This is a particularly difficult question given the description of both ascent and return back into the cave as arduous, painful, and as subjecting one to derision and danger from the prisoners. What benefit could make good of undergoing such difficulties to leave the cave? We have been assuming here that the compulsion Plato describes as motivating the **ascent is a force external to the ascendant, but internal forces motivate us as well.** Why take the treacherous journey out of the cave? Perhaps simply because we *want* to. Our motivation upwards may be a desire for knowledge, as opposed to mere beliefs. If desire is the impetus for the ascent, this places <u>responsibility</u> for one's <u>education squarely on the shoulders of the individual.</u> We may have <u>assistance, encouragement</u> and <u>sometimes</u> even external forces compelling us upwards, but ultimately, our <u>success</u> depends <u>upon</u> our own <u>desire</u> for <u>knowledge and truth,</u> and our willingness to give up what we are accustomed

probably not

hard to understand
(read slow!)

!

Aha-again!

This sounds like my dad!

The cave makes sense here

to—the passive life and familiar comforts of cave-dwelling—for the rewards of rational and grounded knowledge.

important phrase

We are now able to locate ourselves on the trajectory of enlightenment. Looking at and discussing images are a first stage in education according to Plato and indeed that is precisely what we have done here thus far. The next

Here's the main point

One of those essays that leads up to it— doesn't state it at the beginning the way my English teacher wants us to do

step then seems to be turning away from the images we accept unreflectively and towards questions as to why we believe what we do, who or what are the sources of these beliefs, and how reliable are these sources, which can distinguish unfounded beliefs from substantiated knowledge. Maybe this ascent is undertaken by us on a regular basis, rather than simply once, in our lives.

Thinking ↔Writing Activity

Your Reactions

1 Write your reactions to the strategies for active and critical reading in this chapter. Which have you used before? How do they work for you? Which do you want to try now as you do your college reading?

2. How would you annotate "On Plato's Cave?"

3. Do you think that Joshua wrote an accurate summary of it? Would you summarize it differently?

If you can, share your reactions with classmates and notice agreements and disagreements.

USING METACOGNITIVE STRATEGIES

Metacognition is a process we have been working on throughout this book. While *cognition* refers to the process of thinking, *metacognition* refers to a form of thinking *about* the thinking process. For example, think about what you will be doing this evening, and as you are thinking about this, make a special effort to stand outside your thinking process and observe it while it is going on. This process of becoming an observer to your own thinking process—"reflecting" on your thinking—may feel strange, but it is well within your power if you concentrate. In the space below, describe some of the characteristics of the thinking process that you observed yourself engaging in. For instance, did you find you were talking to yourself? Did your thinking make use of still or moving visual images? Did you feel ideas were rushing through your mind like a river, or were your thoughts organized in an orderly fashion? Did you find one idea led to another idea, which led to another idea, through a series of associations?

Characteristics of My Thinking Process:

    1. _____

    2. _____

    3. _____

By participating in this activity you were actually engaging in the process of *metacognition,* working to become aware of the process you use to think about something.

While the process of reading is a thinking (cognitive) activity, expert readers also engage in metacognition while they are reading. In other words, they are aware of their thinking process as they are reading, and they use this awareness to improve their thinking. This awareness can be expressed as a variety of questions:

Goals What are my goals in reading this passage? How well am I meeting these goals?

Comprehension How well do I understand what I am reading? What parts do I understand, and what parts am I confused about?

Anticipation What events are going to take place following the ones I am reading about? How will the author develop and elaborate on these ideas?

Author's Purpose What is the author's point of view, and why did she adopt this particular perspective? How has her point of view affected the information she selected and the manner in which she presented this information?

Evaluation Is this information accurate? Do the ideas make sense? What evidence and reasons does the author provide to support her perspective?

As you work to answer these questions, you are likely to find that you are *rereading* key sections, and this rereading is an essential part of the process of reading effectively.

Practicing Metacognition

Although developing metacognitive reading abilities is a complex process that takes place over time, you can begin using these strategies immediately. Select a chapter from one of your textbooks. As you read, make a conscious effort to ask—and to answer—the metacognitive questions noted above. Record your experience, identifying the questions that you found yourself asking, and how the process of asking—and trying to answer—these questions while you were reading affected your understanding of the material. The metacognitive questions are part of a reading worksheet located below that you can use for reference later.

Reading Worksheet

Reading Assignment: _____

Reading Environment: _____

Reading Schedule: _____

Date Due: _____

Day   *Time Planned for Reading*

_____   _____

_____   _____

Reading Strategies
Problem Solving

Step 1: What is the problem in understanding the reading?

Step 2: What are the possible meanings and interpretations?

Step 3: What are the contextual clues, reasons, or evidence?

Step 4: What meaning or interpretation is most likely?

Step 5: How well is my conclusion working?

Metacognition

What are my *goals* in reading this passage, and how well am I meeting these goals?

What parts do I *understand*, and what parts are *confusing*?

How will the author *elaborate* and *develop* ideas I am reading about?

What is the author's *point of view*, and why did she adopt this particular perspective?

Do the ideas *make sense?* What *evidence* and *reasons* support the ideas presented?

Annotation

Grounds for Fiction

BY JULIA ALVAREZ (b. 1950)

Poet, novelist, and teacher Julia Alvarez was born in New York City but raised in the Dominican Republic. Her parents were involved in the underground resistance movement against Dominican dictator Rafael Trujillo, and when Alvarez was ten years old her family fled the country, settling again in New York City. "When I'm asked what made me into a writer, I point to the watershed experience of coming to this country," Alvarez notes in a biography on her web site. "Not understanding the language, I had to pay close attention to each word—great training for a writer. I also discovered the welcoming world of the imagination and books. . . . As a kid, I loved stories, hearing them, telling them. Since ours was an oral culture, stories were not written down. It took coming to this country for writing and storytelling to become allied in my mind."

Alvarez continues to reach out to diverse populations of readers, writing books for children and young adults and teaching writing in settings as diverse as bilingual elementary school programs and creative writing workshops for senior citizens. In her poems and novels, Alvarez mines her rich engagement with her family's history, cultures, and languages. Her novel In the Time of the Butterflies *(1994) is based on the true story of the four Mirabal sisters who fought against the brutal Trujillo dictatorship, and her enormously popular* How the Garcia Girls Lost Their Accents *(1991) deftly explores the relationships between sisters. Both novels were critically acclaimed, nominated for and winning several important prizes.*

In 2004 Alvarez returned to her poetic roots with her collection, The Woman I Kept to Myself. *"For me," she writes on her web site, "poetry is that cutting edge of the self, the part which moves out into experience ahead of every other part of the self. It's a way of saying what can't be put into words, our deepest and most secret and yet most universal feelings." Alvarez and her husband have started an organic coffee farm in the Dominican Republic; she recently brought a group of her American college students to the farm to work alongside local farmers and teach literacy classes in the community.*

Every once in a while after a reading, someone in the audience will come up to me. *Have I got a story for you!* They will go on to tell me the story of an aunt or sister or next-door neighbor, some moment of mystery, some serendipitous occurrence, some truly incredible story. "You should write it down," I always tell them. They look at me as if they've just offered me their family crown jewels and I've refused them. "I'm no writer," they tell me. "You're the writer."

"Oh, you never know," I reply, so as to encourage them. What I should tell them is that writing ideas can't really be traded in an open market. If they could be, writers would be multimillionaires. Who knows what mystery (or madness) it is that drives us to our computers for two, three, four years, in pursuit of some sparkling possibility that looks like dull fact to everyone else's eyes. One way to define a writer is she who is able to make what obsesses her into everyone's obsession. I am thinking of Goethe, whose *Sorrows of Young Werther,* published in 1774, caused a spate of suicides in imitation of its young hero. Young Werther's blue frock coat and yellow waistcoat became the fad. We have all been the victims of someone's too-long slide show of their white-water rafting trip or their recounting of a convoluted, boring dream. But a Mark Twain can turn that slide show into the lively backdrop of a novel, or a Jorge Luis Borges can take the twist and turn of a dream and wring the meaning of the universe from it.

But aside from talent—and granted, that is a big aside, one that comes and goes and shifts and grows and diminishes, so it is also somewhat unpredictable—how can we tell when we've got it: that seed of experience, of memory, that voice of a character or fleeting image that might just be grounds for fiction? The answer is that we can never tell. And so another way to define a writer is someone who is willing to find out. As James Dickey once explained to an audience, "I work on the process of refining low-grade ore. I get maybe a couple of nuggets of gold out of fifty tons of dirt. It is tough for me. No, I am not inspired."

"Are you all here because you want to muck around in fifty tons of dirt?" I ask my workshop of young writers the first day. Not one hand goes up unless I've told them the Dickey story first.

5   In fact, my students want to know ahead of time if some idea they have will make a good story. "I mean, before I spend hours and hours on it," one young man explained. I told my students what Mallarmé told his friend the painter Degas, when Degas complained that he couldn't seem to write well although he was "full of ideas." Mallarmés's famous answer was, "My dear Degas, poems are not made out of ideas. Poems are made out of words." I told my student that if a young writer had come up to me and told me that he was going to write a story about a man who wakes up one morning and finds out that he has been turned into a cockroach, I would have told him to forget it. That story would never work. "And I would have stopped Kafka from writing his 'Metamorphosis,'" I concluded, smiling at my student, as if he might be a future Kafka.

"Well, it's just two pages," he grumbled. "And I have this other idea that might be better. About a street person who is getting Alzheimer's."

"Write both stories, and I'll read them and tell you what I think of them," I said. He looked alarmed. So I leveled with him. I told him that if he didn't want to spend hours and hours finding out if the kernel of an idea, the glimmer of an inspiration, the flash of a possibility would make a good story, he should give up the *idea* of wanting to be a writer.

As much as I can break down the process of writing stories, I would say that this is how it begins. I find a detail or image or character or incident or cluster of events. A certain luminosity surrounds them. I find myself attracted. I come forward. I pick it up, turn it around, begin to ask questions, and spend hours and weeks and months and years trying to answer them.

I keep a folder, a yellow folder with pockets. For a long time it had no label because I didn't know what to label it: WHATCHAMACALLITS, filed under *W*, or also under *W*, STORY-POEM-WANNABES. Finally, I called the folder CURIOSIDADES, in Spanish so I wouldn't have to commit myself to what I was going to do in English with these random little things. I tell my students this, too, that writing begins before you ever put pen to paper or your fingers down on the keyboard. It is a way of being alive in the world. Henry James's advice to the young writer was to be someone on whom nothing is lost. And so this is my folder of the little things that have not been lost on me; news clippings, headlines, inventory lists, bits of gossip that I've already sensed have an aura about them, the beginnings of a poem or a short story, the seed of a plot that might turn into a novel or a query that might needle an essay out of me.

10
Periodically, when I'm between writing projects and sometimes when I'm in the middle of one and needing a break, I go through my yellow folder. Sometimes I discard a clipping or note that no longer holds my attention. But most of my *curiosidades* have been in my folder for years, though some have migrated to new folders, the folders of stories and poems they have inspired or found a home in.

Here's one of these *curiosidades* that is now in a folder that holds drafts of a story that turned into a chapter of my novel ¡*YO!* This chapter is in the point of view of Marie Beaudry, a landlady who, along with other narrators, gets to tell a story on Yolanda García, the writer. The little curiosity that inspired Marie's voice was a note I found in the trash of an apartment I moved into. It has nothing at all to do with what happens in my story.

> Re and Mal: Here's the two keys to your father's apt. Need I say more excepting that's such a rotten thing you pulled on him. My doing favors is over as of this morning. Good luck to you two hard-hearted hannahs. I got more feeling in my little finger than the two of you got in your whole body.
>
> Jinny

I admit that when I read this note, I wanted to move out of that apartment. I felt the place was haunted by the ghost of the last tenant against whom some violation had been perpetrated by these two hard-hearted hannahs, Re and Mal. Over the years that handwritten note stayed in my yellow folder and eventually gave me the voice of my character Marie Beaudry.

Here's another scrap from deep inside one of the pockets. It's the title of an article in one of my husband's ophthalmological journals: "Treatment of Chronic Postfiltration Hypotony by Intrableb Injection of Autologous Blood." I think I saved that choice bit of medical babble because of the delight I took in the jabberwocky phenomenon of that title.

> 'Twas brillig and the slithy toves
> Did gyre and postfiltrate the wabe;
> All hypotonious was the blood,
> And autologous the intrableb.

I have not yet used it in a story or poem, but who knows, maybe someday you will look over the shoulder of one of my characters and see that he is reading this article or writing it. I can tell you that this delight in words and how we use and misuse them is a preoccupation of mine.

Maybe because I began my writing life as a poet, the naming of things has always interested me:

> Mother, unroll the bolts and name
> the fabrics from which our clothing came,
> dress the world in vocabulary:
> broadcloth, corduroy, denim, terry.

Actually, that poem, "Naming the Fabrics," besides being inspired, of course, by the names of fabrics, was also triggered by something I picked up while reading *The 1961 Better Homes and Garden Sewing Book,* page 45: "During a question and answer period at a sewing clinic, a woman in the audience asked this question: 'I can sew beautifully; my fitting is excellent; the finished dress looks as good as that of any professional—but how do I get up enough courage to cut the fabric?'" I typed out this passage and put it away. A few months later, this fear found its way from my yellow folder to my poem, "Naming the Fabrics":

> I pay a tailor to cut his suits
> from seersucker, duck, tweed, cheviot,
> those names make my cutting hand skittish—
> either they sound like sex or British.

Since I myself have no sewing skills to speak of, I didn't know about this fear that seamstresses experience before cutting fabric. Certainly, the year 1961, when this sewing book was published, brings other fears to mind: the Berlin Wall going up; invaders going down to the Bay of Pigs; Trujillo, our dictator of thirty-one years, being assassinated in the Dominican Republic. But this housewife in Indiana had her own metaphysical fears to work out on cloth. "How do I get up enough courage to cut the fabric?" Her preoccupation astonished me and touched me for all kinds of reasons I had to work out on paper.

15   You might wonder what a "serious writer" was doing reading *The 1961 Better Homes and Garden Sewing Book.* Wouldn't my time have been better spent perusing Milton or Emily Dickinson or even the *New York Review of Books* or *The Nation?* All I can say in my defense is that I believe in Henry James's advice: be someone on whom nothing is lost. Or what Deborah Kerr said in *Night of the Iguana,* "Nothing human disgusts me." I once heard a writer on *Fresh Air* tell Terry Gross that one of the most important things he had ever learned in his life was that you could learn a lot from people who were dumber than you. You can also learn a lot from publications that are below your literary standards: housekeeping books, cookbooks, manuals, cereal boxes, and the local newspapers of your small town.

These last are the best. Even if some of this "news" is really glorified gossip—so what? Most of our classics are glorified gossip. Think of the Wife of Bath's inventory of husbands or the debutante's hair-rape in "The Rape of the Lock." How about Madame Bovary's steamy affair? Is what happened to Abelard over his Héloïse or to Jason for pissing off Medea any less infamous than the John and Lorena Bobbit story of several years ago? The wonderful

Canadian writer Alice Munro admits that she likes reading *People* magazine, and "not just at the checkout stand. I sometimes buy it." She goes on to say that gossip is "a central part of my life. I'm interested in small-town gossip. Gossip has that feeling in it, that one wants to know about life."

I've gotten wonderful stories from the *Addison Independent*, the *Valley Voice*, even the *Burlington Free Press* that would never be reported in the *Wall Street Journal* or the *New York Times*:

11-Year-Old Girls Take Car on Two-State Joyride

Two 11-year-old girls determined to see a newborn niece secretly borrowed their grandfather's car, piled clothes on the front seat so they could see over the steering wheel and drove more than 10 hours.

Neither one of them had ever driven a car before, said Michael Ray, Mercer County's juvenile case worker. The youngsters packed the Dodge Aries with soda, snacks, and an atlas for their trek from West Virginia to the central Kentucky town of Harrodsburg. "They were determined to see that baby," said caseworker Ray.

You could write a whole novel about that. In fact, in Mona Simpson's latest novel, *A Regular Guy,* eleven-year-old Jane di Natali is taught by her mother to drive their pickup with wood blocks strapped to the pedals so her short legs can reach them. Little Jane takes off on her own to see her estranged father hundreds of miles away. I wonder if Mona Simpson got her idea for Jane's odyssey from reading about these two eleven-year-olds.

Here's another article I've saved in my yellow folder:

Misdiagnosed Patient Freed After 2 Years

A Mexican migrant worker misdiagnosed and kept sedated in an Oregon mental hospital for two years because doctors couldn't understand his Indian dialect is going home.

Adolfo Gonzales, a frail 5-foot-4-inch grape picker who doesn't speak English or Spanish, had been trying to communicate in his native Indian dialect of Trique.

Gonzales, believed to be in his 20s, was born in a village in Oaxaca, Mexico. He was committed in June 1990 after being arrested for indecent exposure at a laundromat. Charges later were dropped.

I couldn't get this story out of my head. First, I was—and am—intensely interested in the whole Scheherazade issue of how important it is to be able to tell our stories to those who have power over us. Second, and more mundanely, I was intensely curious about those charges that were later dropped: indecent exposure at a laundromat. What was Adolfo Gonzales doing taking his clothes off in a laundromat? Why was he in town after a hard day of grape picking? I had to find answers to these questions, and so I started writing a poem. "It's a myth that writers write what they know," the writer Marcie Hershman has written. "We write what it is that we need to know."

The next payday you went to town
to buy your girl and to wash your one
set of working clothes.
In the laundromat, you took them off
to wring out the earth you wanted
to leave behind you.
                    from "Two Years Too Late"

20   Of course, you don't even have to go to your local paper. Just take a walk
downtown, especially if you live in a small town, as I do. All I have to do is have
a cup of coffee at Steve's Diner or at Jimmy's Weybridge Garage and listen to my
neighbors talking. Flannery O'Connor claimed that most beginners' stories
don't work because "they don't go very far inside a character, don't reveal very
much of the character. And this problem is in large part due to the fact that these
characters have no distinctive speech to reveal themselves with." Here are some
examples of my fellow Vermonters talking their very distinctive and revealing
speech.

> He's so lazy he married a pregnant woman.
>
> I'm so hungry I could eat the north end out of a southbound skunk.
>
> The snow's butt-high to a tall cow.
>
> More nervous than a long-tailed cat in a room full of rocking chairs.
>
> I'm so sick that I'd have to get well to die.

Of course if, like Whitman, you do nothing but listen, you will also hear all
kinds of bogus voices these days, speaking the new doublespeak. In our liti-
gious, politically overcorrected, dizzily spin-doctored age, politicians and public figures have to use language so that it doesn't say anything that might upset
anyone. Here's a list of nonterms and what they really stand for:

Sufferer of fictitious disorder syndrome:	Liar
Suboptimal:	Failed
Temporarily displaced inventory:	Stolen
Negative gain in test scores:	Lower test scores
Substantive negative outcome:	Death

We're back to "Treatment of Chronic Postfiltration Hypotony by Intrableb Injection of Autologous Blood," what Ken Macrorie in his wonderful book about
expository writing, *Telling Writing*, calls "Engfish"—homogenized, doctored-up,
approximate language that can't be traced to a human being.
        I tend to agree with what Dickinson once said about poetry, "There are no
approximate words in a poem." Auden even went so far as to say that he could
pick out a potential poet by a student's answer to the question, "Why do you
want to write poetry?" If the student answered, "I have important things to

say," then he was not a poet. If he answered, "I like hanging around words listening to what they say," then maybe he was going to be a poet.

I got enmeshed in one such string of words when I visited the United Nations to hear my mother give a speech on violation of human rights. At the door an aide handed me the list of voting member countries and the names caught my eye: Dem Kampuchea, Dem Yemen, Denmark, Djibouti, Dominica, Dominican Republic, Ecuador, Egypt. . . . When I got home, I started writing a poem, ostensibly about hearing my mother give that speech, but really because I wanted to use the names of those countries:

> I scan the room for reactions,
> picking out those countries
> guilty of her sad facts.
> Kampuchea is absent,
> absent, too, the South African delegate.
> I cannot find the United States.
> Nervous countries predominate,
> Nicaragua and Haiti,
> Iraq, Israel, Egypt.
> *from* "Between Dominica and Ecuador"

But of course, it's not just words that intrigue writers, but the stories, the possibilities of human character that cluster around a bit of history, trivia, gossip.

For instance, Anne Macdonald's book, *Feminine Ingenuity*, inspired a character trait of the mother in *How the García Girls Lost Their Accents*. According to Macdonald, at the beginning of the twentieth century, 5,535 American women were granted patents for inventions, including a straw-weaving device, an open-eye needle for sewing hot-air balloons, and special planking designed to discourage barnacles from attaching themselves to warships. These intriguing facts gave me a side of the mother's character I would never have thought up on my own. Inspired by the gadgetry of her new country, Laura García sets out to make her mark: soap sprayed from the nozzle head of a shower when you turn the knob a certain way; instant coffee with creamer already mixed in; time-released water capsules for your potted plants when you were away; a key chain with a timer that would go off when your parking meter was about to expire. (And the ticking would help you find your keys easily if you mislaid them.)

Sometimes the inspiration is history. History . . . that subject I hated in school because it was so dry and all about dead people. I wish now my teachers had made me read novels to make the past spring alive in my imagination. For years, I wanted to write about the Mirabal sisters, but I admit I was put off by these grand historical abstractions. It wasn't until I began to accumulate several yellow folders' worth of vivid little details about them that these godlike women became accessible to me. One of my first entries came from my father, who had just returned from a trip to the Dominican Republic: "I met the man who sold the girls pocketbooks at El Gallo before they set off over the mountain.

He told me he warned them not to go. He said he took them out back to the stockroom supposedly to show them inventory and explained they were going to be killed. But they did not believe him." I still get goosebumps reading my father's letter dated June 5, 1985. It went in my yellow folder. That pocketbook-buying scene is at the end of the novel I published nine years later.

25   So what are you to conclude from this tour of my yellow folder? That this essay is just an excuse to take you through my folder and share my little treasures with you? Well, one thing I don't want you to conclude is that this preliminary woolgathering is a substitute for the real research that starts once you have a poem or story going. In "Naming the Fabrics," for instance, though I was inspired by the plaintive question asked at a sewing clinic, I still had to go down to the fabric store and spend an afternoon with a very kind and patient saleslady who taught me all about gingham and calico, crepe and gauze. I spent days reading fabric books, and weeks working on the poem, and years going back to it, revising it, tinkering with it. For my story, "The Tent," I had to call up the National Guard base near Champaign, Illinois, and get permission from the base commander to go observe his men setting up a tent. ("What exactly do you need this for?" he asked at least half a dozen times.) Sometimes I think the best reason for a writer to have a reputable job like being a professor at a university or a vice president of Hartford Insurance Company is so you can call up those base commanders or bother those salesladies in fabric stores as if you do have a real job. Otherwise, they might think you are crazy and lock you up like poor Adolfo Gonzales.

       On the whole, I have found people to be kind and generous with their time, especially when you ask them to talk about something they know and care about. Many people have actually gone beyond kindness in helping me out. I remember calling up the local Catholic priest, bless his heart, who really deserves, I don't know, a plenary indulgence for tolerance in the face of surprise. Imagine getting an early-morning call (my writing day starts at 6:30, but I really don't do this kind of phone calling till about 7:30 since I do want my sources to be lucid). Anyhow, imagine an early-morning call at your rectory from a woman you don't know who asks you what is the name of that long rod priests have with a hole on one end to sprinkle people with holy water? I'd be lying if I tried to make drama out of the phone call and say there was a long pause. Nope. Father John spoke right up, "Ah yes, my aspergill."

       One thing I should add—the bad news part of all this fun, but something writers do have to think about in this litigious age—what is grounds for fiction can also be, alas, grounds for suing. All three of my novels have been read by my publisher's lawyer for what might be libelous. Thank goodness Algonquin's lawyer is also a reader who refuses to vacuum all the value out of a book in order to play it safe. Still, I have had to take drinks out of characters' hands and make abused ladies disabused and make so many changes in hair coloring and hairstyle that I could start a literary beauty parlor.

       But even if your fictional ground is cleared of litigious material, there might still be grounds for heartache. Your family and friends might feel wounded when they can detect—even if no one else can—the shape of the real behind the form of your fiction. And who would want to hurt those very people you write for, those very people who share with you the world you are struggling to understand in your fiction for their sake as well as your own?

I don't know how to get around this and I certainly haven't figured out what the parameters of my responsibility are to the real people in my life. One of my theories, which might sound defensive and self-serving, is that there is no such thing as straight-up fiction. There are just levels of distance from our own life experience, the thing that drives us to write in the first place. In spite of our caution and precaution, bits of our lives will get into what we write. I have a friend whose mother finds herself in all his novels, even historical novels set in nineteenth-century Russia or islands in the Caribbean where his mother has never been. A novelist writing about Napoleon might convey his greedy character by describing him spooning gruel into his mouth, only to realize that her image of how a greedy man eats comes from watching her fat Tío Jorge stuff his face with sweet habichuelas.

30   I think that if you start censoring yourself as a novelist—*this is out of bounds, that is sacrosanct*—you will never write anything. My advice is to write it out, and then decide, by whatever process seems fair to you—three-o'clock-in-the-morning insomniac angst sessions with your soul, or a phone call with your best friend, or a long talk with your sister—what you are going to do about it. More often than not, an upset reaction has more to do with people's wounded vanity or their own unresolved issues with *you* rather than what you've written. I'm not speaking now of meanness or revenge thinly masquerading as fiction, but of a writer's serious attempts to render justice to the world she lives in, which includes, whether she wants it to or not, the people she loves or has tried to love, the people who have been a part of the memories, details, life experiences that form the whole cloth of her reality—out of which, with fear and a trembling hand, she must perforce cut her fiction.

But truly, this is a worry to put out of your head while you are writing. You'll need your energy for the hard work ahead: tons and tons of good *ideas* to process in order to get those nuggets of pure prose. What Yeats once said in his poem, "Dialogue of Self and Soul," could well be the writer's pledge of allegiance:

> I am content to follow to its source,
> every event in action or in thought.

And remember, no one is probably going to pay you a whole lot of money to do this. You also probably won't save anyone's life with anything you write. But so much does depend on seeing a world in a grain of sand and a heaven in a wildflower. Maybe we are here only to say: house, bridge, aspergill, gingham, calico, gauze. "But to say them," as Rilke said, "remember oh, to say them in a way that the things themselves never dreamed of existing so intensely."

But this is too much of an orchestral close for the lowly little ditty that starts with a newspaper clipping or the feel of a bolt of gingham or a cup of coffee at the Weybridge Garage. The best advice I can give writers is something so dull and simple you'd never save it in your yellow folder. But go ahead and engrave it in your writer's heart. If you want to be a writer, anything in this world is grounds for fiction.

Questions for Active Reading

1. In rereading the essay, highlight all the cultural allusions Alvarez makes—the writers she cites, the paintings she mentions, the literary characters who obsess her, even the tabloid news stories she finds entertaining. Using the Internet (and working with partners, if you like), look up any allusions that are unfamiliar, and annotate your text by writing explanations of those allusions in the margins. What is Alvarez's purpose for all these allusions? How do you, as a reader, respond to the breadth of her interests?

2. How does Alvarez demonstrate the four qualities of an active, thoughtful, and critical reader? In what ways is she curious, open-minded, knowledgeable, and creative in her reading and her use of what she reads?

3. After you have annotated the essay to clarify any unfamiliar allusions, respond to any or all the previous metacognitive reading questions. Do any portions of the essay resist your questioning? Compare notes with your classmates—what is most difficult about Alvarez's essay, and why?

Questions for Thinking Critically

1. An *apologia* is a kind of argument, a defense that someone writes to explain and justify his or her actions, beliefs, or opinions. It's different from an *apology,* in which someone admits wrongdoing. In what ways does Alvarez present an apologia for herself as a writer? How, conversely, would she respond to a writer who might feel compelled to offer an apology for something he or she had written?

2. What does it mean to be inspired? (Look the word up; are you surprised by its etymology?) Where does Alvarez find inspiration? Look into the creative habits of another artist (in any medium) whose work you admire. From where does she draw her inspiration?

3. Get an empty folder. For one week, make an effort to put anything in that folder that catches your interest—an email from a friend, a photograph from the newspaper, the menu from a coffee shop, the stub from a movie ticket. At the end of the week, dump the contents of the folder on your desk. What story do these scraps tell you about your-

self? about your life? Can you arrange them into any sort of "narrative," either creative or very close to true?

You could also exchange folders with a classmate. What stories could you tell about your classmate based on what's in his folder?

Making Meaning

Words are not simple entities with one clear meaning that everyone agrees on. Instead, most words are complex, multidimensional carriers of meaning; their exact meaning often varies from person to person. These differences in meaning can lead to disagreements and confusion. To understand how words function, you have to examine the way that words serve as vehicles to express meaning.

Words arouse a variety of ideas, feelings, and experiences. Taken together, these responses express the total meaning of the words for each individual. Linguists believe that this total meaning is actually composed of four different types of meaning:

- semantic meaning
- perceptual meaning
- syntactic meaning
- pragmatic meaning

Let us examine each of them in turn.

SEMANTIC MEANING (DENOTATION)

The **semantic meaning** of a word expresses the relationship between a **linguistic event** (speaking or writing) and a **nonlinguistic event** (an object, idea, or feeling). For example, saying "chair" relates to an object you sit in while saying "college education" relates to the experience of earning an academic degree through postsecondary study.

The semantic meaning of a word, also referred to as its **denotative meaning,** expresses the general properties of the word, and these properties determine how the word is used within its language system. How do you discover the general properties that determine word usage? Besides examining your own knowledge of the meaning and use of words, you can check dictionary definitions. They tend to focus on the general properties that determine word usage. For example, a dictionary definition of *chair* might be "a piece of furniture consisting of a seat, legs, and back, and often arms, designed to accommodate one person."

However, to understand a word's semantic meaning fully, you often need to go beyond defining its general properties to identifying examples that embody those properties. If you are sitting in a chair or can see one from where you are, examine its design. Does it embody all the properties identified in the definition? (Sometimes unusual examples embody most, but not all, the properties of a word's dictionary definition—for example, a beanbag chair lacks legs and arms.) If you are trying to understand the semantic meaning of a word, it is generally useful to see both the word's general properties and examples that illustrate them.

PERCEPTUAL MEANING (CONNOTATION)

The total meaning of a word also includes its **perceptual meaning,** which expresses the relationship between a linguistic event and an individual's consciousness. For each of us, words elicit personal thoughts and feelings based on previous experiences and past associations. A person might relate saying "chair" to his favorite chair in his living room or the small chair that he built for his daughter. Perceptual meaning also includes an individual's positive and negative responses to the word. When you read or hear the word *book,* what positive or negative feelings does it arouse? What about *textbook? mystery book? comic book? cookbook?* In each case, the word probably elicits distinct feelings, and these contribute to the meaning each word has for you. For this reason, perceptual meaning is also sometimes called **connotative meaning,** the literal or basic meaning of a word plus all it suggests or connotes to you.

SYNTACTIC MEANING

A third component of a word's total meaning is its **syntactic meaning,** which defines its relation to other words in a sentence. The syntactic meaning defines three relationships among words:

- *Content:* words that express the major message of the sentence
- *Description:* words that elaborate or modify the major message of the sentence
- *Connection:* words that join the major message of the sentence

For example, in the sentence "The two novice hikers crossed the ledge cautiously," *hikers* and *crossed* represent the content, or major message, of the sentence. *Two* and *novice* describe *hikers,* and *cautiously* elaborates on *crossed.*

At first, you may think that this sort of relationship among words involves nothing more than semantic meaning. The following sentence, however, clearly demonstrates the importance of syntactic meaning in language: "Invisible fog rumbles in on lizard legs." Although *fog* does not *rumble,* and it is not *invisible,* and the notion of moving on *lizard legs* seems incompatible with *rumbling,* the sentence does "make sense" at some level of meaning—namely, at the syntactic level. One reason it does is that there are three basic content words—*fog, rumbles,* and *legs*—and two descriptive words—*invisible* and *lizard.*

The third major syntactic relationship is connection. Connective words join ideas, thoughts, or feelings being expressed. For example, you could connect content meaning to either of the two sentences in the following ways:

> The two novice hikers crossed the ledge cautiously *after* one of them slipped.
>
> Invisible fog rumbles in on lizard legs, *but* acid rain doesn't.

When you add the content words *one slipped* and *rain doesn't,* you join the ideas, thoughts, and feelings they represent to the ideas, thoughts, or feelings expressed earlier (*hikers crossed* and *fog rumbles*) by using the connective words *after* and *but.*

The second reason that "Invisible fog rumbles in on lizard legs" makes sense at the syntactic level of meaning is that the words of that sentence obey the syntax, or order, of English. Most English speakers would have trouble making sense of "Invisible rumbles legs lizard on fog in"—or of "Barks big endlessly dog brown the," for that matter. Because of syntactic meaning, each word in the sentence derives part of its total meaning from the ways in which it is combined with the other words in that sentence. Look at the following sentences and explain the difference in meaning between the two in each pair.

1. a. The process of obtaining an *education at college* changes a person's future possibilities.
   b. The process of obtaining a *college education* changes a person's future possibilities.

2. a. She felt *happiness* for her long-lost brother.
   b. She felt the *happiness* of her long-lost brother.

3. a. The most important thing to me is *freedom from* the things that restrict my choices.
   b. The most important thing to me is *freedom* to make my choices without restrictions.

4. a. Michelangelo's painting of the Sistine Chapel ceiling represents his *creative* genius.
   b. The Sistine Chapel ceiling represents the *creative* genius of Michelangelo's greatest painting.

5. a. I *love* the person I have been involved with for the past year.
   b. I am *in love* with the person I have been involved with for the past year.

PRAGMATIC MEANING

The fourth element that contributes to the total meaning of a word is its **pragmatic meaning.** The pragmatic meaning of a word involves the person who is writing and the situation in which the word is written. For example, the statement "That student likes to borrow books from the library" allows a number of pragmatic interpretations:

1. Was the writer outside looking at *that student* carrying books out of the library?

2. Did the writer have this information because he or she is a classmate of *that student* but did not actually see the student carrying books?

3. Was the writer in the library watching *that student* check the books out?

The correct interpretation or meaning of the sentence depends on what was actually taking place in the situation—in other words, its pragmatic meaning, which is also called its **situational meaning.** For each of the following sentences, try describing a pragmatic context that identifies the person writing and the situation for which it is being written.

1. A *college education* is currently necessary for many careers that formerly only required high school preparation.

2. The utilitarian ethical system is based on the principle that the right course of action is that which brings the greatest *happiness* to the greatest number of people.

3. The laws of this country attempt to balance the *freedom* of the individual with the rights of society as a whole.

4. "You are all part of things, you are all part of *creation,* all kings, all poets, all musicians, you have only to open up, to discover what is already there."—Henry Miller

5. "If music be the food of *love,* play on."—Shakespeare

After completing the activity, compare your answers with those of your classmates. In what ways are the answers similar or different? Analyze the ways in which different pragmatic contexts (persons speaking and situations) affect the meanings of the italicized words.

The four types of meanings you just examined—semantic, perceptual, syntactic, and pragmatic—create the total meaning of a word. That is, all the dimensions of a word—all the relationships that connect linguistic events with nonlinguistic events, with your consciousness, with other linguistic events, and with situations in the world—make up the meaning you assign to the word. Later, we will build on the ideas of this section.

3

Thinking Critically, Writing Thoughtfully

"The mere process of writing is one of the most powerful tools we have for clarifying our own thinking."
—James Van Allen

Critical Thinking Focus: Thinking about thinking

Writing Focus: Reflecting on experiences

Reading Theme: Experiences that have affected beliefs

Writing Project: Recalling the impact of experience on a belief

From Insight to Writing to Informed Beliefs (and Back Again)

Thinking, writing, reading: these are the tools that you have to understand your world, develop relationships with others, and make intelligent decisions in your quest to live a meaningful life. The underlying theme of this book is the way these potentially powerful tools are intrinsically related to one another. Every day you make choices in many areas of your life, choices that are guided by the beliefs you have developed. Successful choices are generally the product of enlightened beliefs that we have developed as a result of thinking critically, reading actively, and writing thoughtfully, as well as through lived experience. Whether the choices involve how best to write a term paper, enliven your social life, or earn some additional money, these fundamental abilities provide you with the means to construct beliefs that will guide your choices.

Developing informed beliefs involves nurturing the four core qualities that we have been exploring:

- **Curiosity**   This is the catalyst that inspires excellence in thinking and writing, leading to informed beliefs that are accurate and reliable. Lack of curiosity, on the other hand, encourages people to be complacent in their limited understanding, resulting in beliefs that are misdirected, inadequate, and mistaken.

- **Open-minded**   Informed beliefs result from actively exploring diverse ideas and perspectives, reading widely in many subject areas, and using writing as a tool to stretch our intellects and expand our understanding. In contrast, closed-minded individuals remain incarcerated in a limited vision of the world defined by narrow and biased beliefs.

- **Knowledgeable**   Informed beliefs are knowledgeable, the result of in-depth reading, productive discussions, thoughtful reflection, and writing that both analyzes and synthesizes ideas. Uninformed beliefs, on the other hand, lack a sound grounding and meaningful content: they are often vague, confused, rootless, and misguided.

- **Creative**   Being inventive, actively seeking unique connections, presenting a fresh point of view on a standard topic—these are all instances of approaches that lead to creative breakthroughs in thinking; vital, lively writing; and insightful, informed beliefs. In contrast, thinking and writing that is unimaginative, conventional, and clichéd inevitably leads to beliefs that embody these same qualities.

Using these four core qualities as a framework, this chapter extends and deepens them by exploring other related qualities that characterize critical thinkers, active readers, and thoughtful writers, including the following:

- Thinking actively
- Thinking independently
- Viewing a situation from different perspectives
- Supporting diverse perspectives with evidence and reasons

The chapter then presents readings in which authors think critically by reflecting on experiences that have affected their beliefs. Concluding the chapter is a Writing Project which asks you to think critically and write thoughtfully about an experience that had an important impact on a belief that you held or hold. You should keep this Writing Project in mind as you read the chapter and work on Thinking-Writing Activities.

Thinking Actively and Writing

When you think critically, you are *actively* using your intelligence, knowledge, and abilities to deal effectively with life's situations. Similarly, when you write thoughtfully, you act in the following ways:

- You *become involved* in the subject you are writing about, and because the writing process stimulates your thinking, you often discover ideas that you were unaware of until you started writing. Also, if you keep a journal or notebook and make writing part of your daily life, you find yourself more involved in and more reflective about your world.

- You *take initiative* as you develop confidence in your writer's voice, so you express your own perspectives instead of imitating the ideas of others.

- You *follow through* as you revise and edit in order to produce your best effort.

- You *take responsibility* for your work. That is, you begin assignments promptly and budget enough time to complete them. Though your professors will guide you, and your classmates and writing center tutors will make suggestions about your drafts, you are in charge of your writing, and it is up to you to complete it honestly and well.

When you are thinking actively, you are not just waiting for something to happen. You are engaged in the process of achieving goals, making decisions, analyzing issues, and writing thoughtfully.

INFLUENCES ON YOUR THINKING

As our minds grow and develop, we are exposed to influences that encourage us to think actively. We also, however, have many experiences that encourage us to think passively. For example, some analysts believe that when people, especially children, spend much of their time watching television instead of reading and writing, they are being encouraged to think passively, thus inhibiting their intellectual growth. Listed next are some of the influences we all experience in our lives, along with space for adding others you are aware of. As you read through the list, place an *A* next to items that you believe influence you to think actively and a *P* next to items that make you more passive.

Activities	People
Reading	Family members
Writing	Friends
Watching television	Employers

Surfing the Internet	Advertisers
Drawing and painting	Teachers
Playing video games	Police officers
Playing sports	Religious leaders
Listening to music	Politicians
_____	_____
_____	_____

Of course, certain people or activities can act as either active or passive influences, depending on specific situations and your individual responses. For example, consider employers. If you are performing a routine, repetitive task—such as a summer job in a peanut-butter cracker plant, hand-scooping 2,000 pounds of peanut butter a day—the very nature of the work encourages passive, uncritical thinking (although it might also lead to creative daydreaming!). You are also influenced to think passively if an employer gives you detailed instructions for performing every task that permit no exception or deviation. On the other hand, when an employer gives you general areas of responsibility within which you are expected to make thoughtful and creative decisions, you are being stimulated to think actively and independently.

Similar experiences occur in college. You will probably find that some of your professors will encourage you to think actively by expecting you to apply, analyze, synthesize, and evaluate the information you are acquiring. These professors may assign independent research projects, give essay exams, and require you to write papers in which you must bring your informed perspective to the course material. Other professors may expect you to represent the information from class lectures and the textbooks but not ask for your perspective—an approach that may not encourage active thinking.

Thinking ↔ Writing Activity

Active and Passive Influences

Identify one important influence in your life that stimulates you to think actively; then identify one that encourages you to think passively. Write explanations of how each has affected your thinking. Provide at least two specific examples for each influence.

Thinking Independently

Answer the following questions on the basis of what you believe to be true.

	Yes	No	Not Sure
1. Is the earth flat?			
2. Is the soul immortal?			
3. Should marijuana be legalized?			
4. Should music lyrics and videos be censored?			
5. Should we follow "The Golden Rule" ("do unto others as you would have them do unto you") in our relationships with others?			

Your responses to these questions reveal aspects of the way your mind works, beliefs you have developed that you express in your speaking and writing. How did you arrive at these conclusions? Your views on these and many other issues probably had their beginnings with your family, especially your parents or other adults who raised you. When you were little, you were very dependent on those adults, and you were influenced by the way they saw the world. As you grew up, you learned how to think, feel, and behave in various situations. Very likely your teachers included your brothers and sisters, friends, religious leaders, instructors, books, television, and so on. You absorbed most of what you learned without even being aware of doing so. Many of your ideas about the issues raised in the five questions you just answered probably were shaped by experiences you had while growing up.

"I keep my core beliefs written on my palm for easy reference."

As a result of your ongoing experiences, however, your mind—and your thinking—have continued to mature. Instead of simply accepting the views of others, you have gradually developed the ability to examine your earlier thinking and to decide how much of it still makes sense to you and whether you should accept it. Now, when you think through important ideas, use this standard when making a decision: Are there good reasons or evidence that support this thinking? If there are, you can actively decide to adopt the ideas. If not, you can modify or reject them.

Of course, you may not *always* examine your own thinking or the thinking of others so carefully. In fact, people often continue to believe the same ideas they were brought up with, without ever examining and deciding for themselves what to think. Or they may blindly reject the beliefs they were brought up with, without really examining them.

How do you know when you have examined and adopted beliefs yourself instead of simply borrowing them from others? One indication of having thought your beliefs through is being able to explain why you believe in them, giving the reasons that led you to your conclusions.

Still, not all reasons and evidence are equally strong or accurate. For example, in Europe before the fifteenth century, the common belief that the earth was flat was supported by the following reasons and evidence:

People of Authority: Many educational and religious authorities taught that the earth was flat.

Recorded References: The written opinions of scientific experts supported belief in a flat earth.

Observed Evidence: No person had ever circumnavigated the earth.

Personal Experience: From a normal vantage point, the earth *looks* flat.

Thinking ↔ Writing Activity

Evaluating Beliefs

For each of the five beliefs you expressed at the beginning of this section, explain how you arrived at it and state the reasons and evidence that you believe support it.

1. *Example:* Is the earth flat?

   Belief: No, it is round.

   Reasons/Evidence:

   a. People of Authority: My parents and teachers taught me this.

   b. Recorded References: What references support your beliefs? I read about the earth in science textbooks and saw films and videos.

c. Observed Evidence: I have seen a sequence of photographs taken from outer space that show the earth as a globe.

d. Personal Experience: When I flew across the country, I could see the horizon line changing.

2. Is the soul immortal?

3. Should marijuana be legalized?

4. Should music lyrics and videos be censored?

5. Should we follow "the Golden Rule" in our relationships with others?

To evaluate the strengths and accuracy of the reasons and evidence you identified for holding your beliefs on the five issues, address questions such as the following:

People of Authority: Are the authorities knowledgeable in this area? Are they reliable? Have they ever given inaccurate information? Do other authorities disagree with them?

Recorded References: What references support your belief? What are the credentials of the authors? Do other authors disagree with their opinions? On what reasons and evidence do the authors base their opinions?

Observed Evidence: What is the source and foundation of the evidence? Can the evidence be interpreted differently? Does the evidence support the conclusion?

Personal Experience: What were the circumstances under which the experiences took place? Were distortions or mistakes in perception possible? Have other people had either similar or conflicting experiences? Are there other explanations for your experiences?

As a college writer, you are going to apply these questions to material you encounter while gathering information for papers or reports. The opposite of thinking for yourself is simply accepting the thinking of others without examining or questioning it. Learning to become an independent thinker is a complex, ongoing process.

VIEWING A SITUATION FROM DIFFERENT PERSPECTIVES

Critical thinkers listen to other views and new ideas and examine them carefully. No one person has *all* the answers! Your beliefs represent just one perspective on whatever problem you want to solve or situation you are trying to understand. In addition to your own particular viewpoint, there may be others, equally important, that you need to consider if you are to develop a more complete understanding of the problem or situation. Learning to think and write at a high level, in fact, requires this.

Perspective-taking is essential to becoming a thoughtful writer. To begin with, exploring topics from a variety of vantage points is often the best way to present a comprehensive analysis of the subject you are writing about. When you are tied to only one perspective, your writing tends to be one-sided and superficial. Second, effective writing depends on always having a clear sense of your readers, the audience for whom you are writing. The ability to remain focused on that audience includes being able to see things from their point of view, to think empathetically within their frame of reference, and to understand their perspective. Finally, in order to produce your most accomplished writing, you need to be open to the informed comments and suggestions of others and flexible enough to use that feedback to refine your writing.

For most of the important issues and problems in your life, one viewpoint is simply not adequate to provide a full and satisfactory understanding. To increase and deepen your knowledge, you must seek other perspectives. Sometimes you can accomplish this by using your imagination to visualize other viewpoints. Usually, however, you need to seek actively (and *listen to*) other people's viewpoints. It is often very difficult to see things from points of view other than your own; if you are not careful, you can make the serious mistake of assuming that the way you see things is the way they really are.

In order to identify with perspectives other than your own, then, you also have to work to grasp the reasons for these alternate viewpoints. This approach, which stimulates you to evaluate your beliefs critically, is enhanced by writing. Writing about beliefs encourages people to explain their reasons for holding them and provides a vehicle for sharing their thinking with those who have contrasting points of view.

Thinking ↔ Writing Activity

Two Sides of a Belief

Describe in detail a belief about which you feel very strongly. Then explain the reasons or experiences that led you to this belief. Next, describe a point of view that differs from your belief. Identify some of the reasons someone would have that point of view.

Being open to new ideas and different viewpoints means being *flexible* enough to change or modify one's own ideas in the light of new information or better insight. People do have a tendency to cling to the beliefs they were brought up with and the conclusions they have arrived at. If you are going to continue to grow and develop as a thinker, however, you have to be willing to change or modify your beliefs when evidence suggests that you should.

For example, imagine that you have been brought up with certain views concerning an ethnic group—African American, Euroamerican, Hispanic,

Asian, Native American, or any other. As you mature and your experiences increase, you may find that the evidence of your experiences conflicts with those earlier views. As a critical thinker, you will become open to receiving new evidence and flexible enough to change and modify your ideas.

In contrast to open and flexible thinking, *un*critical thinking tends to be one-sided and closed-minded. People who think uncritically are convinced that they alone see things as they really are and that everyone who disagrees with them is wrong. It is very difficult for them to step outside their own viewpoints and look at issues from other people's perspectives. Words often used to describe this type of person include *dogmatic, subjective,* and *egocentric.*

Supporting Diverse Perspectives with Reasons and Evidence

When you are thinking critically, you can offer sound reasons for your views. As a thoughtful writer, you cannot simply take a position on an issue or make a claim; you have to back up your views, reinforce them with information that you feel supports your position. There is an important distinction between *what* you believe and *why* you believe it.

As critical thinkers and thoughtful writers we have an obligation to appreciate diverse perspectives on complex issues and develop informed opinions that are supported by compelling reasons. © Reuters/CORBIS

If you want to know all sides of an issue, you have to be able to give supporting reasons and evidence not just for your own views but also for the views of others.

Consider the issue of whether side air bags should be standard equipment for cars. As you try to make sense of this issue, you should attempt to identify not just the reasons for your view but also the reasons for other views. Following are reasons that support each view of this issue.

Issues

Side air bags should be standard equipment.

Side air bags should not be standard equipment.

Supporting Reasons

1. Studies show that side air bags save lives in accidents.

2. Studies show that side air bags reduce injury in accidents.

Supporting Reasons

1. Side air bags sometimes injure and even kill children and small adults.

2. Side air bags should not be forced on citizens of a free country.

Now see if you can identify additional supporting reasons for each position on making air bags standard equipment. For each of the following issues, identify reasons that support each side.

Issues

1. Multiple-choice and true/false exams should be given in college-level courses.

2. It is better to live in a society in which the government plays a major role in citizens' lives.

3. The best way to deal with crime is to impose long prison sentences.

4. When a couple divorce, the children should choose the parent with whom they wish to live.

1. Multiple-choice and true/false exams should *not* be given in college-level courses.

2. It is better to live in a society that minimizes the role of the government in citizens' lives.

3. Long prison sentences will not reduce crime.

4. When a couple divorce, the court should decide all custody issues regarding the children.

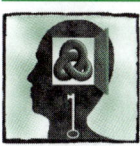

Viewing Different Perspectives

Seeing different perspectives is crucial to getting a more complete understanding of ideas expressed in passages you read. Read the two passages that follow. Then, for each passage, do these four things:

1. Identify the main idea of each passage.
2. List the reasons that support the main idea.
3. Develop another view of the main issue.
4. List the reasons that support the other view.

If we want auto safety but continue to believe in auto profits, sales, styling, and annual obsolescence, there will be no serious accomplishments. The moment we put safety ahead of these other values, something will happen. If we want better municipal hospitals but are unwilling to disturb the level of spending for defense, for highways, or for household appliances, hospital service will not improve. If we want peace but still believe that countries with differing ideologies are threats to one another, we will not get peace. What is confusing is that up to now, while we have wanted such things as conservation, auto safety, hospital care, and peace, we have tried wanting them without changing consciousness; that is, while continuing to accept those underlying values that stand in the way of what we want. The machine can be controlled at the "consumer" level only by people who change their whole value system, their whole worldview, their whole way of life. One cannot favor saving our wildlife and wear a fur coat.

◆

Most wicked deeds are done because the doer proposes some good to himself. The liar lies to gain some end; the swindler and thief want things which, if honestly got, might be good in themselves. Even the murderer may be removing an impediment to normal desires or gaining possession of something his victim keeps from him. None of these people usually does evil for evil's sake. They are selfish or unscrupulous, but their deeds are not gratuitously evil. The killer for sport has no such comprehensible motive. He prefers death to life, darkness to light. He gets nothing except the satisfaction of saying, "Something which wanted to live is dead. There is that much less vitality, consciousness, and, perhaps, joy in the universe. I am the Spirit that Denies." When a human wantonly destroys one of humankind's own works, we call him Vandal. When he wantonly destroys one of the works of God, we call him Sportsman.

DEVELOPING INFORMED BELIEFS

The process of developing informed beliefs is ongoing and lifelong. It is also a process that is essential for you to achieve success and happiness, since your beliefs constitute the "map" you use to guide your choices. If your belief map is accurate, your choices will reflect a clear understanding of the world. However, if your belief map is inaccurate or incomplete, you are in jeopardy of making ineffective or wrong-headed choices.

Developing informed beliefs involves the core qualities of a critical thinker and thoughtful writer to which we have been referring: *Curious Open-minded, Knowledgeable, Creative.* The themes of this chapter complement these qualities:

- **Thinking actively** provides the impetus for asking questions, keeping an open mind, seeking knowledge, and being inventive.
- **Thinking independently** is achieved by being curious, going beyond familiar points of view, engaging in research to develop your own informed opinions, and transcending conventional norms to achieve creative insights.
- **Viewing situations from different perspectives** is the essence of questioning narrow points of view in order to become truly open-minded. Perspective-taking is also the vehicle we use to develop genuine knowledge and achieve creative insights.
- **Supporting diverse perspectives with reasons and evidence** is the outgrowth of questioning, open-minded explorations, and utilizing one's knowledge.

EXPERIENCES THAT AFFECTED BELIEFS

In the following narratives, four writers reflect on learning experiences that caused them to evaluate and in some cases revise beliefs about themselves, about other people, and about ways to live their lives.

As you read the selections, keep in mind one set of critical reading questions that we identified in the second chapter.

- Who is the *writer* and what perspective does he or she bring to the writing selection?
- What is the *subject* of the selection, and how would you evaluate its cogency and reliability?
- Who is the intended *audience,* and what assumptions is the writer making about it?
- What is the *purpose* of the selection, and how is the author trying to achieve it?

Following each selection are questions designed to stimulate and guide your critical thinking, active reading, and thoughtful writing.

FROM

An American Childhood

BY ANNIE DILLARD (b. 1945)

Annie Dillard's engagement with nature and its reflection of the spiritual life informs her extensive creative and nonfiction writing. A poet, novelist, and essayist, Dillard won the Pulitzer Prize for her memoir Pilgrim at Tinker Creek *(1974). Her close observations of the environment and her ongoing spiritual quests combine in her views on writing, as in this passage from "Write Till You Drop": "The sensation of writing a book is the sensation of spinning, blinded by love and daring. It is the sensation of a stunt pilot's turning barrel rolls, or an inchworm's blind rearing from a stem in search of a route. At its worst, it feels like alligator wrestling, at the level of the sentence." In the following memoir, she describes how her parents encouraged her early explorations of the natural world.*

After I read *The Field Book of Ponds and Streams* several times, I longed for a microscope. Everybody needed a microscope. Detectives used microscopes, both for the FBI and at Scotland Yard. Although usually I had to save my tiny allowance for things I wanted, that year for Christmas my parents gave me a microscope kit.

In a dark basement corner, on a white enamel table, I set up the microscope kit. I supplied a chair, a lamp, a batch of jars, a candle, and a pile of library books. The microscope kit supplied a blunt black three-speed microscope, a booklet, a scalpel, a dropper, an ingenious device for cutting thin segments of fragile tissue, a pile of clean slides and cover slips, and a dandy array of corked test tubes.

One of the test tubes contained "hay infusion." Hay infusion was a wee brown chip of grass blade. You added water to it, and after a week it became a jungle in a drop, full of one-celled animals. This did not work for me. All I saw in the microscope after a week was a wet chip of dried grass, much enlarged.

Another test tube contained "diatomaceous earth." This was, I believed, an actual pinch of the white cliffs of Dover. On my palm it was an airy, friable chalk. The booklet said it was composed of the silicaceous bodies of diatoms—one-celled creatures that lived in, as it were, small glass jewelry boxes with fitted lids. Diatoms, I read, come in a variety of transparent geometrical shapes. Broken and dead and dug out of geological deposits, they made chalk, and a fine abrasive used in silver polish and toothpaste. What I saw in the microscope must have been the fine abrasive—grit enlarged. It was years before I saw a recognizable, whole diatom. The kit's diatomaceous earth was a bust.

5   All that winter I played with the microscope. I prepared slides from things at hand, as the books suggested. I looked at the transparent membrane inside an onion's skin and saw the cells. I looked at a section of cork and saw the cells, and at scrapings from the inside of my cheek, ditto. I looked at my blood and saw not much; I looked at my urine and saw long iridescent crystals, for the drop had dried.

All this was very well, but I wanted to see the wildlife I had read about. I wanted especially to see the famous amoeba, who had eluded me. He was supposed to live in the hay infusion, but I hadn't found him there. He lived outside in warm ponds and streams, too, but I lived in Pittsburgh, and it had been a cold winter.

Finally late that spring I saw an amoeba. The week before, I had gathered puddle water from Frick Park, it had been festering in a jar in the basement. This June night after dinner I figured I had waited long enough. In the basement at my microscope table I spread a scummy drop of Frick Park puddle water on a slide, peeked in, and lo, there was the famous amoeba. He was as blobby and grainy as his picture; I would have known him anywhere.

Before I had watched him at all, I ran upstairs. My parents were still at table, drinking coffee. They, too, could see the famous amoeba. I told them, bursting, that he was all set up, that they should hurry before his water dried. It was the chance of a lifetime.

Father had stretched out his long legs and was tilting back in his chair. Mother sat with her knees crossed, in blue slacks, smoking a Chesterfield. The dessert dishes were still on the table. My sisters were nowhere in evidence. It was a warm evening; the big dining-room windows gave onto blooming rhododendrons.

10   Mother regarded me warmly. She gave me to understand that she was glad I had found what I had been looking for, but that she and Father were happy to sit with their coffee, and would not be coming down.

She did not say, but I understood at once, that they had their pursuits (coffee?) and I had mine. She did not say, but I began to understand then, that you do what you do out of your private passion for the thing itself.

I had essentially been handed my own life. In subsequent years my parents would praise my drawings and poems, and supply me with books, art supplies, and sports equipment, and listen to my troubles and enthusiasms, and supervise my hours, and discuss and inform, but they would not get involved with my detective work, nor hear about my reading, nor inquire about my homework or term papers or exams, nor visit the salamanders I caught, nor listen to me play the piano, nor attend my field hockey games, nor fuss over my insect collection with me, or my poetry collection or stamp collection or rock collection. My days and nights were my own to plan and fill.

When I left the dining room that evening and started down the dark basement stairs, I had a life, I sat with my wonderful amoeba, and there he was, rolling his grains more slowly now, extending an arc of his edge for a foot and drawing himself along by that foot, and absorbing it again and rolling on. I gave him some more pond water.

I had hit pay dirt. For all I knew, there were paramecia, too, in that pond water, or daphniae, or stentors, or any of the many other creatures I had read about and never seen: volvox, the spherical algal colony; euglena with its one red eye; the elusive glassy diatom; hydra, rotifers, water bears, worms. Anything was possible. The sky was the limit.

Questions for Active Reading

1. Examine the structure of Dillard's essay. How much time passes over the course of the essay, and how can you tell? When does she "pause" in her narrative, and why?

2. Compare the vocabulary of the final paragraph with the rest of the essay. Why do you think Dillard concludes her essay with this kind of language?

3. In paragraph 11, Dillard asks a rhetorical question (a question that a writer does not answer, but leaves to the reader). Although it's just one word, what is the full meaning of that question? How would you, as a reader, answer it, based on what you know of Dillard's parents? based on your own parents, or your own experience as a parent?

Questions for Thinking Critically

1. When Annie Dillard rushed to share her discovery of the amoeba with her parents, they politely declined. What reaction had she expected, and what did this reveal about her beliefs regarding her relationship with her parents?

2. Her parents' lack of interest in this and other passions in her life led her to a conclusion: "I had essentially been handed my own life." Explain why you think she reached this conclusion.

3. Based on your own experience, do you believe that the best way to achieve "your own life" is through your parents' lack of involvement in your life?

4. The author states that "you do what you do out of your private passion for the thing itself." This "private passion" is a kind of curiosity, a key characteristic of a critical thinker. Describe a "private passion" of your own that you pursue not to please others but because of your personal curiosity and enthusiasm.

FROM

The Blank Slate

BY STEVEN PINKER (b. 1954)

Experimental psychologist Steven Pinker, Johnstone Family Professor of Psychology at Harvard, is well known (and widely read) for his explorations of how human beings have developed—or evolved—language skills, first elaborated in his 1994 book The Language Instinct: How the Mind Creates Language. *In subsequent books, including* How The Mind Works *(a finalist for the 1998 Pulitzer Prize), Pinker has continued to explain and examine the field of evolutionary psychology. This relatively new field seeks to explain human behaviors as biologically based and favored by evolution. As Pinker explained in an interview published in* The New York Times, *"it's a fallacy to think that hunger and thirst and a sex drive are biological but that reasoning and decision making and learning are something else, something nonbiological. They're just a different kind of biology." In the following selection from his book* The Blank Slate: The Modern Denial of Human Nature, *Pinker contests the idea that people are born as "blank slates" to be molded and shaped by their parents and other environmental factors, arguing instead for an innate "human nature" that, even though biologically based, accounts for our common moral and ethical beliefs and responses.*

If you read the pundits in newspapers and magazines, you may have come across some remarkable claims about the malleability of the human psyche. Here are a few from my collection of clippings:

- Little boys quarrel and fight because they are encouraged to do so.
- Children enjoy sweets because their parents use them as rewards for eating vegetables.
- Teenagers get the idea to compete in looks and fashion from spelling bees and academic prizes.
- Men think the goal of sex is an orgasm because of the way they were socialized.

If you find these assertions dubious, your skepticism is certainly justified. In all cultures little boys quarrel, children like sweets, teens compete for status, and men pursue orgasms without the slightest need of encouragement or socialization. In each case, the writers made their preposterous claims without a shred of evidence—without even a nod to the possibility that they were saying something common sense might call into question.

Intellectual life today is beset with a great divide. On one side is a militant denial of human nature, a conviction that the mind of a child is a blank slate that is subsequently inscribed by parents and society. For much of the past century, psychology has tried to explain all thought, feeling, and behavior with a few simple mechanisms of learning by association. Social scientists have tried to explain all customs and social arrangements as a product of the surrounding culture. A long list of concepts that would seem natural to the human way of thinking—emotions, kinship, the sexes—are said to have been "invented" or "socially constructed."

At the same time, there is a growing realization that human nature won't go away. Anyone who has had more than one child, or been in a heterosexual relationship, or noticed that children learn language but house pets don't has recognized that people are born with certain talents and temperaments. An acknowledgment that we humans are a species with a timeless and universal psychology pervades the writings of great political thinkers, and without it we cannot explain the recurring themes of literature, religion, and myth. Moreover, the modern sciences of mind, brain, genes, and evolution are showing that there is something to the commonsense idea of human nature. Although no scientist denies that learning and culture are crucial to every aspect of human life, these processes don't happen by magic. There must be complex innate mental faculties that enable human beings to create and learn culture.

5   Sometimes the contradictory attitudes toward human nature divide people into competing camps. The blank slate camp tends to have greater appeal among those in the social sciences and humanities than it does among biological scientists. And until recently, it was more popular on the political left than it was on the right.

But sometimes both attitudes coexist uneasily inside the mind of a single person. Many academics, for example, publicly deny the existence of intelligence. But privately, academics are *obsessed* with intelligence, discussing it endlessly in admissions, in hiring, and especially in their gossip about one another. And despite their protestations that it is a reactionary concept, they quickly invoke it to oppose executing a murderer with an I.Q. of 64 or to support laws requiring the removal of lead paint because it may lower a child's I.Q. by five points. Similarly, those who argue that gender differences are a reversible social construction do not treat them that way in their advice to their daughters, in their dealings with the opposite sex, or in their unguarded gossip, humor, and reflections on their lives.

No good can come from this hypocrisy. The dogma that human nature does not exist, in the face of growing evidence from science and common sense that it does, has led to contempt among many scholars in the humanities for the concepts of evidence and truth. Worse, the doctrine of the blank slate often distorts science itself by making an extreme position—that culture alone determines behavior—seem moderate, and by making the moderate position—that behavior comes from an interaction of biology and culture—seem extreme.

For example, many policies on parenting come from research that finds a correlation between the behavior of parents and of their children. Loving parents have confident children, authoritative parents (neither too permissive nor too punitive) have well-behaved children, parents who talk to their children have children with better language skills, and so on. Thus everyone concludes that parents should be loving, authoritative, and talkative, and if children don't turn out well, it must be the parents' fault.

Those conclusions depend on the belief that children are blank slates. It ignores the fact that parents provide their children with genes, not just an environment. The correlations may be telling us only that the same genes that make adults loving, authoritative, and talkative make their children self-confident, well behaved, and articulate. Until the studies are redone with adopted children (who get only their environment from their parents), the data are compatible with the possibility that genes make all the difference, that parenting makes all the difference, or anything in between. Yet the extreme position—that parents are everything—is the only one researchers entertain.

10   The denial of human nature has not just corrupted the world of intellectuals but has harmed ordinary people. The theory that parents can mold their children like clay has inflicted child-rearing regimes on parents that are unnatural and

sometimes cruel. It has distorted the choices faced by mothers as they try to balance their lives, and it has multiplied the anguish of parents whose children haven't turned out as hoped. The belief that human tastes are reversible cultural preferences has led social planners to write off people's enjoyment of ornament, natural light, and human scale and forced millions of people to live in drab cement boxes. And the conviction that humanity could be reshaped by massive social engineering projects has led to some of the greatest atrocities in history.

The phrase "blank slate" is a loose translation of the medieval Latin term *tabula rasa*—scraped tablet. It is often attributed to the seventeenth-century English philosopher John Locke, who wrote that the mind is "white paper void of all characters." But it became the official doctrine among thinking people only in the first half of the twentieth century, as part of a reaction to the widespread belief in the intellectual or moral inferiority of women, Jews, nonwhite races, and non-Western cultures.

Part of the reaction was a moral repulsion from discrimination, lynchings, forced sterilizations, segregation, and the Holocaust. And part of it came from empirical observations. Waves of immigrants from southern and eastern Europe filled the cities of America and climbed the social ladder. African Americans took advantage of "Negro colleges" and migrated northward, beginning the Harlem Renaissance. The graduates of women's colleges launched the first wave of feminism. To say that women and minority groups were inferior contradicted what people could see with their own eyes.

Academics were swept along by the changing attitudes, but they also helped direct the tide. The prevailing theories of mind were refashioned to make racism and sexism as untenable as possible. The blank slate became sacred scripture. According to the doctrine, any differences we see among races, ethnic groups, sexes, and individuals come not from differences in their innate constitution but from differences in their experiences. Change the experiences—by reforming parenting, education, the media, and social rewards—and you can change the person. Also, if there is no such thing as human nature, society will not be saddled with such nasty traits as aggression, selfishness, and prejudice. In a reformed environment, people can be prevented from learning these habits.

In psychology, behaviorists like John B. Watson and B. F. Skinner simply banned notions of talent and temperament, together with all the other contents of the mind, such as beliefs, desires, and feelings. This set the stage for Watson's famous boast: "Give me a dozen healthy infants, well-formed, and my own specified world to bring them up in, and I'll guarantee to take any one at random and train him to become any type of specialist I might select—doctor, lawyer, artist, merchant-chief, and yes, even beggar-man and thief, regardless of his talents, penchants, tendencies, abilities, vocations, and race of his ancestors."

15   Watson also wrote an influential child-rearing manual recommending that parents give their children minimum attention and love. If you comfort a crying baby, he wrote, you will reward the baby for crying and thereby increase the frequency of crying behavior.

In anthropology, Franz Boas wrote that differences among human races and ethnic groups come not from their physical constitution but from their *culture*. Though Boas himself did not claim that people were blank slates—he only argued that all ethnic groups are endowed with the same mental abilities—his students, who came to dominate American social science, went further. They insisted not just that *differences* among ethnic groups must be explained in terms of culture (which is reasonable) but that *every aspect* of human existence must be explained in terms of culture (which is not). "Heredity cannot be allowed to have acted any part in history," wrote Alfred Kroeber. "With the exception of the instinctoid reactions in infants to sudden withdrawals of support and to sudden loud noises, the human being is entirely instinctless," wrote Ashley Montagu.

In the second half of the twentieth century, the ideals of the social scientists of the first half enjoyed a well-deserved victory. Eugenics, social Darwinism, overt expressions of racism and sexism, and official discrimination against women and minorities were on the wane, or had been eliminated, from the political and intellectual mainstream in Western democracies.

At the same time, the doctrine of the blank slate, which had been blurred with ideals of equality and progress, began to show cracks. As new disciplines such as cognitive science, neuroscience, evolutionary psychology, and behavioral genetics flourished, it became clearer that thinking is a biological process, that the brain is not exempt from the laws of evolution, that the sexes differ above the neck as well as below it, and that people are not psychological clones. Here are some examples of the discoveries.

Natural selection tends to homogenize a species into a standard design by concentrating the effective genes and winnowing out the ineffective ones. This suggests that the human mind evolved with a universal complex design. Beginning in the 1950s, the linguist Noam Chomsky of the Massachusetts Institute of Technology argued that a language should be analyzed not in terms of the list of sentences people utter but in terms of the mental computations that enable them to handle an unlimited number of new sentences in the language. These computations have been found to conform to a universal grammar. And if this universal grammar is embodied in the circuitry that guides babies when they listen to speech, it could explain how children learn language so easily.

20 Similarly, some anthropologists have returned to an ethnographic record that used to trumpet differences among cultures and have found an astonishingly detailed set of aptitudes and tastes that all cultures have in common. This shared way of thinking, feeling, and living makes all of humanity look like a single tribe, which the anthropologist Donald Brown of the University of California at Santa Barbara has called the universal people. Hundreds of traits, from romantic love to humorous insults, from poetry to food taboos, from exchange of goods to mourning the dead, can be found in every society ever documented.

One example of a stubborn universal is the tangle of emotions surrounding the act of love. In all societies, sex is at least somewhat "dirty." It is conducted in private, pondered obsessively, regulated by custom and taboo, the subject of gossip and teasing, and a trigger for jealous rage. Yet sex is the most concentrated source of physical pleasure granted by the nervous system. Why is it so fraught with conflict? For a brief period in the 1960s and 1970s, people dreamed of an erotopia in which men and women could engage in sex without hang-ups and inhibitions. "If you can't be with the one you love, love the one you're with," sang Stephen Stills. "If you love somebody, set them free," sang Sting.

But Sting also sang, "Every move you make, I'll be watching you." Even in a time when, seemingly, anything goes, most people do not partake in sex as casually as they partake in food or conversation. The reasons are as deep as anything in biology. One of the hazards of sex is a baby, and a baby is not just any seven-pound object but, from an evolutionary point of view, our reason for being. Every time a woman has sex with a man, she is taking a chance at sentencing herself to years of motherhood, and she is forgoing the opportunity to use her finite reproductive output with some other man. The man, for his part, may be either implicitly committing his sweat and toil to the incipient child or deceiving his partner about such intentions.

On rational grounds, the volatility of sex is a puzzle, because in an era with reliable contraception, these archaic entanglements should have no claim on our feelings. We should be loving the one we're with, and sex should inspire no more gossip, music, fiction, raunchy humor, or strong emotions than eating or talking does. The fact that people are tormented by the Darwinian economics of babies they are no longer having is testimony to the long reach of human nature.

Although the minds of normal human beings work in pretty much the same way; they are not, of course, identical. Natural selection reduces generic variability but never eliminates it. As a result, nearly every one of us is genetically unique. And these differences in genes make a difference in mind and behavior, at least quantitatively. The most dramatic demonstrations come from studies of the rare people who *are* genetically identical, identical twins.

25   Identical twins think and feel in such similar ways that they sometimes suspect they are linked by telepathy. They are similar in verbal and mathematical intelligence, in their degree of life satisfaction, and in personality traits such as introversion, agreeableness, neuroticism, conscientiousness, and openness to experience. They have similar attitudes toward controversial issues such as the death penalty, religion, and modern music. They resemble each other not just in paper-and-pencil tests but in consequential behavior such as gambling, divorcing, committing crimes, getting into accidents, and watching television. And they boast dozens of shared idiosyncrasies such as giggling incessantly, giving interminable answers to simple questions, dipping buttered toast in coffee, and in the case of Abigail van Buren and the late Ann Landers, writing indistinguishable syndicated advice columns. The crags and valleys of their electroencephalograms (brain waves) are as alike as those of a single person recorded on two occasions, and the wrinkles of their brains and the distribution of gray matter across cortical areas are similar as well.

Identical twins (who share all their genes) are far more similar than fraternal twins (who share just half their genes). This is as true when the twins are separated at birth and raised apart as when they are raised in the same home by the same parents. Moreover, biological siblings, who also share half their genes, are far more similar than adoptive siblings, who share no more genes than strangers. Indeed, adoptive siblings are barely similar at all. These conclusions come from massive studies employing the best instruments known to psychology. Alternative explanations that try to push the effects of the genes to zero have by now been tested and rejected.

People sometimes fear that if the genes affect the mind at all they must determine it in every detail. That is wrong, for two reasons. The first is that most effects of genes are probabilistic. If one identical twin has a trait, there is often no more than an even chance that the other twin will have it, despite having a complete genome in common (and in the case of twins raised together, most of their environment in common as well).

The second reason is that the genes' effects can vary with the environment. Although Woody Allen's fame may depend on genes that enhance a sense of humor, he once pointed out that "we live in a society that puts a big value on jokes. If I had been an Apache Indian, those guys didn't need comedians, so I'd be out of work."

Studies of the brain also show that the mind is not a blank slate. The brain, of course, has a pervasive ability to change the strengths of its connections as the result of learning and experience—if it didn't, we would all be permanent amnesiacs. But that does not mean that the structure of the brain is mostly a product of experience. The study of the brains of twins has shown that much of the variation in the amount of gray matter in the prefrontal lobes is genetically caused. And these variations are not just random differences in anatomy like fingerprints; they correlate significantly with differences in intelligence.

30   People born with variations in the typical brain plan can vary in the way their minds work. A study of Einstein's brain showed that he had large, unusually shaped inferior parietal lobules, which participate in spatial reasoning and intuitions about numbers. Gay men are likely to have a relatively small nucleus in the anterior hypothalamus, a nucleus known to have a role in sex differences. Convicted murderers and other violent, antisocial people are likely to have a relatively small and inactive prefrontal cortex, the part of the brain that governs decision making and inhibits impulses. These gross features of the brain are almost certainly not sculpted by information coming in from the senses. That, in turn, implies that diffences in intelligence, scientific genius, sexual orientation, and impulsive violence are not entirely learned.

The doctrine of the blank slate had been thought to undergird the ideals of equal rights and social improvement, so it is no surprise that the discoveries undermining it have often been met with fear and loathing. Scientists challenging the doctrine have been libeled, picketed, shouted down, and subjected to searing invective.

This is not the first time in history that people have tried to ground moral principles in dubious factual assumptions. People used to ground moral values in the doctrine that Earth lay at the center of the universe and that God created mankind in his own image in a day. In both cases, informed people eventually reconciled their moral values with the facts, not just because they had to give a nod to reality, but also because the supposed connections between the facts and morals—such as the belief that the arrangement of rock and gas in space has something to do with right and wrong—were spurious to begin with.

We are now living, I think, through a similar transition. The blank slate has been widely embraced as a rationale for morality, but it is under assault from science. Yet just as the supposed foundations of morality shifted in the centuries following Galileo and Darwin, our own moral sensibilities will come to terms with the scientific findings, not just because facts are facts but because the moral credentials of the blank slate are just as spurious. Once you think through the issues, the two greatest fears of an innate human endowment can be defused.

One is the fear of inequality. Blank is blank, so if we are all blank slates, the reasoning goes, we must all be equal. But if the slate of a newborn is not blank, different babies could have different things inscribed on their slates. Individuals, sexes, classes, and races might differ innately in their talents and inclinations. The fear is that if people do turn out to be different, it would open the door to discrimination, oppression, or eugenics.

35   But none of this follows. For one thing, in many cases the empirical basis of the fear may be misplaced. A universal human nature does not imply that *differences* among groups are innate. Confucius could have been right when he wrote, "Men's natures are alike; it is their habits that carry them far apart."

More important, the case against bigotry is not a factual claim that people are biologically indistinguishable. It is a moral stance that condemns judging an *individual* according to the average traits of certain *groups* to which the individual belongs. Enlightened societies strive to ignore race, sex, and ethnicity in hiring, admissions, and criminal justice because the alternative is morally repugnant. Discriminating against people on the basis of race, sex, or ethnicity would be unfair, penalizing them for traits over which they have no control. It would perpetuate the injustices of the past and could rend society into hostile factions. None of these reasons depends on whether groups of people are or are not genetically indistinguishable.

Far from being conducive to discrimination, a conception of human nature is the reason we oppose it. Regardless of I.Q. or physical strength or any other trait that might vary among people, all human beings can be assumed to have certain traits in common. No one likes being enslaved. No one likes being humiliated. No one likes being treated unfairly. The revulsion we feel toward discrimination and slavery comes from a conviction that however much people vary on some traits, they do not vary on these.

A second fear of human nature comes from a reluctance to give up the age-old dream of the perfectibility of man. If we are forever saddled with fatal flaws and deadly sins, according to this fear, social reform would be a waste of time. Why try to make the world a better place if people are rotten to the core and will just foul it up no matter what you do?

But this, too, does not follow. If the mind is a complex system with many faculties, an antisocial desire is just one component among others. Some faculties may endow us with greed or lust or malice, but others may endow us with sympathy, foresight, self-respect, a desire for respect from others, and an ability to learn from experience and history. Social progress can come from pitting some of these faculties against others.

40   For example, suppose we are endowed with a conscience that treats certain other beings as targets of sympathy and inhibits us from harming or exploiting them. The philosopher Peter Singer of Princeton University has shown that moral improvement has proceeded for millennia because people have expanded the mental dotted line that embraces the entities considered worthy of sympathy. The circle has been poked outward from the family and village to the clan, the tribe, the nation, the race, and most recently to all of humanity. This sweeping change in sensibilities did not require a blank slate. It could have arisen from a moral gadget with a single knob or slider that adjusts the size of the circle embracing the entities whose interests we treat as comparable to our own.

     Some people worry that these arguments are too fancy for the dangerous world we live in. Since data in the social sciences are never perfect, shouldn't we err on the side of caution and stick with the null hypothesis that people are blank slates? Some people think that even if we were certain that people differed genetically or harbored ignoble tendencies, we might still want to promulgate the fiction that they didn't.

     This argument is based on the fallacy that the blank slate has nothing but good moral implications and a theory that admits a human nature has nothing but bad ones. In fact, the dangers go both ways. Take the most horrifying example of all, the abuse of biology by the Nazis, with its pseudoscientific nonsense about superior and inferior races. Historians agree that bitter memories of the Holocaust were the main reason that human nature became taboo in intellectual life after the Second World War.

     But historians have also documented that Nazism was not the only ideologically inspired holocaust of the twentieth century. Many atrocities were committed by Marxist regimes in the name of egalitarianism, targeting people whose success was taken as evidence of their avarice. The kulaks ("bourgeois peasants") were exterminated by Lenin and Stalin in the Soviet Union. Teachers, former landlords, and "rich peasants" were humiliated, tortured, and murdered during China's Cultural Revolution. City dwellers and literate professionals were worked to death or executed during the reign of the Khmer Rouge in Cambodia.

     And here is a remarkable fact: Although both Nazi and Marxist ideologies led to industrial-scale killing, *their biological and psychological theories were opposites.* Marxists had no use for the concept of race, were averse to the notion of genetic inheritance, and were hostile to the very idea of a human nature rooted in biology. Marx did not explicitly embrace the blank slate, but he was adamant that human nature has no enduring properties: "All history is nothing but a continuous transformation of human nature," he wrote. Many of his followers did embrace it. "It is on a blank page that the most beautiful poems are written," said Mao. "Only the newborn baby is spotless," ran a Khmer Rouge slogan. This philosophy led to the persecution of the successful and of those who produced more crops on their private family plots than on communal farms. And it made these regimes not just dictatorships but totalitarian dictatorships, which tried to control every aspect of life from art and education to child rearing and sex. After all, if the mind is structureless at birth and shaped by its experience, a society that wants the right kind of minds must control the experience.

45   None of this is meant to impugn the blank slate as an evil doctrine, any more than a belief in human nature is an evil doctrine. Both are separated by many steps from the evil acts committed under their banners, and they must be evaluated on factual grounds. But the fact that tyranny and genocide can come from an anti-innatist belief system as readily as from an innatist one does upend the common misconception that biological approaches to behavior are uniquely sinister. And the reminder that human nature is the source of our interests and needs as well as our flaws encourages us to examine claims about the mind objectively, without putting a moral thumb on either side of the scale.

Questions for Active Reading

1. Construct an outline of Pinker's argument, demonstrating how he moves from one point to the next; you could begin by just listing the topic sentences of each paragraph. (This is a useful active reading strategy for understanding difficult or complex texts.) What do you notice about the structure of his essay, once you've reduced it to its basic structure? Does this exercise help you better understand how Pinker moves from one point to the next?

2. Pinker often uses *definition* as a rhetorical strategy, ensuring that his audience is comfortable with specific scientific or philosophical concepts. Find two or three places in his essay where he uses definition. Why does he define these particular terms? How does he use example or illustration to define them?

3. Although Pinker's essay is based on considerable scientific research, and is structurally complex, his introduction is compelling for entirely different reasons. How would you characterize the tone of Pinker's introduction? For whom do you think it was written?

Questions for Thinking Critically

1. Pinker makes a compelling—and controversial—argument about why there is such a universal "tangle of emotions" around sex. Do you agree with his observations? Do you think that men and women might interpret Pinker's observation differently?

2. Why, in Pinker's view, have scientists who work to debunk the "blank slate" idea of human behavior been subject to so much ferocious criticism?

3. Throughout this chapter, you have been examining your beliefs and how you came to hold them. How does Pinker's essay change your understanding of your beliefs? Return to the Thinking-Writing Activity, Evaluating Beliefs, on pages 62 and 63. Could any of those "beliefs" be due to innate human nature? Explain your answer.

Under Water

BY ANNE FADIMAN (b. 1953)

Journalist and essayist Anne Fadiman, the editor of the American Scholar *magazine, won the 1997 National Book Critics Circle Award for* The Spirit Catches You and You Fall Down, *her study of a Hmong immigrant community and their interaction with the American medical establishment. Her writing has appeared in* Harper's Magazine, The New Yorker, *and the* Washington Post, *among other periodicals. In 1987, Fadiman won the National Magazine Award for a series of articles in* Life *magazine on suicide among the elderly. In the following spare, striking essay, Fadiman describes a moment that changed forever a way of believing about the world.*

When I was eighteen, I was a student on a month-long wilderness program in western Wyoming. On the third day, we went canoeing on the Green River, a tributary of the Colorado that begins in the glaciers of the Wind River Range and flows south across the sagebrush plains. Swollen by warm-weather runoff from an unusually deep snowpack, the Green was higher and swifter that month—June of 1972—than it had been in forty years. A river at flood stage can have strange currents. There is not enough room in the channel for the water to move downstream in an orderly way, so it collides with itself and forms whirlpools and boils and souse holes. Our instructors decided to stick to their itinerary nevertheless, but they put in at a relatively easy section of the Green, one that the flood had merely upgraded, in the international system of white-water classification, from Class I to Class II. There are six levels of difficulty, and Class II was not an unreasonable challenge for novice paddlers.

The Green River did not seem dangerous to me. It seemed magnificently unobstructed. Impediments to progress—the rocks and stranded trees that under normal conditions would protrude above the surface—were mostly submerged. The river carried our aluminum canoe high and lightly, like a child on a broad pair of shoulders. We could rest our paddles on the gunwales and let the water do our work. The sun was bright and hot. Every few minutes, I dipped my bandanna in the river, draped it over my head, and let an ounce or two of melted glacier run down my neck.

I was in the bow of the third canoe. We rounded a bend and saw, fifty feet ahead, a standing wave in the wake of a large black boulder. The students in the lead canoe were backferrying, slipping crabwise across the current by angling their boat diagonally and stroking backward. Backferrying allows paddlers to hover midstream and carefully plan their course instead of surrendering to the water's pace. But if they lean upstream—a natural inclination, for few people choose to lean toward the difficulties that lie ahead—the current can overflow the lowered gunwale and flip the boat. And that is what happened to the lead canoe.

I wasn't worried when I saw it go over. Knowing that we might capsize in the fast water, our instructors had arranged to have our gear trucked to our next campsite. The packs were all safe. The water was little more than waist-deep, and the paddlers were both wearing life jackets. They would be fine. One was already scrambling onto the right-hand bank.

5   But where was the second paddler? Gary, a local boy from Rawlins, a year or two younger than I, seemed to be hung up on something. He was standing at a strange angle in the middle of the river, just downstream from the boulder. Gary was the only student on the course who had not brought sneakers, and one of his mountaineering boots had become wedged between two rocks. The other canoes would come around the bend in a moment, and the instructors would pluck him out.

But they didn't come. The second canoe pulled over to the bank and ours followed. Thirty seconds passed, maybe a minute. Then we saw the standing wave bend Gary's body forward at the waist, push his face underwater, stretch his arms in front of him, and slip his orange life jacket off his shoulders. The life jacket lingered for a moment at his wrists before it floated downstream, its long white straps twisting in the current. His shirtless torso was pale and undulating, and it changed shape as hills and valleys of water flowed over him, altering the curve of the liquid lens through which we watched him. I thought, He looks like the flayed skin of St. Bartholomew in the Sistine Chapel. As soon as I had the thought, I knew that it was dishonorable. To think about anything outside the moment, outside Gary, was a crime of inattention. I swallowed a small, sour piece of self-knowledge: I was the sort of person who, instead of weeping or shouting or praying during a crisis, thought about something from a textbook (H. W. Janson's *History of Art*, page 360).

Once the flayed man had come, I could not stop the stream of images: Gary looked like a piece of seaweed, Gary looked like a waving handkerchief, Gary looked like a hula dancer. Each simile was a way to avoid thinking about what Gary was, a drowning boy. To remember these things is dishonorable, too, for I have long since forgotten Gary's last name and the color of his hair and the sound of his voice.

I do not remember a single word that anyone said. Somehow, we got into one of the canoes, all five of us, and tried to ferry the twenty feet or so to the middle of the river. The current was so strong, and we were so incompetent, that we never got close. Then we tried it on foot, linking arms to form a chain. The water was so cold that it stung. And it was noisy — not the roar and crash of white water but a groan, a terrible bass grumble, from the stones that were rolling and leaping down the riverbed. When we got close to Gary, we couldn't see him; all we could see was the reflection of the sky. A couple of times, groping blindly, one of us touched him, but he was as slippery as soap. Then our knees buckled and our elbows unlocked, and we rolled downstream, like the stones. The river's rocky load, moving invisibly beneath its smooth surface, pounded and scraped us. Eventually, the current heaved us, blue-lipped and panting, onto the bank. In that other world above the water, the only sounds were the buzzing of bees and flies. Our wet sneakers kicked up red dust. The air smelled of sage and rabbitbrush and sunbaked earth.

We tried again and again, back and forth between the worlds. Wet, dry, cold, hot, turbulent, still.

10   At first, I assumed that we would save him. He would lie on the bank and the sun would warm him while we administered mouth-to-mouth resuscitation. If we couldn't get him out, we would hold him upright in the river, and maybe he could still breathe. But the Green River was flowing at nearly three thousand cubic feet—about ninety tons—per second. At that rate, water can wrap a canoe around a boulder like tinfoil. Water can uproot a tree. Water can squeeze the air out of a boy's lungs, undo knots, drag off a life jacket, lever a boot so tightly into the riverbed that even if we had had ropes—the ropes that were in the packs that were in the trucks—we could never have budged him.

We kept going in, not because we had any hope of rescuing Gary after the first ten minutes, but because we had to save face. It would have been humiliating if the instructors came around the bend and found us sitting in the sagebrush, a docile row of five with no hypothermia and no skinned knees. Eventually, they did come. The boats had been delayed because one had nearly capsized, and the instructors had made the other students stop and practice backferrying until they learned not to lean upstream. Even though Gary had already drowned, the instructors did all the same things we had done, more competently but no more effectively, because they, too, would have been humiliated if they hadn't skinned their knees. Men in wet suits, belayed with ropes, pried the body out the next morning.

When I was eighteen, I wanted to hurry through life as fast as I could. Twenty-seven years have passed, and my life now seems too fast. I find myself wanting to backferry, to hover midstream, suspended. I might then avoid many things: harsh words, foolish decisions, moments of inattention, regrets that wash over me, like water.

Questions for Active Reading

1. What is "backferrying," and in what two senses does Fadiman use this specialized term in this essay?

2. How does Fadiman build suspense and use foreshadowing?

3. What do you make of the similes in paragraphs 6 and 7? Why does Fadiman write these similes, use this language, if she considers it "dishonorable" to do so?

4. Paragraph 9 contains only two sentences, and yet it is the hinge of the essay. What makes these two sentences so striking, in terms of both their structure and their content?

Questions for Thinking Critically

1. In retrospect, what does Fadiman believe motivated the rescue attempts that she, her friends, and her instructors made to save Gary? How is this realization reflected in her concluding paragraph?

2. What did Fadiman believe in before this experience that she no longer believed in—or, perhaps, wished she still believed in—after the drowning?

3. In some systems or traditions of belief, confession is said to be good for the soul. According to the Oxford English Dictionary, a "confession" is "the disclosing of something the knowledge of which by others is considered humiliating or prejudicial to the person confessing." Is this essay a kind of confession? Who, then, is its true audience?

Writing Project: An Experience That Affected a Belief

The Thinking-Writing Activities and the readings and questions in this chapter have encouraged you to become an active thinker, to examine your beliefs, and to observe how some thoughtful people have reflected on their learning experiences. As you work on this project, reread what you wrote for the activities and think about the events discussed in the readings.

THE WRITING SITUATION

Begin by considering the elements discussed in the Writing Situation section of the Thinking-Writing Model.

Purpose   Your primary purpose in writing this essay is to make clear to your readers what your belief is, narrate your experience in an interesting way, and connect the two effectively. You are not trying to convince your readers that they

> Write an essay telling of an experience that had an important impact on a belief that you held or hold. The belief might be about yourself, about another person involved in the experience, or about the issue that the experience illustrates. The experience may have helped form your belief, changed or strengthened it.
>
> You should explain your belief, of course, and describe the experience, reflecting on what happened as you tell of its effects. You may want to discuss the sources of the belief (see pages 62 and 63). Follow your instructor's directions for length, format, and so forth.

should adopt your belief. You are showing them what your belief is and the impact of your experience. A second purpose is your own increased understanding of your belief, your ability to evaluate that belief, and your larger understanding of other people's beliefs.

Audience When you write about your own experiences, you are an important part of the audience. This form of writing acts as a catalyst for self-discovery by encouraging you to reflect on your past experiences. As you write, your guiding ideas should include these questions:

- How effectively am I communicating the reality of this experience?
- How effectively have I analyzed the significance of this experience and the impact that it had?

You will also be writing for the other readers with whom you'll share this piece of writing. Consider these questions when thinking about their needs:

- How much information about my belief should I include to help my readers to understand it and know where it came from?
- How much would my readers be likely to know about the background of the experience I am writing about? What in that background is important for them to understand?
- What details of the experience should I include to make it real for my readers? What details can I leave out?

In other words, you need to put yourself in your readers' position and view your writing through their eyes.

Subject When you write about your own experience or create an autobiographical narrative, you are using a common and effective means of communication. Real experiences provide living examples, not abstract or hypothetical ideas. Think of how often speakers, writers, and people you know tell about experiences in order to illustrate a point. This assignment demonstrates that interaction. The belief you are writing about is probably a somewhat abstract idea; your experience is real. In a later chapter you will consider narration again and be reminded that a story illuminates an idea, but does not really prove that the idea is true.

Most of us like to learn about what someone did and what they think it means, and most of us enjoy telling of our own experiences. As you think about your many beliefs and your many experiences, try to identify a belief that will interest an audience and an experience that you can represent in sharp detail.

Writer This Writing Project, like the others in Part One of this book, asks you to use your own experience as the basis of an essay. This makes you the authority on the subject, which should give you confidence. Your challenges are to shape your story and to connect it directly to your belief.

THE WRITING PROCESS

One of this book's main goals is to help you know your own writing process, to tap its strengths and to reduce its weaknesses. This project provides a good opportunity for you to reflect on your writing process.

Generating Ideas   Think about a suitable experience to write about. Look for an experience that had a profound effect on your belief and that may have implications for other people's lives. Once you have found your topic, ask yourself questions and make notes about your responses. Questions you might ask include these:

- What happened? Outline the major events of the experience.
- How did you respond? What were your thoughts, reactions, feelings?
- What roles did other people play? Was the location important? Recall specific details about what people did and said, and about the setting, to make your retelling vivid for your audience.
- What was the result of the experience? How did it affect your belief?
- As you reflect on it, what was the experience's value for you? How has it influenced your life?

You may also refer to the questions for generating ideas in Chapter 4.

Defining a Focus   In a few sentences, summarize the main point you wish to make in your essay, given your subject, audience, and purpose. Then evaluate your focus: Is it specific enough for you to convey it clearly in an essay? Is it interesting so that your audience will find it worth reading about? Is it thoughtful so that it serves the purpose of reflection?

At this point, consider whether or not the experience you have chosen is an appropriate subject. If not, you can begin again by looking for another experience to write about.

Organizing Ideas   Think about how you can order the elements of your experience. Will you start at the beginning and describe them chronologically? Or will you start at a later point in time and use a flashback to the beginning of the experience? Where will you include your observations and reflections about the experience: at the end, or at various places throughout?

Drafting   As you translate your ideas, notes, and early versions into coherent writing, you will need to decide how to draft in ways that will help you revise your work effectively. Because the essay you are about to write will have three distinct components—your belief, your experience, and their connections—you may want to draft each component separately and then think about connecting them.

Drafting Hints

1. Spread out all the work you did while generating ideas and drafting a focus so that you can see it while you write the sections of your draft.

2. Draft briskly. You will revise and correct later.

3. If you stop or are interrupted while drafting, be sure to save what you have written.

4. When you return to drafting, reread what you saved to resume the flow of your ideas.

5. Reward yourself when you complete a section of your draft: Take a short break; exercise; have a snack.

Revising One of the very best strategies is to get an audience's reactions to your draft. Your classmates, or peers, can help you see where your draft is already successful and where it needs improvement. If your instructor allows class time for peer review, be sure to have a draft ready so that you can benefit from this activity.

Revising Strategy: Peer Response Groups This activity works best with groups of three or four.

1. The group selects a timekeeper who allots ten minutes to each writer. Regardless of how many response process steps have been completed, after ten minutes the group goes on to the next writer's work.

2. One person begins by reading aloud his or her draft while group members listen.

3. The writer next reads his or her writing aloud a second time. *Do not skip this step.*

4. Group members listen and write notes or comments.

5. The writer then asks each group member this question and jots down their responses: "What questions do you have about my original belief and its sources?"

6. The writer next asks each member these questions and takes notes as each answers: "What questions do you have about the experience I described? What else do you need to know about it?"

7. The writer then asks each member these questions and records their responses: "Do you understand why my belief changed as a result of this experience and what my belief is now? What could I add to make my writing clearer?"

As soon as possible after peer review, you should revise your draft based on your peers' questions and comments. Then, if possible, put it aside for a day or two before continuing with revision.

Reread your revised draft out loud, slowly. Then think about each of the following questions. As you consider ways to improve your draft based on your answers, stop and make changes to your draft before you move on to the next question.

1. How could you improve the first paragraph? How could you get your readers' attention and make them want to read on?

2. How could you improve the order of your draft? Could you rearrange some paragraphs?

3. How could you improve the flow of your draft? Where would transitions help your audience?

4. How could you improve your sentences? Pay particular attention to sentences that are difficult to read aloud. Your audience will have trouble following them! Could you shorten hard-to-read long sentences or write them as two sentences? Where could you use parallel structure to make your sentences more graceful?

Proofreading After you prepare a final draft, check for standard grammar and punctuation. Proofread carefully for omitted words and punctuation marks. Run your spell-checker program, but be aware of its limitations. Proofread again to detect the kinds of errors the computer can't catch.

Your essay should now be completed to the very best of your ability, and, of course, you will need to submit a copy to your instructor by the due date. But also try to share it with other audiences. Would members of your family enjoy reading it? Would other people who were involved in the experience want to know how it affected you? Would someone with whom you currently have a relationship understand you better by reading it?

The following essay shows how a student responded to this assignment.

STUDENT WRITING

HIROMI ISHII'S WRITING PROCESS

When Hiromi Ishii was *generating ideas,* she participated in a class discussion of possible topics, she read student essays done for this assignment last year—which her instructor provided—and she talked with her instructor after class. Several of her classmates and her instructor were quite interested in what she told them about her new belief in logic. They encouraged her to develop that idea. Then Ishii re-enacted part of the experience that she wrote about in her essay. She decided to use the method that she had learned in her previous writing class. This helped with *Defining a Focus and Organizing Ideas.*

Ishii had learned what is regularly taught in composition classes in U.S.

middle schools, high schools, and colleges. You are surely familiar with the clearly stated thesis, the paragraphs with topic sentences, the transitional expressions pointing out connections, and the interesting introduction and strong conclusion. This pattern is sometimes called the "no-fail" method of organization because it usually works and because anybody can learn to use it, as Ishii tells us and then shows us.

A Changed Belief: Using Logic in Study

BY HIROMI S. ISHII

When people tackle difficult subjects of study, what kinds of approaches can they take? I used to take an intuitive approach; all I did was to input information as much as possible and to wait for an idea to come out. However, studying English writing and art history in the United States convinced me of the importance of logic.

When I studied in Japan, the results of my study largely depended on an intuitive approach. There were two reasons for my attitude: my university major and my enlightenment experiences. I majored in Chinese poetry at Nanzan University in Japan. Most of the lectures and assignments were readings of Chinese poems and translations of them. We were expected to be open-minded about the words, but we didn't have to analyze them. In addition, I regarded enlightenment as the Almighty of study. When I struggled with a difficult problem, sudden enlightenment often led me to comprehension of the point. I didn't know how I had gotten an idea, but the result was not bad. Therefore, I tended to rely on my inspirations although I felt that something was missing.

Last year, I came to the United States from Japan and began to study at Montgomery College. The way of study there rocked my attitude to its foundation because I had to face logic.

First, I took courses for reading and writing in English simply because I was a nonnative, and these courses demanded that I think about a process that I had skipped previously. I needed to give strong supporting details for my opinions and to understand methods for writing.

In the writing class, I learned to compose my ideas into paragraphs more strategically than before. In Japan, I used to believe that ability in writing was a kind of gift and the only way to improve was to practice. However, in the English class, using the methods consciously, everyone could achieve a certain writing quality. One method I learned was to put a topic sentence and supporting details in every paragraph. I learned to analyze my writing.

After I finished ESL classes, I took an art history class, and I was convinced again how logic was important. To tell the truth, I started the class still thinking that an intuitive approach was more important than a logical approach in certain areas of study, such as arts and humanities.

The art class instructed me to see art works within their context, to identify the techniques that were used in them, and to understand influences from society and other artists. It was fun to be able to say more than "I love it" about a favorite painting. For example, I learned that using perspective techniques was an important theme for many European artists during the Renaissance period. I learned that Leonardo da Vinci's *Last*

Supper was not only a famous, well-depicted religious painting but also an experimental artwork with the one-point perspective technique. Then, I could compare and contrast the painting with others that had been made during the same period or on the same subject.

Furthermore, I found that setting my own perspective was a great way of organizing information. Previously, after leaving a museum, sometimes I couldn't remember what I had seen because I tried to be neutral about the paintings. In other words, I didn't have a system of organizing them. If I used a certain perspective, such as the period of art history—like impressionism or modernism, I could pick out key paintings and classify them, so it was easier to consult my memory later.

Now, I believe both intuition and logic are necessary to thinking. I still trust an intuitive approach because experience makes me familiar with a subject and enlightenment can come. However, I realize the importance of a logical approach as a very suitable way to work effectively and objectively. For me, using logic is a new way to explain things, and it leads me to the joy of the academic world. With the discovery of logic, my true study has begun at last.

ALTERNATIVE WRITING PROJECTS

- An Author's Change in Belief

  Explain how one of the authors of the readings in Chapter 3 changed, or strengthened one or more beliefs. Be sure to present the author's original belief, what circumstances changed or strengthened it, and what it was after these circumstances. Be sure to give the title and author's name, probably at the beginning of your essay, and be very sure to put quotation marks around any of the author's words that you use.

- A Friend's or Relative's Belief

  Interview a friend or relative about one of that person's most important beliefs. Be sure to prepare your questions ahead of time and write down the answers carefully. Look ahead to later chapters for some guidelines to conducting an interview. Use what your friend or relative tells you as the basis for an essay about this belief, how it developed, and what it means in the life of the person who holds it.

- A Belief That You Have Observed

  Look around your neighborhood or your community. Can you see evidence of some belief in action? For example, is there evidence that people believe in keeping up (or showing off) their homes or gardens or cars? Is there evidence of a belief in helping one's neighbors or in keeping to oneself? Is there evidence of belief in the importance of education? Or political action? Or sports? Or nice clothes? Use your observation as the basis for an explanation of the belief that you have noticed and your thinking about its significance.

4

Thinking Creatively About Writing

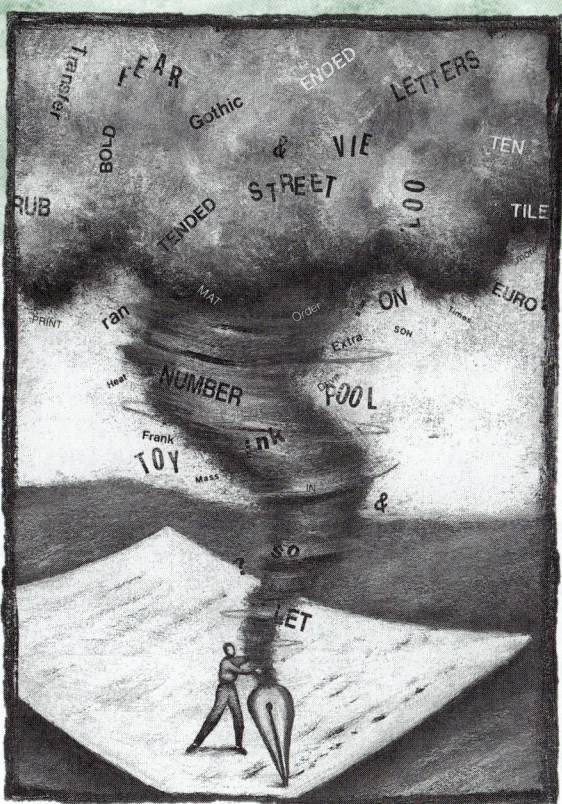

"You must expect the unexpected, because it cannot be found by search or trial." —Heraclitus

Critical Thinking Focus: The qualities of a creative thinker

Writing Focus: Generating original ideas

Reading Theme: The creative thinking process

Writing Project: Imagining your life lived more creatively

Creative Thinking for Expository Writing

Creative writing is often thought of as imaginative fiction, poetry, or drama, for which the author invents characters and situations. So the question naturally arises, what part does creativity have in *expository writing*, in which facts, ideas, and concepts are explored, developed, and argued? The answer: a very large part.

You can use your creative thinking in selecting and narrowing your topic (if you are allowed to pick your own topic), in the way you generate and research ideas, in the way you organize your ideas, and in the way you focus on your ideas with your thesis. You can also use creative thinking to develop your ideas with carefully chosen specific details and examples. You can use creative thinking to develop analogies and metaphors to help your readers grasp your ideas. Finally, you can use creative thinking to write imaginative, inviting introductions that will make your readers eager to read further, and you can use it to write carefully crafted conclusions that tie in elegantly with your introductions. Of course, your critical thinking abilities are also involved in all these steps, helping you to decide which of your creative ideas to include and which to discard.

The challenge to be creative in your writing is a difficult one, but the possibilities for creativity are vast. Focusing on the following four areas for creativity in expository writing will help you further develop the creative thinking abilities you may already have. This chapter deals with the first two.

- Creativity in topic selection
- Creativity in generating ideas, researching, and drafting
- Creativity in using specific details and examples
- Creativity in writing introductions and conclusions

CREATIVITY IN TOPIC SELECTION

The topic of an essay is the subject you write about, one of the four components of the writing situation. Some topics are personal and ask you to draw on your own life experiences, others are impersonal and clearly require research, and still others are a blend of the personal and impersonal. Furthermore, some topics are fairly specific, such as, "Write about your favorite sports figure," or "Write about the effects of the war in Vietnam." Others are more general: "Write about some aspect of political science." A first step is to think creatively about how to shape an assigned topic into one that interests you and that you can handle in the assigned length. A visual way to do this is to "narrow with arrows."

My favorite sports figure → my favorite football player → my favorite quarterback → Brett Favre

Effects of the war in Vietnam → different types of effects → social effects → effects on families of the military → effects on families of MIAs

Political science → elections → recent recall in California → Schwarzenegger's victory → why he won

Notice that at any point, the arrows could take you in a different direction.

My favorite sports figure → my favorite baseball player → my favorite batter → Barry Bonds

Effects of the war in Vietnam → different types of effects → financial effects → effects on the stock market → long-term effects on the stock market

Political science → the last presidential election → what went wrong with the process → intervention by the Supreme Court → constitutional issues raised by the intervention of the Supreme Court.

MOVING FROM TOPIC TO THESIS

A topic is what you are going to write about, and a thesis is what you are going to say about it. Once you have narrowed your topic, try stating it as a question.

Why is Brett Favre my favorite sports figure?

What are the effects of the war in Vietman on the families of MIAs?

How did Arnold Schwarzenegger manage to win the election in California?

If the answer to your question will require research, read as much as you can about the general topic area, looking for ways to modify your tentative topic question or even to change your question altogether. If you are working with a personal topic, begin making notes whether or not you have enough information to answer your question. You can broaden or narrow your topic question as you proceed.

When you think that you have enough information, try answering your question in a complete sentence.

Brett Favre's amazing athletic ability, great leadership skills, and generous contributions to our community make him my favorite sports figure.

The war in Vietnam continues to cast a shadow over our country: the devastating psychological effects on the families of the MIAs.

Arnold Schwarzenegger won the California recall because of the widespread dislike of Gray Davis, Schwarzenegger's prior fame and fortune, and his strategy of avoiding the political press in favor of the entertainment media.

Treat the answer to your question as a tentative thesis, but expect false starts! The fact that your original question needs to be modified or even discarded does not mean that you are doing something wrong. Becoming aware of the need to make these changes is a normal development that most writers experience, so don't become discouraged when it occurs. Instead, congratulate yourself for being willing to put in the time and effort needed for the creative process as you shape your topic.

CREATIVITY IN GENERATING IDEAS

Books about writing sometimes speak as though generating ideas, researching, and drafting are three entirely separate stages, and the writer finishes one stage before beginning the next. This may even be true in some cases, but often writers find themselves getting new ideas while researching or beginning to draft only to realize the need for more research or brainstorming.

Here are some strategies your open and curious mind can use to develop creative ideas in your writing. Your journal or notebook is a good place to practice these strategies.

Brainstorming   **Brainstorming** is an activity in which, working individually or with a group of people, you list all the ideas you can think of related to a given topic. The goal is to produce as many ideas as possible in a specific time period. While you are engaged in this idea-generating process, it is important to relax and let your mind run free.

These guidelines should help you:

- Set a timer and keep thinking until it goes off.
- Go for quantity. You want to generate as many ideas as you can.
- Write down *all* the ideas you generate.
- Build on ideas.
- Don't criticize or discard any ideas.

Imagine, for example, that you are assigned the following topic for a research paper:

There are many problems that students face on college campuses. Identify one such problem and then write a research paper that analyzes the causes of and possible solutions to the problem. Why does the problem occur, and what can be done to deal with it? Your paper should include relevant research findings as well as your own perspective on this problem.

Using the brainstorming strategy with a friend, you might come up with a list that includes the following student problems on your campus:

parking	poor quality of campus food
cafeteria too noisy	classes too large
library closed too early	no comfortable places to study
racial tensions	date rape
abuse of alcohol	use of other drugs
registration a nightmare	tests and papers coming in clumps
not enough social activities	some teachers just lecturing
increasing thefts	books too expensive
not enough financial aid	curriculum not well organized

Mind Maps   **Mind maps** are visual presentations of the various ways ideas can be related to one another. For example, the Thinking-Writing Model is represented as a mind map in Figure 4.1. Mind maps are also a powerful approach for writing, helping you to generate ideas and to begin organizing them into various relationships. They are well suited to the writing process for a number of reasons. First, the organization grows naturally, reflecting the way your mind naturally makes associations and arranges information. Second, the organization can easily be revised to reflect new information and your developing understanding of how it should be organized. Third, you can express a range of relationships among the various ideas. Fourth, instead of being identified once and then forgotten, each idea remains an active part of the overall pattern, suggesting new possible relationships. Fifth, you do not have to decide initially on a beginning, subpoints, and so on; you can do this after your pattern is complete, so you save time and avoid frustration.

These guidelines should help you:

- Draw a circle in the middle of the page, and write your topic in the circle.

- Draw a few lines coming out from the circle, and label them with ideas about your topic.

- See which of your lines you could develop further. Then draw more lines from those, and label them with ideas and details about those aspects of your topic.

- Keep going until you have no more ideas about the topic, or until you see a section of your map developing into a cluster of ideas that you could write about.

For example, imagine that from your list of problems on campus you select "abuse of alcohol" as a paper topic. Your mind map might resemble Figure 4.1.

Freewriting **Freewriting** is a sort of written brainstorming in which you write with a minimum of conscious reflection. But rather than simply list ideas, freewriters usually write in sentences. The goal is to let your ideas flow freely, without inhibition, giving your mind the opportunity to develop creative ideas in unique combinations.

These guidelines should help you:

- Set a timer and keep writing until it goes off.

- Write at a steady, comfortable pace for the entire time. If you get stuck, it is OK to write, "I am stuck, I can't think of any more ideas, I hope I get another idea," until a new idea comes to you. *Don't stop writing!*

- Don't criticize or make corrections.

- After the time limit is up, read carefully what you have written. Think about it for a few minutes. Then try the process again, starting with the most interesting ideas from your first try.

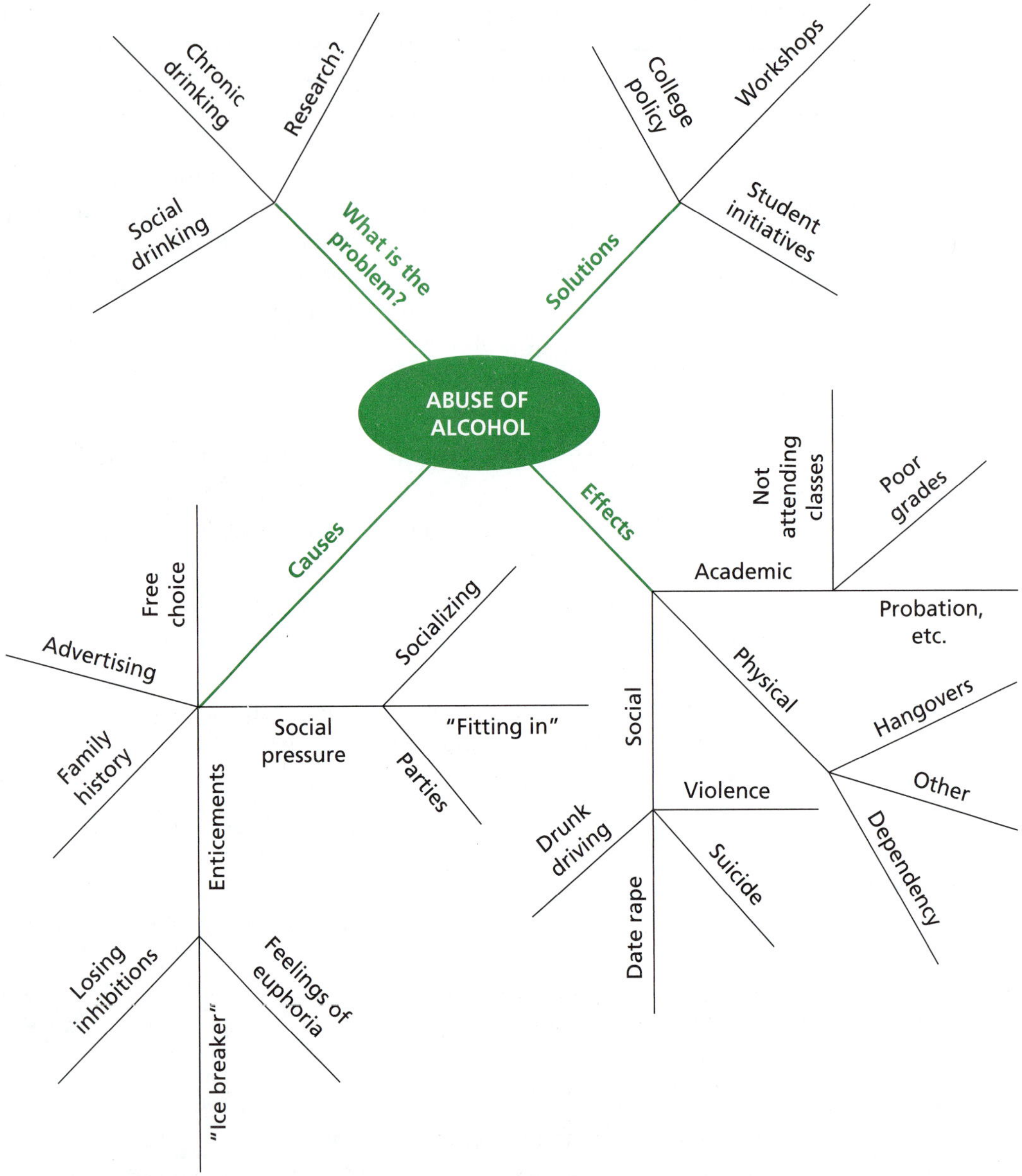

Figure 4.1 Mind Map

An example of freewriting about the problem of alcohol abuse might begin something like this:

Alcohol is a real problem on campus. Every party, that's all people do, is drink too much and then get silly. I think it's ok for people to drink some if they want to. They say it relaxes them and makes it easier to talk to strangers. But it's out of control, and that's a problem. There are a lot of students that drink all the time. They must be failing their classes, they sleep until noon, and they look lousy. There's got to be a better way to socialize and have fun with people besides getting bombed out of your mind. . . .

Questioning **Asking questions** that explore a topic provides another strategy for generating ideas, just as asking questions about a topic supports critical reading. In fact, the ability to ask appropriate and penetrating questions is one of the most powerful thinking/language tools we possess. Asking questions enables us to go beyond the obvious, to think, read, and write in ways that are in-depth, complex, and articulate. Questions come in many different forms and are used for many different purposes. For instance, questions can be classified in terms of the ways people organize and interpret information. The following are six such categories of questions:

1. Fact
2. Interpretation
3. Analysis
4. Synthesis
5. Evaluation
6. Application

Thoughtful writers are able to ask appropriate questions from all of these categories in a very natural and flexible way. Listed next is a summary of the six categories of questions, along with sample forms of questions from each category.

1. **Questions of Fact.** Questions of fact seek to determine the basic information of a situation: who, what, when, where, how, why. These following seek information that is relatively straightforward and objective:

   Who, what, when, where, how, why?

   Describe _____.

2. **Questions of Interpretation.** Questions of interpretation seek to select and organize facts and ideas, discovering the relationships among them. Examples of such relationships include the following:

   Chronological relationships—relating things in time sequence

   Process relationships—relating aspects of growth, development, or change

   Comparison/contrast relationships—relating things in terms of their similar or different features

   Causal relationships—relating events in terms of the way some are responsible for causing others

   These questions can help you discover relationships:

   Can you retell _____ in your own words?

What is the *main idea* of _____?

What is the *time sequence* relating the following events: _____?

What are the steps in the *process of growth* or *development* in _____?

How would you *compare* and *contrast* the features of _____ and _____?

What was/were the *cause(s)* of _____? What was/were the *effect(s)* of _____?

3. **Questions of Analysis.** Questions of analysis seek to separate an entire process or situation into its component parts and understand the relation of these parts to the whole. These questions or statements attempt to classify various elements, outline component structures, articulate various possibilities, and clarify the reasoning being presented:

    What are the *parts* or *features* of _____?

    Classify according to _____.

    Outline/diagram/web _____.

    What *evidence* can you present to support _____?

    What are the *possible alternatives* for _____?

    Explain the *reasons* you think _____.

4. **Questions of Synthesis**. The goal of questions of synthesis is to combine ideas to form a new whole or to arrive at a conclusion, making inferences about future events, creating solutions, and designing plans of action:

    What would you *predict/infer* from _____?

    What ideas can you *add to* _____?

    How would you *create/design* a new _____?

    What might happen if you *combined* _____ with _____?

    What *solutions/decisions* would you suggest for _____?

5. **Questions of Evaluation.** The aim of evaluation questions is to help you make informed judgments and decisions by determining the relative value, truth, or reliability of things. The process of evaluation involves identifying your criteria or standards and then determining to what extent the things being evaluated meet those standards.

    How would you evaluate _____ and what *standards* would you use?

    Do you *agree* with _____? *Why or why not?*

    How would you *decide* about _____?

    What *criteria* would you use to *assess* _____?

6. **Questions of Application.** The purpose of application questions is to help you take the knowledge or concepts you have gained in one situation and apply them to other situations.

How is _____ *an example* of _____?

How would you *apply* this rule/principle to _____?

Thinking ↔ Writing Activity

Generating Ideas

To practice the strategies just presented (brainstorming, mind mapping, freewriting, and asking questions), spend five minutes applying each strategy (choose one set of questions) to one of the following:

Changes you'd like to make in your life

A creative solution to a social problem, such as homelessness or drug use

A creative plan for the perfect house, the perfect party, or the perfect vacation

Additional Tips for Generating Ideas

- When brainstorming, write down every idea, no matter how unusable it may seem at the time.
- When brainstorming, write each idea on a separate Post-it note. (This makes it easy to rearrange them into groups later when organizing them.)
- Phone your voice mail and leave yourself a message if an idea strikes you while you're away from home.
- Speak into a tape recorder and later listen to what you said.
- Talk to other people about your topic. Knowledgeable people will add information; those unfamiliar with the topic will ask useful questions.
- Ask a librarian for research suggestions.
- Note conflicting information or opinions. They are the heart of academic discussion.
- Look in the Yellow Pages for businesses or organizations that can provide information.

- Identify and interview experts on your topic. (Be sure to acknowledge them as sources.)
- Scan the TV schedule, including cable and PBS channels, for related programs.
- Surf the Internet for sources of information.
- When drafting, don't necessarily begin with the introduction. Instead, begin with whatever section is easiest to write.
- Be willing to modify your thesis as you go along so that you don't lock yourself into a position too early.
- Avoid premature organization; draft sections on separate pages or as separate computer files. Then try arranging them in various orders.
- If you are interrupted while drafting, read what you have already written to get back into the flow.

Living Creatively

Human beings have a nearly limitless capacity to be creative; our imaginations give us the power to conceive of new possibilities and to put these innovative ideas into action. Using creative resources in this way enriches our lives and brings a special meaning to our activities. Although we might not go to the extreme of saying that the uncreative life is not worth living, it is surely preferable to live a life enriched by the joys of creativity.

Many people think that being creative is beyond them, that creativity is a mysterious gift bestowed on only a chosen few. One reason for this misconception is that people often confuse being "creative" with being "artistic"—skilled at art, music, poetry, imaginative writing, drama, or dance. Although artistic people are certainly creative, there are an infinite number of ways to be creative that are *not* artistic. Being creative is a state of mind and a way of life. As the writer Eric Gill expresses it: "The artist is not a different kind of person, but each one of us is a different kind of artist."

Are you creative? Yes! Think of all the activities that you enjoy: cooking, creating a wardrobe, raising children, playing sports, cutting or braiding hair, dancing, playing music. Whenever you are investing your own personal ideas, applying your own personal stamp, you are being creative. For example, imagine that you are cooking your favorite dish. To the extent that you are expressing your unique ideas developed through inspiration and experimentation, you are being creative. If, of course, you are simply following someone else's recipe without significant modification, your dish may be tasty—but it is not creative.

Similarly, if your moves on the dance floor or the basketball court express your distinctive personality, you are being creative, as you are when you stimulate the original thinking of your children or make your friends laugh with your own brand of humor.

Thinking ↔ Writing Activity

Recalling a Creative Writing Experience

1. Write about a time when you expressed yourself creatively in writing. It may have been in an important letter, a memorable poem, or even a paper for a school course. Respond to the following questions as you recall the writing experience.

   - What was the writing situation that required your creativity?
   - How did you go about finding a creative idea or approach?
   - Was it successful?
   - How do you feel as you recall this experience?

2. Share your experience with the class and listen carefully to the experiences of other students. On the basis of your own writing experience and those of your peers, make some inferences or general statements about creativity.

Living life creatively means bringing your perspective and creative talents to all the areas of your life. Following are five passages written by students about creative areas in their lives. After reading the passages, complete the Thinking-Writing Activity, which gives you the opportunity to describe a creative area in your own life.

STUDENT PARAGRAPHS ABOUT LIVING CREATIVELY

Creative Cooking

One of the most creative aspects of my life is my diet. I have been a vegetarian for the past five years, while the rest of my family has continued to eat meat. I had to overcome many obstacles to make this lifestyle work for me, including family dissension. The solution was simple: I had to learn how to cook creatively. I have come to realize that my diet is an ongoing learning process. The more I learn about and experiment with different foods, the healthier and happier I become. I feel like an explorer setting out on my own to discover new things about food and nutrition. I slowly evolved from a person who could cook food only if it came from a can into someone who could make bread from scratch and grow yogurt cultures. I find learning new things about nutrition and cooking healthful foods very relaxing and rewarding. I like being alone in my house baking bread; there is something very comforting about the aroma. Most of all, I like to experiment with different ways to prepare foods, because the ideas are my own. Even when an effort is less than successful, I find pleasure in the knowledge that I gained from the experience. I discovered recently, for example, that eggplant is terrible in soup! Making mistakes seems to be a natural way to increase creativity, and I now firmly believe that people who say that they do not like vegetables simply have not been properly introduced to them!

Inventive Child-Rearing

As any parent knows, children have an abundance of energy to spend, and toys or television do not always meet their needs. In response, I create activities to stimulate their creativity and preserve my sanity. For example, I involve them in the process of cooking, giving them the skin from peeled vegetables and a pot so they make their own "soup." Using catalogs, we cut out pictures of furniture, rugs, and curtains, and they paste them onto cartons to create their own interior decor: vibrant living rooms, plush bedrooms, colorful family rooms. I make beautiful boats from aluminum paper, and my children spend hours in the bathtub playing with them. We "go bowling" with empty soda cans and a ball, and they star in "track meets" by running an obstacle course we set up. When it comes to raising children, creativity is a way of survival!

Braiding Hair with Originality

My area of creativity is hair braiding, an activity that requires skill, talent, and patience that is difficult for most people to accomplish. Braiding hair in styles that are being worn today consists of braiding small to tiny braids, and it may include adding artificial hair to make the hair look fuller. It takes anywhere from ten to sixteen hours, depending on the type of style that is desired: the smaller the braids, the longer it takes. In order to braid, I had to learn how to determine the right hair and color for people who wanted extensions, pick out the right style that would fit perfectly on my customers' faces, learn to cut hair in an asymmetrical fashion, put curls in the braids, and know the sequence of activities. Doing hair is a rewarding experience for me because when I am through with my work, my customers think the result is gorgeous!

Creative Construction

After quitting the government agency I was working at because of too much bureaucracy, I was hired as a carpenter at a construction site, although I had little knowledge of this profession. I learned to handle a hammer and other tools by watching co-workers, and within a matter of weeks I was skilled enough to organize my own group of workers for projects. Most of my fellow workers used the old-fashioned method of construction carpentry, building panels with inefficient and poorly made bracings. I redesigned the panels in order to save construction time and materials. My supervisor and site engineer were thrilled with my creative ideas, and I was assigned progressively more challenging projects, including the construction of an office building that was completed in record time.

Imaginative Writing

The most creative area in my life is my writing. I love the thrill of inventing a new person or location, and, although I have a host of characters and story lines, there is one character named Pynthe that I am particularly proud of. Pynthe is not only my favorite character; she is also my most creative. When I invented Pynthe, I did more than just arrange a few words on paper. I gave her dimension. I took a daydream, a glimmer of an idea, and turned it into an individual. From my imagination, I created a fantasy world and religion for my character. I also gave her a past with its share of heartaches and happiness, and a future full of dreams. There is nothing more exhilarating than creating with language. In the extreme, I can destroy my character with two words, or let her lead a long and satisfying life. I can best describe this feeling of creation as a euphoric rush. I love letting my imagination roam, and I easily lose myself in writing, absorbed in the process.

Thinking ↔ Writing Activity

A Creative Area of Your Life

1. Describe a creative area of your life in which you are able to express your personality and talents. Be specific and give examples.

2. Analyze your creative area by answering the following questions:

   - Why do you feel that this activity is creative? Give examples.

   - How would you describe the experience of being engaged in this activity? Where do your creative ideas come from? How do they develop?

   - What strategies do you use to increase your creativity? What obstacles block your creative efforts? How do you try to overcome these blocks?

Spellbound by the Eternal Riddle, Scientists Revel in Their Captivity

BY ALAN LIGHTMAN (b. 1948)

A physicist as well as a writer of fiction and nonfiction, Alan Lightman, a professor at the Massachusetts Institute of Technology, has been fascinated by the intersections of science and art since he was a small boy growing up in Tennessee. As an astrophysicist, he has focused his research on gravitation theory, the structure and behavior of accretion disks, stellar dynamics, radiative processes, and relativistic plasmas. As an educator, however, Lightman has been just as fundamentally engaged with how such arcane and technical concepts can be made comprehensible, even entrancing, to a general audience. "I feel that to most people the scientific culture is like a foreign country," Lightman has said. "I take special delight when I can read a good writer from another culture, bringing me into that world. That's something I would like to do with the scientific culture." Lightman's 1993 novel Einstein's Dreams *has inspired plays and musical compositions, and was a runner-up for the 1994 PEN New England/Boston Globe Winship Award. In 1996 Lightman was elected a fellow of the American Academy of Arts and Sciences and also won the 1996 American Institute of Physics Andrew Gemant Award for linking science to the humanities.*

From an early age, I loved to solve puzzles. When my math teachers assigned homework, most students groaned, but I relished the job. I would save my math problems for last, right before bedtime, like bites of chocolate cake awaiting me after a long and dutiful meal of history and Latin. Then, I would devour my cake.

In geometry, I took pleasure in finding the inexorable and irrefutable relations between lines, angles and curves. In algebra, I delighted in the idea of abstraction, letting x's and y's stand for the number of nickels in a jar or the distance traveled by a train. And then solving a set of connected equations, one logical step after another. Sometimes, when the assigned problems were not challenging enough, I would make up my own problems and seek the solutions.

The biologist Barbara McClintock also enjoyed solving puzzles. In an interview with Evelyn Fox Keller, McClintock recalled that as a child she "used to love to be alone . . . just thinking about things." In high school science classes in Brooklyn, "I would solve some of the problems in ways that weren't the answers the instructor expected," she said. "It was a tremendous joy, the whole process of finding that answer, just pure joy."

Still pursuing that childlike joy in her early 40's, McClintock wondered why some kernels of Indian corn have a mixture of colors, with scattered spots of blue, red and brown. An odd puzzle, seemingly unimportant to anyone except a geneticist.

5   Realizing that the peculiar phenomenon could not be explained by the standard principles of genetic heredity, she began experiments to find an explanation. After five years of work—patient, brilliant, solitary work during which McClintock sometimes spent the fitful nights sleeping on a cot in her lab—she was

led to the unorthodox conclusion that genes are not fixed links in the chain of a chromosome, but instead can change positions, rearrange themselves, and in doing so alter their function. For this revelation, she was awarded a Nobel Prize in 1983.

I believe that scientists of average abilities, like myself, and the great scientists, like McClintock, are propelled by the same forces. Why do I enjoy solving puzzles? I love the mental freedom, letting my mind roam and play. Like an athlete who gets pleasure simply from jogging around the quarter-mile track, I delight in letting my mind run. It feels good to use a machine for what it was designed to do.

I love the purity of problems with a logical solution. And the certainty, which contrasts with so much that is ambiguous and bedraggled in the world of people and society. I guiltily admit that sometimes I have closed the door on a screaming daughter, refused to listen to a dejected friend, and escaped to my little desk with its white pad of paper and lovely equations.

With most problems in mathematics and science, you are guaranteed an answer, as clean and crisp as a new $20 bill. Ever wonder how busy the traffic is on your street at different times of the day? When a scientist ponders such a question, he or she sits by the window with a pencil, paper and clock and records the number of passing cars in each minute interval throughout the day.

Even though science is constantly revising itself, constantly adapting to new information and ideas, at any moment a scientist is studying a more or less definite problem, formulated to lead to a definite answer. That answer is waiting, beckoning, challenging the scientist to find it.

10   In looking back on his early days in science, Einstein wrote that "the nothingness of the hopes and strivings which chases most men restlessly through life came to my consciousness with considerable vitality."

"Out yonder," he continued, "there was this huge world, which exists independently of us human beings and which stands before us like a great, eternal riddle, at least partially accessible to our inspections and thinking. The contemplation of this world beckoned like a liberation . . ."

In addition to the joy of solving riddles, there is the pleasure in craftsmanship. The pleasure in building good and useful things with one's hands. As a professional scientist, I've built only ideas, with equations, but as a child I often built various gadgets, using resistors and capacitors, coils of wire, batteries, switches, photoelectric cells, magnets, chemicals of various kinds. With a thermostat, a light bulb and a padded cardboard box, I constructed an incubator for the cell cultures in my biology experiments.

After seeing the Boris Karloff "Frankenstein" movie, I felt compelled to build a spark-generating induction coil, requiring tedious weeks upon weeks of winding a mile's length of wire around an iron core. Every night, I asked myself the question: Could I make the thing work?

It was a personal question. And that is a paradox of science. Although the truths of science lie outside of human beings, as Einstein said, the motivations for doing science are not only human but intensely personal. Each scientist challenges him or herself at a personal level. Each scientist seeks that challenge, indeed craves that challenge. Each scientist wants to feel his or her own machine revving and rumbling under the hood. Can I build this induction coil? Can I solve this equation? Can I discover the organization of genes?

15   It is a curious I. It is an I that comes in the warm-ups but oddly not during the heat of the race. And there lies another paradox of science. Although some scientists do indeed have astronomical egos and launch themselves toward honors and fame, during the actual moments of scientific discovery, as in all creative discoveries, the ego magically vanishes.

Something else gets under your skin, keeps you working days and nights at the sacrifice of your sleeping and eating and attention to your family and friends, something beyond the love of puzzle solving. And that other force is the anticipation of understanding something about the world that no one has ever understood before you.

Einstein wrote that when he first realized that gravity was equivalent to acceleration—an idea that would underlie his new theory of gravity—it was the "happiest thought of my life." On projects of far smaller weight, I have experienced that pleasure of discovering something new. It is an exquisite sensation, a feeling of power, a rush of the blood, a sense of living forever. To be the first vessel to hold this new thing.

All of the scientists I've known have at least one more quality in common: they do what they do because they love it, and because they cannot imagine doing anything else. In a sense, this is the real reason a scientist does science. Because the scientist must. Such a compulsion is both blessing and burden. A blessing because the creative life, in any endeavor, is a gift filled with beauty and not given to everyone, a burden because the call is unrelenting and can drown out the rest of life.

This mixed blessing and burden must be why the astrophysicist Chandrasekhar continued working until his mid-80's, why a visitor to Einstein's apartment in Bern found the young physicist rocking his infant with one hand while doing mathematical calculations with the other. This mixed blessing and burden must have been the "sweet hell" that Walt Whitman referred to when he realized at a young age that he was destined to be a poet. "Never more," he wrote, "shall I escape."

Questions for Active Reading

1. What similes and metaphors does Lightman use to try to capture the essence of what it's like to have a scientific mind, or to think scientifically? How effective is that figurative language? Could you apply any of that language to some aspect of your own life?

2. Lightman uses an *implied* thesis—that is, a controlling idea that isn't explicitly stated in the first paragraph. In your own words, what is Lightman's thesis?

3. In the last paragraph of his essay, Lightman borrows an *oxymoron* from the poet Walt Whitman. What is an oxymoron (and where is it in that paragraph)? Create an oxymoron of your own to accurately describe a personal passion.

1. In paragraph 15, Lightman describes the "curious I." Throughout this book, we have been examining curiosity as a key characteristic of a critical thinker and thoughtful writer. How does Lightman demonstrate his own curiosity?

2. Lightman describes two paradoxes about being a scientist (in paragraph 14, and in paragraphs 18–19). In your own words, describe those paradoxes. Do either of them apply to an area of your own life? Illustrate your own personal paradox with examples from your own experience, as Lightman does.

3. Does Lightman convince you—if you needed convincing—that scientists are just as "creative" as artists? Why, or why not?

Becoming More Creative: Understand and Trust the Process

Although the forces that discourage you from being creative are powerful, they can nevertheless be overcome with four productive strategies:

- Understand and trust the creative process.
- Eliminate the "Voice of Judgment."
- Make creativity a priority.
- Establish a creative environment.

We each have nearly limitless potential to live creatively, but most people use only a small percentage of their creative gifts. In fact, there is research to suggest that people typically achieve their highest creative point as young children, after which there is a long, steady decline into uncreativity. Why? Well, to begin with, young children are immersed in the excitement of exploration and discovery. They are eager to try out new things, act on their impulses, and make unusual connections between disparate ideas. They are not afraid to take risks by trying out untested solutions; they do not feel compelled to identify the socially acceptable "correct answer." They are not afraid to write stories for fear of making grammar or spelling errors. Children are willing to play with ideas, creating improbable scenarios and imaginative ways of thinking, without fear of being ridiculed.

Reflecting on Past Inhibitions to Creativity

Reflect on your own creative development and describe some of the fears and pressures that inhibit your own creativity. For example, have you ever been penalized for trying a new idea that didn't work out? Have you ever suffered the wrath of the group for daring to be different and violating the group's unspoken rules? Do you feel that your life is so filled with responsibilities and demands that you don't have time to be creative?

Discovering your creative talents requires that you understand how the creative process operates and then have confidence in the results it produces. There are no fixed procedures or formulas for generating creative ideas because creative ideas by definition go beyond established ways of thinking to the unknown and the innovative. As the ancient Greek philosopher Heraclitus once said, "You must expect the unexpected, because it cannot be found by search or trial."

Although there is no fixed path to creative ideas, there are activities you can pursue that make the birth of creative ideas possible. In this respect, generating creative ideas is similar to gardening. You need to prepare the soil; plant the seeds; ensure proper watering, light, and food; and then be patient until the ideas begin to sprout. Following are some steps for cultivating your creative garden.

Absorb yourself in the task: Creative ideas don't occur in a vacuum. They emerge after a great deal of work, study, and practice. For example, if you want to come up with creative ideas in the kitchen, you need to learn more about the art of cooking. The more knowledgeable you are, the better prepared you will be to create innovative dishes. Similarly, if you are developing a creative perspective for a college research paper, you need to immerse yourself in the subject, becoming knowledgeable about the central concepts and issues. Absorbing yourself in the task "prepares the soil" for your creative ideas.

Allow time for ideas to incubate: After absorbing yourself in the task or problem, the next stage is to stop working on it. When your conscious mind stops actively working on the task, the unconscious dimension of your mind continues working—processing, organizing, and ultimately generating innovative ideas and solutions. This process is known as *incubation* because it mirrors the process in which baby chicks gradually evolve inside the egg until the moment when they break out through the shell. In the same way, your creative mind is at work while you are going about your business until the moment of *illumination*, when the incubating idea finally erupts to the surface of your conscious mind. People report that these illuminating moments—when their mental light bulbs go on—often occur when they are engaged in activities completely unrelated to the task. For example, you may suddenly realize how to organize your research paper while you are working out at the gym.

Seize on the ideas when they emerge and follow them through: Generating creative ideas is of little use unless you recognize them when they appear and then act on them. Too often people don't pay much attention to these ideas when they occur, or they dismiss them as too impractical. Have confidence in your ideas, even if they seem a little strange. Many of the most valuable inventions in history began as improbable ideas ridiculed by the popular wisdom. For example, the idea of Velcro started with burrs covering the pants of the inventor as he walked through a field, and Post-it notes resulted from the accidental invention of an adhesive that was weaker than normal. In other words, thinking effectively means thinking creatively and thinking critically. After you use your *creative thinking* abilities to generate innovative ideas, you must employ your *critical thinking* abilities to evaluate and refine those ideas and design a practical plan for implementing them. For example, you should write down your creative idea about organizing your research paper and then begin drafting to see if it will work.

ELIMINATE THE VOICE OF JUDGMENT

The biggest threat to your creativity lies within yourself, the negative **Voice of Judgment (VOJ)**. This term was coined by Michael Ray and Rochelle Myers, the authors of *Creativity in Business*, a book based on a Stanford University course. The VOJ can undermine your confidence in every area of your life, including your creative activities. For example, when you are drafting a paper, the VOJ may whisper:

"This is a stupid idea, and no one will like it."

"Even if I could pull this idea off, it probably won't amount to much."

These statements, and countless others like them, have the ongoing effect of making you doubt yourself and the quality of your creative thinking. As you lose confidence, you become more timid, reluctant to follow through on ideas and present them to others. After a while your cumulative insecurity will discourage you from even generating ideas in the first place, and you will end up simply conforming to established ways of thinking and the expectations of others. In so doing, you surrender an important part of yourself, the vital and dynamic creative core of your personality.

How do you eliminate this unwelcome and destructive inner voice? There are a number of effective strategies. Remember, though, that the fight, although worth the effort, will not be easy.

Become aware of the VOJ: You have probably been listening to the negative messages of the VOJ for so long that you may not even consciously be aware of it. To conquer the VOJ, you first need to recognize it when it speaks.

Restate the judgment in a more accurate or constructive way: Sometimes there is an element of truth in our self-judgments, but we may have blown the reality out of proportion. For example, if you receive a low grade on a writing assignment , your VOJ may say, "You're a failure." But you need to assess the situation accurately: "I got a low grade on this paper—I wonder what went wrong and how I can improve my performance in the future."

Get tough with the VOJ: You can't be a wimp if you hope to overcome the VOJ. Instead, you have to be strong and determined, responding as soon as the VOJ appears: "I'm throwing you out and not letting you back in!" You may feel peculiar at first, but this will soon become an automatic response when those negative judgments appear.

Create positive voices and visualizations: The best way to destroy the VOJ for good is to replace it with positive encouragement. As soon as you have stomped on, say, the judgment "You're a jerk," replace it with "No, I'm an intelligent, valuable person with many positive qualities and talents." Similarly, make extensive use of positive visualization—"see" yourself performing well on assignments, being entertaining and insightful with other people, and succeeding gloriously in your courses and activities.

Use other people for independent confirmation: The negative judgments coming from the VOJ are usually irrational, but until they are dragged out into the light of day for examination, they can be very powerful. Sharing your VOJ with people you trust is an effective strategy because they can provide an objective perspective that will reveal the irrationality and destructiveness of negative judgments.

ESTABLISH A CREATIVE ENVIRONMENT

An important part of eliminating the negative voice in your mind is to establish environments in which your creative resources can flourish. This means finding or developing physical environments conducive to creative expression as well as supportive social environments. Sometimes, working with other people can be stimulating and energizing to your creative juices; at other times, you may need a private place to work without distraction. One writer says, "I have a specific location in which I do much of my writing: sitting on a comfortable couch, with a calm, pleasing view, music on the stereo, a cold drink, a supply of Tootsie Roll Pops. I'm ready for creativity to strike me, although I sometimes have to wait for some time." Different environments work for different writers: You have to find the environment(s) best suited to your own creative process; then make a special effort to do your work there.

The people in your life who form your social environment play an even more influential role in encouraging or inhibiting your creative process. When you are surrounded by people who are positive and supportive, their presence will increase your confidence and encourage you to risk expressing your creative vision. They can stimulate your creativity by providing you with fresh ideas and new perspectives. By engaging in brainstorming, they can help you generate ideas and then later can help you figure out how to refine and implement the most valuable ones.

MAKE CREATIVITY A PRIORITY

Having diminished the negative Voice of Judgment in your mind, established a creative environment, and committed yourself to trusting your creative gifts, you are now in a position to live and write more creatively. But how do you actually do this? Start small. Identify some habitual patterns in your life and break out of them. Choose new experiences whenever possible—for example, order unfamiliar items from a menu, get to know people outside your circle of friends, or deliberately choose a new type of introduction for a paper—and strive to develop fresh perspectives on aspects of your life. Resist falling back into the ruts you were in previously; remember that living things are supposed to be continually growing, changing, and evolving, *not* acting in repetitive patterns like machines.

Where Do Ideas Come From?

Creativity is the process we use to discover and develop ideas that are unusual and worthy of further elaboration. But how do we get creative ideas? Where do they come from? The following reading by a highly creative writer may give us some clues.

FROM

"Experience"

RALPH WALDO EMERSON (1803–1882)

Born in Boston to a distinguished Unitarian family, Ralph Waldo Emerson studied at Harvard University before becoming a Unitarian minister himself. He married young, but after just eighteen months his beloved wife, Ellen Tucker, died of tuberculosis. Emerson's faith was deeply shaken, and he moved to Europe for a brief period. Upon his return to America, he remarried and settled in Concord, Massachusetts. There, Emerson became the philosophical center of a circle of writers, artists, and thinkers who became known as "Transcendentalists." This uniquely American approach to art and the life of the mind is based on the premise that each individual human is uniquely responsible for his or her own happiness, and that mutual respect and individual independence can be balanced in an ideal society. Emerson was an ardent Abolitionist who also spoke out against abuses of Native Americans. His philosophical writings, especially his Essays, *and his political commitments were enormously popular in both the United States and in Europe.*

Where do we find ourselves? In a series of which we do not know the extremes, and believe that it has none. We wake and find ourselves on a stair; there are stairs below us, which we seem to have ascended; there are stairs above us, many a one, which go upward and out of sight. But the Genius which, according to the old belief, stands at the door by which we enter, and gives us the lethe to drink, that we may tell no tales, mixed the cup too strongly, and we cannot shake off the lethargy now at noonday. Sleep lingers all our lifetime about our eyes, as night hovers all day in the boughs of the fir-tree. All things swim and glitter. Our life is not so much threatened as our perception. . . .

If any of us knew what we were doing, or where we are going, then when we think we best know! We do not know today whether we are busy or idle. In times when we thought ourselves indolent, we have afterwards discovered, that much was accomplished, and much was begun in us. All our days are so unprofitable while they pass, that 'tis wonderful where or when we ever got anything of this which we call wisdom, poetry, virtue. We never got it on any dated calendar day. . . . It is said, all martyrdoms looked mean when they were suffered. Every ship is a romantic object, except that we sail in. Embark, and the romance quits our vessel, and hangs on every other sail in the horizon. Our life looks trivial, and we shun to record it. Men seem to have learned of the horizon the art of perpetual retreating and reference. 'Yonder uplands are rich pasturage, and my neighbor has fertile meadow, but my field,' says the querulous farmer, 'only holds the world together.' I quote another man's saying; unluckily, that other withdraws himself in the same way, and quotes me. 'Tis the trick of nature thus to degrade today; a good deal of buzz, and somewhere a result slipped magically in. Every roof is agreeable to the eye, until it is lifted; then we find tragedy and moaning women, and hard-eyed husbands, and deluges of lethe, and the men ask, 'What's the news?' as if the old were so bad. How many individuals can we count in society? how many actions? how many opinions? So much of our time is preparation, so much is routine, and so much retrospect, that the pith of each man's genius contracts itself to a very few hours. The history of literature . . . is a sum of very few ideas, and of very few original tales,— all the rest being variation of these. So in this great society wide lying around us, a critical analysis would find very few spontaneous actions. It is almost all custom and gross sense. There are even few opinions, and these seem organic in the speakers, and do not disturb the universal necessity. . . .

Dream delivers us to dream, and there is no end to illusion. Life is a train of moods like a string of beads, and, as we pass through them, they prove to be many-colored lenses which paint the world their own hue, and each shows only what lies in its focus. From the mountain you see the mountain. We animate what we can, and we see only what we animate. Nature and books belong to the eyes that see them. It depends on the mood of the man, whether he shall see the sunset or the fine poem. There are always sunsets, and there is always genius; but only a few hours so serene that we can relish nature or criticism. The more or less depends on structure or temperament. Temperament is the iron wire on which the beads are strung. Of what use is fortune or talent to a cold and defective nature? Who cares what sensibility or discrimination a man has at some time shown, if he falls asleep in his chair? or if he laugh and giggle? or if he apologize? or is affected with egotism? or thinks of his dollar? or cannot go by food? or has gotten a child in his boyhood? Of what use is genius, if the organ is too convex or too concave, and cannot find a focal distance within the actual horizon of human life? Of what use, if the brain is too cold or too hot, and the man does not care enough for results, to stimulate him to experiment, and hold him up in it? or if the web is too finely woven, too irritable by pleasure and pain, so that life stagnates from too much reception, without due outlet? Of what use to make heroic vows of amendment, if the same old law-breaker is to keep them? What cheer can the religious sentiment yield, when that is suspected to be secretly dependent on the seasons of the year, and the state of the blood? I knew a witty physician who found theology in the biliary duct, and used to affirm that if there was disease in the liver, the man became a Calvinist, and if that organ was sound, he became a Unitarian. Very mortifying is the reluctant experience that some unfriendly excess or imbecility neutralizes the promise of genius. We see young men who owe us a new world, so readily and lavishly they promise, but they never acquit the debt; they die young and dodge the account: or if they live, they lose themselves in the crowd. . . .

The secret of the illusoriness is in the necessity of a succession of moods or objects. Gladly we would anchor, but the anchorage is quicksand. This onward trick of nature is too strong for us: *Pero si muove.* When, at night, I look at the moon and stars, I seem stationary, and they to hurry. Our love of the real draws us to permanence, but health of body consists in circulation, and sanity of mind in variety or facility of association. We need change of objects. Dedication to one thought is quickly odious . . . So with pictures; each will bear an emphasis of attention once, which it cannot retain, though we fain would continue to be pleased in that manner. How strongly I have felt of pictures, that when you have seen one well, you must take your leave of it; you shall never see it again. I have had good lessons from pictures, which I have since seen without emotion or re-mark. A deduction must be made from the opinion, which even the wise express of a new book or occurrence. Their opinion gives me tidings of their mood, and some vague guess at the new fact but is nowise to be trusted as the lasting rela-tion between that intellect and that thing. The child asks, 'Mamma, why don't I like the story as well as when you told it me yesterday?' Alas, child, it is even so with the oldest cherubim of knowledge. But will it answer thy question to say, Because thou wert born to a whole, and this story is a particular? The reason of the pain this discovery causes us (and we make it late in respect to works of art and intellect), is the plaint of tragedy which murmurs from it in regard to persons, to friendship and love. . . .

5   But what help from these fineries or pedantries? What help from thought? Life is not dialectics. We, I think, in these times, have had lessons enough of

the futility of criticism. Our young people have thought and written much on labor and reform, and for all that they have written, neither the world nor themselves have got on a step. Intellectual tasting of life will not supersede muscular activity. If a man should consider the nicety of the passage of a piece of bread down his throat, he would starve. At Education-Farm, the noblest theory of life sat on the noblest figures of young men and maidens, quite powerless and melancholy. It would not rake or pitch a ton of hay; it would not rub down a horse; and the men and maidens it left pale and hungry. A political orator wittily compared our party promises to western roads, which opened stately enough, with planted trees on either side, to tempt the traveller, but soon became narrow and narrower, and ended in a squirrel-track, and ran up a tree. So does culture with us; it ends in head-ache. Unspeakably sad and barren does life look to those, who a few months ago were dazzled with the splendor of the promise of the times. . . . Objections and criticism we have had our fill of. There are objections to every course of life and action, and the practical wisdom infers an indifferency, from the omnipresence of objection. The whole frame of things preaches indifferency. Do not craze yourself with thinking, but go about your business anywhere. Life is not intellectual or critical, but sturdy. Its chief good is for well-mixed people who can enjoy what they find, without question. Nature hates peeping, and our mothers speak her very sense when they say, "Children, eat your victuals, and say no more of it." To fill the hour,—that is happiness; to fill the hour, and leave no crevice for a repentance or an approval. We live amid surfaces, and the true art of life is to skate well on them. Under the oldest mouldiest conventions, a man of native force prospers just as well as in the newest world, and that by skill of handling and treatment. He can take hold anywhere. Life itself is a mixture of power and form, and will not bear the least excess of either. To finish the moment, to find the journey's end in every step of the road, to live the greatest number of good hours, is wisdom. It is not the part of men, but of fanatics, or of mathematicians, if you will, to say, that, the shortness of life considered, it is not worth caring whether for so short a duration we were sprawling in want, or sitting high. Since our office is with moments, let us husband them. Five minutes of today are worth as much to me, as five minutes in the next millennium. Let us be poised, and wise, and our own, today. Let us treat the men and women well: treat them as if they were real: perhaps they are. Men live in their fancy, like drunkards whose hands are too soft and tremulous for successful labor. It is a tempest of fancies, and the only ballast I know, is a respect to the present hour. Without any shadow of doubt, amidst this vertigo of shows and politics, I settle myself ever the firmer in the creed, that we should not postpone and refer and wish, but do broad justice where we are, by whomsoever we deal with, accepting our actual companions and circumstances, however humble or odious, as the mystic officials to whom the universe has delegated its whole pleasure for us. . . .

I know that the world I converse with in the city and in the farms, is not the world I *think*. I observe that difference and shall observe it. One day, I shall know the value and law of this discrepance. But I have not found that much was gained by manipular attempts to realize the world of thought. Many eager persons successively make an experiment in this way, and make themselves ridiculous. They acquire democratic manners, they foam at the mouth, they hate and deny. Worse, I observe, that, in the history of mankind, there is never a solitary example of success,—taking their own tests of success. I say this polemically, or in reply to the inquiry, why not realize your world? But far be from me the despair which prejudges the law by a paltry empiricism,—since there never was a right endeavor, but it succeeded. Patience and patience, we shall win at the last. We must be very suspicious of the deceptions of the element of time. It takes a good deal of time to eat or to sleep, or to earn a hundred dollars, and a very little time to entertain a hope and an insight which becomes the light of our life. We dress our garden, eat our dinners, discuss the household with our wives, and these things make no impression, are forgotten next week; but in the solitude to which every man is always returning, he has a sanity and revelations, which in his passage into new worlds he will carry with him. Never mind the ridicule, never mind the defeat: up again, old heart!—it seems to say,—there is victory yet for all justice; and the true romance which the world exists to realize, will be the transformation of genius into practical power.

Questions for Active Reading

1. What anecdotes, examples, and illustrations from everyday life does Emerson give to support his argument? Do these examples make it easier to understand his argument?

2. Emerson asks many rhetorical questions in this essay, especially in paragraph 3. Does he intend for you, the reader, to answer these questions? Are they provocative or troubling?

3. Using the reading strategies in Chapter 2, annotate these excerpts from "Experience." How does rereading the essay assist you in better understanding Emerson's argument? What do you perceive more clearly after a deliberate second (or third) reading?

Questions for Thinking Critically

1. Emerson advises: "Do not craze yourself with thinking, but go about your business anywhere. Life is not intellectual, but sturdy." Where does Emerson find his own inspiration, his own will to keep on living? Is this a kind of "creativity"?

2. Emerson makes a keen observation about human nature and the tricks of the imagination in paragraph 2. What is his main point? Do you agree? Can you think of other sayings or proverbs that capture this same idea?

3. How would you summarize Emerson's approach to balancing the life of the mind and the life of "the city and in the farms"? Why is this balance important to Emerson, and how does it encourage creativity (or "sanity and revelations," as Emerson says)?

Writing Project: Imagining Your Life Lived More Creatively

According to a French proverb, "Only he who does nothing makes a mistake." The chapter's Writing Project asks you to think creatively to imagine changes in your life. Doing this can, in fact, be very difficult. But it is important to do to avoid future regrets; often people most regret the things they did not do as they lived their lives.

> Imagine how some part of your life could be more satisfying or exciting. You will need to focus on one or more specific areas of your life, such as an important relationship, your college work, or a job that would be ideal for you. Visualize how your future will be when you creatively transform this part of your life, and think about what you must do in the present to achieve this imagined goal. Follow your instructor's directions for length, format, and so on.

THE WRITING SITUATION

Begin by considering the key elements of the Thinking-Writing Model.

Purpose   Your purpose is to use the strategies for thinking, living, and writing this chapter presents to create a new vision of your own life. Doing this will require you to step back from your life, to become an observer of how you have lived, or are living, or might be living, and then to create a potentially different vision.

Audience   You have an interesting and varied audience. You are your own most important audience, for who else could be more interested in the subject? Beyond yourself, you may choose to show your writing to key people in your life, especially if any of them would be affected by the changes you propose. Their reactions to early drafts could be very helpful as you revise.

Your classmates may be part of your audience if your writing is going to be shared with them. All the readers mentioned so far will be interested in what you say, and especially in the changes you propose, so include enough background information about how your life was, or is, for them to understand the impact of those changes.

Subject Thinking and writing about our own lives can be exciting yet challenging. Often we are so busy just living our lives that we don't take time to think about how they might be different. We begin to think that whatever *is* has to be.

A potential problem is that you may believe that there is little in your life that can be changed. You are not necessarily being asked to propose major changes. What you end up writing about could be a different life or simply a richer, more fully realized version of your life now.

Writer As the expert on your own life, you write with authority on this project. If you are the creative type, you should welcome the chance to let your imagination go! If you consider yourself unimaginative, take this opportunity to develop your creative side.

THE WRITING PROCESS

The following sections guide you through the stages of the writing process. Try to be particularly conscious of how creative thinking can help you discover and connect ideas.

Generating Ideas Review your responses to the Thinking-Writing Activities in this chapter. You will probably see a number of ideas that pertain to this project. Then, to discover more ideas and a possible focus, follow these suggestions and jot down your responses.

- Think about two or three things you do that are particularly important to you. How might they become more satisfying if you became more creative in your approach?
- Envision your life five years from now. What activities do you hope to be involved in? How could they be shaped by creative thinking? What would your ideal job situation be?
- Recall an event from the past in which you experienced a creative breakthrough. What was your flash of insight? Can you apply that creative insight to your current situation or future life?
- Choose a situation and brainstorm or ask questions about it.
- Talk to friends or family members about your ideas to see if they have suggestions.
- Ask yourself if you have enough ideas to begin drafting your paper. If not, you may want to try again by examining another aspect of your life.

Defining a Focus After reviewing the material you created, consider which area of your life would be most exciting to focus on. Then write a few sentences about that change. For example:

> I think that I would like to be a more creative cook. Why? How? So that my housemates and I can have more enjoyable meals when it's my turn in the kitchen; so that I can really enjoy cooking. . . . Some ways that I can do this is to take a cooking course, check some really different cookbooks out of the library—like from other countries or other regions, or vegan, or barbecue. I should spend some time with my uncle who makes such good one-dish meals, find some tasty web sites, and watch some of those cooking shows instead of surfing away.

This writer has a focus: becoming a more creative cook. She can now decide how to draft the thesis—as a simple statement or a "blueprinted" sentence that lays out the organization of the paper.

Simple statement: I want to change my life by becoming a more creative cook.

Blueprinted sentence: I plan to become a more creative cook by taking a cooking course, checking some good cookbooks out of the library, spending more time with my uncle, finding some tasty web sites, and watching some cooking shows.

If you do write a blueprinted sentence, consider whether you have listed the changes in an order that your audience can easily comprehend. Once you have established an order, use it to structure your essay.

Organizing Ideas After you have decided on a focus, you can

- describe your current or past situation
- describe some changes you would like to make or wish you had made
- describe the improved situation

Does this thinking suggest a method of organization? Is that organization effective, or is it too stodgy for a paper about creative thinking? How about narrating the events from a future perspective, after you have made some changes?

Map out an organizational plan that you think might work. Consult with your instructor if you are taking a creative approach to organization.

Drafting As you translate your ideas into coherent writing, you need to draft in ways that will help you revise effectively. Because the essay you are about to write will have three distinct components—your present situation, the changes you would make, and how your life would be different—you may want to draft each component separately and then think about connecting them.

Drafting Hints

1. If you are drafting on a word processor, double or even triple space. Be sure to save your work every few minutes if your program does not do so automatically.

2. Consider drafting the three components of this essay as three separate files. You could name them "Present Situation," "Changes," and "New and Different Life." Then you can easily copy and paste them to see what organization would work best.

3. If you are drafting by hand, skip lines and write on only one side of the paper. That way you can easily rearrange them if you decide to re-organize.

Revising One of the best revision strategies is to get an audience's reactions to your draft. Your classmates can help you see where your draft is already successful and where it needs improvement. If your instructor allows class time for peer review, have a draft ready.

Revising Strategy: Peer Response with Silent Writer This activity, which works best with groups of three or four, introduces a different method for peer review than the one in Chapter 3. In this method, the writer is silent after reading the draft aloud twice and listens as peers respond. Follow all the steps of the directions carefully.

1. The group selects a timekeeper, who allots ten minutes to each writer. Regardless of how many steps in the response process have been completed, after ten minutes the group moves on to consider the next writer's work.

2. One person begins by reading his or her draft aloud while group members listen, giving the writer their full attention.

3. The writer then reads the draft aloud a second time. Group members listen again, this time taking notes.

4. Group members read their comments to the writer. Responses that are stated as "I" messages and are geared to helping the writer to revise work well:

   Weak response: "I like it. It sounds okay to me." (*no specific help given to writer*)

   Marginally useful: "I thought the description of your new neighborhood was entertaining." (*encouragement for the writer*)

   Useful: "Can you give me an example of the kind of task you would perform in your new job?" (*The writer learns what information the reader needs.*)

Very useful: "I was confused when you said your aunt came into the room. I thought you said earlier that you were alone in the house." (*Again, the writers hear from someone who wasn't there when it happened, someone who needs more information.*)

5. The writer listens to questions and comments and may take notes but does *not* answer or respond aloud. The writer may ask questions after all group members have commented.

6. Continue the process until each group member has used ten minutes of response time.

As soon as possible after peer review, you should revise your draft based on your peers' questions and comments. Then, if possible, put it aside for a day or two before continuing.

Reread your revised draft out loud, slowly. Think about each of the following questions.

1. How could you improve your thesis?

2. How could you improve the order of your draft? Here you need to balance creativity against the needs of your readers. Is there a more creative way to arrange your essay without sacrificing the needs of your readers?

3. Could you provide transitions between sections of your essay to help your readers follow your ideas?

4. Is your use of language creative? Could you provide more specific adjectives and adverbs?

5. Have you given your essay an inventive title that will make your readers want to read it?

Editing and Proofreading To prepare a final draft, edit for standard grammar and punctuation. Proofread carefully to detect omitted words and punctuation marks. Run your spell-checker program, but be aware of its limitations. Finally, ask someone you trust to proofread after you are finished.

The following essays show how two students responded to the idea of living their lives more creatively. Before writing, each of them used one of the methods on pages 108–109 for generating ideas.

STUDENT WRITING

JESSIE LANGE'S WRITING PROCESS: FREE WRITING

I have to write a paper about a legend I didn't even understand. There are stairs going up a tower to a place that is a kind of nirvana, a place of happiness, but you can only reach the top if you don't believe in the legend itself. Hello? If you don't believe it, why would you spend your time climbing up? OK, OK, I needed to think. Usually getting out-side helps me think better so I tried that up at our place in the country. I did have a great experience. I saw some deer in the mist at night. They were really hard to see and when I put up my lamp to get more light, instead of seeing them better, they almost disappeared in the light. So I turned out the light and I could see them better in the dark. I'm thinking that maybe this is like the legend. The opposite of what you would ex-pect happens. Maybe the legend is about trying too hard. I'll try this angle and see what happens.

Discovering Creativity by Not Looking for It

BY JESSIE LANGE

There have been numerous times when I have sat in front of a blank computer screen, a writing assignment in hand, feeling completely uninspired and uncreative. Without hav-ing even begun I think, "Now what?" There have been numerous times when I've just started filling up that screen with meaningless, dry words that really have no effect on me or anyone else. Yes, I'm getting the job done, but not the job I'd like—not my best work, not anywhere near it. One thing that I've found in my life is that in your most uncreative ruts sometimes you can't pull yourself out all on your own. You can't always, sitting in an idea-less vacuum, turn on the creativity. Sometimes you will save yourself time and produce a much more fulfilling piece of work if you take the time out to go *out* of the world of your blank screen. For me this has always meant literally getting outdoors, be-cause somehow it always seems that I find *outside* what I've been looking for *inside*.

It was the first English assignment of my senior year of high school—an interpreta-tion of a Buddhist legend—and I was struggling with its meaning. The legend is about a set of stairs leading to the top of the tower from where you can see the "whole horizon" and the "loveliest landscape"—a symbol of attaining nirvana. The paradox in the legend is that you can only reach the top if you do not believe in the legend itself. How would those who believe, then, ever reach the top? How can you even start the climb without making the conscious decision to do so?

Being in the country on weekends has many benefits, one of them being that I could go outside to clear my head. I lit my Williams Sonoma oil lamp and walked out into the night that offered the occasional drizzle and a strong breeze that ruffled the leaves of the tree I lay down under. I was there for an hour, feeling the drops on my face and the damp-ness settling into my body, before it happened. I rolled over and looked out into the field, because I sensed something the way that you can and will when you're listening with your entire body. Farther out, right before the lawn becomes high grass and eventually woods, were four white shapes moving across my line of vision. The same deer I casually glance at during the day were like ghosts grazing out there at night. Just faint, light vaporous fig-ures against the pitch black. That moment was like seeing the "whole horizon." Those an-imals, moving with such grace, were unaware of my presence. For all they knew, I was another tree silently overseeing their nightly ritual. Watching these beasts—because that's what they are, wonderfully wild animals—I was witnessing a scene that could have taken place in this same spot on this same night hundreds or thousands of years before.

I reached for my lantern and turned up the flame, holding it in front of me for a better view. This light, however, obstructed my vision rather than illuminating it. It was only when I put the flame aside and cupped my hands around my eyes, creating a deeper darkness, that I could really see the deer.

And then I realized that perhaps that was why only those who do not believe the legend ever climb the stairs of the tower—because when you actively search for things, like holding the light, perhaps you prevent yourself from seeing them. Had I not put my writing aside and taken that walk, I would never have found this answer, the answer I was looking for. I wrote my English essay and I also learned something about creativity in my own life. Some of your most creative moments happen when you're not looking. In the journey up the steps of the tower toward creativity, sometimes it is not those who are keenly searching for a victory of sorts, but those who are instead turning down the light, that begin the climb.

STUDENT WRITING

STEPHANIE MOSES'S WRITING PROCESS: BRAINSTORMING

the creative voice inside my head
keeps me up, makes me mad
has a big head, wants attention
wants to be listened to, to get out
lies
or not?
comes up with fiction?
my occasional lies—dentist, SAT scores
lying to people you don't know
future creative writing classes
fiction professor lies about job
a writing job

The Voice

BY STEPHANIE H. MOSES

I lie in my bed. For the last two hours I have been trying to fall asleep. My roommates are being too loud. It isn't all their fault that I'm still awake, though. It's the voice. From within I hear many different dialogues. Words pop in and out of my head to form sentences that mean nothing to me. Without proper guidance, the voice can be a nuisance. It beckons me to go to my computer. *I am talking to you,* it says. *I want to say something important. Get up and let me be realized!* But I stay in bed. I fight it. I once learned to give the dialogues a representation, and visualize picking them up and putting them in a jar one at a time. Then close the jar, and the voices will be silent. This doesn't work for me. The voice always fights back. *I am stronger than this jar. I can break it to pieces from within, and your head will be filled with pieces of broken glass forever.* So I let it talk to me with the hope that it will either run out of things to say or develop laryngitis. If

I am lucky and it stops before three a.m., I can still get five hours of sleep before class in the morning.

Next quarter I will be taking two writing classes, and I know that I will not be kept awake at night by the voice. I will have to go in search of it, and the blank Word document will mock my pain and remind me of the time when the voice came without summons. *Remember when you lay in your bed all night, trying to ignore the voice,* my computer will say. *You had so much to write, but not one single creative writing assignment.* I could've opened my journal and written something. I could've turned on the computer and let the voice free flow. I could've reworked an old piece with the hope of submitting it to a contest or a magazine. Even reading a book would've turned down the voice's tenacious spirit and quenched my creative desires.

For me writing is not only a necessity—the alternative being insanity—it is also a private realm in which I can create an outcome to my liking. I interweave experiences from real life that I dislike with fantasy and the hypothetical. This induces in me a sense of justice. The person who was wronged is avenged. The world is set right once again.

Every person I have met that wants to be a serious writer is intrigued with lying. A poet once told me that he lies about everything when he gives speeches to people that he doesn't know. My fiction professor is the same way: when he meets people, he tells them that he works for NASA. I too am captivated by telling the occasional lie. I have been known to tell people that I am a dentist, my mother is Spanish and this is why I am bilingual, and that I got a perfect score on the SATs. Being able to pull off a lie is living fiction. After all, it is not me that comes up with these ideas; it is the voice inside. It fights with reality and wins.

My voice has a big head. It wants to be doted on, adored; it wants to be the main focus of my life and the only source of my income. This is the path that I want to follow into the future, not the path to insanity. I will submit my short stories to literary magazines. I will apply to MFA programs throughout the country. I will listen to my voice and feed it with creativity. I know it will give me sensational writings in return. If I cannot get by just writing novels, I hope to find a job in which writing is a major component. For me, the type of writing doesn't matter, so long as the voice is being heard and is communicating with me at decent hours.

ALTERNATIVE WRITING PROJECTS

1. Write an essay explaining your original, creative solution to a physical problem, one involving a piece of equipment, the use of space, overcoming some barrier, and so on. Here are some examples:

   - Crowd control or better seating at concerts and sporting events
   - A device that makes some activity easier or more accessible for the disabled
   - New design or redesign of highways and roads in your area
   - An imaginative new tool or transportation device

2. Write an essay explaining your original, creative solution to a social problem, such as homelessness, tensions between racial groups, or drug use among young teenagers.

3. Write an essay explaining your original, creative plan for the perfect house, the perfect party, or the perfect vacation.

5

Making Decisions and Drafting

"The strongest principle of growth lies in human choice." —George Eliot

Critical Thinking Focus: Decision making in writing and in life

Writing Focus: Making decisions about drafts

Reading Themes: Extraordinary decisions

Writing Project: Analyzing a decision to be made

A decision is a kind of commitment. You make decisions, of varying degrees of importance and impact, every day of your life. How carefully you approach that moment of decision, how thoughtfully you evaluate your choices, and how meaningfully you follow through on your commitment to what you have decided varies with the degree of that decision's importance. For example, a knowledgeable and open-minded evaluation of your current lifestyle might lead you to decide to make a few fundamental changes—you might get more exercise, resolve to drink less on the weekends, opt for salad instead of fries. Your decision to live more healthfully might be based on the advice of your doctor and the example set by an athletic friend, but until you *commit* yourself to that decision, you're never going to succeed at lowering your cholesterol or waking up refreshed on Monday morning.

When you decide on a topic for an essay, you are also making a commitment. In the previous chapter, we looked at the process of deciding on a topic—engaging your creativity, your curiosity, your open-mindedness and your knowledge in order to *decide* on the most engaging and appropriate topic for you to write about. In this chapter, we'll examine strategies for following through on that decision, applying those same four qualities to the decision making inherent in each stage of the drafting process.

In addition, this chapter includes essays by and about people forced to make extraordinary decisions under the most perilous circumstances. Their insight, creativity, strength, and thoughtfulness are truly inspiring.

Decisions While Drafting

Most decisions made while drafting a piece of writing are not made in a first this, then that, sequential order. As Chapter 1 points out, writing processes are usually recursive. Ideas are generated, drafts are made, more ideas come, revisions are necessary, more planning, maybe more drafting—back and forth until the writer says this is it. However, throughout this recursive process, writers must make decisions on subjects, audiences, purposes, and specific ideas and words.

Actually, there is a *first decision*. That is, of course, to take the step from generating ideas to drafting. Some people do this easily; others postpone it. You need to understand your own tendency here and be sure to have some strategies that get you going. Some of the strategies in Chapter 4 used to generate ideas are also useful for beginning to draft. For example,

- *Focused freewriting.* Writing freely on the selected topic can get a draft started, especially if the writer resolves to write and not stare at the screen or the blank page.
- *Listing ideas about the topic and then expressing the ideas in sentences.*
- *Deciding to write on the topic for a set amount of time,* maybe one-half hour.
- *Deciding to draft a specific section first,* usually the one you know most about.

Once you start drafting, you will face other decisions.

Decide What Your Purpose Is   Usually in college and at work, the purpose is clear. You want to complete the lab report or the English paper to fulfill the assignment as well as you can; or you want your proposal or your application to be accepted. However, if you are composing an email to go to your family list about reunion plans or a letter to the editor about a community problem, you might need to define your purpose. Do you want family members to help? Do you want the city council to act?

In your notebook or a separate file, write a sentence beginning "My purpose(s) for this (essay, email, memo) are . . ." and list them. Then write a sentence beginning "In order to fulfill my purpose, I should . . ." You are the audience for these sentences and those following the other decisions. These sentences will almost surely not be part of your draft. They will help you decide what to include.

Decide Who Your Audience Is and What Its Needs Are

As with purpose, the primary audience is often obvious in college and workplace writing—the professor or the supervisor—but your classmates and fellow workers might be an audience, too. You often know what those audiences expect since assignments and office formats are usually explicit. If you are writing for family members or community groups, as you draft you should think about what background information is necessary or superfluous, what tone is suitable, what level of vocabulary is appropriate, and what special needs that audience may have.

In your notebook or a separate file, write a sentence beginning "My audience is . . . Then write a sentence beginning, "My audience will expect . . .; my audience will need to know . . .; my audience will already know . . ."

Decide on a Tentative Thesis

This is a time to be open-minded. After some drafting, you need to think again about the thesis you may have started with or think about formulating one if you have not yet done so. Reread the material in Chapter 4 about moving from a topic to a thesis statement. As you continue to draft, you will decide exactly how to state it and where to place it.

In your notebook or a separate file, write a sentence beginning "As I see it now, the thesis for this piece is . . ." Then write "Or perhaps it is better said as . . ."

Decide What Information to Use and What More You Need

Review your idea-generating activities. Look again at your tentative thesis. What information do you need to support it and to fulfill your purpose? Think about what you know; think about what you should know more about. Think about what your audience needs to know. The Critical Reading Questions of Interpretation, Analysis, and Evaluation in Chapter 2 can be helpful in this decision.

In your notebook or a separate file, write a sentence beginning "The ideas about . . . are important to my thesis." Then a sentence beginning "I need to know more about . . ." Then a sentence beginning "My audience needs to know . . ."

Decide When to Outline to Bring Order to Your Draft

Some writers make an outline or a plan before drafting; some writers outline after drafting; some writers do not outline but revise and redraft until they are satisfied with the organization of the piece.

A rough outline, which indicates the order of sections but is not carefully formatted, usually helps a draft get into shape. Sometimes, a draft benefits from being outlined more than once. Formal outlines, with logical patterns of letters, numbers, sentences, and phrases, can be done when a piece is close to finished. See your handbook for formal outline specifications if you are asked to do one or if you want to be very sure about your paper's organization.

In your notebook or a separate file, outline the material in your draft, using an informal or a formal system as you find helpful.

Decide on an Introduction and a Conclusion   Although you will look carefully at these parts of your draft as you revise and probably refine them then, don't forget to work out possible beginnings and endings as you draft.

Explore as many different types of introductions and conclusions as you can if you are writing something for which there can be choices. (Some kinds of writing, such as lab reports, have expected formats that include types of beginnings and endings.)

Following are some types of beginnings:

- Background information or context
- A relevant anecdote
- A quotation or proverb that relates to the topic
- A striking statement (to be contradicted or supported)
- The problem to be addressed in the paper
- Questions connected to the content of the paper
- The who, what, where, when, how, and why of the paper's focus
- The claim, thesis, or main point
- Combinations of these types

Explore the many possibilities for endings, such as:

- A summary of the paper's information
- A recommendation or call for action
- An apt quotation or proverb
- A telling anecdote
- The thesis or main point restated or stated at the end instead of the beginning
- A suggestion of the need for more discussion of the issue

A conclusion must provide a sense of closure to the piece; readers should recognize it as an ending (you should not have to write "The End"!).

Neither introductions nor conclusions should be apologetic ("I don't know much about this, but . . ."); nor should their tone differ from that of the body of the paper.

Decisions in Your Life

Throughout your life you will continue to make decisions and to deal with decisions others make that affect your life. Recalling a previous decision about your education, your relationships, your athletic activities, or any other part of your life will remind you of how important those choices are.

Analyzing a Previous Decision

Think back to an important decision you made that turned out well and describe the experience as specifically as possible by reconstructing the reasoning process you used to make your decision.

- How did you *define* the decision to be made?
- What *choices* did you consider?
- What were the various *pros and cons* of each possible choice?
- What specific plan of action did you use to implement your ideas?
- How did you review your decision to make any necessary adjustments?

Using a method to help you decide about important issues will help you make intelligent decisions and avoid poor choices.

AN ORGANIZED APPROACH TO MAKING DECISIONS

As you were reflecting on the successful decision you wrote about in the previous Thinking-Writing Activity, you probably noticed your mind working in a systematic way as you thought your way through the decision-making process. Of course, we often make important decisions with less thoughtful analysis by acting impulsively and are later forced to cope with the consequences. Our intuitions can be a useful guide to success when they are *informed intuitions*—based on lessons learned from past experience and thoughtful reflection. Naturally, there are no guarantees that careful analysis will lead to a successful result—there are often too many unknown elements and factors beyond our control. But we can certainly improve our success rate by becoming more knowledgeable about the decision-making process.

This approach consists of five steps. As you master these steps, you will be able to apply them in a natural and flexible way.

STEP 1: DEFINE THE DECISION AND ITS GOALS CLEARLY

This seems like an obvious step, but decision making frequently goes wrong at the starting point. For example, imagine that you are trying to decide on a major. In order to make an informed decision, you have to project yourself into the future, imagining the career that will be right for you. Your goals will likely include

- financial security
- personal fulfillment
- an opportunity to make use of your special talents
- employment opportunities and job security

Keeping these goals in mind as you consider various majors will give you the greatest success in discovering the field that best suits you. The more specific your definition of the decision—and its goals—is, the clearer your analysis and the greater the likelihood of your success will be. Here's a strategy you can use to best define your decision:

   Strategy: *Write a one-page analysis describing your decision-making situation that defines your goals as clearly and specifically as possible.*

STEP 2: CONSIDER ALL POSSIBLE CHOICES

Successful decision makers explore all possible choices, not simply the obvious ones. In fact, the less obvious choices often turn out to be the most effective ones. For instance, one student couldn't decide whether to major in accounting or business management. While discussing his situation with his friends, he revealed that his real interest was in graphic design and illustration. Although he was very talented, he considered this area only a hobby, not a possible career choice. His friends pointed out that design and illustration could prove to be his best career opportunity, but he first needed to see it as a possibility.

   Strategy: *List as many possible choices for your situation as you can—obvious and not obvious, practical and impractical. Ask other people for additional suggestions and keep an open mind—don't censor or prejudge any ideas.*

STEP 3: GATHER ALL RELEVANT INFORMATION AND EVALUATE THE PROS AND CONS OF EACH POSSIBLE CHOICE

Each of the possible choices you identified will have certain advantages and disadvantages, so it is essential that you analyze these pros and cons in an organized fashion. In the case of the student discussed in Step 2, the career choice of accounting might on the one hand offer advantages like ready employment opportunities, the flexibility of working in many different situations and geographical locations, a moderate to high income, and job security. On the other hand, disadvantages might be that accounting does not reflect the student's deep and abiding interest, that he might become bored with it over time, and that the career might not result in the personal challenge and fulfillment that he needs.

   Strategy: *Using a format similar to the following, analyze the pros and cons of each of your possible choices.*

   In many cases, you may lack sufficient information to make an informed choice. Unfortunately, this has never prevented people from plunging ahead anyway, making a decision that is more a gamble than an informed choice. But it makes much more sense to seek out the information you need in order to determine which of your choices has the best chance of success. In the case of the student, he would need certain crucial information to determine which career would be best for him: What sort of academic preparation and experience is required for the various careers? What are the prospects for employment in these areas, and how well do the positions pay? What are the day-to-day activities in each career? How happy are the people in the various careers?

Strategy: For each possible choice that you have identified, create questions regarding information you need; then obtain that information.

STEP 4: SELECT THE CHOICE THAT SEEMS BEST SUITED TO THE SITUATION

The first three steps are designed to help you analyze your decision situation: to define clearly the decision in terms of your goals, to generate possible choices, and to evaluate the pros and cons of the choices you have identified. In the fourth step, you must synthesize what you have learned, weaving together all the various threads into a conclusion that you consider your best choice. How do you do this? There is no one simple way to identify your best choice, but the following are two useful strategies for guiding your deliberations.

Strategy: Identify and prioritize the goal(s) of your decision situation and determine which of your choices best meets these goals. This process will probably involve reviewing and perhaps refining your definition of the decision situation. For example, for the student we have been discussing, goals included choosing a career that would (a) provide financial security, (b) provide personal fulfillment, (c) make use of special talents, and (d) offer plentiful work opportunities along with job security.

Once identified, these goals can be ranked in order of priority, which will then suggest what the best choice would be. If the student ranks goals *a* and *d* at the top of the list, a choice of accounting or business administration may make sense. However, if the student ranks goals *b* and *c* at the top, pursuing a career in graphic design and illustration may be the best selection.

Project yourself into the future, imagining as realistically as you can the consequences of each possible choice. Write your thoughts down and discuss them with your friends or colleagues.

STEP 5: IMPLEMENT A PLAN OF ACTION AND MONITOR THE RESULTS, MAKING NECESSARY ADJUSTMENTS

Once you have made your best choice, you need to develop and implement a plan of action. The more specific your plan, the greater the likelihood of its success. If, for instance, the student in the example decides to pursue a career in graphic design and illustration, his plan should include reviewing the major that best meets his needs, discussing his situation with students and faculty in that department, planning what courses to take, and perhaps speaking with people working in the field.

Strategy: Create a plan that details the steps you would take to implement your decision, along with a time line for taking these steps. Naturally, your plan is merely a starting point. As you actually begin taking the steps in your plan, you may discover that you need to make changes and adjustments. You might find new information which suggests that your choice may be wrong. For example, as the student takes courses in graphic design and illustration, he may realize that his interest in the field is not as serious as he once thought and that although he liked this area as a hobby, he does not want it to be his life's work. In this case, he should reconsider his other choices, perhaps adding some choices that he did not contemplate before.

Strategy: After implementing your choice, evaluate its success by identifying what is working and what is not; then make the necessary adjustments to improve the situation.

Summary for Making Decisions

1. Define the decision clearly.
2. Consider all possible choices.
3. Gather all relevant information and evaluate the pros and cons of each possible choice.
4. Select the choice that seems best suited to the situation.
5. Implement a plan of action and monitor the results, making necessary adjustments.

ANALYZING DECISIONS

The following readings illustrate decisions of tremendous, life-altering import. Frederick Douglass describes how he and fellow slaves made the momentous decision to escape to the North in 1835. Journalist Sara Corbett depicts the long and difficult journey teenaged refugees from the Sudanese civil war are making toward freedom, and the often mundane but critical decisions they make as they adjust to a completely new culture and geography.

FROM

Narrative of the Life of Frederick Douglass, an American Slave

BY FREDERICK DOUGLASS (1818–1895)

Frederick Bailey was born into slavery in 1818, his mother a field worker and his father rumored to be her white master. He spent his early childhood with his grandmother.

When he was six years old, his grandmother brought him to the Lloyd Plantation, one of the oldest and largest plantations in Maryland. Frederick only saw his mother once more; she died when he was seven years old.

In 1825 Frederick was sent to live at the Baltimore home of Hugh and Sophia Auld. Sophia, a religious woman, began to teach Bailey (not yet known as Douglass) to read—until she was abruptly forbidden to continue the lessons by her husband, who believed that teaching a slave to read and write was too dangerous. Douglass quickly realized that literacy was a powerful tool for gaining his freedom.

Deaths and squabbles in the Auld family led to Douglass, at the age of fifteen, being sent back as a field hand to the plantation run by Hugh Auld's brother Thomas. When he discovered that Douglass was leading other slaves in religious services, Thomas Auld sent him to a local farmer, Edward Covey, known as a "slave-breaker" for his particularly vicious and brutal treatment of slaves. One hot August day, as Covey prepared to whip Douglass, Douglass fought back. In his autobiographical Narrative, *Douglass recalled that he and Covey fought for nearly two hours, and that Douglass finally won— his dignity, perhaps, but not yet his freedom. Still, he had learned a critical lesson: in his own words, "Men are whipped oftenist who are whipped easiest." At the age of fifteen, Douglass could have been put to death for the crime of rebelling against his master; Covey, however, perhaps not wanting it known that he could be beaten by a boy, did not make the incident public.*

Douglass then spent a year working for William Freeland (described in the following excerpt). After the incident described in this excerpt, Douglass went back to the Auld family and was placed in an apprenticeship program in a Baltimore shipyard. In 1838 Douglass decided to flee the Auld household and go north to New York City. Through the Underground Railroad, Douglass and his wife moved further north to New Bedford, Massachusetts, a prosperous whaling town. To further protect himself from bounty hunters looking for runaway slaves, Frederick Bailey changed his name to Frederick Douglass. In 1845, he published the autobiographical Narrative *of the Life of Frederick Douglass, an American Slave, which quickly became a bestseller.*

During the Civil War, Douglass met several times with President Abraham Lincoln. He urged black men to join the Union Army, editorialized his joy at Lincoln's Emancipation Proclamation, and worked with the president to ensure continued work for genuine equality for the freed slaves. After the Civil War, Douglass was perhaps the most important black advocate for equal rights and suffrage (the right to vote) in America. Between 1858 and 1870, blacks were being elected to both the Senate and the House of Representatives. In later years, Douglass moved to Washington, D.C., and was offered posts with both the Hayes and the Garfield presidential administrations. He continued to tour and lecture—and to provoke controversy, when after his wife Anna died he married a white woman, Helen Pitts, who was some twenty years his junior.

Douglass died in Washington, D.C., on February 20, 1895.

At the close of the year 1834, Mr. Freeland again hired me of my master, for the year 1835. But, by this time, I began to want to live ~upon free land~ as well as ~with freeland;~ and I was no longer content, therefore, to live with him or any other slave-holder. I began, with the commencement of the year, to prepare myself for a final struggle, which should decide my fate one way or the other. My tendency was upward. I was fast approaching manhood, and year after year had passed, and I was still a slave. These thoughts roused me—I must do something. I therefore resolved that 1835 should not pass without witnessing an attempt, on my part, to secure my liberty. But I was not willing to cherish this determination alone. My fellow-slaves were dear to me. I was anxious to have them participate with me in this, my life-giving determination. I therefore, though with great prudence, commenced early to ascertain their views and feelings in regard to their condition, and to imbue their minds with thoughts of freedom. I bent myself to devising ways and means for our escape, and meanwhile strove, on all fitting occasions, to impress them with the gross fraud and inhumanity of slavery. I went first to Henry, next to John, then to the others. I found, in them all, warm hearts and noble spirits. They were ready to hear, and ready to act when a feasible plan should be proposed. This was what I wanted. I talked to them of our want of manhood, if we submitted to our enslavement without at least one noble effort to be free. We met often, and consulted frequently, and told our hopes and fears, recounted the difficulties, real and imagined, which we should be called on to meet. At times we were almost disposed to give up, and try to content ourselves with our wretched lot; at others, we were firm and unbending in our determination to go. Whenever we suggested any plan, there was shrinking—the odds were fearful. Our path was beset with the greatest obstacles; and if we succeeded in gaining the end of it, our right to be free was yet questionable—we were yet liable to be returned to bondage. We could see no spot, this side of the ocean, where we could be free. We knew nothing about Canada. Our knowledge of the north did not extend farther than New York; and to go there, and be forever harassed with the frightful liability of being returned to slavery—with the certainty of being treated tenfold worse than before—the thought was truly a horrible one, and one which it was not easy to overcome. The case sometimes stood thus: At every gate through which we were to pass, we saw a watchman—at every ferry a guard—on every bridge a sentinel—and in every wood a patrol. We were hemmed in upon every side. Here were the difficulties, real or imagined—the good to be sought, and the evil to be shunned. On the one hand, there stood slavery, a stern reality, glaring frightfully upon us,—its robes already crimsoned with the blood of millions, and even now feasting itself greedily upon our own flesh. On the other hand, away back in the dim distance, under the flickering light of the north star, behind some craggy hill or snow-covered mountain, stood a doubtful freedom—half frozen—beckoning us to come and share its hospitality. This in itself was sometimes enough to stagger us; but when we permitted ourselves to survey the road, we were frequently appalled. Upon either side we saw grim death, assuming the most horrid shapes. Now it was starvation, causing us to eat our own flesh;—now we were contending with the waves, and were drowned;—now we were overtaken, and torn to pieces by the fangs of the terrible bloodhound. We were stung by scorpions, chased by wild beasts, bitten by snakes, and finally, after having nearly reached the desired spot,—after swimming rivers, encountering wild beasts, sleeping in the woods, suffering hunger and nakedness,—we were overtaken by our pursuers, and, in our resistance, we were shot dead upon the spot! I say, this picture sometimes appalled us, and made us

> rather bear those ills we had,
> Than fly to others, that we knew not of.

In coming to a fixed determination to run away, we did more than Patrick Henry, when he resolved upon liberty or death. With us it was a doubtful liberty at most, and almost certain death if we failed. For my part, I should prefer death to hopeless bondage.

Sandy, one of our number, gave up the notion, but still encouraged us. Our company then consisted of Henry Harris, John Harris, Henry Bailey, Charles Roberts, and myself. Henry Bailey was my uncle, and belonged to my master. Charles married my aunt: he belonged to my master's father-in-law, Mr. William Hamilton.

The plan we finally concluded upon was, to get a large canoe belonging to Mr. Hamilton, and upon the Saturday night previous to Easter holidays, paddle directly up the Chesapeake Bay. On our arrival at the head of the bay, a distance of seventy or eighty miles from where we lived, it was our purpose to turn our canoe adrift, and follow the guidance of the north star till we got beyond the limits of Maryland. Our reason for taking the water route was, that we were less liable to be suspected as runaways; we hoped to be regarded as fishermen; whereas, if we should take the land route, we should be subjected to interruptions of almost every kind. Any one having a white face, and being so disposed, could stop us, and subject us to examination.

5   The week before our intended start, I wrote several protections, one for each of us. As well as I can remember, they were in the following words, to wit:–

> This is to certify that I, the undersigned, have given the bearer, my servant, full liberty to go to Baltimore, and spend the Easter holidays. Written with mine own hand, & c., 1835.
>   "WILLIAM HAMILTON,
> Near St. Michael's, in Talbot county, Maryland.

We were not going to Baltimore; but, in going up the bay, we went toward Baltimore, and these protections were only intended to protect us while on the bay.

As the time drew near for our departure, our anxiety became more and more intense. It was truly a matter of life and death with us. The strength of our determination was about to be fully tested. At this time, I was very active in explaining every difficulty, removing every doubt, dispelling every fear, and inspiring all with the firmness indispensable to success in our undertaking; assuring them that half was gained the instant we made the move; we had talked long enough; we were now ready to move; if not now, we never should be; and if we did not intend to move now, we had as well fold our arms, sit down, and acknowledge ourselves fit only to be slaves. This, none of us were prepared to acknowledge. Every man stood firm; and at our last meeting, we pledged ourselves afresh, in the most solemn manner, that, at the time appointed, we would certainly start in pursuit of freedom. This was in the middle of the week, at the end of which we were to be off. We went, as usual, to our several fields of labor, but with bosoms highly agitated with thoughts of our truly hazardous undertaking. We tried to conceal our feelings as much as possible; and I think we succeeded very well.

After a painful waiting, the Saturday morning, whose night was to witness our departure, came. I hailed it with joy, bring what of sadness it might. Friday night was a sleepless one for me. I probably felt more anxious than the rest, because I was, by common consent, at the head of the whole affair. The responsibility of success or failure lay heavily upon me. The glory of the one, and the confusion of the other, were alike mine. The first two hours of that morning were such as I never experienced before, and hope never to again. Early in the morning, we went, as usual, to the field. We were spreading manure; and all at once, while thus engaged, I was overwhelmed with an indescribable feeling, in the fulness of which I turned to Sandy, who was near by, and said, "We are betrayed!" "Well," said he, "that thought has this moment struck me." We said no more. I was never more certain of any thing.

The horn was blown as usual, and we went up from the field to the house for breakfast. I went for the form, more than for want of any thing to eat that morning. Just as I got to the house, in looking out at the lane gate, I saw four white men, with two colored men. The white men were on horseback, and the colored ones were walking behind, as if tied. I watched them a few moments till they got up to our lane gate. Here they halted, and tied the colored men to the gate-post. I was not yet certain as to what the matter was. In a few moments, in rode Mr. Hamilton, with a speed betokening great excitement. He came to the door, and inquired if Master William was in. He was told he was at the barn. Mr. Hamilton, without dismounting, rode up to the barn with extraordinary speed. In a few moments, he and Mr. Freeland returned to the house. By this time, the three constables rode up, and in great haste dismounted, tied their horses, and met Master William and Mr. Hamilton returning from the barn; and after talking awhile, they all walked up to the kitchen door. There was no one in the kitchen but myself and John. Henry and Sandy were up at the barn. Mr. Freeland put his head in at the door, and called me by name, saying, there were some gentlemen at the door who wished to see me. I stepped to the door, and inquired what they wanted. They at once seized me, and, without giving me any satisfaction, tied me—lashing my hands closely together. I insisted upon knowing what the matter was. They at length said, that they had learned I had been in a "scrape," and that I was to be examined before my master; and if their information proved false, I should not be hurt.

[Douglass and his companions were caught, jailed, and released to their owners.]

Questions for Active Reading

1. Frederick Douglass and many other nineteenth-century abolitionist writers used biblical metaphors to describe the experience of slavery and the quest for freedom. (In the next chapter, on page 181, you'll see how Martin Luther King also uses biblical imagery to describe the moral imperative for civil rights.) How effective are the religious images and allusions that Douglass makes? (Some of these allusions are quite subtle; for example, why does he specify "thirty-nine lashes" of the whip that slaves who dared attend Sabbath school risked? or his use of the word "betrayed" in paragraph 8?) What does this language suggest about Douglass's audience?

2. In this excerpt Douglass describes at least one major decision that he makes. Describe, in your own words, one such decision. What steps did he take before making a commitment to that decision? Which factors were most important to him in making that decision?

3. In academic writing, students are often discouraged from using the first person in making an argument. How would the impact of Douglass's argument be affected if he had written in the third person? When is one person's experience enough for an argument to be completely authoritative and effective?

Questions for Thinking Critically

1. Throughout his *Narrative,* Douglass emphasizes the power of literacy. What does literacy mean to Douglass, and why does he make an effort (even at great personal danger) to teach other slaves to become literate? Would Douglass and Malcolm X (page 155) share a common definition of "literacy"?

2. Douglass says of his "fellow-slaves": "We were linked and interlinked with each other. I loved them with a love stronger than anything I have experienced since." Given Douglass's audience for his autobiography, why does he feel it so necessary to describe the intensity of these feelings? (Remember, too, that at the time he wrote this autobiography, Douglass was married and a father.)

3. To inspire his close friends and fellow slaves at the Freeland home, Douglass "talked to them of our want of manhood, if we submitted to our enslavement without at least one noble effort to be free." What does he mean? What is a "noble effort to be free," and have you ever made such an effort? Are *you* truly "free" to make decisions about how you live your life?

The Lost Boys

BY SARA CORBETT

Journalist Sara Corbett received an MFA degree from the University of Iowa's highly regarded Iowa Writer's Workshop, and as a journalist has covered subjects ranging from the reintroduction of wolves to Yellowstone to the nursing shortage to snowboarding. The author of Venus to the Hoop: A Gold-Medal Year in Women's Basketball *(1997) for which she closely followed the 1995 Women's Olympic basketball team, Corbett covered basketball for* Conde Nast Sports for Women *magazine. Her work has also appeared in the magazines* Outside *and* Skiing Magazine. *Corbett is married to journalist Michael Paterniti.*

One evening in late January, Peter Dut, twenty-one, leads his two teenage brothers through the brightly lit corridors of the Minneapolis airport, trying to mask his confusion. Two days earlier, the brothers, refugees from Africa, encountered their first light switch and their first set of stairs. An aid worker in Nairobi demonstrated the flush toilet to them—also the seat belt, the shoelace, the fork. And now they find themselves alone in Minneapolis, three bone-thin African boys confronted by a swirling river of white faces and rolling suitcases.

Finally, a traveling businessman recognizes their uncertainty. "Where are you flying to?" he asks kindly, and the eldest brother tells him in halting, bookish English. A few days earlier, they left a small mud hut in a blistering hot Kenyan refugee camp, where they had lived as orphans for nine years after walking for hundreds of miles across Sudan. They are now headed to a new home in the U.S.A. "Where?" the man asks in disbelief when Peter Dut says the city's name. "Fargo? North Dakota? You gotta be kidding me. It's too cold there. You'll never survive it!"

And then he laughs. Peter Dut has no idea why.

In the meantime, the temperature in Fargo has dropped to 15 below. The boys tell me that until now, all they have ever known about cold is what they felt grasping a bottle of frozen water. An aid worker handed it to them one day during a "cultural orientation" session at the Kakuma Refugee Camp, a place where the temperature hovers around 100 degrees.

5   Peter Dut and his two brothers belong to an unusual group of refugees referred to by aid organizations as the Lost Boys of Sudan, a group of roughly 10,000 boys who arrived in Kenya in 1992 seeking refuge from their country's fractious civil war. The fighting pits a northern Islamic government against rebels in the south who practice Christianity and tribal religions.

The Lost Boys were named after Peter Pan's posse of orphans. According to U.S. State Department estimates, some 17,000 boys were separated from their families and fled southern Sudan in an exodus of biblical proportions after fighting intensified in 1987. They arrived in throngs, homeless and parentless, having trekked about 1000 miles, from Sudan to Ethiopia, back to Sudan, and finally to Kenya. The majority of the boys belonged to the Dinka and Nuer tribes, and most were then between the ages of eight and eighteen. (Most of the boys don't know for sure how old they are; aid workers assigned them approximate ages after they arrived in 1992.)

Along the way, the boys endured attacks from the northern army and marauding bandits as well as lions, who preyed on the slowest and weakest among them. Many died from starvation or thirst. Others drowned or were eaten by crocodiles as they tried to cross a swollen Ethiopian river. By the time the Lost Boys reached the Kakuma Refugee Camp, their numbers had been cut nearly in half.

Now, after nine years of subsisting on rationed corn mush and lentils and living largely ungoverned by adults, the Lost Boys of Sudan are coming to America. In 1999, the United Nations High Commissioner for Refugees, which handles refugee cases around the world, and the U.S. government agreed to send 3600 of the boys to the United States—since going back to Sudan was out of the question. About 500 of the Lost Boys still under the age of eighteen will be living in apartments or foster homes across the United States by the end of this year. The boys will start school at a grade level normal for their age, thanks to a tough English-language program at their refugee camp. The remaining 3100 Lost Boys will be resettled as adults. After five years, each boy will be eligible for citizenship, provided he has turned twenty-one.

Nighttime in America?

On the night that I stand waiting for Peter Dut and his brothers to land in Fargo, tendrils of snow are snaking across the tarmac. The three boys file through the gate without money or coats or luggage beyond their small backpacks. The younger brothers, Maduk, seventeen, and Riak, fifteen, appear petrified. As a social worker passes out coats, Peter Dut studies the black night through the airport window. "Excuse me," he says worriedly. "Can you tell me, please, is it now night or day?"

10   This is a stove burner. This is a can opener. This is a brush for your teeth. The new things come in a tumble. The brothers' home is a sparsely furnished two-bedroom apartment in a complex on Fargo's south side. Rent is $445 a month. It has been stocked with donations from area churches and businesses: toothpaste, bread, beans, bananas.

A caseworker empties a garbage bag full of donated clothing, which looks to have come straight from the closet of an elderly man. I know how lucky the boys are: the State Department estimates that war, famine, and disease in southern Sudan have killed more than 2 million people and displaced another 4 million. Still I cringe to think of the boys showing up for school in these clothes.

The next day, when I return to the apartment at noon, the boys have been up since five and are terribly hungry. "What about your food?" I ask, gesturing to the bread and bananas and the box of cereal sitting on the counter.

Peter grins sheepishly. I suddenly realize that the boys, in a lifetime of cooking maize and beans over a fire pit, have never opened a box. I am placed in the role of teacher. And so begins an opening spree. We open potato chips. We open a can of beans. We untwist the tie on the bagged loaf of bread. Soon the boys are seated and eating a hot meal.

Living on Leaves and Berries

The three brothers have come a long way since they fled their village in Sudan with their parents and three sisters, all of whom were later killed by Sudanese army soldiers. The Lost Boys first survived a six- to ten-week walk to Ethiopia, often subsisting on leaves and berries and the occasional boon of a warthog carcass. Some boys staved off dehydration by drinking their own urine. Many fell behind; some were devoured by lions or trampled by buffalo.

15   The Lost Boys lived for three years in Ethiopia, in UN-supported camps, before they were forced back into Sudan by a new Ethiopian government no longer sympathetic to their plight. Somehow, more than 10,000 of the boys miraculously trailed into Kenya's UN camps in the summer of 1992—as Sudanese government planes bombed the rear of their procession.

For the Lost Boys, then, a new life in America might easily seem to be the answer to every dream. But the real world has been more complicated than that. Within weeks of arriving, Riak is placed in a local junior high; Maduk starts high school classes; and Peter begins adult education classes.

Refugee Blues

Five weeks later, Riak listens quietly through a lesson on Elizabethan history at school, all but ignored by white students around him.

Nearby, at Fargo South High School, Maduk is frequently alone as well, copying passages from his geography textbook, trying not to look at the short skirts worn by many of the girls.

Peter Dut worries about money. The three brothers say they receive just $107 in food stamps each month and spend most of their $510 monthly cash assistance on rent and utilities.

20   Resettlement workers say the brothers are just undergoing the normal transition. Scott Burtsfield, who coordinates resettlement efforts in Fargo through Lutheran Social Services, says, "The first three months are always the toughest. It really does get better."

The Lost Boys can only hope so; they have few other options. A return to southern Sudan could be fatal. "There is nothing left for the Lost Boys to go home to—it's a war zone," says Mary Anne Fitzgerald, a Nairobi-based relief consultant.

Some Sudanese elders have criticized sending boys to the United States. They worry that their children will lose their African identity. One afternoon an eighteen-year-old Lost Boy translated a part of a tape an elder had sent along with many boys: "He is saying, 'Don't drink. Don't smoke. Don't kill. Go to school every day, and remember, America is not your home.'"

But if adjustment is hard, the boys also experience consoling moments. One of these came on a quiet Friday night last winter. As the boys make a dinner of rice and lentils, Peter changes into an African outfit, a finely woven green tunic with a skullcap to match, bought with precious food rations at Kakuma.

Just then the doorbell rings unexpectedly. And out of the cold tumble four Sudanese boys—all of whom have resettled as refugees over the past several years. I watch one, an eighteen-year-old named Sunday, wrap his arms encouragingly around Peter Dut. "It's a hard life here," Sunday whispers to the older boy, "but it's a free life, too."

Questions for Active Reading

1. Unlike Frederick Douglass, Sara Corbett writes here from an objective perspective; not having directly experienced what the "Lost Boys" have gone through, she can only report on what she observes and share what they reveal to her. How does she express the strangeness and difficulties of Peter Dut's experiences by using her own powers of observation?

2. Corbett describes episodes and circumstances that would appear to be ironic, even comic, and "stranger than fiction." However, she reports these things objectively, without judgment or editorializing. What do you, as a reader, make of the irony that Peter Dut and thousands of children like him are called "Lost Boys" by aid organizations? (To understand the irony, be sure that you know where the term "Lost Boys" comes from.) What about the contrast described in paragraph 4?

3. Despite her journalistic objectivity, Corbett does eventually appear in the first person. Where, and why? How does this change your perception of her as a writer, a journalist, a person? Do journalists have an ethical responsibility toward their subjects?

Questions for Thinking Critically

1. From the information about the Sudanese civil war and the Kenyan refugee camps in Corbett's article, how much choice do you think the "Lost Boys" had in determining their fates? When one of the boys, Sunday, says to Peter Dut "It's a hard life here, but it's a free life, too," what do you think he means?

2. In what ways are Peter Dut and his friends courageous, and sources of inspiration, to each other? How did Frederick Douglass inspire courage in his own friends? What is the connection between courage and inspiration?

3. Is it ever easier to let circumstances make a decision for you? What do you think takes over when you give up control of your own destiny?

Thinking ↔ Writing Activity

Preparing for Decisions

1. Make a list of whatever important decisions in your academic or personal life you have to make now or will have to make in the near future.

2. Select one decision and apply the five-step decision-making method that begins on page 129. As you think through your decision, be sure to identify all your possible choices and to follow your thoughts wherever they lead.

There are no guarantees in life. Our decisions may or may not turn out well. Still, following an organized method for making decisions can at least assure us of having explored and evaluated many possible choices and then selected the one that seemed to best meet our needs. In other words, we will know that we made the best decision that we could have at the time.

Writing Project: Analyzing a Decision to Be Made

This chapter includes both readings and Thinking-Writing Activities that encourage you to reflect on drafting and decision making. Be sure to reread what you wrote for those activities; you may be able to use your responses to complete this project.

Write an essay in which you analyze a decision you must make now or in the near future. Be sure to select a decision for which you already have considerable information or want to obtain more. Include all five steps of the decision-making method. After you have drafted your essay, revise it as best you can. Follow your instructor's directions for length, format, and so on.

THE WRITING SITUATION

Begin by considering the key elements in the Thinking-Writing Model.

Purpose Use this opportunity to work through an important real-life decision to obtain the best possible outcome. If others will be involved in or affected by this decision, your paper can show them your best thinking about it, making them more likely to agree with your decision. Also, in writing this paper, you can practice the creative and critical thinking involved in the five-step decision-making method. You can hone your revision skills both by carefully working through the revision questions on page 145 and by using ideas about revision from Chapter 6 as well as ideas from this chapter.

Audience An essay about a decision implies at least two potential audiences. In describing a decision you made and the process of making that decision, you could be writing for people who are faced with similar circumstances or a closely related predicament. For example, people in communities that welcome refugees from distant lands would learn a great deal from Sara Corbett's article about the many small but important adjustments refugees must learn to make. Through describing your commitment to a decision, even at its most difficult, you can inspire people who have made a similar decision.

Subject Decisions can be challenging to think about and difficult to make. Sometimes we haven't enough information to make an intelligent choice; sometimes we *think* we know what the right decision is yet are reluctant to actually make it. Therefore, we often tend to put off decision making for as long as possible. Keep in mind that not making a decision is, in a way, making a decision to do nothing. For this assignment, try to identify a decision that will have significant consequences. It may be what area to major in, whether to get a part-time job, whether to participate in a sport or other extracurricular activity, or whether to get a dog. The more significant the decision, the more helpful this assignment will be to you.

Writer You approach this Writing Project as the expert on the subject since you are analyzing one of your own decisions. One challenge here is to distinguish between your own expertise about the decision-making situation and your audience's needs for enough background and information. Another challenge is to focus on the material provided earlier in this chapter because this assignment moves away from recollecting experience and asks you to apply the decision-making process to a decision you need to make soon. For example, Frederick Douglass writes with the authority of personal experience. Although Sara Corbett is not a refugee, she establishes her authority through scrupulous observation, insightful interviews, and background research.

THE WRITING PROCESS

The following sections will guide you through the stages of generating, planning, drafting, and revising as you work on an essay about making a decision.

Generating Ideas   Try to be particularly conscious of both the creative and the critical thinking you do while making your decision and of the critical thinking and decision making you do as you revise.

- Is there a decision you must make in the near future? If so, this is a good opportunity for you to accomplish two things at once: writing your paper and making your decision.

- Think about how much additional information you would need to evaluate possible choices for this decision. Do you have time to locate and absorb all of it?

- Describe the decision-making situation and your goals as clearly as you can.

- Brainstorm as many possible choices as you can. Ask others involved in the decision to help.

- Eliminate choices that you know are impractical or undesirable.

- Determine what information you must find for each choice. Locate that information.

- Write each choice on a separate sheet of paper. Then divide the paper into two columns: pros and cons. Write as much as you can in each column.

- For each, freewrite for five minutes on what would happen and how you would feel if you selected that choice.

- Freewrite for five minutes on how you would know if any given choice was the right one.

Defining a Focus   Write a tentative thesis statement that clarifies your decision-making situation. You might write something like "After thinking about the situation carefully, I realize that I have only two possible choices." Or you might "blueprint" your paper by naming the possible choices: "My choices for housing next year come down to these three: living with my aunt, sharing an apartment with my friend, or looking for a live-in job situation." You may even decide to announce your decision in your thesis statement: "After carefully weighing my options, I have decided to major in business administration." Or you may find a more creative way to state your thesis.

Organizing Ideas   The five-step method for making decisions fits well with essay structure. Your description of the decision-making situation might be the beginning of an introduction, to be completed by your thesis statement. You could include your goals in the introduction or state them in a separate paragraph.

Each of the possible choices, explained in as much detail as possible along with the pros and cons of that choice, could serve as a body paragraph. Your decision of the best choice and your plan for monitoring it could be the essay's conclusion.

Drafting Begin with the easiest part to draft. Your description of the decision-making situation could begin the introduction, but consider what, if any, additional information your audience might need in order to understand the situation. The introduction can end with your tentative thesis statement.

In your conclusion or thesis statement, name the choice you have selected. You may want to explain why if you think your reason may not be obvious to your audience. Remember to explain how you will monitor the results of your decision.

Revising One of the best revision strategies is to get an audience's reactions to your draft. Here are some questions to ask your peers about this assignment:

- What questions do you have about my decision-making situation and my goals?
- What questions do you have about the alternative choices I described? What else do you need to know about them? Can you suggest any others?
- Do you understand why I am making this decision?
- What could I add to clarify why this choice is best for me?

Armed with the information from peer review, you are now ready to begin revising by using the revision method presented on page 160 in Chapter 6 (and included on the inside back cover). If possible, use the following directions for revising with a word processor as you work through the revision process.

Revising Strategy: Using a Computer to Revise Use the revision method by creating a series of files, one for each time you revise using your word processor. This system will give you a complete record of your work so that you can track how each draft changes.

- Call your first draft Decision 1 and print and save it.
- Later, create a new file called Decision 2 by copying and pasting Decision 1. Then make changes to the draft as a whole, being guided by your answers from the peer review and your answers to the Think Big questions on page 160. Print and save this draft.
- Now, consider the Think Medium questions to evaluate your individual paragraphs. Create a new file called Decision 3 by copying and pasting Decision 2. Then make whatever changes are suggested by your answers to the Think Medium questions on page 160. Print and save this draft.
- Next, consider the Think Small questions. Create a new file called Decision 4 by copying and pasting Decision 3. Then make whatever changes

at the sentence level that are suggested by your answers to the Think Small questions on page 161. Print and save this draft.

- Finally, consider the Think "Picky" questions. Create a new file called Decision 5 by copying and pasting Decision 4. Then make whatever changes are suggested by your answers to the Think "Picky" questions on page 161. Run the spelling and grammar checking features of your word processing program, and use your judgment about which suggested changes to make. Print and save this draft. Decision 5 should present your very best work. It is now ready to be submitted to your instructor and any other audience you select.

Editing and Proofreading Your essay should now have been completed to the best of your ability, and, of course, you will need to submit it to your instructor by the due date. But also consider other possible audiences for this essay. Do you want to share your ideas with other people involved in your decision-making situation? Would members of your family or your close friends benefit by reading it? If your paper is about a decision that others must also make, such as selecting a major, perhaps your student newspaper would be interested in publishing it as a model of good decision making that others could emulate.

The following essays show how two students responded to this assignment.

STUDENT WRITING
WENDY AGUDO'S WRITING PROCESS

Wendy Agudo began to compose the following essay after a chance remark her philosophy professor made in class. Wendy had already completed the Thinking-Writing assignment on page 129, reflecting on her decision in junior high to overcome her learning disability and earn the high grades she would need to go to college and pursue a career in television journalism. The day after she completed that assignment, her philosophy professor told her class that the French philosopher Jean-Paul Sartre had said that we were "condemned to be free." Wendy began with a freewriting to sort out her feelings about how that quote related to her own experience, and then used the five steps to organized decision making (pages 129–132) to begin to plan her paper.

Jean-Paul Sartre "we are condemned to be free"—it wasn't anyone's fault, the accident. I don't blame my parents. I don't blame anyone, and they don't blame each other. It just happened. Moving to America when I was really little was probably the best thing they could have done for me. Back in Ecuador it would have been really hard for me to get the help I needed. But still I wouldn't have had to learn a new language, and mami and papa wouldn't have had to work so hard and leave me alone for so much time when I really needed them. I'm angry with Lidia because she doesn't even know how easy she has it.

Lidia has always had the family support and the money and the time to do whatever she wants, but all she wants to do is sit around talking on her celly to her boy. We're at work together and we're on deadline and I'm trying to get her to shut up and pay attention and she just rolls her eyes and says something in Albanian over the phone. She has no respect but I can't be jealous, that's not right either. Does she think about where she'll be in two years? in ten years?

1. *Define the decision.* I decided not to let my brain injury get in the way of my goals.

2. *Consider all possible choices.* I didn't have a choice. Either I succeed or I fail. It's up to me.

3. *Gather all relevant information and evaluate the pros and cons of each choice.*

   - I could have stayed in the remedial class in junior high. PRO—less work. CON—where would I be today?

   - I could ignore Lidia and let her screw up. PRO—not having to confront Lidia. CON—it's my job to confront her and make sure she's learning skills. If I don't help her then I fail at some level.

   - I could let Lidia learn for herself. It worked for me. You need to take responsibility for your own life.

4. *Select the choice that seems best suited to the situation.* I can't boss Lidia around. She needs to find out for herself what the consequences of her lack of responsibility will be. Besides she won't listen to me. I can be a better example for everyone in the peer training program if I just get my own work done and set a high standard for myself.

5. *Implement a plan of action.* I owe it to my parents and to myself to succeed. I can't get jealous of Lidia or let her own decisions make my own work look bad.

Freedom

BY WENDY AGUDO

It's funny how some people always seem to have an excuse for everything, refusing to take responsibility for their actions. All of us have, at some point, shrugged our shoulders and made an excuse for behavior we should have regretted, or at least apologized for—being late to meet a friend, not having an assignment completed on time, not visiting an elderly relative. But making these excuses implies that we are not really in control of our own lives. When we make an excuse for our behavior, we are really saying that some other force—a train conductor, the weather, a computer, whatever—has more control over our lives than we do. To make excuses is to place limits on the extent of your personal freedom.

I see this kind of refusal to take responsibility all the time at my job. I work as a peer trainer for a small non-profit television station, teaching other young people (high school through age 25) how to use field and studio digital cameras, digital and analog video editing, and media literacy. I was fortunate enough to begin this work at the age of 18, and now at the age of 20 I consider myself very skilled and motivated. Because of my experience in a professional environment I tend to have high expectations for my peers in this training program, who are my own age and often a little older. When they are late for a meeting, or careless with their work, or would rather go out and have fun than stay late and edit a story, I am very disappointed. I hear excuses like "I have no time because of school," or "my family this" and "my intelligence that." I could come up with many more compelling excuses myself, but yet I don't.

I believe that we all make choices in life, and that there is no reason for failure or self-pity. Many factors have contributed to my sense of responsibility, my stubbornness, and my loyalty to my family. But the most significant challenge I have faced—and that I could use as an excuse, but don't—has to do with my health.

I was born in Ecuador. When I was two years old, I accidentally fell from the second-story window of my parents' house. I landed on a pile of broken concrete and suffered brain damage, which the doctor said would be permanent. My parents could have allowed this to be a limit on my freedom, but they refused. I know I was too young to think this, but I do know that somewhere around this time I didn't allow myself to let this keep me down. As I grew I got better. It was my choice to continue and get past it.

Or maybe it was just luck.

My story doesn't have an accidentally happy ending. After I recovered from the fall there were still limitations. I was slow to walk and speak, and was dyslexic. Then, when I was four years old, my family immigrated to the United States. I was enrolled in an English-speaking public school. Between my difficulties in reading, walking, and speaking, I had to work three times as hard as anyone else just to keep up. I stuttered and had a lisp, so even when I did manage to speak English, other children teased me. Due to my dyslexia I had trouble focusing and concentrating, so I had trouble reading. Eventually I was afraid to read anything. I saw all of the other kids round me finishing with two books before I was able to get through even one. I was so discouraged that I wanted to give up.

This is another example of freedom of choice. I could have chosen to work harder, to study more, but I allowed outside circumstances—my disability—to make the choice for me. I gave up, but giving up was my own choice. It wasn't determined for me and it wasn't something I couldn't avoid. I chose to give up out of my own free will. And that choice had consequences. For many years I had very low grades and was passed from one "special" classroom to another.

At some point during junior high I realized that I wasn't going to get anywhere with such low grades. I worked harder and harder and eventually got better. I defeated the dyslexia, but it hasn't gone away. I still have dyslexia, but it doesn't control me. At least now it's something that doesn't hold me back. Eventually, I graduated from high school with honors, and I am now enrolled in college and earning "A" grades. Not bad for someone with a damaged brain!

This brings me back to the high expectations I have for other people in my peer training program. Due to the fact that I had to work so hard to develop myself, I also developed what I call high standards. I look at another peer trainer, whom I will call Lidia, as a comparison. Lidia is five months older than I am, and is also an immigrant. Her family came to the United States from Albania when she was four years old, just like me. Her parents are both doctors, and she was raised with many privileges. Although we both grew up in the same New York City neighborhood, our lives were very different. For my parents to get here from Ecuador, they had to make a dangerous and lonely journey across South America by car and on foot. We had no family in America to welcome us, and my parents had to work illegally in sweatshops for many years. But Lidia's parents joined a large family of uncles, aunts, and cousins, and her parents were able to begin practicing medicine again within a year or two of their arrival.

I have read that the environment you grow up in determines the kind of life you lead. I guess that, based on that evidence, I should have been a mother when I was still a teenager, and shouldn't have gone to college at all. But environment doesn't determine everything, and freedom to choose your own destiny isn't limited because of one or two aspects. Even in poverty, even in prison—even with a damaged brain!—you still have the freedom to choose to work hard and to make the best of your circumstances.

Lidia is always complaining at work. She takes fewer college classes than I do, and only works ten hours at the television station each week (I work 30 hours, sometimes more). Yet she is always late for meetings, loses track of equipment, and doesn't take her work assignments seriously. She assumes that everything will be easy for her, and doesn't realize that that complacency limits the choices she can make about her life. When things go wrong, she makes excuses—her car broke down, or she was out late the night before. She doesn't know how fortunate she is, and she'll never achieve as much as she could.

I believe that freedom is unlimited, and your life is determined by matters of choice. If you choose to give up, to accept less of yourself, then you will forever limit your choices and your freedom. But if you choose to continue, no matter what the obstacles, you will eventually achieve your goals. I may be disappointed in other people, but I have never been disappointed in myself. My family has sacrificed too much for me to come this far, and I will not let them down.

STUDENT WRITING
CYNTHIA BROWN'S WRITING PROCESS

Cynthia Brown's approach to this writing project exhibits those qualities of creativity, open-mindedness, knowledge, and curiosity that are the hallmarks of a critical thinker. Rather than writing about a specific decision, Cynthia reflected on a key factor—time—and how her relationship to time shaped all the major decisions she had made in her life. Cynthia drew on readings from her writing class (especially her responses to Sara Corbett's "The Lost Boys" on page 138) and notes from her philosophy class to inform her essay.

When I moved to New York, I thought I was going to go insane. As much as I loved the city, I could not bear to live here. However, I came to New York to attend college and decided it would be best to allow myself time to make this decision based on rationale as opposed to emotion. I spent the next two years carefully analyzing and weighing my options. With the passage of time, I have come to the conclusion that I cannot live the kind of life I want to live as a student if I stay in New York. I decided to transfer, upon graduation from my current college, to a small liberal arts college in the middle of nowhere. I used time to help me explore my options instead of feeling trapped within its confines. This allowed me to move through the two years with ease and come to a truly authentic decision regarding my life.

Freedom and the Constraint of Time

BY CYNTHIA BROWN

Do I believe that I am free?

The 18th-century French philosopher Baron d'Holbach says that we are drowning in a river, desperately trying to keep our heads above water, sinking, rising, sinking again, until we die. The American writer William James argued that we are free to act, to drag ourselves out of that river of circumstance any time we choose and set our own course. I believe that whatever your personal belief about the nature of your freedom, we are all captured and held by the whims of Time. Time is universal, preceding both existence and essence.

Take, for example, measurement. Everything we know about the material world, everything we experience, is measured by time. Distance, stability, stamina, progress, relationships . . . the list is endless. We run, not a mile, but ten minutes. We travel, not by miles, but by hours. We wait, not with patience but in days. To an imaginary objective observer, an angel or an alien, humans would all seem to be motivated not by internal desires or the pursuit of knowledge, but by the hands of the clock. An alien wouldn't know that you decided to stop speaking with your boyfriend because you had fallen in love with someone else; the alien would notice that the clock on your bedroom wall said 3:37 pm, and could just as easily assume that the time determined your heart's action.

People wear wristwatches, follow the sun across the sky, track the phases of the moon. New technology helps us to process time faster so we don't waste a moment of it. We have cell phones and computers so we can work faster, multitask, move several concepts and relationships through time simultaneously. We are racing time, desperate to control it, bend it to our will. Yet time is a universal law, a rule we must abide by. We might think that we are free to make decisions about our own lives, but whatever we "choose" is ultimately changed, decayed, or unraveled by the passage of time.

When we look into the heavens, we see stars and wonder just how small we are. How long would it take me to travel to the next galaxy, the next universe? Ask a physicist and she will answer you in increments of time: light years. Our imaginations can travel as far into the universe as they may please in the shortest segment time has to give us. We feel we can take a shortcut and go where we please, sometimes inventing new universes where time does not exist. We feel, briefly, ecstatically, that we have beaten time—and then we wake up, or come down, and find ourselves in a place where we are alone and helpless, desperate to come back to the places and people we know.

Suppose we were to look back at our lives and what has shaped us. Wouldn't it be nice to go back and change everything, to disappear without knowledge of our present life and be given a chance to start all over again? Alan Lightman, a renowned physicist, explores this idea in his novel *Einstein's Dreams*. Many of his stories claim that time is an endless cycle, never giving in or relenting to our wishes. Our clocks repeat themselves in a circle. We fall in and out of love, looking back at time spent in our relationships as so much wasted time, hardly daring to allow ourselves to experience the emotion itself. We are simultaneously anticipating the future and regretting the past. We move forward, waiting for time to heal our wounds.

Although we created a calendar to help us move through and keep track of time, it is an endless cycle. Day into night. Hour into hour. The refugee boy from Sudan, lost on the dark North Dakota prairie, asks a friend: "Can you tell me, please, is it now night or day?" We ask Time to be responsible, ignoring our own role in our destiny. While we are thinking of everything that has gone wrong with our lives, Time is passing through us, creating us, owning us. We are creating ourselves in Time. Are we really making our decisions based on our experience and careful analysis, or are we allowing Time to take control and be our guide?

We slip in and out of awareness of time. We wake in the morning fresh from our dreams and instinctively look at the clock. Some mornings we rise and say "Shit, I'm late for class. My professor is going to be so mad. He wears a watch." And here, we have a choice. Do we go late, or not go at all? Both of these decisions come with consequences. We weigh them as we brush our teeth and pull a sweater over our heads. Is the decision we make truly free, or are we simply responding to the urgency of the ticking clock?

It's possible to leave the technology of clocks and cell phones behind, but just like the Lost Boys of Sudan, we are still instinctively aware of the cycles of the sun. We cannot live without sunlight; we cannot imagine the universe without darkness. Our secrets are kept in the dark, and we reveal ourselves to each other by shining a light on our deepest truths. We are determined to live in light and shadow, and from an early age we are trained to respond to the shifts from day to night and back again.

One of the earliest lessons I remember from preschool was how to tell time (tell it what? I wonder now . . .) We learned how to read the hands on a clock, and what the numbers on a digital dial meant; we were taught to "be on time," and were punished if we were late. As schoolchildren, responding to bells, we were taught to be driven by forces beyond what we can truly see—only measure (and isn't it ironic that we are not allowed to pray in schools? But that's another argument entirely). Were we learning because we were curious, eating because we were hungry, jumping up from our desks because we couldn't wait to get home? Or were we just responding, like a bunch of trained rats, to the sound of the bell?

And so we wait. We wait for time to tell us what will be and where we will end up next. Whether or not the alarm clock will let us live another day. All of our teachings and still we wait, for something as old as the universe itself, a force that will long outlast any choices or commitments or decisions we make. Time moves forward, carrying us with it whether we ask it to or not. For surely if we exist outside of this concept of time, lock ourselves in a windowless room for what we suspect are minutes, days, or years, we are certain to be driven to madness.

So when I am asked, "Are you free?"

I answer, "Well, I don't wear a wristwatch. Do you?"

ALTERNATIVE WRITING PROJECTS

1. Write an essay in which you analyze a decision that must be made soon by a community or group to which you belong. Describe the circumstances leading up to this decision, and follow through the five steps of the decision-making method discussed in this chapter. When you consider alternate choices and their pros and cons, be sure to include the perspectives of several members of your community who will be affected by this decision.

2. The theme of the wandering pilgrim, or the prodigal son, is found in literature across cultures and time periods. What does it mean to "come home" after a life-changing experience? Is it more difficult to decide to run away, or to decide to come home? Think about how a tribal elder urged the Lost Boys to maintain their "African identity" in a strange new land. Have you had a comparable experience? What led you away? Why did you decide to go home? How did the experience change you?

3. Have you ever talked someone out of what you knew was a bad decision? What were the circumstances of that decision? What was your relationship to the person making the decision? What was the most effective, or surprising, argument that you made to change that person's mind?

6

"Only where there is language is there world." —Adrienne Rich

Revising Thoughtfully, Using Language Ethically

Critical Thinking Focus: Language and power

Writing Focus: Revising language to clarify thinking

Reading Theme: Using language ethically

Writing Project: The impact of language on our lives

Every time we use language, we send a message about our thinking. When we speak or write, we are not simply making sounds or writing symbols; we are conveying ideas, sharing feelings, and describing experiences. At the same time, language itself shapes and influences thinking. When language use is sloppy—vague, general, indistinct, imprecise, foolish, inaccurate—it leads to the same sort of thinking. The reverse is also true: clear, precise language leads to clear, precise thinking, speaking, and writing.

The careless or imprecise use of language can be more consequential than a mediocre grade or a boring essay. When you write, you are assuming an audience; even if your audience is "only" your teacher, you still take on the responsibility of enlightening, entertaining, and truth telling. That assumption of an audience, so fundamental to rhetoric, implies that you are writing from an *ethical* perspective. The word *ethics* comes from the Greek term *ethos,* or "character." What you say, and how you say it, reveals to your audience what kind of person you are.

To write ethically also implies that you have a *responsibility* toward your reader, your subject, and yourself. To be responsible to your reader means that you write clearly, choosing the most appropriate language, constructing a logical argument that your reader can easily follow. To be responsible to your subject requires you to be as truthful as you can, given what you know. If you are writing an argument, it is your responsibility as an ethical writer to present opposing viewpoints fairly and accurately. Finally, you are responsible to your *ethos,* or how you appear in your writing. A carefully written, logically organized, interestingly illustrated essay reveals the presence of a thoughtful, interesting, curious mind.

This chapter explores the ethical implications of language—how it is used on both a personal and a social level to provoke, to haunt, to challenge, and to heal. Activities in this chapter discuss the *revision* part of the writing process, that careful reconsideration of your sources, organization, and word choice before you present your "final" paper to your audience.

Thinking ↔ Writing Activity

Language That Offends

Has your attention been drawn to the ethical or responsible use of language on your campus, or in your workplace? For example, does your campus have a speech code that defines hate speech or otherwise proscribed language? Are there words you are uncomfortable to use, or to hear, in the classroom or the office? Are you uncomfortable with that language because it offends you, or because you worry about offending someone?

Recognizing Effective Use of Language

One effective way to develop your ability to use language ethically and responsibly in communicating your thoughts, feelings, and experiences is to read widely. Highly regarded writers use word meanings accurately. They also often use many action verbs, concrete nouns, and vivid adjectives to communicate effectively. Another way to become a more sensitive and responsive writer is by seeking feedback from readers. In this section, you will be using all these strategies.

The following passage by Malcolm X chronicles his discovery of the power of language while he was serving time in prison. Frustrated by not being able to communicate his ideas in writing, he commited himself to mastering the use of words by copying the dictionary. As you read, pay special attention to the way Malcolm X uses language to share his experiences with us. Do you find his personal quest inspiring? Why?

FROM

The Autobiography of Malcolm X
BY MALCOLM X (1925–1965) WITH ALEX HALEY

Born as Malcolm Little in Omaha, Nebraska, the son of an activist Baptist preacher and a mother busy with her eight children, Malcolm X saw racial injustice and violence from a very young age. His father, Earl Little, was outspoken in his support for Black Nationalist leader Marcus Garvey; as a result, the family was the target of harassment and forced to move frequently. In 1931, Earl Little's body was found on the town's trolley tracks; although the local police dismissed it as an accident, Earl Little's death was widely believed to have been murder at the hands of white supremacists.

Malcolm dropped out of high school after a teacher's contemptuous discouragement of his ambitions to be a lawyer. For the next several years he moved between Boston and New York, becoming profitably involved in various criminal activities. After a conviction for burglary in Boston, he was sentenced to prison for ten years. (In the following excerpt from his autobiography, Malcolm X describes how he used this time for reflection and intellectual growth.) His brother, Reginald, visited him there and shared with him his conversion to Islam, brought about by the black nationalist organization the Nation of Islam, founded by Elijah Muhammad. Paroled in 1952, Malcolm dropped the name "Little" (which he now referred to as his "slave name") and took up the name "X" to symbolize his lost African heritage.

Articulate and charismatic, Malcolm X quickly rose to prominence in the Nation of Islam. As the racial tensions of the 1960s began to flare, he attracted the attention of American mainstream media—and the watchful surveillance of the FBI. In 1964, following a period of disappointment and disillusion with Elijah Muhammad, Malcolm X broke with the Nation of Islam. Returning to the spiritual roots of his conversion to Islam, he made a hajj, *or pilgrimage, to Mecca in Saudi Arabia. The sight of so many Muslims of so many different races and colors was deeply moving to Malcolm X, and upon his return to America he began working toward healing and reconciliation for all Americans of all races. "I am not a racist," he declared; "I am against every form of racism and segregation, every form of discrimination. I believe in human beings, and that all human beings should be respected as such, regardless of their color."*

Unfortunately, the enemies he had made and the fears he had provoked did not leave Malcolm X much time to share this message; three assassins took him down as he spoke at the Audubon Ballroom in Harlem on February 15, 1965.

I became increasingly frustrated at not being able to express what I wanted to convey in letters that I wrote, especially those to Mr. Elijah Muhammad. In the street, I had been the most articulate hustler out there—I had commanded attention when I said something. But now, trying to write simple English, I not only wasn't articulate, I wasn't even functional. How would I sound writing in slang, the way I would *say* it, something such as, "Look, daddy, let me pull your coat about a cat, Elijah Muhammad—"

Many who today hear me somewhere in person, or on television, or those who read something I've said, will think I went to school far beyond the eighth grade. This impression is due entirely to my prison studies.

It had really begun back in the Charlestown Prison, when Bimbi first made me feel envy of his stock of knowledge. Bimbi had always taken charge of any conversation he was in, and I had tried to emulate him. But every book I picked up had few sentences which didn't contain anywhere from one to nearly all of the words that might as well have been in Chinese. When I just skipped those words, of course, I really ended up with little idea of what the book said. So I had come to the Norfolk Prison Colony still going through only book-reading motions. Pretty soon, I would have quit even these motions, unless I had received the motivation that I did.

I saw that the best thing I could do was get hold of a dictionary—to study, to learn some words. I was lucky enough to reason also that I should try to improve my penmanship. It was sad. I couldn't even write in a straight line. It was both ideas together that moved me to request a dictionary along with some tablets and pencils from the Norfolk Prison Colony school.

5   I spent two days just riffling uncertainly through the dictionary's pages. I'd never realized so many words existed! I didn't know *which* words I needed to learn. Finally, just to start some kind of action, I began copying.

In my slow, painstaking, ragged handwriting, I copied into my tablet everything printed on that first page, down to the punctuation marks.

I believe it took me a day. Then, aloud, I read back, to myself, everything I'd written on the tablet. Over and over, aloud, to myself, I read my own handwriting.

I woke up the next morning, thinking about those words—immensely proud to realize that not only had I written so much at one time, but I'd written words that I never knew were in the world. Moreover, with a little effort, I also could remember what many of these words meant. I reviewed the words whose meaning I didn't remember. Funny thing, from the dictionary's first page right now, that "aardvark" springs to my mind. The dictionary had a picture of it, a long-tailed, long-eared, burrowing African mammal, which lives off termites caught by sticking out its tongue as an anteater does for ants.

I was so fascinated that I went on—I copied the dictionary's next page. And the same experience came when I studied that. With every succeeding page, I also learned of people and places and events from history. Actually the dictionary is like a miniature encyclopedia. Finally the dictionary's A section had filled a whole tablet—and I went on into the B's. That was the way I started copying what eventually became the entire dictionary. It went a lot faster after so much practice helped me to pick up handwriting speed. Between what I wrote in my tablet, and writing letters, during the rest of my time in prison I would guess I wrote a million words.

10   I suppose it was inevitable that as my word-base broadened, I could for the first time pick up a book and read and now begin to understand what the book was saying. Anyone who has read a great deal can imagine the new world that opened. Let me tell you something: from then until I left the prison, in every free moment I had, if I was not reading in the library, I was reading on my bunk. You couldn't have gotten me out of books with a wedge. Between Mr. Muhammad's teachings, my correspondence, my visitors—usually Ella and Reginald—and my reading of books, months passed without my even thinking about being imprisoned. In fact, up to then, I never had been so truly free in my life.

The Norfolk Prison Colony's library was in the school building. A variety of classes was taught there by instructors who came from such places as Harvard and Boston universities. The weekly debates between inmate teams were also held in the school building. You would be astonished to know how worked up convict debaters and audiences would get over subjects like "Should Babies Be Fed Milk?"

Available on the prison library's shelves were books on just about every general subject. Much of the big private collection that Parkhurst had willed to the prison was still in crates and boxes in the back of the library—thousands of old books. Some of them looked ancient: covers faded, old-time parchment-looking binding. Parkhurst, I've mentioned, seemed to have been principally interested in history and religion. He had the money and the special interest to have a lot of books that you wouldn't have in general circulation. Any college library would have been lucky to get that collection.

As you can imagine, especially in a prison where there was heavy emphasis on rehabilitation, an inmate was smiled upon if he demonstrated an unusually intense interest in books. There was a sizable number of well-read inmates, especially the popular debaters. Some were said by many to be practically walking encyclopedias. They were almost celebrities. No university would ask any student to devour literature as I did when this new world opened to me, of being able to read and *understand*.

I read more in my room than in the library itself. An inmate who was known to read a lot could check out more than the permitted maximum number of books. I preferred reading in the total isolation of my own room.

15   When I had progressed to really serious reading, every night at about ten (P.M.) I would be outraged with the "lights out." It always seemed to catch me right in the middle of something engrossing.

Fortunately, right outside my door was a corridor light that cast a glow into my room. The glow was enough to read by, once my eyes adjusted to it. So when "lights out" came, I would sit on the floor where I could continue reading in that glow.

At one-hour intervals the night guards paced past every room. Each time I heard the approaching footsteps, I jumped into bed and feigned sleep. And as soon as the guard passed, I got back out of bed onto the floor area of that light-glow, where I would read for another fifty-eight minutes—until the guard approached again. That went on until three or four every morning. Three or four hours of sleep a night was enough for me. Often in the years in the streets I had slept less than that.

Questions for Active Reading

1. How does Malcolm X organize this excerpt from his autobiography? Why is this method of organization particularly effective? Create a simile to describe this organization strategy (for example, "it's like a light going on," or "it's like a tree putting out leaves after a long winter).

2. For whom is Malcolm X writing, and what is his purpose? (In fact, if you read closely, you might detect more than one assumed audience, and many layers of purpose.) What language does he use, and images does he create, to appeal to a specific audience?

3. Malcolm X uses contrast throughout this excerpt—especially the contrast between what his audience might *expect*, and what actually *occurs*. These contrasts are occasionally humorous, and often moving. Find three examples of these contrasts in this excerpt, and explain what makes them effective.

Questions for Thinking Critically

1. Malcolm X states that, although he was an articulate "street hustler," this ability was of little help in expressing his ideas in writing. Explain the differences between expressing your ideas orally and in writing, including the advantages and disadvantages of each form of language expression.

2. Malcolm X envied one of the other inmates, Bimbi, because his stock of knowledge enabled him to take charge of any conversation he was in. Explain why knowledge—and our ability to use it—leads to power in our dealings with others. Describe a situation from your own experience in which having expert knowledge about a subject enabled you, through writing, to influence the thinking of other people.

3. About pursuing his mastery of language and exploring books, Malcolm X states, "Up to then, I never had been so truly free in my life." Explain what you think he means by this statement. Then describe a time in your life when you felt "truly free."

Making Decisions When Revising Drafts

Revising your writing is the key to producing your best possible work. It is very rare for a first draft to represent the most effective writing of which a person is capable. Most accomplished writers expect their work to undergo a number of revisions based on their own re-evaluation and on feedback from others. The difference between outstanding and mediocre writing often depends on revision.

Many of the concepts in the five-step decision-making approach can be applied to revising your drafts.

- You *define the decision and your goals* by identifying what in a draft needs to be revised and what should be left as it is.

- You *consider possible choices* for improving a draft, especially with major components such as composing and placing the thesis statement, presenting evidence, and arranging material in sequences, sections, or paragraphs. You also often have various choices among words and sentence patterns when you work at the editing level of revision.

- You *gather relevant information* and *evaluate the pros and cons* of the different choices in order to select the one that best meets the needs of the writing situation. Sometimes you may want to write down the different possibilities; in other instances, you may just try them out in your mind.

- After *implementing* your choices by revising a draft, you *evaluate* your writing by *reading it again,* slowly and completely, to be sure that the whole piece is as good as you can make it.

Collaborating with classmates or other trusted readers in all these decisions will usually be very helpful. Other readers can see your drafts more objectively and can help you "re-see" and revise them.

SPECIFIC DECISIONS TO MAKE AT SEVERAL LEVELS

The following suggestions should help you revise your drafts.

Read your entire draft slowly and carefully. You may find, as many writers do, that reading out loud helps you to identify parts that don't sound right. Also, ask someone whose judgment you trust to read the draft and help you to decide what improvement is needed. If your class allows peer review, be prepared for this opportunity by having a draft ready.

If you determine that improvement is required, you need to make a decision immediately. At what level should you begin to make changes? Some people think that revision means correcting grammar, punctuation, and spelling. Revision can indeed include those corrections, but it usually means much more. In fact, those corrections are often made separately, as editing and proofreading, to distinguish them from larger aspects of revision.

A helpful way to decide where to begin revising is to move through the following hierarchy of concerns and questions about your draft. If you find yourself answering any of the questions in a manner that suggests ways to improve your writing, *stop and try to make the changes or additions to your draft before you move on to the next level.* There is no point in worrying about punctuation if your draft lacks focus or good examples.

However, remember that revision, like all activities in a writing process, is recursive. You may detect content, organization, or wording problems while you are checking punctuation; you may fix a typo while you're rewording the thesis statement. The following hierarchy emphasizes the importance of looking first at major concerns, but you should be prepared to move around among the levels of revision as you make your decisions about a draft.

A Step-by-Step Method for Revising Any Assignment

The following method can be used both for revising your own papers and for reviewing your classmates' papers. It can be applied to any assignment. For easy reference as you move through the assignments in this book and those for other courses, an edited version of this method is reprinted on the inside back cover of this text. It will be referred to in the Revising section of each Writing Project in the following chapters.

1. **Think big.** Look at the draft as a whole.

   ❑ Does it fulfill the assignment in terms of topic and length?

   ❑ Does it have a clear focus?

   ❑ What parts of the draft, if any, do not relate to its focus?

   ❑ How could the draft be reorganized to make it more logical?

   ❑ What evidence could be added to help to accomplish your purpose?

   ❑ How could the flow between paragraphs be made smoother?

   ❑ Is your point of view consistent throughout?

   Develop alternatives based on the answers to these questions, decide which alternatives will improve your draft, and then make changes to your draft before proceeding to the next level of revision.

2. **Think medium.** Look at the draft paragraph by paragraph.

   First consider the *introduction*.

   ❑ How could you rewrite your lead to make the audience more interested in reading on? (See the suggestions for being creative with introductions in Chapter 5.)

❏ How could you make the introduction more appropriate for the rest of the draft—that is, can you make the tone of the introduction match the tone of the rest of the draft?

❏ How could you indicate the focus more effectively?

Then look at each of your *body paragraphs.*

❏ Does each support the thesis?

❏ Does each present relevant, specific evidence not presented elsewhere?

❏ Which, if any, body paragraphs should be combined or eliminated?

❏ Which body paragraphs use topic sentences effectively? Which don't?

❏ Where could you use transitions to improve the flow within or between body paragraphs?

Now look at your *conclusion.* This is your last chance to accomplish your purpose with your intended audience.

❏ How could you make your conclusion more effective? (See the suggestions for being creative with conclusions in Chapter 5.)

❏ Is the tone of the conclusion appropriate?

Again, develop alternatives and make changes to your draft before proceeding to the next level.

3. **Think small.** Look at your draft sentence by sentence.

❏ Which sentences are difficult to understand? How could you reword them?

❏ Which, if any, sentences are so long that your audience could get lost in them?

❏ Where are there short, choppy sentences that can be combined?

❏ Which sentences seem vague? How could you clarify them?

❏ Which, if any, sentences have errors in standard English grammar or usage? How could you correct them?

Make necessary changes to your draft before proceeding to the next level.

4. **Think "picky."** Look at your draft as the fussiest critic might.

❏ Which words are not clear or not quite right for your meaning? What words could you use instead?

❏ Are any words spelled incorrectly? (Run the spell-checker program on your computer, but don't rely on it alone.)

❏ Are the pages numbered consecutively?

❏ Does the physical appearance of your draft make a good impression?

❏ Is there anything else you can do to improve your draft?

Thinking ↔ Writing Activity

Using the Revision Method

Apply the revision method to an essay you have written for this course (your instructor will advise you about which one to select). Be sure to complete each of the steps in the method. Although this process may initially seem time-consuming and rather mechanical, you will soon begin to integrate these ideas in a more natural and flexible way. As you become more experienced as a writer, the revision method will eventually become an integral part of your composing process.

Beyond considering your own earlier experiences, you can deepen your understanding of revision by reading the following selection by an expert writer.

The Maker's Eye: Revising Your Own Manuscripts

BY DONALD M. MURRAY (b. 1924)

Known as both a professional journalist and a brilliant teacher, Donald M. Murray won the Pulitzer Prize for his editorials in the Boston Herald *in 1954. Since then, he has taught writing at the University of New Hampshire and Boston University and is now a columnist for* The Boston Globe. *He has acted as a writing coach for several national newspapers and written poetry for many journals. Now in retirement, he published his memoir,* My Twice-Lived Life, *in 2001.*

Murray has also authored several books on the craft of writing and teaching writing, including Learning by Teaching, Expecting the Unexpected, *and* Crafting a Life in Essay, Story, Poem. *His work has been highly influential in the way writing is taught. In this selection, he describes his own revision process, one that has served him well.*

When students complete a first draft, they consider the job of writing done—and their teachers too often agree. When professional writers complete a first draft, they usually feel that they are at the start of the writing process. When a draft is completed, the job of writing can begin.

That difference in attitude is the difference between amateur and professional, inexperience and experience, journeyman and craftsman. Peter F.

Drucker, the prolific business writer, calls his first draft "the zero draft"—after that he can start counting. Most writers share the feeling that the first draft, and all of those which follow, are opportunities to discover what they have to say and how best they can say it.

To produce a progression of drafts, each of which says more and says it more clearly, the writer has to develop a special kind of reading skill. In school we are taught to decode what appears on the page as finished writing. Writers, however, face a different category of possibility and responsibility when they read their own drafts. To them the words on the page are never finished. Each can be changed and rearranged, can set off a chain reaction of confusion or clarified meaning. This is a different kind of reading, which is possibly more difficult and certainly more exciting.

Writers must learn to be their own best enemy. They must accept the criticism of others and be suspicious of it; they must accept the praise of others and be even more suspicious of it. Writers cannot depend on others. They must detach themselves from their own pages so that they can apply both their caring and their craft to their own work.

5   Such detachment is not easy. Science fiction writer Ray Bradbury supposedly puts each manuscript away for a year to the day and then rereads it as a stranger. Not many writers have the discipline or the time to do this. We must read when our judgment may be at its worst, when we are close to the euphoric moment of creation.

Then the writer, counsels novelist Nancy Hale, "should be critical of everything that seems to him most delightful in his style. He should excise what he most admires, because he wouldn't thus admire it if he weren't . . . in a sense protecting it from criticism." John Ciardi, the poet, adds, "The last act of writing must be to become one's own reader. It is, I suppose, a schizophrenic process, to begin passionately and to end critically, to begin hot and to end cold; and, more important, to be passion-hot and critic-cold at the same time."

Most people think that the principal problem is that writers are too proud of what they have written. Actually, a greater problem for most professional writers is one shared by the majority of students. They are overly critical, think everything is dreadful, tear up page after page, never complete a draft, see the task as hopeless.

The writer must learn to read critically but constructively, to cut what is bad, to reveal what is good. Eleanor Estes, the children's book author, explains: "The writer must survey his work critically, coolly, as though he were a stranger to it. He must be willing to prune, expertly and hard-heartedly. At the end of each revision, a manuscript may look . . . worked over, torn apart, pinned together, added to, deleted from, words changed and words changed back. Yet the book must maintain its original freshness and spontaneity."

Most readers underestimate the amount of rewriting it usually takes to produce spontaneous reading. This is a great disadvantage to the student writer, who sees only a finished product and never watches the craftsman who takes the necessary steps back, studies the work carefully, returns to the task, steps back, returns, steps back, again and again. Anthony Burgess, one of the most prolific writers in the English-speaking world, admits, "I might revise a page twenty times." Roald Dahl, the popular children's writer, states, "By the time I'm nearing the end of a story, the first part will have been reread and altered and corrected at least 150 times. . . . Good writing is essentially rewriting. I am positive of this."

10   Rewriting isn't virtuous. It isn't something that ought to be done. It is simply something that most writers find they have to do to discover what they have to say and how to say it. It is a condition of the writer's life.

There are, however, a few writers who do little formal rewriting, primarily because they have the capacity and experience to create and review a large number of invisible drafts in their minds before they approach the page. And some writers slowly produce finished pages, performing all the tasks of revision simultaneously, page by page, rather than draft by draft. But it is still possible to see the sequence followed by most writers most of the time in rereading their own work.

Most writers scan their drafts first, reading as quickly as possible to catch the larger problems of subject and form, then move in closer and closer as they read and write, reread and rewrite.

The first thing writers look for in their drafts is *information.* They know that a good piece of writing is built from specific, accurate, and interesting information. The writer must have an abundance of information from which to construct a readable piece of writing.

Next, writers look for meaning in the information. The specifics must build a pattern of significance. Each piece of specific information must carry the reader toward meaning.

15   Writers reading their own drafts are aware of *audience.* They put themselves in the reader's situation and make sure that they deliver information which a reader wants to know or needs to know in a manner which is easily digested. Writers try to be sure that they anticipate and answer the questions a critical reader will ask when reading the piece of writing.

Writers make sure that the *form* is appropriate to the subject and the audience. Form, or genre, is the vehicle which carries meaning to the reader, but form cannot be selected until the writer has adequate information to discover its significance and an audience which needs or wants that meaning.

Once writers are sure the form is appropriate, they must then look at the *structure,* the order of what they have written. Good writing is built on a solid framework of logic, argument, narrative, or motivation which runs through the entire piece of writing and holds it together. This is the time when many writers find it most effective to outline as a way of visualizing the hidden spine by which the piece of writing is supported.

The element on which writers may spend a majority of their time is *development.* Each section of a piece of writing must be adequately developed. It must give readers enough information so that they are satisfied. How much information is enough? That's as difficult as asking how much garlic belongs in a salad. It must be done to taste, but most beginning writers underdevelop, underestimating the reader's hunger for information.

As writers solve development problems, they often have to consider questions of *dimension*. There must be a pleasing and effective proportion among all the parts of the piece of writing. There is a continual process of subtracting and adding to keep the piece of writing in balance.

20   Finally, writers have to listen to their own voices. *Voice* is the force which drives a piece of writing forward. It is an expression of the writer's authority and concern. It is what is between the words on the page, what glues the piece of writing together. A good piece of writing is always marked by a consistent, individual voice.

As writers read and reread, write and rewrite, they move closer and closer to the page until they are doing line-by-line editing. Writers read their own pages with infinite care. Each sentence, each line, each clause, each phrase, each word, each mark of punctuation, each section of white space between the type has to contribute to the clarification of meaning.

Slowly the writer moves from word to word, looking through language to see the subject. As a word is changed, cut, or added, as a construction is rearranged, all the words used before that moment and all those that follow that moment must be considered and reconsidered.

Writers often read aloud at this stage of the editing process, muttering or whispering to themselves, calling on the ear's experience with language. Does this sound right—or that? Writers edit, shifting back and forth from eye to page to ear to page. I find I must do this careful editing in short runs, no more than fifteen or twenty minutes at a stretch, or I become too kind with myself. I begin to see what I hope is on the page, not what actually is on the page.

This sounds tedious if you haven't done it, but actually it is fun. Making something right is immensely satisfying, for writers begin to learn what they are writing about by writing. Language leads them to meaning, and there is the joy of discovery, of understanding, of making meaning clear as the writer employs the technical skills of language.

25   Words have double meanings, even triple and quadruple meanings. Each word has its own potential for connotation and denotation. And when writers rub one word against the other, they are often rewarded with a sudden insight, an unexpected clarification.

The maker's eye moves back and forth from word to phrase to sentence to paragraph to sentence to phrase to word. The maker's eye sees the need for variety and balance, for a firmer structure, for a more appropriate form. It peers into the interior of the paragraph, looking for coherence, unity, and emphasis, which make meaning clear.

I learned something about this process when my first bifocals were prescribed. I had ordered a large section of the reading portion of the glass because of my work, but even so, I could not contain my eyes within this new limit of vision. And I still find myself taking off my glasses and bending my nose towards the page, for my eyes unconsciously flick back and forth across the page, back to another page, forward to still another, as I try to see each evolving line in relation to every other line.

When does this process end? Most writers agree with the great Russian writer Tolstoy, who said, "I scarcely ever reread my published writings, if by chance I come across a page, it always strikes me: all this must be rewritten; this is how I should have written it."

The maker's eye is never satisfied, for each word has the potential to ignite new meaning. This article has been twice written all the way through the writing process, and it was published four years ago. Now it is to be republished in a book. The editors make a few small suggestions, and then I read it with my maker's eye. Now it has been re-edited, re-vised, re-read, re-re-edited, for each piece of writing to the writer is full of potential and alternatives.

30   A piece of writing is never finished. It is delivered to a deadline, torn out of the typewriter on demand, sent off with a sense of accomplishment and shame and pride and frustration. If only there were a couple more days, time for just another run at it, perhaps then . . .

Questions for Active Reading

1. Murray identifies elements for writers to examine when critically reading their drafts: information, audience, form, structure, development, dimension, and voice. Reread any essay you have written for this course, paying attention to each of these elements. How would you revise the essay further to better express your meaning?

2. Reread that same essay aloud to yourself and see if your "ear's experience with language" suggests any additional changes.

3. Murray quotes several authors in his essay, identifying each with a short phrase. Does that additional information influence how you read that quote and "listen" to its speaker? In what way?

Questions for Thinking Critically

1. Murray begins by contrasting the "student" and the "professional" writer. How do you, as a member of his audience, feel about your place in this comparison?

2. Compare the kind of writing that Murray is discussing to the writing that Malcolm X describes. How might Malcolm X interpret Murray's idea that "the words on the page are never finished?"

3. How does Murray establish his authority as a writer? Are you satisfied that he is someone whose advice you should follow? Why or why not?

Talking in the New Land
BY EDITE CUNHÃ (b. 1953)

The whaling and manufacturing towns of Massachusetts have long-established Portuguese communities, with some families tracing their roots back to sailors from the Azores who signed on to American whaling ships in the early nineteenth century, when Massachusetts towns like New Bedford were flourishing centers of the whaling industry. Edite Cunhã immigrated to Peabody, Massachusetts, with her family when she was seven years old. In this essay, originally published in The New England Monthly, *Cunhã describes the responsibilities assumed by many children in immigrant families. With their quick facility for language and their immersion in local school systems, many immigrant children find themselves serving as translators for their parents, taking on a kind of maturity and responsibility that can sometimes seem overwhelming.*

In her current writing, Cunhã continues to explore the Portuguese-American community. She is working on a novel and a collection of short stories. In addition, she is an established artist, working in a medium called pique-assiette, *which uses fragments of broken glass and china as raw material for complex and beautiful mosaics. On her gallery web site, Cunhã recalls that, as a child, she "combed the hillside below the central Portuguese village where my grandparents lived searching for potsherds. They were my favorite playthings. I have an old fading photograph of myself as a small girl, playing in the courtyard with my cousins. Spread before us on a makeshift table are our treasures—fascinating bits of colored porcelain and pottery." As you read "Talking in the New Land," take note of how she uses a kind of mosaic or collage effect in the arrangement of her anecdotes—as well as an evocative, and heartbreaking, appearance of old china.*

Before I started school in America I was Edite. Maria Edite dos Anjos Cunha. Maria, in honor of the Virgin Mary. In Portugal it was customary to use Maria as a religious and legal prefix to every girl's name. Virtually every girl was so named. It had something to do with the apparition of the Virgin to three shepherd children at Fatima. In naming their daughters Maria, my people were expressing their love and reverence for their Lady of Fatima.

Edite came from my godmother, Dona Edite Baetas Ruivo. The parish priest argued that I could not be named Edite because in Portugal the name was not considered Christian. But Dona Edite defended my right to bear her name. No one had argued with her family when they had christened her Edite. Her family had power and wealth. The priest considered privileges endangered by his stand, and I became Maria Edite.

The dos Anjos was for my mother's side of the family. Like her mother before her, she had been named Maria dos Anjos. And Cunha was for my father's side. Carlos dos Santos Cunha, son of Abilio dos Santos Cunha, the tailor from Saíl.

I loved my name. "Maria Edite dos Anjos Cunha," I'd recite at the least provocation. It was melodious and beautiful. And through it I knew exactly who I was.

5   At the age of seven I was taken from our little house in Sobreira, São Mart-inho da Cortiça, Portugal, and brought to Peabody, Massachusetts. We moved into the house of Senhor João, who was our sponsor in the big land. I was in America for about a week when someone took me to school one morning and handed me over to the teacher, Mrs. Donahue.

    Mrs. Donahue spoke Portuguese, a wondrous thing for a woman with a funny, unpronounceable name.

    "Como é que te chamas?" she asked as she led me to a desk by big windows.

    "Maria Edite dos Anjos Cunha," I recited, all the while scanning Mrs. Don-ahue for clues. How could a woman with such a name speak my language?

    In fact, Mrs. Donahue was Portuguese. She was a Silva. But she had married an Irishman and changed her name. She changed my name, too, on the first day of school.

10   "Your name will be Mary Edith Cunha," she declared. "In America you only need two or three names. Mary Edith is a lovely name. And it will be easier to pronounce."

    My name was Edite. Maria Edite. Maria Edite dos Anjos Cunha. I had no trouble pronouncing it.

    "Mary Edith, Edithhh, Mary Edithhh," Mrs. Donahue exaggerated it. She wrinkled up her nose and raised her upper lip to show me the proper position-ing of the tongue for the *th* sound. She looked hideous. There was a big pain in my head. I wanted to scream out my name. But you could never argue with a teacher.

    At home I cried and cried. *Mãe* and *Pai* wanted to know about the day. I couldn't pronounce the new name for them. Senhor João's red face wrinkled in laughter.

    Day after day Mrs. Donahue made me practice pronouncing that name that wasn't mine. Mary Edithhhhh. Mary Edithhh. Mary Edithhh. But weeks later I still wouldn't respond when she called it out in class. Mrs. Donahue became cross when I didn't answer. Later my other teachers shortened it to Mary. And I never knew quite who I was. . . .

15   Mrs. Donahue was a small woman, not much bigger than my seven-year-old self. Her graying hair was cut into a neat, curly bob. There was a smile that she wore almost every day. Not broad. Barely perceptible. But it was there, in her eyes, and at the corners of her mouth. She often wore gray suits with jackets neatly fitted about the waist. On her feet she wore matching black leather shoes, tightly laced. Matching, but not identical. One of them had an extra-thick sole, because like all of her pupils, Mrs. Donahue had an oddity. We, the children, were odd because we were of different colors and sizes, and did not speak in the accepted tongue. Mrs. Donahue was odd because she had legs of different lengths.

    I grew to love Mrs. Donahue. She danced with us. She was the only teacher in all of Carroll School who thought it was important to dance. Every day after recess she took us all to the big open space at the back of the room. We stood in a circle and joined hands. Mrs. Donahue would blow a quivering note from the little round pitch pipe she kept in her pocket, and we became a twirling, singing wheel. Mrs. Donahue hobbled on her short leg and sang in a high trembly voice, "Here we go, loop-de-loop." We took three steps, then a pause. Her last "loop" was always very high. It seemed to squeak above our heads, bouncing on the ceiling. "Here we go, loop-de-lie." Three more steps, another pause, and on we whirled. "Here we go, loop-de-loop." Pause. "All on a Saturday night." To anyone looking in from the corridor we were surely an irregular sight, a circle of children of odd sizes and colors singing and twirling with our tiny hobbling teacher.

I'd been in Room Three with Mrs. Donahue for over a year when she decided that I could join the children in the regular elementary classes at Thomas Carroll School. I embraced the news with some ambivalence. By then the oddity of Mrs. Donahue's classroom had draped itself over me like a warm safe cloak. Now I was to join the second-grade class of Miss Laitinen. In preparation, Mrs. Donahue began a phase of relentless drilling. She talked to me about what I could expect in second grade. Miss Laitinen's class was well on its way with cursive writing, so we practiced that every day. We intensified our efforts with multiplication. And we practiced pronouncing the new teacher's name.

"Lay-te-nun." Mrs. Donahue spewed the *t* out with excessive force to demonstrate its importance. I had a tendency to forget it.

"Lay-nun."

20   "Mary Edith, don't be lazy. Use that tongue. It's Lay-te"—she bared her teeth for the *t* part—"nun."

One morning, with no warning, Mrs. Donahue walked me to the end of the hall and knocked on the door to Room Six. Miss Laitinen opened the door. She looked severe, carrying a long rubber-tipped pointer which she held horizontally before her with both hands. Miss Laitinen was a big, masculine woman. Her light, coarse hair was straight and cut short. She wore dark cardigans and very long, pleated plaid kilts that looked big enough to cover my bed.

"This is Mary Edith," Mrs. Donahue said. Meanwhile I looked at their shoes. Miss Laitinen wore flat, brown leather shoes that laced up and squeaked on the wooden floor when she walked. They matched each other perfectly, but they were twice as big as Mrs. Donahue's.

"Mary Edith, say hello to Miss Laitinen." Mrs. Donahue stressed the *t*—a last-minute reminder.

"Hello, Miss Lay-te-nun," I said, leaning my head back to see her face. Miss Laitinen was tall. Mrs. Donahue's head came just to her chest. They both nodded approvingly before I was led to my seat.

25   Peabody, Massachusetts. "The Leather City." It is stamped on the city seal, along with the image of a tanned animal hide. And Peabody, an industrial city of less than fifty thousand people, has the smokestacks to prove it. They rise up all over town from sprawling, dilapidated factories. Ugly, leaning, wooden buildings

that often stretch over a city block. Strauss Tanning Co. A. C. Lawrence Leather Co. Gnecco & Grilk Tanning Corp. In the early sixties, the tanneries were in full swing. The jobs were arduous and health-threatening, but it was the best-paying work around for unskilled laborers who spoke no English. The huge, firetrap factories were filled with men and women from Greece, Portugal, Ireland, and Poland.

In one of these factories, João Nunes, who lived on the floor above us, fed animal skins into a ravenous metal monster all day, every day. The pace was fast. One day the monster got his right arm and wouldn't let go. When the machine was turned off João had a little bit of arm left below his elbow. His daughter Teresa and I were friends. She didn't come out of her house for many days. When she returned to school, she was very quiet and cried a lot.

"Rosa Veludo's been hurt." News of such tragedies spread through the community fast and often. People would tell what they had seen, or what they had heard from those who had seen. *"She was taken to the hospital by ambulance. Someone wrapped her fingers in a paper bag. The doctors may be able to sew them back on."*

A few days after our arrival in the United States, my father went to work at the Gnecco & Grilk leather tannery, on the corner of Howley and Walnut streets. Senhor João had worked there for many years. He helped *Pai* get the job. Gnecco & Grilk was a long, rambling, four-story factory that stretched from the corner halfway down the street to the railroad tracks. The roof was flat and slouched in the middle like the back of an old workhorse. There were hundreds of windows. The ones on the ground floor were covered with a thick wire mesh.

Pai worked there for many months. He was stationed on the ground floor, where workers often had to stand ankle-deep in water laden with chemicals. One day he had a disagreement with his foreman. He left his machine and went home vowing never to return. . . .

30   *Pai* and I stood on a sidewalk in Salem facing a clear glass doorway. The words on the door were big. Division of Employment Security. There was a growing coldness deep inside me. At Thomas Carroll School, Miss Laitinen was probably standing at the side blackboard, writing perfect alphabet letters on straight chalk lines. My seat was empty. I was on a sidewalk with *Pai* trying to understand a baffling string of words. Division had something to do with math, which I didn't particularly like. Employment I had never seen or heard before. Security I knew. But not at that moment.

Pai reached for the door. It swung open into a little square of tiled floor. We stepped in to be confronted by the highest, steepest staircase I had ever seen. At the top, we emerged into a huge, fluorescently lit room. It was too bright and open after the dim, narrow stairs. *Pai* took off his hat. We stood together in a vast empty space. The light, polished tiles reflected the fluorescent glow. There were no windows.

Far across the room, a row of metal desks lined the wall. Each had a green vinyl-covered chair beside it. Off to our left, facing the empty space before us, was a very high green metal dm, esk. It was easily twice as high as a normal-size desk. Its odd size and placement in the middle of the room gave it the appearance of a kind of altar that divided the room in half. There were many people working at desks or walking about, but the room was so big that it still seemed empty.

The head and shoulders of a white-haired woman appeared to rest on the big desk like a sculptured bust. She sat very still. Above her head the word CLAIMS dangled from two pieces of chain attached to the ceiling. As I watched the woman she beckoned to us. *Pai* and I walked toward her.

The desk was so high that *Pai's* shoulders barely cleared the top. Even when I stood on tiptoe I couldn't see over it. I had to stretch and lean my head way back to see the woman's round face. I thought that she must have very long legs to need a desk that high. The coldness in me grew. My neck hurt.

35   "My father can't speak English. He has no work and we need money."

She reached for some papers from a wire basket. One of her fingers was encased in a piece of orange rubber.

"Come around over here so I can see you." She motioned to the side of the desk. I went reluctantly. Rounding the desk I saw with relief that she was a small woman perched on a stool so high it seemed she would need a ladder to get up there.

"How old are you?" She leaned down toward me.

"Eight."

40   "My, aren't you a brave girl. Only eight years old and helping daddy like that. And what lovely earrings you have."

She liked my earrings. I went a little closer to let her touch them. Maybe she would give us money.

"What language does your father speak?" She was straightening up, reaching for a pencil.

"Portuguese."

"What is she saying?" Pai wanted to know.

45   *"Wait,"* I told him. The lady hadn't yet said anything about money.

"Why isn't your father working?"

"His factory burned down."

"What is she saying?" Pai repeated.

"She wants to know why you aren't working."

50   *"Tell her the factory burned down."*

"I know. I did." The lady was looking at me. I hoped she wouldn't ask me what my father had just said.

"What is your father's name?"

"Carlos S. Cunha. C-u-n-h-a." No one could ever spell *Cunha. Pai* nodded at the woman when he heard his name.

"Where do you live?"

55   "Thirty-three Tracey Street, Peabody, Massachusetts." *Pai* nodded again when he heard the address.

"When was your father born?"

"Quando é que tu naçestes?"

"When was the last day your father worked?"

"Qual foi o último dia que trabalhastes?"

60 "What was the name of the factory?"

"Qual éra o nome da fábrica?"

"How long did he work there?"

"Quanto tempo trabalhastes lá?"

"What is his Social Security number?"

65 I looked at her blankly, not knowing what to say. What was a Social Security number?

"What did she say?" Pai prompted me out of silence.

"I don't know. She wants a kind of number." I was feeling very tired and worried. But *Pai* took a small card from his wallet and gave it to the lady. She copied something from it onto her papers and returned it to him. I felt a great sense of relief. She wrote silently for a while as we stood and waited. Then she handed some paper to *Pai* and looked at me.

"Tell your father that he must have these forms filled out by his employer before he can receive unemployment benefits."

I stared at her. What was she saying? Employer? Unemployment benefits? I was afraid she was saying we couldn't have any money. Maybe not, though. Maybe we could have money if I could understand her words.

70 *"What did she say? Can we have some money?"*

"I don't know. I can't understand the words."

"Ask her again if we can have money," Pai insisted. *"Tell her we have to pay the rent."*

"We need money for the rent," I told the lady, trying to hold back tears.

"You can't have money today. You must take the forms to your father's employer and bring them back completed next week. Then your father must sign another form which we will keep here to process his claim. When he comes back in two weeks there may be a check for him." The cold in me was so big now, I was trying not to shiver.

75 "Do you understand?" The lady was looking at me.

I wanted to say, "No, I don't," but I was afraid we would never get money and *Pai* would be angry.

"Tell your father to take the papers to his boss and come back next week." Boss. I could understand boss.

"She said you have to take these papers to your 'bossa' and come back next week."

80 *"We can't have money today?"*

"No. She said maybe we can have money in two weeks."

"Did you tell her we have to pay the rent?"

"Yes, but she said we can't have money yet."

The lady was saying good-bye and beckoning the next person from the line that had formed behind us.

85 I was relieved to move on, but I think *Pai* wanted to stay and argue with her. I knew that if he could speak English, he would have. I knew that he thought it was my fault we couldn't have money. And I myself wasn't so sure that wasn't true.

That night I sat at the kitchen table with a fat pencil and a piece of paper. In my second-grade scrawl I wrote: Dear Miss Laitinen, Mary Edith was sick.

I gave the paper to *Pai* and told him to sign his name.

"What does it say?"

"It says that I was sick today. I need to give it to my teacher."

90 *"You weren't sick today."*

"Ya, but it would take too many words to tell her the truth."

Pai signed the paper. The next morning in school, Miss Laitinen read it and said that she hoped I was feeling better.

When I was nine, *Pai* went to an auction and bought a big house on Tremont Street. We moved in the spring. The yard at the side of the house dipped downward in a gentle slope that was covered with a dense row of tall lilac bushes. I soon discovered that I could crawl in among the twisted trunks to hide from my brothers in the fragrant shade. It was paradise. . . .

I was mostly wild and joyful on Tremont Street. But there was a shadow that fell across my days now and again.

95 *"Ó Ediiiite."* *Pai* would call me without the least bit of warning, to be his voice. He expected me to drop whatever I was doing to attend him. Of late, I'd had to struggle on the telephone with the voice of a woman who wanted some old dishes. The dishes, along with lots of old furniture and junk, had been in the house when we moved in. They were in the cellar, stacked in cardboard boxes and covered with dust. The woman called many times wanting to speak with *Pai.*

"My father can't speak English," I would say. "He says to tell you that the dishes are in our house and they belong to us." But she did not seem to understand. Every few days she would call.

"Ó Ediiiite." *Pai*'s voice echoed through the empty rooms. Hearing it brought on a chill. It had that tone. As always, my first impulse was to pretend I had not heard, but there was no escape. I couldn't disappear into thin air as I wished to do at such calls. We were up in the third-floor apartment of our new house. *Pai* was working in the kitchen. Carlos and I had made a cavern of old cushions and were sitting together deep in its bowels when he called. It was so dark and comfortable there I decided not to answer until the third call, though that risked *Pai*'s wrath.

"Ó Ediiite." Yes, that tone was certainly there. *Pai* was calling me to do something only I could do. Something that always awakened a cold beast deep in my gut. He wanted me to be his bridge. What was it now? Did he have to talk to someone at City Hall again? Or was it the insurance company? They were al-

ways using words I couldn't understand: liability, and premium, and dividend. It made me frustrated and scared.

"You wait. My dotta come." *Pai* was talking to someone. Who could it be? That was some relief. At least I didn't have to call someone on the phone. It was always harder to understand when I couldn't see people's mouths.

100 "*Ó Ediiiiite.*" I hated Carlos. *Pai* never called his name like that. He never had to do anything but play.

"*Que éééé?*"

"*Come over here and talk to this lady.*"

Reluctantly I crawled out from the soft darkness and walked through the empty rooms toward the kitchen. Through the kitchen door I could see a slim lady dressed in brown standing at the top of the stairs in the windowed porch. She had on very skinny high-heeled shoes and a brown purse to match. As soon as *Pai* saw me he said to the lady, "Dis my dotta." To me he said, "*See what she wants.*"

The lady had dark hair that was very smooth and puffed away from her head. The ends of it flipped up in a way that I liked.

105 "Hello. I'm the lady who called about the dishes."

I stared at her without a word. My stomach lurched.

"*What did she say?*" Pai wanted to know.

"*She says she's the lady who wants the dishes.*"

Pai's face hardened some.

110 "*Tell her she's wasting her time. We're not giving them to her. Didn't you already tell her that on the telephone?*"

I nodded, standing helplessly between them.

"*Well, tell her again.*" Pai was getting angry. I wanted to disappear.

"My father says he can't give you the dishes," I said to the lady. She clutched her purse and leaned a little forward.

"Yes, you told me that on the phone. But I wanted to come in person and speak with your father because it's very important to me that—"

115 "My father can't speak English," I interrupted her. Why didn't she just go away? She was still standing in the doorway with her back to the stairwell. I wanted to push her down.

"Yes, I understand that. But I wanted to see him." She looked at *Pai*, who was standing in the doorway to the kitchen holding his hammer. The kitchen was up one step from the porch. *Pai* was a small man, but he looked kind of scary staring down at us like that.

"*What is she saying?*"

"*She says she wanted to talk to you about getting her dishes.*"

"*Tell her the dishes are ours. They were in the house. We bought the house and everything in it. Tell her the lawyer said so.*"

120 The brown lady was looking at me expectantly.

"My father says the dishes are ours because we bought the house and the lawyer said everything in the house is ours now."

"Yes, I know that, but I was away when the house was being sold. I didn't know . . ."

"*Eeii.*" There were footsteps on the stairs behind her. It was *Mãe* coming up from the second floor to find out what was going on. The lady moved away from the door to let *Mãe* in.

"Dis my wife," *Pai* said to the lady. The lady said hello to *Mãe,* who smiled and nodded her head. She looked at me, then at *Pai* in a questioning way.

125 "*It's the lady who wants our dishes,*" *Pai* explained.

"*Ó.*" *Mãe* looked at her again and smiled, but I could tell she was a little worried.

We stood there in kind of a funny circle; the lady looked at each of us in turn and took a deep breath.

"I didn't know," she continued, "that the dishes were in the house. I was away. They are very important to me. They belonged to my grandmother. I'd really like to get them back." She spoke this while looking back and forth between *Mãe* and *Pai.* Then she looked down at me, leaning forward again. "Will you tell your parents, please?"

The cold beast inside me had begun to rise up toward my throat as the lady spoke. I knew that soon it would try to choke out my words. I spoke in a hurry to get them out.

130 "*She said she didn't know the dishes were in the house she was away they were her grandmother's dishes she wants them back.*" I felt a deep sadness at the thought of the lady returning home to find her grandmother's dishes sold.

"*We don't need all those dishes. Let's give them to her,*" *Mãe* said in her calm way. I felt relieved. We could give the lady the dishes and she would go away. But *Pai* got angry.

"*I already said what I had to say. The dishes are ours. That is all.*"

"*Pai, she said she didn't know. They were her grandmother's dishes. She needs to have them.*" I was speaking wildly and loud now. The lady looked at me questioningly, but I didn't want to speak to her again.

"*She's only saying that to trick us. If she wanted those dishes she should have taken them out before the house was sold. Tell her we are not fools. Tell her to forget it. She can go away. Tell her not to call or come here again.*"

135 "What is he saying?" The lady was looking at me again.

I ignored her. I felt sorry for *Pai* for always feeling that people were trying to trick him. I wanted him to trust people. I wanted the lady to have her grandmother's dishes. I closed my eyes and willed myself away.

"*Tell her what I said!*" *Pai* yelled.

"*Pai, just give her the dishes! They were her grandmother's dishes!*" My voice cracked as I yelled back at him. Tears were rising.

I hated *Pai* for being so stubborn. I hated the lady for not taking the dishes before the house was sold. I hated myself for having learned to speak English.

Questions for Active Reading

1. In this essay, Edite Cunhã shifts gracefully between two perspectives—that of a child, and that of an adult reflecting back upon her childhood. Identify at least three places in the text where she is clearly writing from a child's perspective. How can you tell, in those passages, that she is writing with the viewpoint and understanding of a very young girl? What effect does that perspective convey? What does the child perceive, from that perspective, that the adults around her seem to miss?

2. Think about the structure of the interpreted dialogue between Edite, her *Pai,* and the caseworker at the Division of Employment Security. What is missing from this transcription of the dialogue, and why?

3. In reflecting back upon her childhood and her relationship to her father, Cunhã likely had many years of experiences and stories from which to draw. Why did she choose to describe these specific episodes and conversations?

Questions for Thinking Critically

1. Both Edite Cunhã and Malcolm X understand something profound not only about language, but about *literacy*—the ability to use written and spoken language in a socially functional and acceptable fashion. They both realize that those who cannot attain literacy (or who are denied literacy) lose power and self-determination. What kind of "literacy" do you expect to gain from your college education? Are there other literacies that cannot be "taught," but only learned through experience?

2. Cunhã's use of a child's perspective makes for some especially wrenching moments for us as adult readers. For example, take another look at paragraph 41. What is the caseworker really assessing? What does this brief anecdote suggest about the immigrant experience with bureaucracy, particularly when it comes to seeking aid or assistance?

3. What is the difference between explanation and interpretation?

Using Language Ethically

Language reflects thinking, and thinking is shaped by language. Language not only provides multiple ways of expressing the same ideas, thoughts, and feelings but also helps to structure those thoughts, weaving into them nuances of focus. In turn, patterns of thinking breathe life into language, giving both processes power.

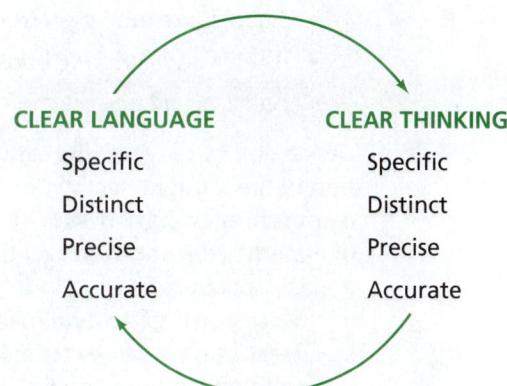

The relationship between thinking and language is *interactive;* both processes are continually influencing each other in many ways. The interactive qualities of language also extend, of course, to its communicative purpose. We use language to persuade, to entertain, to inform, and to delight; yet we also know that language can be used to conceal the truth, to foment hatred, to create terror. As a critical thinker, it is your ethical responsibility to continually evaluate the quality and reliability of what you communicate to others through text, visuals, and speech. Malcolm X and Edite Cunhã both recognized, at a personal level, how powerful language can be; later in this chapter, writers George Orwell and William Lutz explain how language, used for unethical purposes, can cause tremendous damage.

When language use is sloppy—vague, general, indistinct, imprecise, foolish, inaccurate, and so on—it leads to the same sort of thinking. And the reverse is also true. Clear and precise language leads to clear and precise thinking, as shown in Figure 6.1.

The opposite of clear, effective language is language that fails to help the reader picture or understand what the writer means because it is vague or ambiguous. Most of us are guilty of using such ineffective language in speech ("It was a great party!"), but for college and work writing, we need to be as precise as possible. And our writing can gain clarity and power if we use our creative thinking skills to develop fresh, striking figures of speech to illuminate our ideas. Martin Luther King, Jr. gives an extraordinary demonstration of the power of clear language to illuminate an ethical issue in his "I Have a Dream" speech later in this chapter.

IMPROVING VAGUE LANGUAGE

Although our ability to name and identify gives us the power to describe the world in a precise way, we often tend to describe it in words that are imprecise and general. Such nonspecific words are termed *vague* words. Consider the following sentences:

- I had a *nice* time yesterday.
- That is an *interesting* book.
- She is an *old* person.

In each of these cases, the italicized word does not provide a precise description of the thought, feeling, or experience that the writer or speaker is trying to communicate. Vagueness occurs whenever a word is used to represent an area of experience without clearly defining it. A **vague word** is one that lacks a clear and distinct meaning.

Most words of general measurement—*short, tall, big, small, heavy, light,* and so on—are vague. The exact meanings of these words depend on the specific situation in which they are used and on the particular perspective of the person using them. For example, give specific definitions for the following italicized words by filling in the blanks. Then compare your responses with those of your classmates. Can you account for the differences in meaning?

1. A *middle-aged* person is one who is _____ years old.
2. A *tall* person is one who is over _____ feet _____ inches tall.
3. It's *cold* when the temperature is _____ degrees.
4. A person is *wealthy* when he or she is worth _____ dollars.

Although the vagueness of general measurement terms can lead to confusion, other forms of vagueness are more widespread and often more problematic. Terms such as *good* and *enjoyable,* for example, are imprecise and unclear. Vagueness of this sort permeates every level of human discourse, undermines clear thinking, and is extremely difficult to combat. To use language clearly and precisely, you must develop an understanding of the way language functions and commit yourself to breaking the entrenched habit of using vague expression.

For example, read the following opinion of a movie and circle all the vague, general words that do not express a clear meaning.

Pulp Fiction is a really funny movie about some really unusual characters in California. The movie consists of several different stories that connect at different points. Some of the stories are nerve-wracking and others are hilarious, but all of them are very well done. The plots are very interesting, and the main characters are excellent. I liked this movie a lot.

Because of the vague language in this passage, it expresses only general approval—it does not explain in exact or precise terms what the experience of seeing the movie was like. Thus, the writer of the passage has not successfully communicated the experience.

Vagueness is always a matter of degree. In fact, you can think of your descriptive/informative use of language as falling somewhere on a scale between extreme generality and extreme specificity. The following statements move from the general to the specific.

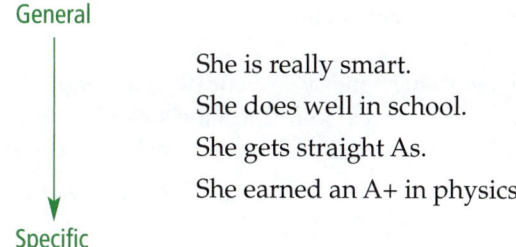

General

She is really smart.

She does well in school.

She gets straight As.

She earned an A+ in physics.

Specific

Although different situations require various degrees of specificity, you should work to become increasingly more precise in your use of language.

When you are revising your own work, try to recognize and improve vague language, remembering your obligation to your audience to be as clear as possible. Be on the lookout for words such as *nice, good, fine, interesting, well, special, bad, really, very, old, young, situation,* and so on. Resist the temptation to improve vague words by putting *very* or *really* in front of them. Instead, if you have written, "The dessert was good," ask yourself, "How or why was it good?" Then substitute your answer for the vague word: "The dessert was full of fresh, plump strawberries flavored with orange juice and bits of mint." Now your audience can enjoy it with you!

USING FIGURATIVE LANGUAGE

Thus far in this section, we have been concerned with saying and writing exactly what we mean as precisely as possible. However, there is another way to use language to express thinking: to say something we do not literally mean. Of course, there are some writing situations for which figurative language is inappropriate. When in doubt, check with your instructor. But when we do use figurative language effectively, our readers or listeners understand that we are not speaking literally but rather that we are speaking *figuratively*, using a *figure of speech.* There are many different figures of speech; some literary experts have identified as many as 250. Here, though, we will focus on two that may already be familiar: *simile* and *metaphor.*

Both simile and metaphor are based on a special kind of comparative thinking called an **analogy,** which is a limited comparison of two essentially unlike things for the purpose of illuminating or enriching our understanding. Analogies differ from the more common comparisons that examine the similarities and differences of two items in the same general category, such as two items on a menu or two methods of birth control. Similes and metaphors focus on unexpected likenesses between items from different categories. Thus, when we compare a baby's skin to velvet, we may be calling attention to the skin's color or softness, but we are not suggesting that it has pile or can be dyed different shades.

Consider the following example:

Life's but a walking shadow, a poor player
That struts and frets his hour upon the stage,
And then is heard no more.. . .

—Shakespeare, Macbeth

In this famous metaphor, Shakespeare is comparing two things that at first seem to have nothing in common: life and an actor. Yet a closer look reveals that even though they are dissimilar in many ways, they share some undeniable similarities.

It is simple to distinguish similes from metaphors. Similes are explicitly stated comparisons, so they include the words *as, like,* or *than.* For example, "To the goalie, Mia Hamm's shot appeared as a photon of light." On the other hand, metaphors are implicitly stated comparisons, usually using some part of the verb *to be,* and do not include the words *as, like,* or *than.* Thus, it would be a metaphor to say, "To the goalie, Mia Hamm's shot was a photon of light."

When should you use figurative language in your writing? Extensive reading will help you develop a feel for opportunities, but here are four suggestions:

- When you are having trouble finding the right words. Powerful or complex emotions can make you speechless or make you say things like, "Words cannot express what I feel." For example, if you are trying to describe your feelings of love for someone, you might write, "As breathtaking as the first rose in spring, this is the first great love of my life," or "Like the fragile yet supple petals of the rose, my feelings are tender and sensitive."

- When you want to express a profound thought in a strikingly original way. For example, you want to express an idea about the meaning of life, which the simple word *life* does not convey. Shakespeare wrote, "(Life) is a tale/ Told by an idiot, full of sound and fury,/ Signifying nothing." Forrest Gump said, "Life is like a box of chocolates." You might write, "Life is a football game," or "Life is an earthquake."

- When you want to add an extra dimension to a description. Edite Cunhã wrote, "By then the oddity of Mrs. Donahue's classroom had draped itself over me like a warm safe cloak," and "The roof was flat and slouched in the middle like the back of an old work horse." You might write, "The spilled flour settled all over the apartment like a soft snow."

- When you want to be clever and amuse your audience. The great pool hustler Minnesota Fats wrote, "A pool player in a tuxedo is like a hotdog with whipped cream on it." By putting together two things that don't go together, like hotdogs and whipped cream, Minnesota Fats made his audience smile. You might write, "My twin brothers get along like ice cream and sauerkraut."

Thinking ↔ Writing Activity

Creating Similes and Metaphors

1. Use your creative thinking skills to create a simile for a subject of your own choosing, noting at least two points of comparison.

2. Now use your creative thinking skills to create a metaphor (implied analogy) for a subject of your own choosing, noting at least two points of comparison.

3. Create a metaphor for life that represents your feelings and explain the points of similarity.

Figurative language that has become cliché is not effective. "He runs like a deer" and "I slept like a baby" were wonderful similes the first time they were used, but they have become old and tired: clichés. Use your creative thinking skills to write original, striking figures of speech.

Very skillful speakers and writers are able to weave similes and metaphors together into a striking tapestry. As you read the following selection by Martin Luther King Jr., notice now he uses figurative language effectively while being clear and precise about both the problem and the solution.

I Have a Dream

BY MARTIN LUTHER KING JR. (1929–1968)

The son of an influential Baptist minister, Martin Luther King Jr. was a gifted and driven student, entering college at the age of fifteen and eventually completing studies for a doctorate in theology at Boston University. His involvement with the civil rights movement began in 1955, when as a Baptist minister in Montgomery, Alabama, he led the Montgomery bus boycott (after Rosa Parks, an African-American woman, heroically refused to give up her seat at the front of a public bus; at that time in Alabama, African Americans were forced to ride in the back of city buses). From 1960, King moved to Atlanta to be co-pastor with his father at Ebenezer Baptist Church. King also founded and became president of the Southern Christian Leadership Conference.

The American South in the middle of the last century was a segregated society, with the separation of African Americans and white citizens enforced not only by law, but by intimidation and violence. King's extraordinary strategy was to meet violence with the force of peace. Greatly influenced by the nonviolent resistance of Mohandas K. Ghandi, King advocated an approach to protesting injustice that continues to resonate in progressive movements worldwide. Through education and outreach, marches, silent sit-ins at segregated lunch counters, and other acts of nonviolent resistance, King and his followers consistently met acts of barbarism with gestures of peace. Films from this period show crowds of peaceful marchers being attacked by police dogs and blasted by fire hoses, and yet the powerful appeal of King's message won the moral victory. He was awarded the Nobel Peace Prize in 1964.

And yet the violence he so peacefully—but forcefully—resisted eventually claimed him (as it did Ghandi). Dr. King was assassinated while standing on the balcony of the Lorraine Motel in Memphis, Tennessee, on April 4, 1968. He was in Memphis to help lead sanitation workers in a protest against low wages and intolerable working conditions.

The speech that follows was delivered during the great March on Washington in 1963. That peaceful march and demonstration for human rights remains one of the most indelible images of twentieth-century American culture.

Five score years ago, a great American, in whose symbolic shadow we stand, signed the Emancipation Proclamation. This momentous decree came as a great beacon light of hope to millions of Negro slaves who had been seared in the flames of withering injustice. It came as a joyous daybreak to end the long night of captivity.

But one hundred years later, we must face the tragic fact that the Negro is still not free. One hundred years later, the life of the Negro is still sadly crippled by the manacles of segregation and the chains of discrimination. One hundred years later, the Negro lives on a lonely island of poverty in the midst of a vast ocean of material prosperity. One hundred years later, the Negro is still languishing in the corners of American society and finds himself an exile in his own land. So we have come here today to dramatize an appalling condition.

In a sense we have come to our nation's capital to cash a check. When the architects in our republic wrote the magnificent words of the Constitution and the Declaration of Independence, they were signing a promissory note to which every American was to fall heir. This note was a promise that all men would be guaranteed the unalienable rights of life, liberty, and the pursuit of happiness.

It is obvious today that America has defaulted on this promissory note insofar as her citizens of color are concerned. Instead of honoring this sacred obligation, America has given the Negro people a bad check; a check which has come back marked "insufficient funds." But we refuse to believe that the bank of justice is bankrupt. We refuse to believe that there are insufficient funds in the great vaults of opportunity of this nation. So we have come to cash this check—a check that will give us upon demand the riches of freedom and the security of justice. We have also come to this hallowed spot to remind America of the fierce urgency of *now*. This is no time to engage in the luxury of cooling off or to take the tranquilizing drugs of gradualism. *Now* is the time to make real the promises of Democracy. *Now* is the time to rise from the dark and desolate valley of segregation to the sunlit path of racial justice. *Now* is the time to open the doors of opportunity to all of God's children. *Now* is the time to lift our nation from the quicksands of racial injustice to the solid rock of brotherhood.

It would be fatal for the nation to overlook the urgency of the moment and to underestimate the determination of the Negro. This sweltering summer of the Negro's legitimate discontent will not pass until there is an invigorating autumn of freedom and equality. 1963 is not an end, but a beginning. Those who hope that the Negro needed to blow off steam and will now be content will have a rude awakening if the nation returns to business as usual. There will be neither rest nor tranquillity in America until the Negro is granted his citizenship rights. The whirlwinds of revolt will continue to shake the foundations of our nation until the bright day of justice emerges.

But there is something that I must say to my people who stand on the warm threshold which leads into the palace of justice. In the process of gaining our rightful place we must not be guilty of wrongful deeds. Let us not seek to satisfy our thirst for freedom by drinking from the cup of bitterness and hatred. We must forever conduct our struggle on the high plane of dignity and discipline. We must not allow our creative protest to degenerate into physical violence. Again and again we must rise to the majestic heights of meeting physical force with soul force. The marvelous new militancy which has engulfed the Negro community must not lead us to a distrust of all white people, for many of our white brothers, as evidenced by their presence here today, have come to realize that their destiny is tied up with our destiny and their freedom is inextricably bound to our freedom. We cannot walk alone.

And as we walk, we must make the pledge that we shall march ahead. We cannot turn back. There are those who are asking the devotees of civil rights, "When will you be satisfied?" We can never be satisfied as long as the Negro is the victim of the unspeakable horrors of police brutality. We can never be satisfied as long as our bodies, heavy with the fatigue of travel, cannot gain lodging in the motels of the highways and the hotels of the cities. We cannot be satisfied as long as the Negro's basic mobility is from a smaller ghetto to a larger one. We can never be satisfied as long as a Negro in Mississippi cannot vote and a Negro in New York believes he has nothing for which to vote. No, no, we are not satisfied, and we will not be satisfied until justice rolls down like waters and righteousness like a mighty stream.

I am not unmindful that some of you have come here out of great trials and tribulations. Some of you have come fresh from narrow jail cells. Some of you have come from areas where your quest for freedom left you battered by the storms of persecution and staggered by the winds of police brutality. You have been the veterans of creative suffering. Continue to work with the faith that un-earned suffering is redemptive.

Go back to Mississippi, go back to Alabama, go back to South Carolina, go back to Georgia, go back to Louisiana, go back to the slums and ghettos of our northern cities, knowing that somehow this situation can and will be changed. Let us not wallow in the valley of despair.

10   I say to you today, my friends, that in spite of the difficulties and frustrations of the moment I still have a dream. It is a dream deeply rooted in the American dream.

I have a dream that one day this nation will rise up and live out the true meaning of its creed: "We hold these truths to be self-evident; that all men are created equal."

I have a dream that one day on the red hills of Georgia the sons of former slaves and the sons of former slaveowners will be able to sit down together at the table of brotherhood.

I have a dream that one day even the state of Mississippi, a desert state sweltering with the heat of injustice and oppression, will be transformed into an oasis of freedom and justice.

I have a dream that my four little children will one day live in a nation where they will not be judged by the color of their skin but by the content of their character.

15   I have a dream today.

I have a dream that one day the state of Alabama, whose governor's lips are presently dripping with the words of interposition and nullification, will be transformed into a situation where little black boys and black girls will be able to join hands with little white boys and white girls and walk together as sisters and brothers.

I have a dream today.

I have a dream that one day every valley shall be exalted, every hill and mountain shall be made low, the rough places will be made plain, and the crooked places will be made straight, and the glory of the Lord shall be revealed, and all flesh shall see it together.

This is our hope. This is the faith with which I return to the South. With this faith we will be able to hew out of the mountain of despair a stone of hope. With this faith we will be able to transform the jangling discords of our nation into a beautiful symphony of brotherhood. With this faith we will be able to work together, to pray together, to struggle together, to go to jail together, to stand up for freedom together, knowing that we will be free one day.

20   This will be the day when all of God's children will be able to sing with new meaning:

My country, 'tis of thee, Sweet land of liberty, Of thee I sing: Land where my fathers died, Land of the pilgrims' pride, From every mountain-side Let freedom ring.

And if America is to be a great nation, this must become true. So let freedom ring from the prodigious hilltops of New Hampshire. Let freedom ring from the mighty mountains of New York. Let freedom ring from the heightening Alleghenies of Pennsylvania!

Let freedom ring from the snowcapped Rockies of Colorado!

Let freedom ring from the curvaceous peaks of California!

25   But not only that; let freedom ring from Stone Mountain of Georgia!

Let freedom ring from Lookout Mountain of Tennessee!

Let freedom ring from every hill and molehill of Mississippi. From every mountainside, let freedom ring.

When we let freedom ring, when we let it ring from every village and every hamlet, from every state and every city, we will be able to speed up that day when all of God's children, black men and white men, Jews and Gentiles, Protestants and Catholics, will be able to join hands and sing in the words of the old Negro spiritual, "Free at last! free at last! thank God almighty, we are free at last!"

Questions for Active Reading

1. Of the rich metaphors King uses, which two or three do you find most effective or striking? Why?

2. This text is at once a speech and a sermon. Locate a recording of King's delivery of this great sermon, and listen to his delivery. How does King's voice, his emphasis on particular phrases, his call-and-response engagement with his audience, change the way you silently "read" the printed text?

3. The cadences and the figurative language of "I Have a Dream" are profoundly influenced by King's lifelong immersion in the African-American Baptist church. Are those rhythms and biblical allusions familiar to you? Do you need to understand those allusions in order to fully appreciate the ethical and moral implications of his call to action?

Questions for Thinking Critically

1. King exhorts the marchers to "continue to work with the faith that unearned suffering is redemptive." In the same year as the March on Washington, Malcolm X delivered a speech in Detroit in which he noted that "there is nothing in our book, the Koran, that teaches us to suffer peacefully. Our religion teaches us to be intelligent. Be peaceful, be courteous, obey the law, respect everyone; but if someone puts his hands on you, send him to the cemetery." Can these two views be reconciled? How do you think injustice should best be fought?

2. Do you have faith in individual people, or in society as a whole, to address and correct a specific injustice? Describe an injustice that you have witnessed, and evaluate how either individuals or a community has responded to that injustice.

3. King dreams of a nation where people are judged by the "content of their character"—their *ethic*. What is the content of your own character? How do you measure up to your own ethical ideals?

Using Language to Influence

Because of the intimate relationship between language and thinking, people naturally use language to influence the thinking of others. One of the reasons Dr.

King's speech was so influential was that he invoked the cadences and the vocabulary of the Bible. President William Jefferson Clinton used the same strategy when he promised Americans "a new covenant" between the government and the people. Later, George W. Bush became president after promoting an agenda of "compassionate conservatism." Conversely, the term "weapons of mass destruction" was so terrifying that many people believe it was one of the reasons that Congress voted to support the war in Iraq.

Manufacturers and advertising professionals choose language just as carefully to influence buying decisions. Americans are told that the Energizer bunny "keeps going and going." We are invited to "Join the Pepsi generation" and challenged to stop eating chips: "I bet you can't eat just one." And we are told over and over, "It's Miller time."

Whatever your political positions or buying habits, there are people who make a profession of using language to influence others' thinking. They are interested in influencing—and sometimes in controlling—your thoughts, feelings, and behavior. To avoid being unconsciously manipulated by these efforts, you need to be aware of how language functions. This knowledge will help you to distinguish actual arguments, information, and reasons from techniques of persuasion that others use to get you to accept their views without thinking critically. Three types of language often used to promote the uncritical acceptance of views are euphemistic language, clichés, and emotive language.

EUPHEMISTIC LANGUAGE

The term *euphemism* is derived from a Greek word meaning "to speak with good words." Using a **euphemism** involves substituting a pleasanter, less objectionable expression for a blunt or more direct one. For example, an entire collection of euphemisms exists to disguise the unpleasantness of death: *passed away, went to her reward, departed this life,* and *blew out the candle.*

Why do people use euphemisms? Probably to help smooth out the "rough edges" of life, to make the unbearable bearable and the offensive inoffensive. Sometimes people use them to make their occupations sound more dignified (a garbage collector, for instance, might be called a "sanitation engineer"). Sometimes euphemisms can be humorous, as are the following "New Euphemisms for Bad Stuff at School."

Course failure	Unrequested course reregistration
Incomplete course grade	An unrequited educational encounter
Suspension	Mandatory discontinued attendance
Absence	A non-school learning experience

Euphemisms can become dangerous, though, when they are used to evade or to create misperceptions of serious issues. An alcoholic may describe herself as a "social drinker," thus denying her problem and need for help. A politician may indicate that one of his statements was "somewhat at variance with the truth"—meaning that he lied. Another example would be to describe rotting slums as "substandard housing," making deplorable conditions appear reasonable and the need for action less urgent. One of the most devastating examples of the destructive power of euphemisms was Nazi Germany's characterizing the slaughter of millions of men, women, and children as "the final solution" and "the purification of the race." The "ethnic cleansing" in Bosnia in the 1990s is a similar example.

Thinking ↔ Writing Activity

Thinking Critically About Euphemisms

Select an important social problem such as drug use, crime, poverty, juvenile delinquency, support for wars in other countries, racism, unethical or illegal behavior in government. List several euphemisms commonly used to describe the problem; then explain how these euphemisms can lead to dangerous misperceptions and serious consequences.

CLICHÉS

Clichés function in a similar way to *euphemisms* in that they tend to dilute meaning and avoid the complexities of an issue. A cliché is an overused phrase, usually employing figurative language, and so often repeated that the phrase becomes an automatic pattern. For example, if someone says "Sly as a . . .," what word comes next? Or "Sharp as a . . ."? On page 181, in the discussion of figurative language, the point was made that clichés usually start off as fresh wordings. People like the way the phrase sounds and repeat it over and over, year after year. After a while, the phrase loses its freshness and also its clear reference to what is being discussed. George Orwell calls clichés "dying metaphors."

What does it really mean to be "drunk as a skunk"? First of all, skunks do not imbibe alcohol. But, more important, this cliché is not helpful to a discussion of intoxication. The issue may be a drinker's health or safety—or the safety of those around that person. What does it really mean to say that someone is "sly as a fox"? The issue may be manipulative behavior that can cause serious problems, not just wily strategies.

In addition, the use of clichés indicates lazy thinking. Imagine how clever it must have seemed the first time someone said in a meeting that the group should "think outside the box." Yet a person who uses that phrase now is not being clever, just repeating a tired phrase, and will probably be considered inarticulate. Clichés may not create serious problems in casual conversation, but they do cloud meaning and should not be used in your academic writing.

Cliché and Proverb

Of course, different societies and different time periods give rise to different clichés.

1. Write down two or three phrases that you consider to be clichés. Try to recall where you have read or heard them. Share this writing with classmates to see if they know these phrases and if they think that they are clichés.

   Proverbs and famous quotations are also often repeated, but they function differently from clichés because they tend to encourage thinking.

2. Write down a proverb or a famous quotation that you know and write a few sentences about how it stimulates your thinking.

3. Select a cliché and write a few sentences about how it does not help you think clearly about an issue to which it could apply.

EMOTIVE LANGUAGE

What is your immediate reaction to each of the following words?

tyrant	*peaceful*	*disgusting*	*God*	*filthy*
mouthwatering	*bloodthirsty*	*freedom*	*Nazi*	

Most of these words probably arouse strong feelings in you. In fact, this ability to evoke feelings accounts for the extraordinary power of language.

Certain words (like those just listed) are used to stand for the emotive areas of your experience. These emotive words symbolize the whole range of human feelings from powerful emotions ("I detest you!") to the subtlest of feelings.

Emotive language often plays a double role: it not only symbolizes and expresses our feelings but also arouses or *evokes* feelings in others. When you tell someone, "You're my best friend," you usually are not simply expressing your feelings for the person; you also hope to inspire that person to have similar feelings for you. Even when communicating factual information, we make use of the emotive influence of language to interest other people in what we are saying. For example, compare the *New York Times* account (page 313) of the events of 9/11 with the *People's Daily* account (page 316). Which account do you find more emotive? Which seems more objective? Which do you find more engaging? Why?

Although an emotive word may be an accurate description of feelings, it is not the same as a factual statement because it is true only for the speaker—not for others. For instance, even though you may feel that a movie is "tasteless" and "repulsive," someone else may find it "exciting" and "hilarious." By describing your feelings about the movie, you are giving your personal evaluation, which often may differ from the personal evaluations of others (it is not unusual to see conflicting reviews of the same movie). A factual statement, on the other hand, is a statement with which rational people will agree, providing that suitable evidence to verify it is available (for example, the fact that mass transit uses less energy than automobiles).

In some ways, symbolizing emotions is more difficult than representing factual information about the world. For example, expressing your feelings about a person often is more challenging than stating facts about him or her.

When emotive words are used in larger groups (such as sentences, paragraphs, compositions, poems, plays, or novels), they become even more powerful. The pamphlets of Thomas Paine helped to inspire American patriots in the Revolutionary War, and Abraham Lincoln's Gettysburg Address has endured as an expression of Americans' most cherished values. In horrifying contrast were the vehement speeches of Adolf Hitler that influenced German people before and during World War II.

One way to think about the meaning and power of emotive words is to see them on a scale or continuum, from mild to strong. For example:

overweight	fat	obese

The thinker Bertrand Russell used this continuum to illustrate how we perceive the same trait in various people:

- I am *firm.*
- You are *stubborn.*
- He/she is *pigheaded.*

We usually tend to perceive ourselves favorably ("I am firm"). I am speaking to you face to face, so I view you only somewhat less favorably ("You are stubborn"). But since a third person is not present, I can use stronger emotive language ("He/she is pigheaded"). Try this technique with two other emotive words:

1. I am . . .   You are . . .   He/she is . . .

2. I am . . .   You are . . .   He/she is . . .

Emotive words can be used to confuse opinions with facts, a situation that commonly occurs when we combine emotive uses of language with informative uses. Although people may appear to be giving factual information, they actually may be adding personal evaluations that are not factual. These opinions are often emotional, biased, unfounded, or inflammatory. Consider the following statement: "New York City is the filthiest and most dangerous city; only idiots would want to live there." Although the speaker at first appears to be giving factual information, she is really using emotive language to advance an opinion. Yet emotive uses of language are not always negative. The statement "He's the most generous, wise, honest, and warm friend anyone could have" also illustrates the potential confusion of the emotive and the informative uses of language, except that in this case the feelings are positive.

Emotive words usually signal that a personal opinion or evaluation, rather than a fact, is being stated. Speakers occasionally do identify their opinions as opinions, using phrases like "In my opinion" or "I feel that." Often, however, speakers do not identify their opinions as such because they want you to treat their judgments as facts. In these cases, the combination of the informative use and the emotive use of language can be misleading and even dangerous.

Thinking ↔ Writing Activity

Evaluating Emotive Language

Identify examples of emotive language in the following passages and explain how the writer is using it to influence people's thoughts and feelings.

We need another and a wiser and perhaps a more mystical concept of animals. Remote from universal nature, and living by complicated artifice, man in civilization surveys the creature through the glass of his knowledge and sees thereby a feather magnified and the whole image in distortion. We patronize them for their incompleteness, for their tragic fate of having taken form so far below ourselves. And therein we err, and greatly err. For the animal shall not be measured by man. In a world older and more complete than ours they move finished and complete, gifted with senses that you have lost or never attained, living by voices you shall never hear.—Henry Beston, *The Outermost House*

Every criminal, every gambler, every thug, every libertine, every girl ruiner, every home wrecker, every wife beater, every dope peddler, every moonshiner, every crooked politician, every pagan Papist priest, every shyster lawyer, every white slaver, every brothel madam, every Rome-controlled newspaper, every black spider—is fighting the Klan. Think it over. Which side are you on? —From a Ku Klux Klan circular

A final point to consider about emotive language is that it can be used in a reverse way, as we have seen in the section on euphemism. George Orwell gives examples of this in the following essay, his classic "Politics and the English Language." He points out that such usages deliberately drain the emotion from terms in order to lessen the shock of the information being conveyed. "Defenseless villages are bombarded from the air, the inhabitants driven out into the country-side, the cattle machine-gunned, the huts set on fire with incendiary bullets: this is called *pacification*."

Politics and the English Language

BY GEORGE ORWELL (1903–1950)

Born in India in 1903, George Orwell was christened Eric Blair but later took on his famous pen name. He did most of his writing in the last twenty years of his life, publishing Animal Farm *in 1945 and* Nineteen Eighty-Four *in 1949.* Animal Farm *satirized the Russian Revolution and was initially rejected by publishers who feared that it might disrupt relations between the United States and Russia.* Nineteen Eighty-Four *chillingly laid out what the future would be like if totalitarianism were to prevail. Beyond these two famous works, Orwell produced a wide range of essays, literary criticism, journalism, and poetry. In addition to his fine writing style, he is remembered as a brilliant social critic. His legacy was complicated, however, with the 1996 revelation that Orwell had been an informer to the covert Information Research Department, a British intelligence agency that produced anti-Communist propaganda during the Cold War. As you read "Politics and the English Language," notice that Orwell is criticizing not just certain uses of language, but also the motives of those who use them.*

Most people who bother with the matter at all would admit that the English language is in a bad way, but it is generally assumed that we cannot by conscious action do anything about it. Our civilization is decadent and our language—so the argument runs—must inevitably share in the general collapse. It follows that any struggle against the abuse of language is a sentimental archaism, like preferring candles to electric light or hansom cabs to aeroplanes. Underneath this lies the half-conscious belief that language is a natural growth and not an instrument which we shape for our own purposes.

Now, it is clear that the decline of a language must ultimately have political and economic causes: it is not due simply to the bad influence of this or that individual writer. But an effect can become a cause, reinforcing the original cause and producing the same effect in an intensified form, and so on indefinitely. A man may take to drink because he feels himself to be a failure, and then fail all the more completely because he drinks. It is rather the same thing that is happening to the English language. It becomes ugly and inaccurate because our thoughts are foolish, but the slovenliness of our language makes it easier for us to have foolish thoughts. The point is that the process is reversible. Modern English, especially written English, is full of bad habits which spread by imitation and which can be avoided if one is willing to take the necessary trouble. If one gets rid of these habits one can think more clearly, and to think clearly is a necessary first step towards political regeneration: so that the fight against bad English is not frivolous and is not the exclusive concern of professional writers. I will come back to this presently, and I hope that by that time the meaning of what I have said here will have become clearer. Meanwhile here are five specimens of the English language as it is now habitually written.

These five passages have not been picked out because they are especially bad—I could have quoted far worse if I had chosen—but because they illustrate various of the mental vices from which we now suffer. They are a little below the average, but are fairly representative samples. I number them so that I can refer back to them when necessary:

(1) I am not, indeed, sure whether it is not true to say that the Milton who once seemed not unlike a seventeenth-century Shelley had not become, out of an experience ever more bitter in each year, more alien [*sic*] to the founder of that Jesuit sect which nothing could induce him to tolerate.

—Professor Harold Laski (Essay in *Freedom of Expression*)

(2) Above all, we cannot play ducks and drakes with a native battery of idioms which prescribes such egregious collocations of vocables as the Basic *put up with* for *tolerate* or *put at a loss* for *bewilder.*

—Professor Lancelot Hogben (*Interglossa*)

(3) On the one side we have the free personality: by definition it is not neurotic, for it has neither conflict nor dream. Its desires, such as they are, are transparent, for they are just what institutional approval keeps in the forefront of consciousness; another institutional pattern would alter their number and intensity; there is little in them that is natural, irreducible, or culturally dangerous. But *on the other side,* the social bond itself is nothing but the mutual reflection of these self-secure integrities. Recall the definition of love. Is not this the very picture of a small academic? Where is there a place in this hall of mirrors for either personality or fraternity?

—Essay on psychology in *Politics* (New York)

(4) All the "best people" from the gentlemen's clubs, and all the frantic fascist captains, united in common hatred of Socialism and bestial horror of the rising tide of the mass revolutionary movement, have turned to acts of provocation, to foul incendiarism, to medieval legends of poisoned wells, to legalize their own destruction of proletarian organizations, and rouse the agitated petty-bourgeoisie to chauvinistic fervor on behalf of the fight against the revolutionary way out of the crisis.

—Communist pamphlet

(5) If a new spirit *is* to be infused into this old country, there is one thorny and contentious reform which must be tackled, and that is the humanization and galvanization of the B.B.C. Timidity here will bespeak canker and atrophy of the soul. The heart of Britain may be sound and of strong beat, for instance, but the British lion's roar at present is like that of Bottom in Shakespeare's *Midsummer Night's Dream*—as gentle as any sucking dove. A virile new Britain cannot continue indefi-

nitely to be traduced in the eyes or rather ears, of the world by the effete languors of Langham Place, brazenly masquerading as "standard English." When the voice of Britain is heard at nine o'clock, better far and infinitely less ludicrous to hear aitches honestly dropped than the present priggish, inflated, inhibited, school-ma'amish arch braying of blameless bashful mewing maidens!

—Letter in *Tribune*

Each of these passages has faults of its own, but, quite apart from avoidable ugliness, two qualities are common to all of them. The first is staleness of imagery; the other is lack of precision. The writer either has a meaning and cannot express it, or he inadvertently says something else, or he is almost indifferent as to whether his words mean anything or not. This mixture of vagueness and sheer incompetence is the most marked characteristic of modern English prose, and especially of any kind of political writing. As soon as certain topics are raised, the concrete melts into the abstract and no one seems able to think of turns of speech that are not hackneyed: prose consists less and less of *words* chosen for the sake of their meaning, and more and more of *phrases* tacked together like the sections of a prefabricated henhouse. I list below, with notes and examples, various of the tricks by means of which the work of prose-construction is habitually dodged:

5   ### Dying Metaphors

A newly invented metaphor assists thought by evoking a visual image, while on the other hand a metaphor which is technically "dead" (e.g., *iron resolution*) has in effect reverted to being an ordinary word and can generally be used without loss of vividness. But in between these two classes there is a huge dump of worn-out metaphors which have lost all evocative power and are merely used because they save people the trouble of inventing phrases for themselves. Examples are: *Ring the changes on, take up the cudgels for, toe the line, ride roughshod over, stand shoulder to shoulder with, play into the hands of, no axe to grind, grist to the mill, fishing in troubled waters, on the order of the day, Achilles' heel, swan song, hotbed.* Many of these are used without knowledge of their meaning (what is a "rift," for instance?), and incompatible metaphors are frequently mixed, a sure sign that the writer is not interested in what he is saying. Some metaphors now current have been twisted out of their original meaning without those who use them even being aware of the fact. For example, *toe the line* is sometimes written *tow the line.* Another example is the *hammer and the anvil,* now always used with the implication that the anvil gets the worst of it. In real life it is always the anvil that breaks the hammer, never the other way about: a writer who stopped to think what he was saying would be aware of this, and would avoid perverting the original phrase.

Operators or Verbal False Limbs

These save the trouble of picking out appropriate verbs and nouns, and at the same time pad each sentence with extra syllables which give it an appearance of symmetry. Characteristic phrases are *render inoperative, militate against, make contact with, be subjected to, give rise to, give grounds for, have the effect of, play a leading part (role) in, make itself felt, take effect, exhibit a tendency to, serve the purpose of,* etc., etc. The keynote is the elimination of simple verbs. Instead of being a single word, such as *break, stop, spoil, mend, kill,* a verb becomes a *phrase,* made up of a noun or adjective tacked on to some general-purposes verb such as *prove, serve, form, play, render.* In addition, the passive voice is wherever possible used in preference to the active, and noun constructions are used instead of gerunds (*by examination of* instead of *by examining*). The range of verbs is further cut down by means of the *-ize* and *de-*formations, and the banal statements are given an appearance of profundity by means of the *non un*-formation. Simple conjunctions and prepositions are replaced by such phrases as *with respect to, having regard to, the fact that, by dint of, in view of, in the interests of, on the hypothesis that;* and the ends of sentences are saved from anticlimax by such resounding commonplaces as *greatly to be desired, cannot be left out of account, a development to be expected in the near future, deserving of serious consideration, brought to a satisfactory conclusion,* and so on and so forth.

Pretentious Diction

Words like *phenomenon, element, individual* (as noun), *objective, categorical, effective, virtual, basic, primary, promote, constitute, exhibit, exploit, utilize, eliminate, liquidate,* are used to dress up simple statements and give an air of scientific impartiality to biased judgments. Adjectives like *epoch-making, epic, historic, unforgettable, triumphant, age-old, inevitable, inexorable, veritable,* are used to dignify the sordid processes of international politics, while writing that aims at glorifying war usually takes on an archaic color, its characteristic words being: *realm, throne, chariot, mailed fist, trident, sword, shield, buckler, banner, jackboot, clarion.* Foreign words and expressions such as *cul de sac, ancien régime, deus ex machina, mutatis mutandis, status quo, gleichschaltung, weltanschauung,* are used to give an air of culture and elegance. Except for the useful abbreviations *i.e., e.g.,* and *etc.,* there is no real need for any of the hundreds of foreign phrases now current in English. Bad writers, and especially scientific, political and sociological writers, are nearly always haunted by the notion that Latin or Greek words are grander than Saxon ones, and unnecessary words like *expedite, ameliorate, predict, extraneous, deracinated, clandestine, subaqueous* and hundreds of others constantly gain ground from their Anglo-Saxon opposite numbers.[1] The jargon peculiar to Marxist writing (*hyena, hangman, cannibal, petty bourgeois, these gentry, lacquey, flunkey, mad dog, White Guard,* etc.) consists largely of words and phrases translated from Russian, German or French; but the normal way of coining a new word is to use a Latin or Greek root with the appropriate affix and, where nec-

---

1. An interesting illustration of this is the way in which the English flower names which were in use till very recently are being ousted by Greek ones, *snapdragon* becoming *antirrhinum, forget-me-not* becoming *myosotis,* etc. It is hard to see any practical reason for this change of fashion: it is probably due to an instinctive turning-away from the more homely word and a vague feeling that the Greek word is scientific.

essary, the *-ize* formation. It is often easier to make up words of this kind (*deregionalize, impermissible, extramarital, non-fragmentary* and so forth) than to think up the English words that will cover one's meaning. The result, in general, is an increase in slovenliness and vagueness.

Meaningless Words

In certain kinds of writing, particularly in art criticism and literary criticism, it is normal to come across long passages which are almost completely lacking in meaning.[2] Words like *romantic, plastic, values, human, dead, sentimental, natural, vitality,* as used in art criticism, are strictly meaningless, in the sense that they not only do not point to any discoverable object, but are hardly ever expected to do so by the reader. When one critic writes, "The outstanding feature of Mr. X's work is its living quality," while another writes, "The immediately striking thing about Mr. X's work is its peculiar deadness," the reader accepts this as a simple difference of opinion. If words like *black* and *white* were involved, instead of the jargon words *dead* and *living,* he would see at once that language was being used in an improper way. Many political words are similarly abused. The word *Fascism* has now no meaning except in so far as it signifies "something not desirable." The words *democracy, freedom, patriotic, realistic, justice,* have each of them several different meanings which cannot be reconciled with one another. In the case of a word like *democracy,* not only is there no agreed definition, but the attempt to make one is resisted from all sides. It is almost universally felt that when we call a country democratic we are praising it: consequently the defenders of every kind of regime claim that it is a democracy, and fear that they might have to stop using the word if it were tied down to any one meaning. Words of this kind are often used in a consciously dishonest way. That is, the person who uses them has his own private definition, but allows his hearer to think he means something quite different. Statements like, *Marshal Pétain was a true patriot, The Soviet Press is the freest in the world, The Catholic Church is opposed to persecution,* are almost always made with intent to deceive. Other words used in variable meanings, in most cases more or less dishonestly, are: *class, totalitarian, science, progressive, reactionary, bourgeois, equality.*

Now that I have made this catalogue of swindles and perversions, let me give another example of the kind of writing that they lead to. This time it must of its nature be an imaginary one. I am going to translate a passage of good English into modern English of the worst sort. Here is a well-known verse from *Ecclesiastes:*

> I returned and saw under the sun, that the race is not to the swift, nor the battle to the strong, neither yet bread to the wise, nor yet riches to

---

2. Example: "Comfort's catholicity of perception and image, strangely Whitmanesque in range, almost the exact opposite in aesthetic compulsion, continues to evoke that trembling atmospheric accumulative hinting at a cruel, an inexorably serene timelessness. . . . Wrey Gardiner scores by aiming at simple bull's-eyes with precision. Only they are not so simple, and through this contented sadness runs more than the surface bittersweet of resignation." (*Poetry Quarterly*)

men of understanding, nor yet favour to men of skill; but time and chance happeneth to them all.

10   Here it is in modern English:

> Objective consideration of contemporary phenomena compels the conclusion that success or failure in competitive activities exhibits no tendency to be commensurate with innate capacity, but that a considerable element of the unpredictable must invariably be taken into account.

This is a parody, but a very gross one. Exhibit (3), above, for instance, contains several patches of the same kind of English. It will be seen that I have not made a full translation. The beginning and ending of the sentence follow the original meaning fairly closely, but in the middle the concrete illustrations—race, battle, bread—dissolve into the vague phrase "success or failure in competitive activities." This had to be so, because no modern writer of the kind I am discussing—no one capable of using phrases like "objective consideration of contemporary phenomena"—would ever tabulate his thoughts in that precise and detailed way. The whole tendency of modern prose is away from concreteness. Now analyse these two sentences a little more closely. The first contains forty-nine words but only sixty syllables, and all its words are those of everyday life. The second contains thirty-eight words of ninety syllables: eighteen of its words are from Latin roots, and one from Greek. The first sentence contains six vivid images, and only one phrase ("time and chance") that could be called vague. The second contains not a single fresh, arresting phrase, and in spite of its ninety syllables it gives only a shortened version of the meaning contained in the first. Yet without a doubt it is the second kind of sentence that is gaining ground in modern English. I do not want to exaggerate. This kind of writing is not yet universal, and outcrops of simplicity will occur here and there in the worst-written page. Still, if you or I were told to write a few lines on the uncertainty of human fortunes, we should probably come much nearer to my imaginary sentence than to the one from *Ecclesiastes.*

As I have tried to show, modern writing at its worst does not consist in picking out words for the sake of their meaning and inventing images in order to make the meaning clearer. It consists in gumming together long strips of words which have already been set in order by someone else, and making the results presentable by sheer humbug. The attraction of this way of writing is that it is easy. It is easier—even quicker, once you have the habit—to say *In my opinion it is not an unjustifiable assumption that* than to say *I think.* If you use ready-made phrases, you not only don't have to hunt about for words; you also don't have to bother with the rhythms of your sentences, since these phrases are generally so arranged as to be more or less euphonious. When you are composing in a hurry—when you are dictating to a stenographer, for instance, or making a public speech—it is natural to fall into a pretentious, Latinized style. Tags like *a consideration which we should do well to bear in mind* or *a conclusion to which all of us would readily assent* will save many a sentence from coming down with a bump. By using stale metaphors, similes and idioms, you save much mental effort, at the cost of leaving your meaning vague, not only for your reader but for yourself. This is the significance of mixed metaphors. The sole aim of a metaphor is to call up a visual image. When these images clash—as in *The Fascist octopus has sung its swan song, the jackboot is thrown into the melting pot*—it can be taken as certain that the writer is not seeing a mental image of the objects he is naming; in other words he is not really thinking. Look again at the examples I gave at the beginning of this essay. Professor Laski (1) uses five negatives in fifty-three words. One of these is superfluous, making nonsense of the whole passage, and in addition there is the slip *alien* for *akin*, making further nonsense, and several avoidable pieces of clumsiness which increase the general vagueness. Professor Hogben (2) plays ducks and drakes with a battery which is able to write prescriptions, and, while disapproving of the everyday phrase *put up with*, is unwilling to look *egregious* up in the dictionary and see what it means; (3), if one takes an uncharitable attitude towards it, is simply meaningless: probably one could work out its intended meaning by reading the whole of the article in which it occurs. In (4), the writer knows more or less what he wants to say, but an accumulation of stale phrases chokes him like tea leaves blocking a sink. In (5), words and meaning have almost parted company. People who write in this manner usually have a general emotional meaning—they dislike one thing and want to express solidarity with another—but they are not interested in the detail of what they are saying. A scrupulous writer, in every sentence that he writes, will ask himself at least four questions, thus: What am I trying to say? What words will express it? What image or idiom will make it clearer? Is this image fresh enough to have an effect? And he will probably ask himself two more: Could I put it more shortly? Have I said anything that is avoidably ugly? But you are not obliged to go to all this trouble. You can shirk it by simply throwing your mind open and letting the ready-made phrases come crowding in. They will construct your sentences for you—even think your thoughts for you, to a certain extent—and at need they will perform the important service of partially concealing your meaning even from yourself. It is at this point that the special connection between politics and the debasement of language becomes clear.

In our time it is broadly true that political writing is bad writing. Where it is not true, it will generally be found that the writer is some kind of rebel, expressing his private opinions and not a "party line." Orthodoxy, of whatever color, seems to demand a lifeless, imitative style. The political dialects to be found in pamphlets, leading articles, manifestos, White Papers and the speeches of under-secretaries do, of course, vary from party to party, but they are all alike in that one almost never finds in them a fresh, vivid, homemade turn of speech. When one watches some tired hack on the platform mechanically repeating the familiar phrases—*bestial atrocities, iron heel, bloodstained tyranny, free peoples of the world, stand shoulder to shoulder*—one often has a curious feeling that one is not watching a live human being but some kind of dummy: a feeling which suddenly becomes stronger at moments when the light catches the speaker's spectacles and turns them into blank discs which seem to have no eyes behind them. And this is not altogether fanciful. A speaker who uses that kind of phraseology has gone some distance towards turning himself into a machine. The appropriate noises are coming out of his larynx, but his brain is not involved as it would be if he were choosing his words for himself. If the speech he is making is one that he is accustomed to make over and over again, he may be almost unconscious of what he is saying, as one is when one utters the responses in church. And this reduced state of consciousness, if not indispensable, is at any rate favorable to political conformity.

In our time, political speech and writing are largely the defence of the indefensible. Things like the continuance of British rule in India, the Russian purges and deportations, the dropping of the atom bombs on Japan, can indeed be defended, but only by arguments which are too brutal for most people to face, and which do not square with the professed aims of political parties. Thus political language has to consist largely of euphemism, question-begging and sheer cloudy vagueness. Defenceless villages are bombarded from the air, the inhabitants driven out into the countryside, the cattle machine-gunned, the huts set on fire with incendiary bullets: this is called *pacification*. Millions of peasants are robbed of their farms and sent trudging along the roads with no more than they can carry: this is called *transfer of population* or *rectification of frontiers*. People are imprisoned for years without trial, or shot in the back of the neck or sent to die of scurvy in Arctic lumber camps: this is called *elimination of unreliable elements*. Such phraseology is needed if one wants to name things without calling up mental pictures of them. Consider for instance some comfortable English professor defending Russian totalitarianism. He cannot say outright, "I believe in killing off your opponents when you can get good results by doing so." Probably, therefore, he will say something like this:

> While freely conceding that the Soviet régime exhibits certain features which the humanitarian may be inclined to deplore, we must, I think, agree that a certain curtailment of the right to political opposition is an unavoidable concomitant of transitional periods, and that the rigors which the Russian people have been called upon to undergo have been amply justified in the sphere of concrete achievement.

15   The inflated style is itself a kind of euphemism. A mass of Latin words falls upon the facts like soft snow, blurring the outlines and covering up all the details. The great enemy of clear language is insincerity. When there is a gap between one's real and one's declared aims, one turns as it were instinctively to long words and exhausted idioms, like a cuttlefish squirting out ink. In our age there is no such thing as "keeping out of politics." All issues are political issues, and politics itself is a mass of lies, evasions, folly, hatred and schizophrenia. When the general atmosphere is bad, language must suffer. I should expect to find—this is a guess which I have not sufficient knowledge to verify—that the

German, Russian and Italian languages have all deteriorated in the last ten or fifteen years, as a result of dictatorship.

But if thought corrupts language, language can also corrupt thought. A bad usage can spread by tradition and imitation, even among people who should and do know better. The debased language that I have been discussing is in some ways very convenient. Phrases like *a not unjustifiable assumption, leaves much to be desired, would serve no good purpose, a consideration which we should do well to bear in mind,* are a continuous temptation, a packet of aspirins always at one's elbow. Look back through this essay, and for certain you will find that I have again and again committed the very faults I am protesting against. By this morning's post I have received a pamphlet dealing with conditions in Germany. The author tells me that he "felt impelled" to write it. I open it at random, and here is almost the first sentence that I see: "[The Allies] have an opportunity not only of achieving a radical transformation of Germany's social and political structure in such a way as to avoid a nationalistic reaction in Germany itself, but at the same time of laying the foundations of a cooperative and unified Europe." You see, he "feels impelled" to write—feels, presumably, that he has something new to say—and yet his words, like cavalry horses answering the bugle, group themselves automatically into the familiar dreary pattern. The invasion of one's mind by ready-made phrases (*lay the foundations, achieve a radical transformation*) can only be prevented if one is constantly on guard against them, and every such phrase anaesthetizes a portion of one's brain.

I said earlier that the decadence of our language is probably curable. Those who deny this would argue, if they produced an argument at all, that language merely reflects existing social conditions, and that we cannot influence its development by any direct tinkering with words and constructions. So far as the general tone or spirit of a language goes, this may be true, but it is not true in detail. Silly words and expressions have often disappeared, not through any evolutionary process but owing to the conscious action of a minority. Two recent examples were *explore every avenue* and *leave no stone unturned,* which were killed by the jeers of a few journalists. There is a long list of fly-blown metaphors which could similarly be got rid of if enough people would interest themselves in the job; and it should also be possible to laugh the *not un-*formation out of existence,[3] to reduce the amount of Latin and Greek in the average sentence, to drive out foreign phrases and strayed scientific words, and, in general, to make pretentiousness unfashionable. But all these are minor points. The defence of the English language implies more than this, and perhaps it is best to start by saying what it does *not* imply.

To begin with, it has nothing to do with archaism, with the salvaging of obsolete words and turns of speech, or with the setting up of a "standard English" which must never be departed from. On the contrary, it is especially concerned with the scrapping of every word or idiom which has outworn its usefulness.

3. One can cure oneself of the *not un-*formation by memorizing this sentence: *A not unblack dog was chasing a not unsmall rabbit across a not ungreen field.*

It has nothing to do with correct grammar and syntax, which are of no importance so long as one makes one's meaning clear, or with the avoidance of Americanisms, or with having what is called a "good prose style." On the other hand it is not concerned with fake simplicity and the attempt to make written English colloquial. Nor does it even imply in every case preferring the Saxon word to the Latin one, though it does imply using the fewest and shortest words that will cover one's meaning. What is above all needed is to let the meaning choose the word, and not the other way about. In prose, the worst thing one can do with words is to surrender to them. When you think of a concrete object, you think wordlessly, and then, if you want to describe the thing you have been visualizing you probably hunt about till you find the exact words that seem to fit it. When you think of something abstract you are more inclined to use words from the start, and unless you make a conscious effort to prevent it, the existing dialect will come rushing in and do the job for you, at the expense of blurring or even changing your meaning. Probably it is better to put off using words as long as possible and get one's meaning as clear as one can through pictures or sensations. Afterwards one can choose—not simply *accept*—the phrases that will best cover the meaning, and then switch round and decide what impression one's words are likely to make on another person. This last effort of the mind cuts out all stale or mixed images, all prefabricated phrases, needless repetitions, and humbug and vagueness generally. But one can often be in doubt about the effect of a word or a phrase, and one needs rules that one can rely on when instinct fails. I think the following rules will cover most cases:

1. Never use a metaphor, simile, or other figure of speech which you are used to seeing in print.
2. Never use a long word where a short one will do.
3. If it is possible to cut a word out, always cut it out.
4. Never use the passive where you can use the active.
5. Never use a foreign phrase, a scientific word or a jargon word if you can think of an everyday English equivalent.
6. Break any of these rules sooner than say anything outright barbarous.

These rules sound elementary, and so they are, but they demand a deep change of attitude in anyone who has grown used to writing in the style now fashionable. One could keep all of them and still write bad English, but one could not write the kind of stuff that I quoted in those five specimens at the beginning of this article.

I have not here been considering the literary use of language, but merely language as an instrument for expressing and not for concealing or preventing thought. Stuart Chase and others have come near to claiming that all abstract words are meaningless, and have used this as a pretext for advocating a kind of political quietism. Since you don't know what Fascism is, how can you struggle against Fascism? One need not swallow such absurdities as this, but one ought to recognize that the present political chaos is connected with the decay of language, and that one can probably bring about some improvement by starting at the verbal end. If you simplify your English, you are freed from the worst follies of orthodoxy. You cannot speak any of the necessary dialects, and when you make a stupid remark its stupidity will be obvious, even to yourself. Political language—and with variations this is true of all political parties, from Conservatives to Anarchists—is designed to make lies sound truthful and murder respectable, and to give an appearance of solidity to pure wind. One cannot change this all in a moment, but one can at least change one's own habits, and from time to time one can even, if one jeers loudly enough, send some worn-out and useless phrase—some *jackboot, Achilles' heel, hotbed, melting pot, acid test, veritable inferno* or other lump of verbal refuse—into the dustbin where it belongs.

Questions for Active Reading

1. Sixty years ago, when Orwell's essay was published, its references to historical figures and political circumstances were urgent and well-known. Highlight all allusions and references to people, places, and circumstances that are unfamiliar to you, and use the Internet to find the information you need for context and definitions. How does this deeper understanding of Orwell's own time influence your reading of his essay?

2. In your own words, paraphrase the cause-and-effect argument that Orwell makes for the decay of the English language.

3. After the highly detailed and clearly outrageous examples that Orwell gives—and the urgent, almost despairing argument that he makes for an ethical clarity in language—Orwell offers six very simple rules for writing ethically and responsibly. Reread one of your own essays, and revise according to Orwell's guidelines. How useful and effective are his suggestions? Does he follow his own advice?

Questions for Thinking Critically

1. Compare your and Orwell's views on a specific topic, such as euphemism or the view that "if thought corrupts language, language can also corrupt thought." To what extent do they agree or disagree?

2. Orwell would agree with Murray that clarity is essential to effective writing, but Murray doesn't connect that clarity to the greater ethical imperatives that Orwell implies. Given the kinds of writing that you do for school, in your workplace, or perhaps on a blog or personal web site, do you think that Orwell's urgent ethical concerns apply to your own work? Or is Murray's editorial advice on revision strategies

adequate for your concerns? What ethical responsibilities do you have toward any one audience for your own writing?

3. What does Orwell mean, in paragraph 19, by "political quietism"? Does that concept apply to you, your friends, your colleagues, or your community? How did Malcolm X and Martin Luther King Jr.—and, at a much more personal and intimate level, Edite Cunhã—use language to combat quietism?

Writing Project: The Impact of Language on Our Lives

This chapter explores the essential role of language in developing sophisticated thinking abilities. The goal of clear, effective thinking and communication is accomplished through the joint efforts of thought and language. Learning to use the appropriate language style, which depends on the social context in which you are operating, requires both critical judgment and flexible expertise with various language forms. Critically evaluating the pervasive attempts of advertisers and others to by-pass your critical faculties and influence your thinking involves insight into the way language and thought create and express meaning. We will be examining these relationships between language and thought further in upcoming chapters.

The following Writing Project provides an opportunity for you to apply what you have learned in this chapter to your own writing.

Write a paper in which you discuss some specific aspect of your experience with language. Analyze some way or ways in which words have affected you. You could write about a favorite poem or song lyric, about how the language of a religious ceremony or political statement influenced you, or about advertisements that made you desire or reject a product. You might tell of the impact of statements made by your parents, grandparents, teachers, or friends. You could recount one event or several situations, positive or negative effects. Whenever possible, connect your experience to concepts explained in this chapter. Follow your instructor's directions for topic limitations, length, format, and so on.

The guidelines you need to consider are those involved in writing any paper that connects your personal experience with a complex issue.

1. Present your experience vividly and use specific details.

2. Clearly state your point or thesis about the effect(s) the experience had on you. Think about the best place in your paper to do this.

3. Be explicit about the connections you see between your experience and the concepts about language that they illustrate. You may want to quote from the chapter. If you do, cite material as directed by your instructor.

4. Consider using some of the language techniques explored in this chapter (such as figurative language).

THE WRITING SITUATION

Begin by considering the key elements in the Thinking-Writing Model (illustrated in Chapter 1.)

Purpose One purpose you have here is to connect abstract ideas about language with real-life experiences so that you and your readers can understand the concepts better. As with any writing project another major purpose is to make your points clear and convincing to your audience.

Audience As always, consider who could benefit from reading your paper. Perhaps your ideas would appeal to a larger audience, in which case you could submit your writing for publication, possibly in the "My Turn" column in *Newsweek*, the opinion pages of your campus newspaper, or some other publication or web site.

Subject Because language is such a large subject, one involving fairly simple as well as very complex ideas, writing about a real-life experience can clarify—and test—the ideas you choose to write about.

Writer Because this project draws on your own experience, you are in a position of authority. However, the project asks you to focus on an aspect of your experience that you might not have thought about before, and it requires an analytical approach rather than a narrative one, even though you may decide to tell of an event. Therefore, you will need a sort of double consciousness as a writer: you first want to recall your experience as directly as you can, but then you will have to distance yourself as you analyze the effect of language on the experience.

THE WRITING PROCESS

The following sections will guide you through the stages of generating, planning, drafting, and revising as you work on this writing assignment.

Generating Ideas

1. Think of times when something you heard, read, or even said had an impact on you. Did someone use harsh language that upset you or

comforting language that soothed you? Did you say something funny, helpful, embarrassing, or astute? Has a particular phrase ever made you want to do or try something? Why?

2. Do you find any common denominator among several experiences, or does one experience stand out and ask to be told as a single story?

3. Have your significant language experiences involved spoken words more often than written ones?

4. Have any of your experiences involved more than one language or more than one dialect or level of usage?

Defining a Focus   What do you want your audience to understand about the way the experience has affected you? If you are going to recount several experiences, is it important to make that clear in your thesis? Draft a thesis statement that makes a point about your experience(s).

Share your tentative thesis with classmates. Do they consider your idea worthwhile? Next, list things you might say to develop your thesis. How do your peers respond?

Organizing Ideas   The organization of this paper will depend on whether you are discussing one or more experiences. However you approach it, you will need to consider what arrangement will best help your audience understand the effects of your experience. If you are using specific concepts from the chapter, you will have to think about how and where to present them so that their relevance is clear. Using a mind map or a web may help you organize your ideas. Here is one possible format:

First experience	Second experience	Why the two experiences are related
Circumstances	Circumstances	_____
What was said	What was said	_____
How it affected you	How it affected you	_____

Drafting   Start with the part that will be easiest to write. Look at your freewriting, your possible thesis statement, and your list or map of ideas. Now, work those early-stage writings into a coherent draft. Remember that shaping ideas is your biggest concern at this stage. Trust yourself to speak about your own experiences and to explain what they mean to you.

After you have drafted enough material, give attention to paragraphs. Where does your material cluster into divisions? Which paragraphs need topic sentences? Where in the paragraphs should topic sentences be placed?

Draft an opening paragraph and a conclusion. What connections exist between them? Will they create an effective beginning and a good ending for your essay?

Revising   Each author included in this chapter offers guidelines and inspiration for revising and clarifying your writing. What advice would Orwell offer? What would Murray draw your attention to? Are your word choices as specific, insightful, and sharp-eyed as Malcolm X's engagement with a dictionary would provide?

The following essay shows how one student responded to this assignment. While revising, she applied concepts about language she learned in this chapter. Her essay is followed by a poem by Roberto Obregon.

STUDENT WRITING

JESSIE LANGE'S WRITING PROCESS

One student, Jessie Lange, decided to write about an experience she had with her younger brother. She took the advice given, to start with the part that would be easiest to write. She began to describe her experience, which would become the third paragraph of her essay below, this way:

> After my first four months of college, I returned home for the winter break. After all this, I returned home to be more affected by one word uttered by my younger brother than I had been by my classes.

Then Jessie thought about the precise language used in the readings in this chapter, and she realized that her readers would not know what "all this" meant and her readers also would not know how much younger her brother was. So she revised in this way:

> After my first four months of college, I returned home for the winter break. After four months of reading inspirational writers, attending the lectures of powerful speakers, learning about language itself in my linguistics course, speaking French, and having discussions with intelligent professors who are at the top of their field, I returned home to be more affected by one word uttered by my twelve-year-old brother than I had been by any of the speaking and listening I'd engaged in first semester.

Jessie continued this process as she drafted and revised, and finally produced this essay.

The Power of Language

BY JESSIE LANGE

Language is indeed one of the most powerful things we possess. It is how we communicate our ideas, how we put our abstract feelings for others into words, and it is what we use to describe and evaluate our human experience. Being a "good speaker" in public is something we value highly as we do effective communication in our personal lives. One of the most incredible things about language is the power that just a phrase or even a single word can have. In fact, just a few words often have more of an impact than long speeches and rambling sentences. How does it happen that a small combination of letters can have such a tremendous effect on us?

In the play *Kiss of the Spider Woman* by Manuel Puig, one of the characters, Molina, comments on the power of language. Molina, a gentle soul and an expert storyteller, is desperately in love with the man with whom he is sharing a prison cell. "How does it happen that sometimes someone says something and wins someone else over forever?" he wonders. If only he knew, he could win the love of his cell-mate, Valentin. What Molina is acknowledging is that it doesn't take an infinite number of words to say something powerful. It can be a phrase or even a single word that has the most profound impact on others. In this case, it is the "one thing" uttered that causes another to fall in love with you. In the everyday, there are particular words and phrases that stay with us, that we roll over in our minds, repeating them to ourselves again and again. There are certain words that have such an impact that they stay with us eternally longer than the time it took to utter them. I recently had a personal experience with the effects of this.

After my first four months of college, I returned home for the winter break. After four months of reading inspirational writers, attending the lectures of powerful speakers, learning about language itself in my linguistics course, speaking French, and having discussions with intelligent professors who are at the top of their field, I returned home to be more affected by one word uttered by my twelve-year-old brother than I had been by any of the speaking or listening I'd engaged in first semester. My brother and I have always been extremely close. We do not have the "sibling rivalry" I so often hear about from others. And so being apart had been a struggle. The fact that we had been apart so long and the impending separation just a few weeks away were probably much of the reason his words had such an effect on me. We were saying goodnight one night and my brother who, in many ways, is a miniature me, was holding my hand. I'd just finished assuring him that he was the "bomb" and he was smiling at me. Somewhere out of his slim twelve-year-old frame a thought emerged in the form of speech: "I wish I could take you with me," he said. "Where?" I asked, thoroughly confused. His smile broadened. "Everywhere," he said matter-of-factly. Such a simple word but, to me, so profoundly meaningful, causing a complete overflow of emotion. I had visions of never letting go of his hand. Of bringing him to college with me, of going to school with him, of bringing him all through my life and never missing a day or a second of his getting older. Just one word: *Everywhere.*

If I've learned anything about language, it's that the cliché "quality, not quantity" definitely applies. It took one utterance from my brother to almost bring me to tears. With one word, I could imagine myself holding his fingers in mine wherever I went, wherever we went.

ALTERNATIVE WRITING PROJECTS

1. Write an essay about the most current uses of doublespeak. Be sure to have a focus, a main point that your examples support.

2. Write an essay about how names define or don't define who we are. You might refer back to Edite Cunhã's essay for help. If you decide to include any of her material, talk to your instructor about how to do so.

Thinking and Writing to Shape Our World

All of us actively shape, as well as discover, the world of our experience in which we live. Our world does not exist as a finished product waiting for us to perceive it, think about it, and describe it with words and pictures. Instead, we are active participants in composing our world—selecting, organizing, and interpreting sensations into a coherent whole. Many times, our shaping of this world will reflect basic thinking patterns that we rely on constantly whenever we think, act, speak, or write.

Part Two explores four basic ways of relating and organizing: relationships in space and time, relationships of comparison, relationships of cause, and relationships of classification and definition. The Writing Projects at the end of each chapter ask you to integrate ideas from one, two, or three other sources into your essays as you explore these relationships, and the thinking/organizing patterns that develop from them.

7

Exploring Perceptions

"... a thing is not seen because it is visible, but conversely, visible because it is seen ..." —Plato

Writing to Describe and Narrate

Critical Thinking Focus: Understanding perceptions

Writing Focus: Detail and order in chronologies

Reading Theme: Narratives and process descriptions

Writing Project: Narrative showing the effect of a perception

The way we make sense of the world is through thinking, but our first experiences of the world come to us through our senses: sight, hearing, smell, touch, and taste. These senses are our bridges to the world, making us aware of what occurs outside us. The process of becoming aware of the world through our senses is known as *perceiving*.

This chapter and Chapter 11 will explore the way the perceiving process operates and how it relates to the ability to think, read, and write effectively. In particular, these chapters examine the way each of us shapes personal experience by actively selecting from, organizing, and interpreting the information provided by our senses. In a way, we each view the world through a pair of individual "contact lenses" that reflect our past experiences and our unique personalities. As critical thinkers, we want to become aware of the nature of our own lenses in order to offset any bias or distortion they may be causing. We also want to become aware of the lenses of others so that we can better understand why they view things the way that they do.

Developing insight into the nature of people's lenses—our own and others'—is essential to becoming an effective writer. When we write, it's helpful to understand our own point of view, to be aware of our own biases. That doesn't mean that we should strive to be completely "objective." In fact, such absolute objectivity is not possible because we can never completely remove our personal lenses. However, understanding our lenses helps us achieve our goals as writers. For example, if we want to present our ideas objectively, then we can work to compensate for our inherent bias. On the other hand, if our intention is to persuade others, we may choose to enhance and strengthen our point of view.

Analogously, we need to understand our audience's lenses if we are to communicate our thoughts and feelings effectively through our writing. This involves appreciating their point of view and understanding their biases. We can then use this knowledge to craft our writing, shape our language, and utilize the appropriate terminology and logic.

Once again, we can see the essential union of writing and thinking, communicating and knowing. This chapter will provide you with a foundation for understanding how you develop your beliefs and knowledge about the world and how you can communicate your ideas through clear, expressive, and compelling writing. Let's begin by exploring our main source of information—the perceiving process. Some of the most basic patterns of thinking and of presenting ideas draw directly on perceptions. This chapter will focus on three such patterns: description, process, and narrative.

Thinking Critically About Perceptions

BECOMING AWARE OF YOUR OWN PERCEPTIONS

At almost every waking moment of life, our senses are being bombarded by a tremendous number of stimuli: images to see, noises to hear, odors to smell, textures to feel, and flavors to taste. Experiencing all such sensations at once could create what the nineteenth-century American philosopher William James called "a bloomin' buzzin' confusion." Yet to us, the world usually seems much more orderly and understandable. Why is this so?

In the first place, our sense equipment can receive sensations only within certain limited ranges. For example, there are many sounds and smells that animals can detect but we cannot; animals' sense organs have broader ranges in these areas than ours do. A second reason we can handle sensory bombardment is that from the stimulation available, we select only a small amount on which to focus our attention. To demonstrate this, complete the following Thinking-Writing Activity.

Thinking ↔ Writing Activity

What Do You Sense Right Now?

Respond to the following questions in writing, using a spontaneous, free-flowing style. Record your sensations as you experience them rather than first taking time to reflect and deliberate.

1. What can you *see?* (for example, the shape of the letters on the page, the design of the clothing on your arm)

2. What can you *hear?* (for example, the hum of the air circulator, the rustling of a page)

3. What can you *feel?* (for example, the pressure of the clothes against your skin, the texture of the page on your fingers)

4. What can you *smell?* (for example, the perfume someone is wearing, the odor of stale cigarette smoke)

5. What can you *taste?* (for example, the aftertastes of your last meal)

Compare your responses with those of your classmates. Did they perceive sensations different from the ones you perceived? If so, how do you explain these differences?

This simple exercise demonstrates that for every sensation on which you focus, there are countless others that you are simply ignoring. If you were aware of everything that was happening at every moment, you would be completely overwhelmed. By selecting particular sensations, you are able to make sense of your world in a relatively orderly way. That is, you are **perceiving,** a process by which you actively select, organize, and interpret what is experienced by the senses.

It is tempting to think that our senses simply record what is happening out in the world, as if we were human camcorders. We are not, however, passive receivers of information, containers into which sense experience is poured. Instead, we are active participants who are always trying to understand the sensations we are encountering. As we perceive the world, our experiences are the result of combining the sensations we receive with our understanding of these sensations. For instance, examine the collection of markings in Figure 7.1. What do you see? If all you see is a collection of green spots, try turning the illustration sideways; you will probably perceive a familiar animal.

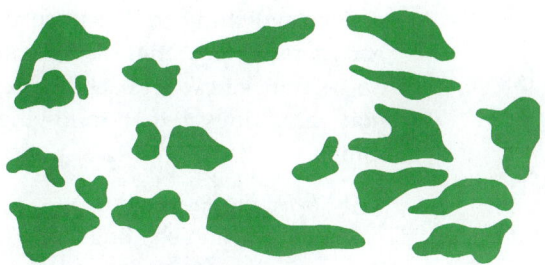

Figure 7.1 Recognizing a Pattern

From this example you can grasp how, when you perceive the world, you are doing more than simply recording what your senses experience; instead, you are actively making sense of these sensations. The collection of green spots suddenly became the figure of an animal because your mind was able to actively organize the spots into a pattern you recognized. Or think about times when you looked up at white, billowy clouds and saw different figures and designs. The figures you were perceiving were not actually in the clouds but were the result of your giving meaningful form to shapes you were experiencing.

The same is true for virtually everything we experience. Our perceptions of the world result from combining information provided by our senses with the way we actively make sense of this information. And since making sense of information is what we are doing when we are thinking, perceiving the world involves using our minds in an active way. Of course, we are usually not aware that we are using our minds to interpret sensations we are experiencing. We simply see the animal or the figures in the clouds as if they were really there.

ACTIVELY SELECTING, ORGANIZING, AND INTERPRETING SENSATIONS

When we actively perceive the sensations we are experiencing, we are usually engaged in three distinct activities:

- *Selecting* certain sensations to pay attention to
- *Organizing* these sensations into a design or pattern
- *Interpreting* what this design or pattern means

In the case of Figure 7.1, you were able to perceive an animal because you selected certain markings to concentrate on, organized these markings into a pattern, and interpreted this pattern as representing a dog.

Of course, when we perceive, the three operations of selecting, organizing, and interpreting are usually performed quickly, automatically, and often simultaneously. Also, because they are so rapid and automatic, we are not normally aware of performing these operations.

Take a few moments to explore more examples that illustrate how you actively select, organize, and interpret your perceptions of the world. Carefully examine Figure 7.2. Do you see both the young woman and the old woman? If you do, try switching back and forth between the two images. As you do so, notice how for each image, you are doing the following things:

Figure 7.2 Young Woman/Old Woman

- *Selecting* certain lines, shapes, and shadings on which to focus your attention

- *Organizing* these lines, shapes, and shadings into different patterns

- *Interpreting* these patterns as representing things you can recognize—a hat, a nose, a chin

So far, we have been exploring how the mind actively participates in the ways we perceive the world. By combining the sensations we are receiving with the way our minds select, organize, and interpret these sensations, we perceive a world that is stable and familiar. Thus, each of us develops a perspective on the world, one that usually makes sense to us.

The process of perceiving takes place on various levels. At the most basic level, *perceiving* refers to the selection, organization, and interpretation of sensations: for example, being able to perceive various objects such as a basketball. However, we also perceive larger patterns of meaning at more complex levels, as in watching the action of a group of people engaged in a basketball game. Although these are different situations, both engage us in the process of perceiving.

NOTING DIFFERENCES IN PEOPLE'S PERCEPTIONS

As we have noted, we are not usually aware of our active participation in perceiving the world. We normally assume that what we are perceiving is what is actually taking place. Only when we find that our perception of an event differs from others' perceptions of it are we forced to examine the manner in which we are selecting, organizing, and interpreting the event. Many artists and photographers believe that what an individual viewer sees in a picture mirrors something within the viewer himself.

Thinking ↔ Writing Activity

Comparing Your Perceptions with Others'

Carefully examine this photograph of twins and then explore your reactions. What do you think is happening in this picture? Explain by answering the following questions.

© Image Bank/Getty Images.

1. Describe as specifically as possible what you perceive as taking place in the picture.

2. Describe what you think will take place next.

3. Identify which details of the picture inform your perceptions.

4. Compare your perceptions with those of your classmates. List several perceptions that differ from yours.

In most cases, people in a group will have a variety of perceptions about what is taking place in the photograph. Some will see the twins simply as identical, dressed up for a family event. Others will focus on differences, especially in the eyes, smile, and posture. In each case, the perception depends on how the viewer is actively using his or her mind to organize and interpret what is taking place.

Writing Thoughtfully About Perceptions

Although the verb *describe* can be used to mean the giving of any detailed account, it more precisely indicates the reporting of sensory impressions: what you see, hear, feel, smell, or taste—your perceptions. Look back at the questions on page 210 to note how your five senses responded; also, reflect on what you have been reading about selecting, organizing, and interpreting sensations. This material should help you understand the two types of descriptions that you will be writing about in the Thinking-Writing Activity on pages 224–225, descriptions that you might also write in other college courses or in work situations.

WRITING OBJECTIVELY AND SUBJECTIVELY

Descriptions can be broadly divided into two categories: *objective*, involving as little judgment as possible, or *subjective,* involving whatever personal judgment is appropriate to a writer's purpose.

   Objective descriptions are often expected in scientific, medical, engineering, and law enforcement writing. The purpose of an objective description is to help the audience sense an object or situation as it is. Later, judgments and implications can be drawn from objective descriptions, but the cleanest possible rendering is needed as a starting point. Of course, the selection and presentation of *any* ideas or information involve conscious and unconscious judgments. However, when objectivity is the purpose, you should try to perceive with as little bias as you can and to describe in language that is as neutral as possible.

   In other writing situations, descriptions are intended to be more subjective. Then the explicit purpose is to shape the audience's opinion of the object under scrutiny. Subjective descriptions occur in literary texts of all kinds: stories, poems, personal essays, and biographies; in argumentative pieces; and in personal writing such as letters to friends and journal entries. Think of how a novelist describes characters or settings; think of how an attorney might reword the police report's objective description of a victim in order to influence a jury; think of how you would describe your new special person to a close friend! You may want to use the first person (I) when writing subjective description to help your audience realize that this description is how you see it. When writing a subjective description, you will be selecting details purposefully and using language that creates the effect that you want your audience to experience.

Objective Language	Subjective Language
A German shepherd	A vicious, snarling dog
A lake at night	A shimmering mirror of moonlight
Drove at 85 mph	Recklessly tore down the road
A six-foot five-inch man	A towering man
Quit my job	Told them to take their job and shove it
Filed for divorce	Got revenge on the lowlife
Won the election	Stole victory from the real winner

CONTRASTING OBJECTIVE AND SUBJECTIVE WRITING

The two readings which follow both have, as their subject, the building of a wall to divide a room. However, the purpose and audience for each reading is quite different; as a result, one reading is obviously "objective," while the other reading is "subjective." (Each reading also uses process analysis, chronological organization, description, and narration; these concepts will be discussed later in this chapter.)

Lowe's Home Improvement Warehouse: Dividing a Room

An unfinished basement or other large room can feel cold and impersonal. Add visual interest and a sense of warmth by breaking up the space with a non-load-bearing wall. Because this task is almost always part of a larger project, it is appropriate for intermediate-level do-it-yourselfers who have a good command of their tools. It would be good to have a helper, as some of the materials to be lifted are heavy.

Click a text link below to shop for that item.

Tools	Materials
• Circular saw	• 2×4 lumber
• Reciprocating saw	• Shims
• Level	• 16d nails or 2-1/2" wood screws
• Framing square	• 8d nails
• Combination square	
• Drill/driver	
• Hammer	
• Tape measure	
• Safety goggles	

Identify the Location for the Wall

Lay out the location for the wall on the floor and ceiling. Determine whether it runs parallel with or perpendicular to the joists above it. If the wall is perpendicular to the joists, you can nail the top plate directly to the joists. If the wall is parallel with the joists and falls directly under a joist, the top plate can be nailed directly to the joist. If the wall is parallel with the joists and not directly under a joist, follow the instructions below for blocking.

Blocking Instructions

If the area where the wall is going has a finished ceiling, remove the ceiling material between the two joists on either side of the wall to a point half the width of the joist (see Figure A). If there isn't a finished ceiling in place, proceed directly to the next section.

*SAFETY These instructions are for the construction of non-load-bearing walls only. If you need to construct load-bearing walls, contact your local building authorities or a licensed contractor in your area.

1. Cut lengths of 2×4 blocking to fit snugly between the exposed joists.

2. Use 8d nails to toenail a length of blocking between the joists at one end of the wall. Ensure that the bottom of the blocking is level with the bottoms of the joists.

3. Continue installing blocking at 12" intervals until you reach the end of the wall. Be sure to put a blocking board directly over the far end of the wall, regardless of the interval (see Figure B).

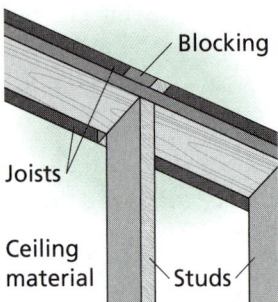

Figure A

5   ### Laying Out and Assembling the Wall

A completed stud wall can be heavy and awkward. Always lay out the wall in the room where it is to be used.

1. Cut two pieces of 2×4 the length of the wall and lay them side by side. Use these as the top and bottom plates.

2. Starting at the left end of one of the plates and measuring to the right, make a mark at 1-1/2", then make an X on the left side of the mark (see Figure C). Continue measuring to the right from the 1-1/2" mark, making a new mark every 24" until you reach the end of the plate. Be sure to allow for a stud at the far right end of the wall regardless of the interval.

3. Align the top and bottom plates and use a combination square to draw a line across the face of each one at the marks. Put an X to the left of each line on each plate. The X indicates the location of the studs in the completed wall.

4. Cut 2×4× 8s to length for the wall studs. Measure the distance from the floor to the ceiling. Subtract 3" from this distance to allow for the top and bottom plates. Subtract another 1/4" to allow for raising the wall into place.

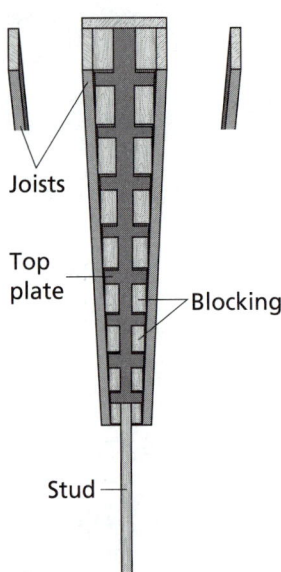

Figure B

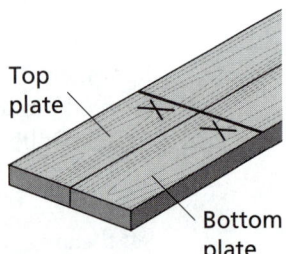

Figure C

5. Align each stud flush with the lines on the top and bottom plates, covering the X's. Use 16d nails to nail through the plates into the ends of the studs.

Securing the Wall in Place

After the wall is assembled, raise it and secure it to the floor and ceiling.

1. Stand the wall in place. Use a framing square to square the new wall to the wall or walls it abuts. Then use a level to plumb the wall.

2. Secure the new wall to the floor with 2 1/2" wood screws or 16d nails. If your floor is concrete use concrete anchors or masonry nails.

3. Shim the top of the wall at each point where the top plate crosses a stud or blocking board. Secure the top plate with 2 1/2" wood screws or 16d nails.

Once the wall is up and the openings are framed, drill for and install electrical wiring or plumbing pipe as needed. Finish with paneling or wallboard, and install the door and any trim you want.

Questions for Active Reading

1. Would you describe this text as "objective"? What examples of "objectivity" would you give? Is there anything "subjective" about this text?

2. How is this text organized? What does that organization suggest about the audience for this text?

3. This text originally appeared on a web site. Words and phrases that are underlined are "linked" to information about other projects and specific tools sold by Lowe's. In what other ways can you tell that this text was written for a web site?

Questions for Thinking Critically

1. This text has one obvious audience, but several purposes. How many different purposes can you determine for this text?

2. Have you ever undertaken, or assisted with, a complex project? Whose instructions did you follow? What kind of guidance do you find most helpful as you work through a complex task: listening to someone explain the steps; reading about each step to take; or seeing visual diagrams of what you need to do? Compare the effectiveness of different teaching styles for different classes you are taking. (For example, some professors might use PowerPoint to highlight key points during a lecture, while other professors might ask you to work with small groups of other students to solve problems.)

3. How many terms in this article were completely unfamiliar to you?
   Could you find those terms in a dictionary, or did you need to turn to
   a more specialized source (and, if so, what was that source)?

The Inheritance of Tools

BY SCOTT RUSSELL SANDERS (b.1945)

A native of Ohio, Scott Russell Sanders writes fiction, science fiction, biography, and personal essays. His essay collections include Writing from the Center *(1995) and* Hunting for Hope *(1998). These essays, which often focus on life in the Midwest, deal with the daily problems of living and with the relationships and values passed on between generations. In the following essay he uses an overall narrative frame, the story of the day he heard the news that his father had died, to enclose a number of other, smaller, narratives. His narratives are made stronger by the detailed description he uses. Note especially his description of his own pain and his family's reaction to it in the hours immediately following the phone call from his mother.*

At just about the hour when my father died, soon after dawn one February morning when ice coated the windows like cataracts, I banged my thumb with a hammer. Naturally I swore at the hammer, the reckless thing, and in the moment of swearing I thought of what my father would say: "If you'd try hitting the nail it would go in a whole lot faster. Don't you know your thumb's not as hard as that hammer?" We both were doing carpentry that day, but far apart. He was building cupboards at my brother's place in Oklahoma; I was at home in Indiana, putting up a wall in the basement to make a bedroom for my daughter. By the time my mother called with news of his death—the long distance wires whittling her voice until it seemed too thin to bear the weight of what she had to say—my thumb was swollen. A week or so later a white scar in the shape of a crescent moon began to show above the cuticle and month by month it rose across the pink sky of my thumbnail. It took the better part of a year for the scar to disappear, and every time I noticed it I thought of my father.

The hammer had belonged to him, and to his father before him. The three of us have used it to build houses and barns and chicken coops, to upholster chairs and crack walnuts, to make doll furniture and bookshelves and jewelry boxes. The head is scratched and pockmarked, like an old plowshare that has been working rocky fields, and it gives off the sort of dull sheen you see on fast creek water in the shade. It is a finishing hammer, about the weight of a bread loaf, too light, really, for framing walls, too heavy for cabinet work, with a curved claw for pulling nails, a rounded head for pounding, a fluted neck for looks, and a hickory handle for strength.

The present handle is my third one, bought from a lumberyard in Tennessee, down the road from where my brother and I were helping my father build his retirement house. I broke the previous one by trying to pull sixteen-penny nails out of floor joists—a foolish thing to do with a finishing hammer, as my father pointed out. "You ever hear of a crowbar?" he said. No telling how many handles he and my grandfather had gone through before me. My grandfather used to cut down hickory trees on his farm, saw them into slabs, cure the planks in his hayloft, and carve handles with a drawknife. The grain in hickory is crooked and knotty, and therefore tough, hard to split, like the grain in the two men who owned this hammer before me.

After proposing marriage to a neighbor girl, my grandfather used this hammer to build a house for his bride on a stretch of river bottom in northern Mississippi. The lumber for the place, like the hickory for the handle, was cut on his own land. By the day of the wedding he had not quite finished the house, and so right after the ceremony he took his wife home and put her to work. My grandmother had worn her Sunday dress for the wedding, with a fringe of lace tacked on around the hem in honor of the occasion. She removed this lace and folded it away before going out to help my grandfather nail siding on the house. "There she was in her good dress," he told me some fifty-odd years after that wedding day, "holding up them long pieces of clapboard while I hammered, and together we got the place covered up before dark." As the family grew to four, six, eight, and eventually thirteen, my grandfather used this hammer to enlarge his house room by room, like a chambered nautilus expanding its shell.

5   By and by the hammer was passed along to my father. One day he was up on the roof of our pony barn nailing shingles with it, when I stepped out the kitchen door to call him for supper. Before I could yell, something about the sight of him straddling the spine of that roof and swinging the hammer caught my eye and made me hold my tongue. I was five or six years old, and the world's commonplaces were still news to me. He would pull a nail from the pouch at his waist, bring the hammer down, and a moment later the *thunk* of the blow would reach my ears. And that is what had stopped me in my tracks and stilled my tongue, that momentary gap between seeing and hearing the blow. Instead of yelling from the kitchen door, I ran to the barn and climbed two rungs up the ladder—as far as I was allowed to go—and spoke quietly to my father. On our walk to the house he explained that sound takes time to make its way through air. Suddenly the world seemed larger, the air more dense, if sound could be held back like any ordinary traveler.

By the time I started using this hammer, at about the age when I discovered the speed of sound, it already contained houses and mysteries for me. The smooth handle was one my grandfather had made. In those days I needed both hands to swing it. My father would start a nail in a scrap of wood, and I would pound away until I bent it over.

"Looks like you got ahold of some of those rubber nails," he would tell me. "Here, let me see if I can find you some stiff ones." And he would rummage in a drawer until he came up with a fistful of more cooperative nails. "Look at the head," he would tell me. "Don't look at your hands, don't look at the hammer. Just look at the head of that nail and pretty soon you'll learn to hit it square."

Pretty soon I did learn. While he worked in the garage cutting dovetail joints for a drawer or skinning a deer or tuning an engine, I would hammer nails. I made innocent blocks of wood look like porcupines. He did not talk much in the midst of his tools, but he kept up a nearly ceaseless humming, slipping in and out of a dozen tunes in an afternoon, often running back over the same stretch of melody again and again, as if searching for a way out. When the humming did cease, I knew he was faced with a task requiring great delicacy or concentration, and I took care not to distract him.

He kept scraps of wood in a cardboard box—the ends of two-by-fours, slabs of shelving and plywood, odd pieces of molding—and everything in it was fair game. I nailed scraps together to fashion what I called boats or houses, but the results usually bore only faint resemblance to the visions I carried in my head. I would hold up these constructions to show my father, and he would turn them over in his hands admiringly, speculating about what they might be. My cobbled-together guitars might have been alien spaceships, my barns might have been models of Aztec temples, each wooden contraption might have been anything but what I had set out to make.

10   Now and again I would feel the need to have a chunk of wood shaped or shortened before I riddled it with nails, and I would clamp it in a vise and scrape at it with a handsaw. My father would let me lacerate the board until my arm gave out, and then he would wrap his hand around mine and help me finish the cut, showing me how to use my thumb to guide the blade, how to pull back on the saw to keep it from binding, how to let my shoulder do the work.

"Don't force it," he would say, "just drag it easy and give the teeth a chance to bite."

As the saw teeth bit down, the wood released its smell, each kind with its own fragrance, oak or walnut or cherry or pine—usually pine because it was the softest, easiest for a child to work. No matter how weathered and gray the board, no matter how warped and cracked, inside there was this smell waiting, as of something freshly baked. I gathered every smidgen of sawdust and stored it away in coffee cans, which I kept in a drawer of the workbench. When I did not feel like hammering nails, I would dump my sawdust on the concrete floor of the garage and landscape it into highways and farms and towns, running miniature cars and trucks along miniature roads. Looming as huge as a colossus, my father worked over and around me, now and again bending down to inspect my work, careful not to trample my creations. It was a landscape that smelled dizzyingly of wood. Even after a bath my skin would carry the smell, and so would my father's hair, when he lifted me for a bedtime hug.

I tell these things not only from memory but also from recent observation, because my own son now turns blocks of wood into nailed porcupines, dumps cans full of sawdust at my feet and sculpts highways on the floor. He learns how to swing a hammer from the elbow instead of the wrist, how to lay his thumb beside the blade to guide a saw, how to tap a chisel with a wooden mallet, how to mark a hole with an awl before starting a drill bit. My daughter did the same before him, and even now, on the brink of teenage aloofness, she will occasionally drag out my box of wood scraps and carpenter something. So I have seen my apprenticeship to wood and tools reenacted in each of my children, as my father saw his own apprenticeship renewed in me.

The saw I use belonged to him, as did my level and both of my squares, and all four tools had belonged to his father. The blade of the saw is the bluish color of gun barrels, and the maple handle, dark from the sweat of hands, is inscribed with curving leaf designs. The level is a shaft of walnut two feet long, edged with brass and pierced by three round windows in which air bubbles float in oil-filled tubes of glass. The middle window serves for testing if a surface is horizontal, the others for testing if a surface is plumb or vertical. My grandfather used to carry this level on the gun rack behind the seat in his pickup, and when I rode with him I would turn around to watch the bubbles dance. The larger of the two squares is called a framing square, a flat steel elbow, so beat up and tarnished you can barely make out the rows of numbers that show how to figure the cuts on rafters. The smaller one is called a try square, for marking right angles, with a blued steel blade for the shank and a brass-faced block of cherry for the head.

15   I was taught early on that a saw is not to be used apart from a square: "If you're going to cut a piece of wood," my father insisted, "you owe it to the tree to cut it straight."

Long before studying geometry, I learned there is a mystical virtue in right angles. There is an unspoken morality in seeking the level and the plumb. A house will stand, a table will bear weight, the sides of a box will hold together, only if the joints are square and the members upright. When the bubble is lined up between two marks etched in the glass tube of a level, you have aligned yourself with the forces that hold the universe together. When you miter the corners of a picture frame each angle must be exactly forty-five degrees, as they are in the perfect triangles of Pythagoras, not a degree more or less. Otherwise the frame will hang crookedly, as if ashamed of itself and of its maker. No matter if the joints you are cutting do not show. Even if you are butting two pieces of wood together inside a cabinet, where no one except a wrecking crew will ever see them, you must take pains to ensure that the ends are square and the studs are plumb.

I took pains over the wall I was building on the day my father died. Not long after that wall was finished—paneled with tongue-and-groove boards of yellow pine, the nail holes filled with putty and the wood all stained and sealed—I came close to wrecking it one afternoon when my daughter ran howling up the stairs to announce that her gerbils had escaped from their cage and were hiding in my brand new wall. She could hear them scratching and squeaking behind her bed. Impossible! I said. How on earth could they get inside my drum-tight wall? Through the heating vent, she answered. I went downstairs, pressed my ear to the honey-colored wood, and heard the *scritch scritch* of tiny feet.

"What can we do?" my daughter wailed. "They'll starve to death, they'll die of thirst, they'll suffocate."

"Hold on," I soothed. "I'll think of something."

20   While I thought and she fretted, the radio on her bedside table delivered us the headlines: Several thousand people had died in a city in India from a poisonous cloud that had leaked overnight from a chemical plant. A nuclear-powered submarine had been launched. Rioting continued in South Africa. An airplane had been hijacked in the Mediterranean. Authorities calculated that several thousand homeless people slept on the streets within sight of the Washington Monument. I felt my usual helplessness in the face of all these calamities. But here was my daughter, weeping because her gerbils were holed up in a wall. This calamity I could handle.

"Don't worry," I told her. "We'll set food and water by the heating vent and lure them out. And if that doesn't do the trick, I'll tear the wall apart until we find them."

She stopped crying and gazed at me. "You'd really tear it apart? Just for my gerbils? The *wall*?" Astonishment slowed her down only for a second, however, before she ran to the workbench and began tugging at drawers, saying, "Let's see, what'll we need? Crowbar. Hammer. Chisels. I hope we don't have to use them—but just in case."

We didn't need the wrecking tools. I never had to assault my handsome wall, because the gerbils eventually came out to nibble at a dish of popcorn. But for several hours I studied the tongue-and-groove skin I had nailed up on the day of my father's death, considering where to begin prying. There were no gaps in that wall, no crooked joints.

I had botched a great many pieces of wood before I mastered the right angle with a saw, botched even more before I learned to miter a joint. The knowledge of these things resides in my hands and eyes and the webwork of muscles, not in the tools. There are machines for sale—powered miter boxes and radial-arm saws, for instance—that will enable any casual soul to cut proper angles in boards. The skill is invested in the gadget instead of the person who uses it, and this is what distinguishes a machine from a tool. If I had to earn my keep by making furniture or building houses, I suppose I would buy powered saws and pneumatic nailers; the need for speed would drive me to it. But since I carpenter only for my own pleasure or to help neighbors or to remake the house around the ears of my family, I stick with hand tools. Most of the ones I own were given to me by my father, who also taught me how to wield them. The tools in my workbench are a double inheritance, for each hammer and level and saw is wrapped in a cloud of knowing.

25   All of these tools are a pleasure to look at and to hold. Merchants would never paste NEW NEW NEW! signs on them in stores. Their designs are old because they work, because they serve their purpose well. Like folk songs and aphorisms and the grainy bits of language, these tools have been pared down to essentials. I look at my claw hammer, the distillation of a hundred generations of carpenters, and consider that it holds up well beside those other classics—Greek vases, Gregorian chants, *Don Quixote*, barbed fish hooks, candles, spoons.

Knowledge of hammering stretches back to the earliest humans who squatted beside fires, chipping flints. Anthropologists have a lovely name for those un-worked rocks that served as the earliest hammers. "Dawn stones," they are called. Their only qualification for the work, aside from hardness, is that they fit the hand. Our ancestors used them for grinding corn, tapping awls, smashing bones. From dawn stones to this claw hammer is a great leap in time, but no great distance in design or imagination.

On that iced-over February morning when I smashed my thumb with the ham-mer, I was down in the basement framing the wall that my daughter's gerbils would later hide in. I was thinking of my father, as I always did whenever I built anything, thinking how he would have gone about the work, hearing in mem-ory what he would have said about the wisdom of hitting the nail instead of my thumb. I had the studs and plates nailed together all square and trim, and was lifting the wall into place when the phone rang upstairs. My wife answered, and in a moment she came to the basement door and called down softly to me. The stillness in her voice made me drop the framed wall and hurry upstairs. She told me my father was dead. Then I heard the details over the phone from my mother. Building a set of cupboards for my brother in Oklahoma, he had knocked off work early the previous afternoon because of cramps in his stom-ach. Early this morning, on his way into the kitchen of my brother's trailer, maybe going for a glass of water, so early that no one else was awake, he slumped down on the linoleum and his heart quit.

    For several hours I paced around inside my house, upstairs and down, in and out of every room, looking for the right door to open and knowing there was no such door. My wife and children followed me and wrapped me in arms and backed away again, circling and staring as if I were on fire. Where was the door, the door, the door? I kept wondering. My smashed thumb turned purple and throbbed, making me furious. I wanted to cut it off and rush outside and scrape away at the snow and hack a hole in the frozen earth and bury the shameful thing.

    I went down into the basement, opened a drawer in my workbench, and stared at the ranks of chisels and knives. Oiled and sharp, as my father would have kept them, they gleamed at me like teeth. I took up a clasp knife, pried out the longest blade, and tested the edge on the hair of my forearm. A tuft came away cleanly, and I saw my father testing the sharpness of tools on his own skin, the blades of axes and knives and gouges and hoes, saw the red hair shaved off in patches from his arms and the backs of his hands. "That will cut bear," he would say. He never cut a bear with his blades, now my blades, but he cut deer, dirt, wood. I closed the knife and put it away. Then I took up the hammer and went back to work on my daughter's wall, snugging the bottom plate against a chalk line on the floor, shimming the top plate against the joists overhead, plumbing the studs with my level, making sure before I drove the first nail that every line was square and true.

Questions for Active Reading

1. Compare the details Sanders gives (paragraphs 17 and 26–28, especially) about building a wall to divide a room with the instructions given on the Lowe's web site. Can you clearly visualize what Sanders is doing at each step? Do you need to? Why, at the end of the essay, does Sanders feel the need to describe so clearly each step in the process?

2. How does Sanders use chronological order in this essay? What objects, images, or ideas connect the different periods of time that he describes?

3. What is a "dawn stone"? Why does Sanders describe it in this essay, and what does it represent to him?

Questions for Thinking Critically

1. In paragraphs 16–23, Sanders describes an ethical obligation in carpentry. What, in your own words, is that obligation? Is there any similar ethic implied by the Lowe's instructions? How does Sanders relate that obligation to larger problems in the world? Is carpentry, for Sanders, a metaphor for some greater lesson or world-view? (The very last words of the essay should provide a clue; there might also, of course, be more than one metaphor.)

2. Sanders describes a kind of "apprenticeship" that has been passed down in his family for generations. Is there a skill, or a kind of knowledge, that has been passed down in your family? How was that knowledge or skill imparted to you? How do you intend to pass it along to your own children?

3. What do you make of Sanders's description of his grief, and his early attempt to come to terms with that grief, in paragraphs 27 and 28?

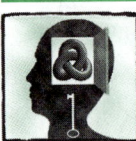

Thinking ↔ Writing Activity

Creating Objective and Subjective Descriptions

Write two separate paragraphs in which you describe the same person or object in two different ways. Make one paragraph as objective as possible; make the other primarily subjective in order to create a particular impression for your readers. Each paragraph should have about six to eight sentences.

Which of these paragraphs will have a strong topic sentence? Why? Which may not have a topic sentence or may have one that makes no claim? Why?

Chronological Relationships

Chronological forms of writing organize events or ideas in a time sequence. The focus in chronological writing is on using description to illustrate growth, development, or change—from a person's life story to the steps in creating a favorite dish. The **chronological pattern** organizes a topic into a series of events in the time sequence in which they occurred. Many chronologies are narratives or stories. For example, Scott Russell Sanders uses chronology to describe how carpentry skills are passed, in his family, from father to son. The process mode of thinking organizes an activity into a series of steps necessary for reaching a certain end. Here the focus is on describing aspects of growth, development, or change, as you might do when explaining how to prepare a favorite dish or perform a new dance.

NARRATIVES

Perhaps the oldest and most universal form of chronological expression is the *narrative,* a story about real or fictional experiences. Many people who study communication believe that narrative is the starting point for other patterns of presentation because we often process our perceptions in storylike ways.

Every human culture has used narratives to pass on values and traditions from one generation to the next, as exemplified by such enduring works as the *Odyssey*, the Bible, and the Koran. One of America's great storytellers, Mark Twain, once said that a good story has to accomplish something and arrive somewhere. In other words, if a story is to be effective in engaging the interest of the audience, it has to have a purpose. The purpose may be to provide more information on a subject, to illustrate an idea, to lead the audience to a particular way of thinking, or to entertain. An effective narrative does not merely record the complex, random, and often unrelated events of life. Instead, it has focus, an ordered structure, and a meaningful point of view.

WRITING ABOUT PROCESSES

A second type of time-ordered thinking pattern is the *process relationship*, which describes events or experiences in terms of their development. From birth, we are involved with processes in every facet of life. They can be classified in various ways: *natural* (such as growing physically), *mechanical* (such as assembling a bicycle), *physical* (such as learning a sport), *mental* (such as developing a way of thinking), and *creative* (such as writing a poem).

Writing about a process involves two basic tasks. The first is to divide the process being analyzed into parts or stages. The second is to explain the movement of the process through these parts or stages from beginning to end. The stages identified should be separate and distinct and should involve no repetition or significant omissions.

Processes are explained for two purposes. One is to give instructions on how to do something, such as build a wall or set up a computer. Instructions will often use the pronoun "you" and imperative or command verb forms. This is an excellent example of grammar, meaning, and purpose working together; the Lowe's web site instructions clearly illustrate this kind of process writing. The other purpose of process writing, as demonstrated by Scott Russell Sanders, is to describe a process but not necessarily teach someone to do it.

In your academic reading, you'll notice both kinds of process writing. For example, a biology textbook will explain the process of photosynthesis—something that your professor might expect you to understand, but certainly not to do yourself! (If you could, you'd be green.) On the other hand, when your biology professor gives you instructions for dissecting a frog, those instructions describe a process that you are expected to do.

EXAMPLES OF PROCESS WRITING

Read the following two examples of process writing. What is the purpose of each? How can you tell? What are some words in each that indicate sequence?

> Jacketing was a sleight-of-hand I watched with wonder each time, and I have discovered that my father was admired among sheepmen up and down the valley for his skill at it: He was just pretty catty at that, the way he could get that ewe to take on a new lamb every time. Put simply, jacketing was a ruse played on a ewe whose lamb had died. A substitute lamb quickly would be singled out, most likely from a set of twins. Sizing up the tottering newcomer, Dad would skin the dead lamb, and into the tiny pelt carefully snip four leg holes and a head hole. Then the stand-in lamb would have the skin fitted onto it like a snug jacket on a poodle. The next step of disguise was to cut out the dead lamb's liver and smear it several times across the jacket of pelt. In its borrowed and bedaubed skin, the new baby lamb then was presented to the ewe. She would sniff the baby impostor endlessly, distrustful but pulled by the blood-smell of her own. When in a few days she made up her dim sheep's mind to accept the lamb, Dad snipped away the jacket and recited his victory: Mother him like hell now, don't ye? See what a hellava dandy lamb I got for ye, old sister? Who says I couldn't jacket day onto night if I wanted to, now-I-ask-ye?

> —Ivan Doig, *This House of Sky*

If you are inexperienced in relaxation techniques, begin by sitting in a comfortable chair with your feet on the floor and your hands resting easily in your lap. Close your eyes and breathe evenly, deeply, and gently. As you exhale each breath let your body become more relaxed. Starting with one hand direct your attention to one part of your body at a time. Close your fist and tighten the muscles of your forearm. Feel the sensation of tension in your muscles. Relax your hand and let your forearm and hand become completely limp. Direct all your attention to the sensation of relaxation as you continue to let all tension leave your hand and arm. Continue this practice once or several times each day, relaxing your other hand and arm, your legs, back, abdomen, chest, neck, face, and scalp. When you have this mastered and can relax completely, turn your thoughts to scenes of natural tranquillity from your past. Stay with your inner self as long as you wish, whether thinking of nothing or visualizing only the loveliest of images. Often you will become completely unaware of your surroundings. When you open your eyes you will find yourself refreshed in mind and body.

—Laurence J. Peter, *The Peter Prescription*

Thinking ↔ Writing Activity

Writing Process Descriptions

Write two substantive paragraphs about two processes that you understand very well. In one, give instructions to a specific audience who would benefit from learning how to perform this activity. In the other, explain a process—but do not give instructions.

In the following essay, surgeon and writer Atul Gawande uses the description of a technical medical procedure to describe the ways in which young surgical residents become experienced, confident practitioners of their art.

The Learning Curve

BY ATUL GAWANDE (b.1965)

Atul Gawande received his M.D. from Harvard Medical School and an M.P.H. from the Harvard School of Public Health. He is a doctor at a Boston hospital and a staff writer for The New Yorker, *contributing essays on public health issues as well as spe-*

cific cases and experiences from his own practice. A collection of these essays, Complications: A Surgeon's Notes on an Imperfect Science, *was published in 2002. "The
thing that most startled me upon entering the medical profession is how human an endeavor it is," Gawande observed in an interview about the book on the web site of* The
Atlantic *magazine. "We have all the technology and studies and science and know-
how and yet, in the end, it's still this tiny pair—the individual doctor and the individual patient—who are left to try to sort through it all. It's the decisions that are really
critical. And those decisions are inherently imperfect because both doctor and patient are
fallible, because there are still mysteries in medicine—things that we don't understand—and because there is always going to be uncertainty."*

The patient needed a central line. "Here's your chance," S., the chief resident,
said. I had never done one before. "Get set up and then page me when you're
ready to start."

It was my fourth week in surgical training. The pockets of my short white
coat bulged with patient printouts, laminated cards with instructions for doing
CPR and reading EKGs and using the dictation system, two surgical handbooks,
a stethoscope, wound-dressing supplies, meal tickets, a penlight, scissors, and
about a dollar in loose change. As I headed up the stairs to the patient's floor, I
rattled.

This will be good, I tried to tell myself: my first real procedure. The patient—fiftyish, stout, taciturn—was recovering from abdominal surgery he'd
had about a week earlier. His bowel function hadn't yet returned, and he was
unable to eat. I explained to him that he needed intravenous nutrition and that
this required a "special line" that would go into his chest. I said that I would put
the line in him while he was in his bed, and that it would involve my numbing
a spot on his chest with a local anesthetic, and then threading the line in. I did
not say that the line was eight inches long and would go into his vena cava, the
main blood vessel to his heart. Nor did I say how tricky the procedure could
be. There were "slight risks" involved, I said, such as bleeding and lung collapse; in experienced hands, complications of this sort occur in fewer than one
case in a hundred.

But, of course, mine were not experienced hands. And the disasters I knew
about weighed on my mind: the woman who had died within minutes from
massive bleeding when a resident lacerated her vena cava; the man whose chest
had to be opened because a resident lost hold of a wire inside the line, which
then floated down to the patient's heart; the man who had a cardiac arrest when
the procedure put him into ventricular fibrillation. I said nothing of such things,
naturally, when I asked the patient's permission to do his line. He said, "OK."

5   I had seen S. do two central lines; one was the day before, and I'd attended
to every step. I watched how she set out her instruments and laid her patient
down and put a rolled towel between his shoulder blades to make his chest arch
out. I watched how she swabbed his chest with antiseptic, injected lidocaine,
which is a local anesthetic, and then, in full sterile garb, punctured his chest near

his clavicle with a fat three-inch needle on a syringe. The patient hadn't even flinched. She told me how to avoid hitting the lung ("Go in at a steep angle," she'd said. "Stay *right* under the clavicle"), and how to find the subclavian vein, a branch to the vena cava lying atop the lung near its apex ("Go in at a steep angle. Stay *right* under the clavicle"). She pushed the needle in almost all the way. She drew back on the syringe. And she was in. You knew because the syringe filled with maroon blood. ("If it's bright red, you've hit an artery," she said. "That's not good.") Once you have the tip of this needle poking in the vein, you somehow have to widen the hold in the vein wall, fit the catheter in, and snake it in the right direction—down to the heart, rather than up to the brain— all without tearing through vessels, lung, or anything else.

To do this, S. explained, you start by getting a guide wire in place. She pulled the syringe off, leaving the needle in. Blood flowed out. She picked up a two-foot-long twenty-gauge wire that looked like the steel D string of an electric guitar, and passed nearly its full length through the needle's bore, into the vein, and onward toward the vena cava. "Never force it in," she warned, "and never, ever let go of it." A string of rapid heartbeats fired off on the cardiac monitor, and she quickly pulled the wire back an inch. It had poked into the heart, causing momentary fibrillation. "Guess we're in the right place," she said to me quietly. Then to the patient: "You're doing great. Only a few minutes now." She pulled the needle out over the wire and replaced it with a bullet of thick, stiff plastic, which she pushed in tight to widen the vein opening. She then removed this dilator and threaded the central line—a spaghetti-thick, flexible yellow plastic tube—over the wire until it was all the way in. Now she could remove the wire. She flushed the line with a heparin solution and sutured it to the patient's chest. And that was it.

Today, it was my turn to try. First, I had to gather supplies—a central-line kit, gloves, gown, cap, mask, lidocaine—which took me forever. When I finally had the stuff together, I stopped for a minute outside the patient's door, trying to recall the steps. They remained frustratingly hazy. But I couldn't put it off any longer. I had a page-long list of other things to get done: Mrs. A needed to be discharged; Mr. B needed an abdominal ultrasound arranged; Mrs. C needed her skin staples removed. And every fifteen minutes or so I was getting paged with more tasks: Mr. X was nauseated and needed to be seen; Miss Y's family was here and needed "someone" to talk to them; Mr. Z needed a laxative. I took a deep breath, put on my best don't-worry-I-know-what-I'm-doing look, and went in.

I placed the supplies on a bedside table, untied the patient's gown, and laid him down flat on the mattress, with his chest bare and his arms at his sides. I flipped on a fluorescent overhead light and raised his bed to my height. I paged S. I put on my gown and gloves and, on a sterile tray, laid out the central line, the guide wire, and other materials from the kit. I drew up five cc's of lidocaine in a syringe, soaked two sponge sticks in the yellow-brown Betadine, and opened up the suture packaging.

S. arrived. "What's his platelet count?"

My stomach knotted I hadn't checked. That was bad: too low and he could have a serious bleed from the procedure. She went to check a computer. The count was acceptable.

Chastened, I started swabbing his chest with the sponge sticks. "Got the shoulder roll underneath him?" S. asked. Well, no, I had forgotten that, too. The patient gave me a look. S., saying nothing, got a towel, rolled it up, and slipped it under his back for me. I finished applying the antiseptic and then draped him so that only his right upper chest was exposed. He squirmed a bit beneath the drapes. S. now inspected my tray. I girded myself.

"Where's the extra syringe for flushing the line when it's in?" Damn. She went out and got it.

I felt for my landmarks. *Here?* I asked with my eyes, not wanting to undermine the patient's confidence any further. She nodded. I numbed the spot with lidocaine. ("You'll feel a stick and a burn now, sir.") Next, I took the three-inch needle in hand and poked it through the skin. I advanced it slowly and uncertainly, a few millimeters at a time. This is a big goddamn needle, I kept thinking. I couldn't believe I was sticking it into someone's chest. I concentrated on maintaining a steep angle of entry, but kept spearing his clavicle instead of slipping beneath it.

"Ow!" he shouted.

"Sorry," I said. S. signaled with a kind of surfing hand gesture to go underneath the clavicle. This time, it went in. I drew back on the syringe. Nothing. She pointed deeper. I went in deeper. Nothing. I withdrew the needle, flushed out some bits of tissue clogging it, and tried again.

"*Ow!*"

Too steep again. I found my way underneath the clavicle once more. I drew the syringe back. Still nothing. He's too obese, I thought. S. slipped on gloves and a gown. "How about I have a look?" she said. I handed her the needle and stepped aside. She plunged the needle in, drew back on the syringe, and, just like that, she was in. "We'll be done shortly," she told the patient.

She let me continue with the next steps, which I bumbled through. I didn't realize how long and floppy the guide wire was until I pulled the coil out of its plastic sleeve, and, putting one end of it into the patient, I very nearly contaminated the other. I forgot about the dilating step until she reminded me. Then, when I put in the dilator, I didn't push quite hard enough, and it was really S. who pushed it all the way in. Finally, we got the line in, flushed it, and sutured it in place.

Outside the room, S. said that I could be less tentative the next time, but that I shouldn't worry too much about how things had gone. "You'll get it," she said. "It just takes practice." I wasn't so sure. The procedure remained wholly mysterious to me. And I could not get over the idea of jabbing a needle into someone's chest so deeply and so blindly. I awaited the X-ray afterward with trepidation. But it came back fine: I had not injured the lung and the line was in the right place.

20

My second try at placing a central IV line went no better than the first. The patient was in intensive care, mortally ill, on a ventilator, and needed the line so that powerful cardiac drugs could be delivered directly to her heart. She was also heavily sedated, and for this I was grateful. She'd be oblivious of my fumbling.

My preparation was better this time. I got the towel roll in place and the syringes of heparin on the tray. I checked her lab results, which were fine. I also made a point of draping more widely, so that if I flopped the guide wire around by mistake again, it wouldn't hit anything unsterile.

For all that, the procedure was a bust. I stabbed the needle in too shallow and then too deep. Frustration overcame tentativeness and I tried one angle after another. Nothing worked. Then, for one brief moment, I got a flash of blood in the syringe, indicating that I was in the vein. I anchored the needle with one hand and went to pull the syringe off with the other. But the syringe was jammed on too tightly, so that when I pulled it free I dislodged the needle from the vein. The patient began bleeding into her chest wall. I held pressure the best I could for a solid five minutes, but still her chest turned black and blue around the site. The hematoma made it impossible to put a line through there anymore. I wanted to give up. But she needed a line and the resident supervising me—a second-year this time—was determined that I succeed. After an X-ray showed that I had not injured her lung, he had me try on the other side, with a whole new kit. I missed again, and he took over. It took him several minutes and two or three sticks to find the vein himself, and that made me feel better. Maybe she was an unusually tough case.

When I failed with a third patient a few days later, though, the doubts really set in. Again, it was stick, stick, stick, and nothing. I stepped aside. The resident watching me got it on the next try.

Surgeons, as a group, adhere to a curious egalitarianism. They believe in practice, not talent. People often assume that you have to have great hands to become a surgeon, but it's not true. When I interviewed to get into surgery programs, no one made me sew or take a dexterity test or checked to see if my hands were steady. You do not even need all ten fingers to be accepted. To be sure, talent helps. Professors say that every two or three years they'll see someone truly gifted come through a program—someone who picks up complex manual skills unusually quickly, sees tissue planes before others do, anticipates trouble before it happens. Nonetheless, attending surgeons say that what's most important to them is finding people who are conscientious, industrious, and boneheaded enough to keep at practicing this one difficult thing day and night for years on end. As a former residency director put it to me, given a choice between a Ph.D. who had cloned a gene and a sculptor, he'd pick the Ph.D. every time. Sure, he said, he'd bet on the sculptor's being more physically talented; but he'd bet on the Ph.D.'s being less "flaky." And in the end that matters more. Skill, surgeons believe, can be taught; tenacity cannot. It's an odd approach to recruitment, but it continues all the way up the ranks, even in top surgery departments. They start with minions with no experience in surgery, spend years training them, and then take most of their faculty from these homegrown ranks.

25   And it works. There have now been many studies of elite performers—concert violinists, chess grand masters, professional ice skaters, mathematicians, and so forth—and the biggest difference researchers find between them and lesser performers is the amount of deliberate practice they've accumulated. Indeed, the most important talent may be the talent for practice itself. K. Anders Ericsson, a cognitive psychologist and an expert on performance, notes that the most important role that innate factors play may be in a person's *willingness* to engage in sustained training. He has found, for example, that top performers dislike practicing just as much as others do. (That's why, for example, athletes and musicians usually quit practicing when they retire.) But, more than others, they have the will to keep at it anyway.

I wasn't sure I did. What good was it, I wondered, to keep doing central lines when I wasn't coming close to hitting them? If I had a clear idea of what I was doing wrong, then maybe I'd have something to focus on. But I didn't. Everyone, of course, had suggestions. Go in with the bevel of the needle up. No, go in with the bevel down. Put a bend in the middle of the needle. No, curve the needle. For a while, I tried to avoid doing another line. Soon enough, however, a new case arose.

The circumstances were miserable. It was late in the day, and I'd had to work through the previous night. The patient weighed more than three hundred pounds. He couldn't tolerate lying flat because the weight of his chest and abdomen made it hard for him to breathe. Yet he had a badly infected wound, needed intravenous antibiotics, and no one could find veins in his arms for a peripheral IV. I had little hope of succeeding. But a resident does what he is told, and I was told to try the line.

I went to his room. He looked scared and said he didn't think he'd last more than a minute on his back. But he said he understood the situation and was willing to make his best effort. He and I decided that he'd be left sitting propped up in bed until the last possible minute. We'd see how far we got after that.

I went through my preparations: checking his blood counts from the lab, putting out the kit, placing the towel roll, and so on. I swabbed and draped his chest while he was still sitting up. S., the chief resident, was watching me this time, and when everything was ready I had her tip him back, an oxygen mask on his face. His flesh rolled up his chest like a wave. I couldn't find his clavicle with my fingertips to line up the right point of entry. And already he was looking short of breath, his face red. I gave S. a "Do you want to take over?" look. Keep going, she signaled. I made a rough guess about where the right spot was, numbed it with lidocaine, and pushed the big needle in. For a second, I thought it wouldn't be long enough to reach through, but then I felt the tip slip underneath his clavicle. I pushed a little deeper and drew back on the syringe.

30   Unbelievably, it filled with blood. I was in. I concentrated on anchoring the needle firmly in place, not moving it a millimeter as I pulled the syringe off and

threaded the guide wire in. The wire fed in smoothly. The patient was struggling hard for air now. We sat him up and let him catch his breath. And then, laying him down one more time, I got the entry dilated and slid the central line in. "Nice job" was all S. said, and then she left.

I still have no idea what I did differently that day. But from then on my lines went in. That's the funny thing about practice. For days and days, you make out only the fragments of what to do. And then one day you've got the thing whole. Conscious learning becomes unconscious knowledge, and you cannot say precisely how.

I have now put in more than a hundred central lines. I am by no means infallible. Certainly, I have had my fair share of complications. I punctured a patient's lung, for example—the right lung of a chief of surgery from another hospital, no less—and, given the odds, I'm sure such things will happen again. I still have the occasional case that should go easily but doesn't, no matter what I do. (We have a term for this. "How'd it go?" a colleague asks. "It was a total flog," I reply. I don't have to say anything more.)

But other times everything unfolds effortlessly. You take the needle. You stick the chest. You feel the needle travel—a distinct glide through the fat, a slight catch in the dense muscle, then the subtle pop through the vein wall—and you're in. At such moments, it is more than easy; it is beautiful.

It is 2 P.M. I am in the intensive-care unit. A nurse tells me Mr. G.'s central line has clotted off. Mr. G. has been in the hospital for more than a month now. He is in his late sixties, from South Boston, emaciated, exhausted, holding on by a thread—or a line, to be precise. He has several holes in his small bowel, and the bilious contents leak out onto his skin through two small reddened openings in the concavity of his abdomen. His only chance is to be fed by vein and wait for these fistulae to heal. He needs a new central line.

35   I could do it, I suppose. I am the experienced one now. But experience brings a new role: I am expected to teach the procedure instead. "See one, do one, teach one," the saying goes, and it is only half in jest.

There is a junior resident on the service. She has done only one or two lines before. I tell her about Mr. G. I ask her if she is free to do a new line. She misinterprets this as a question. She says she still has patients to see and a case coming up later. Could I do the line? I tell her no. She is unable to hide a grimace. She is burdened, as I was burdened, and perhaps frightened, as I was frightened.

She begins to focus when I make her talk through the steps—a kind of dry run, I figure. She hits nearly all the steps, but forgets about checking the labs and about Mr. G.'s nasty allergy to heparin, which is in the flush for the line. I make sure she registers this, then tell her to get set up and page me.

I am still adjusting to this role. It is painful enough taking responsibility for one's own failures. Being handmaiden to another's is something else entirely. It occurs to me that I could have broken open a kit and had her do an actual dry run. Then again, maybe I can't. The kits must cost a couple of hundred dollars each. I'll have to find out for next time.

Half an hour later, I get the page. The patient is draped. The resident is in her gown and gloves. She tells me that she has saline to flush the line with and that his labs are fine.

40   "Have you got the towel roll?" I ask.

She forgot the towel roll. I roll up a towel and slip it beneath Mr. G.'s back. I ask him if he's all right. He nods. After all he's been through, there is only resignation in his eyes.

The junior resident picks out a spot for the stick. The patient is hauntingly thin. I see every rib and fear that the resident will puncture his lung. She injects the numbing medication. Then she puts the big needle in, and the angle looks all wrong. I motion for her to reposition. This only makes her more uncertain. She pushes in deeper and I know she does not have it. She draws back on the syringe: no blood. She takes out the needle and tries again. And again the angle looks wrong. This time, Mr. G. feels the jab and jerks up in pain. I hold his arm. She gives him more numbing medication. It is all I can do not to take over. But she cannot learn without doing, I tell myself. I decide to let her have one more try.

Questions for Active Reading

1. Why does Gawande conclude this essay as he does? How do you, as a reader, respond?

2. Obviously, Gawande is not writing for an audience who are about to perform the insertion of a large intravenous tube into the main blood vessel of the heart. Yet he gives a significant amount of detail as he describes the process of doing so. Each time he describes the insertion of such a tube, or "central line," his perceptions of the procedure change. What are the differences in Gawande's perceptions of each incident? What is Gawande's purpose for each description?

3. How does Gawande use chronology to organize his essay? Why is this a particularly effective organizational choice, given his subject and purpose?

Questions for Thinking Critically

1. Both Gawande and Scott Russell Sanders describe a kind of apprenticeship, a way in which knowledge and skills are passed along from one generation to another through example and practice. What are the similarities between the apprenticeships each writer describes? What are the differences? Is apprenticeship always the best way to learn, or teach, a particular skill or body of knowledge?

2. "Skill, surgeons believe, can be taught; tenacity cannot." Do you agree, or disagree? Describe a time in your life when being *tenacious* helped you to overcome an obstacle, to master a skill, or to solve a problem.

3. Why does Gawande describe the experience in paragraph 33 as "beautiful"? What, exactly, is "beautiful" about it? Have you experienced that same kind of "beauty" in accomplishing something difficult?

Writing Project: A Narrative Showing the Effect of a Perception

The readings and Thinking-Writing activities in this chapter encourage you to become more aware of your perceptions, to use description to convey those perceptions, and to choose the appropriate organizing structure (chronology, narrative, and/or process) for writing about those perceptions.

> Write a narrative essay describing the influence another person's perceptions had on your understanding of yourself, on a skill or body of knowledge you are learning, or on a significant decision you have made (or are in the process of making). When were you first made aware of this issue, conflict, idea, or skill? How did this other person (or persons) make their perceptions known to you? Were you initially in conflict with that other person, or have you always been in agreement? If there have been points of conflict in your relationship, did you learn and grow from them? How have your own perceptions grown and changed since knowing this other person (or persons)?
>
> As part of your preparation for writing your essay, find a magazine or newspaper article dealing with the perception and quote from it at least once in your essay. Document the quoted material according to your instructor's directions. If an academic documentation format such as that of the Modern Language Association (MLA) or American Psychological Association (APA) is required, be sure that your entry conforms exactly to the models in a writing handbook.

Principles for Writing Narratives

The following principles for writing narratives are not fixed rules; you may have good reasons for not following some of them. In general, though, they should help you to write an effective essay.

1. Identify the relevant issue fully so that the narrative has a meaningful context.

2. State your thesis well; place it effectively in your paper.

3. Use description to introduce your readers to the people involved and to let them visualize the place. Consider whether subjective or objective description, or a combination of the two, will best serve your purpose.

4. Tell the story as fully as seems appropriate for your intended audience, without either rambling excessively or leaving out important details or events.

5. Be sure to begin and end effectively. The conclusion is likely to be especially important in this essay since you may want to reiterate your main point there.

THE WRITING SITUATION

Begin by considering the key elements in the Thinking-Writing Model in Chapter 1 on page 6 .

Purpose You have a variety of purposes here. You have the opportunity to recall and relate a significant experience. You also can think about an issue that concerns you and learn more about it by finding the required article. In addition, you will be improving your ability to connect what you read with your own ideas, something you must do regularly as a college student. Most important, you can inform your classmates, your instructor, and your other readers about an issue that concerns you or skill that interests you and about the impact of another person's perception of that same issue.

Audience As always, you are a member of your own audience and perhaps the person who will enjoy the narrative most since it is connected with your life. Your classmates will be a good audience, both to learn from your narrative and to share your experience. In addition, they are valuable as peer reviewers of your draft, reacting as intelligent readers who are also immersed in the assignment. Of course, anyone else who has had a similar experience would also benefit from reading your essay. Perhaps your campus newspaper would be interested. Finally, your instructor remains the audience who will judge how well you have planned, drafted, and revised. As a writing teacher, he or she cares about a clear focus, logical organization, specific details, and correctness. Keep these aspects in mind as you revise, edit, and proofread.

Subject Although you and your readers are probably concerned about many perceptual issues, both you and they may need to be reminded of how an issue and a person's perceptions of it can affect someone else.

Writer You are in a dual position here. You are, of course, the expert on your own story. This is both an advantage and a disadvantage: no one can argue with you about your story, but you still need to remember that your audience was not there. You must provide them with sufficient background and description to make them feel as if they did share your experience, but you don't want to overwhelm them with details. Therefore, you will need to be selective as you decide what to include and what to omit. Also, remember that you are not the expert on the article from which you plan to quote, so do think carefully about what it says and where to use it in your own work.

THE WRITING PROCESS

The following sections will guide you through the stages of generating, planning, drafting, and revising as you work on a descriptive and illustrative narrative.

Generating Ideas

1. You may immediately recall a meaningful experience that you want to narrate. If not, think about past events that were worrisome, frightening, amusing, or exciting and then think again about the context of the event.

2. You may be deeply involved in dealing with others' perceptions of issues because of who you are, where you live, or which organizations you support. If so, you should have no problem identifying a concern you want to address. If not, look around, talk with friends and family members, read newspapers and magazines, and watch the news.

3. Think locally. Look at issues in your community or those connected with your college or job. Then try to recall any experiences in which another person's perceptions had an impact on you.

Defining a Focus Draft a thesis statement that connects your experience with the perception you plan to write about. You may want to emphasize the directness of the connection, or you may need to show that what is not obvious is indeed related. Perhaps you may wish to emphasize a time element: "I didn't understand at the time, but now I see that . . ." or "I knew at that moment that . . ." You may want to focus on the impact this perception has had on your life.

Organizing Ideas You could tell the story first and then connect it with the perceptual stereotype. Or you might make statements about the perception regularly throughout the narration as different events illustrate various aspects of the situation. In either case, your use of chronological order will help your audience follow the events of your story. Therefore, unless you see some serious reason not to do so, give background information first and then guide your audience through the time sequence of the events. You need to consider what arrangements will best help your audience see their connection to the issue. Be sure to select and place carefully the material quoted from your source and to incorporate it smoothly into your writing by introducing and commenting on it.

If you are using process writing in your essay, determine if the process itself can provide the organizational structure for the entire essay. Otherwise, be sure that each step of the process is clearly explained within each relevant paragraph.

Drafting   Begin with the easiest part to write, possibly the experience itself. Tell it fully; then plan to increase its effectiveness by including sharp details and a tight sequence of events at the revision stage. The paragraphs within the narrative may or may not have topic sentences. This is one of the differences between narration and exposition. Since your purpose is to connect the experience with others' perceptions, you may want to have topic sentences for the paragraphs that do that.

After you have drafted the narrative, draft the paragraphs that state the thesis and make the connection between the experience and the issue. Then establish and write any necessary transitions.

Revising, Editing, and Proofreading   Use the step-by-step method on page 160 to revise your essay and prepare a final draft.

The following two essays demonstrate how student writers used a combination of description, process writing, and chronological ordering to illustrate how the perceptions of other people influenced their own decisions.

STUDENT WRITING
JOSHUA CHAFFEE'S WRITING PROCESS

Living so close to "Ground Zero," the site where the World Trade Center used to stand in New York City, Joshua Chaffee had an overwhelming amount of perceptions, emotions, and experiences to sort through as he contemplated this essay. Like Maria Muniz, whose essay follows Joshua's, this experience was to define both his perceptions of his community and how he understood himself. Joshua knew he wanted to draw upon that experience as he approached this essay, but he also knew that he had to be careful with his organization and his descriptions. Often, when writing about something so overwhelming—and something experienced, even at a distance, by so many people—it becomes difficult to stay focused on your audience and your purpose. Joshua brought in the perceptions of other people to balance his own feelings. Here is an excerpt from Joshua's rough outline for this essay.

1. How did New Yorkers respond to 9/11?—keep it personal and specific; what did I personally witness? (Probably keep my emotions out of it—stick to what I perceived, not how I "felt"—that's too subjective and probably overwhelming. . . .)

2. Connect those perceptions to why I want to be a journalist. Can I talk to or find an article by another New York journalist who covered 9/11?—need to make a logical connection between 9/11 and why I want to be a journalist . . .

3. Incorporate as assignment for the "Feature Writing" course—how writing about New York (the La Frieda interview? the profile I did of Alan Kaufman and his pickle shop?) can give a voice to all New Yorkers, and connect that to my response to 9/11.

4. Conclusion?—maybe connect whatever I choose from "Feature Writing" to the behavior I witnessed on 9/11? A larger observation about why I love New York and want to stay here and do something for New Yorkers. . . .

We're All at Ground Zero

BY JOSHUA CHAFFEE

From my bedroom window, I can see the six-story remainder of the World Trade Center's steel siding, forked in the ground, shooting up towards its former resting place in the New York City skyline. The site is lit through the entire night with an otherworldly glow, and men are working there, at "Ground Zero," when I go to sleep and when I wake up.

Outside my house, hundreds of people gather to cheer and offer their gratitude towards the workers. Each night I have joined them. At one point, a truck stops beside the crowd and a fireman inside exclaims, "We've just contacted two Port Authority Police Officers on the second floor and we're digging them out right now!" What follows is an eruption of yelling and cheering far greater than I have ever heard.

In an interview I did with former *New York Times* columnist turned novelist Anna Quindlen, she told me, "September 11th was a time that made me proud of the journalism profession. Journalists provided a huge public service to people because they created an instant sense of community. It was a time when I seriously considered writing columns again." After 9/11, Anna Quindlen re-affirmed her passion for journalism, while I discovered mine for the first time. It hit me on a Monday in late October of 2001.

About a month into the journalism course I was taking junior year, I found myself wedged in between Pat and Lisa La Frieda, scribbling madly onto a notepad because the air coolers in the meat locker were too loud for me to use my tape recorder. Outside the sun had yet to come up and, only weeks after September 11th, the air still smelled of ash. Inside, Pat La Frieda wore the same long, bloodstained white jacket and black knit cap characteristic of Italian-American butchers generations ago, when his grandparents owned La Frieda Meats. As he spoke to me, men hoisted sides of beef onto their shoulders while others sprayed the floor tiles with hoses to flush the blood into drains. The smell of cold, fresh meat permeated every corner of the long white room, a smell Pat relished as he slowly strolled past the lockers.

La Frieda Meats is located in Greenwich Village, one block east of the Hudson River and across the street from a controversial empty lot where an 18-story, luxury high-rise is planned to go up. The high-rise would be eight stories taller than any building near it, thus casting a long six-block shadow over the neighborhood. Pat had a lot to say on the topic. One question and he took off like a racehorse: "People have got to welcome advancement. You can't live in the past, saying how the Village used to be. Look, when my grandparents owned this meat packing business, they delivered the meat by horse drawn wagons every morning. Where would I be if I still used horses today!"

However, on the other side of me, his sister Lisa had a different point of view. Lisa is a large woman with heavy dark makeup. She jumped in, cutting off Pat, "Yeah, but you know what'll happen when they put in a luxury building? All the tenants will start screaming about my trucks coming in at four in the morning. And paying that much for an apartment, they probably got the right to complain." Sandwiched between Pat and Lisa, I tried to keep up with their words, which were barely audible above the meat coolers. I couldn't hold back a smile, though. Walking around a meat packing warehouse at six in the morning before school and talking to Pat and Lisa—I would rather be here than anywhere else, including my bed.

That Monday night I wrote about Pat and Lisa La Frieda, piecing their ideas into my article on the effects of the anticipated luxury high-rise. Hours later, I found myself still at my computer with a bowl of Chex Mix, writing and thinking about the interviews that morning. I understood what I had felt when I was standing in that frigid warehouse. I had realized my passion, and knew exactly what I wanted to be doing in the future. As a journalist, I have the opportunity to go out and have a half-hour conversation with some of the most interesting people—people I might otherwise never speak to. Then I come home and write about them; I give Pat and Lisa La Frieda a voice that they might never have used before—a voice that can be heard by hundreds of people.

The city is too big to know everyone's story. Most people don't know Alan Kaufman, the owner of the only remaining fresh pickle shop in the Lower East Side; or Joe Oliva, the 16-year security guard at Night Court, where every criminal arrested in Manhattan comes to be arraigned; or Chef José, the chef at a private Manhattan school, who was the head chef at United Airlines for most of his life. But, by opening up the worlds of everyone around us, journalists can unite a community.

This, I believe, is what Anna Quindlen meant by journalists creating "an instant sense of community," and this is what attracts me to the profession. Immediately after September 11, we all felt alone and frightened. But journalists showed us that everyone else was experiencing the same feelings, and that together we could help each other to understand and move on from what happened. When we are alone, our surroundings can seem overwhelming and unfriendly. But, through the telling of people's stories and the revealing of the true fabric of the city, New York can begin to feel as intimate as your family, and as small as a Village. All around the city people have come together. The city has united in a community of shared pain, devoted to its country and to each other. Everyone felt his or her hearts come down with those towers, but as we start to rebuild, we have each other for support.

STUDENT WRITING

MARIA MUNIZ'S WRITING PROCESS

Maria Muniz initially approached this assignment intending to describe the process of immigrating to America as experienced by her family. But then she returned to her written responses to Edite Cunhã's essay, "Talking in the New Land," in Chapter 6. She had been especially drawn to Cunhã's use of her childhood perceptions to describe the immigrant experience. Maria decided to use her own childhood memories of Cuba to answer the question: "Would you ever go back?"

> Would I ever go back? I haven't been in Cuba since I was five years old. I think part of me is still there, with my aunts and my grandmothers. Part of me, the adult me, feels very American, but I always tell people that I'm Cuban, even though my Spanish isn't as good as my English anymore. I don't know, sometimes, who I am, because I can't go back to my childhood home. Everyone else can go back to the source of what they know and I can't. How can I know who I am if I don't know that source? I don't think I can write an essay that describes a specific "process" because I'm still <u>in</u> the process, I'm still becoming someone. Can I write about how having two very different kinds of perceptions— I'm as American as I am Cuban—influences how I answer that question "would you ever go back"?

Back, But Not Home

BY MARIA MUNIZ

With all the talk about resuming diplomatic relations with Cuba, and with the increasing number of Cuban exiles returning to visit friends and relatives, I am constantly being asked, "Would you ever go back?" In turn, I have asked myself, "Is there any reason for me to go?" I have had to think long and hard before finding my answer. *Yes.*

I came to the United States with my parents when I was almost five years old. We left behind grandparents, aunts, uncles and several cousins. I grew up in a very middle-class neighborhood in Brooklyn. With one exception, all my friends were Americans. Outside of my family, I do not know many Cubans. I often feel awkward visiting relatives in Miami because it is such a different world. The way of life in Cuban Miami seems very strange to me and I am accused of being too "Americanized." Yet, although I am now an American citizen, whenever anyone has asked me my nationality, I have always and unhesitatingly replied, "Cuban."

Outside American, inside Cuban.

I recently had a conversation with a man who generally sympathizes with the Castro regime. We talked of Cuban politics and although the discussion was very casual, I felt an old anger welling inside. After 16 years of living an "American" life, I am still unable to view the revolution with detachment or objectivity. I cannot interpret its results in social, political or economic terms. Too many memories stand in my way.

And as I listened to this man talk of the Cuban situation, I began to remember how as a little girl I would wake up crying because I had dreamed of my aunts and grandmothers and I missed them. I remembered my mother's trembling voice and the sad look on her face whenever she spoke to her mother over the phone. I thought of the many letters and photographs that somehow were always lost in transit. And as the conversation continued, I began to remember how difficult it often was to grow up Latina in an American world.

It meant going to kindergarten knowing little English. I'd been in this country only a few months and although I understood a good deal of what was said to me, I could not express myself very well. On the first day of school I remember one little girl saying to the teacher: "But how can we play with her? She's so stupid she can't even talk!" I felt so helpless because inside I was crying, "Don't you know I can understand everything you're saying?" But I did not have words for my thoughts and my inability to communicate terrified me.

As I grew a little older, Latina meant being automatically relegated to the slowest reading classes in school. By now my English was fluent, but the teachers would always assume I was somewhat illiterate or slow. I recall one teacher's amazement at discovering I could read and write just as well as her American pupils. Her incredulity astounded me. As a child, I began to realize that being Latina would always mean proving I was as good as the others. As I grew older, it became a matter of pride to prove I was better than the others.

As an adult I have come to terms with these memories and they don't hurt as much. I don't look or sound very Cuban. I don't speak with an accent and my English is far better than my Spanish. I am beginning my career and look forward to the many possibilities ahead of me.

But a persistent little voice is constantly saying, "There's something missing. It's not enough." And this is why when I am now asked, "Do you want to go back?" I say "yes" with conviction.

I do not say to Cubans, "It is time to lay aside the hurt and forgive and forget." It is impossible to forget an event that has altered and scarred all our lives so profoundly.

But I find I am beginning to care less and less about politics. And I am beginning to remember and care more about the child (and how many others like her) who left her grandma behind. I have to return to Cuba one day because I want to know that little girl better.

When I try to review my life during the past 16 years, I almost feel as if I've walked into a theater right in the middle of a movie. And I'm afraid I won't fully understand or enjoy the rest of the movie unless I can see and understand the beginning. And for me, the beginning is Cuba. I don't want to go "home" again; the life and home we all left behind are long gone. My home is here and I am happy. But I need to talk to my family still in Cuba.

Like all immigrants, my family and I have had to build a new life from almost nothing. It was often difficult, but I believe the struggle made us strong. Most of my memories are good ones.

But I want to preserve and renew my cultural heritage. I want to keep "la Cubana" within me alive. I want to return because the journey back will also mean a journey within. Only then will I see the missing piece.

"Our life is what our thoughts make it." —Marcus Aurelius

Exploring Concepts

Writing to Classify and Define

Critical Thinking Focus: The conceptualizing process

Writing Focus: Defining and applying concepts

Reading Theme: Gender issues

Writing Project: Defining an important concept

---

nternet, beauty, hip-hop culture, channel surfing, truth, bungee jumping, attitude, and *thinking* are only a few examples of concepts in a world filled with them. As you speak and write, you refer to concepts you have formed. Your academic study involves learning new concepts as well, and being successful in college and in your career requires understanding the conceptualizing process.

When you read textbooks or listen to lectures and take notes, you have to grasp key concepts and follow them as they are developed and supported. Many course examinations involve applying the key concepts you have learned to new sets of circumstances. When you write papers, you are usually expected to focus on certain concepts, develop a thesis around them, present the thesis (itself a concept), and back it up with specific evidence.

Your college writing will often require the definition of terms or concepts. Chapter 6 discussed the fact that words are complex carriers of meaning—with meanings varying from person to person. This chapter will explore further implications of this complexity as it pertains to your writing.

The Writing Project in the chapter asks you to write a full definition of a concept that is important to your life. As you write this paper, you will see that definition usually involves using all the patterns of thinking that the previous chapter in Part Two discussed.

Definition is a very important thinking and writing pattern. The analytical activity of classification, which underlies defining, is essential to good thinking. Definition and classification rely on comparative relationships in order to establish categories by means of similarities and in order to distinguish among concepts within categories by identifying differences. Definitions usually include descriptions and sometimes employ causal, chronological, or process analyses to make distinctions or to show the development of a concept. Understanding the thinking patterns that you have already worked with and being able to use them effectively can ease the difficult task of defining concepts.

To help you define significant concepts, this chapter will explain the conceptualizing process, present readings that involve definitions, and give you opportunities to define some terms that are significant in various aspects of your life.

What Are Concepts?

Concepts are general ideas that you use to organize your experience and, in so doing, bring order to your life. In the same way that words are the vocabulary of language, concepts are the vocabulary of thought. As organizers of your experience, concepts work in conjunction with language to identify, describe, distinguish, and relate all the various aspects of your world.

Developing expertise in the conceptualizing process improves your ability to form, apply, and relate concepts. This complex conceptualizing process is going on all the time in your mind, enabling you to think in a distinctly human way. When you form opinions or make judgments, you are applying and relating concepts.

How do you use concepts to organize and make sense of experience? Think back to the first day of the semester. For most students, this is a time to evaluate their courses by trying to determine which concepts apply.

- Will this course be interesting? useful? challenging?
- Is the instructor stimulating? demanding? understanding?
- Are the other students friendly? intelligent? conscientious?

Each of these descriptive words or phrases represents a concept you are attempting to apply so that you can understand what is occurring at the moment and also anticipate what will occur. As the course progresses, you gather more information from experiences in class. This information may support your initial concepts, or it may conflict with them. If it supports them, you tend to maintain them ("Yes, I can see that this is going to be a difficult course"). When the information you receive conflicts with your initial concepts, you tend to find new concepts to explain the situation ("No, I can see that I was wrong—this course isn't going to be as difficult as I first thought"). A diagram of this process might look something like the one in Figure 8.1.

Throughout this thinking process you are making evaluations that establish classifications of kinds or types: What *kind* of course—difficult? easy? What *kind* of teacher? What *kind* of reading? What *kind* of student am I in relation to this course? And you are consciously or unconsciously using definitions that you have formulated: When I say "difficult course," I mean one that . . . When I say "demanding teacher," I mean one who . . . And so on.

Figure 8.1 Experience Leads to Action

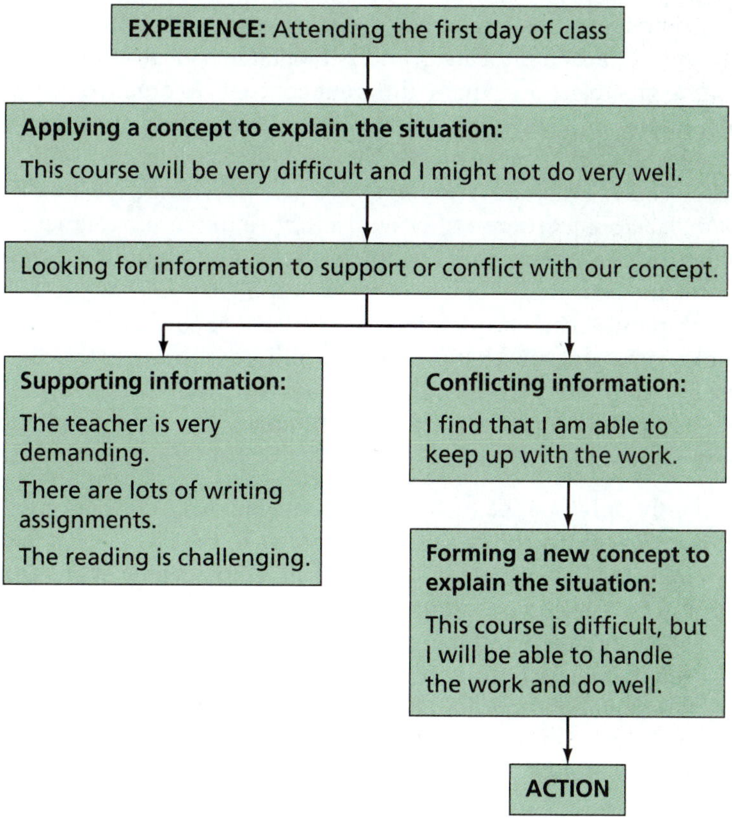

Changing Your Concepts

Identify an initial concept you had about an event in your life (a new job, attending college, getting married, and so on). After identifying your initial concept, describe the experiences that led you to change or modify the concept; then explain the new concept you formed to explain the situation. Your response should include the following elements.

- The initial concept
- New information provided by additional experiences
- The new concept formed to explain the situation

THE IMPORTANCE OF CONCEPTS

Learning to understand and write about concepts will help you in every area of your life: academic, career, and personal. In college study, each academic discipline or subject uses many different concepts to organize experience, give explanations, and solve problems. Here is a sampling of college-level concepts: *entropy, subtext, Gemeinschaft, cell, metaphysics, relativity, parallel processing, prehistory, unconscious, aesthetic, minor key, interface, health, quantum mechanics, schizophrenia.* To make sense of how disciplines function, you need to understand what the concepts of that discipline mean, how to define them, how to apply them, and how they relate to other concepts.

Although each academic discipline has its own unique and specific concepts, some concepts change their definition according to the disciplinary "lens" used to interpret it. In the following passage from *Colour: Art & Science*, physiologist Trevor Lamb describes how the concept of "color" is understood by different academic disciplines.

Although the idea of "colour" may seem a simple concept, it conjures up very different ideas for each of us. To the physicist, colour is determined by the wavelength of light. To the physiologist and psychologist, our perception of colour involves neural responses in the eye and the brain, and is subject to the limitations of our nervous system. To the naturalist, colour is not only a thing of beauty but also a determinant of survival in nature. To the social historian and linguist, our understanding and interpretation of colour are inextricably linked to our own culture. To the art historian, the development of colour in painting can be traced both in artistic and technological terms. And for the painter, colour provides a means of expressing feelings and the intangible, making possible the creation of a work of art. . . . In the field of colour, the arts and the sciences now travel in unison, and together they provide a rich and comprehensive understanding of the subject.

You will regularly present your understanding of definitions, of applications, and of relationships among concepts in your written work. You will also need to learn the methods of investigation, patterns of thought, and forms of reasoning that various disciplines use to form larger conceptual theories and methods. Successful completion of writing assignments in the courses that you will take will depend on your understanding of the key concepts that form the core of each discipline.

Regardless of their specific knowledge content, all careers require conceptual abilities, whether you are trying to apply a legal principle, develop a promotional theme, or devise a new computer program. Similarly, expertise in forming and applying concepts helps you to make sense of your personal life, understand others, and make informed decisions. The Greek philosopher Aristotle said that the intelligent person is a "master of concepts."

THE STRUCTURE OF CONCEPTS

Concepts, in addition to being general ideas that you use to identify and organize your experience, are useful for distinguishing and connecting one thing to another. Concepts allow you to organize your world into patterns that make sense to you.

In their role of organizers of experience, concepts act to group aspects of your experience on the basis of their similarity. Consider the object that you usually write with: a pen. The concept *pen* represents an instrument that you use for writing. Now look around the classroom at other instruments people are using to write. You use the concept *pen* to identify these as well, even though they may look quite different from yours. Thus, the concept *pen* not only helps you to make distinctions in your experience by indicating how pens differ from pencils, crayons, or markers; it also helps you to determine which items are similar enough to all be called pens. When you put items into a group with a single description—such as *pen*—you are focusing on their similarities:

- They use ink.
- They are used for writing.
- Each is held in one hand.

Being able to see and name the similarities among certain things in your experience is the way you form concepts and is crucial for making sense of your world. If you were not able to do this, everything in the world would appear to be different, with its own individual name.

THE PROCESS OF CLASSIFYING

The process by which you group things on the basis of their similarities is known as **classifying**. Classifying is a natural human activity that goes on all the time. In most cases, however, you are not conscious of classifying something in a particular sort of way; you do so automatically. The process of classifying is one of the main ways that you order, organize, and make sense of your world. Because no two things or experiences are exactly alike, your ability to classify things into various groups is what enables you to recognize things in your experience. When you perceive a pen, you recognize it as a *kind* of object you have seen before. Even though you may not have seen this particular pen, you recognize that it belongs to a category of things that is familiar.

The best way to understand the structure of concepts is to visualize them by means of a model. Examine Figure 8.2. The **sign** is the word or symbol used to name or designate the concept; for example, the word *triangle* is a sign. The **referents** represent all the various examples of the concept; the three-sided figure we are using as our model is an example of the concept *triangle*. The **properties** of the concept are the features that all things named by the word or sign share in common; all examples of the concept *triangle* share the characteristics of being a polygon and having three sides. These are the properties that we refer to when we define concepts; thus, "A triangle is a three-sided polygon."

Let's take another example. Suppose you wanted to explore the structure of the concept *automobile*. The sign that names the concept is the word *automobile* or the symbol 🚗 . Referents of the concept include the 1954 MG "TF" currently residing in the garage as well as the Ford Explorer parked in front of the house. The properties that all things named by the sign *automobile* include are wheels, a chassis, an engine, seats, and so on. Figure 8.3 shows a conceptual model of the concept *automobile*.

Figure 8.2 Model of a Concept

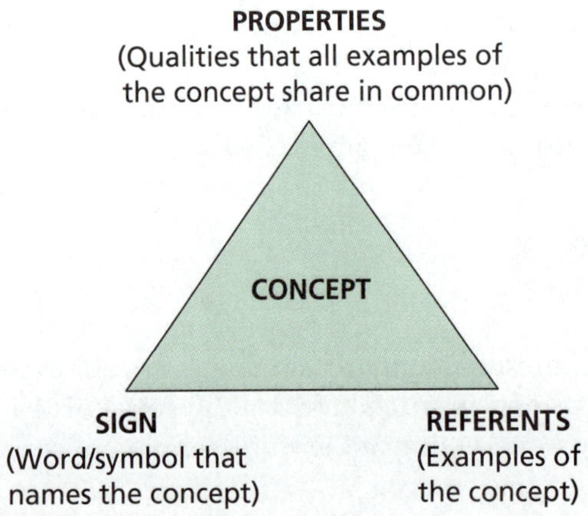

PROPERTIES
(Qualities that all examples of
the concept share in common)

CONCEPT

SIGN
(Word/symbol that
names the concept)

REFERENTS
(Examples of
the concept)

Figure 8.3 Model of Concept "Automobile"

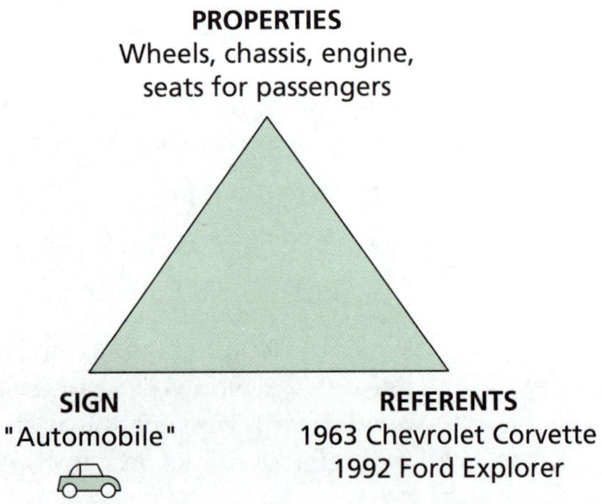

PROPERTIES
Wheels, chassis, engine,
seats for passengers

SIGN
"Automobile"

REFERENTS
1963 Chevrolet Corvette
1992 Ford Explorer

Diagramming Concepts

Using the model we have developed, diagram the structure of three of the following concepts as well as those of two concepts of your own choice: *dance, success, student, religion, music, friend.*

Forming Concepts

You form—and apply—concepts to organize your experience, make sense of what is happening, and anticipate what may happen in the future. You form concepts by the interactive processes of **generalizing** (focusing on the common properties shared by a group of things) and **interpreting** (finding examples of the concept). The common properties form the necessary requirements that must be met in order for you to be able to apply the concept to your experience. If you examine the diagrams of concepts in the last section, you can see that the process of forming concepts involves moving back and forth between the referents (examples) of the concept and the properties (common features) shared by all examples of the concept. Let's further explore the way this interactive process of forming concepts operates.

Consider the following conversation between two people trying to form and clarify the concept *philosophy.*

A: What is your idea of what philosophy *means*?

B: Well, I think philosophy involves expressing important beliefs that you have—like discussing the meaning of life, assuming that there is a meaning.

A: Is explaining my belief about who's going to win the Super Bowl engaging in philosophy? After all, this is a belief that is very important to me—I've got a lot of money riding on the outcome!

B: I don't think so. A philosophical belief is usually a belief about something that is important to everyone—like what standards we should use to guide our moral choices.

A: What about the message that was in my fortune cookie last night: "Eat, drink, and be merry, for tomorrow we diet!"? This is certainly a belief that most people can relate to, especially during a holiday season! Is this philosophy?

B: I think that's what my grandmother used to call "foolosophy"! Philosophical beliefs are usually deeply felt views to which we have given a great deal of thought—not something plucked out of a cookie.

A: What about my belief in the golden rule: "Do unto others as you would have them do unto you" because "What goes around comes around"? Doesn't that have the qualities that you mentioned?

B: Now you've got it!

As we review this dialogue, we can see that forming the concept *philosophical belief* works hand in hand with applying the concept to different examples. When two or more things work together in this way, we say that they *interact*. In this case, there are two parts of this interactive process.

We form concepts by generalizing, by focusing on the similar features among different things. In the previous dialogue, the things about which generalizations are being made are types of beliefs—beliefs about the meaning of life or about standards we use to guide our moral choices. By focusing on the similar features of these beliefs, the dialogue's two participants develop a list of properties philosophical beliefs share, including (1) beliefs dealing with important issues in life about which everyone is concerned and (2) beliefs reflecting deeply felt views—views to which people have given much thought. These common properties act as the requirements a viewpoint must meet to be considered a philosophical belief.

We apply concepts by interpreting, by looking for different examples of a concept and seeing if they meet the requirements of the concept we are developing. In the preceding dialogue, one participant attempts to apply the concept *philosophical belief* to the following examples:

a belief about the outcome of the Super Bowl

a fortune cookie message: "Eat, drink, and be merry, for tomorrow we diet."

Each of these proposed examples suggests the development of new requirements for the concept to help clarify how the concept can be applied. Applying a concept to different possible examples thus becomes the way we develop and gradually sharpen our idea of it.

Even when a proposed example turns out not to be a valid one, we have often clarified our understanding of that concept. For instance, although the proposed example of a belief about the outcome of the Super Bowl turned out not to be an example of the concept *philosophical belief*, examining it helped to clarify the concept and suggest other examples.

The process of developing concepts involves a constant back-and-forth movement between generalizing and interpreting. As the back-and-forth movement progresses, we gradually develop a list of specific requirements for an example of the concept; at the same time, we gain a clearer sense of how the concept is defined. We are also developing a collection of examples that embody the qualities of the concept and demonstrate situations in which the concept applies. This interactive process is illustrated in Figure 8.4.

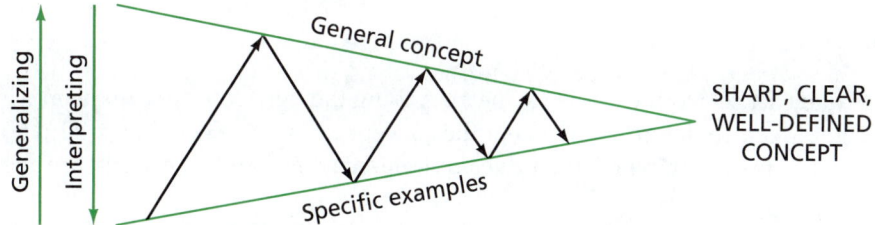

Figure 8.4 Movement from General Concept to Well-Defined Concept

Thinking ↔ Writing Activity

Forming a Concept

Select a type of music with which you are familiar and write a dialogue similar to the one just examined. In the course of the dialogue, be sure to include the following:

1. Examples from which you are generalizing (such as specific bands).

2. General properties shared by various types of this music (e.g., "Jazz is a uniquely American form of music which uses complex rhythms and improvisation.").

3. Examples to which you are trying to apply the developing concept (such as the music of Marian McPartland, Miles Davis, or Thelonius Monk).

Forming concepts involves performing the operations of generalizing and interpreting together for two reasons.

1. You cannot form a concept unless you know how it might apply. If you have absolutely no idea what *jazz* or *philosophy* might exemplify, you cannot begin to form the concept, even in vague or general terms.

2. You cannot gather examples of the concept unless you know what they might be examples of. Until you begin to develop some idea of what the concepts *jazz* or *philosophy* might be (based on certain similarities among various things), you won't know where to look for examples of the concept (or how to evaluate them).

This interactive process is the way that you usually form all concepts, particularly the complicated ones. In school, much of your education is focused on carefully forming and exploring key concepts such as *democracy, dynamic equilibrium,* and *personality.*

Applying Concepts

Making sense of our experience means finding the right concept to explain what is going on. To determine whether the concept we have selected fits a situation, we have to determine whether the requirements that form the concept are being met.

To figure out which concept applies to the situation, we must do the following:

1. Be aware of the properties that form the boundaries of the concept.
2. Determine whether the experience meets those requirements, for only if it does can we apply the concept to it.

If we have the requirements of the concept clearly in mind, we can proceed to figure out which of these requirements are met by the experience. This is how we apply concepts, which is one of the most important ways we have for figuring out what is taking place in our experience.

DETERMINING THE REQUIREMENTS OF A CONCEPT

In determining the requirements of a concept we ask ourselves: *Would something still be an example of this concept if that thing did not meet this requirement?* If the answer to this question is *no*—that something would not be an example of this concept if it did not meet this requirement—we can say the requirement is a necessary part of the concept.

Consider the concept *dog*. Which of the following descriptions are requirements that must be met by an example of this concept?

1. Is an animal
2. Normally has four legs and a tail
3. Bites the mail carrier

It is clear that descriptions 1 and 2 are requirements that must be met to apply the concept *dog* because if we apply our test question—"Would something be an example of this concept if that thing did not meet this requirement?"—we can say that the thing would not be an example of the concept *dog* if it did not fit the first two descriptions: if it was not an animal and did not normally have four legs and a tail.

This does not seem to be the case, however, with description 3. If we ask ourselves the same test question, we can see that the thing might still be an example of the concept *dog* even if it did not bite the mail carrier. Even though some dogs do in fact bite mail carriers, this is not a requirement for being a dog.

Of course, there may be other things that meet these requirements but are not dogs. For example, a cat is an animal (description 1) that normally has four legs and a tail (description 2). What this means is that the requirements of a concept tell us only what attributes something must have to be an example of the concept. As a result, we often have to identify additional requirements that will define the concept more sharply. These requirements determine when the concept can be applied and indicate those things that qualify as examples of it. When we are able to identify all the requirements of the concept, we say these requirements are both necessary and sufficient for applying the concept.

ANALYZING COMPLEX CONCEPTS

Although dealing with concepts like *dog* and *cat* may seem simple, matters become somewhat confusing when you start analyzing the more complex concepts you will encounter in your academic study. For example, consider the concepts of *masculinity* and *femininity*, two of the more emotionally charged and politically contentious concepts in our culture. There are many different perspectives on what these concepts mean, what they should mean, or whether we should be using them at all. See if you can identify properties and examples of these two concepts by completing the following Thinking-Writing Activity.

Thinking ↔ Writing Activity

Exploring the Concepts of *Masculine* and *Feminine*

Identify what you consider the essential properties (specific requirements that must be met to apply the concept) for each of these concepts as well as examples of people or behavior that illustrates these properties. For example, you might identify physical risk taking as a property of the concept *masculinity* and identify Bruce Willis as a person who illustrates this quality. Or you might identify intuition as a property of the concept *femininity*, illustrating this with the behavior "knowing without the conscious use of rational processes."

General Properties   Specific Examples

FEMININITY

1. _____   1. _____

2. _____   2. _____

3. _____   3. _____

MASCULINITY

1. _____   1. _____

2. _____   2. _____

3. _____   3. _____

Compare your list with those of your classmates. What similarities and differences do you notice? What factors might account for these similarities and differences? Look back at your responses after you have read the following selections.

A Casebook on Gender and Sexuality

It would seem to be the easiest characteristic to define, the most basic classification into which we can sort human beings: Are you a man or a woman? Is your behavior feminine or masculine? And yet the dazzling variety of human responses, preferences, fears, and favors blurs these apparently simple distinctions into a never-ending source of pleasure and conflict. Not surprisingly, the similarities and differences between men and women have inspired poets and storytellers as well as provoked the interests of social scientists and essayists. In the following casebook, writers across genres and perspectives attempt to define and classify issues of gender and sexuality.

Standing His Ground

BY MICHAEL NORMAN

Michael Norman, a former marine, is an associate professor of journalism and mass communication at New York University. A former reporter and columnist for the New York Times, *where this essay first appeared, he is the author of* These Good Men: Friendships Forged in War, *a memoir of his experience in Vietnam (1990). A review of the book in* Newsweek *magazine observed that "*These Good Men *is really about the consolations of friendship, and if it ends affirmatively, it is never foolish, because Norman understands the irony of his territory: that love as intense and lasting as anything produced in peacetime should arise out of the awful circumstances of war. "*

I have bruised a knuckle and bloodied another man's nose, but I am not, by most measures, a fighter. The last time I broke the peace was more than a decade ago in a small restaurant on the west slope of the Rocky Mountains in Colorado.

My stepfather had encountered an old nemesis. Words were exchanged and the distance between the two narrowed. I stepped in to play the peacemaker and ended up throwing the first punch. For the record, my target, a towering 230-pound horseman, easily absorbed the blow and then dispatched the gnat in front of him.

The years since have been filled with discretion—I preach it, embrace it and hide behind it. I am now the careful watchman who keeps his eye on the red line and reroutes pressure before it has a chance to blow. Sometimes, I backslide and turn a domestic misdemeanor into a capital case or toss the cat out of the house without bothering to see where he lands. But I do not punch holes in the plaster or call my antagonists to the woodshed. The Furies may gather, but the storm always stays safely out to sea. And yet, lately, I have been struggling with this forced equanimity. The messenger of reason, the advocate of accord, once again has the urge to throw the first punch—in spirit at least.

All of this began rather quietly, a deep stirring that would come and go and never take form, an old instinct, perhaps, trying to reassert itself. I was angry, restless, combative, but I could not say why. It was a mystery of sorts. I was what I was expected to be, the very model of a modern man, a partner instead of a husband, a proponent of peace over action, thin-skinned rather than thick, a willow instead of a stone. And yet there was something about this posture that did not fit my frame. Then, an acquaintance, a gentle man who spent his Peace Corps days among the villagers of Nepal, suddenly acted out of character. He got into an argument with a local brute in a neighborhood tavern and instead of walking away from trouble, stood his ground. It was, he said, a senseless confrontation, but he had no regrets, and it made me think of Joey.

Joey, the bully of the sixth grade, used to roam the hallways picking victims at random and slugging them on the arm. When he rounded a corner, we scattered or practiced a crude form of mysticism and tried to think ourselves invisible in the face of the beast. Since I was slow and an inept mystic, my mother kept on hand an adequate supply of Ben Gay to ease the bruises and swelling.

5   One day, a boy named Tony told the marauder that he had had enough and an epic duel was scheduled in the playground after school. Tony had been taking boxing lessons on the sly. He had developed a stinging left jab and when the appointed hour arrived, he delivered it in the name of every bruised shoulder in the school.

The meek pack of which Tony was once a part took courage from his example and several weeks later when a boy at my bus stop sent me sprawling, I returned the favor.

There were only a few challenges after that. On the way up, a Joey would occasionally round the corner. But in the circles I traveled, he was the exception rather than the rule. In the Marine Corps in Vietnam, we were consumed by a much larger kind of warfare. In college, faculty infighting and bullying aside, violence was considered anti-intellectual. And in the newsrooms where I have practiced my trade, reporters generally have been satisfied with pounding a keyboard instead of their editors.

And then came Colorado and the battle of the west slope. For years, I was embarrassed by the affair. I could have walked away and dragged my stepfather with me. As it was, we almost ended up in jail. I had provoked a common brawl, a pointless, self-destructive exercise. The rationalist had committed the most irrational of acts. It was not a matter of family or honor, hollow excuses. I had simply succumbed to instinct, and I deeply regretted it. But not any longer. Now I see virtue in that vulgar display of macho. It disqualifies me from the most popular male club—the brotherhood of nurturers, fraternity sensitivus.

From analyst's couch to tavern booth, their message is the same: The male animus is out of fashion. The man of the hour is supposed to be gentle, thoughtful, endearing and compassionate, a wife to his woman, a mother to his son, an androgynous figure with the self-knowledge of a hermaphrodite. He takes his lumps on the psyche, not the chin, and bleeds with emotion. Yes, in the morning, he still puts on a three-piece suit, but his foulard, the finishing touch, is a crying towel.

10   He is so ridden with guilt, so pained about the sexist sins of his kind, he bites at his own flanks. Not only does he say that he dislikes being a man, but broadly proclaims that the whole idea of manhood in America is pitiful.

He wants to free himself from the social conditioning of the past, to cast off the yoke of traditional male roles and rise above the banality of rituals learned at boot camp or on the practice field. If science could provide it, he would swallow an antidote of testosterone, something to stop all this antediluvian thumping and bashing.

And he has gone too far. Yes, the male code needs reform. Our rules and our proscriptions have trapped us in a kind of perpetual adolescence. Why else would a full-grown rationalist think he could get even with Joey by taking a poke at another bully 25 years later in a bar in Colorado? No doubt there is something pitiful about that.

But the fashion for reform, the drive to emasculate macho, has produced a kind of numbing androgyny and has so blurred the lines of gender that I often find myself wanting to emulate some of the women I know—bold, aggressive, vigorous role models.

It sometimes seems that the only exclusively male trait left is the impulse to throw a punch, the last male watermark, so to speak, that is clear and readable. Perhaps that is why the former Peace Corps volunteer jumped into a brawl and why I suspect that the new man—the model of sensitivity, the nurturer—goes quietly through the day with a clenched fist behind his back.

Questions for Active Reading

1. According to Norman, what are the properties of the concept masculinity? What are some examples he gives of the properties that he has identified?

2. Do you agree with the properties that Norman has identified? Explain why or why not. Does Norman achieve a definition of *masculinity*, or a partial definition? What thinking-writing patterns has he used?

3. How does Norman describe "discretion" (paragraph 2)? Shakespeare wrote that "The better part of valor is discretion;" what is "valor," and could Norman be referring, in this paragraph, to Shakespeare's well-known observation?

Questions for Thinking Critically

1. Some people believe that the concepts of *masculinity* and *femininity* were formed by earlier cultures, are outdated in our current culture, and should be revised. Other people believe that these concepts reflect essential qualities of the human species and should not be excessively tampered with. Where do you stand on this issue?

2. Do you see connections among the concepts *feminism/feminist* and *masculism/masculinist* and the concepts of *femininity* and *masculinity*? What are some differences among these related concepts? Where does *machismo* fit in?

3. To what extent is our popular culture, especially that aimed at kids and teenagers, dependent on violence? Think about music videos, on-line or video games, and other popular distractions that depict violence randomly or without apparent consequence. Do these games, videos, movies, and songs appeal (in your opinion) primarily to young men, to young women, or both? Why is violence entertaining?

FROM *The Collected Poems of Theodore Roethke*

My Papa's Waltz
BY THEODORE ROETHKE (1908–1963)

The theme of fathers lost and found, fatherhood as conflicted and yearned for, permeates the work of Theodore Roethke. His German father, grandfather, and uncles owned and operated greenhouses in Saginaw, Michigan; the image of the greenhouse as a fragile shelter, a transparent place of life even in the most brutal of climates, gives a poignant force to several poems in his second volume of verse, The Lost Son and Other Poems *(1948). The death of Roethke's father from cancer in 1923 shaped his adolescence and may have contributed to the severe bouts of depression that periodically shook him for the rest of his life. In an autobiographical essay, Roethke observed that "I believe that the spiritual man must go back in order to go forward"; this regression into the personal as well as poetic past in order to develop his own voice and persona shaped his poetic project.*

Roethke held several university teaching appointments and was widely published during his life. He was awarded the Guggenheim Fellowship (1950), Poetry *magazine's Levinson Prize (1951), and major grants from the Ford Foundation and the National Institute of Arts and Letters in 1952. His posthumously published and final book,* The Far Field *(1964), received the National Book Award.*

The whiskey on your breath
Could make a small boy dizzy;
But I hung on like death:
Such waltzing was not easy.

5   We romped until the pans
Slid from the kitchen shelf;
My mother's countenance
Could not unfrown itself.

The hand that held my wrist
10   Was battered on one knuckle;
At every step you missed
My right ear scraped a buckle.

You beat time on my head
With a palm caked hard by dirt,
15   Then waltzed me off to bed
Still clinging to your shirt.

Questions for Active Reading

1. Although poets often use figurative language in richly imaginative ways, there is just one simile in this poem. Where is that simile, and what does it reveal about the relationship between the father and the son?

2. Reading the poem out loud (to yourself, or to each other in the classroom), what do you notice about its rhyming and its rhythm? Do these patterns remind you of other kinds of poems, rhymes, or songs? In what way?

3. Is the narrator of the poem a small boy, or an adult writing from the perspective of a small boy? How can you tell?

Questions for Thinking Critically

1. Fatherhood, and the loss of or search for a father figure, is an overarching theme of Roethke's work. Based on this poem, how would you define Roethke's concept of fatherhood (not the specific father described here)?

2. In what ways do the father and the mother in this poem evoke the "masculine" and "feminine" qualities described by Michael Norman?

3. Compare and contrast the ways in which Roethke, Norman, and (in a later reading) Carol Tavris describe how men express love and caring. Of these authors, whose perspective do you think is most accurate? Are you basing your assessment on your own personal experience and relationships, or on more abstract classifications of behavior?

FROM *The Blue Jay's Dance*

The Names of Women

BY LOUISE ERDRICH (b. 1954)

A member of the Turtle Mountain band of the Chippewa nation of Native Americans, writer Louise Erdrich (born in 1954) explores the fragmented, sorrowful, and ongoing conflict between Native Americans and the larger American culture in her novels, poetry, and essays. Raised in a family of seven children, and the mother of six children herself, Erdrich finds within the entanglements of family all of the story and metaphor necessary to tell larger truths about the ways in which men and women, Native American and "American," and adults and children relate to and conflict with one another. Her first novel, Love Medicine *(1984), won the National Book Critics Circle Award, and her subsequent novels* The Beet Queen *(1986) and* Tracks *(1988) were also best-sellers. Her recent novel,* The Last Report on the Miracles at Little No Horse *(2001), was a finalist for the National Book Award. In an interview with the online magazine* Salon, *Erdrich described how growing up in a household of storytellers influences her writing: "My mother read, my father told them to me. Lots of stories. That's the way they are. They're always making stories out of things—'This happened today and he is connected to so and so.' It's a small town thing." Erdrich lives in Minneapolis and runs a small independent bookstore.*

Ikwe is the word for woman in the language of the Anishinabe, my mother's people, whose descendants, mixed with and married to French trappers and farmers, are the Michifs of the Turtle Mountain reservation in North Dakota. Every Anishinabe *Ikwe*, every mixed-blood descendant like me, who can trace her way back a generation or two, is the daughter of a mystery. The history of the woodland Anishinabe—decimated by disease, fighting Plains Indian tribes to the west and squeezed by European settlers to the east—is much like most other Native American stories, a confusion of loss, a tale of absences, of a culture that was blown apart and changed so radically in such a short time that only the names survive,

And yet, those names.

The names of the first women whose existence is recorded on the rolls of the Turtle Mountain Reservation, in 1892, reveal as much as we can ever recapture of their personalities, complex natures, and relationships. These names tell stories, or half stories, if only we listen closely.

There once were women named *Standing Strong, Fish Bones, Different Thunder*. There once was a girl called *Yellow Straps*. Imagine what it was like to pick berries with *Sky Coming Down*, to walk through a storm with *Lightning Proof*. Surely, she was struck and lived, but what about the person next to her? People always avoided *Steps Over Truth*, when they wanted a straight answer, and *I Hear*, when they wanted to keep a secret. *Glittering* put coal on her face and watched for enemies at night. The woman named *Standing Across* could see things moving far across the lake. The old ladies gossiped about *Playing Around*, but no one dared say anything to her face. *Ice* was good at gambling. *Shining One Side* loved to sit and talk to *Opposite the Sky*. They both knew *Sounding Feather, Exhausted Wind*, and *Green Cloud*, daughter of *Seeing Iron*. *Center of the Sky* was a widow. *Rabbit, Prairie Chicken*, and *Daylight* were all little girls. *She Tramp* could make great distance in a day of walking. *Cross Lightning* had a powerful smile. When *Setting Wind* and *Gentle Woman Standing* sang together the whole tribe listened. *Stop the Day* got her name when at her shout the afternoon went still. *Log* was strong, *Cloud Touching Bottom* weak and consumptive. *Mirage* married *Wind*. Everyone loved *Musical Cloud*, but children hid from *Dressed in Stone*. *Lying Down Grass* had such a gentle voice and touch, but no one dared to cross *She Black of Heart*.

5   We can imagine something of these women from their names. Anishinabe historian Basil Johnston notes that "such was the mystique and force of a name that it was considered presumptuous and unbecoming, even vain, for a person to utter his own name. It was the custom for a third person, if present, to utter the name of the person to be identified. Seldom, if ever, did either husband or wife speak the name of the other in public."

Shortly after the first tribal roll, the practice of renaming became an ecclesiastical exercise, and, as a result, most women in the next two generations bear the names of saints particularly beloved by the French. *She Knows the Bear* became Marie. *Sloping Cloud* was christened Jeanne. *Taking Care of the Day* and *Yellow Day Woman* turned into Catherines. Identities are altogether lost. The daughters of my own ancestors, *Kwayzancheewin—Acts Like a Boy* and *Striped Earth Woman*—go unrecorded, and no hint or reflection of their individual natures comes to light through the scatter-shot records of those times, although they must have been genetically tough in order to survive: there were epidemics of typhoid, flu, measles and other diseases that winnowed the tribe each winter. They had to have grown up sensible, hard-working, undeviating in their attention to their tasks. They had to have been lucky. And if very lucky, they acquired carts.

It is no small thing that both of my great-grandmothers were known as women with carts.

The first was Elise Eliza McCloud, the great-granddaughter of *Striped Earth Woman*. The buggy she owned was somewhat grander than a cart. In her photograph, Elise Eliza gazes straight ahead, intent, elevated in her pride. Perhaps she and her daughter Justine, both wearing reshaped felt fedoras, were on their way to the train that would take them from Rugby, North Dakota, to Grand Forks, and back again. Back and forth across the upper tier of the plains, they peddled their hand-worked tourist items—dangling moccasin brooches and little beaded hats, or, in the summer, the wild berries, plums, and nuts that they had gathered from the wooded hills. Of Elise Eliza's industry there remains in the family only an intricately beaded pair of buffalo horns and a piece of real furniture, a "high-boy," an object once regarded with some awe, a prize she won for selling the most merchandise from a manufacturer's catalogue.

The owner of the other cart, Virginia Grandbois, died when I was nine years old: she was a fearsome and fascinating presence, an old woman seated like an icon behind the door of my grandparents' house. Forty years before I was born, she was photographed on her way to fetch drinking water at the reservation well. In the picture she is seated high, the reins in her fingers connected to a couple of shaggy fetlocked draft ponies. The barrel she will fill stands behind her. She wears a man's sweater and an expression of vast self-pleasure. She might have been saying *Kaygoh*, a warning, to calm the horses. She might have been speaking to whomever it was who held the camera, still a novel luxury.

10   Virginia Grandbois was known to smell of flowers. In spite of the potato picking, water hauling, field and housework, she found the time and will to dust her face with pale powder, in order to look more French. She was the great-great-granddaughter of the daughter of the principal leader of the *A-waus-e*, the Bullhead clan, a woman whose real name was never recorded but who, on marrying a Frenchman, was "recreated" as Madame Cadotte. It was Madame Cadotte who acted as a liaison between her Ojibway relatives and her husband so that, even when French influence waned in the region, Jean-Baptiste Cadotte stayed on as the only trader of importance, the last governor of the fort at Sault St. Marie.

By the time I knew Virginia Grandbois, however, her mind had darkened, and her body deepened, shrunk, turned to bones and leather. She did not live in the present or in any known time at all. Periodically, she would awaken from dim and unknown dreams to find herself seated behind the door in her daughter's house. She then cried out for her cart and her horses. When they did not materialize, Virginia Grandbois rose with great energy and purpose. Then she walked towards her house, taking the straightest line.

That house, long sold and gone, lay over one hundred miles due east and still Virginia Grandbois charged ahead, no matter what lay in her path—fences, sloughs, woods, the yards of other families. She wanted home, to get home, to be home. She wanted her own place back, the place she had made, not her daughter's, not anyone else's. Hers. There was no substitute, no kindness, no reality that would change her mind. She had to be tied to the chair, and the chair to the wall, and still there was no reasoning with Virginia Grandbois. Her entire life, her hard-won personality, boiled down in the end to one stubborn, fixed, desperate idea.

I started with the same idea—this urge to get home, even if I must walk straight across the world. Only, for me, the urge to walk is the urge to write. Like my great-grandmother's house, there is no home for me to get to. A mixed-blood, raised in the Sugarbeet Capital, educated on the Eastern seaboard, married in a tiny New England village, living now on a ridge directly across from the Swan Range in the Rocky Mountains, my home is a collection of homes, of wells in which the quiet of experience shales away into sweet bedrock.

Elise Eliza pieced the quilt my mother slept under, a patchwork of shirts, pants, other worn-out scraps, bordered with small rinsed and pressed Bull Durham sacks. As if in another time and place, although it is only the dim barrel of a four-year-old's memory, I see myself lying wrapped under smoky quilts and dank green army blankets in the house in which my mother was born. In the fragrance of tobacco, some smoked in home-rolled cigarettes, some offered to the Manitous whose presence still was honored, I dream myself home. Beneath the rafters, shadowed with bunches of plants and torn calendars, in the nest of a sagging bed, I listen to mice rustle and the scratch of an owl's claws as it paces the shingles.

15   Elise Eliza's daughter-in-law, my grandmother Mary LeFavor, kept that house of hand-hewed and stacked beams, mudded between. She managed to shore it up and keep it standing by stuffing every new crack with disposable diapers. Having used and reused cloth to diaper her own children, my grandmother washed and hung to dry the paper and plastic diapers that her granddaughters bought for her great-grandchildren. When their plastic-paper shredded, she gathered them carefully together and one day, on a summer visit, I woke early to find her tamping the rolled stuff carefully into the cracked walls of that old house.

It is autumn in the Plains, and in the little sloughs ducks land, and mudhens, whose flesh always tastes greasy and charred. Snow is coming soon, and after its first fall there will be a short, false warmth that brings out the sweet-sour odor of highbush cranberries. As a descendant of the women who skinned buffalo and tanned and smoked the hides, of women who pounded berries with the dried meat to make winter food, who made tea from willow bark and rosehips, who gathered snakeroot, I am affected by the change of seasons. Here is a time when plants consolidate their tonic and drop seed, when animals store energy and grow thick fur. As for me, I start keeping longer hours, writing more, working harder, though I am obviously not a creature of a traditional Anishinabe culture. I was not raised speaking the old language, or adhering to the cycle of religious ceremonies that govern the Anishinabe spiritual relationship to the land and the moral order within human configurations. As the wedding of many backgrounds, I am free to do what simply feels right.

My mother knits, sews, cans, dries food and preserves it. She knows how to gather tea, berries, snare rabbits, milk cows, and churn butter. She can grow squash and melons from seeds she gathered the fall before. She is, as were the women who came before me, a repository of all of the homey virtues, and I am the first in a long line who has not saved the autumn's harvest in birch bark *makuks* and skin bags and in a cellar dry and cold with dust. I am the first who scratches the ground for pleasure, not survival, and grows flowers instead of potatoes. I record rather than practice the arts that filled the hands and days of my mother and her mother, and all the mothers going back into the shadows, when women wore names that told us who they were.

Questions for Active Reading

1. Erdrich describes a culture, the Anishinabe nation of Native Americans, for whom names and naming carried a "mystique." What is the connection, in this essay, between defining and naming a person?

2. Study Erdrich's description of her great-grandmother Virginia Grandbois. How does Erdrich use classification—or, more specifically, the impossibility of classification—to describe this woman who seems to "not live in the present or in any known time at all"? In how many ways is this elderly woman neither here nor there, neither completely Ojibwe nor French, neither at home nor away? What does Virginia Grandbois's story suggest about the fate of Native Americans?

3. In many traditional cultures men and women have more than one "name"—a name they were given at birth; another (often secret) name given at adolescence or initiation; a public name that links them to some adventure or characteristic (as in "The Names of Women"). How many different names are you known by? To what extent do you believe your name defines your character?

Questions for Thinking Critically

1. What are the "homey virtues" that Erdrich lovingly describes in paragraph 17, and what is Erdrich's own attitude toward those "virtues"?

2. What does the list of names in paragraph 4 suggest about the place of women in the traditional Anishinabe culture?

3. A "tribal roll" (paragraph 6) is a listing registered with the Bureau of Indian Affairs of all the members of a specific Native American "tribe" (or "nation," which has come to be a more widely accepted term than "tribe"). What, according to Erdrich, was lost in the transcription of Anishinabe women's names onto official government documents? What other factors caused the changing, blurring, or loss of these women's identities and their stories?

Men and Their Hidden Feelings

BY RICHARD COHEN

Richard Cohen has been a columnist for the Washington Post *since 1976. Born in New York City, he graduated from New York University and began his career as a journalist in New York. He joined* The Washington Post *in 1968 after attending the Columbia University Graduate School of Journalism, and after doing, as he puts it, "some postgraduate work" at Fort Dix, New Jersey, and Fort Leonard Wood, Missouri. At the* Post *he covered all sorts of stories—night police, city hall, education, state government, and national politics. His reporting has carried him into perilous situations in the Middle East and Africa, and Ground Zero immediately after the September 11 attacks. Cohen's graceful writing and engagement with topics of intimate interest as well as global import have earned him a devoted readership.*

My friends have no friends. They are men. They think they have friends, and if you ask them whether they have friends they will say yes, but they don't really. They think, for instance, that I'm their friend, but I'm not. It's OK. They're not my friends either.

The reason for that is that we are all men—and men, I have come to believe, cannot or will not have real friends. They have something else—companions, buddies, pals, chums, someone to drink with and someone to wench with and someone to lunch with, but no one when it comes to saying how they feel—especially how they hurt.

Women know this. They talk about it among themselves. I heard one woman describe men as the true Third World people—still not yet emerged. To women, this inability of men to say what they feel is a source of amazement and then anguish and then, finally, betrayal. Women will tell you all the time that they don't know the men they live with. They talk of long silences and drifting off and of keeping feelings hidden and never letting on that they are troubled or bothered or whatever.

If it's any comfort to women, they should know that it's nothing personal. Men treat other men the same way.

5   For instance, I know men who have suffered brutal professional setbacks and never mentioned it to their friends. I know of a guy who never told his best friend that his own son had a rare childhood disease. And I know others who

never have sex with their wives, but talk to their friends as though they're living in the Playboy Mansion, either pretending otherwise or saying nothing.

This is something men learn early. It is something I learned from my father, who taught me, the way fathers teach sons, to keep my emotions to myself. I watched him and learned from him. One day we went to the baseball game, cheered and ate and drank, and the next day he was taken to the hospital with yet another ulcer attack. He had several of them. My mother said he worried a lot, but I saw none of this.

Legend has it that men talk a lot about sex. They don't. They talk about it only in the sense that it is treated like sports. They joke about it and rate women from 1 to 10. But they almost never talk about it in a way that matters—the quality of it. They almost never talk in real terms, in terms other than a cartoon, in terms that apply to them and the woman or women with whom they have a relationship.

Women do talk that way. Women talk about fulfillment, and they admit—maybe complain is the better word—to nonexistent sex lives. No man would admit to having virtually no sex life, yet there are plenty who do.

When I was a kid, I believed that it was men who had real friendships and women who did not. This seemed to be the universal belief, and boys would talk about this. We wondered about girls, about what made them so catty that they could not have friendships, and we really thought we were lucky to be men and have real friends.

10   We thought our friendships would last forever; we talked about them in some sort of Three Musketeer fashion—all for one and one for all. If one of us needed help, all of us would come running. We are still good friends, some of us, anyway, and I still feel that I will fight for them, but I don't think I could confide in them. No—not that.

Sometimes I think that men are walking relics—outmoded and outdated, programmed for some other age. We have all the essential qualities for survival in the wild and for success in battle, but we run like hell from talking about our feelings. We are, as the poet said in a different context, truly a thing of wonder.

Some women say that they have always had this ability to confide in one another—to talk freely. Others say that this is something relatively new—yet another benefit of the women's movement. I don't know. All I know is that they have it, and most men don't, and even the men who do—the ones who can talk about how they feel—talk to women. Have we been raised to think of feelings and sentiment as feminine? Can a man talk intimately with another man and not wonder about his masculinity? I don't know. I do know it sometimes makes the other men feel uncomfortable.

I know this is a subject that concerns me, and yet I find myself bottling it all up—keeping it all in. I've been on automatic pilot for years now.

It would be nice to break out of it. It would be nice to join the rest of the human race, connect with others in a way that makes sense, in a way that's meaningful—in a way that's more than a dirty joke and a slap on the back. I wonder whether it can be done.

15   If it can, it will happen because women will insist on it, because they themselves have shown the way, come out of the closet as women, talked about it, organized, defined an agenda, set their goals and admitted that as women—just as women—they have problems in common. So do men. It's time to talk about them.

Questions for Active Reading

1. According to Cohen, what are the properties of men's relationships? Why does he think that these properties do not fit a definition of *friendship?*

2. What fundamental distinction does Cohen make between men and women? That is, how does he *classify* men and women? Do you agree with his classification? Why, or why not?

3. Examine the kind of evidence that Cohen offers in paragraph 5 to support his thesis. Would his argument be stronger if he had talked about, or named, *specific* men? What are the risks of generalizing about human behavior?

Questions for Thinking Critically

1. How do you think those men who might have considered themselves to be Cohen's "friends" felt after reading this column (which appeared in the *Washington Post*)? What are the risks a journalist—or any writer, really—takes when they use material from their personal life in their work?

2. Richard Cohen and Michael Norman make broad generalizations about categories of people (men "cannot or will not have real friends;" women are "dominated by emotion;" men are confused by "the drive to emasculate macho"). What are the inherent risks of making an argument based on very broad classifications or categories (such as "all men" or "all women")? How does each writer successfully—or unsuccessfully—address those risks?

3. What are these "feelings" that Cohen describes? Is he arguing that men don't *have* feelings, or just that men don't *discuss* feelings? Do you think it's as important to discuss feelings as to have them? To what extent is your response to that question based on your upbringing? On your current peer group or profession?

FROM *At the Bottom of the River*

Girl

BY JAMAICA KINCAID (B. 1949)

Born on the Caribbean island of Antigua and named Elaine Potter Richardson by her parents, Jamaica Kincaid left home for America at the age of sixteen to work as an au pair in the wealthy New York City suburbs of Westchester. She moved to New York City to study photography, and then spent a year at Franconia College in New Hampshire. In 1973, facing her family's disapproval over her published writing, she changed her first name to Jamaica, to evoke her Caribbean heritage, and her last name to Kincaid, simply because she liked the sound of it. Her articles in such magazines as Ingenue *led, eventually, to a staff writing position at* The New Yorker, *where she wrote on a wide range of subjects (including gardening, her great passion). Her first novel,* A Small Place *(1988), delves into the painful legacy of colonization in the Caribbean, a theme that recurs throughout her fiction. She has also explored the impact of colonialism's legacy at the more intimate level of family, in such novels as* Lucy *(1990),* The Autobiography of My Mother *(1996), and* My Brother *(1997). In an interview with* Mother Jones *magazine upon publication of* My Brother, *Kincaid described why she felt compelled to share the story of her little brother, who died of AIDS in 1996: ". . . Americans find difficulty very hard to take. They are inevitably looking for a happy ending. Perversely, I will not give the happy ending. I think life is difficult and that's that. I am not at all—absolutely not at all—interested in the pursuit of happiness. I am not interested in the pursuit of positivity. I am interested in pursuing a truth, and the truth often seems to be not happiness but its opposite."*

Wash the white clothes on Monday and put them on the stone heap; wash the color clothes on Tuesday and put them on the clothesline to dry; don't walk barehead in the hot sun; cook pumpkin fritters in very hot sweet oil; soak your little cloths right after you take them off; when buying cotton to make yourself a nice blouse, be sure that it doesn't have gum on it, because that way it won't hold up well after a wash; soak salt fish overnight before you cook it; is it true that you sing benna in Sunday school?; always eat your food in such a way that it won't turn someone else's stomach; on Sundays try to walk like a lady and not like the slut you are so bent on becoming; don't sing benna in Sunday school; you mustn't speak to wharf-rat boys, not even to give directions; don't eat fruits on the street—flies will follow you; *but I don't sing benna on Sundays at all and never in Sunday school*; this is how to sew on a button; this is how to make a buttonhole for the button you have just sewed on; this is how to hem a dress when you see the hem coming down and so to prevent yourself from looking like the slut I know you are so bent on becoming; this is how you iron your father's khaki shirt so that it doesn't have a crease; this is how you iron your father's khaki pants so they don't have a crease; this is how you grow okra—far from the house, because okra tree harbors red ants; when you are growing dasheen, make sure it gets plenty of water or else it makes your throat itch when you are eating it; this is how you sweep a corner; this is how you sweep a whole house; this is how you sweep a yard; this is how you smile to someone you don't like too much; this is how you smile to someone you don't like at all; this is how you smile to someone you like completely; this is how you set a table for tea; this is how you set a table for dinner; this is how you set a table for dinner with an important guest; this is how you set a table for lunch; this is how you set a table for breakfast; this is how to behave in the presence of men who don't know you very well, and this way they won't recognize immediately the slut I have warned you against becoming; be sure to wash every day, even if it is with your own spit; don't squat down to play marbles—you are not a boy, you know; don't pick people's flowers—you might catch something; don't throw stones at blackbirds, because it might not be a blackbird at all; this is how to make a bread pudding; this is how to make doukona; this is how to make pepper pot; this is how to make a good medicine for a cold; this is how to make a good medicine to throw away a child before it even becomes a child; this is how to catch a fish; this is how to throw back a fish you don't like, and that way something bad won't fall on you; this is how to bully a man; this is how a man bullies you; this is how to love a man, and if this doesn't work there are other ways, and if they don't work don't feel too bad about giving up; this is how to spit up in the air if you feel like it, and this is how to move quick so that it doesn't fall on you; this is how to make ends meet; always squeeze bread to make sure it's fresh; *but what if the baker won't let me feel the bread?*; you mean to say that after all you are really going to be the kind of woman who the baker won't let near the bread?

Questions for Active Reading

1. Who is speaking in this monologue, and who is being spoken to? How can you tell?

2. What are the properties of correct behavior for a "girl," according to this speaker, and what are the consequences of defying that behavior?

3. There's a phrase that's repeated three times in this monologue. What is that sentence? Why is it repeated, and how does it foreshadow the very last lines of this monologue?

Questions for Thinking Critically

1. When you were growing up, who told you how to behave? Did anyone ever tell you (either explicitly, or by implication) that there were correct ways to behave like a "lady" or a "gentleman"? Were these household rules, or just friendly guidelines? Is there anything that the speaker of this monologue says that reminds you of something you were told when you were a child?

2. What kind of future does the speaker of this monologue foresee for the listener? Is there anything surprising in the advice given?

3. Did you find anything comic in this monologue? If so, what made you laugh, and why?

How Friendship Was "Feminized"

BY CAROL TAVRIS (b. 1944)

Social psychologist Carol Tavris earned her Ph.D. from the University of Michigan. She has long been interested in exploring human relationships and conveying and explaining the results of her observations to a wider audience. For many years, Tavris was the editor of the influential magazine Psychology Today, *and her articles on human behavior have appeared in magazines as diverse as* The New York Times, Discover, Science Digest, Human Nature, New York, Vogue, *and* Harper's. *She is also the author of widely adopted college-level psychology textbooks, and teaches in the department of psychology at UCLA. Among her books for a general audience are* Anger: The Misunderstood Emotion *(1989) and* Mismeasure of Women: Why Women Are Not the Better Sex, the Inferior Sex, or the Opposite Sex *(1993), which won the American Association for Applied and Preventive Psychology's Distinguished Media Contribution Award. In a review published in* The Chronicle of Higher Education *of books about women and anger, Tavris noted that "of course, gender differences are eternally fascinating, a source of amusement, anger, and exasperation; trying to understand one's own and the "other sex" is America's second-favorite indoor sport. (And it's part of the job description if you're female.)" Tavris is a Fellow of the American Psychological Association. She lives in Los Angeles, California.*

Once upon a time and not so very long ago, everyone thought that men had the great and true-blue friendships. The cultural references stretched through time and art. Damon and Pythias, Hamlet and Horatio, Butch Cassidy and the Sundance Kid. The Lone Ranger never rode off with anyone but Tonto, and Laurel never once abandoned Hardy in whatever fine mess he got them into.

Male friendships were said to grow from the deep roots of shared experience and faithful camaraderie, whereas women's friendships were portrayed as shallow, trivial and competitive, like Scarlett O'Hara's with her sisters. Women, it was commonly claimed, would sell each other out for the right guy, and even for a good time with the wrong one.

Some social scientists told us that this difference was hard wired, a result of our evolutionary history. In the early 1970's, for example, the anthropologist Lionel Tiger argued in "Men in Groups" that "male bonding" originated in prehistoric male hunting groups and was carried on today in equivalent pack-like activities: sports, politics, business and war.

Apparently, women's evolutionary task of rummaging around in the garden to gather the odd yam or kumquat was a solo effort, so females do not bond in the same way. Women prattle on about their feelings, went the stereotype, but men act.

5   My, how times have changed. Today, we are deluged in the wave of best-selling books that celebrate female friendships—"Girlfriends," "Sisters," "Mothers and Daughters" and its clever clone, "Daughters and Mothers." The success of this genre is partly because the book market is so oriented to female readers these days.

But it is also a likely result of two trends that began in the 1970's and 1980's: Female scholars began to dispel the men-are-better stereotype in all domains and women became the majority of psychotherapists. The result was a positive reassessment of the qualities associated with women, including a "feminizing" of definitions of intimacy and friendship.

Accordingly, female friendships are now celebrated as the deep and abiding ones, based as they are on shared feelings and confidences. Male friendships are scorned as superficial, based as they are on shared interests in, say, the Mets and Michelle Pfeiffer.

In our psychologized culture, "intimacy" is defined as what many women like to do with their friends: talk, express feelings and disclose worries. Psychologists, most of whom are good talkers, validate this definition as the true measure of intimacy. For example, in a study of "intimacy maturity" in marriage, published in the *Journal of Personality and Social Psychology*, researchers equated "most mature" with "most verbally expressive." As a woman, I naturally think this is a perfectly sensible equation, but I also know it is an incomplete one. To label people mature or immature, you also have to know how they actually behave toward others.

What about all the men and women who support their families, put the wishes of other family members ahead of their own or act in moral and considerate ways when conflicts arise? They are surely mature, even if they are inarticulate or do not express their feelings easily. Indeed, what about all the men and women who define intimacy in terms of deeds rather than words: sharing activities, helping one another or enjoying companionable silence? Too bad for them. That's a "male" definition, and out of favor in these talky times.

10   Years ago, my husband had to have some worrisome medical tests, and the night before he was to go to the hospital we went to dinner with one of his best friends who was visiting from England. I watched, fascinated, as male stoicism combined with English reserve produced a decidedly unfemale-like encounter. They laughed, they told stories, they argued about movies, they reminisced. Neither mentioned the hospital, their worries or their affection for each other. They didn't need to.

It is true that women's style of intimacy has many benefits. A large body of research in health psychology and social psychology finds that women's greater willingness to talk about feelings improves their mental and physical health and makes it easier to ask for help.

But as psychologists like Susan Nolen-Hoeksema of Stanford University have shown, women's fondness for ruminating about feelings can also prolong depression, anxiety and anger. And it can keep women stuck in bad jobs or relationships, instead of getting out of them or doing what is necessary to make them better.

Books and movies that validate women's friendships are overdue, and welcome as long as they don't simply invert the stereotype. Playing the women-are-better game is fun, but it blinds us to the universal need for intimacy and the many forms that friendship takes. Maybe men could learn a thing or two about friendship from women. But who is to say that women couldn't learn a thing or two from them in exchange?

Questions for Active Reading

1. What perspectives does Tavris present that are different from those of Richard Cohen? What ideas in her essay are similar to those in his?

2. In your own words, paraphrase both Cohen's and Tavris's definitions of friendship. Then, write your own definition of friendship, in which you explicitly agree or disagree with the ideas of Cohen and/or Tavris.

3. How does Tavris suggest classifying people as either "mature" or "immature"? Why does she make this distinction? What other characteristics would you say define someone (male or female) as "mature" or "immature"?

Questions for Thinking Critically

1. What is Tavris's larger point in the final paragraph of her essay? Is she the only author in this casebook to suggest a resolution, or at least a compromise? How does she use examples and illustrations to support this conclusion?

2. To a certain extent, both Tavris's and Cohen's views on the expression of feelings are culturally determined—they are both writing from a modern, middle-class, educated American perspective. In what ways does American popular culture support either Tavris's or Cohen's view of the expression of "feelings" by men and women? For example, think about the explosion of "confessional" television talk shows—why do such shows attract such large audiences, even though practically no one in the audience is personally acquainted with the "guests" and really has no reason to care about their "feelings"?

3. Do you look for the same qualities in a friend as you do in a romantic partner? What are the similarities and the differences, for you, in these two categories of relationships?

Using Concepts to Classify

When you apply a concept to an object, idea, or experience, you are in effect classifying it by placing it in a group of things that are defined by the properties or requirements of the concept. In fact, the same things can often be classified in many different ways. For example, if someone handed you a tomato and asked, "Which category does this tomato belong in, fruit or vegetable?" how would you respond? The fact is that a tomato can be classified as both a fruit and a vegetable because its botanical definition does not seem consistent with its uses as a food.

Let's consider another example. Imagine that you are walking on undeveloped land with some other people when you come across an area of soggy ground with long grass and rotting trees. One person in your group surveys the parcel and announces, "That's a smelly marsh. All it does is breed mosquitoes. It ought to be covered with landfill and built on so that we can use it productively." Another member of your group disagrees with the classification "smelly marsh," stating, "This is a wetland of great ecological value. There are many plants and animals that need this area and other areas like it to survive.

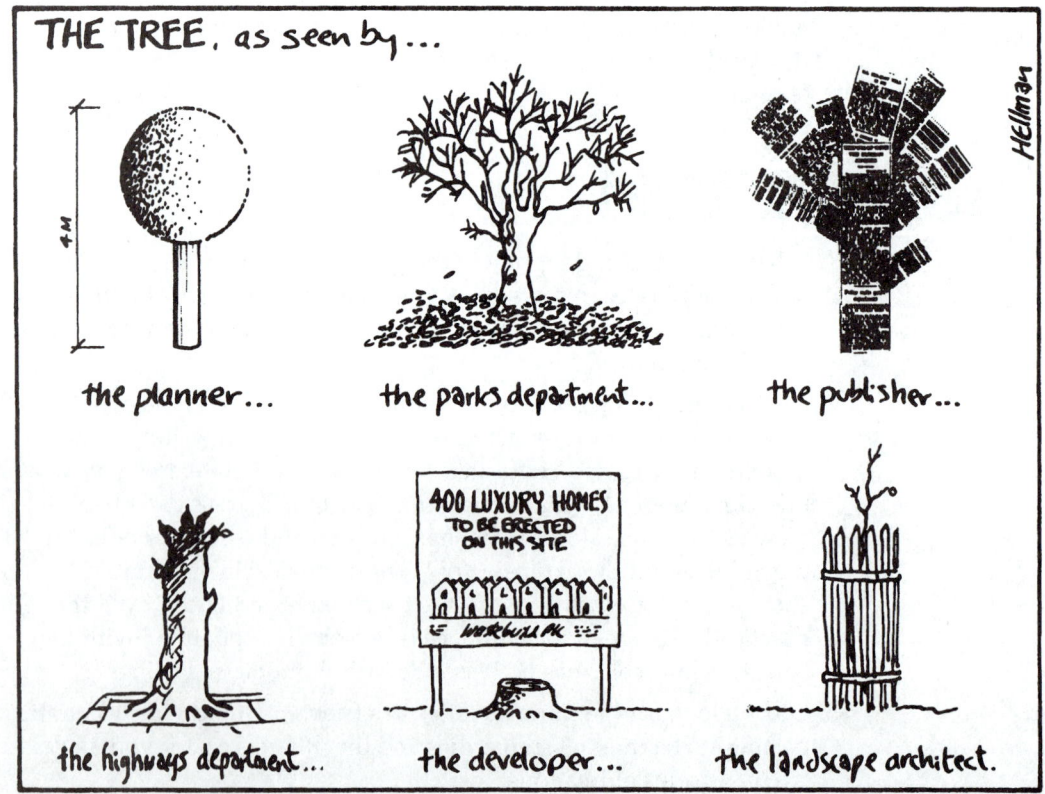

From *Pulp!* Used by permission of Louis Hellman.

Wetland areas also help to prevent the rivers from flooding, by absorbing excess water during heavy rains." Which person is right? Should the wet area be classified as a "smelly marsh" or as a "valuable wetland"? Actually, the wet area can be classified both ways. The classification that you select depends on your needs and your interests.

These examples illustrate how the way you classify reflects and influences the way you see the world, the way you think about the world, and the way you behave in the world. You classify many of the things in your experience differently than others do because of your individual needs, interests, and values. For instance, smoking marijuana might be classified by some as "use of a dangerous drug" and by others as a "harmless good time." Some view SUVs as "gas guzzlers"; others see the same cars as "safer, more comfortable vehicles." Some people categorize body piercing as "perverse abuse" while others think of it as "creative fashion." The way you classify aspects of your experience reflects the kind of individual you are and the way you think and feel about the world.

CLASSIFYING PEOPLE AND THEIR ACTIONS

You also place people in various categories. The specific categories you select depend on who you are and how you see the world. Similarly, each of us is placed in a variety of classifications by other people. Here, for instance, are some of the categories in which certain people have placed one of this book's authors:

Classification	People Who Classify Him
First-born son	His parents
Taxpayer	Internal Revenue Service
Tickler	His son/daughter
Bagel with cream cheese	Restaurant where he picks up his breakfast

List some of the different ways that you can be classified and identify the people who would classify you that way.

Not only do you continually classify things and people and place them in various groups on the basis of common properties you choose to focus on; you also classify ideas, feelings, actions, and experiences. Explain, for instance, why the killing of another person might be classified in different ways, depending on the circumstances.

Classification	Circumstance	Example
1. Manslaughter	Killing someone accidentally	Driving while intoxicated
2. Self-defense	_____	_____

3. Premeditated murder   _____   _____

4. Mercy killing   _____   _____

5. Diminished capacity   _____   _____

Each of these classifications represents a separate legal concept, one with its own properties and referents (examples). Of course, even when you clearly understand what the concept means, the complexity of the circumstances often makes it difficult to determine which concept applies. Court cases raise complex and disturbing issues. During a trial, trying first to identify the appropriate concept of the crime and then to determine which of the related concepts—*guilty* or *not guilty*—also applies is a challenging process. This is also true of many of life's other complex situations: you must work hard at identifying appropriate concepts to apply to the circumstances you are trying to make sense of, then be prepared to change or modify these concepts on the basis of new information or better insights.

WRITING AND CLASSIFYING

The intellectual act of classifying is an essential part of writing in three ways.

First, writings themselves are classified into many different forms. You know this already, of course. Novels, poems, essays, news stories, letters, emails, lab reports—the list is almost endless. And each of these forms of writing has subclassifications: science fiction, historical novels, romance novels, and so forth. Different classifications of writing have different purposes and styles. You are aware of this as a reader. As a college writer, you must become more aware of using styles and formats appropriate to the kind of writing that you are doing for your classes.

Second, almost any piece of writing is organized by classifying material into sections, chapters, or paragraphs in which the content is sorted out and arranged in logical ways. Usually, writers put similar material together so that readers can think about related items that have been assembled for their easy comprehension. You—and other writers—do this when you revise drafts to create good paragraphs that each focus on one idea. You do this when you are sorting your research notes into topics (or categories) in order to organize a paper, report, or speech.

Third, much writing concentrates on presenting *kinds, categories, types,* or *classifications* of concepts. The readings by Cohen and Tavris in this chapter discuss different classifications of friendship. "What Is Religion?" is organized around different kinds of questions to ask about conceptions of religion. This book itself is divided into different categories of approaches to thinking and writing.

Thinking ↔ Writing Activity

Identifying Classifications

1. Think of any reading selection in this book that you recall as being well organized. Turn to it and see how the writer classified or sorted the material into logical arrangements. Note the classifications of information. Perhaps topic sentences of paragraphs will show you what the writer has done.

2. Share your observations with classmates. See if they agree.

3. How did analyzing this piece of writing provide ideas about organizing your own work?

Defining Concepts

When you define a concept, you usually identify the necessary properties or requirements that determine when the concept can be applied. In fact, the word *definition* is derived from a Latin word meaning "boundary." A definition provides the boundaries of whatever territory in your experience can be described by the concept.

Definitions also use examples of the concept being defined. Consider the following:

Oxymoron   A rhetorical figure in which incongruous or contradictory terms are combined as in *a deafening silence* and *a mournful optimist.*

                     —*The American Heritage Dictionary of the English Language*

An edible   Good to eat and wholesome to digest, as a worm to a toad, a toad to a snake, a snake to a pig, a pig to a man, and a man to a worm.

                     —Ambrose Bierce

Facts, theories   Facts and theories are different things, not rungs in a hierarchy of increasing certainty. Facts are the world's data. Theories are structures of ideas that explain and interpret facts. Facts do not go away when scientists debate rival theories to explain them. Einstein's theory of gravitation replaced Newton's, but apples did not suspend themselves in mid-air pending the outcome.

—Stephen Jay Gould

Contrast these definitions with the one illustrated in the following passage from Charles Dickens's Hard Times:

> "Bitzer," said Thomas Gradgrind. "Your definition of a horse." "Quadruped. Graminivorous. Forty teeth, namely twenty-four grinders, four eye teeth, and twelve incisive. Sheds coat in the spring; in marshy countries sheds hoofs, too. Hoofs hard, but requiring to be shod with iron. Age known by marks in mouth." That (and much more) Bitzer. "Now girl number twenty," said Mr. Gradgrind, "you know what a horse is."

Although Bitzer has certainly done an admirable job of listing some of the necessary properties or requirements of the concept *horse*, it is unlikely that "girl number twenty" has any better idea of what a horse is than she had before since Bitzer's definition relies exclusively on a technical listing of the properties characterizing the concept *horse* without giving any examples that might illustrate the concept more completely. Definitions like this which rely exclusively on a technical description of the concept's properties are not very helpful unless you already know what the concept means. A more concrete way of communicating the concept *horse* would be to point out various animals that qualify as horses and other animals that do not. You could also explain why they do not. (For example, "That can't be a horse because it has two humps and its legs are far too long.")

Although examples do not take the place of a clearly understood definition, they are often very useful in clarifying, supplementing, and expanding such a definition. If someone asked you, "What is a horse?" and you replied by giving examples of different kinds of horses (thoroughbred racing horses, plow horses for farming, quarter horses for cowhands, circus horses), you certainly would be communicating a good portion of the meaning of *horse*. Giving examples of a concept complements and clarifies the necessary requirements for the correct use of that concept.

Giving an effective definition of a concept requires

- Identifying the general qualities of the concept, which determine when it can be correctly applied
- Classifying it, which means identifying its category, type, or "family"
- Using appropriate examples that embody its general qualities
- Differentiating it from other items in its classification

The process of providing definitions of concepts is basically the same process that you use to develop concepts.

Thinking ↔ Writing Activity

Trying to Define a Concept

Before you read the next selections, try to write a short definition of one of the concepts that they discuss. One reading is about *religion*, and the other is about *poverty*.

1. Identify and list the general qualities or properties of *religion* or of *poverty*.

2. Classify it. In what category of human activity does it belong? Write the classification. (Is religion an expression of belief or a system? Is poverty an economic state or an insufficiency of any kind?)

3. Write down an example or two.

4. Now try to write a definition in one, two, or three sentences. You might want to begin your definition with the classification or category that you have decided upon.

5. Then read the selection about the concept you have defined. What did you write that is similar to what you read? What was different?

There are few concepts more complex and emotionally charged than that of *religion*. The following passage is taken from the book *Ways of Being Religious* and presents a thoughtful introduction to the concepts of *religion* and *religious experience*.

What Is Religion?

BY FREDERICK J. STRENG, CHARLES L. LLOYD, AND JAY T. ALLEN

An African proverb, from the Ganda tribe in central Uganda, states, "He who never visits thinks his mother is the only cook." As with most proverbs, its meaning is larger than the explicit subjects referred to—in this case food and visiting. It suggests that a person is much the poorer for not having had exposure to and acquaintance with the ways of other people.

All of us have had some acquaintance with religious people, just as we have tasted our mother's food. But do we really understand very well what it means to be religious? The "Father of the Scientific Study of Religion," Max Mueller, once said: "He who knows one religion understands none." That is perhaps too extreme a statement as it stands, and yet it says about the study of religion what the African proverb says about the knowledge of life in general—that we sacrifice much if we confine ourselves to the familiar.

If a visit is to be fruitful, the "traveler" must do more than just move from place to place. He must respond to what he sees. But what is it that shapes the way we respond to new experiences? Our perception of things is often colored by our previous attitudes toward them. In this case, what do you, the reader, expect from an exposure to various expressions of religion? What sorts of things do you expect to see? How do you think you will respond to them? If you were asked to define, illustrate, or to characterize religious behavior, how would you do so? The answers to these questions, of course, reflect your pre-conceptions. To become conscious of your pre-conceptions, ask yourself the following four questions:

Does your definition *reduce* religion to what you happen to be acquainted with by accident of birth and socialization? Perhaps that goes without saying. It may be true of anyone's "off-the-cuff" definition of religion. However, we ask this question to encourage you to consider whether your definition has sufficient *scope.* Is it broad enough to include the religious activities of human beings throughout the world? In surveying university students we have commonly gotten responses to the question, "What is religion?" as follows: "Being Christian, I would define it [religion] as [a] personal relationship with Christ." "Religion [is]: God, Christ, and Holy Ghost and their meaning to each individual." Other students think of worship rather than belief. In this vein, one edition of Webster's dictionary, in the first of its definitions, describes religion as "the service and adoration of God or a god as expressed in forms of worship." If we were to accept any of the above definitions, many people in the world would be excluded—people who regard some of their most important activities as religious, but who do not focus upon a deity. That is to say, not all religions are theistic. It remains to be seen, of course, whether and to what extent this is true. But let us all be warned of taking our habits or our dictionary as the sole resource for defining religion. In some areas, the main lines of significant understanding are already well established. Therefore we have no serious quarrel with Webster's definition of food as "nutritive material taken into an organism for growth, work, or repair and for maintaining the vital processes." But in religion, interpretive concepts are more problematical. Therefore we are suspicious of the adequacy of the dictionary's definition of religion.

5   Another common way to define religion is to regard it as "morality plus stories," or "morality plus emotion." These are ways of asserting that religion has to do mainly with ethics, or that its myths merely support the particular views of a people. There are, of course, persons for whom religion has been reduced to ethics, as when Thomas Paine stated (in *The Rights of Man)*: "My country is the world, and my religion is to do good." But we should be cautious in assuming that this testimony would do for all religious people.

A final example of a definition that begins with personal experience is one that claims: "Religion is a feeling of security"; or, as one student put it: "Religion is an aid in coping with that part of life which man does not understand, or in some cases a philosophy of life enabling man to live more deeply." In locating the basis of religion in man's need for a sense of security, this approach suggests that the deepest study of religion is through psychology. It has been dramatically expressed by the psychiatrist and writer C. G. Jung when he wrote: "Religion is a relationship to the highest or strongest value . . . the value by which you are possessed unconsciously. That psychological fact which is the greatest power in your system is the god, since it is always the overwhelming psychic factor which is called 'god.'" Although this understanding of religion expresses a very important point, many theologians and religious philosophers point out that an interpretation that reduces all of religious experience to psychological, biological, or social factors omits the central reality exposed in that experience—the Sacred or Ultimate Reality. Thus, a student of religion should keep open the question of whether a familiar interpretation of religious life that fits into a conventional, social science perspective of man is adequate for interpreting the data.

Does your definition reflect a *bias* on your part—positive or negative—toward religion as a whole, or toward a particular religion? There are many examples of biased definitions that could be cited. Some equate religion with superstition, thus reflecting a negative evaluation. One man defined religion as "the sum of the scruples which impede the free exercise of the human faculties." Another hostile view of religion is to see religion as a device of priests to keep the masses in subjection and themselves in comfort. Similarly, Karl Marx, while not actually attempting to define religion, called it "the opiate of the people," again reflecting a bias against (all) religion.

Still others, in defining religion, are stating their concept of *true* religion as opposed to what they regard as false or pagan faiths. Henry Fielding, in his novel *Tom Jones*, has the provincial parson Mr. Thwackum saying, "When I mention religion I mean the Christian religion; and not only the Christian religion, but the Protestant religion; and not only the Protestant religion; but the Church of England." Some Christians assume that their personal conviction comprises a definition of religion, so the religion is regarded as "the worship of God through his Son Jesus Christ," or "a personal relationship with Christ." A Muslim can point out that the essence of religion is to make peace with God through complete submission to God's will, a submission that he will insist is brought to fulfillment in Islam. (In Arabic the word "Islam" means "submission," "peace," "safety," and "salvation.")

Therefore the student interested in reflecting on religious experience that includes more than a single institutional or cultural expression should remember the distinction between descriptive (neutral) and evaluative definitions. A descriptive definition attempts to be as inclusive as possible about a class of items, such as religious forms. An evaluative definition, on the other hand, reflects one's own criteria for truth or falsity, for reality or illusion. In "visiting" religious people, we suggest that you delay making an evaluation until you have understood why their expressions and processes have profound meaning for them—however strange those expressions may seem to you. In the final analysis, each person must evaluate different religious alternatives; but one of our goals in bringing together the material in this volume is to provide you with a variety of options—a variety that is reduced if you limit religion to any single historical expression.

10   Obviously the believer who advocates one religion to the exclusion of all others differs sharply from one who rejects all. Nevertheless, if either accepts his own convictions about what is best or worst in religion as a description of what religion in fact is everywhere and for everyone, he exhibits a common indifference to unfamiliar, and therefore potentially surprising, religious patterns. As a believer (or skeptic), you have a right to declare your own understanding of what is most important, most real, in religion. This declaration is, in fact, essential, for it guides you in your quest for whatever is most real in life. As a student, on the other hand, you have an obligation to carry your studies as far as necessary to include relevant data. In this role, your obligation is not only to your own perception of value but also to a common world of understanding in which men of many religious persuasions can converse with each other.

Does your definition *limit* religion to what it has been in the past, and nothing else, or does your definition make it possible to speak of emerging forms of religion? In asking this question, we should observe two striking facts of the history of religion: there was a time when some present religions did not exist, and some of the religions which once emerged no longer exist (for example, the Egyptian and Babylonian religions). Human history, then, has witnessed the emergence and abandonment of several religions.

Even religious traditions that have maintained a sense of continuity over vast stretches of time (Hinduism, Buddhism, Judaism, Christianity, for example) have undergone important changes. Is it really as obvious as we tend to think that they are essentially the same now as they were at their origins? Do the terms naming these traditions even today point to a single entity, however complex? You are familiar with at least some instances of religious warfare *within* the Christian tradition. Roman Catholics have persecuted and killed Lutherans; Lutherans have persecuted and killed Calvinists; Calvinists, Anglicans; Anglicans, Quakers; and most have returned the act with interest. Are all of these groups expressions of "the one true church"? Are some more Christian than others? Is there only one form of Christianity? Are new movements violations of the tradition? Or is the one who speaks to his own time the one who is most faithful to the genius of his tradition? These questions can be asked of all religious traditions. All have experienced change and diversity. Furthermore, it seems likely that this will continue, and that new religious traditions will emerge. Therefore, the conventions of the past cannot be regarded as the limits of future religious forms.

In part because history has witnessed the emergence and internal changes of many religions, anthropologists and cultural historians commonly suggest that religion (and human culture in general) has attained only its adolescence.

Likewise, philosophers and religious thinkers in both East and West point to the anxiety and tensions today that are expressed in political, social, economic, and intellectual upheaval. They raise a question of whether or not man's moral, psychic, and evaluative resources can catch up with his self-destructive potential seen in technologically advanced weapons and psychological-chemical techniques for social control. The most hopeful of these philosophers perceive the present turmoil as a lack of "maturity" in human consciousness, and express the hope that it is not too late (quite) to change the direction of man from self-destruction to self-fulfillment.

From this perspective most of mankind's experience is still in the future. The history of religious life to the present is only a beginning. But the basis of these projections is the recognition that man's survival requires him to recognize religious dynamics and processes for evaluations as major forces in human life. Should not a definition of religion aid us in looking at contemporary phenomena to see if any new ways of being religious are emerging? At least it should not inhibit persons with an interest in this matter, and we think an introduction to religion should encourage such reflection.

15   **Does your definition have sufficient *precision*?** Are there any limits to the scope of religion, or are the limits so vague that they fail to mark out an object of study? In an attempt to be as broadminded as possible, many definitions are like a student's statement that religion is "the means man has of coping with his world." Or they are similar to the claim that religion is "believing in a way of life which involves understanding and caring for others," or "religion is love." Such definitions tell us a good deal, but without some qualification they might refer to many other expressions of human life than specifically religious ones. In order to find a focus and a set of limitations at the outer circumference of that focus, we need to designate what are those essential elements of religion that will expose the *religious* meaning of the evidence we look at.

When one has "visited" (seen) a wide range of religious life, from all parts of the world and throughout human history, it becomes apparent that religion is a way of life that involves many processes—all of which, in different ways, are directed toward a common end. The goal is to reach a state of being that is conceived to be the highest possible state or condition. Religion is the general term for the various ways by which people seek to become changed into that highest state. We understand *religion as a means toward ultimate transformation*. By this we are not claiming that every activity you think of as religious will in fact transform you ultimately. It might, but that is not our point. We mean that *any* reasonably specific means that *any* person adopts with the serious hope and intention of moving toward ultimate transformation should be termed "religious." We think it possible to speak of all religious activity (Eastern and Western, past, present, and emerging) without reducing *religion* to what is merely familiar to us and without putting a value judgment on one or more religions.

Questions for Active Reading

1. Where in this excerpt is the definition of *religion* given? Do you find that placement effective? If so, why?

2. What do you find helpful about the questions at the beginning of many of the paragraphs?

3. Apply one of those questions to a different concept and write a paragraph modeled on the one following the question, substituting this other concept for *religion*.

Questions for Thinking Critically

1. Would you make a distinction between "religion" and "faith"? Is it possible to have one without the other?

2. The writers of this essay, originally intended for an audience of college students, attempt to be objective and fairly neutral about the topic; do they succeed? How would you characterize the tone of this textbook excerpt?

3. In paragraph 9, the authors offer a useful distinction between "descriptive" and "evaluative" definitions. Select another broad, abstract term, such as "love," "democracy," or "globalization." In an essay, create both a *descriptive* and an *evaluative* definition of that term, using your descriptive definition to support your evaluation.

Poverty might seem easy to define, particularly if you think only in terms of money. The following essay takes a subtler approach to defining what could be classified as an economic problem.

FROM *The Working Poor: Invisible in America*

A Poor Cousin of the Middle Class

BY DAVID K. SHIPLER (b. 1942)

The Pulitzer Prize-winning author of Arab and Jew: Wounded Spirits in a Promised Land *(1987), David Shipler spent more that twenty years reporting for the* New York Times *from Saigon, Moscow, Jerusalem, New York, and Washington. Among Shipler's other works is the best-seller* Russia: Broken Idols, Solemn Dreams, *published in 1983 and updated in 1989. Widely acclaimed by critics, it won the Overseas Press Club Award in 1983 as the best book that year on foreign affairs. Shipler was also executive producer, writer, and narrator of a two-hour PBS documentary on Arab and Jew, which won a 1990 Dupont-Columbia award for broadcast journalism. He was a guest scholar at the Brookings Institution, a senior associate at the Carnegie Endowment for International Peace, and Ferris Professor of Journalism and Public Affairs at Princeton University.* The Working Poor: Invisible in America, *from which the following essay is excerpted, was published in 2004.*

Caroline Payne embraces the ethics of America. She works hard and has no patience with those who don't. She has owned a house, pursued an education and deferred to the needs of her child. Yet she can barely pay her bills. Her earnings have hovered in a twilight between poverty and minimal comfort, usually between $8,000 and $12,000 a year.

She is the invisible American, unnoticed because she blends in. Like millions at the bottom of the labor force who contribute to the country's prosperity, Caroline's diligence is a camouflage. At the convenience store where she works, customers do not see that she struggles against destitution.

Others of the unseen sew clothes, clean offices and harvest fruit. They serve Big Macs and stack merchandise at Wal-Mart. In a California factory, they package lights for kids' bikes. In a New Hampshire plant, they assemble books of wallpaper samples.

They cannot afford the wallpaper themselves, just as the man who washes cars does not own one. The assistant teacher cannot pay the fees to put her own children in the day-care center where she works. The clerk in the back room of a bank, filing canceled checks, may have $2.02 in her own account, as Caroline had when she briefly did that job. The clientele never saw her. She was out of sight, part of the hidden America.

5   Always in search of something better somewhere else, Caroline has moved from job to job, from place to place, from New England to Florida and back— and now to Indiana—without anchoring herself solidly in a community that can offer support.

Just over a year after arriving in Muncie, where she lives in a small apartment in a public housing project, she remains unconnected. "I don't know many people here still," she told me recently. "I just get out to go to work and do errands." Her hours at the store provide only a trickle of cash. "I just can't get ahead," she declared. "There's no good jobs, and I'm just not happy here." She has spent her life in perpetual motion while standing still.

Futility has nagged at Caroline for a long time. Four years ago, at the dawn of the new millennium, she sat at her kitchen table in Claremont, N.H., and added up her life. It was the height of the economic boom. The nation wallowed in luxury, burst with microchips, consumed with abandon, swaggered globally. Everything grew larger: homes, vehicles, stock portfolios, life expectancy. Never before in the sweep of human history had so many people been so utterly comfortable.

Caroline was not one of them. She had achieved two of her three goals. She had earned a college diploma (a two-year associate's degree), and she had gone from a homeless shelter into her own house (owned mostly by a bank). The third objective, "a good paying job," as she put it, still eluded her. Back in the mid-70's, she earned $6 an hour in a Vermont factory that made plastic cigarette lighters and cases for Gillette razors. A quarter century later, she earned $6.80 an hour stocking shelves and working cash registers at a vast Wal-Mart superstore.

"And that's sad," she declared. "I'm only making 80 cents more than I did more than 20 years ago." Or less, taking into account the rise in the cost of living.

10   She was not the victim of racial discrimination; she was white. She was not lazy; she was caustic about colleagues who were. She was punctual, rarely out sick, willing to do night shifts and assiduous in her work habits. The Wal-Mart manager, Mark Brown, called her "a nice lady" with lots of enthusiasm. "She's self-driven," he observed. "She's always willing to learn and better herself. She's got potential. She can definitely move up."

But she did not move up. She had never moved up. And that ceased to amaze her; it had been going on for so long, in job after job after job. She was astonished only by Mark Brown's praise. "I'm surprised," she remarked when I told her what he said. She was stacking blank videotapes on a shelf. "I didn't think they liked me here. People don't usually say nice things about me."

Somewhere along this track that leads nowhere, a good many Americans give up on the dream. They sink back onto welfare, or they stop imagining themselves as foremen or managers. Caroline was then 50, with so many years of disappointment that her bouts of depression, for which she was occasionally treated, seemed unsurprising.

Still, she kept striving. She called herself "luckylady" in her e-mail address. She said, "Have a wonderful day," on her answering machine. She did not have big thoughts about corporate profits or dark judgments about society's unfairness. She just tried for basic financial security. Her persistence played like a dissonant melody against the monotone of job stagnation.

Again and again, she applied to manage one sales department or another at Wal-Mart, and again and again she was passed over in favor of men—or, she observed wryly, women who were younger and slimmer.

15   "I work my butt off, excuse my language," she said sharply. "I'm there most of the time, but that don't matter to them." She was paid a dollar an hour more during nighttime shifts, nothing close to what her flexibility was worth to a store that stayed open around the clock. Trying to get ahead, she always made herself available to change hours and fill in, even during evenings when she had to leave her 14-year-old daughter, Amber, home alone. Without a car, Caroline had a 20-minute walk each way, trekking back and forth at odd times of night in all kinds of weather. One cold February day, walking gingerly along icy streets, worried about her temperamental back, she trudged from her house to her job at her normal time of 10 a.m., only to be told to come for a shift beginning at 1 p.m. instead. So she made her way home and then returned to the store: three trips consuming one hour before earning her first dime of the day.

The people who received promotions tend to have something that Caroline did not. They had teeth. Caroline's teeth had succumbed to poverty, to the years when she could not afford a dentist. Most of them decayed and abscessed, and when she lived on welfare in Florida, she had them all pulled in a grueling two-hour session that left her looking bruised and beaten. Under the state's Medicaid rules as she understood them, a set of dentures would have been covered only if she had been without any teeth at all; while some of them could have been saved, she couldn't afford to do less than everything. In the end, the dentures paid for by Medicaid didn't fit and made her gag, so she couldn't wear them. An adjustment would have cost about $250, money she didn't have.

Probably no employer would ever admit to passing her over because she was missing that radiant, tooth-filled smile that Americans have been taught to prize as highly as their right to vote. Caroline had learned to smile with her whole face, a sweet look that didn't show her gums, yet it came across as wistful, something less than the thousand-watt beam of friendly delight that the culture requires. Where showing teeth was an unwritten part of the job description, she did not excel. She was turned down for a teller's position with the Claremont Savings Bank, which then hired her for back-room filing and eventually fired her from that. Wal-Mart considered her for customer-service manager and then promoted someone else, someone with teeth.

Caroline's is the face of the working poor, marked by a poverty-generated handicap more obvious than most deficiencies but no different, really, from the less visible deficits that reflect and reinforce destitution. If she were not poor, she would not have lost her teeth, and if she had not lost her teeth, perhaps she would not have remained poor. Poverty is a peculiar, insidious thing, not just one problem but a constellation of problems: not just inadequate wages but also inadequate education, not just dead-end jobs but also limited abilities, not just insufficient savings but also unwise spending, not just the lack of health insurance but also the lack of healthy households. The villains are not just exploitative employers but also incapable employees, not just overworked teachers but also defeated and unruly pupils, not just bureaucrats who cheat the poor but also the poor who cheat themselves. . . .

Two months after graduating from high school—the only one of three siblings to do so—Caroline married. "Now there's times I wished I hadn't," she declared. "I think it was so easy for me to latch onto people because I haven't had lots of love and security and communication and things. It was almost like if a guy gave me affection, I'd latch onto almost like the first one that come along. And that's not good. I've learnt over the years, it's not good."

20   The marriage produced three children, lasted 14 years and finally sank into a swamp of suspicions that her husband was unfaithful. Because she could not afford a lawyer and just wanted out, she ended up with only $400 a month in child support and a modest amount for her share in their house. So she moved with her children into a small apartment and bounced between welfare and dead-end jobs, supplementing her income by scavenging for cans. "We'd go and

watch a ballgame at school, and I'd take bags and stuff them in my pocketbook," she recalled. "After the ballgame I'd be going around poring through the garbage cans picking out 5-cent cans." Her first daughter would ride her bike as far ahead of her mother as possible to avoid any hint of association. "I figured that a few cents buys some milk, buys some bread, things that you need, you know what I'm saying? It all helps. But it embarrassed her. She hated it as she got older."

Determined to move up, Caroline applied for good office jobs and, when she failed to be hired, called to find out why. The answer was always the same: the winning candidate had a college degree. So she decided to get one, too. Gathering credits from community colleges in Vermont and Florida, she ended up with a two-year associate's degree in office technology and information processing. She also ran up a debt of $17,000 in student loans, a sum that rose to $20,000 as she deferred payments. It turned out to be a bad investment; she never landed a job in her field of training, never got one that required anything more than a high-school diploma. A full bachelor's degree would have been a door-opening credential, of course, but the associate's degree proved useless.

Perhaps if Caroline's personal life had been stable and content, she could have concentrated more intently on her work; perhaps she could have found the focus to stay in a job long enough to advance. But family turbulence can rarely be walled out of the workplace. An employer may tolerate a distracted employee who has crucial skills or a powerful position, but Caroline had no such capital to purchase a boss's patience. . . .

As her life at home got tense, her life at work got perilous. That meant marginal performance, no promotions and a rolling career of short stays in jobs with no accumulation of seniority. "You're all nerved up, you're stressed, you don't know what somebody's gonna pull on you next," she said. Even at the factory in the middle of the night, she would cry and cry, "and people would know things were wrong."

Anyone who walked all the way around the outside of the Wal-Mart superstore on Route 103 would walk a mile, Caroline said. The place was immense. But it didn't seem to have room for Caroline to progress. She bounced from one department to another, from one shift to another, while her pay stayed within a narrow range, beginning at $6.15 an hour, going to $6.80, sometimes up to $7.50 if she worked at night. So unpredictable were her hours that she couldn't work a second job to help her cash flow. She kept applying for higher positions and kept hearing that she needed a bit more experience. When asked to work odd shifts, "I never said no to them," she insisted. "But why couldn't they have the decency to pay me a little bit more?"

25   She won recognition. "I did make Cashier of the Month for November," she reported happily, for collecting more than $1,500 for the World War II veterans memorial in Washington. She also persuaded customers who checked out at her register to buy a total of 72 tickets to a Boston Bruins game to raise money for the Claremont Fire Department, and that won her a weekend getaway from Pepsi.

She could take herself and three other people to a paid stay in any Marriott she chose, anywhere.

"But I have to get there," she said, and she had no money to travel. So Hawaii never entered her mind, not even New York; she considered only places in New Hampshire. "I think there's one up here in Lebanon," she said. "If I could get somebody to take me to Manchester, Amber likes to look at the malls. I've never been down there. Just to look at things." In the end, she and Amber rode with a friend north to a hotel in Bethlehem, N.H., where they visited a small shopping center in North Conway. For $31.99, Caroline bought a winter coat to replace a jacket that she had torn two years before.

Her anemic paycheck failed to improve. The Wal-Mart manager who liked her, Mark Brown, was transferred, and no promotion seemed in the offing. When a temp agency found her a $7.50-an-hour job assembling books of wallpaper samples, she took pleasure in telling Wal-Mart's assistant manager that she was leaving. "I'm just hoping they'll be sorry someday," Caroline said.

Unwittingly, Caroline then stepped into the vortex that drags numbers of low-wage single mothers down into the great chasm between decent work and decent parenting, a place where a child's safety has to be balanced against survival in the labor market.

After a month at the wallpaper plant, the temp agency offered Caroline a job back at the Tampax factory for $10 an hour, the most she had ever earned. She took it, but there was a problem: Procter & Gamble had organized the factory on rotating shifts. One week she left the house at 5:30 A.M. and got home at 2:30 P.M., the next week she was gone from 1:30 P.M. to 10:30 P.M., and the third from 9:30 P.M. to 6:30 A.M.

30 "I'm trying to do the best I can and get caught up on little bills," she said. "And now I don't have a job, and I'm gonna have to go apply for welfare. You pull yourself up, and then somebody has to knock you down. If I don't work, it's neglect: not feeding or clothing my child."

Perhaps the most curious and troubling facet of this confounding puzzle was everybody's failure to pursue the most obvious solution: if the factory had just let Caroline work day shifts, her problem would have disappeared. She asked a supervisor and got brushed off, but nobody else—not the school principal, not the doctor, not the myriad agencies she contacted—nobody in the profession of helping thought to pick up the phone and appeal to the factory manager or the foreman or anybody else in authority at her workplace.

Indeed, this solemn regard for the employer as untouchable and beyond the realm of persuasion unless in violation of the law permeates the culture of American antipoverty efforts, with only a few exceptions. The most socially minded physicians and psychologists who treat malnourished children, for example, will advocate vigorously with government agencies to provide food stamps, health insurance, housing and the like. But when they are asked if they ever urge the parents' employers to raise wages enough to pay for nutritious food, the doctors express surprise at the notion. First, it has never occurred to them, and second, it seems hopeless. Wages and hours are set by the marketplace, and you cannot expect magnanimity from the marketplace. It is the final arbiter from which there is no appeal. . . .

As the New Hampshire winter arrived after Thanksgiving, Caroline left with pockets nearly empty. To escape from $10,000 to $12,000 in credit-card debt, she had declared bankruptcy earlier that year, much to her shame. She could not even afford to rent a truck without a $700 loan from her older daughter. A couple of friends donated their vacation time to drive the truck and Caroline to Indiana, by way of a slashing blizzard in upstate New York. She was on the move again, as she had been since childhood, but she was happy to see a little of the country.

Muncie has not been gentle, though. She found her first, shabby apartment in a neighborhood riddled with drug dealers and prostitutes, her first job in a convenience store at $5.45 an hour, a downward slide from the Vermont plastics factory in the 1970's. In April she moved into a two-bedroom apartment in a newer, safer public housing project, but she can't get more than part-time work at the store, for about $10,000 a year.

35   She has a new set of dentures, courtesy of $400 from Medicaid, plus a $322 loan from her older daughter. She is still trying to get used to wearing them. She misses her house and her friends in New Hampshire. "I used to go out with some of the girls, you know," she recalled. In Muncie, "I don't get out much," she said. "I'm broke." . . .

Money may not always cure, but it can often insulate one problem from another. In the house of the poor, however, the walls are thin and fragile, and troubles seep into one another.

Into Caroline's spirit, hopes also filter. Her latest is that WorkOne, a job-training agency, will pay $403 for a course to make her a certified nursing assistant. She knows she would do well in a nursing home. "I've got the personality," she said. "It's helping people, and I feel sorry for them."

Questions for Active Reading

1. How does Shipler define the "invisible American"?

2. Instead of speaking generally about poverty in America, Shipler focuses on the story of one specific woman. How effective is this strategy in conveying the larger issues of poverty in America? What are the risks of using one person's story as an example or symbol of a larger, more abstract concept?

3. In what ways does Caroline Payne not fit a preconceived or stereotyped definition of "poverty"? Review the discussion of semantic, perceptual, syntactic, and pragmatic meaning in Chapter 2. For each kind of meaning, create a definition (in your own words, but drawing on Shipler's essay if you like) of "poverty."

1. Does Shipler refrain from making judgments in this newspaper story, either about Caroline Payne or about the way she has experienced the work force, the government, and the school system? Is his narrative completely objective? Illustrate your answer by making reference to specific paragraphs or images.

2. Why do you think Caroline Payne has been poor all her life? After you have explored the critical thinking strategies of causal analysis in Chapter 10, return to this essay and see if you can establish a causal chain that led Caroline Payne to her current situation.

3. Review the final paragraph of this essay. Shipler obviously spent a great deal of time with Caroline Payne, observing her at home and at work. Why, then, of all the quotations and anecdotes he collected, does he choose to conclude his essay with this particular quote?

Writing Thoughtfully to Define Concepts

Writing a full definition, often called an *extended definition,* is among the most important and most difficult of writing activities. Defining terms is a necessary part of college-level writing and speaking. For productive discussions about complex issues, all involved must agree on the meanings of significant terms, so clear definitions are often required. Difficulties arise because significant terms related to complex issues are usually abstract concepts, with possibilities of different definitions for different people. For example, the common political terms *conservative* and *liberal* often have varied meanings, even to people who identify themselves as one or the other.

No one has much trouble agreeing on definitions of physical objects. A table, a tree, a television set—not many arguments arise about what these objects are. But like *liberal* and *conservative*, concepts such as *religion, love, democracy, femininity,* and *masculinity* can be defined in different ways. If people discussing ideas like these do not establish definitions, their discussions will not be productive. Worse, these discussions sometimes lead to disagreements, arguments, and even wars. The readings and Thinking-Writing Activities in this chapter have been selected and planned to demonstrate the importance of definitions.

Notice how with both simple objects and complex concepts, defining is somewhat easier as long as a single word is being examined. As soon as modifying and classifying ideas are added, defining becomes more challenging and more significant to critical thinking. A *beautiful* table, a *good* tree to plant in a *small* yard, the *best* television set to buy for *your family room*—now these objects call for fuller definitions. The *kind* of democracy that can work in a country with a *history of despotism,* the *kind* of love that a *parent* might have for an *adult child*—these are the types of concepts that people must define in order to present arguments, to make decisions, to solve problems. These are the kinds of terms that you might want to define in the Writing Project in this chapter because they are the kinds that involve judgments; they are important to our lives because they influence our actions.

Clear, satisfying definitions can be as extended as book chapters, articles, or entire books; however, a definition often will be developed in a paragraph or two as a vital part of a paper or report. In the Writing Project for this chapter, you will write an essay that defines; you will see the need for using a variety of thinking/organizing patterns as you develop it. The guidelines for writing definitions are not fixed rules; there may be times when you would have good reasons for varying or adapting some of them. Try to use them, though, unless you have good reason not to.

Guidelines for Writing Definitions

1. Establish the need for a definition. Why is it needed? Do people disagree on the meaning of the concept? Are there multiple meanings? Are earlier definitions no longer satisfactory? Is this a new concept or new terminology?

2. Choose carefully the word or words in which you state the concept. Definitions provide precision, so you need to be sure that you have presented the concept in the words that are most indicative.

3. Incorporate two kinds of dictionary definitions: the short one that gives meaning, as in a regular college dictionary, and a longer one giving the history of the word's usage, which can be found in the *Oxford English Dictionary*. Word origins and past meanings can often illuminate the meaning that you want to present.

4. Be sure that you identify the category into which the concept fits.

5. Show comparative thinking. Point out similar concepts, but then make clear how your concept is distinct. Think of analogies that can illuminate the meaning of the concept.

6. Provide specific examples to show what the concept means. Illustrative anecdotes are often effective.

7. Include the meaning of the concept in the thesis statement. Give careful thought to where you state the thesis.

8. Throughout your definition, emphasize that you are establishing the meaning you believe the concept has within the context that you have identified.

9. Address the foregoing principles in separate paragraphs or sections of the definition. Provide each paragraph with a clear topic sentence whenever appropriate.

10. Document any sources that you use. Introduce source material into your definition, explain and comment on it, and cite it correctly.

Writing Project: Defining an Important Concept

This chapter has included readings, questions, and Thinking-Writing Activities that encourage you to define concepts that affect your life. Be sure to reread what you wrote for the activities; you may be able to use some of that material in completing this project.

Write an essay in which you define a concept that is important to your life now or to your future life. Include explanations of why this concept is significant for you and why it needs defining or redefining. You may want to think of a concept that is expressed in a phrase rather than in a single word. Include material from two sources in addition to any dictionaries that you consult. Integrate your sources into your essay and document them as your instructor advises. After you have drafted your essay, revise it to the best of your ability. Follow your instructor's directions for topic limits, length, format, and so on.

Begin by considering the key elements in the Thinking-Writing Model on page 6.

THE WRITING SITUATION

Purpose You have several purposes here. You want to think about and formulate a definition that will be significant as you continue your college studies, decide on your profession, or enter a new phase in your personal life. Indeed, all of us need to be able to define the complex terms that are foundations for our thinking, our decisions, and our actions in life. In addition, you can improve your ability to present a full definition in order to clarify your own thinking and to increase your audience's understanding.

Audience You have a multilevel audience. *You* are an important audience, for in facing the challenge of defining a complex concept, you can think more clearly about some aspect of your life. Your classmates can learn from your definition and also can be a valuable audience in peer reviews of a draft, reacting as intelligent readers who are not as knowledgeable as you about the concept that pertains to your life. In addition, you should think about and identify people outside your class who might enjoy or profit from reading your definition. If you are writing about a concept that impacts people in your community or on your campus, your paper can both share information and urge action.

Subject All of us need to be able to define abstract, complex terms that are foundations for our thinking, our decisions, and our actions in life. College courses, family life, spiritual concerns, and romantic relationships all involve concepts that need to be well defined. Clear definitions help us understand what we mean when we speak and write, understand what others mean when they communicate with us, and—most important—avoid confusion and conflict. For this assignment, try to identify an important concept that is central to how you see yourself and your future. Concepts like *creative expression, enlightened free choice, authentic person, fulfillment, achieving potential, meaningful empathy, social responsibility, critical thinker*, and (of course) *thoughtful writer* are all examples with broad implications in a person's life.

Writer This project provides you with the opportunity to participate in the "conversation of ideas" that is the lifeblood of thoughtful, reflective people in a society. By defining a complex concept, you are explaining how the concept you have selected has personal meaning for you. You are also suggesting to others—your audience—how they might think about your analysis of the concept. The definition you propose may help them understand something in their experience more clearly, or it may provide an added meaning they have not previously considered. The outside sources integrated into your analysis ensure that your definition is grounded in a common understanding that goes beyond your own experience.

THE WRITING PROCESS

The following sections will guide you through the recursive stages of generating, planning, drafting, and revising as you work on an essay in which you define a significant concept. Try to be particularly conscious of both the critical thinking you do as you articulate your definition and the critical thinking and decision making you do as you revise.

Generating Ideas

- Refer back to the responses you wrote for the Thinking-Writing Activities for the readings on gender issues and the essays on defining religion and poverty. These concepts are important in many people's lives, so perhaps you will write about one of them—or perhaps what you read and wrote will lead you to another concept to define.
- Think about the activities or concerns that are central to your life. Some of these are probably rather serious, as are the subjects discussed in this chapter, but some parts are surely more lighthearted, like sports you play or watch, television comedies, thriller movies, or parties.

- Next, think of concepts inherent in some of your activities, such as a satisfying relationship or what it means to be a good athlete, college student, or practitioner of your religion.

- Now, list the properties of two or three concepts that you have identified. Include specific examples. How should each example be classified?

- Think about why any of these concepts need to be defined or redefined. Do people agree on the meaning? Have you formulated a meaning that is more precise and accurate?

- Share your lists and thinking with classmates and, if you can, with people involved in the area in which the concept is important.

- Use as many thinking patterns as you can to discover ideas about your concept. What is it different from? similar to? analogous to? Describe it; think about what causes it; think about what effects it has.

- Look up the concept's key words in a good college-level dictionary and also in the *Oxford English Dictionary*. Ask your instructor or one of your college librarians to explain the OED to you. See if you can use any of your concept's word history in your definition.

- Freewrite for at least five minutes about why the concept is important to your life, why it needs to be defined, and what information needs to be in your definition.

Defining a Focus

- Look at your freewriting and lists to see what main idea you are moving toward in your definition. Write this idea in any way that you can.

- Now draft a thesis statement that gives the key ideas in your definition. Recently a student defining *freedom of religion* had this as her thesis sentence: "To me, freedom of religion means more than simply being able to practice our religions as we believe that we should; it also means that we must understand and respect other people's religions." Another student, working on a definition of today's *superwoman*, wrote, "The main properties of a superwoman are being capable, tenacious, and independent."

- Be sure that your thesis statement emphasizes the meaning of the concept that you are defining.

Organizing Ideas
Essays emphasizing definition are not easy to organize because there are so many approaches to a clear definition of a complex concept. Because the thesis—the essence of the definition—needs to be placed in a context and explained in a number of ways, the question of where to state the thesis is especially crucial. This is the kind of essay in which it might come at the end. (Reread "What Is Religion?" on pages 277–282 to see how this organizing technique is used.) When you state the thesis at the end, you need to lead up to it or preview it throughout the essay. However, you will want to think of stating the thesis

provisionally near the beginning and referring to it elsewhere in the paper as you establish your definition.

Identify the approaches that you have used in your generative writing and early drafts. Where have you used contrast, comparison, analogy, narration, and so on? The material developed by each of these approaches is likely to form a paragraph. The definitions that you have found in your dictionary and in the OED will need a paragraph or two to connect them with the definition that you are developing. As always, give careful thought to paragraphing. Try your drafted paragraphs in different orders to discover which will best help your readers understand your definition.

Because it is important that your readers understand the need for a definition, explaining that need is an effective way to begin. Explaining the significance of this concept in your life might be part of the beginning or conclusion.

Drafting Be sure to identify source material as you include it in your draft. See the Appendix for further guidelines on citing source material

Begin with the easiest paragraph to draft. Explaining the concept's significance in your life is likely to be easy since you are writing about your thoughts and feelings; showing the need for a definition should not be difficult because you are writing about one of your convictions. As you draft, be sure that each paragraph contains real-life examples that pertain to the meaning of the concept—unless for some good reason a specific paragraph does not need examples.

After you draft your paragraphs, make every effort to write topic sentences that focus on how the material in each paragraph helps to establish the meaning of your concept.

As you draft the conclusion, be sure that it provides a satisfying ending with some reference to the thesis and emphasis on the meaning of the concept.

Revising, Editing, and Proofreading Use the step-by-step method on pages 160–162 to revise and polish your essay.

The following two essays use definition and classification to define concepts. The first essay explores the meaning of the term "freedom"; the second uses an extended definition to explore the politically charged concept of "workfare."

STUDENT WRITING
NAWANG DOMA SHERPA'S WRITING PROCESS

An immigrant from the Himalayan nation of Nepal, student Nawang Doma Sherpa's perspective on "freedom" is informed both by the extraordinary choices and challenges she has made in her life as well as by her strong Buddhist faith. In her essay, she examines the concept of "freedom" through the lenses of both her immigrant experience and her faith, describing how achieving a sense of "freedom" has allowed her to define herself and her life. To generate ideas for her essay, she returned to her journal notes on the Thinking-Writing activity "Defining a Concept."

<u>General qualities of religion</u>: I know what I believe, but everyone has their own very private reasons for what they believe in—it seems like everyone in my class has a different religion, but their faith—*why* they believe, or *how* they believe is the same. I think we're all looking for reasons for our lives. Why are we here?

<u>Classification? What kind of human activity is it?</u>: It's a mysterious activity. There has always been religion just as there have always been dreams. In Nepal our religion, Buddhism, determined so much—from how our days were structured to how we treated our parents and our neighbors. Here it seems like everyone has a different religion, or no religion at all. American society sometimes seems very religious—there's lots of talk about God and religion in politics for example—but it's not like the kind of everyday practice and discipline that I grew up with

<u>What is my definition of religion?</u>: For me Buddhism is what I practice as well as what I believe. I live my life as a Buddhist, and it helps me to make rational choices about my life. Being free and contributing to make this world a better and more peaceful place is the only aim of Buddhism.

Freedom for Enlightenment

BY NAWANG DOMA SHERPA

Human freedom is dependent upon two qualities: our relationships with others, and our need to believe in a higher purpose for our lives. All the different roles that each of us play in this world—child, student, peer, parent, and countless other relations—are intricate and interwoven with each other. In addition to the roles we each play, the mysterious phenomenon of religion both brings people together (as families and as entire societies) and drives them apart. In my own life, I have struggled with determining my freedom both in relationship to my family's traditions and expectations, and to my Buddhist faith.

I define myself on the basis of my achievements and flaws. In other words, I am who I am because of what I have done in my past—not because of the high goals and beautiful dreams I have set for my future. Both my own experience and the teachings of Buddhism have shown me that the future is both unpredictable and unknowable, but the past and present are reality and fact. The philosopher Jean-Paul Sartre noted that "man is nothing else but what he makes of himself," and I have come to share this view. We are free to determine our own fates, but we are not always fully aware of the responsibilities that come with this freedom. For me, religion and family duties helped me to acknowledge both my freedom and my responsibilities. However, it has not always been easy to accept these things.

I was born in Nepal into a middle class Sherpa family. They allowed me to pursue an education by attending a private girl's school for nine years and then a co-education school for another two years. After I graduated, I decided on my own to come to the United States. I moved to New York City, applied to college, and I now work to support myself and pay my tuition. This was a very unusual decision for a young girl from a traditional Nepalese family to make. Even though I am grown up, I still miss the love and care of my parents, especially the comfort of my mother's embrace and our home. My parents wanted me to stay in Nepal after I graduated, because it is traditional for girls of my social class to get married after they complete high school. But I made the decision to leave, to travel halfway around the world and live on very little money, entirely of my own free will. But if you ask me if I plan to spend the rest of my life away from Nepal, my family, and my home, I would not be able to answer you. I can only say that I will continue to make decisions based on my experience and my faith.

I practiced Buddhism, like most people in Nepal, and I feel free as a Buddhist. I could change my religion if I wanted to, because Buddhism encourages people to determine their own best choices for themselves rather than adhere strictly to one "perfect" or "correct" God. For me, Buddhism is rational. Ancestors have passed along the teaching of Buddha from generation to generation, and the core of that teaching is that we can free ourselves by understanding our inner self. The "eight-fold path" that all Buddhists follow determines how we relate to our selves and to each other: right speech, understanding, good deeds, determination, effort, awareness, thinking, and living. By understanding and accepting responsibility for our actions and beliefs, we achieve freedom. This makes us more responsible for who we are because by following this eight-fold path we will never hurt others and we will never fail in creating our image. Being free and contributing to make this world a better and more peaceful place is the only aim of Buddhism.

Freedom is possible, but with it comes responsibility. Freedom allows us to be conscious and aware, to explore and create new options and make choices that define us in the future. To deny your freedom is to deny responsibility for the choices that you make. I exercised free choice, and at the same time achieved freedom from my society's conservative expectations, by choosing to pursue a college education in America rather than getting married and staying in Nepal. But I have to accept the responsibility for this decision: my family misses me terribly, and I sometimes find it very difficult to balance work and school and to support myself financially. I am fortunate to have both the support of my family and the strength of my religion as I move forward into my future.

STUDENT WRITING

Vicki Diaz decided on her topic for this Writing Project after reading David K. Shipler's essay "A Poor Cousin of the Middle Class." As a New Yorker, Diaz explained how the city's implementation of "workfare" affected people in her neighborhood. In rereading Shipler's essay, she noted that he relied not only on his own reporting and observations but also on research into things like Medicaid rules and labor issues. As she thought about the development of her essay, Vicki was especially concerned with her potential audience. She decided that she wanted to write for other New Yorkers, both to share information about workfare and to encourage them to get involved with reforming the program so that its effects would be more positive.

Workfare: Moral or Immoral?

BY VICKI DIAZE

Over the last several years, New York City has worked to implement a policy of "workfare" in order to move people off the welfare roles and into the workforce. If you haven't applied for welfare, you might not understand what workfare is and how it affects people who live in our neighborhoods. In this paper, I will attempt to explain what workfare is, as well as explain why I (and many other community activists) believe that in its current incarnation workfare is not working. However, there are groups who are working to reform workfare in such a way that it will provide genuine assistance and motivation to people who need it most.

Workfare is a program that was first instituted by Mayor Rudolph Giuliani. The program was designed to move welfare recipients into skilled jobs in exchange for their welfare checks. However, this didn't happen for the majority of people who signed up for the program. Many people making the transition from welfare to workfare hoped for "real jobs" with real salaries and benefits, and yet all they received were basic, low-skilled jobs for minimum wage or less. This program not only hurt welfare recipients, but it also hurt the workers who were displaced from those low-wage jobs, according to a report in the *New York Times* (Bernstein).

Another problem with the current workfare program is that the government wants to involve religious or "faith-based" organizations to help offset an individual's needs, such as assistance with housing or food programs, that would normally be met by state- or city-funded welfare programs. According to Cathlin Baker, co-director of the non-profit organization Employment Project, "Churches feel caught between advocating for the people they serve and being contractors for the city" (Mickulas and Berkley-Gerard). Part of the reason that New York's churches feel this way is that they have to get approval for every social service they provide from the city's Human Resources Administration (HRA). Churches aren't as free as they used to be to help those in need as they are with other programs they run without the HRA. In addition, many churches, synagogues, and non-profit groups believe that workfare is morally wrong (because it unfairly exploits labor) and will not accept workfare employees (PBS.org). Rabbi Brenton-Granatoor stated that workfare recipients are "treated inhumanely . . . there is no way to address their grievances. That to me is enslavement" (PBS.org).

Individual recipients of workfare have their own horror stories to tell. One such story is that of Laura Morales, who was forced to work outdoors in order to receive her benefits. The problem was that Ms. Morales was asthmatic, and because of the workfare rules, she was not able to go to her doctor for treatment for fear that she would lose benefits. She wound up dying from complications after an asthma attack exacerbated by having to work outside (Jordan). Another case is that of Nancy Nay, a 41-year-old woman who suffered from cancer, sickle cell anemia, asthma, and a fractured skull from a car accident. In an article in the *New York Times*, Ms. Nay said that "I was in one of their work programs and was constantly sick—I would have to get up and excuse myself to vomit. It all came to the point that the supervisor said, 'We're going to cut you off, you're going to lose your apartment and be on the street'" (Bernstein). The problem is that people who administer workfare benefits—and the employers who take advantage of this very vulnerable workforce—do not care about the well-being of families or individuals. In addition, welfare recipients who were unable to begin workfare jobs when their benefits expired spent from a few weeks to several months without any benefits at all, and many of them were left homeless and hungry as a result.

Some policymakers and thinkers believe that workfare, as a concept, can be both useful and helpful if it is thoughtfully reformed and managed. In a story about workfare in New York City on NBC's *Nightly News*, Professor Lawrence Mead of New York University noted that "although many people remain poor, they're less poor than they were before. There's progress. Even though we haven't got everyone up to the poverty line, there's progress." Another woman interviewed on that broadcast described how she went from being a welfare recipient to making a living as a receptionist. She was now able to live independently and support both herself and her daughter. However, her case was unusual in that she received employment training, childcare assistance, and even help in how to dress for an office interview — benefits that are sparsely available to most workfare recipients. She is an example of what workfare *might* be able to accomplish, *if* it is properly funded and managed; but she cannot be held up as an example of the current system's overall success.

Another supporter of workfare, journalist John Tierney, wrote in the *Gotham Gazette* about a block in Harlem where "over the course of five years it was transformed from a dangerous place where few people worked to a safe street where former welfare recipients now go to work in the morning. It was revived thanks to welfare reform" (Tierney). I personally resent this opinion, because it makes it seem like crime was created by people on welfare and that because of workfare crime has gone down. I live in East Harlem, a neighborhood where many people are on welfare or who have depended at some point in their lives on public assistance. I can personally tell you that although crime has gone down, it is still an issue. Drugs are also a problem, and the services that addicts need to get clean and receive training and support to move into the workforce are simply not available through the HRA.

It is shameful that so many people have to work for less than minimum wage and work in conditions in which unionized workers would not be caught dead. Yet people trapped in the welfare/workfare cycle have no choice. Either they take these low-wage, dead-end jobs, or they lose their benefits and go homeless and hungry. I agree with advocates against workfare who say it is "akin to slavery because it forces poor people to work without pay and drives down wages for other workers" (PBS.org). I feel that if the Human Resources Administration took the time to review cases more closely, and that if people received proper training and support (like the receptionist interviewed on NBC's *Nightly News*), workfare might be a legitimate transition from public assistance to the workplace. Currently, however, it is a flawed solution to a broken system.

Works Cited

Bernstein, Nina. "As Welfare Deadline Looms, Answers Don't Seem So Easy." *New York Times* 25 June 2001, edu.sec.: *General News. Lexis-Nexis Academic Universe.* La-Guardia Community College Library, Long Island City, NY. 26 Mar 2002 <http://www.lexis-nexis.com/universe>.

"Is WorkFare Moral?: Join the Debate Over Whether Workfare Is Modern Slavery." *PBS Online NewsHour: Online Forums.* 6 Aug 1997. 27 Mar 2002 <http://www.pbs.org/newshour/forum/august97/slavery_8-6.html>.

Jordan, Howard. "Not All Black and White." *Gotham Gazette* 9 Jan 2002. 27 Mar 2002 <http://www.gothamgazette.com/commentary/85.jordan.shtml>.

Mickulas, P., and M. Berkley-Gerard. "Turning to Faith-Based Organizations." *Gotham Gazette* 18 Dec 2000. 27 Mar 2002 <http://www.gothamgazette.com/iotw/faith/index/shtml>.

Tierney, John. "Giuliani's Legacy: A Change in the Way New Yorkers Think About Crime, Welfare, Quality of Life, Squeegee Men." *Gotham Gazette* 9 Jan 2002. 27 Mar 2002 <http://gothamgazette.com/commentary/commentary_printable/ fixed/91.Tierney.shtml>.

9

"Nothing that God ever made is the same thing to more than one person." —Zora Neale Hurston

Exploring Perspectives and Relationships

Writing to Compare and Evaluate

Critical Thinking Focus: Critically evaluating perceptions and perspectives

Writing Focus: Using comparative thinking

Reading Theme: Differing perspectives from history

Writing Project: Comparing perspectives on an issue or an event

Chapter 7 introduced the concept of perceptions and showed how writers use their perceptions when they describe, narrate, and explain processes. As critical thinkers, active readers, and thoughtful writers, however, we need to go beyond simply recognizing that people have different perceptions. We have to think carefully about perceptions. In addition, we need to see how *perceptions*—messages from the senses—are connected to *perspectives*—points of view that develop from and also influence perceptions.

This chapter emphasizes critical evaluation and comparison of perceptions and perspectives. It will help you think about the differing points of view that people bring to what they say and write. Perspectives often conflict with one another, so you then must try to determine which one makes the most sense. You need to be able to analyze the differences and similarities that you find.

Because so many life situations and college assignments involve comparing and contrasting perspectives in an organized way, this chapter presents strategies for using comparative analysis in thinking and writing. The Writing Project asks you to analyze different perspectives on one event or issue.

Perceptions and Perspectives

Perspectives, or points of view, are what people express when they speak and write and also the vantage points from which they perceive events or issues. So a complex interaction exists between perceptions and perspectives. People's perspectives are formed by beliefs, interests, needs, age, gender, nationality, ethnicity, health, education—the multiple factors of life. These factors of perspective influence perceptions; at the same time, perceptions continuously influence perspectives.

To understand how various people can be exposed to the same stimuli or events and yet have different perceptions, it helps to imagine that each of us views the world through personal "contact lenses," an analogy from the previous chapter. (You might think of the factors that go into forming perspectives as the prescription for the lenses!)

We aren't usually aware that we are wearing these lenses. Instead, without our realizing it, our lenses act as filters that select and shape what we perceive.

To understand how people perceive the world, we have to understand their individual lenses, which influence how they actively select, organize, and interpret the events in their experience. A diagram of the process might look like Figure 9.1.

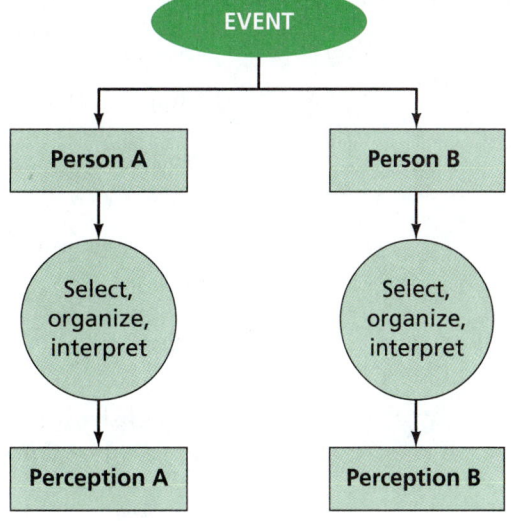

Figure 9.1 Differing Perceptions of an Event

301

Examine the following pairs of statements. In each pair, two people are being exposed to the same basic stimulus or event, yet the perception of one differs greatly from that of the other. Explain how the various perceptions might have developed.

   1. a. That chili was much too spicy to eat.

      Explanation: _____

      b. That chili needed more hot peppers and chili powder to spice it up a little.

      Explanation: _____

   2. a. People who wear lots of makeup and jewelry are very sophisticated.

      Explanation: _____

      b. People who wear lots of makeup and jewelry are ostentatious and overdressed.

      Explanation: _____

   3. a. The music young people enjoy listening to is a highly creative cultural expression.

      Explanation: _____

      b. The music young people enjoy listening to is obnoxious noise.

      Explanation: _____

   4. a. I really enjoy how stimulating and intellectually challenging this English class is.

      Explanation: _____

      b. This English class is too much work. All the teacher wants to do is make us think, think, think. It makes my head hurt.

      Explanation: _____

Effective critical thinkers are aware of the lenses that they—and others—are wearing. People unaware of the nature of their own lenses can often mistake their own perceptions for objective truth, not having examined either the facts or others' perceptions of a given issue.

In the cartoon "The Investigation," each witness is giving what he or she (or it!) believes is an accurate description of the man in the center, and all are unaware that their descriptions are being influenced by who they are and the way that they perceive things.

SELECTING PERCEPTIONS: WHY DO WE NOTICE THE THINGS WE NOTICE?

We tend to select perceptions about subjects that have been called to our attention. For instance, at the age of three, one author's child suddenly became aware of beards. On entering a subway car, she would ask in a penetrating voice, "Any beards here?" and proceed to count them out loud. In so doing, she naturally focused her parents' attention—as well as that of other passengers—on beards.

Another aspect of our perceiving lenses is our tendency to notice what we need, desire, or otherwise find interesting. When we go shopping, we focus on whatever items we are looking for. Walking down the street, we tend to notice certain kinds of people or events while completely ignoring others. Even while watching a movie or reading a book, we tend to concentrate on and remember the elements most meaningful to us. Another person can perform *exactly* the same actions— shop at the same store, walk down the same street, read the same book, or go to the same movie—and yet notice and remember entirely different things.

Although we tend to focus on what is familiar, normally

THE INVESTIGATION

HE WAS A REAL TALL GUY DRESSED NORMALLY, WITH LIGHT, DRY HAIR.

HE WAS A HEALTHY, GOOD LOOKING YOUNG KID... BUT DRESSED RATHER SHABBILY.

HE WAS REAL BIG AND REAL OLD.

HE WAS A WELL-DRESSED SORT, A LITTLE OVERWEIGHT AND WITH A LOT OF HAIR.

I REMEMBER HE HAD A LARGE HEAD AND HE SMELLED FUNNY.

HE WAS SURELY A WESTERNER.

HE WAS A SCRAWNY LITTLE SHORT-HAIRED TWERP FROM BACK EAST.

HE HAD DARK HAIR AND A CUTE NOSE. A REAL DOLL.

HE WAS A ROUGH, FURRY GUY WITH LITTLE BEADY EYES PROBABLY INEDIBLE

© John Jonik from cartoonbank.com.

we are not aware of doing so. In fact, we often take for granted what is familiar to us—the taste of chili or eggs, the street that we live on, our family or friends—and normally don't think about how we perceive it. When something happens that makes the familiar seem strange and unfamiliar, though, we do become aware of our perceptions and start to evaluate them.

To sum up, we actively select our perceptions on the basis of

- What has been called to our attention
- What our needs or interests are
- What our moods or feelings are
- What seems familiar or unfamiliar
- What our backgrounds are

The way in which we select perceptions is a paramount factor in shaping the lenses through which we view the world and it influences our writing to a great extent. Our writing is based on the points we choose to make, the details we select to include. Even when different people are writing about the same subject, the results are often very different because their lenses and their perspectives lead them to make different selections.

ORGANIZING PERCEPTIONS

Not only do you actively select certain perceptions; you also actively organize them into meaningful relationships and patterns. Carefully examine Figure 7.2 from page 212, Chapter 7. Do you see both the young woman and the old woman? If you do, try switching your perspective back and forth between the two images. As you do so, notice how for each image, you are doing the following things:

- *Selecting* certain lines, shapes, and shadings on which to focus your attention
- *Organizing* these lines, shapes, and shadings into different patterns
- *Interpreting* these patterns as representing things you can recognize—a hat, a nose, a chin

We naturally try to order and organize what we are experiencing into patterns and relationships that make sense to us. When we succeed in doing so, the completed whole means more than the sum of the individual parts. We are continually organizing the world in this way during virtually every waking moment. We do not live in a world of isolated sounds, patches of color, random odors, and individual textures. Instead, we live in a world of objects and people, language and music—a world in which all these individual stimuli are woven together. We are able to perceive this world of complex experiences because we can organize the individual stimuli we are receiving into relationships that have meaning for us.

This organizing process is integral to the writing process. When you write an essay, compose a letter, or create a story, you are actively organizing the ideas you selected to include into various relationships. Instead of simply stringing together words, you are developing a coherent structure through which to communicate thoughts and feelings.

INTERPRETING PERCEPTIONS

Besides selecting and organizing perceptions, we also actively interpret what we perceive: we are figuring out what something means. One of the elements that influences interpretations is the *context,* or overall situation, within which the perception is occurring. For example, imagine that you see a man running down the street. Your interpretation of his action will depend on the specific context. For example, is there a bus waiting at the corner? Is a police officer running behind him? Is the man wearing a jogging suit?

We are continually trying to interpret what we perceive, whether it is a design, someone else's behavior, or a social situation. As in the example of someone running down the street, many perceptions can be interpreted in more than one way. When a situation has more than one possible interpretation, it is ambiguous. The more ambiguous a situation is, the greater its possible meanings or interpretations.

Feelings often influence our interpretations of experience. When we feel happy and optimistic, the world often seems friendly and the future full of possibilities, so we interpret problems as challenges to be overcome. When we are depressed or unhappy, we may perceive the world entirely differently. The future can appear filled with problems that are trying to overwhelm us. In both cases the outer circumstances may be very similar; it is our own interpretations of the world through our lenses that vary so completely.

Perceptions of the world are also influenced by the perspectives that come from training and education. Consider two people watching a football game. One of them, who has very little understanding of football, sees merely a bunch of grown men hitting each other for no apparent reason. The other person, who loves football, sees complex play patterns, daring coaching strategies, effective blocking and tackling techniques, and zone defenses with seams that the receivers are trying to split. Both spectators have their eyes focused on the same event, but they are perceiving two entirely different situations. Their perceptions differ because each person is actively selecting, organizing, and interpreting the available stimuli in different ways.

The same is true of any situation in which we are perceiving something about which we have special knowledge or expertise. The following are examples.

- A builder examining the construction of a new house
- A musician attending a concert

- A naturalist experiencing the outdoors
- A chef tasting a dish just prepared
- A lawyer examining a contract

Naturally, your knowledge (or lack thereof) influences your writing in significant ways. When you are very familiar with a subject, your writing expresses an informed perspective, a knowledgeable point of view.

Thinking ↔ Writing Activity

How Knowledge Influences Perceptions

1. Think about one of your special areas of interest or expertise and about how your perceptions in that area might differ from those of people who don't share your knowledge. List some specific things that you would notice that others might not. Note how your knowledge influences what you see, hear, or otherwise perceive.

2. Write a paragraph telling of what you've noticed. Share it with classmates and see what they think about what you've said.

3. Respond to classmates' paragraphs. How do you perceive things in their areas of expertise?

4. Does this activity help you to understand perspectives?

Understanding Different Perspectives

The perceptions of a knowledgeable person usually differ substantially from those of a person who lacks such specialized knowledge. The following reading illuminates this point.

Two Ways of Viewing the River
BY SAMUEL CLEMENS (MARK TWAIN) (1835–1910)

Samuel Clemens, who took the pen name "Mark Twain" to commemorate his work as a river-boat pilot on the Mississippi (the term "mark twain" means the river's depth is safe for the boat's passage), was raised in the Mississippi river town of Hannibal, Missouri. He later immortalized the town as "St. Petersburg" in his novels The Adventures of Tom Sawyer *(1876) and* Adventures of Huckleberry Finn *(1883).*

Although Tom Sawyer *depicted a seemingly idyllic, small-town way of life,* Huckleberry Finn *is one of the darkest and most complex explorations of the American character, especially the American attitude toward race, ever written.*

As a journalist Twain traveled widely, becoming famous for his humorous (and frequently sarcastic) dispatches from Europe, in which he spoofed relationships between Old World tradition and the burgeoning (if uncouth) power of the New World. In 1870 Twain married his beloved Olivia Langdon, settling with her in Hartford, Connecticut, and beginning the most productive years of his writing career. The Prince and the Pauper *appeared in 1881, and* Life on the Mississippi *in 1883.*

Financial speculation led Twain into bankruptcy in the 1890s, and to recoup some of his family's financial security he embarked on a world lecture tour. His books from this time, including The Tragedy of Pudd'head Wilson *(1894) and* A Connecticut Yankee in King Arthur's Court *(1889), continued to explore the issues of race and the emerging American identity. A series of personal tragedies, especially the death of his adored eldest daughter Susy, darkened Twain's later perspective, which is seen in his posthumously published autobiography (1924). Twain died on April 21, 1910.*

Now when I had mastered the language of this water and had come to know every trifling feature that bordered the great river as familiarly as I knew the letters of the alphabet, I had made a valuable acquisition. But I had lost something, too. I had lost something which could never be restored to me while I lived. All the grace, the beauty, the poetry, had gone out of the majestic river! I still kept in mind a certain wonderful sunset which I witnessed when steamboating was new to me. A broad expanse of the river was turned to blood; in the middle distance the red hue brightened into gold, through which a solitary log came floating, black and conspicuous; in one place a long, slanting mark lay sparkling upon the water; in another the surface was broken by boiling, tumbling rings that were as many-tinted as an opal; where the ruddy flush was faintest, was a smooth spot that was covered with graceful circles and radiating lines, ever so delicately traced; the shore on our left was densely wooded and the somber shadow that fell from this forest was broken in one place by a long, ruffled trail that shone like silver; and high above the forest wall a clean-stemmed dead tree waved a single leafy bough that glowed like a flame in the unobstructed splendor that was flowing from the sun. There were graceful curves, reflected images, woody heights, soft distances, and over the whole scene, far and near, the dissolving lights drifted steadily, enriching it every passing moment with new marvels of coloring.

I stood like one bewitched. I drank it in, in a speechless rapture. The world was new to me and I had never seen anything like this at home. But as I have said, a day came when I began to cease from noting the glories and the charms which the moon and the sun and the twilight wrought upon the river's face; another day came when I ceased altogether to note them. Then, if that sunset scene had been repeated, I should have looked upon it without rapture, and should have commented upon it inwardly after this fashion: "This sun means that we are going to have wind tomorrow; that floating log means that the river is rising, small thanks to it; that slanting mark on the water refers to a bluff reef which is going to kill somebody's steamboat one of these nights, if it keeps on stretching out like that; those tumbling 'boils' show a dissolving bar and a changing channel there; the lines and circles in the slick water over yonder are a warning that the troublesome place is shoaling up dangerously; that silver streak in the shadow of the forest is the 'break' from a new snag and he has located himself in the very best place he could have found to fish for steamboats; that tall dead tree, with a single living branch, is not going to last long, and then how is a body ever going to get through this blind place at night without the friendly old landmark?"

No, the romance and beauty were all gone from the river. All the value any feature of it had for me now was the amount of usefulness it could furnish toward compassing the safe piloting of a steamboat. Since those days, I have pitied doctors from my heart. What does the lovely flush in a beauty's cheek mean to a doctor but a "break" that ripples above some deadly disease? Are not all her visible charms sown thick with what are to him the signs and symbols of hidden decay? Does he ever see her beauty at all, or doesn't he simply view her professionally and comment upon her unwholesome condition all to himself? And doesn't he sometimes wonder whether he has gained most or lost most by learning his trade?

Questions for Active Reading

1. Examine Twain's use of simile and metaphor in this essay (reviewing the discussion of figurative language on page 178). Which similes and metaphors do you find most effective, and why?

2. Why does Twain use the word "viewing" in his title, rather than "seeing" or "describing"?

3. What key words and phrases does Twain use to indicate the "before and after" structure of his essay?

Questions for Thinking Critically

1. In this passage Twain provides a compelling description of the way developing a knowledgeable perspective as a river pilot influenced his perceptions of the river. How did his perceptions change? Why did he feel that his shift of perspective caused him to both gain and lose in his experience of the river?

2. Describe how your perception of something changed because you had learned more about it. Did you, like Twain, both lose and gain? Explain why or why not.

Thinking ↔ Writing Activity

Five Accounts of the Assassination of Malcolm X, 1965

Let's examine a situation in which a number of different people had differing perceptions about an event they were describing. Chapter 6 of this book contains a passage by Malcolm X (pages 154–157), written when he was just beginning his life's work. A few years later, this work came to a tragic end with his assassination at a meeting in Harlem. As you read through the various accounts, pay particular attention to the perceptions each presents. After reading the accounts, analyze some of the differences in these perceptions by writing answers to the questions that follow.

1. What details of the events has each writer selected to focus on?

2. How has each writer organized the selected details? Remember that most newspapers give what they consider the most important information first.

3. How does each writer depict Malcolm X, his followers, the gunmen, and the significance of the assassination?

The *New York Times* (February 22, 1965)

Malcolm X, the 39-year-old leader of a militant Black Nationalist movement, was shot to death yesterday afternoon at a rally of his followers in a ballroom in Washington Heights. The bearded Negro extremist had said only a few words of greeting when a fusillade rang out. The bullets knocked him over backwards.

A 22-year-old Negro, Thomas Hagan, was charged with the killing. The police rescued him from the ballroom crowd after he had been shot and beaten.

Pandemonium broke out among the 400 Negroes in the Audubon Ballroom at 160th Street and Broadway. As men, women and children ducked under tables and flattened themselves on the floor, more shots were fired. The police said seven bullets struck Malcolm. Three other Negroes were shot. Witnesses reported that as many as 30 shots had been fired. About two hours later the police said the shooting had apparently been a result of a feud between followers of Malcolm and members of the extremist group he broke with last year, the Black Muslims. . . .

Life (March 5, 1965)

His life oozing out through a half dozen or more gunshot wounds in his chest, Malcolm X, once the shrillest voice of black supremacy, lay dying on the stage of a Manhattan auditorium. Moments before, he had stepped up to the lectern and 400 of the faithful had settled down expectantly to hear the sort of speech for which he was famous—flaying the hated white man. Then a scuffle broke out in the hall and Malcolm's bodyguards bolted from his side to break it up—only to discover that they had been faked out. At least two men with pistols rose from the audience and pumped bullets into the speaker, while a third cut loose at close range with both barrels of a sawed-off shotgun. In the confusion the pistol man got away. The shotgunner lunged through the crowd and out the door, but not before the guards came to their wits and shot him in the leg. Outside he was swiftly overtaken by other supporters of Malcolm and very likely would have been stomped to death if the police hadn't saved him. Most shocking of all to the residents of Harlem was the fact that Malcolm had been killed not by "whitey" but by members of his own race.

The *New York Post* (February 22, 1965)

They came early to the Audubon Ballroom, perhaps drawn by the expectation that Malcolm X would name the men who firebombed his home last Sunday. . . . I sat at the left in the 12th row and, as we waited, the man next to me spoke of Malcolm and his followers: "Malcolm is our only hope. You can depend on him to tell it like it is and to give Whitey hell."

There was a prolonged ovation as Malcolm walked to the rostrum. Malcolm looked up and said "A salaam aleikum (Peace be unto you)" and the audience replied "We aleikum salaam (And unto you, peace)."

Bespectacled and dapper in a dark suit, sandy hair glinting in the light, Malcolm said: "Brothers and sisters . . ." He was interrupted by two men in the center of the ballroom, who rose and, arguing with each other, moved forward. Then there was a scuffle at the back of the room. I heard Malcolm X say his last words: "Now, brothers, break it up," he said softly. "Be cool, be calm."

Then all hell broke loose. There was a muffled sound of shots and Malcolm, blood on his face and chest, fell limply back over the chairs behind him. The two men who had approached him ran to the exit on my side of the room, shooting wildly behind them as they ran. I heard people screaming, "Don't let them kill him." "Kill those bastards." At an exit I saw some of Malcolm's men beating with all their strength on two men. I saw a half dozen of Malcolm's followers bending over his inert body on the stage. Their clothes stained with their leader's blood.

Four policemen took the stretcher and carried Malcolm through the crowd and some of the women came out of their shock and one said: "I hope he doesn't die, but I don't think he's going to make it."

Associated Press (February 22, 1965)

A week after being bombed out of his Queens home, Black Nationalist leader Malcolm X was shot to death shortly after 3 (P.M.) yesterday at a Washington Heights rally of 400 of his devoted followers. Early today, police brass ordered a homicide charge placed against a 22-year-old man they rescued from a savage beating by Malcolm X supporters after the shooting. The suspect, Thomas Hagan, had been shot in the left leg by one of Malcolm's bodyguards as, police said, Hagan and another assassin fled when pandemonium erupted. Two other men were wounded in the wild burst of firing from at least three weapons. The firearms were a .38, a .45 automatic and a sawed-off shotgun. Hagan allegedly shot Malcolm X with the shotgun, a double-barrelled sawed-off weapon on which the stock also had been shortened, possibly to facilitate concealment. Cops charged Reuben Frances, of 871 E. 179th St., Bronx, with felonious assault in the shooting of Hagan, and with Sullivan Law violation—possession of the .45. Police recovered the shotgun and the .45.

The *Amsterdam News* (February 27, 1965)

"We interrupt this program to bring you a special newscast . . . ," the announcer said as the Sunday afternoon movie on the TV set was halted temporarily. "Malcolm X was shot four times while addressing a crowd at the Audubon Ballroom on 166th Street." "Oh no!" That was my first reaction to the shocking event that followed one week after the slender, articulate leader of the Afro-American Unity was routed from his East Elmhurst home by a bomb explosion. Minutes later we alighted from a cab at the corner of Broadway and 166th St. just a short 15 blocks from where I live on Broadway. About 200 men and women, neatly dressed, were milling around, some with expressions of awe and disbelief. Others were in small clusters talking loudly and with deep emotion in their voices. Mostly they were screaming for vengeance. One woman, small, dressed in a light gray coat and her eyes flaming with indignation, argued with a cop at the St. Nicholas corner of the block. "This is not the end of it. What they were going to do to the Statue of Liberty will be small in comparison. We black people are tired of being shoved around." Standing across the street near the memorial park one of Malcolm's close associates commented: "It's a shame." Later he added that "if it's war they want, they'll get it." He would not say whether Elijah Muhammed's followers had anything to do with the assassination. About 3:30 P.M. Malcolm X's wife, Betty, was escorted by three men and a woman from the Columbia Presbyterian Hospital. Tears streamed down her face. She was screaming, "They killed him!" Malcolm X had no last words. . . . The bombing and burning of the No. 7 Mosque early Tuesday morning was the first blow by those who are seeking revenge for the cold-blooded murder of a man who at 39 might have grown to the stature of respectable leadership.

Thinking ↔ Writing Activity

Analyzing Different Accounts of the 2001 World Trade Center and Pentagon Attacks

This perspective-taking activity involves critical thinking about the terrorist attacks on the World Trade Center and Pentagon in 2001. The various accounts appeared in news sources in the United States and around the world. After you have finished reading these accounts, analyze some of the differences in perceptions by answering the following questions:

1. What details of the events has each writer *selected* to focus on?

2. How has each writer *organized* the details that have been selected? Bear in mind that most news organizations present what they consider the most important information first and the least important information last.

3. How does each writer *interpret* the significance of the attacks?

4. How has each writer used *language* to express his or her perspective and to influence the thinking of the reader? Which language styles do you find most effective?

The *New York Times* (New York City, September 12, 2001)

Hijackers rammed jetliners into each of New York's Trade Center towers yesterday, toppling both in a hellish storm of ash, glass, smoke and leaping victims, while a third jetliner crashed into the Pentagon in Virginia. There was no official count, but President Bush said thousands had perished, and in the immediate aftermath the calamity was already being ranked the worst and most audacious terror attack in American history.

The attacks seemed carefully coordinated. The hijacked planes were all en route to California, and therefore gorged with fuel, and their departures were spaced within an hour and 40 minutes. The first, American Airlines Flight 11, a Boeing 767 out of Boston for Los Angeles, crashed into the north tower at 8:48 A.M. Eighteen minutes later, United Airlines Flight 175, also headed from Boston to Los Angeles, plowed into the south tower. Then an American Airlines Boeing 757, Flight 77, left Washington's Dulles International Airport bound for Los Angeles, but instead hit the western part of the Pentagon, the military headquarters where 24,000 people work, at 9:40 A.M. Finally, United Airlines Flight 93, a Boeing 757 flying from Newark to San Francisco, crashed near Pittsburgh, raising the possibility that its hijackers had failed in whatever their mission was.

In all, 266 people perished in the four planes and several score more were known dead elsewhere. Numerous firefighters, police officers and other rescue workers who responded to the initial disaster in Lower Manhattan were killed or injured when the buildings collapsed. Hundreds were treated for cuts, broken bones, burns and smoke inhalation. But the real carnage was concealed for now by the twisted, smoking, ash-choked carcasses of the twin towers, in which thousands of people used to work on a weekday. The collapse of the towers caused another World Trade Center building to fall 10 hours later, and several other buildings in the area were damaged or aflame. "I have a sense it's a horrendous number of lives lost," said Mayor Rudolph W. Giuliani. "Right now we have to focus on saving as many lives as possible."

Le Monde (Paris, September 12, 2001)

The United States underwent, Tuesday, September 11, the worst attack of their history. The financial, military and policy centers of the country were reached. Terrorists destroyed the two towers of the World Trade Center in New York and tackled the Pentagon. As in Pearl Harbour, the American power was taken by surprise. The dream of invulnerable America definitively ended.

Hamburger Morgenpost (Hamburg, September 12, 2001)

New York, 8:42 A.M.: It is a sunny morning, as the millions-metropolis wakes up, a morning that will change America, and perhaps the entire world, forever. As eyewitnesses later reported, a jetliner flies in a straight line towards the southern of the two 411-meter high towers of the World Trade Center. Flying debris falls in as far as a 5 kilometer radius to the ground, hitting pedestrians in the well-visited streets of Manhattan.

Still the world, which will be informed within only minutes, goes about its business. The news network CNN, whose reach is worldwide, runs live footage with photos of the smoking skyscraper. The damage appears terrible, but overcomable. This impression changes a mere 18 minutes later, as the public, via television, witnesses a second jetliner flying into the second, still stable tower. Incomprehensible: like the special effects in the Hollywood film "Independence Day" the jet penetrates the glass giant, almost slicing all the way through it. TV viewers see how the still-intact glass façade of the opposite side of the tower is destroyed, obviously caused by the jet's explosion in the inside of the tower.

It is only now that the suspicion rises up to awareness: this is the work of terrorists, whose horrific dimensions have until now not been known. Yet for America, the nightmare has not yet ended: Barely an hour after the first attack, there comes a report from the nation's capital, Washington: flames are erupting from the Pentagon. The cause: a passenger aircraft, probably a Boeing 767. Now the terror has struck America's central nervous system. A few minutes later, the Mall outside Congress burns also. A car bomb is the suspected cause. CNN switches from a burning Manhattan to the burning capital—this is war, and the victims are civilians. With the world as a witness, the people behind the shattered glass façade of the WTC gesticulate as the desperate leap out of the burning buildings. A little while later, both towers collapse, transformed in an instant from New York's giants to empty shells.

Pakistani newspaper (Pakistan, September 12, 2001)

A Pakistani newspaper said on Wednesday that Saudi militant Osama bin Laden had issued a denial of responsibility for the devastating terror attacks on the United States. "The terrorist act is the action of some American group. I have nothing to do with it," the newspaper quoted bin Laden as saying through "sources close to the Taliban." The Urdu-language newspaper has a reputation for sensational reporting and there was no independent confirmation of the claim.

Time.com (September 12, 2001)

Morning came, and everything was changed. The sun rose Wednesday over the absence of a national landmark, a smoldering ruin in lower Manhattan where the World Trade Center towers had stood. In Washington the Pentagon, still on fire, was deeply scarred, along with America's collective sense of security. After a day in which terrorists had managed to effectively shut down both cities, suspend all air traffic in the U.S. and force evacuations across the country and in U.S. facilities worldwide, a day in which President George W. Bush warned that "the United States will hunt down and punish those responsible for these cowardly acts," there was nothing to do in the bright, crisp fall sunshine but to clean up, search for those responsible, and mourn the dead.

In a tragic and spectacular explosion that engulfed lower Manhattan in thick smoke and gray powder debris, two airplanes crashed into the World Trade Center in New York City at around 9 A.M. EST. . . . The planes were loaded with fuel for transcontinental flights, and that jet fuel ignited a hellish blaze that sent temperatures at the point of impact soaring to an estimated 2000 degrees F. Within an hour, the intense heat caused the seemingly invincible steel beams of the towers to melt like cotton candy. At 10 A.M. EST, the southern tower of the World Trade Center was enveloped in smoke after a second gigantic explosion, and part of that tower collapsed and was destroyed. About twenty minutes later, the northern tower imploded.

In Washington, the Pentagon was evacuated after another commercial airliner crashed into the building. A short time later, part of the building collapsed. A fire was also reported on the Mall. The White House, the Capitol and other government buildings were also evacuated, and Washington became a ghost town. If the terrorists sought to undermine the conduct of government, they succeeded at least for the day. They may not, however, have hit all of their targets: Wednesday afternoon, White House officials reported that both the White House and Air Force One were targets of the terrorist attacks; officials speculate the plane that crashed into the Pentagon may have been intended to destroy the White House instead.

The *London Times* (London, September 11, 2001)

It was terrorism by timetable. Morning in America became the darkest of national catastrophes after a carefully co-ordinated attack of grotesque barbarity. The first the world knew of what was to become an unfolding tragedy, which stretched human powers of understanding to breaking point, was just before 9 A.M. U.S. Eastern time (1400 BST). Inside the World Trade Centre, New York's public servants, bankers and industrialists would have been settling into their second working hour. When disaster struck. An American Airlines flight crashed direct into the 100-storey building, not just a symbol of American corporate power and capitalism's global sway but the workplace for thousands of New Yorkers. The large passenger jet was careering towards the tower before it embedded itself in the building. Heavy black smoke billowed into the sky above one of New York City's most famous landmarks and debris rained down on the street, one of its busiest work areas.

Before any rational reaction could come, before any judgment about the cause of the disaster could be made, as emergency services were being scrambled and newsrooms alerted, a second jet plunged into the World Trade Centre just after 9 A.M. When the second plane hit, a fireball of flame and smoke erupted, leaving a huge hole in the glass and steel tower. Television stations, alerted to the first crash, caught the second plane ploughing into the second of the twin towers, exploding in a fireball a few minutes after the first impact. The scenario of a Tom Clancy thriller or Spielberg blockbuster was now unfolding live on the world's television screens.

For eyewitnesses, the scale of the devastation was already incomprehensible. John Axisa, who was getting off a commuter train to the World Trade Centre, said he saw "bodies falling out of the building." He ran outside and watched people jump out of the first building. Other witnesses on the street were screaming every time another person leapt. For those below the point of impact, the only thought was flight. People ran down the stairs in panic and fled from the building. And in a grotesque parody of the tickertape parades that characterize New York celebrations, thousands of pieces of office paper were carried on the gusting wind to Brooklyn, about three miles away.

People's Daily (Beijing, September 12, 2001)

At least one Chinese national was injured in the terror attacks against the World Trade Center in New York and the fate of roughly 30 others was unknown on Wednesday morning, China's Foreign Trade Ministry said. China had 14 companies with offices in the building at the heart of the global financial centre which was hit by two aircraft on Tuesday, the ministry said in a statement on its Web site.

Chinese police blocked off the road past the U.S. embassy in Beijing to all but American embassy cars and personnel and doubled the number of guards to about 30.

Ordinary Chinese scrambled for more information, with many trying to access foreign news Web sites. Many condemned the attacks, first reported on the Sina.com, a NASDAQ listed Chinese portal, just several minutes after the event. "I think no matter what, if you play with people's lives, it is too tragic," said Chen Xiao, who works for a Beijing publishing firm, as she bought a morning newspaper. "It doesn't matter who did it or what they were upset about, but taking that many innocent lives is a price that's barbaric." Feng Chang-lin, 63, owner of a downtown hardware store in Shanghai, said the world would never be the same again. "This is just a cowardly act by terrorists," he said. "No matter what problems you might have with another country, you should never resort to such tactics."

China's stock markets dropped sharply at the open on Wednesday, with Shanghai B shares down more than six percent. Chinese investors, who routinely ignore everything from U.S. Fed rate cuts to tumbling Asian bourses, would be unable to shrug off the attacks, brokers and analysts said.

All four flights scheduled from China to the United States on Wednesday had been cancelled. Air China flight CA985 to San Francisco and China Eastern flight MU583 to Los Angeles were both diverted to Vancouver on Tuesday night and China Eastern cargo flight MU5787 was diverted to an American military airport in Anchorage, Alaska.

Chinese President Jiang Zemin sent a message of sympathy to U.S. President George W. Bush at Tuesday's midnight. Jiang also expressed condolences to the family members of the victims of the attacks and "grave concern" for the safety of tens of thousands of Chinese in the United States. Foreign Ministry spokesman Zhu Bangzao said in a statement the Chinese people were "deeply shocked" by the attacks. "The Chinese government has consistently condemned and opposed all manner of terrorist violence," Zhu said.

The *Washington Post* (Washington, D.C., September 12, 2001)

Terrorists unleashed an astonishing air assault on America's military and financial power centers yesterday morning, hijacking four commercial jets and then crashing them into the World Trade Center in New York, the Pentagon and the Pennsylvania countryside. There were no reliable estimates last night of how many people were killed in the most devastating terrorist operation in American history. The number was certainly in the hundreds and could be in the thousands.

It was the most dramatic attack on American soil since Pearl Harbor, and it created indelible scenes of carnage and chaos. The commandeered jets obliterated the World Trade Center's twin 110-story towers from their familiar perch above Manhattan's skyline and ripped a blazing swath through the Defense Department's imposing five-sided fortress, grounding the domestic air traffic system for the first time and plunging the entire nation into an unparalleled state of anxiety. U.S. military forces at home and abroad were placed on their highest state of alert, and a loose network of Navy warships was deployed along both coasts for air defense.

None of the 266 people aboard the four planes survived. There were even more horrific but still untallied casualties in the World Trade Center and the Pentagon, which together provided office space for more than 70,000 people. At just one of the firms with offices in the World Trade Center, the Marsh & McLennan insurance brokerage, 1,200 of its 1,700 employees were unaccounted for last night. The spectacular collapse of the Trade Center's historic twin towers and another less recognizable skyscraper during the rescue operations caused even more bloodshed. At least 300 New York firefighters and 85 police officers are presumed dead. The preliminary list of victims included the conservative commentator Barbara K. Olson, "Frasier" executive producer David Angell and two hockey scouts from the Los Angeles Kings.

No one claimed responsibility for the attacks, but federal officials said they suspect the involvement of Islamic extremists with links to fugitive terrorist Osama bin Laden, who has been implicated in the 1998 bombings of two U.S. embassies in Africa and several other attacks. Law enforcement sources said there is already evidence implicating bin Laden's militant network in the attack, and politicians from both parties predicted a major and immediate escalation in America's worldwide war against terrorism. In a grim address to the nation last night, President Bush denounced the attacks as a failed attempt to frighten the United States, and promised to hunt down those responsible. "We will make no distinction," he said, "between the terrorists who committed these acts and those who harbor them."

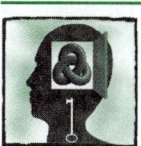

Thinking ↔ Writing Activity

Seven Accounts of Events at Tiananmen Square, 1989

In the spring of 1989, a vigorous pro-democracy movement erupted in Beijing, the capital of China. Protesting the authoritarian control of the Communist regime, thousands of students staged demonstrations, engaged in hunger strikes, and organized marches involving hundreds of thousands of people. The geographical heart of these activities was the historic Tiananmen Square, taken over by the demonstrators who had erected a symbolic "Statue of Liberty." On June 4, 1989, the fledgling pro-democracy movement came to a bloody end when the Chinese army entered Tiananmen Square and seized control of it. The following are various accounts of this event from different sources. After analyzing these accounts, construct your own version of what you believe took place on that day. Use the questions on page 312 to guide your analysis.

The *New York Times* (June 4, 1989)

Tens of thousands of Chinese troops retook the center of the capital from pro-democracy protesters early this morning, killing scores of students and workers and wounding hundreds more as they fired submachine guns at crowds of people who tried to resist. Troops marched along the main roads surrounding central Tiananmen Square, sometimes firing in the air and sometimes firing directly at crowds who refused to move. Reports on the number of dead were sketchy. Students said, however, that at least 500 people may have been killed in the crackdown. Most of the dead had been shot, but some had been run over by personnel carriers that forced their way through the protesters' barricades.

Days before their violent confrontation, demonstrating students surround police-men near Tiananmen Square, calling for freedom and democracy. What is your per-ception of what is taking place? © Associated Press.

A report on the state-run radio put the death toll in the thousands and de-nounced the Government for the violence, the Associated Press reported. But the station later changed announcers and broadcast another report supporting the governing Communist party. The official news programs this morning re-ported that the People's Liberation Army had crushed a "counter-revolutionary rebellion." They said that more than 1,000 police officers and troops had been in-jured and some killed, and that civilians had been killed, but did not give de-tails.

Deng Xiaoping, Chairman of the Central Military Commission, as reported in *Beijing Review* (July 10–16, 1989)

The main difficulty in handling this matter lay in that we had never experienced such a situation before, in which a small minority of bad people mixed with so many young students and onlookers. Actually, what we faced was not just some ordinary people who were misguided, but also a rebellious clique and a large number of the dregs of society. The key point is that they wanted to overthrow our state and the Party. They had two main slogans: to overthrow the Commu-nist Party and topple the socialist system. Their goal was to establish a bour-geois republic entirely dependent on the West.

During the course of quelling the rebellion, many comrades of ours were in-jured or even sacrificed their lives. Some of their weapons were also taken from them by the rioters. Why? Because bad people mingled with the good, which made it difficult for us to take the firm measures that were necessary. Handling this matter amounted to a severe political test for our army, and what happened

Aftermath of the bloody clash between a pro-democracy student movement and the Chinese army on June 4, 1989. Based on this photograph, what is your perception of what took place? Why? © Patrick Durand/SYGMA

shows that our People's Liberation Army passed muster. If tanks were used to roll over people, this would have created a confusion between right and wrong among the people nationwide. That is why I have to thank the PLA officers and men for using this approach to handle the rebellion. The PLA losses were great, but this enabled us to win the support of the people and made those who can't tell right from wrong change their viewpoint. They can see what kind of people the PLA are, whether there was bloodshed at Tiananmen, and who were those that shed blood.

This shows that the people's army is truly a Great Wall of iron and steel of the Party and country. This shows that no matter how heavy the losses we suffer and no matter how generations change, this army of ours is forever an army under the leadership of the Party, forever the defender of the country, forever the defender of socialism, forever the defender of the public interest, and they are the most beloved of the people. At the same time, we should never forget how cruel our enemies are. For them we should not have an iota of forgiveness.

Additional Chinese Government Accounts

"Comrades, thanks for your hard work. We hope you will continue with your fine efforts to safeguard security in the capital."

—Prime Minister Li Peng (addressing a group of soldiers after the Tiananmen Square event)

"It never happened that soldiers fired directly at the people."

—General Li Zhiyun

"Not a single student was killed in Tiananmen Square."
—Chinese army commander

"The People's Liberation Army crushed a counter-revolutionary rebellion. More than 1,000 police officers and troops were injured and killed, and some civilians were killed."
—Official Chinese news program

"At most 300 people were killed in the operation, many of them soldiers."
—Yuan Mu, official government spokesman

"My government has stated that a mob led by a small number of people prevented the normal conduct of the affairs of state. There was, I regret to say, loss of life on both sides. I wonder whether any other government confronting such an unprecedented challenge would have handled the situation any better than mine did."
—Han Xu, Chinese ambassador to the United States

Reporter (*eyewitness account*), reported in the *New York Times* (June 4, 1989)

Changan Avenue, or the Avenue of Eternal Peace, Beijing's main east-west thoroughfare, echoed with screams this morning as young people carried the bodies of their friends away from the front lines. The dead or seriously wounded were heaped on the backs of bicycles or tricycle rickshaws and supported by friends who rushed through the crowds, sometimes sobbing as they ran.

The avenue was lit by the glow of several trucks and two armed personnel carriers that students and workers set afire, and bullets swooshed overhead or glanced off buildings. The air crackled almost constantly with gunfire and tear gas grenades.

Students and workers tried to resist the crackdown, and destroyed at least sixteen trucks and two armored personnel carriers. Scores of students and workers ran alongside the personnel carriers, hurling concrete blocks and wooden staves into the treads until they ground to a halt. They then threw firebombs at one until it caught fire, and set the other alight after first covering it with blankets soaked in gasoline. The drivers escaped the flames, but were beaten by students. A young American man, who could not be immediately identified, was also beaten by the crowd after he tried to intervene and protect one of the drivers.

Clutching iron pipes and stones, groups of students periodically advanced toward the soldiers. Some threw bricks and firebombs at the lines of soldiers, apparently wounding many of them. Many of those killed were throwing bricks at the soldiers, but others were simply watching passively or standing at barricades when soldiers fired directly at them.

It was unclear whether the violence would mark the extinction of the seven-week-old democracy movement, or would prompt a new phase in the uprising, like a general strike. The violence in the capital ended a period of remarkable restraint by both sides, and seemed certain to arouse new bitterness and antagonism among both ordinary people and Communist Party officials for the Government of Prime Minister Li Peng.

"Our Government is already done with," said a young worker who held a rock in his hand, as he gazed at the army forces across Tiananmen Square. "Nothing can show more clearly that it does not represent the people." Another young man, an art student, was nearly incoherent with grief and anger as he watched the body of a student being carted away, his head blown away by bullets. "Maybe we'll fail today," he said. "Maybe we'll fail tomorrow. But someday we'll succeed. It's a historical inevitability."

The *New York Times* (June 5, 1989)

It was clear that at least 300 people had been killed since the troops first opened fire shortly after midnight on Sunday morning but the toll may be much higher. Word-of-mouth estimates continued to soar, some reaching far into the thousands. . . . The student organization that coordinated the long protests continued to function and announced today that 2,600 students were believed to have been killed. Several doctors said that, based on their discussions with ambulance drivers and colleagues who had been on Tiananmen Square, they estimated that at least 2,000 had died. Soldiers also beat and bayoneted students and workers after daybreak on Sunday, witnesses said, usually after some provocation but sometimes entirely at random. "I saw a young woman tell the soldiers that they are the people's army, and that they mustn't hurt the people," a young doctor said after returning from one clash Sunday. "Then the soldier shot her, and ran up and bayoneted her."

Xiao Bin (*eyewitness account immediately after the event*)

Tanks and armored personnel carriers rolled over students, squashing them into jam, and the soldiers shot at them and hit them with clubs. When students fainted, the troops killed them. After they died, the troops fired one more bullet into them. They also used bayonets. They were too cruel. I never saw such things before.

Xiao Bin (*account after being taken into custody by Chinese authorities*)

I never saw anything. I apologize for bringing great harm to the party and the country.

Thinking ↔ Writing Activity

Analyzing Multiple Perspectives in the News

1. Analyze the perceiving lenses of each account by using the questions on page 312 as a framework.
2. If you were to compose your own account of either of these catastrophes

- Which details would you select to be included?
- How would you organize the details?
- What would your interpretation of the significance of the event be? What themes would you want to suggest and elaborate on?
- Of the language styles displayed in the previous accounts, which style would you choose?

3. Compose your own account of this event, as if you were writing for a major news organization with an international audience.

CHANGES IN PERCEPTIONS AND PERSPECTIVES

Just as Mark Twain's perceptions of the river were changed by his perspective of increased knowledge, your ways of viewing the world will develop and change through the experiences you have, the knowledge you acquire, and your reflections on your experiences and knowledge. As you think critically about perceptions, you will learn more about how you make sense of the world. This understanding may strengthen your perceptions, or it may change them.

Obtaining More Accurate Perceptions: Adjusting the Lenses

So far, we have emphasized the great extent to which, by selecting, organizing, and interpreting, we directly affect our perceptions. We have suggested that each of us views the world through his or her own unique lenses, that no two of us perceive the world in exactly the same way.

Because we actively participate in selecting, organizing, and interpreting the sensations we experience, our perceptions are often incomplete, inaccurate, or subjective. To complicate the situation further, our own limitations in perceiving are not the only factors that can cause us problems. Other people often purposefully create perceptions and misperceptions. An advertiser who wants to sell a product may try to create the impression that our lives will be changed if we use it. Or a person who wants to discredit someone else may spread untrue rumors about her.

DEVELOP AWARENESS

The only way to correct the mistakes, distortions, and incompleteness of our perceptions is to become aware of the ordinarily unconscious process by which we perceive and make sense of the world. By doing so, we will be able to think critically about what is going on and to correct our mistakes and distortions. In other words, we can use our critical thinking abilities to create a clearer and more informed idea of what is taking place. We cannot rely on the validity of our perceptions alone. If we remain unaware of how our process of perceiving operates and of our active role in it, we will be unable to control it. We will be convinced that the way we see the world is the way the world is, even when our perceptions are mistaken, distorted, or incomplete.

Besides asking questions, we have to become aware of the personal perspectives that we bring to our perceptions. Each of us brings to every situation a whole collection of expectations, interests, fears, and hopes that can influence what we are perceiving.

Consider the following situations:

- You've been fishing all day without a nibble. Suddenly you get a strike! You reel the fish in, but just as you're about to pull it into the boat, it frees itself from the hook and swims away. When you get home later, your friends ask you, "How large was the fish that got away?"

- Your teacher asks you to evaluate the performance of a classmate who is giving a report to the class. You don't like this other student because he acts as if he's superior to everyone else in the class. How do you evaluate his report?

- You are asked to estimate the size of an audience attending an event that your organization has sponsored. How many people are there?

In each of these cases, your perceptions might be influenced by whatever hopes, fears, or prejudices you brought to the situation, causing your observations to be distorted or inaccurate. Although you usually cannot eliminate the personal feelings that influence your perceptions, you can become aware of these feelings and try to control them.

GET INPUT FROM OTHERS

The first step in critically examining your perceptions is to be willing to ask questions about them. As long as you believe that the way you see things is the only way to see them, you will not be able to recognize when your perceptions are distorted or inaccurate.

For instance, if you believe that your interpretation of the twins shown in the photo in the Thinking-Writing Activity on page 213 is the only correct one, you will probably not consider other interpretations. But if you are willing to entertain other possible interpretations, you will open the way to more fully developing your perception of what is taking place.

As noted in Chapter 7, critical thinkers strive to see things from different perspectives. One of the best ways to do so is by communicating with others. This means exchanging and critically examining ideas in an open and organized way. Engaging in dialogue is one of the main ways to check your perceptions—

by asking others what their perceptions are and comparing and contrasting them with yours.

This is exactly what you did when you discussed the various possible interpretations of the twins in the photo. By comparing your perceptions with those of your classmates, you developed a more complete sense of how differently events can be viewed as well as an appreciation of the reasons supporting the different perspectives.

FIND EVIDENCE

Also, you should try to discover independent proof or evidence regarding your perceptions. You can evaluate the accuracy of your perceptions when evidence is available in the form of records, photographs, videotapes, or the results of experiments. What independent forms of evidence could verify your perceptions about the twins?

KEEP AN OPEN MIND

Thinking critically about perceptions means trying to avoid developing impulsive or superficial ones that you are unwilling to change. As explained in Chapter 3, a critical thinker is *thoughtful* in approaching the world and open to modifying his or her views in light of new information or better insights. Consider the following perceptions:

- Women are very emotional.
- Politicians are corrupt.
- Teenagers are wild and irresponsible.
- People who are good athletes are usually poor students.
- Men are thoughtless and insensitive.

These types of general perceptions are known as *stereotypes* because they express a belief about an entire group of people without recognizing the individual differences among members of the group.

For instance, it is probably accurate to say that there are some politicians who are corrupt, but this is not the same as saying that all, or even most, politicians are corrupt. Stereotypes affect our perceptions of the world because they encourage us to form inaccurate and superficial ideas about a whole group of people ("Teenagers are reckless drivers"). When we meet someone who falls into this group, we automatically perceive that person as possessing a stereotyped quality ("This person is a teenager, so he is a reckless driver"). Even if we find that the person does not fit our stereotyped perception ("This teenager is not a reckless driver"), this sort of superficial and thoughtless labeling does not encourage us to change our perceptions of the group as a whole. Instead, it encourages us to overlook the conflicting information in favor of our stereotyped perceptions ("All teenagers are reckless drivers—except this one"). In contrast, when we are perceiving in a thoughtful fashion, we try to see what a person is like as an individual instead of trying to fit him or her into a pre-existing category.

Sometimes stereotypes are so built into a culture that it is difficult for a person to be aware of them until they are brought to his or her attention. The perspective, or view of the world, that the culture presents may not even acknowledge the possibility of other perspectives, so it can be very difficult for an individual to become aware of them and then to "switch lenses" to try to see a situation from those viewpoints.

True critical thinkers can and do switch lenses, and in their writing they help others to do so as well. The following two readings present varying perspectives on Native Americans. One was written by a famous eighteenth-century American; the other was written in the early twentieth century by a member of the Sioux nation. As you read these accounts, think about what factors probably contributed to the writers' perspectives.

Remarks Concerning the Savages of North America

BY BENJAMIN FRANKLIN (1706–1790)

Perhaps no other figure so captures the American imagination—or the America as once imagined—as Benjamin Franklin. Born into a family of Boston soapmakers, Franklin became a printer's apprentice to his brother, James, at the age of twelve. As brothers tend to do, Benjamin and James quarreled repeatedly; in 1723, Benjamin ran away to Philadelphia. Very young, very poor, and with the stigma of having run away both from his professional and his family obligations, Franklin was very fortunate to find work again in Philadelphia as a printer's apprentice. After several difficult years of hard work, including a stint in England, Franklin was established enough in his own printing business to marry Deborah Read in 1730. He began publishing and contributing to a newspaper, the Pennsylvania Gazette, *and in 1733 he started publishing* Poor Richard's Almanack.

Franklin used his prominent position as a businessman and journalist to undertake civic initiatives that are still cornerstones of American communities. Franklin helped to establish the first free lending library, the first public hospital, and the first organized firefighting company in America. Politically, Franklin was elected to the Second Continental Congress in 1775 and helped to draft the Declaration of Independence. In 1776 Franklin was appointed the ambassador to the Court of Louis XVI for the American colonies. His diplomatic savvy helped to secure French support for the colonies during the American Revolution. Franklin died at the age of eighty-four, back home in Philadelphia. His funeral was attended by 20,000 people.

In the following essay, excerpted from a longer work published in 1784, Franklin uses the term "savages" ironically. His admiration and respect for Native Americans is rooted in the diplomatic relationships he established with the Iroquois Nation in the

1760s.When, in 1763, a vigilante army of white settlers massacred a settlement of Conestoga Iroquois—including women and children—Franklin responded by mustering an army of Quakers and other citizens, including Governor Penn himself. The action probably saved more than one hundred Conestoga lives.

Savages we call them, because their Manners differ from ours, which we think the Perfection of Civility; they think the same of theirs.

Perhaps, if we could examine the Manners of different Nations with Impartiality, we should find no People so rude, as to be without any Rules of Politeness; nor any so polite, as not to have some Remains of Rudeness.

The Indian Men, when young, are Hunters and Warriors; when old, Counsellors; for all their Government is by Counsel of the Sages; there is no Force, there are no Prisons, no Officers to compel Obedience, or inflict Punishment. Hence they generally study Oratory, the best Speaker having the most Influence. The Indian Women till the Ground, dress the Food, nurse and bring up the Children, and preserve and hand down to Posterity the Memory of public Transactions. These Employments of Men and Women are accounted natural and honourable. Having few artificial Wants, they have abundance of Leisure for Improvement by Conversation. Our laborious Manner of Life, compared with theirs, they esteem slavish and base; and the Learning, on which we value ourselves, they regard as frivolous and useless. An Instance of this occurred at the Treaty of Lancaster, in Pennsylvania, *anno* 1744, between the Government of Virginia and the Six Nations. After the principal Business was settled, the Commissioners from Virginia acquainted the Indians by a Speech, that there was at Williamsburg a College, with a Fund for Educating Indian youth; and that, if the Six Nations would send down half a dozen of their young Lads to that College, the Government would take care that they should be well provided for, and instructed in all the Learning of the White People. It is one of the Indian Rules of Politeness not to answer a public Proposition the same day that it is made; they think it would be treating it as a light matter, and that they show it Respect by taking time to consider it, as of a Matter important. They therefore deferr'd their Answer till the Day following; when their Speaker began, by expressing their deep Sense of the kindness of the Virginia Government, in making them that Offer; "for we know," says he, "that you highly esteem the kind of Learning taught in those Colleges, and that the Maintenance of our young Men, while with you, would be very expensive to you. We are convinc'd, therefore, that you mean to do us Good by your Proposal; and we thank you heartily. But you, who are wise, must know that different Nations have different Conceptions of things; and you will therefore not take it amiss, if our Ideas of this kind of Education happen not to be the same with yours. We have had some Experience of it; Several of our young People were formerly brought up at the Colleges of the Northern Provinces; they were instructed in all your Sciences; but, when they came back to us, they were bad Runners, ignorant of every means of living in the Woods, unable to bear either Cold or Hunger, knew neither how to build a Cabin, take a Deer, or kill an Enemy, spoke our Language imperfectly, were therefore neither fit for Hunters, Warriors, nor Counsellors; they were totally good for nothing. We are however not the less oblig'd by your kind Offer, tho' we decline accepting it; and, to show our grateful Sense of it, if the Gentlemen of Virginia will send us a Dozen of their Sons, we will take great Care of their Education, instruct them in all we know, and make *Men* of them."

Having frequent Occasions to hold public Councils, they have acquired great Order and Decency in conducting them. The old Men sit in the foremost Ranks, the Warriors in the next, and the Women and Children in the hindmost. The Business of the Women is to take exact Notice of what passes, imprint it in their Memories (for they have no Writing), and communicate it to their Children. They are the Records of the Council, and they preserve Traditions of the Stipulations in Treaties 100 Years back; which, when we compare with our Writings, we always find exact. He that would speak, rises. The rest observe a profound Silence. When he has finish'd and sits down, they leave him 5 to 6 Minutes to recollect, that, if he has omitted anything he intended to say, or has anything to add, he may rise again and deliver it. To interrupt another, even in common Conversation, is reckon'd highly indecent. How different this is from the conduct of a polite British House of Commons, where scarce a day passes without some Confusion, that makes the Speaker hoarse in calling *to Order*; and how different from the Mode of Conversation in many polite Companies of Europe, where, if you do not deliver your Sentence with great Rapidity, you are cut off in the middle of it by the Impatient Loquacity of those you converse with, and never suffer'd to finish it!

5   The Politeness of these Savages in Conversation is indeed carried to Excess, since it does not permit them to contradict or deny the Truth of what is asserted in their Presence. By this means they indeed avoid Disputes; but then it becomes difficult to know their Minds, or what Impression you make upon them. The Missionaries who have attempted to convert them to Christianity, all complain of this as one of the great Difficulties of their Mission. The Indians hear with Patience the Truths of the Gospel explain'd to them, and give their usual Tokens of Assent and Approbation; you would think they were convinc'd. No such matter. It is mere Civility.

A Swedish Minister, having assembled the chiefs of the Susquehanah Indians, made a Sermon to them, acquainting them with the principal historical Facts on which our Religion is founded; such as the Fall of our first Parents by eating an Apple, the coming of Christ to repair the Mischief, his Miracles and Suffering, &c. When he had finished, an Indian Orator stood up to thank him. "What you have told us," says he, "is all very good. It is indeed bad to eat Apples. It is better to make them all into Cyder. We are much oblig'd by your kindness in coming so far, to tell us these Things which you have heard from your Mothers. In return, I will tell you some of those we had heard from ours. In the Beginning, our Fathers had only the Flesh of Animals to subsist on; and if their Hunting was unsuccessful, they were starving. Two of our young Hunters, having kill'd a Deer, made a Fire in the Woods to broil some Part of it. When they were about to satisfy their Hunger, they beheld a beautiful young Woman descend from the Clouds, and seat herself on that Hill, which you see yonder among the blue Mountains. They said to each other, it is a Spirit that has smelt our broiling Venison, and wishes to eat of it; let us offer some to her. They presented her with the Tongue; she was pleas'd with the Taste of it, and said, 'Your kindness shall be rewarded; come to this Place after thirteen Moons, and you shall find something that will be of great Benefit in nourishing you and your Children to the latest Generations.' They did so, and, to their Surprise, found Plants they had never seen before; but which, from that ancient time, have been constantly cultivated among us, to our great Advantage. Where her right Hand had touched the Ground, they found Maize; where her left hand had touch'd it, they found Kidney-Beans; and where her Backside had sat on it, they found Tobacco." The good Missionary, disgusted with this idle Tale, said, "What I delivered to you were sacred Truths; but what you tell me is mere Fable, Fiction, and Falshood." The Indian, offended, reply'd, "My brother, it seems your Friends have not done you Justice in your Education; they have not well instructed you in the Rules of common Civility. You saw that we, who understand and practise those Rules, believ'd all your stories; why do you refuse to believe ours?"

When any of them come into our Towns, our People are apt to crowd round them, gaze upon them, and incommode them, where they desire to be private; this they esteem great Rudeness, and the Effect of the Want of Instruction in the Rules of Civility and good Manners. "We have," say they, "as much Curiosity as you, and when you come into our Towns, we wish for Opportunities of looking at you; but for this purpose we hide ourselves behind Bushes, where you are to pass, and never intrude ourselves into your Company."

Their Manner of entering one another's village has likewise its Rules. It is reckon'd uncivil in travelling Strangers to enter a Village abruptly, without giving Notice of their Approach. Therefore, as soon as they arrive within hearing, they stop and hollow, remaining there till invited to enter. Two old Men usually come out to them, and lead them in. There is in every Village a vacant Dwelling, called *the Strangers' House*. Here they are plac'd, while the old Men go round from Hut to Hut, acquainting the Inhabitants, that Strangers are arriv'd, who are probably hungry and weary; and every one sends them what he can spare of Victuals, and Skins to repose on. When the Strangers are refresh'd, Pipes and Tobacco are brought; and then, but not before, Conversation begins, with Enquiries who they are, whither bound, what News, &c.; and it usually ends with offers of Service, if the Strangers have occasion of Guides, or any Necessaries for continuing their Journey; and nothing is exacted for the Entertainment.

The same Hospitality, esteem'd among them as a principal Virtue, is practis'd by private Persons; of which Conrad Weiser, our Interpreter, gave me the following Instance. He had been naturaliz'd among the Six Nations, and spoke well the Mohock Language. In going thro' the Indian Country, to carry a Message from our Governor to the Council at Onondaga, he call'd at the Habitation of Canassatego, an old Acquaintance, who embrac'd him, spread Furs for him to sit on, plac'd before him some boil'd Beans and Venison, and mix'd some

Rum and Water for his Drink. When he was well refresh'd, and had lit his Pipe, Canassatego began to converse with him; ask'd how he had far'd the many Years since they had seen each other; whence he then came; what occasion'd the Journey, &c. Conrad answered all his Questions; and when the Discourse began to flag, the Indian, to continue it, said, "Conrad, you have lived long among the white People, and know something of their Customs; I have been sometimes at Albany, and have observed, that once in Seven Days they shut up their Shops, and assemble all in the great House; tell me what it is for? What do they do there?" "They meet there," says Conrad, "to hear and learn *good Things.*" "I do not doubt," says the Indian, "that they tell you so; they have told me the same; but I doubt the Truth of what they say, and I will tell you my Reasons. I went lately to Albany to sell my Skins and buy Blankets, Knives, Powder, Rum, &c. You know I us'd generally to deal with Hans Hanson; but I was a little inclin'd this time to try some other Merchant. However, I call'd first upon Hans, and asked him what he would give for Beaver. He said he could not give any more than four Shillings a Pound; 'but,' says he, 'I cannot talk on Business now; this is the Day when we meet together to learn *Good Things,* and I am going to the Meeting.' So I thought to myself, 'Since we cannot do any Business to-day, I may as well go to the meeting too,' and I went with him. There stood up a Man in Black, and began to talk to the People very angrily. I did not understand what he said; but, perceiving that he look'd much at me and at Hanson, I imagin'd he was angry at seeing me there; so I went out, sat down near the House, struck Fire, and lit my Pipe, waiting till the Meeting should break up. I thought too, that the Man had mention'd something of Beaver, and I suspected it might be the Subject of their Meeting. So, when they came out, I accosted my Merchant. 'Well, Hans,' says I, 'I hope you have agreed to give more than four Shillings a Pound.' 'No,' says he, 'I cannot give so much; I cannot give more than three shillings and sixpence.' I then spoke to several other Dealers, but they all sung the same song,—Three and sixpence,—Three and sixpence. This made it clear to me, that my Suspicion was right; and, that whatever they pretended of meeting to learn *good Things,* the real purpose was to consult how to cheat Indians in the Price of Beaver. Consider but little, Conrad, and you must be of my Opinion. If they met so often to learn *good Things,* they would certainly have learnt some before this time. But they are still ignorant. You know our Practice. If a white Man, in travelling thro' our Country, enters one of our Cabins, we all treat him as I treat you; we dry him if he is wet, we warm him if he is cold, we give him Meat and Drink, that he may allay his Thirst and Hunger; and we spread soft Furs for him to rest and sleep on; we demand nothing in return. But, if I go into a white Man's House at Albany, and ask for Victuals and Drink, they say, 'Where is your Money?' and if I have none, they say, 'Get out, you Indian Dog.' You see they have not yet learned those little *Good Things,* that we need no Meetings to be instructed in, because our Mothers taught them to us when we were Children; and therefore it is impossible their Meetings should be, as they say, for any such purpose, or have any such Effect; they are only to contrive *the Cheating of Indians in the Price of Beaver.*"

Questions for Active Reading

1. What is Franklin's definition of "savage"? This term has long since ceased to be appropriate when used to refer to indigenous peoples; do you think that Franklin, writing two hundred years ago, was also aware of how inappropriate this term could be? Explain your answer with reference to Franklin's own examples and argument.

2. What two ideals is Franklin comparing in this essay? How does he use comparison to structure this essay?

3. Franklin was widely known for his wit, of which there is a sly example in paragraph 6. Identify the joke. Why does Franklin include it? Is he simply being sarcastic, or is he making a much larger and subtler comparison of perspectives?

Questions for Thinking Critically

1. What does Franklin mean when he says, "Perhaps, if we could examine the Manners of different Nations with Impartiality, we should find no People so rude, as to be without any Rules of Politeness; nor any so polite, as not to have some Remains of Rudeness"?

2. What does the Iroquois speaker mean when he says, "If the Gentlemen of Virginia will send us a Dozen of their Sons, we will take great Care of their Education, instruct them in all we know, and make *Men* of them"?

3. In paragraph 9, Franklin recounts the experience of the Iroquois elder Canassatego when he went to a "great House" to "hear and learn *good Things*." Why does Franklin use Canassatego's exact language, rather than explaining or translating his perspective for his English-speaking colonial audience? What is the tremendous irony that Canassatego's perspective gives to the concept of *"good Things"*?

The School Days of an Indian Girl

BY ZITKALA-SA (GERTRUDE SIMMONS BONNIN) (1876–1938)

A member of the Yankton Sioux nation, Zitkala-Sa was born on the Pine Ridge Reservation in South Dakota and raised in a traditional tipi on the Missouri River. At the end of the nineteenth and beginning of the twentieth centuries, many surviving Native American nations were forced from their traditional lands onto "reservations," lands managed by the American government. Children on these reservations were forced to sacrifice their native languages, cultures, and traditions, often sent away from their families to religious or secular boarding schools. In the following autobiographical essay,

Zitkala-Sa recounts her time spent at a Quaker boarding school for Native American children in Wabash, Indiana. The experience left her feeling divided between identities and cultures, a division that galvanized her into pursuing further education and devoting her life to justice for Native Americans. She graduated from Earlham College with plans to become a teacher, and her musical talents brought her to the Boston Conservatory. In 1900 she went to Paris with the Carlisle Indian Industrial School (CIIS) as violin soloist for the Paris Exposition. But the loss and destruction of her own culture haunted her, and led to her first book, the 1901 collection Old Indian Legends.*

Zitkala-Sa became increasingly active politically, along with her husband, Ray Bonnin of the Sioux nation. She worked to increase voter participation by Native Americans, and in 1930, she formed the National Council of American Indians, where she served as president until her death in 1938.*

The Land of Red Apples

There were eight in our party of bronzed children who were going East with the missionaries. Among us were three young braves, two tall girls, and we three little ones, Judewin, Thowin, and I.

We had been very impatient to start on our journey to the Red Apple Country, which, we were told, lay a little beyond the great circular horizon of the Western prairie. Under a sky of rosy apples we dreamt of roaming as freely and happily as we had chased the cloud shadows on the Dakota plains. We had anticipated much pleasure from a ride on the iron horse, but the throngs of staring palefaces disturbed and troubled us.

On the train, fair women, with tottering babies on each arm, stopped their haste and scrutinized the children of absent mothers. Large men, with heavy bundles in their hands, halted near by, and riveted their glassy blue eyes upon us.

I sank deep into the corner of my seat, for I resented being watched. Directly in front of me, children who were no larger than I hung themselves upon the backs of their seats, with their bold white faces toward me. Sometimes they took their forefingers out of their mouths and pointed at my moccasined feet. Their mothers, instead of reproving such rude curiosity, looked closely at me, and attracted their children's further notice to my blanket. This embarrassed me, and kept me constantly on the verge of tears.

5   I sat perfectly still, with my eyes downcast, daring only now and then to shoot long glances around me. Chancing to turn to the window at my side, I was quite breathless upon seeing one familiar object. It was the telegraph pole which strode by at short paces. Very near my mother's dwelling, along the edge of a road thickly bordered with wild sunflowers, some poles like these had been planted by white men. Often I had stopped, on my way down the road, to hold my ear against the pole, and, hearing its low moaning, I used to wonder what the paleface had done to hurt it. Now I sat watching for each pole that glided by to be the last one.

In this way I had forgotten my uncomfortable surroundings, when I heard one of my comrades call out my name. I saw the missionary standing very near, tossing candies and gums into our midst. This amused us all, and we tried to see who could catch the most of the sweetmeats. The missionary's generous distribution of candies was impressed upon my memory by a disastrous result which followed. I had caught more than my share of candies and gums, and soon after our arrival at the school I had a chance to disgrace myself, which, I am ashamed to say, I did.

Though we rode several days inside of the iron horse, I do not recall a single thing about our luncheons.

It was night when we reached the school grounds. The lights from the windows of the large buildings fell upon some of the icicled trees that stood beneath them. We were led toward an open door, where the brightness of the lights within flooded out over the heads of the excited palefaces who blocked the way. My body trembled more from fear than from the snow I trod upon.

Entering the house, I stood close against the wall. The strong glaring light in the large whitewashed room dazzled my eyes. The noisy hurrying of hard shoes upon a bare wooden floor increased the whirring in my ears. My only safety seemed to be in keeping next to the wall. As I was wondering in which direction to escape from all this confusion, two warm hands grasped me firmly, and in the same moment I was tossed high in midair. A rosy-cheeked paleface woman caught me in her arms. I was both frightened and insulted by such trifling. I stared into her eyes, wishing her to let me stand on my own feet, but she jumped me up and down with increasing enthusiasm. My mother had never made a plaything of her wee daughter. Remembering this I began to cry aloud.

10 They misunderstood the cause of my tears, and placed me at a white table loaded with food. There our party were united again. As I did not hush my crying, one of the older ones whispered to me, "Wait until you are alone in the night."

It was very little I could swallow besides my sobs, that evening.

"Oh, I want my mother and my brother Dawee! I want to go to my aunt!" I pleaded; but the ears of the palefaces could not hear me.

From the table we were taken along an upward incline of wooden boxes, which I learned afterward to call a stairway. At the top was a quiet hall, dimly lighted. Many narrow beds were in one straight line down the entire length of the wall. In them lay sleeping brown faces, which peeped just out of the coverings. I was tucked into bed with one of the tall girls, because she talked to me in my mother tongue and seemed to soothe me.

I had arrived in the wonderful land of rosy skies, but I was not happy, as I had thought I should be. My long travel and the bewildering sights had exhausted me. I fell asleep, heaving deep, tired sobs. My tears were left to dry themselves in streaks, because neither my aunt nor my mother was near to wipe them away.

The Cutting of My Long Hair

15 The first day in the land of apples was a bitter-cold one; for the snow still covered the ground, and the trees were bare. A large bell rang for breakfast, its loud

metallic voice crashing through the belfry overhead and into our sensitive ears. The annoying clatter of shoes on bare floors gave us no peace. The constant clash of harsh noises, with an undercurrent of many voices murmuring an unknown tongue, made a bedlam within which I was securely tied. And though my spirit tore itself in struggling for its lost freedom, all was useless.

A paleface woman, with white hair, came up after us. We were placed in a line of girls who were marching into the dining room. These were Indian girls, in stiff shoes and closely clinging dresses. The small girls wore sleeved aprons and shingled hair. As I walked noiselessly in my soft moccasins, I felt like sinking to the floor, for my blanket had been stripped from my shoulders. I looked hard at the Indian girls, who seemed not to care that they were even more immodestly dressed than I, in their tightly fitting clothes. While we marched in, the boys entered at an opposite door. I watched for the three young braves who came in our party. I spied them in the rear ranks, looking as uncomfortable as I felt.

A small bell was tapped, and each of the pupils drew a chair from under the table. Supposing this act meant they were to be seated, I pulled out mine and at once slipped into it from one side. But when I turned my head, I saw that I was the only one seated, and all the rest at our table remained standing. Just as I began to rise, looking shyly around to see how chairs were to be used, a second bell was sounded. All were seated at last, and I had to crawl back into my chair again. I heard a man's voice at one end of the hall, and I looked around to see him. But all the others hung their heads over their plates. As I glanced at the long chain of tables, I caught the eyes of a paleface woman upon me. Immediately I dropped my eyes, wondering why I was so keenly watched by the strange woman. The man ceased his mutterings, and then a third bell was tapped. Every one picked up his knife and fork and began eating. I began crying instead, for by this time I was afraid to venture anything more.

But this eating by formula was not the hardest trial in that first day. Late in the morning, my friend Judewin gave me a terrible warning. Judewin knew a few words of English, and she had overheard the paleface woman talk about cutting our long, heavy hair. Our mothers had taught us that only unskilled warriors who were captured had their hair shingled by the enemy. Among our people, short hair was worn by mourners, and shingled hair by cowards!

We discussed our fate some moments, and when Judewin said, "We have to submit, because they are strong," I rebelled.

20

"No, I will not submit! I will struggle first!" I answered.

I watched my chance, and when no one noticed I disappeared. I crept up the stairs as quietly as I could in my squeaking shoes,—my moccasins had been exchanged for shoes. Along the hall I passed, without knowing whither I was going. Turning aside to an open door, I found a large room with three white beds in it. The windows were covered with dark green curtains, which made the room very dim. Thankful that no one was there, I directed my steps toward the corner farthest from the door. On my hands and knees I crawled under the bed, and cuddled myself in the dark corner.

From my hiding place I peered out, shuddering with fear whenever I heard footsteps near by. Though in the hall loud voices were calling my name, and I knew that even Judewin was searching for me, I did not open my mouth to answer. Then the steps were quickened and the voices became excited. The sounds came nearer and nearer. Women and girls entered the room. I held my breath, and watched them open closet doors and peep behind large trunks. Some one threw up the curtains, and the room was filled with sudden light. What caused them to stoop and look under the bed I do not know. I remember being dragged out, though I resisted by kicking and scratching wildly. In spite of myself, I was carried downstairs and tied fast in a chair.

I cried aloud, shaking my head all the while until I felt the cold blades of the scissors against my neck, and heard them gnaw off one of my thick braids. Then I lost my spirit. Since the day I was taken from my mother I had suffered extreme indignities. People had stared at me. I had been tossed about in the air like a wooden puppet. And now my long hair was shingled like a coward's! In my anguish I moaned for my mother, but no one came to comfort me. Not a soul reasoned quietly with me, as my own mother used to do; for now I was only one of many little animals driven by a herder.

The Snow Episode

A short time after our arrival we three Dakotas were playing in the snowdrifts. We were all still deaf to the English language, excepting Judewin, who always heard such puzzling things. One morning we learned through her ears that we were forbidden to fall lengthwise in the snow, as we had been doing, to see our own impressions. However, before many hours we had forgotten the order, and were having great sport in the snow, when a shrill voice called us. Looking up, we saw an imperative hand beckoning us into the house. We shook the snow off ourselves, and started toward the woman as slowly as we dared.

25   Judewin said: "Now the paleface is angry with us. She is going to punish us for falling into the snow. If she looks straight into your eyes and talks loudly, you must wait until she stops. Then, after a tiny pause, say, 'No.'" The rest of the way we practiced upon the little word "no."

As it happened, Thowin was summoned to judgment first. The door shut behind her with a click.

Judewin and I stood silently listening at the keyhole. The paleface woman talked in very severe tones. Her words fell from her lips like crackling embers, and her inflection ran up like the small end of a switch. I understood her voice better than the things she was saying. I was certain we had made her very impatient with us. Judewin heard enough of the words to realize all too late that she had taught us the wrong reply.

"Oh, poor Thowin!" she gasped, as she put both hands over her ears.

Just then I heard Thowin's tremulous answer, "No."

30   With an angry exclamation, the woman gave her a hard spanking. Then she stopped to say something. Judewin said it was this: "Are you going to obey my word the next time?"

Thowin answered again with the only word at her command, "No."

This time the woman meant her blows to smart, for the poor frightened girl shrieked at the top of her voice. In the midst of the whipping the blows ceased abruptly, and the woman asked another question: "Are you going to fall in the snow again?"

Thowin gave her bad password another trial. We heard her say feebly, "No! No!"

With this the woman hid away her half-worn slipper, and led the child out, stroking her black shorn head. Perhaps it occurred to her that brute force is not the solution for such a problem. She did nothing to Judewin nor to me. She only returned to us our unhappy comrade, and left us alone in the room.

35   During the first two or three seasons misunderstandings as ridiculous as this one of the snow episode frequently took place, bringing unjustifiable frights and punishments into our little lives.

Within a year I was able to express myself somewhat in broken English. As soon as I comprehended a part of what was said and done, a mischievous spirit of revenge possessed me. One day I was called in from my play for some misconduct. I had disregarded a rule which seemed to me very needlessly binding. I was sent into the kitchen to mash the turnips for dinner. It was noon, and steaming dishes were hastily carried into the dining room. I hated turnips, and their odor which came from the brown jar was offensive to me. With fire in my heart, I took the wooden tool that the paleface woman held out to me. I stood upon a step, and, grasping the handle with both hands, I bent in hot rage over the turnips. I worked my vengeance upon them. All were so busily occupied that no one noticed me. I saw that the turnips were in a pulp, and that further beating could not improve them; but the order was, "Mash these turnips," and mash them I would! I renewed my energy; and as I sent the masher into the bottom of the jar, I felt a satisfying sensation that the weight of my body had gone into it.

Just here a paleface woman came up to my table. As she looked into the jar she shoved my hands roughly aside. I stood fearless and angry. She placed her red hands upon the rim of the jar. Then she gave one lift and a stride away from the table. But lo! the pulpy contents fell through the crumbled bottom to the floor! She spared me no scolding phrases that I had earned. I did not heed them. I felt triumphant in my revenge, though deep within me I was a wee bit sorry to have broken the jar.

As I sat eating my dinner, and saw that no turnips were served, I whooped in my heart for having once asserted the rebellion within me.

The Devil

Among the legends the old warriors used to tell me were many stories of evil spirits. But I was taught to fear them no more than those who stalked about in material guise. I never knew there was an insolent chieftain among the bad spirits, who dared to array his forces against the Great Spirit, until I heard this white man's legend from a paleface woman.

40   Out of a large book she showed me a picture of the white man's devil. I looked in horror upon the strong claws that grew out of his fur-covered fingers. His feet were like his hands. Trailing at his heels was a scaly tail tipped with a serpent's open jaws. His face was a patchwork: he had bearded cheeks, like some I had seen palefaces wear; his nose was an eagle's bill, and his sharp-pointed ears were pricked up like those of a sly fox. Above them a pair of cow's horns curved upward. I trembled with awe, and my heart throbbed in my throat, as I looked at the king of evil spirits. Then I heard the paleface woman say that this terrible creature roamed loose in the world, and that little girls who disobeyed school regulations were to be tortured by him.

That night I dreamt about this evil divinity. Once again I seemed to be in my mother's cottage. An Indian woman had come to visit my mother. On opposite sides of the kitchen stove, which stood in the centre of the small house, my mother and her guest were seated in straight-backed chairs. I played with a train of empty spools hitched together on a string. It was night, and the wick burned feebly. Suddenly I heard some one turn our door-knob from without.

My mother and the woman hushed their talk, and both looked toward the door. It opened gradually. I waited behind the stove. The hinges squeaked as the door was slowly, very slowly pushed inward.

Then in rushed the devil! He was tall! He looked exactly like the picture I had seen of him in the white man's papers. He did not speak to my mother, because he did not know the Indian language, but his glittering yellow eyes were fastened upon me. He took long strides around the stove, passing behind the woman's chair. I threw down my spools, and ran to my mother. He did not fear her, but followed closely after me. Then I ran round and round the stove, crying aloud for help. But my mother and the woman seemed not to know my danger. They sat still, looking quietly upon the devil's chase after me. At last I grew dizzy. My head revolved as on a hidden pivot. My knees became numb, and doubled under my weight like a pair of knife blades without a spring. Beside my mother's chair I fell in a heap. Just as the devil stooped over me with outstretched claws my mother awoke from her quiet indifference, and lifted me on her lap. Whereupon the devil vanished, and I was awake.

On the following morning I took my revenge upon the devil. Stealing into the room where a wall of shelves was filled with books, I drew forth The Stories of the Bible. With a broken slate pencil I carried in my apron pocket, I began by scratching out his wicked eyes. A few moments later, when I was ready to leave the room, there was a ragged hole in the page where the picture of the devil had once been.

Iron Routine

45   A loud-clamoring bell awakened us at half past six in the cold winter mornings. From happy dreams of Western rolling lands and unlassoed freedom we tumbled out upon chilly bare floors back again into a paleface day. We had short time to jump into our shoes and clothes, and wet our eyes with icy water, before a small hand bell was vigorously rung for roll call.

There were too many drowsy children and too numerous orders for the day to waste a moment in any apology to nature for giving her children such a shock in the early morning. We rushed downstairs, bounding over two high steps at a time, to land in the assembly room.

A paleface woman, with a yellow-covered roll book open on her arm and a gnawed pencil in her hand, appeared at the door. Her small, tired face was coldly lighted with a pair of large gray eyes.

She stood still in a halo of authority, while over the rim of her spectacles her eyes pried nervously about the room. Having glanced at her long list of names and called out the first one, she tossed up her chin and peered through the crystals of her spectacles to make sure of the answer "Here."

Relentlessly her pencil black-marked our daily records if we were not present to respond to our names, and no chum of ours had done it successfully for us. No matter if a dull headache or the painful cough of slow consumption had delayed the absentee, there was only time enough to mark the tardiness. It was next to impossible to leave the iron routine after the civilizing machine had once begun its day's buzzing; and as it was inbred in me to suffer in silence rather than to appeal to the ears of one whose open eyes could not see my pain, I have many times trudged in the day's harness heavy-footed, like a dumb sick brute.

50   Once I lost a dear classmate. I remember well how she used to mope along at my side, until one morning she could not raise her head from her pillow. At her deathbed I stood weeping, as the paleface woman sat near her moistening the dry lips. Among the folds of the bedclothes I saw the open pages of the white man's Bible. The dying Indian girl talked disconnectedly of Jesus the Christ and the paleface who was cooling her swollen hands and feet.

I grew bitter, and censured the woman for cruel neglect of our physical ills. I despised the pencils that moved automatically, and the one teaspoon which dealt out, from a large bottle, healing to a row of variously ailing Indian children. I blamed the hard-working, well-meaning, ignorant woman who was inculcating in our hearts her superstitious ideas. Though I was sullen in all my little troubles, as soon as I felt better I was ready again to smile upon the cruel woman. Within a week I was again actively testing the chains which tightly bound my individuality like a mummy for burial.

The melancholy of those black days has left so long a shadow that it darkens the path of years that have since gone by. These sad memories rise above those of smoothly grinding school days. Perhaps my Indian nature is the moaning wind which stirs them now for their present record. But, however tempestuous this is within me, it comes out as the low voice of a curiously colored seashell, which is only for those ears that are bent with compassion to hear it.

Four Strange Summers

After my first three years of school, I roamed again in the Western country through four strange summers.

During this time I seemed to hang in the heart of chaos, beyond the touch or voice of human aid. My brother, being almost ten years my senior, did not quite understand my feelings. My mother had never gone inside of a schoolhouse, and so she was not capable of comforting her daughter who could read and write. Even nature seemed to have no place for me. I was neither a wee girl nor a tall one; neither a wild Indian nor a tame one. This deplorable situation was the effect of my brief course in the East, and the unsatisfactory "teenth" in a girl's years.

55   It was under these trying conditions that, one bright afternoon, as I sat restless and unhappy in my brother's cabin, I caught the sound of the spirited step of my brother's pony on the road which passed by our dwelling. Soon I heard the wheels of a light buckboard, and Dawee's familiar "Ho!" to his pony. He alighted upon the bare ground in front of our house. Tying his pony to one of the projecting corner logs of the low-roofed cottage, he stepped upon the wooden doorstep.

I met him there with a hurried greeting, and as I passed by, he looked a quiet "What?" into my eyes.

When he began talking with my mother, I slipped the rope from the pony's bridle. Seizing the reins and bracing my feet against the dashboard, I wheeled around in an instant. The pony was ever ready to try his speed. Looking backward, I saw Dawee waving his hand to me. I turned with the curve in the road and disappeared. I followed the winding road which crawled upward between the bases of little hillocks. Deep water-worn ditches ran parallel on either side. A strong wind blew against my cheeks and fluttered my sleeves. The pony reached the top of the highest hill, and began an even race on the level lands. There was nothing moving within that great circular horizon of the Dakota prairies save the tall grasses, over which the wind blew and rolled off in long, shadowy waves.

Within this vast wigwam of blue and green I rode reckless and insignificant. It satisfied my small consciousness to see the white foam fly from the pony's mouth.

Suddenly, out of the earth a coyote came forth at a swinging trot that was taking the cunning thief toward the hills and the village beyond. Upon the moment's impulse, I gave him a long chase and a wholesome fright. As I turned away to go back to the village, the wolf sank down upon his haunches for rest, for it was a hot summer day; and as I drove slowly homeward, I saw his sharp nose still pointed at me, until I vanished below the margin of the hilltops.

60   In a little while I came in sight of my mother's house. Dawee stood in the yard, laughing at an old warrior who was pointing his forefinger, and again waving his whole hand, toward the hills. With his blanket drawn over one shoulder, he talked and motioned excitedly. Dawee turned the old man by the shoulder and pointed me out to him.

"Oh han!" (Oh yes) the warrior muttered, and went his way. He had climbed the top of his favorite barren hill to survey the surrounding prairies, when he spied my chase after the coyote. His keen eyes recognized the pony and driver. At once uneasy for my safety, he had come running to my mother's cabin to give her warning. I did not appreciate his kindly interest, for there was an unrest gnawing at my heart.

As soon as he went away, I asked Dawee about something else.

"No, my baby sister, I cannot take you with me to the party to-night," he replied. Though I was not far from fifteen, and I felt that before long I should enjoy all the privileges of my tall cousin, Dawee persisted in calling me his baby sister.

That moonlight night, I cried in my mother's presence when I heard the jolly young people pass by our cottage. They were no more young braves in blankets and eagle plumes, nor Indian maids with prettily painted cheeks. They had gone three years to school in the East, and had become civilized. The young men wore the white man's coat and trousers, with bright neckties. The girls wore tight muslin dresses, with ribbons at neck and waist. At these gatherings they talked English. I could speak English almost as well as my brother, but I was not properly dressed to be taken along. I had no hat, no ribbons, and no close-fitting gown. Since my return from school I had thrown away my shoes, and wore again the soft moccasins.

65   While Dawee was busily preparing to go I controlled my tears. But when I heard him bounding away on his pony, I buried my face in my arms and cried hot tears.

My mother was troubled by my unhappiness. Coming to my side, she offered me the only printed matter we had in our home. It was an Indian Bible, given her some years ago by a missionary. She tried to console me. "Here, my child, are the white man's papers. Read a little from them," she said most piously.

I took it from her hand, for her sake; but my enraged spirit felt more like burning the book, which afforded me no help, and was a perfect delusion to my mother. I did not read it, but laid it unopened on the floor, where I sat on my feet. The dim yellow light of the braided muslin burning in a small vessel of oil flickered and sizzled in the awful silent storm which followed my rejection of the Bible.

Now my wrath against the fates consumed my tears before they reached my eyes. I sat stony, with a bowed head. My mother threw a shawl over her head and shoulders, and stepped out into the night.

After an uncertain solitude, I was suddenly aroused by a loud cry piercing the night. It was my mother's voice wailing among the barren hills which held the bones of buried warriors. She called aloud for her brothers' spirits to support her in her helpless misery. My fingers grew icy cold, as I realized that my unrestrained tears had betrayed my suffering to her, and she was grieving for me.

70   Before she returned, though I knew she was on her way, for she had ceased her weeping, I extinguished the light, and leaned my head on the window sill.

Many schemes of running away from my surroundings hovered about in my mind. A few more moons of such a turmoil drove me away to the Eastern school. I rode on the white man's iron steed, thinking it would bring me back to my mother in a few winters, when I should be grown tall, and there would be congenial friends awaiting me.

Incurring My Mother's Displeasure

In the second journey to the East I had not come without some precautions. I had a secret interview with one of our best medicine men, and when I left his wigwam I carried securely in my sleeve a tiny bunch of magic roots. This possession assured me of friends wherever I should go. So absolutely did I believe in its charms that I wore it through all the school routine for more than a year. Then, before I lost my faith in the dead roots, I lost the little buckskin bag containing all my good luck.

At the close of this second term of three years I was the proud owner of my first diploma. The following autumn I ventured upon a college career against my mother's will.

I had written for her approval, but in her reply I found no encouragement. She called my notice to her neighbors' children, who had completed their education in three years. They had returned to their homes, and were then talking English with the frontier settlers. Her few words hinted that I had better give up my slow attempt to learn the white man's ways, and be content to roam over the prairies and find my living upon wild roots. I silenced her by deliberate disobedience.

75   Thus, homeless and heavy-hearted, I began anew my life among strangers.

As I hid myself in my little room in the college dormitory, away from the scornful and yet curious eyes of the students, I pined for sympathy. Often I wept in secret, wishing I had gone West, to be nourished by my mother's love, instead of remaining among a cold race whose hearts were frozen hard with prejudice.

During the fall and winter seasons I scarcely had a real friend, though by that time several of my classmates were courteous to me at a safe distance.

My mother had not yet forgiven my rudeness to her, and I had no moment for letter-writing. By daylight and lamplight, I spun with reeds and thistles, until my hands were tired from their weaving, the magic design which promised me the white man's respect.

At length, in the spring term, I entered an oratorical contest among the various classes. As the day of competition approached, it did not seem possible that the event was so near at hand, but it came. In the chapel the classes assembled together, with their invited guests. The high platform was carpeted, and gayly festooned with college colors. A bright white light illumined the room, and outlined clearly the great polished beams that arched the domed ceiling. The assembled crowds filled the air with pulsating murmurs. When the hour for speaking arrived all were hushed. But on the wall the old clock which pointed out the trying moment ticked calmly on.

80   One after another I saw and heard the orators. Still, I could not realize that they longed for the favorable decision of the judges as much as I did. Each contestant received a loud burst of applause, and some were cheered heartily. Too soon my turn came, and I paused a moment behind the curtains for a deep breath. After my concluding words, I heard the same applause that the others had called out.

Upon my retreating steps, I was astounded to receive from my fellow students a large bouquet of roses tied with flowing ribbons. With the lovely flowers I fled from the stage. This friendly token was a rebuke to me for the hard feelings I had borne them.

Later, the decision of the judges awarded me the first place. Then there was a mad uproar in the hall, where my classmates sang and shouted my name at the top of their lungs; and the disappointed students howled and brayed in fearfully dissonant tin trumpets. In this excitement, happy students rushed forward to offer their congratulations. And I could not conceal a smile when they wished to escort me in a procession to the students' parlor, where all were going to calm themselves. Thanking them for the kind spirit which prompted them to make such a proposition, I walked alone with the night to my own little room.

A few weeks afterward, I appeared as the college representative in another contest. This time the competition was among orators from different colleges in our state. It was held at the state capital, in one of the largest opera houses.

Here again was a strong prejudice against my people. In the evening, as the great audience filled the house, the student bodies began warring among themselves. Fortunately, I was spared witnessing any of the noisy wrangling before the contest began. The slurs against the Indian that stained the lips of our opponents were already burning like a dry fever within my breast.

85   But after the orations were delivered a deeper burn awaited me. There, before that vast ocean of eyes, some college rowdies threw out a large white flag, with a drawing of a most forlorn Indian girl on it. Under this they had printed in bold black letters words that ridiculed the college which was represented by a "squaw." Such worse than barbarian rudeness embittered me. While we waited for the verdict of the judges, I gleamed fiercely upon the throngs of palefaces. My teeth were hard set, as I saw the white flag still floating insolently in the air.

Then anxiously we watched the man carry toward the stage the envelope containing the final decision.

There were two prizes given, that night, and one of them was mine!

The evil spirit laughed within me when the white flag dropped out of sight, and the hands which furled it hung limp in defeat.

Leaving the crowd as quickly as possible, I was soon in my room. The rest of the night I sat in an armchair and gazed into the crackling fire. I laughed no more in triumph when thus alone. The little taste of victory did not satisfy a hunger in my heart. In my mind I saw my mother far away on the Western plains, and she was holding a charge against me.

Questions for Active Reading

1. Zitkala-Sa uses a strikingly apt metaphor in paragraph 23. What is that metaphor? How many different layers of meaning does it have here?

2. Zitkala-Sa recounts her experiences through the perspective of a child. What are the advantages to this perspective in telling her story? What are the disadvantages?

3. Why does Zitkala-Sa include the section "The Devil"? In what other ways do the Bible, or representations of Christianity, figure in her narrative?

1. Compare Zitkala-Sa's experience with the missionary school to the conversation between an Iroquois elder and a group of Virginia politicians who offered to educate six young Iroquois men at a Williamsburg, Virginia, college (the college, William and Mary, is today one of the oldest continuing institutions of higher learning in America). In what ways does Zitkala-Sa's experience reflect the observations of the Iroquois elders, both in terms of the perils of assimilation as well as the rifts created between family members?

2. What is the "evil spirit" that Zitkala-Sa refers to in paragraph 88?

3. Did your education—and think broadly here of "education," not just of "school"—involve the taming or controlling of some part of your spirit or personality? What did you give up, and why? What did that loss teach you, if anything?

Writing Thoughtfully About Perspectives

COMPARISON AND CONTRAST

Whenever we place two or more perspectives, or two or more other things, together and examine them for similarities and differences, we are engaging in the powerful thinking pattern called **comparison and contrast.** To be precise, when we *compare,* we are focusing on likenesses or areas of agreement; when we *contrast,* we are focusing on differences or areas of disagreement. Generally, the items examined are from the same category. We will discuss writing about items from the same category in the next section, Thinking in Comparisons. Sometimes, in order to make a point or to explain something, we may compare items from different categories. We will discuss these unusual comparisons in the Analogy section (pages 345–346).

THINKING IN COMPARISONS

We use comparison and contrast informally in our daily lives when we make decisions such as what food to buy or which TV programs to watch. When we use comparison and contrast in a formal way by following certain established principles, we are using it to think critically to arrive at a significant conclusion. That is, we use it not only to list areas of similarity or difference but also to help achieve a clearer understanding or new insight. When we use comparison and contrast to examine different perspectives, we do so in order to understand each perspective, to see if one is superior to another, to see if we ourselves have yet another perspective, and so on.

The principles for using comparison and contrast to think critically are straightforward.

1. *Compare or contrast two or more things that have something essential in common (that is, items from the same category).* Thus, it makes sense to compare two accounts of the same event or two essays on affirmative action.

2. *Establish important bases or points for comparison and contrast.* In everyday situations, it is fairly easy to determine which points are important. In deciding between two cars, the important points may be price, model, and safety features; exterior color or exact trunk capacity may be lesser concerns. But when you are working with written texts, finding points for comparison and contrast and deciding which of them are important require careful thought. When comparing or contrasting two accounts of the same event, important points might include the actual presence of the writers at the event or the writers' reliance on the accounts of others, the language the writers use to describe the participants or actions, and which details the writers have included or omitted. The writer's gender or the length of an account might or might not be significant.

3. *Develop or locate relevant, specific evidence for each point.* Opinions valued by critical thinkers are those supported by evidence. In everyday situations, evidence usually means facts: the prices of two different cars, the presence or absence of air bags, and so on. With written texts, the evidence comes from the texts themselves, in the form of either accurate paraphrases or direct quotations.

4. *Determine the significance of the comparison and contrast: What can be learned from it?* What should be done as a result? In everyday situations, this significance is often a determination: one car is superior to another and is therefore the one to purchase. When you are working with written texts, the significance may be that the texts disagree on important points; therefore, you may decide that one is more persuasive than the other.

Guidelines for Using Comparisons in Writing

When you are ready to present the results of your critical thinking in writing for others to read and consider, you need to present your thinking in such a way that readers will be able to follow it and, hopefully, agree with your conclusion. Therefore, for writing, you should also follow these principles:

1. *Early and accurately, introduce the things to be compared and contrasted.* When you work with written texts, this means identifying what the texts are (personal essays, poems, newspaper accounts, excerpts from books, and so on) and naming the titles and authors, probably in the introductory paragraph.

2. *Develop a thesis which states that you will examine likenesses and differences.* Because you will be discussing two or more things and introducing points about each, the audience will be confronting a difficult reading task. A clear statement of what is to come can offer them a framework to follow.

3. *Organize the comparison or contrast in the way that will be easiest for the audience to follow.* There are three ways to organize a comparison and contrast: block, point-by-point, or a careful combination of the two.

   - *Block* means that after the introduction, you first present all the material about the first subject; then, you present all the material about the second. The selection by Mark Twain on pages 306–308 uses block organization.

   - *Point-by-point* means that for each key point or basis of comparison, you first give information about one of the things being compared and contrasted, then give information about the other. In this way, you can move back and forth between the two things being compared and contrasted. The selection by Benjamin Franklin on pages 325–329 uses point-by-point organization.

   - You can also use a *combination* of these two patterns when there are some items of similarity or difference that you can present in blocks, followed by points that you may want to address separately. Topic sentences and transitions are very important in a combination method!

4. *Bring up the same bases or points of comparison or contrast for each subject, and in the same order.* An incomplete comparison results when, for instance, the language used in one text is addressed but the language used in another is not discussed. If an important detail appears in one text but not in the other, it is reasonable to simply tell the audience this: "No mention is made of a doctor in this account."

5. *Assist the audience by using words, phrases, or sentences that show relationships and shifts.* Logical connections that exist in your mind may not necessarily be apparent to your audience, but you can point them out by using appropriate expressions.

Comparison words and phrases	Contrast words and phrases
Same	Different, differ from, difference
Similar, similarly	In contrast
Like, alike	Unlike
Reminds me of	On the other hand
Resembles	Conversely
Shows connections with	
Both	Is separate from

6. *State the significance of your comparison and contrast at the place in the essay where it will be most effective.* Sometimes writers use the significance as the opening lead, sometimes they incorporate it into the thesis statement, and sometimes they save it for the conclusion. In deciding where to place it, ask yourself where it will have the greatest impact on your audience.

ANALOGY

We noted earlier that comparative relationships involve examining the similarities and differences of two items in the same general category, such as two perspectives, two items on a menu, or two methods of birth control. There is another kind of comparison, however, one that does not focus on things in the same category. Such comparisons are known as *analogies,* and their goal is to clarify or illuminate a concept from one category by saying that in some ways, it resembles a concept from a very different category.

The purpose of an analogy is not the same as the purpose of the comparison we have been discussing. We noted that the goal of comparing similar things is often to make a choice and that the process of comparing can provide us with information on which we can base an intelligent decision. The main goal of analogies, however, is not to choose or decide; it is to illuminate our understanding. Identifying similarities between very different things can often stimulate us to see these things in a new light or from a different perspective.

We often create and use analogies to put a point across. Used appropriately, an analogy can help to illustrate what we are trying to communicate. This device is particularly useful when we have difficulty finding the right words to represent our experiences. Similes and metaphors, two figures of speech based on analogy that help us to "say things for which we have not words," are discussed on pages 179–181 of Chapter 6.

In addition to communicating experiences that resist simple characterization, analogies are useful when a writer is explaining a complicated concept. For instance, we might compare the eye to a camera lens or compare the body's immune system to the National Guard (corpuscles are called to active duty and rush to the scene of danger when undesirable elements threaten the well-being of the organism).

Analogies are often used to describe shape or size. They help our readers to visualize size if we describe an object as "about the size of a dollar bill" or a piece of property as "roughly the size of two football fields."

Analogies enliven discourse by evoking images that illuminate the points of comparison. Consider the following analogies and explain the points of comparison.

> "Laws are like cobwebs, which may catch small flies, but let wasps and hornets break through." —Jonathan Swift

> "Like as the waves make towards the pebbled shore, so do our minutes hasten to their end." —William Shakespeare

> "Some books are to be tasted, others to be swallowed, and some few to be chewed and digested." —Francis Bacon

> "He has all the qualities of a dog, except its devotion." —Gore Vidal

In addition to *simple analogies* like the preceding ones that are designed to make one or two penetrating points, *extended analogies* have a more ambitious purpose. They attempt to illuminate a more complex subject by identifying a number of points of comparison. For example, we might seek to explain the theory of causal determinism by drawing an analogy between the universe and a watch or by analogizing the chemical interaction of molecules to a choreographed dance.

A word of caution about using analogies is in order here. Since they are based on items from different categories and have only limited points of similarity, be very careful when writing or reading arguments based on analogies. The failed U.S. military policy in Vietnam was partially based on the "domino theory," which held that since the countries in Southeast Asia had common borders, if one country became Communist, the other countries would also "fall" to Communism, just as a row of dominoes would all fall if one were knocked down. However, the countries were separate entities, places with people, history, cultures, and policies of their own. They were not small game pieces like dominoes, so the theory proved false. Analogies do have value for describing and explaining, but by their very nature, they have limited value in an argument.

Thinking ↔ Writing Activity

Examining Extended Analogies

1. Identify the items being compared in the following paragraphs and note the points of similarity. How does the analogy help to illuminate the subject being discussed?

2. Where does each analogy fall apart, or, in other words, where do categorical differences in the items cause the analogy to be interesting but not really accurate?

3. Try writing a paragraph-length analogy of your own.

The mountain guide, like the true teacher, has a quiet authority. He or she engenders trust and confidence so that one is willing to join the endeavor. The guide accepts his leadership role, yet recognizes that success (measured by the heights that are scaled) depends upon the close cooperation and active participation of each member of the group. He has crossed the terrain before and is familiar with the landmarks, but each trip is new and generates its own anxiety and excitement. Essential skills must be mastered; if they are lacking, disaster looms. The situation demands keen focus and rapt attention; slackness, misjudgment, or laziness can abort the venture. The teacher is not a pleader, not a performer, not a huckster, but a confident, exuberant guide on expeditions of shared responsibility into the most exciting and least-understood terrain on earth—the mind itself. —Nancy K. Hill, *Scaling the Heights: The Teacher as Mountaineer*

Life's but a walking shadow, a poor player,
That struts and frets his hour upon the stage,
And then is heard no more. It is a tale
Told by an idiot, full of sound and fury,
Signifying nothing. —William Shakespeare, *Macbeth*, V.v

The following extended analogies were written by students in a college composition class.

Love in a good marriage is like an exponential function; it will grow until infinity. As time passes, love increases. It doesn't grow in the shape of a linear function; it grows faster. As I say every day to my husband, I love him more today than yesterday and less than tomorrow. And that is the exponential way.

Becoming a wise shopper is like becoming a smart chef in a fancy restaurant. Everywhere the chef turns in the kitchen, he finds an exotic treat. But he can't taste everything, much less consume it all. A chef who tastes too much will get a stomach ache. A shopper who buys too much will spend a lot of money and then suffer the pain of paying off those credit card bills. A wise shopper can resist the sweet temptations of the shopping life like the smart cook can resist the delicious temptations in the kitchen.

Phone conversations with my stepmother and writing assignments are both difficult for me in similar ways. Finding topics for them is often hard. After I tell my stepmother that I'm fine and ask about her and my father, I sometimes don't know what else to say. When I have an assignment to write about whatever I want, I sometimes can't think of a topic.

Also, I must worry about my vocabulary in both situations. My stepmother doesn't know the new "in" words, and my English papers have to be written correctly. I only increase my difficulty with both of these obligations by putting them off. I wait until Sunday night to call my father's house and then, after the phone call, work on my English paper for Monday morning.

Writing Project: Comparing Perspectives on an Issue or Event

This chapter has included both readings and Thinking-Writing Activities that encourage you to reflect on the nature of perception and on comparing and contrasting different perspectives. Be sure to reread what you wrote for those activities; you may be able to use the material when completing this project.

> Write an essay comparing and contrasting two or more written texts that present different perspectives on the same event or issue. Your primary purpose is to present some significant insights about the perspectives and the texts. Follow your instructor's directions for choosing texts and for the paper's length and format.

Begin by considering the key elements in the Thinking-Writing Model on page 6.

THE WRITING SITUATION

Purpose Along with presenting significant insights about the texts and their subject, you will better understand how to use the thinking patterns of comparison and contrast. Also, you will think more about the implications of different perspectives presented in various accounts. And, since comparative papers invite logical organization, your planning abilities should improve. Finally, you will be sharing your insights about the texts with your audience.

Audience One audience for this paper would be anyone interested in the subject discussed in your choice of texts. This audience might be outside of your college since most events or issues that are written about have community, national, or international significance. If you can, identify such an audience and see if you can share your paper with them by publishing it in a newspaper or newsletter or by otherwise distributing it. If the texts pertain to history, sociology, psychology, or some other academic subject, perhaps people studying those subjects would want to read your essay.

You should consider whether or not your audience has read the texts that you are analyzing. If they have, you will not need to include much summary of content or explanation of context. If your readers have not read the texts, you will have to include a brief summary and perhaps an explanation of why the texts were written.

To communicate with your audience, you will need to include enough evidence from the texts to demonstrate your points. You should not merely *tell* your audience that a likeness or difference exists; you must *show* them the evidence so they can see it for themselves.

Subject If your instructor specifies which texts you should compare and contrast, consider why he or she may have chosen them. A question to ask yourself is what those texts have in common. If your instructor has left the choice to you, remember that you must use texts that have something essential in common. It helps a great deal to pick texts that genuinely interest you, either because of their subject matter or because of their style. Or you may decide to select an issue or event that interests you and use your research skills to locate texts about the topic. In that case, it may be necessary to provide paraphrases or summaries of the texts for your audience.

Writer This project asks you to bring your critical reading and thinking skills to other writers' works and to analyze their perspectives. Your position of authority and your comfort level may depend on how much you know about the subject. However, neither your personal opinions nor your experiences are the focus of this project. You must be as objective as possible as you write and as thoughtful as possible as you establish the significance of your analysis.

THE WRITING PROCESS

The following sections will guide you through the stages of generating, planning, drafting, and revising as you work on your essay. Try to be particularly conscious of applying the principles discussed in this chapter and of the critical thinking you do when you revise.

Generating Ideas Once you have decided which texts you will use, reread each of them several times. Likenesses and differences may not be immediately apparent, nor may any significance strike you at the start. Doing some preliminary writing may help.

- Make a list of the ideas in each text.
- Make a list of what you notice about each text. Are you struck by the opening, the choice of words, the author's bias or objectivity, the presence or absence of specific details, or any other elements or characteristics?

- After you have made these lists, begin to look for bases or points of likeness or difference. Doing this requires abstract thinking on your part, but patience will yield results.

- Collaboration can be productive. Talk with others about the texts.

- Read the student papers at the end of this chapter. They may help you to see what needs to be done.

- Carefully read any other models your instructor provides.

- Try freewriting for five minutes on what the texts have in common, then for five minutes on how they differ.

- Once you have established some bases for comparison or contrast, go back to the texts themselves and look for passages you could quote to illustrate your points.

- If you own the publication(s) in which the texts appear, use a highlighting pen to mark areas you may wish to quote. If you don't own them, copy the quotations or make photocopies to highlight.

- Now begin to think about significance. What are you beginning to observe about the texts? What are you beginning to feel about them?

- Try freewriting for five minutes on any or all of these questions:

Does one text do a better job than the other? If so, in what way or ways?

Do you agree with either or both texts? If not, what *is* your perspective?

Have the texts caused you to re-evaluate or change your own ideas or perspectives?

Do the texts have different styles or vocabularies?

Defining a Focus Write a thesis statement that will clearly inform your audience that you are going to explore similarities, differences, or both. You might decide to write something like "After studying both of these accounts carefully, I saw two distinct differences." Or you might decide to name the areas of likeness or difference: "The authors are similar in their recognition of the need for more education and their determination in pursuing that education." You may even decide to announce the personal significance of your comparisons in your thesis statement: "Seeing the biased way in which one of the texts presented this event made me wary of accepting any printed reports at face value."

Organizing Ideas This assignment fits well with what you have already learned about essay structure but requires you to move a few steps beyond what you have accomplished previously. Your description of the issue or event and of the texts that describe it can give you an introduction that will end with your thesis statement. The actual discussion of likenesses and/or differences will take place in the body paragraphs, and the significance of your analysis can be introduced or expanded upon in the conclusion. The major decision you will have to make is whether to use block or point-by-point organization or some combination of the two.

Drafting Begin with the easiest paragraph to draft. If you are using point-by-point, remember to begin each body paragraph with a topic sentence indicating that this point will be discussed for both (or all) texts: for example, "Both accounts agree on the cause of the contamination." Then provide the audience with as much information as is needed to help them see what you mean. Use the quotations you highlighted to support your points and let the audience see that the texts really do say very similar—or very different—things. You will, of course, have to decide on the most logical order for the body paragraphs: which point to present first, which second, and so on.

Generally, readers have an easier time following point-by-point organization, but some writing situations call for block. Fortunately, word processors make it easy to move material around, so try it both ways to see which will be easier for your audience.

In your conclusion, name or expand upon the significance of your analysis, but be careful not to make too broad a statement. Consideration of two or three texts does not prove, for instance, that all texts are racist or sexist, but discovering racism or sexism in some texts should encourage you and your readers to be aware that these perspectives may be present in others.

Revising, Editing, and Proofreading   Use the Step-by-Step method on pages 160–162 to revise and polish your essay.

STUDENT WRITING
JESSE CHEN'S WRITING PROCESS

Student Jesse Chen felt an immediate and powerful personal connection to this chapter's selection of perspectives on the Tiananmen Square massacre in 1989. Sorting out personal perspective and comparing it to the "official" or "objective" accounts presented in this chapter was a particular challenge for Jesse, and led to a very compelling essay. Many forms of academic and professional writing do not (by convention, or common agreement) allow for the use of the personal voice. In Jesse's case, however, a personal perspective lends this essay a particular authority. The process writing that follows is from Jesse's class notebook, in which Jesse responded to question 4 on page 312 about the ways different writers used language to express their perspectives.

> I made a list of words in the "official" Chinese reports that seemed so false and hurtful:
> dregs of society
> misguided
> bad people
> a mob

but what hurt the most reading these accounts was how Xiao Bin changed his story. How can you use words to tell lies, how can you refuse to tell the truth? Even though I saw on television what actually happened—it was bloody and abhorrent. It was a slaughter. The Chinese government not only isn't telling the truth, but it's using insults to lie. I witnessed innocent students getting shot and run over. They were not "dregs of society." I don't think I could write an "objective" report about what I witnessed because that would be a kind of lying. If I write about Tiananmen Square I have to use words that describe <u>exactly</u> how I feel and how my parents felt. We are all Chinese and we all suffered on June 4, 1989.

Opposing Stories

BY JESSE CHEN

I can never forget what happened to my people at Tiananmen Square in Beijing, China, on the morning of June 4, 1989. My parents and I stayed up all night in our home in Hong Kong watching the news on television. It was broadcasting the quelling of the demonstrators in Tiananmen Square, and it was abhorrent and unbelievable. The Chinese Army entered Tiananmen Square and shot the students who were protesting for the pro-democracy movement. It came to a bloody end in that many innocent students were killed on that blood red morning. I remember that my parents were both crying when they saw their own people being killed by the "People's Army." When I read the accounts in my textbook from the New York Times (June 4, 1989) and the Official Chinese Government Accounts which include quotations from six Chinese persons, I found it incredible that they turned out to be two completely different stories even though they were about the same event. The New York Times tends to focus on reporting the facts of the slaughter while the Official Chinese Government Accounts tend to glorify the People's Liberation Army and the sacrifices made by its members. Because of different backgrounds and perspectives, the New York Times and the Official Chinese Government Accounts have come to two different stories about the slaughter; therefore, we need to think critically and analyze carefully before we can recognize a reliable source.

As a public medium, the *New York Times* plays a neutral role which only reports the fact of the slaughter without adding any biased opinion. It describes the students as "students," a factual title. Moreover, when describing the scene of the slaughter, it reports that the troops "fired submachine guns at the crowd of people who tried to resist." It states, "Troops marched along the roads surrounding central Tiananmen Square, sometimes firing in the air and sometimes firing directly at crowds who refused to move." It reports, "Most of the dead had been shot, but some had been run over by personnel carriers that forced their way through the protestors' barricades." Those descriptions of the scene are very close to the news which I saw and heard broadcast on TV, so the reliability is high. Moreover, in reporting the death toll, the *Times* does not give a very accurate number because it is impossible to be estimated or proved. Therefore, it merely gives a sketchy death toll: "Students said, however, that at least 500 people may have been killed in the crackdown." Furthermore, the *Times* does not render a judgment; it neither praises nor criticizes one side or the other since its responsibility is to report the facts only.

On the contrary, the Official Chinese Government Accounts give a different report, mainly glorifying the People's Liberation Army and sympathizing with the sacrifices made by its soldiers. Unlike the *Times,* these accounts do not name the students as "students." Han Xu, the Chinese ambassador to the United States, criticized them as "a mob led by a small number of people" who were trying to prevent "the normal conduct of the affairs of state." Also, General Lie Zgiyun said, "It never happened that soldiers fired directly at the people." Moreover, the Official Accounts even deny the death of the students: "Not a single student was killed at Tiananmen Square," said a Chinese army commander. However, the Official Chinese news program reported, "More than 1,000 police officers and troops were injured and killed, and some civilians were killed." Yuan Mu, an official government spokesman, said, "At most 300 people were killed in the operation, many of them soldiers." Finally, Prime Minister Li Peng offered his appreciation to the army: "Comrades, thanks for your hard work. We hope you will continue your fine efforts to safeguard security in the capital."

In conclusion, people's perspectives vary according to their backgrounds and status. Because of the differences in the backgrounds and status, the *Times* and the Chinese Government came to two opposed stories. We can measure their reliability by analyzing their backgrounds and status. Being a public medium, the *Times* tends to be neutral, not biased toward either side. However, in order to evade responsibility and cover up the faults, the Official Chinese Government Accounts tend to by-pass the sacrifices of the students and glorify the "hard work" of the army. Even until now, the Chinese Government still denies that they killed any students. Therefore, before we can trust or believe a source, we need to think critically about its perspective before we accept its reliability.

ALTERNATIVE WRITING PROJECT: COMPARING TWO REVIEWS

Find a recent review of a movie that you have seen or of a restaurant at which you have eaten. Compare the review with your experience. Do you agree with the reviewer? Identify specific examples of points you agree with and explain why. Do you disagree with the reviewer? Identify specific examples of these, too. Write an essay presenting your analysis of the review as it relates to your experience with the movie or at the restaurant.

Exploring Cause and Effect

"The present contains nothing more than the past, and what is found in the effect was already in the cause."
—Henri Bergson

Writing to Speculate

Critical Thinking Focus: Causal reasoning

Writing Focus: Presenting causal reasoning

Reading Theme: Ecological relationships

Writing Project: Exploring causes of a recent event

Previous chapters have examined thinking and writing patterns that help us make sense of the world. As we explore our world, we humans tend to ask why things are as they are: Why do some marriages endure for years and others end in divorce? Why does a northern area of the country have relatively mild winters for several years, then experience a record-breaking blizzard? Why do certain political ideas take hold during particular periods of history?

When we contemplate such questions, we are asking about (1) **causes,** factors that contribute to events and bring them about, and (2) **effects,** events that result directly or indirectly from causes or from other events. Much thinking about causes and effects occurs in an impromptu way. For example, about a divorce, we might guess, "I think the marriage failed because of money problems." Though that might in fact be one reason, other factors are probably also involved. Determining causes is complicated because:

- An event may have more than one cause
- An event may have various types of causes
- Determining causes with certainty is often impossible

When we think about causal relationships in an organized way, ever conscious of the difficulty and uncertainty of the task, we are using a critical thinking process called **causal analysis.**

The Writing Project in this chapter asks you to find information about some causes of a recent event and then to write a paper in which you present this information. The chapter should help you to write effectively about causal relationships.

Kinds of Causal Relationships

Causal patterns of thinking involve relating events in terms of the influence or effect they have on one another. The following statements are all examples of causal statements.

- Since I was the last to leave, I turned off the lights.
- Taking plenty of vitamin C really cured that terrible cold I had.
- I accidentally toasted my hand along with the marshmallows by getting too near the campfire.

In these statements, the words *since, turned off, cured,* and *getting too near* all point to the fact that something has caused something else to take place.

Some Words That Indicate Causes and Effects

Cause	Effect
because	because of
reason(s), for this reason (these reasons)	as a result, result, resulted in
affect, effect (verb)	consequently, consequence
bring about	therefore
a factor in	since
cure, infect	thus
lead, lead to	accordingly

produce (verb)

encourage, encouragement

discourage

influence

solve

happens whenever

follows from, follows that

ensues

What additional cause and effect words can you think of?

You are probably realizing that you make causal statements all the time and that you are constantly thinking in terms of causal relationships. In fact, the goal of much of your thinking is to figure out why something happened or how something came about. One advantage of causal analysis is that it enables you to make reasonable predictions because you are able to clarify the causal relationships involved and make predictions based on your understanding.

CAUSAL CHAIN

Although you may think of causes and effects in isolation—A caused B—in reality, causes and effects rarely appear by themselves. There is not just one cause of a resulting effect; there is a whole string of causes, as illustrated by the structures in Figure 10.1. These interrelated causes form more complex patterns, including three that we will examine next: *causal chains, contributory causes,* and *interactive causes.* Consider the following scenario:

Your paper on the topic "life after death" is due on Monday morning. You have reserved the whole weekend to work on it and are just getting started when the phone rings. A favorite childhood friend is in town and wants to stay with you for the weekend. You say *yes.* By Sunday night, you've had a great weekend but have made little progress on your paper. You brew a pot of coffee and get started. At 3:00 A.M. you are too exhausted to continue. Deciding to get a few hours' sleep, you set the alarm clock for 6:00 A.M., giving yourself plenty of time to finish up. When you wake up, it's nine o'clock; the alarm failed to go off. Your class starts in forty minutes. You have no chance of getting the paper done on time. On your way to class, you mentally review the causes of this disaster. No longer concerned about life after death, you are very worried about life after this class!

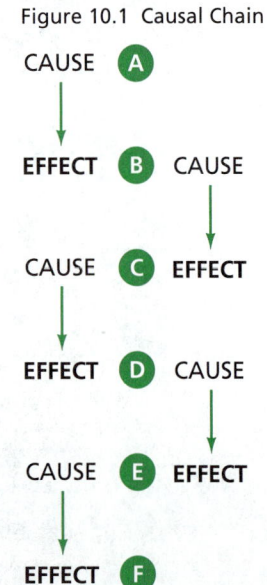

Figure 10.1 Causal Chain

- What causes in this situation are responsible for your paper's being late?
- What do you think is the single most important cause?

- What do you think your instructor will identify as the most important cause? Why?

A **causal chain,** as illustrated by the preceding example, is a situation in which one thing leads to another, which then leads to another, and so on over a period of time. In writing about causal chains, your narrative would use chronological ordering (see page 225). There is not just one cause of the resulting effect. Which event or circumstance in the chain is the "tipping point," the most important contributing factor to the effect? Your answer will depend on your perspective on the situation. You might see the cause of the unfinished paper as a defective alarm clock. Your instructor, though, might see the cause of the problem as overall lack of planning.

Thinking ↔ Writing Activity

Creating a Causal Chain

1. Create a scenario in which you make a series of decisions that culminate in a significant conclusion. For example, your decision to take a course outside of your major might lead to a conversation with the professor, which leads you to explore a career option that you had not previously considered, and so on. The scenario might be based on an actual experience in your life or one created through your imagination.

2. Review the scenario you have just created. Explain how the "real" cause of the final effect could vary, depending on your perspective on the situation.

CONTRIBUTORY CAUSES

In addition to operating in causal chains over a period of time, causes can also work simultaneously to produce an effect. This results in a situation in which a number of different **contributory causes** bring something about. Instead of working in isolation, each cause contributes to bringing about the final effect. When this situation occurs, each cause serves to support and reinforce the action of the other causes, a condition illustrated in Figure 10.2.

Consider the following situation:

It is the end of the term, and you have been working incredibly hard at school—writing papers, preparing for exams, finishing up course projects. You

Figure 10.2 Contributory Causes

CAUSE A

CAUSE B

CAUSE C   EFFECT

CAUSE D

haven't been getting enough sleep, and you haven't been eating regular, well-balanced meals. To make matters worse, you have been under intense pressure in your personal life, having serious arguments with the person you have been dating, and this is constantly on your mind. It is the middle of the flu season, and many people you know have been sick with various respiratory infections. Walking home one evening, you get soaked by an unexpected downpour. By the time you get home, you are shivering. You soon find yourself in bed with a thermometer in your mouth—you are sick!

What was the "cause" of your illness? In this situation, you can see that evidently, a combination of factors led to your physical breakdown: low resistance, getting wet and chilled, being exposed to various germs and viruses, physical exhaustion, lack of proper eating, and so on. Taken by itself, no one factor might have been enough to cause your illness. Together, they all contributed to the final outcome.

Thinking ↔ Writing Activity

Creating a Contributory-Cause Scenario

Create a similar scenario, detailing the contributory causes that led to your asking someone for a date, choosing a major, losing or winning a game, or another effect.

INTERACTIVE CAUSES

Causes rarely operate in isolation but instead often influence (and are influenced by) other factors. Imagine that you are scheduled to give a speech to a large group of people. As your moment in the spotlight approaches, you become anxious, which results in a dry mouth and throat, making your voice sound more like a croak. The prospect of sounding like a bullfrog increases your anxiety, which in turn dries your mouth and constricts your throat further, reducing your croak to something much worse—silence.

Different factors can relate to each other through reciprocal influences that flow back and forth from one to the other. Understanding this type of **interactive causal relationship** helps you to organize and make sense of your experiences. For instance, to comprehend social relationships (families, teams, groups of friends), you consider the complex ways in which each individual influences—and is influenced by—all the other members of the group. Understanding biological systems and other systems is similar to understanding social systems. To comprehend and explain how an organ such as the heart, liver, or brain functions, you have to describe its complex, interactive relationships with all the other parts of the biological system. Figure 10.3 illustrates these dynamic causal relationships.

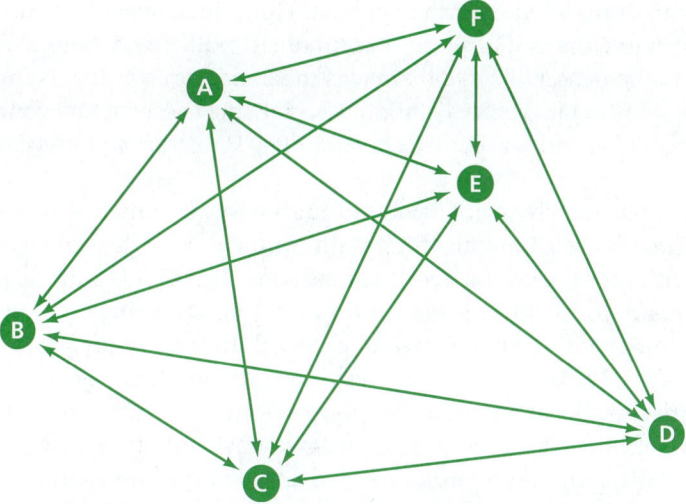

Figure 10.3 Interactive Causes

Thinking ↔ Writing Activity

Identifying Causal Patterns

Read the following passages that illustrate causal patterns of thinking. For each passage, identify the kind of causal relationship (chain, contributory, or interactive), and explain how the causes are related to one another.

Nothing posed a more serious threat to the bald eagle's survival than a modern chemical compound called DDT. Around 1940, a retired Canadian banker named Charles L. Broley began keeping track of eagles nesting in Florida. Each breeding season, he climbed into more than 50 nests, counted the eaglets and put metal bands on their legs. In the late 1940's, a sudden drop-off in the number of young produced led him to conclude that 80 percent of his birds were sterile. Broley blamed DDT. Scientists later discovered that DDE, a breakdown product of DDT, causes not sterility, but a fatal thinning of eggshell among birds of prey. Applied on cropland all over the United States, the pesticide was running off into waterways where it concentrated in fish. The bald eagles ate the fish and the DDT impaired their ability to reproduce. They were not alone, of course. Ospreys and pelicans suffered similar setbacks. —Jim Doherty, "The Bald Eagle and DDT"

It is popularly accepted that Hitler was the major cause of World War II, but the ultimate causes go much deeper than one personality. First, there were long-standing German grievances against reparations levied on the nation following its defeat in World War I. Second, there were severe economic strains that caused resentment among the German people. Third, there were French and English reluctance to work out a sound disarmament policy and American noninvolvement in the matter. Finally, there was the European fear that communism was a much greater danger than National Socialism. These factors contributed to the outbreak of World War II. —Gilbert Muller, *The American College Handbook*

You crunch and chew your way through vast quantities of snacks and confectioneries and relieve your thirst with multicolored, flavored soft drinks, with and without calories, for two basic reasons. The first is simple; the food tastes good, and you enjoy the sensation of eating it. Second, you associate these foods, often without being aware of it, with the highly pleasurable experiences depicted in the advertisements used to promote their sale. Current television advertisements demonstrate this point: people turn from grumpiness to euphoria after crunching a corn chip. Others water ski into the sunset with their loved ones while drinking a popular soft drink. People entertain on the patio with friends, cook over campfires without mosquitoes, or go to carnivals with granddad munching away at the latest candy or snack food. The people portrayed in these scenarios are all healthy, vigorous, and good looking; one wonders how popular the food they convince you to eat would be if they would crunch or drink away while complaining about low back pain or clogged sinuses. —Judith Wurtman, *Eating Your Way Through Life*

Ways of Testing Causes

NECESSARY CONDITION AND SUFFICIENT CONDITION

In addition to the three patterns of causality we have just examined, we need to consider necessary and sufficient conditions. A **necessary condition** is a factor that is required to bring about a certain result: for example, an intact light bulb is required for a lamp's illumination. However, by itself, an intact light bulb is not sufficient to provide illumination: you also need electricity, which is another necessary condition.

A **sufficient condition** is a factor that of itself is always sufficient for bringing about a certain result. For example, a pinch on the arm is a sufficient cause for discomfort. Of course, even with a sufficient condition, there may be an additional necessary condition, or several necessary conditions, for a result to occur. Having healthy nerves in the arm and being conscious are two necessary conditions for someone's feeling a sensation when pinched on the arm.

IMMEDIATE CAUSE AND REMOTE CAUSE

Yet another way to think critically about causes is to classify them by how close in time the cause is to its result. Something that happens just before an event that it causes is called an **immediate cause.** A factor that also helped to bring about this same event but that occurred further back in time is called a **remote cause.** For example, a last-minute touchdown could be the immediate cause of a football championship, but wise trades made for key players before the season began might be remote causes.

Thinking ↔ Writing Activity

Seeing Causal Relationships

1. Study the photograph of young people at a bar and see how many causal relationships are being suggested. What are your perceptions of why they are there and why some of them have the expressions that they do? See what perceptions your classmates have and notice how they differ.

2. Carefully examine the Budweiser ad in the background. What do you think are the causal relationships among advertisements for alcoholic drinks, these young peoples' apparent moods, and the drinking behaviors of college students you know.

3. What are the causes of your attitudes toward drinking alcohol? Have your attitudes changed since attending college? If you wish, share your analysis of your perspectives with your classmates.

© B. Stitzer/PhotoEdit.

Debates over important environmental issues, ranging from global warming to pollution of our water, are dominated by discussions of causes and effects.

Identifying Causal Fallacies

Because causality plays such a dominant role in the way we make sense of the world, it is not surprising that people make many mistakes and many errors in judgment in trying to determine causal relationships. These mistakes and errors can lead to unsound arguments, or **fallacies.** The following are some of the most common fallacies associated with causality.

- Questionable cause
- Misidentification of the cause
- *Post hoc ergo propter hoc*
- Slippery slope

QUESTIONABLE CAUSE

The fallacy of *questionable cause* occurs when someone presents a causal relationship for which no real evidence exists. Superstitious beliefs such as "If you break a mirror, you will have seven years of bad luck" usually fall into this category. Some people feel that astrology, a system of beliefs tying one's personality and fortunes in life to the position of the planets at the moment of birth, also falls into this category.

Consider the following passage from the *Confessions* of St. Augustine. Does it seem to support the causal assertions of astrology or deny them? Why?

> Firminus had heard from his father that when his mother had been pregnant with him, a slave belonging to a friend of his father's was also about to bear. It happened that since the two women had their babies at the same instant, the men were forced to cast exactly the same horoscope for each newborn child down to the last detail, one for his son, the other for the little slave. Yet Firminus, born to wealth in his parents' house, had one of the more illustrious careers in life whereas the slave had no alleviation of his life's burden.

Other examples of this fallacy include beliefs such as:

- Lottery numbers that occur in dreams are more likely to be winners than random choices.
- Spending money is the best way to solve most problems.
- Music CDs and books that sell the most copies are the highest quality and most deserving.

MISIDENTIFICATION OF THE CAUSE

In causal situations we are not always certain about what is causing what—in other words, about what is the cause and what is the effect. For example, in the following pairs of items, which is the cause, and which is the effect? Why?

- Headaches and tension
- Failure in school and personal problems
- Shyness and lack of confidence
- Substance abuse and emotional difficulties

Sometimes a third factor is responsible for two effects that we are examining. Headaches and tension may both be the result of a third element—such as some new medication a person is taking. When we fail to recognize the third element, we commit the fallacy of *ignoring a common cause*. There also exists the fallacy of *assuming a common cause*—such as assuming that a person's sore toe and earache both stem from the same cause.

POST HOC ERGO PROPTER HOC

The translation of the Latin phrase *post hoc ergo propter hoc* is "After that, therefore because of that." It refers to situations in which, because two things occur closely together in time, we assume that one has caused the other. Suppose your team wins the game each time you wear your favorite shirt; you just may be tempted to conclude that the one event (wearing your favorite shirt) has some influence on the other event (winning the game). As a result, you may continue to wear this shirt "for good luck." It is easy to see how this sort of mistaken thinking can lead to all sorts of superstitious beliefs. Consider the following causal conclusion arrived at by Mark Twain's fictional character Huckleberry Finn in the following passage. How would you analyze his conclusion?

> I've always reckoned that looking at the new moon over your left shoulder is one of the carelessest and foolishest things a body can do. Old Hank Bunker done it once, and bragged about it; and in less than two years he got drunk and fell off a shot tower and spread himself out so that he was just a kind of layer. . . . But anyway, it all came of looking at the moon that way, like a fool.

Can you identify any of your own superstitious beliefs or practices that may have resulted from *post hoc* thinking?

SLIPPERY SLOPE

The causal fallacy of *slippery slope* is illustrated in the following advice:

Don't miss that first deadline, because if you do, it won't be long before you're missing all your deadlines. This will spread to the rest of your life, as you will be late for every appointment. This terminal procrastination will ruin your career, and friends and relatives will abandon you. You will end up a lonely failure who is unable to ever do anything on time.

Slippery slope thinking asserts that one undesirable action will inevitably lead to a worse action, which will necessarily lead to still a worse one, all the way down the "slippery slope" to some terrible disaster at the bottom. Although this progression may indeed occur, there certainly is no causal guarantee that it will. Create slippery slope scenarios for one of the following warnings:

- If you get behind on one credit card payment . . .
- If you fail that first test . . .
- If you eat that first fudge square . . .

Summary: Causal Fallacies

Questionable Cause:	Presenting a causal relationship for which no real evidence exists
Misidentification of Cause:	Uncertainty about what is the cause and what is the effect: ignoring a common cause, assuming a false common cause
Post Hoc Ego Propter Hoc:	Assuming a causal relationship between situations occurring closely together in time
Slippery Slope:	Asserting that one undesirable action will lead to a worse action, which will lead to still a worse one—down, down the slippery slope

Thinking ↔ Writing Activity

Diagnosing Causal Fallacies

Review the four causal fallacies just described; then identify and explain the errors of reasoning illustrated in the following examples.

1. The person who won the lottery says she dreamed the winning numbers. I'm going to start writing down the numbers that I dream about.

2. Yesterday I forgot to take my vitamins, and I immediately got sick. That mistake won't occur again!

3. I'm warning you: if you miss a class, it won't be long before you flunk out of school and ruin your future.

4. I always take the first seat in the bus. Today I took another seat, and the bus broke down.

5. I think the reason I'm not doing well in school is that I simply don't have enough time to study, and my classes aren't interesting, either.

Detecting Causal Claims

Sometimes people use causal reasoning because they want us to see cause-and-effect relationships that they believe exist. When they do this, we say they are making **causal claims.** Consider the following examples.

1. Politicians assure us that a vote for them will result in better schools and lower taxes.

2. Advertisers tell us that using a detergent will leave our wash "cleaner than clean, whiter than white."

3. Doctors tell us that eating a balanced diet will result in better health.

4. Educators tell us that a college degree is worth an average of $830,000 additional income over an individual's lifetime.

5. Utility companies inform us that using nuclear energy will result in less pollution.

In each of these examples, certain causal claims are being made about how the world operates in an effort to persuade us to adopt a certain point of view. As critical thinkers, it is our duty to evaluate these various causal claims to determine whether they are valid or questionable.

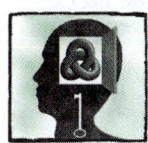

Thinking ↔ Writing Activity

Evaluating Causal Claims

Explain how you might go about evaluating the causal claims previously listed.

- *Example:* Electing politicians and claims about getting better schools and lower taxes.

- *Evaluation:* Speak to teachers and principals about school needs. Understand what a politician in a specific office can and cannot do about education. Learn about budgets for school systems. Remember your own school experiences and think about why they were good or bad. Learn about taxes and schools in your area.

A Casebook on Environmental Issues

The impact of human civilization on the environment has taken on increasing urgency, as global warming, the razing of rainforests, the search for sustainable fuel sources, and our dependence on "factory-farmed" or genetically modified food are discussed and debated in the media and affect the most basic aspects of our lives, from the quality of our air to the safety of our next meal. The writers here consider the various and complicated causal relationships between humans and the natural world. As you read, watch for each writer's development of causal chains and evaluate the clarity and effectiveness of their arguments.

"Worried? Us?"

BY BILL MCKIBBEN (b. 1960)

As a journalist, Bill McKibben has worked for years to raise awareness—and alarm—about the terrifying impact unchecked population growth and consumerism has wrought upon the environment, even as he maintains a fundamental hope in the redemptive qualities of nature. McKibben lives in the Adirondack Mountains of New York State, and practices in his own lifestyle the environmentally sound choices he recommends to others. With The End of Nature *(1989), which he mentions in this essay, McKibben joined Rachel Carson (see page 20) as a critical literary voice linking environmental awareness, scientific research, social policy, and individual ethics. For his second book,* The Age of Missing Information *(1992), McKibben recorded 103 cable television channels over a single twenty-four-hour period and then watched every single hour of every channel—after which he spent a week alone in the mountains. The experience confirmed McKibben's theory that many Americans are completely disconnected from, and indifferent to, the environment because they are so saturated with the media.*

The following essay, published in 2003, is more despairing in tone than McKibben's earlier, more hopeful books, such as his 1995 Hope, Human and Wild: True Stories of Living Lightly on the Earth.

For fifteen years now, some small percentage of the world's scientists and diplomats and activists has inhabited one of those strange dreams where the dreamer desperately needs to warn someone about something bad and imminent; but somehow, no matter how hard he shouts, the other person in the dream—standing smiling, perhaps, with his back to an oncoming train—can't hear him. This group, this small percentage, knows that the world is about to change more profoundly than at any time in the history of human civilization. And yet, so far, all they have achieved is to add another line to the long list of human problems—people think about "global warming" in the way they think about "violence on television" or "growing trade deficits," as a marginal concern to them, if a concern at all. Enlightened governments make smallish noises and negotiate smallish treaties; enlightened people look down on America for its blind pig-gishness. Hardly anyone, however, has fear in their guts.

Why? Because, I think, we are fatally confused about time and space. Though we know that our culture has placed our own lives on a demonic fast-forward, we imagine that the earth must work on some other timescale. The long slow accretion of epochs—the Jurassic, the Cretaceous, the Pleistocene—lulls us into imagining that the physical world offers us an essentially stable background against which we can run our race. Humbly, we believe that the world is big and that we are small. This humility is attractive, but also historic and no longer useful. In the world as we have made it, the opposite is true. Each of us is big enough, for example, to produce our own cloud of carbon dioxide. As a result, we—our cars and our industry—have managed to raise the atmospheric level of carbon dioxide, which had been stable at 275 parts per million throughout human civilization, to about 380 parts per million, a figure that is climbing by one and a half parts per million each year. This increase began with the Industrial Revolution in the eighteenth century, and it has been accelerating ever since. The consequence, if we take a median from several respectable scientific projections, is that the world's temperature will rise by five degrees Fahrenheit (roughly two and a half degrees Celsius) over the next hundred years, to make it hotter than it has been for 400 million years. At some level, these are the only facts worth knowing about our earth.

Fifteen years ago, it was a hypothesis. Those of us who were convinced that the earth was warming fast were a small minority. Science was skeptical, but set to work with rigour. Between 1988 and 1995, scientists drilled deep into glaciers, took core samples from lake bottoms, counted tree rings, and, most importantly, refined elaborate computer models of the atmosphere. By 1995, the almost impossibly contentious world of science had seen enough. The world's most distinguished atmospheric chemists, physicists and climatologists, who had organized themselves into a large collective called the Intergovernmental Panel on Climate Change, made their pronouncement: "The balance of evidence suggests that there is a discernible human influence on global climate." In the eight years since, science has continued to further confirm and deepen these fears, while the planet itself has decided, as it were, to peer-review their work with a succession of ominously hot years (1998 was the hottest ever, with 2002 trailing by only a few hundredths of a degree). So far humanity has raised the planet's temperature by about one degree Fahrenheit, with most of that increase happening after 1970—from about fifty-nine degrees Fahrenheit, where it had been stuck since the first cities rose and the first crops grew, to about sixty degrees. Five more degrees in the offing, as I have said, but already we understand, with an almost desperate clarity, how finely balanced our world has been. One degree turns out to be a lot. In the cryosphere—the frozen portions of the planet's surface—glaciers are everywhere in rapid retreat (spitting out Bronze Age hunter-gatherers). The snows of Kilimanjaro are set to become the rocks of Kilimanjaro by 2015. Montana's Glacier National Park is predicted to lose its last glaciers by 2030. We know how thick Arctic ice is—we know it because Cold War nuclear-powered submarines needed the information for their voyages under the ice cap. When the data was declassified in the waning days of the Clinton administration, it emerged that Arctic ice was forty per cent thinner than it had been forty years before. *Perma*frost is melting. Get it?

"Global warming" can be a misleading phrase—the temperature is only the signal that extra solar radiation is being trapped at the earth's surface. That extra energy drives many things: wind-speeds increase, a reflection of the increasing heat-driven gradients between low and high pressure; sea level starts to rise, less because of melting ice caps than because warm air holds more water vapour than cold; hence evaporation increases and with it drought, and then, when the overloaded clouds finally part, deluge and flood. Some of these effects are linear. A recent study has shown that rice fertility drops by ten per cent for each degree Celsius that the temperature rises above thirty degrees Celsius during the rice plant's flowering. At forty degrees Celsius, rice fertility drops to zero. But science has come to understand that some effects may not follow such a clear progression. To paraphrase Orwell, we may all be hot, but some will be hotter than others. If the Gulf Stream fails because of Arctic melting, some may, during some seasons, even be colder.

5   The success of the scientific method underlines the failure of the political method. It is clear what must happen—the rapid conversion of our energy system from fossil to renewable fuels. And it is clear that it could happen—much of the necessary technology is no longer quixotic, no longer the province of backyard tinkerers. And it is also clear that it isn't happening. Some parts of Europe have made material progress—Denmark has built great banks of windmills. Some parts of Europe have made promises—the United Kingdom thinks it can cut its carbon emissions by sixty per cent by 2050. But China and India are still building power plants and motorways, and the United States has made it utterly clear that nothing will change soon. When Bill Clinton was President he sat by while American civilians traded up from cars to troop-transport vehicles; George Bush has not only rejected the Kyoto treaty, he has ordered the Environmental Protection Agency to replace "global warming" with the less ominous "climate change," and issued a national energy policy that foresees ever more drilling, refining and burning. Under it, American carbon emissions will grow another forty per cent in the next generation.

As satisfying as it is to blame politicians, however, it will not do. Politicians will follow the path of least resistance. So far there has not been a movement loud or sustained enough to command political attention. Electorates demand economic prosperity—more of it—above all things. Gandhianism, the political philosophy that restricts material need, is now only a memory even in the country of its birth. And our awareness that the world will change in every aspect, should we be so aware, is muted by the future tense, even though that future isn't far away, so near in fact that preventing global warming is a lost cause—all we can do now is to try to keep it from getting utterly out of control.

This is a failure of imagination, and in this way a literary failure. Global warming has still to produce an Orwell or a Huxley, a Verne or a Wells, a *Nineteen Eighty-Four* or a *War of the Worlds,* or in film any equivalent of *On The Beach* or *Doctor Strangelove.* It may never do so. It may be that because—fingers crossed—we have escaped our most recent fear, nuclear annihilation via the Cold War, we resist being scared all over again. Fear has its uses, but fear on this scale seems to be disabling, paralysing. Anger has its uses too, but the rage of anti-globalization demonstrators has yet to do more than alienate majorities. Shame sends a few Americans shopping for small cars, but on the whole America, now the exemplar to the world, is very nearly unshameable.

My own dominant feeling has always been sadness. In 1989, I published *The End of Nature,* the first book for a lay audience about global warming. Half of it was devoted to explaining the science, the other half to my unease. It seemed, and still seems, to me that humanity has intruded into and altered every part of the earth (or very nearly) with our habits and economies. Thoreau once said that he could walk half an hour from his home in Concord, Massachusetts, and come to a place where no man stood from one year to the next, and "there consequently politics are not, for politics are but the cigar smoke of a man." Now that cigar smoke blows everywhere.

Paradoxically, the world also seems more lonely. Everything else exists at our sufferance. Biologists guess that the result of a rapid warming will be the greatest wave of extinction since the last asteroid crashed into the earth. Now we are the asteroid. The notion that we live in a God-haunted world is harder to conjure up. God rebuked Job: "Were you there when I wrapped the ocean in clouds . . . and set its boundaries, saying, 'Here you may come but no farther. Here shall your proud waves break . . . Who gathers up the stormclouds, slits them and pours them out?'" Job, and everyone else until our time, had the sweet privilege of shutting up in the face of that boast—it was clearly God or gravity or some force other than us. But as of about 1990 we can answer back, because we set the sea level now, and we run the storm systems. The excretion of our economy has become the most important influence on the planet we were born into. We're what counts.

10   Our ultimate sadness lies in the fact that we know that this is not a preordained destiny; it isn't fate. New ways of behaving, of getting and spending, can still change the future; there is, as the religious evangelist would say, still time, though not much of it, and a miraculous conversion is called for—Americans in the year 2000 produced fifteen per cent more carbon doxide than they had ten years before.

The contrast between two speeds is the key fact of our age: between the pace at which the physical world is changing and the pace at which human society is reacting to this change. In history, if it exists, we shall be praised or damned.

Questions for Active Reading

1. If "global warming" is the effect about which McKibben is writing, how does he go about establishing causation? Does he describe a causal chain, contributory causes, interactive causes, or a combination of all three strategies to organize his argument?

2. How does McKibben use cause and effect to suggest solutions to the problem of global warming? What are those solutions, and what evidence does he offer to support those solutions?

3. McKibben uses the first person, and the occasional colloquialism, in this essay (beginning with the title). What does this suggest about his purpose for writing, and his attitude toward his audience? Does his diction strengthen or undermine his argument?

Questions for Thinking Critically

1. The quality and fairness of an argument are often based on the author's willingness to consider opposing points of view (as you will find in Chapter 13). When an argument—and its author—focuses solely on one viewpoint, it may become a *polemic*. What kind of evidence, or whose viewpoint, is absent from McKibben's essay? If "Worried? Us?" is indeed a polemic, is it effective?

2. The very term "global warming" is fiercely contested. Find at least two different web sites from nongovernmental organizations, think tanks, activist groups, and so on (not individual web pages) that present very different kinds of evidence and conclusions about global warming. How does each "side" of the argument refute the causation claims made by the other?

3. Can you identify—or do you suspect—the presence of causal fallacy in McKibben's argument?

FROM *The Amicus Journal*

Back to the Land

BY WENDELL BERRY (b. 1934)

The novels, essays, poems, and articles of Wendell Berry have profoundly influenced the American environmental movement of the twentieth and twenty-first centuries (Bill McKibben, whose essay appears earlier in this chapter, has cited Berry as a key influence on his own writing and environmental consciousness). Wendell Berry lives and works with his wife, Tanya, on their farm in Port Royal, Kentucky; his family first settled in the region in the early nineteenth century. His deep concerns for stewardship—of the land, of community, and of family—nourish both his creative and his more pragmatic writing; although he is best known for his poetry and novels, Berry is also a contributing editor to such practical journals as New Farm Magazine *and* Organic Gardening and Farming.

As a farmer, Berry is as critical of a kind of romanticism among some environmental activists (who would naively return all land to wilderness) as he is of large-scale industrial agriculture. Small, family-owned farms, Berry believes, represent the most sustainable relationship between communities and the local environment. "We must support what supports local life, which means community, family, household life—the moral capital our larger institutions have to come to rest upon," Berry claimed in a 1992 interview with New Perspectives Quarterly. *"If the larger institutions undermine the local life, they destroy that moral capital just exactly as the industrial economy has destroyed the natural capital of localities—soil fertility and so on. Essential wisdom accumulates in the community much as fertility builds in the soil."*

One of the primary results—and one of the primary needs—of industrialism is the separation of people and places and products from their histories. To the extent that we participate in the industrial economy, we do not know the histories of our families or of our habitats or of our meals. This is an economy, and in fact a culture, of the one-night stand. "I had a good time," says the industrial lover, "but don't ask me my last name." Just so, the industrial eater says to the svelte industrial hog, "We'll be together at breakfast. I don't want to see you before then, and I won't care to remember you afterward."

In this condition, we have many commodities but little satisfaction, little sense of the sufficiency of anything. The scarcity of satisfaction makes of our many commodities an infinite series of commodities, the new commodities invariably promising greater satisfaction than the older ones. In fact, the industrial economy's most marketed commodity is satisfaction, and this commodity, which is repeatedly promised, bought, and paid for, is never delivered.

This persistent want of satisfaction is directly and complexly related to the dissociation of ourselves and all our goods from our and their histories. If things do not last, are not made to last, they can have no histories, and we who use these things can have no memories. One of the procedures of the industrial economy is to reduce the longevity of materials. For example, wood—which, well made into buildings and furniture and well cared for, can last hundreds of years—is now routinely manufactured into products that last just twenty-five years. We do not cherish the memory of shoddy and transitory objects, and so we do not remember them. That is to say that we do not invest in them the lasting respect and admiration that make for satisfaction.

The problem of our dissatisfaction with all the things that we use is not correctable within the terms of the economy that produces those things. At present, it is virtually impossible for us to know the economic history or the ecological cost of the products we buy; the origins of the products are typically too distant and too scattered and the processes of trade, manufacture, transportation, and marketing too complicated. There are, moreover, too many good reasons for the industrial suppliers of these products not to want their histories to be known.

5   Where there is no reliable accounting and therefore no competent knowledge of the economic and ecological effects of our lives, we cannot live lives that are economically and ecologically responsible. This is the problem that has frustrated, and to a considerable extent undermined, the American conservation effort from the beginning. It is ultimately futile to plead and protest and lobby in favor of public ecological responsibility while, in virtually every act of our private lives, we endorse and support an economic system that is by intention, and perhaps by necessity, ecologically irresponsible.

If the industrial economy is not correctable within or by its own terms, then obviously what is required for correction is a countervailing economic idea. And the most significant weakness of the conservation movement is its failure to produce or espouse an economic idea capable of correcting the economic idea of the industrialists. Anybody who has studied with care the issues of conservation knows that our acts are being measured by a real and unyielding standard that was invented by no human. Our acts that are not in harmony with nature are inevitably and sometimes irremediably destructive. The standard exists. But having no opposing economic idea, the conservationists have had great difficulty in applying the standard.

What, then, is the countervailing idea by which we might correct the industrial idea? We will not have to look hard to find it, for there is only one, and that is agrarianism. Our major difficulty (and danger) will be in attempting to deal with agrarianism as "an idea"—agrarianism is primarily a practice, a set of attitudes, a loyalty, and a passion; it is an idea only secondarily and at a remove. I am well aware of the danger in defining things, but if I am going to talk about agrarianism, I am going to have to define it. The definition that follows is derived both from agrarian writers, ancient and modern, and from the unliterary and sometimes illiterate agrarians who have been my teachers.

The fundamental difference between industrialism and agrarianism is this: Whereas industrialism is a way of thought based on monetary capital and technology, agrarianism is a way of thought based on land.

An agrarian economy rises up from the fields, woods, and streams—from the complex of soils, slopes, weathers, connections, influences, and exchanges that we mean when we speak, for example, of the local community or the local watershed. The agrarian mind is therefore not regional or national, let alone global, but local. It must know on intimate terms the local plants and animals and local soils; it must know local possibilities and impossibilities, opportunities and hazards.

10   Because a mind so placed meets again and again the necessity for work to be good, the agrarian mind is less interested in abstract quantities than in particular qualities. It feels threatened and sickened when it hears people and creatures and places spoken of as labor, management, capital, and raw material. It

is not at all impressed by the industrial legendry of gross national products or of the numbers sold and dollars earned by gigantic corporations. It is interested in, and forever fascinated by, questions leading toward the accomplishment of good work: What is the best location for a particular building or fence? What is the best way to plow this field? What is the best course for a skid road in this woodland? Should this tree be cut or spared?—questions that cannot be answered in the abstract, and that yearn not toward quantity but toward elegance. Agrarianism can never become abstract, because it has to be practiced in order to exist.

An agrarian economy is always a subsistence economy before it is a market economy. The center of an agrarian farm is the household. It is the subsistence part of the agrarian economy that assures its stability and its survival. A subsistence economy necessarily is highly diversified, and it characteristically has involved hunting and gathering as well as farming and gardening. These activities bind people to their local landscape by close, complex interests and economic ties.

The stability, coherence, and longevity of human occupation require that the land should be divided among many owners and users. The central figure of agrarian thought has invariably been the small owner or small holder who maintains a significant measure of economic self-determination on a small acreage. The scale and independence of such holdings imply two things that agrarians see as desirable: intimate care in the use of the land and political democracy resting upon the indispensable foundation of economic democracy. A major characteristic of the agrarian mind is a longing for independence—that is, for an appropriate degree of personal and local self-sufficiency. Agrarians wish to earn and deserve what they have. They do not wish to live by piracy, beggary, charity, or luck.

The agrarian mind begins with the love of fields and ramifies in good farming, good cooking, good eating, and gratitude to God. Exactly analogous to the agrarian mind is the sylvan mind, which begins with the love of forests and ramifies in good forestry, good woodworking, good carpentry, etc., and in gratitude to God. These two kinds of mind readily intersect and communicate; neither ever intersects or communicates with the industrial-economic mind. The industrial-economic mind begins with ingratitude and ramifies in the destruction of farms and forests. The "lowly" and "menial" arts of farm and forest are mostly taken for granted or ignored by the culture of the "fine arts" and by "spiritual" religions; they are taken for granted or ignored or held in contempt by the powers of the industrial economy. But in fact they are inescapably the foundation of human life and culture, and their adepts are capable of as deep satisfaction and as high attainments as anybody else.

Having, so to speak, laid industrialism and agrarianism side by side, implying a preference for the latter, I will be confronted by two questions that I had better go ahead and answer.

15   The first is whether or not agrarianism is simply a "phase" that we humans had to go through and then leave behind in order to get onto the track of technological progress toward ever greater happiness. The answer is that although industrialism has certainly conquered agrarianism, and has very nearly destroyed it altogether, in every one of its uses of the natural world industrialism is in the process of catastrophic failure. Industry is now desperately shifting— by means of genetic engineering, global colonialism, and other contrivances—to prolong its control of our farms and forests, but the failure nonetheless continues. It is not possible to argue sanely in favor of soil erosion, water pollution, genetic impoverishment, and the destruction of rural communities and local economies. Industrialism, unchecked by the affections and concerns of agrarianism, becomes monstrous.

The second question is whether or not by espousing the revival of agrarianism we will commit the famous sin of "turning back the clock." The answer to that, for present-day North Americans, is fairly simple. Agrarian people wish to fit the farming to the farm and the forestry to the forest. At times and in places we latter-day Americans may have come close to accomplishing this goal, but we never yet have developed stable, sustainable, locally adapted land-based economies. The good rural enterprises and communities that we will find in our past have been almost constantly under threat from the colonialism, first foreign and then domestic, that has been institutionalized for a long time in the industrial economy. The possibility of an authentically settled country still lies ahead of us.

If we wish to look ahead, we will see, not only in the United States but in the world, two economic programs that conform pretty exactly to the aims of industrialism and agrarianism as I have described them.

The first is the effort to globalize the industrial economy, not merely by the expansionist programs of supra-national corporations within themselves, but also by means of government-sponsored international trade agreements, the most prominent of which is the General Agreement on Tariffs and Trade.

The second program, counter to the first, comprises many small efforts to preserve or improve or establish local economies. These efforts on the part of nonindustrial or agrarian conservatives, local patriots, are taking place in countries both affluent and poor all over the world.

20   The global economists are the great centralizers of our time. The local economists, who have so far attracted the support of no prominent politician, are the true decentralizers and downsizers, for they seek an appropriate degree of self-determination and independence for localities. They seem to be moving toward a radical and necessary revision of our idea of a city. They are learning to see the city, not just as a built and paved municipality set apart by "city limits" to live by trade and transportation from the world at large, but rather as a part of a community that includes also the city's rural neighbors, its surrounding landscape, and its watershed, on which it might depend for at least some of its

necessities, and for the health of which it might exercise a competent concern and responsibility. For though agrarianism proposes that everybody has agrarian responsibilities, it does not propose that everybody should be a farmer or that we do not need cities. Furthermore, any thinkable human economy would have to grant to manufacturing an appropriate and honorable place. Agrarians would insist only that any manufacturing enterprise should be formed and scaled to fit the local landscape, the local ecosystem, and the local community, and that it should be locally owned and employ local people.

Between these two programs—the industrial and the agrarian, the global and the local—the most critical difference is that of knowledge. The global economy institutionalizes a global ignorance, in which producers and consumers cannot know or care about one another, and in which the histories of all products will be lost.

But in a sound local economy, in which producers and consumers are neighbors, nature will become the known standard of work and production. Consumers who understand their economy will not tolerate the destruction of the local soil or ecosystem or watershed as a cost of production. Only a healthy local economy can keep nature and work together in the consciousness of the community. Only such a community can restore history to economics.

What agrarian principles implicitly propose—and what I explicitly propose in advocating these principles at this time—is a revolt of local small producers and local consumers against the global industrialism of the corporations. Do I think that there is a hope that such a revolt can survive and succeed, and that it can have a significant influence upon our lives and our world?

Yes, I do. And to be as clear as possible in arguing for this hope, let me begin with an example. Not long ago I received a phone call from my friend David Kline in Holmes County, Ohio. David is an Amish minister, one of the best farmers I know, and a man of excellent judgment. He told me, among other things, that he and his neighbors are now selling organic milk at a premium of several cents a pound above the price of nonorganic milk, and that a small cheese factory in their community is about to begin marketing organic cheese. He said that industrial excesses and abuses in milk production are "making the market" for these organic products. As a result, the farm economy has improved in Holmes County—where, because of the Amish economic and agricultural practices, the farm economy has been pretty good anyhow.

25   This, I think, gives the pattern of an economic revolt that not only is possible but is in fact happening. It is happening for two reasons: First, as the scale of industrial agriculture increases, so does the scale of its abuses, and it is hard to hide large-scale abuses from consumers. Second, as the food industries focus more and more on gigantic global opportunities, they cannot help but overlook small local opportunities, as is made plain by the increase of "community-supported agriculture," farmers' markets, health-food stores, and so on. In fact, there are some markets that the great corporations by definition cannot supply. The market for so-called organic food, for example, is really a market for good,

fresh, trustworthy food, food from producers known and trusted by consumers, and such food cannot be produced by a global corporation.

But the food economy is only one example. It is also possible to think of good local forest economies. And in the face of much neglect, it is possible to think of local small-business economies—some of them related to the local economies of farm and forest—supported by locally owned, community-oriented banks.

What do these struggling, sometimes failing, sometimes hardly realized efforts of local economy have to do with conservation as we know it? The answer, probably, is everything.

I would like my fellow conservationists to notice how many people and organizations are now working to save something of value—not just wilderness places, wild rivers, wildlife habitats, species diversity, water quality, and air quality, but also agricultural land, family farms and ranches, communities, children and childhood, local schools, local economies, local food markets, livestock breeds and domestic plant varieties, fine old buildings, scenic roads, and so on. I would like my fellow conservationists to understand also that there is hardly a small farm or ranch or locally owned restaurant or store or shop or business anywhere that is not struggling to save itself.

All of these people, who are fighting sometimes lonely battles to preserve things of value that they cannot bear to lose, are the conservation movement's natural allies. Most of them have the same enemies as the conservation movement. There is no necessary conflict among them. Thinking of them, in their great variety, in the essential likeness of their motives and concerns, one thinks almost automatically of the possibility of a defined community of interest among them all, a shared stewardship of all the diversity of good things that are needed for the health and abundance of the world.

30   I don't suppose that this will be easy, given especially the history of conflict between conservationists and land users. I only suppose that it is necessary. Conservationists can't conserve everything that needs conserving without joining the effort to use well the agricultural lands, the forests, and the waters that we must use. To enlarge the areas protected from use without at the same time enlarging the areas of good use is a mistake.

We know better than to expect very soon a working model of a conserving global corporation. But we must begin to expect—and we must, as conservationists, begin working for, and in—working models of conserving local economies. These are possible now. Good and able people are working hard to develop them now. They need the full support of the conservationist movement now. Conservationists need to go to these people, ask what they can do to help, and then help. A little later, having helped, they can in turn ask for help.

Questions for Active Reading

1. Although the fundamental structure of this essay is comparison (between agrarianism and industrialism), Berry uses cause and effect to illustrate his comparison and to argue that one "way of thought" is

preferable to the other. Summarize Berry's essay, giving particular attention to the various effects he attributes to both an agrarian and an industrial approach to the environment. Based on those effects, which way of life does Berry find preferable?

2. With reference to Figures 10.1, 10.2, and 10.3, create a diagram that illustrates the various causes of industrialism (as Berry sees it) that lead to a particular effect. (This is a kind of summary; it may be a more effective way for you to work through and understand a complex reading.)

3. Compare Berry's rhetorical strategies (his use of evidence and his diction, especially) to McKibben's. Are they writing for the same audience, or for different groups of people? Do they share a common purpose? Explain your answers by referring to specific quotes from each essay.

Questions for Thinking Critically

1. Both McKibben and Berry imply an ethical obligation, both individual and collective, to change our habits of consumption. What do these authors think about the effects of American consumer culture on the natural environment and on our relationships with each other? What evidence does each author offer to support their causal claim(s)? How would you balance their ethical demands with the practical (and, frankly, recreational) needs of your own life?

2. In paragraphs 2 and 3, Berry makes a point that reaches across spiritual and ethical traditions—that material goods do not ultimately offer satisfaction. Do you agree, or disagree? Are there different kinds of satisfaction to be had in life, and are any of them more virtuous or important than the others?

3. Think about the most recent meal you ate. Where did it come from? Who grew it, harvested it, shipped it, and sold it? Should you know? Should you care?

Writing Thoughtfully About Causal Relationships

Clearly, because of the complexity of determining cause and effect, writing a causal analysis requires special care. Causal analyses range all the way from rigorous scientific studies that can establish causes with some degree of certainty to theorizing about events in our personal lives. The causal analysis assignments you will encounter in college are likely to be of two types: those for which you conduct some kind of study to determine causality and then report your results, and those for which you research what others have said about the causes of an event and report their findings.

For the first type, you are likely to be given a format, such as for a lab report or an experimental design. It will be important for you to follow directions as you plan and conduct your study, and important for you to observe the conventions of the discipline in which you are writing as you prepare your report. Models are extremely helpful, so study them carefully if your professor provides them. If not, ask a librarian for guidance.

The second type, in which you report what others have said about the causes of an event, can be structured as an essay. If you consult other sources of information, you must properly cite and document those sources (see Appendix).

Principles for Analyzing Causes

1. Be cautious. Causal relationships are difficult to prove. You may have to use wording such as *possible cause* or *may have affected.*

2. Name and describe the event and people's reactions to it in your introduction.

3. In your thesis statement, indicate that you will be analyzing the causes of this event or that you will be reporting what others have said about its causes.

4. Discuss each cause in a separate section (at least one body paragraph for each cause).

5. Amplify how or why each cause brought about the event. Simply naming the cause is not enough.

6. Whenever possible, focus on immediate rather than remote causes.

7. Use the labels in this chapter (contributory, causal chain, interactive, sufficient, and so on) to identify causal relationships if they are suitable for the style of your paper.

8. Represent accurately any sources that you use and document them honestly and correctly.

9. Avoid logical fallacies such as *post hoc ergo propter hoc.*

10. In your conclusion, name the causes and discuss the level of certainty for each of them. You may, of course, wish to do more than this in your conclusion.

Writing Project: Exploring Some Causes of a Recent Event

This chapter has included both readings and Thinking-Writing Activities that encourage you to think about causal relationships in your own life and in the environment. Be sure to reread what you wrote for those activities; you may be able to use some of the material when completing this project.

Write an essay in which you report and discuss some of the causes of a specific local or national event that occurred within the last three years. You might want to choose an event that had an environmental impact, or, depending on your interests or your instructor's assignment, you might want to write about something else that has affected the lives of many people (such as recent Supreme Court decisions or a current international crisis). Include material from two to four sources, being certain to cite and document those sources accurately.

After you have drafted your essay, revise it to the best of your ability. Follow your instructor's directions for topic choices, length, format, documentation style, and so on.

Begin by considering the key elements in the Thinking-Writing Model.

THE WRITING SITUATION

Purpose You have a variety of purposes here. You can satisfy your own curiosity about why an event occurred and explain the causes to others. You can improve your ability to think critically about causal relationships. You can hone your revision skills by working through the revision questions that follow.

Audience You have a range of readers within your audience. *You* are an important audience, for in researching and analyzing causes, you can become a better thinker and possibly a more concerned citizen. Your classmates can be a valuable audience for review of a draft, reacting as intelligent readers who are not as knowledgeable as you about the causes of this event. Others interested in the event may find your paper enlightening. Finally, your instructor remains the audience who will judge how well you have planned, drafted, and revised. As a writing teacher, he or she cares about a clear focus, logical organization, specific details and examples, accurate documentation of sources, and correctness. Your classmates and your instructor will be interested in how you have applied this chapter's ideas.

Subject You should reflect on the event in terms of its causes and effects on the community. For example, if you decide to write about an event affecting the environment, consider that all of us need to be concerned about both positive and negative environmental changes. Not only our future, but our children's and their children's futures depend on our careful stewardship of the earth. At the same time, there are competing economic and political pressures that can act against a strict conservationist view. By researching and analyzing a specific event, we can add to our own knowledge and that of our audience, thereby preparing all for responsible future action.

Writer   You will be using sources for this essay, but your paper should be written in your own voice (it should sound like you). You will report and document the published writers' words and ideas and comment upon them as you think appropriate. If you find disagreement among your sources, don't discard any of them: the lack of agreement gives you a variety of views to report and consider.

THE WRITING PROCESS

The following sections will guide you through the stages of generating, planning, drafting, and revising as you work on your essay. Try to be particularly conscious of both the critical thinking you find in your sources and the critical thinking you do as you examine them.

Generating Ideas

- Within your instructor's parameters for the assignment, begin by finding an event that interests you. If one comes to mind immediately, you can begin to research it. If not, begin by brainstorming a list of all the local and national events you can remember from the last few years. Other good sources for events are encyclopedia yearbooks and December ("The Year in Review") issues of magazines. Then make a tentative choice.

- After you have selected an event, use your college library and the Internet. Consult Chapter 14 and your handbook about locating sources. Search for full texts of articles from reputable publications. Check titles for words like *causes, factors, results in, reasons,* or *underlie.*

- Locate or print the sources that you identify and read them, using the strategies for active and critical reading discussed in Chapter 2. First, check to see that they do indeed discuss the causes of the event, not just the event itself. Then see what causes they identify and how they label them (contributory, interactive, and so on). If they do not label them, try to do that yourself. Also, look for language that indicates the source's level of certainty about these causes ("has been definitely identified as a cause," or "may be partially responsible").

- Highlight sections of the source that you will include (if you own the source or have photocopied it). If you are required to do so, make note cards based on the marked sections.

- Think about how much information you have. Do you need more? If so, continue researching, reading, and marking until you have enough to answer the question "Why did this event take place?"

Defining a Focus Write a thesis statement that will make clear to your audience that you are going to analyze *why* the event occurred. Here are two possible ways to frame this type of thesis.

The first is simply to report what your sources say and whether or not they are in agreement.

A second type of thesis requires you to take a position on the causal relationships involved. For example, you could say, "Having read four sources dealing with the causes of this event, I agree with three of them but reject a theory proposed in the fourth."

Organizing Ideas If you made note cards, read through them two or three times. Then spread them all out on a table or desk so that you can see them all at once. Begin to group them into stacks: one to describe the event and one for each cause mentioned. Ideally, doing this will help you to integrate material from your different sources into various parts of your essay. You may decide not to use a few note cards; this often happens and indicates that you have done a good job of finding sufficient information. If you discover that you don't have enough information, you can do more research.

If you didn't make note cards, spread your marked sources out and try to plan how you will use information from each.

Review the principles for writing an essay of causal analysis on page 378 of this chapter. In addition, you will need to determine the order of your body paragraphs. For a causal chain, you will probably want chronological order. For contributory causes, you may want to use climactic (least to most important) order. For interactive causes, you may want to try different orders until you discover which will make the interaction of the causes easiest for your audience to understand.

Drafting Draft one section from each stack of note cards. A highly specific description of the event could become the introduction. Quotations from eyewitnesses or participants in the event can help to interest your audience. The introduction can conclude with the tentative thesis statement you have written.

Begin each body paragraph with a topic sentence that names the possible or verifiable cause being discussed. Then provide the audience with as much information as necessary to help them understand how that cause actually could or did bring about the event.

Be sure to note the author or title and page any information from a source comes from. Do not trust yourself to add documentation as you revise your paper. It's easy to lose track and therefore to plagiarize accidentally.

In your conclusion, you can summarize the causes and discuss the level of certainty, or uncertainty, about them. If you found considerable disagreement among your sources, you can comment on that. If research is still ongoing about the causes, you can say so. You can, of course, do more than this in your conclusion, depending on your content.

On a separate page, draft a Works Cited list, using the format specified by your instructor.

Revising, Editing, and Proofreading   Use the step-by-step method on pages 160–161 to revise and polish your essay.

The following essay shows how two students responded to this assignment.

STUDENT WRITING
LY TRUC HOANG'S WRITING PROCESS

During the process of planning the organization of her paper, Ly Truc Hoang needed to conceptualize her findings so that she could present them clearly. Notice how writing about the assignment and the ideas generated for it can lead to effective organization:

> The essay has to explain why so many crows live in the parking lot at an upscale shopping mall. The sources say that developers wanted to make money building townhouses at a location where the crows had been living. So the developers cut down all the trees to get ready to build. That was the beginning of a causal chain of events: the birds missed the trees, and because they liked to roost together, they searched for a new location for their nests and found the mall's parking lot.
>
> The chain looks like this: birds miss trees → birds look for new place → birds find big parking lot with many trees at White Flint Mall.
>
> But there was another cause, unrelated to the developer's actions, for the crows going to the mall instead of a nearby park. The parking lot offered a lot of food for the birds from trash and from the rodents the trash attracts, so there has to be a paragraph explaining that. This is a contributory cause. So is the crow's intelligence.

Huang did not use the terms "causal chain" and "contributory causes" in her essay, but using them as she brainstormed led to an understanding of those distinctions and helped her to organize her final draft.

Crows at the Mall
BY LY TRUC HOANG

I am a newcomer to the United States. Amazingly, a bird which I saw on my first day in this country was a crow. I wondered if in America crows are common birds. Now I know that there are thousands of crows which live around my city. Recently, some of these crows have caused concern because they have moved into the trees at White Flint Mall, a large, upscale shopping center.

In the *Washington Post,* an article by reporter Alona Wartofsky has a photo of crows with this caption: "Ruling the roost: Crows are making their presence known and felt at White Flint Mall" (D1). Because people are upset about too many crows at the mall, Wartofsky reports the people tend "to use words like 'eradicate' and 'terminate' " (D8). Why have the crows appeared at White Flint Mall? After reading some articles, I think I can answer this question. Missing the trees in Rockville, seeking spaces to live, and looking for food are some causes that many experts discuss about the crows' taking up residence in the mall parking lot.

First of all, missing the trees in Rockville is a cause for the crows to immigrate to White Flint. Wartofsky believes, "As many as 200,000 crows spent fall and winter around the intersection of Montrose Road and East Jefferson Drive in Rockville. But last November, developers cut down many of the trees there, and most of the birds have moved on" (D1). This is consistent with a national trend. Crows "[have] suffered huge losses in recent decades from disease, predation, logging, and development" (Kelly 107). Since the traditional habitats of crows are being destroyed by development, the birds are increasingly finding new homes. Moreover, Miller observes that "they must rapidly search for new habitat and shelter when critical habitats are disturbed" (32).

Thus, seeking a new place to live is a cause for the crows' coming to White Flint. In "Birds Need Open Space," Miller indicates, "Birds have tried to adapt and seek new shelters and places . . . as our human encroachment continues to grow" (32). They choose places that provide an appropriate habitat for nesting and for spending the winter. Some species, such as crows, prefer to spend the winter in large colonies. "Colonial roosts afford individual crows several advantages, primarily greater awareness of predators, such as owls and hawks" (Wartofsky D8). The same article quotes Audubon Naturalist Society's Mark Garland, who told Wartofsky that "many birds packed together can actually raise the ambient temperature of a particular area" (D8). In the case of White Flint, the displaced crows did not have to go far from their old location; White Flint was only a few blocks away from their old trees.

A good food supply was another cause for the crows' choice of White Flint. Many experts agree that birds' movements are typically motivated by food. In *National Wildlife,* Les Line states, "Migration is the avian solution to the problem of a disappearing food supply" (54). Crows are among the most intelligent and adaptable of birds. "The crow is a flexible omnivore," says Pete Budo, a reporter for the *New York Times* (8:9). Therefore, their food includes garbage as well as eggs and nestlings, small animals, vegetables, and carrion. And, like parking lots in malls all across the country, the lot at White Flint has food dropped by shoppers, trash receptacles, and the small animal life which trash attracts.

For all these reasons, thousands of crows enjoy spending the winter in the White Flint parking lot; that has become a serious problem for this mall. The crows are noisy, and their droppings fall on cars, sidewalks, bushes, benches, and sometimes shoppers.

Human beings intervene in natural environments, perhaps only slightly and with good intentions. However, the results are unforeseen and unwanted effects, like the crows at the mall.

Works Cited

Bodo, Pete. "The Cunning, Resourceful Crow Doesn't Deserve Its Bad Rap." *New York Times* 21 Jan. 1996: 8: 9.

Kelly, Mary Sidney. "A Crow's Last Stand." *Audubon* Sept. 1996: 107.

Line, Les. "Staying the Winter." *National Wildlife* Feb. 1995: 52–59.

Miller, David. "Birds Need Open Space." *New York State Conservationist* Aug. 1996: 32.

Wartofsky, Alona. "Caws for Concern at White Flint." *Washington Post* 2 Apr. 1997: D1+.

PART THREE

Thinking and Writing to Explore Issues and Take Positions

A s you have become more confident in your thinking and writing abilities, you may also have developed more respect for the thinking and writing of others. You have probably observed how academic work and even democracy itself depend on understanding sources of beliefs and various perspectives. You have been learning how to evaluate information and how to express your own perspectives clearly.

Part One of this book helped you focus on yourself as a thinker and a writer, and you wrote from your experiences and observations. Part Two asked you to explore important thinking patterns and to incorporate some ideas from others into your writing. Here in Part Three assignments will lead to the presentation of your ideas and those from sources in well-reasoned writing.

The Writing Projects at the end of each chapter in Part Three ask you to integrate material from several sources into your written work. As you do so, you will learn effective, responsible ways of introducing, commenting on, and documenting ideas from others. You will consider the principles that underlie research and citation, and you will use appropriate formats for academic writing.

11

Believing and Knowing

Writing to Analyze

"A belief is not merely an idea the mind possesses, it is an idea that possesses the mind." —Robert Bolton

Critical Thinking Focus: Analyzing beliefs and their accuracy

Writing Focus: Evaluating evidence and presenting beliefs

Reading Theme: How the media shape our thinking

Writing Project: Analyzing influences on beliefs about a social or academic issue

Writers write about what they believe, and their purposes often include explaining their beliefs and persuading others to adopt them. Yet what exactly are beliefs, and how are they constructed? When should they be kept, when should they be modified, and when should they be discarded? What are the differences between believing and knowing, and how do writers handle these differences? How do writers present beliefs they hold with varying degrees of certainty?

In this information age, we are flooded with data, stories, and pictures from television, radio, newspapers, magazines, books, and computers. Thus, critical thinkers and thoughtful writers face a continuing challenge to evaluate information they receive and to redefine their beliefs accordingly.

Chapter 3 examined the sources of beliefs, especially those related to personal life. This chapter continues that discussion by further examining the structure of beliefs, by presenting guidelines for evaluating beliefs, and by drawing distinctions between believing and knowing and between knowledge and truth. This chapter presents some of the ways in which beliefs take shape and some of the ways in which they are presented. The concepts of *interpretation, evaluation, conclusion, prediction, report, inference,* and *judgment* will provide a vocabulary to help you think about your beliefs and those of others.

The Writing Project at the end of the chapter asks you to analyze some influences on your beliefs about a social or an academic issue.

Ways of Forming Beliefs

Throughout our lives, we form beliefs about the world around us to explain why things happen as they do, to predict how things will happen, and to govern the choices we make. Consider, for example, the extent to which you believe the following statements.

1. Human beings need to eat in order to stay alive.

2. Smoking marijuana is a harmful activity.

3. Every human life is valuable.

4. Developing your mind is as important as taking care of your body.

5. People should care about other people, not just about themselves.

Your responses to these statements reflect certain beliefs you have, beliefs not all people share.

So what exactly are "beliefs"? We can define a **belief** as an interpretation, evaluation, conclusion, or prediction that a person believes to be true. You may not have considered these different representations of beliefs before, but, if you think about it, you might see that most of your beliefs fit into one of these categories. Sometimes it might be important as you consider a belief to see which type it is. For example, *interpretation* suggests that other explanations are possible, and *prediction* makes clear that an event has not yet happened. Such understandings help when thinking critically about your beliefs.

The statement "I believe that the U.S. Constitution's guarantee of 'the right of the people to keep and bear arms' does not prohibit all governmental regulation of firearms" represents an interpretation of the Second Amendment. To say, "I believe that watching daytime talk shows is unhealthy because they focus almost exclusively on the seamy side of human life" expresses an *evaluation* of daytime talk shows. The statement "I believe that one of the main reasons two out of three people in the world go to bed hungry each night is that industrially advanced nations like the United States have not done a satisfactory job of sharing their resources" expresses a *conclusion* about the problem of world hunger. To say, "I believe that if drastic environmental measures are not undertaken to slow the global warming trend, the polar icecaps will melt and the earth will be flooded" is to make a prediction about events that will occur in the future.

Besides expressing an interpretation, evaluation, conclusion, or prediction about the world, a belief also expresses the speaker's *endorsement* of its accuracy—an indication that the belief is held to be true. This endorsement by the speaker is a necessary dimension of a belief. For example, the statement "Astrological predictions are meaningless because there is no persuasive evidence that the position of the planets has any effect on human affairs" expresses a belief even though it doesn't specifically include the words *I believe.*

In addition, it is necessary to recognize that beliefs are not static—at least not if we apply a critical approach. We continually form and re-form our beliefs throughout much of our lives. This process often follows the following sequence:

1. We *form* beliefs in order to explain what is taking place. (These initial beliefs are often based on our past experiences.)

2. We *test* these beliefs by acting on the basis of them.

3. We *revise* (or "re-form") these beliefs if our actions do not achieve our goals.

4. We *retest* these revised beliefs by again using them as a basis for action.

As we actively participate in this ongoing process of forming and re-forming beliefs, we are using our critical thinking abilities to identify and critically examine our beliefs by, in effect, asking the following questions.

- How effectively do these beliefs explain what is taking place?
- To what extent are the beliefs consistent with other beliefs about the world?
- How effectively do the beliefs help us to predict what will happen in the future?
- To what extent are these beliefs supported by sound reasons and compelling evidence derived from reliable sources?

This process of critical exploration enables us to develop more understanding of various situations and to exert more control over them.

Thinking ↔ Writing Activity

Identifying Beliefs

State in a sentence or two one of your beliefs for each of these four categories: interpretation, evaluation, conclusion, and prediction. At least some of your statements should be ones that not everyone would agree with.

1. *Interpretation:* I believe that "X means this."
2. *Evaluation:* I believe that "X is good/bad, harmful/beneficial because . . ."
3. *Conclusion:* I believe that "X is what exists/should exist."
4. *Prediction:* I believe that "X will happen."

BELIEFS BASED ON PERSONAL EXPERIENCE

The introductory discussion of beliefs in Chapter 3 identified four sources of beliefs: people of authority, recorded references, observed evidence, and personal experience. The last two involve direct experience. Yet how we interpret and understand direct experience—what conclusions we draw from what we perceive—depends to some extent on what we already believe. In offering evidence to support their beliefs, people generally choose those perceptions and experiences that fit with their previous beliefs; contradictory experiences may be ignored or downplayed.

In the following pair of readings, two writers offer differing beliefs about the situation of the homeless in the United States, based on their perceptions of direct experience. L. Christopher Awalt's essay appeared as a "My Turn" column in *Newsweek*. Following that is "The Allesandros," a chapter from a book about homelessness by Jonathan Kozol, a long-time advocate for the politically and socially disenfranchised.

Before you begin to read, write down two or three of your beliefs about homelessness and the homeless. After you have read both pieces, write a few sentences about how your beliefs were affected by your reading these articles. If possible, share your statements with your classmates.

Brother, Don't Spare a Dime
BY L. CHRISTOPHER AWALT

L. Christopher Awalt is a writer from Austin, Texas. This essay appeared as a "My Turn" column in Newsweek *magazine.*

Homeless people are everywhere—on the street, in public buildings, on the evening news and at the corner parking lot. You can hardly step out of your house these days without meeting some haggard character who asks you for a cigarette or begs for "a little change." The homeless are not just constant symbols of wasted lives and failed social programs—they have become a danger to public safety.

What's the root of the homeless problem? Everyone seems to have a scapegoat: Advocates of the homeless blame government policy; politicians blame the legal system; the courts blame the bureaucratic infrastructure; the Democrats blame the Republicans; the Republicans, the Democrats. The public blames the economy, drugs, the "poverty cycle," and "the breakdown of society." With all this finger-pointing, the group most responsible for the homeless being the way they are receives the least blame. That group is the homeless themselves.

How can I say this? For the past two years I have worked with the homeless, volunteering at the Salvation Army and at a soup kitchen in Austin, Texas. I have led a weekly chapel service, served food, listened, counseled, given time and money, and shared in their struggles. I have seen their response to troubles, and though I'd rather report otherwise, many of them seem to have chosen the lifestyles they lead. They are unwilling to do the things necessary to overcome their circumstances. They must bear the greater part of the blame for their manifold troubles.

Let me qualify what I just said. Not everyone who finds himself out of a job and in the street is there because he wants to be. Some are victims of tragic circumstances. I met many dignified, capable people during my time working with Austin's homeless: the single father struggling to earn his high-school equivalency and to be a role model for his children; the woman who fled a good job in another city to escape an abusive husband; the well-educated young man who had his world turned upside down by divorce and a layoff. These people deserve every effort to help them back on their feet.

But they're not the real problem. They are usually off the streets and resuming normal lives within a period of weeks or months. Even while "down on their luck," they are responsible citizens, working in the shelters and applying for jobs. They are homeless, true, but only temporarily, because they are eager to reorganize their lives.

For every person temporarily homeless, though, there are many who are chronically so. Whether because of mental illness, alcoholism, poor education, drug addiction, or simple laziness, these homeless are content to remain as they are. In many cases they choose the streets. They enjoy the freedom and consider begging a minor inconvenience. They know they can always get a job for a day or two for food, cigarettes, and alcohol. The sophisticated among them have learned to use the system for what it's worth and figure that a trip through the welfare line is less trouble than a steady job. In a society that has mastered dodging responsibility, these homeless prefer a life of no responsibility at all.

Waste of time.   One person I worked with is a good example. He is an older man who has been on the streets for about 10 years. The story of his decline from respectability to alcoholism sounded believable and I wanted to help. After buying him toiletries and giving him clothes, I drove him one night to a Veterans Administration hospital, an hour and a half away, and put him into a detoxification program. I wrote him monthly to check on his progress and attempted to line up a job for him when he got out. Four months into his program, he was thinking and speaking clearly and talking about plans he wanted to make. At five months, he expressed concern over the life he was about to lead. During the sixth month, I called and was told that he had checked himself out and returned home. A month later I found him drunk again, back on the streets.

Was "society" to blame for this man? Hardly. It had provided free medical care, counseling, and honest effort. Was it the fault of the economy? No. This man never gave the economy a chance to solve his problems. The only person who can be blamed for his failure to get off the streets is the man himself. To argue otherwise is a waste of time and compassion.

Those who disagree will claim that my experience is merely anecdotal and that one case does not a policy make. Please don't take my word for it. The next time you see someone advertising that he'll work for food, take him up on it. Offer him a hard day's work for an honest wage, and see if he accepts. If he does, tell him you'll pay weekly, so that he will have to work for an entire week before he sees any money. If he still accepts, offer a permanent job, with taxes withheld and the whole shebang. If he accepts again, hire him. You'll have a fine employee and society will have one less homeless person. My guess is that you won't find many takers. The truly homeless won't stay around past the second question.

10　　So what are the solutions? I will not pretend to give ultimate answers. But whatever policy we decide upon must include some notion of self-reliance and individual responsibility. Simply giving over our parks, our airports, and our streets to those who cannot and will not take care of themselves is nothing but a retreat from the problem and allows the public property that we designate for their "use" to fall into disarray. Education, drug, and alcohol rehabilitation, treatment for the mentally ill, and job training programs are all worthwhile projects, but without requiring some effort and accountability on the part of the homeless for whom these programs are implemented, all these efforts do is break the taxpayer. Unless the homeless are willing to help themselves, there is nothing anyone else can do. Not you. Not me. Not the government. Not anyone.

FROM *Rachel and Her Children: Homeless Families in America*

The Allesandros

BY JONATHAN KOZOL (b.1936)

Jonathan Kozol has written extensively on education, poverty, and inequity. His 1967 book, Death at an Early Age: The Destruction of the Hearts and Minds of Negro Children in the Boston Public Schools, *attracted much attention. It was based on his experiences as a young teacher in a low-income neighborhood. Kozol himself was educated at a private preparatory school and Harvard University, but his work with poor children caused him to become a spokesperson for disavantaged people. His books include* Savage Inequalities: Children in America's Schools; Amazing Grace: The Lives of Children and the Conscience of a Nation; *and* Blueprint for a Democratic Education. *"The Allesandros: is a chapter from his book* Rachel and her Children: Homeless Families in America.

Far from any zone of safety lives a man named Mr. Allesandro. He's six feet tall and weighs 120 pounds—down 20 pounds from late September. When he came to the hotel a year ago he weighed 165. I first met him in the ballroom before Christmas when I handed him an apple. One bright apple. One week later he does not forget and, when he sees me in the lobby, asks me if I have some time to talk.

His two daughters are asleep. Christopher, his nine-year-old, is lying on the top bunk, fully dressed and wrapped beneath a pile of blankets, but he is awake and vigilant and almost belligerently alert. It's a cold night and the room appears to be unheated. Mr. Allesandro shows me a cracked pane of glass that he has covered over with a sheet of garbage plastic and Scotch tape. The two coils of the hot plate offer a symbolic reassurance ("heat exists") but they do not provide much warmth. He's wearing a coat and woolen hat. His mother, who is seventy-three, lives with them; for some reason, she's not here.

There aren't many men as heads of households in this building; this fact, I think, adds to his feeling of humiliation. His story, quickly told, remains less vivid for me later on than certain details like his trembling hands, the freezing room, the strange sight of his watchful boy, unsleeping on the bed. The boy reminds me of a rabbit staring from a thicket or caught in the headlights of a car.

These, as Mr. Allesandro tells me, are the facts: He was one of several maintenance workers in a high-rise building in Manhattan owned by one of the well-known developers. It was early autumn and his wife, for reasons I don't learn until much later, just picked up one day and disappeared. He tried to keep his job and home by rising early, feeding the children, bringing them to school, then rushing to his job. But his shift required him to be on duty very early. He was reprimanded and, when he explained his problem, was permitted to stay on but cut back to a half-time job. Half-time work was not enough to pay the rent. He was evicted. In the subsequent emergency he had to take leave from his job.

5   "My mother went with me to the EAU. We asked them if we could be placed together. That way, she could get the kids to school and I could keep my job." Instead, they put him in a barracks shelter with the children but would not allow his mother to go with them. As best he understands, this is because she drew a Social Security check and was on a different budget from his own. Eligibility rules are difficult to fathom; but, even where the consequences are calamitous and costly, they are faithfully observed.

"So I'm alone there in this place with about 200 cots packed side by side. Men and women, children," he says, "all together. No dividers. There's no curtains and no screens. I have to dress my kids with people watching. When my girls go to the toilet I can't take them and they're scared to go alone. A lot of women there are frantic. So I stand and wait outside the door."

He went back to the EAU and begged once more. "In my line of work," he says, "you don't earn much of your money from the salary. The people in the building get to know you and you do them favors and they give you money in return. Christmas is a time you get your tips. They'll hand you an envelope. Twenty dollars. Fifty dollars. Some give you a hundred. These are very wealthy people . . . " So his disappointment was intensified by recognition of the fact that he could not get back his job in time to benefit from the expected generosity of people whom he'd known: "Some of those people knew me well. They liked me." He seems desperate to be assured that he was liked, remembered, missed, by people who had frequently befriended him.

The use of barracks shelters as deterrence to the homeless is not absolute. Assignments are made "on an ad hoc basis," as one social worker states it. But nothing that Mr. Allesandro said could bring the EAU to place his mother with him. His former boss, he says, had told him he would take him back if he could start the day at 5:00 A.M. "There's no way that I could do it. Would you leave your kids alone within a place like that at 5:00 A.M.? I couldn't do it."

The upshot is this: He loses the chance to go back to his job a few weeks before Christmas. Although he's worked for many years, he hasn't been on *this* job long enough to have accumulated pension benefits. Dispossession from his home has left him unemployed; unemployment now will render permanent his homelessness.

10   Having finally lost everything he had, he returns a few weeks later to the EAU. This time having undergone "deterrence" and still being homeless, he is granted "temporary" placement at the Martinique. His mother can join him now. But he is no longer a wage earner; he's an AFDC father, broken in spirit, mourning for those lost tips which he will obsessively recall each time we talk. His job has been assigned to someone else. He loses self-control. He thanks God for his mother. This strikes me as a gruesome and enormously expensive instance of municipal assault upon a man's work ethic and familial integrity at the same time.

How does he feel not working?

"It's a nightmare, I'm Italian. You know—I don't mean this to sound prejudiced"—all of the white people here, I notice, are extremely careful and apologetic on this score—"my people work. My father and grandfather worked. My mother worked. I can do construction, carpentry. I can repair things. I'm somebody who's mechanically inclined. I would make beds, I would clean toilets. I'd do anything if I could have a decent job."

He searches the ads, walks the pavement, rides the subway; but he cannot find a job that pays enough to rent a home and feed three children. His rent allowance is $281. He's seen apartments for $350 and $400. If he takes an apartment over his rent limit he will have to make the difference up by cutting back on food and clothes. His mother's pension is too small to offer them a safety margin. "I wouldn't risk it. I'm afraid to take a chance. Even if I got a job, what if I lost it? I'd be back there with the children in the barracks."

So, like everybody else, he's drowning in the squalor of the Martinique Hotel but dreads the thought of being forced to leave.

15   "My mother helps to make it like a home. She tries. We got the kids a kitten, which is something that is not allowed. I don't like to break the rules, but you have got to give them something to remember that they're children."

Thinking of his hunger, I ask how he feeds the cat.

"We don't need to. We have never bought one can. She eats better than we do—on the mice and rats."

Around midnight I notice that Christopher is wide awake and watching from the bed: blue eyes, pale skin, blondish hair. Mrs. Allesandro cuts the children's hair.

Where is Mrs. Allesandro?

20   Mr. Allesandro calls her "grandma" and he speaks of her as if she were *his* grandmother as well. Grandma fell in the stairwell Friday afternoon. There had been a fire and the stairs were still slick from the water left there by the fire hoses. She's in the hospital for an examination of her hip. He tells me that she has a heart condition. "If anything happens to her [pauses] . . . I'd be dead. She's the one that's holding us together."

Other people in this building speak of Mrs. Allesandro in almost identical words. They count on her perhaps even a little more than on the nurse or on the other people in the crisis center. Unlike the crisis workers she is here around the clock. As short of food and money as the Allesandros are, I am told that she is often in the hallways bringing food to neighbors, to a pregnant woman, a sick child living somewhere on the floor. A man who knows her but does not live on this floor speaks of Mrs. Allesandro in these words: "Here she is, an old Italian lady. Here are all these women. Most of them are Puerto Rican, black . . . You will see them holding onto her, crying to her as if she was their mother."

Mrs. Allesandro, however, is not here tonight. Her son is on his own—a skeleton of hunger, disappointment, fear. I look at him, at the two girls, asleep, and at the boy—awake, alert. The boy's persistent gaze unsettles me. I ask him: "Are you sleepy?" He just shakes his head. His father is too proud to tell me that the boy is hungry. I feel embarrassed that it's taken me so long to ask. At my request he opens the refrigerator door. There is one packaged dinner, smuggled out of the lunch program. "There was something wrong with it," he says. It has a rancid smell. "It's spoiled." There's a gallon tin of peanut butter, two part-empty jars of applesauce, some hardened bread. That's it.

Mr. Allesandro takes the $20 that I hand him to the corner store. Christopher sits up halfway and talks with me. He lists for me the ten largest cities of America. I ask him whether he likes school. He does not give the usual perfunctory affirmative response. "I hate it," Christopher says. I ask him what he does for fun. He plays ball on the sidewalk at the corner of the street across from the hotel.

"Is there room to play ball on the sidewalk?"

25   He explains: "We play against the building of the bank—against the wall."

He falls asleep after I think of giving him a candy bar. His father returns in twenty minutes with a box of Kellogg's Special K, a gallon of juice, half-gallon of milk, a loaf of bread, a dozen eggs, a package of sausages, a roll of toilet paper.

He wakes his son. The boy has a bowl of cereal with milk. His father stands before the counter where he placed the food. He looks like a man who has been admitted to an elegant buffet.

Is Mr. Allesandro laden with anxiety? Is Christopher depleted, sick, exhausted? Yes, I suppose both statements are correct. Are they candidates for psychiatric care? Perhaps they are, but I should think a more important observation is that they are starving.

A few months after my evening with the Allesandros, President Reagan meets a group of high school students from New York. Between government help and private charity, he says, "I don't believe there is anyone that is going hungry in America simply by reason of denial. . . ." The president says there is a problem of "people not knowing where or how to get this help." This is what he also says of those who can't find space in public housing that he has stopped building.

His former counselor and now attorney general, Edwin Meese, concedes that people have been turning to soup kitchens but refuses to accept that they are in real need. They go to soup kitchens "because the food is free," he says, and adds, "that's easier than paying for it."

30   Marian Wright Edelman of the Children's Defense Fund makes this interesting calculation: If Defense Secretary Caspar Weinberger were to give up just a single Pentagon budget item, that which pays for him to have a private dining room, one million low-income school children could get back their morning snack—a snack denied them by administration cuts.

Hundreds of miles from Christopher's bedroom in the Martinique, a reporter describes an underground limestone cave near Kansas City: the largest surplus-food repository in the nation. In this cave and in some other large facilities, in the winter of 1986, the government was storing some 2 billion pounds of surplus food. To a child like Christopher, the vision of millions of pounds of milk and cheese and butter secreted in limestone caves might seem beyond belief. Storage of this surplus food costs taxpayers $1 million a day.

Getting surplus food from limestone caves to children's tables calls for modest but essential transportation costs. In an extraordinary action, termed illegal by the General Accounting Office, the president deferred funds allocated by the Congress for transporting food to homeless people. The sum involved, $28 million, is a small amount beside the $365 million spent to store this food in limestone caves and other warehouse areas. The withholding of such funds may possibly make sense to an economist. I do not know whether it would make much sense to Christopher.

November 1986: I'm in New York and visit with the Allesandros. Grandma's back. She says her health is good. But Christopher looks frighteningly thin. Food was scarce before. The situation's worsened since I was here last. Families in the homeless shelters of New York have been cut back on their food-stamp allocations. The White House has decided to consider money paid for rental to the hotel owners as a part of family income. By this standard, families in the

Martinique are very rich. "Tightening of eligibility requirements" has an abstract sound in Washington. On the twelfth floor of the Martinique what does it mean?

I study the computerized receipts that Mr. Allesandro has received. In June, his food-stamp allocation was $145. In August, the first stage in government reductions lowered this to $65. In October: $50. As of December it will be $33.

35   Mrs. Allesandro does not speak in ambiguities about the lives of her grandchildren. I ask her what the cuts will mean. "They mean," she says, "that we aren't going to eat." New York announces it will help make up the difference but, at the time I visit, no supplemental restaurant allowances have been received.

Questions for Active Reading

1. Awalt and Kozol have formed different beliefs about homelessness based on their personal experiences. Awalt states his beliefs directly; Kozol is less direct, but his beliefs seem clear. Try to summarize their differing beliefs in about three sentences for each. Which summary did you find easier to write? Why?

2. What other differences can you find between Awalt's expository presentation and Kozol's narrative approach? What do you see as strengths of each approach? Remember that Awalt's essay was a magazine piece limited to one page and Kozol's is a chapter from a book.

3. Identify passages in each of the readings that express interpretations, evaluations, conclusions, and predictions.

Questions for Thinking Critically

1. Do you find Awalt's and Kozol's experiences with the homeless equally effective as evidence to support each writer's expression of his beliefs? How do these readings contribute to your beliefs about the homeless?

2. Are any of your beliefs about homelessness based on direct experience? If so, whose experiences are closer to yours, Awalt's or Kozol's?

3. How did your beliefs affect your response to each essay?

BELIEFS BASED ON INDIRECT EXPERIENCE

No matter how much we have experienced in our lives, the fact is, of course, that no one person's direct experiences are enough to establish an adequate set of accurate beliefs. We all depend on the experience of others to provide us with beliefs and also to serve as foundations for those beliefs. For example, does Antarctica exist? How do we know? Have we ever been there and seen it with our own eyes? Probably not; nevertheless, we believe in the existence of Antarctica and its ice and penguins. Of all the beliefs each of us has, few are actually based on our direct personal experience. Instead, other people have in some way or form communicated to us virtually all these beliefs and the evidence for them. As we reach beyond our personal experiences to form and revise our beliefs, we find that information is provided by two sources: people of authority and recorded references.

As we have seen in the essays about homelessness by Awalt and Kozol, the beliefs of others cannot be accepted without question. Each of us views the world through individual lenses that shape and influence the way we select and present information. Comparing different sources helps to make these lenses explicit and highlights the different interests and purposes involved. In fact, examining sources may lead us to recognize that there are a variety of competing viewpoints, some fairly similar, some quite contradictory. In critically reviewing the beliefs of others, it is essential for us to pursue the same goals of accuracy and completeness that we set when examining beliefs based on personal experience. As a result, we focus on the reasons or evidence that support the information others are presenting.

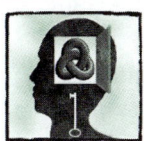

Thinking ↔ Writing Activity

The Origin of a Belief

Select one of the beliefs that you identified in the Thinking-Writing Activity at the beginning of this chapter. What indirect sources helped shape it: your family, friends, teachers, religious leaders, television, radio, the Internet? What direct personal experiences or observations have had an impact on it? Note specifically how some of these influences shaped your belief.

Evaluating Sources and Information

When we depend on information that others provide, we need to ask key questions. The most crucial part of determining the reliability of a source's information is determining the reliability of the source itself.

HOW RELIABLE IS THE SOURCE?

We know that some sources—such as advertising—can be very unreliable whereas other sources, such as *Consumer Reports* magazine (which does not accept advertising), are generally considered reliable. Sometimes, however, the reliability of a source of information is not immediately clear. In those cases, we have to use a variety of standards or criteria to evaluate a source's reliability, whether the source is written or audible.

Special care should be taken when evaluating information from Web sites. See Guidelines for Evaluating the Reliability of a Web Site on page 553 in Chapter 14.

HOW KNOWLEDGEABLE OR EXPERIENCED IS THE SOURCE?

When seeking information from indirect sources, we want to locate people of authority or recorded references that can offer a special understanding of a subject. When a car begins making strange noises, we search for someone who knows cars. When we want to learn more about a social issue such as homelessness, we turn to articles and books written by people who have studied the problem.

In seeking information from sources, it is important to distinguish between nonexpert sources and expert sources who have training, education, and experience in a particular area. Also, any expert source's credentials should be up-to-date. A book about careers in the computer industry published twenty years ago is not likely to be reliable.

Sports and entertainment figures often endorse products in TV commercials, but their testimony is not very convincing if those products have nothing to do with sports or entertainment (and if these "experts" have been paid large sums of money and told exactly what to say). Finally, we should not accept expert opinion without question or critical examination, even if the experts meet all of our criteria.

WAS THE SOURCE ABLE TO MAKE ACCURATE OBSERVATIONS?

You may have heard about an experiment in which an angry student enters a classroom, argues with the professor, then pulls out a gun and apparently shoots the professor before running out. Students in the class are then quickly informed that the situation has been staged to test their powers of observation and asked to record what happened in as much detail as they can remember. Invariably many witnesses are quite mistaken about much of what they remember while others can recall many fine details exactly. The same is true in any kind of eyewitness account: some people have quite sharp memories while others may "remember" many imagined details. In addition, a person's vantage point as a witness may color the reliability of the testimony. The amount of light, obstructions to vision, and other matters can make his or her perceptions less than wholly reliable.

The reliability of an indirect source also depends on the personal viewpoints and beliefs the source brings to a situation. These feelings, expectations, and interests often influence what a witness perceives without his or her full awareness of the process. For example, a group that sponsored an anti-racism rally on a campus might claim a crowd of more than five hundred while campus security issues a report estimating rally attendance at about two hundred. We have seen that two different writers can draw very different conclusions after spending time working in a homeless shelter. What further questions could be asked, and how might additional sources be located to evaluate the reliability of such differing sources?

HOW REPUTABLE IS THE SOURCE?

When evaluating the reliability of sources, it is useful to consider how accurate and reliable their information has been in the past. If someone has consistently given sound information over a period of time, we gradually develop confidence in the accuracy of that person's reports. Police officers and news media reporters must continually evaluate the reliability of information sources. Of course, this works the other way as well. When people consistently give inaccurate or incomplete information, others lose confidence in their reliability. Nevertheless, few people provide information that is either completely reliable or completely unreliable. You probably realize that your own reliability tends to vary, depending on the situation, the type of information you are providing, and the person to whom you are giving it. Thus, in trying to evaluate information offered by others, you have to explore the following factors before arriving at a provisional conclusion, which you may have to revise later in light of additional information.

WHAT ARE THE SOURCE'S PURPOSES AND INTERESTS?

Evaluating information means thinking critically about the perceiving lenses through which the source of the information views the situation. Is this source presenting an argument or giving information? Are you looking at a report, an inference, or a judgment (see pages 412–413)? In other words, what is the rhetorical purpose of the piece? How is the purpose reflected in the selection of details and in wording and tone?

You also need to think about the piece's audience. Who is the intended audience? Is it friendly, neutral, or hostile? Is it informed or new to the subject? Writers or speakers can focus on specific audiences without being dishonorable, but sometimes they can emphasize one point of view or tap emotions in manipulative ways. Can you detect any slanting, or does this source's material seem balanced?

HOW VALUABLE IS INFORMATION FROM THIS SOURCE?

Of course, you also need to assess the credibility of the information itself by asking these questions: What are the main ideas being presented? What evidence is provided? Does the information seem accurate? Is it up-to-date? Does anything seem false? Does anything seem to have been left out?

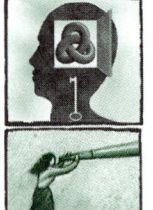

Thinking ↔ Writing Activity

Evaluating a Source of a Belief

Select one of the beliefs that you discussed in the Thinking-Writing Activity on page 389 that is based on sources such as people of authority or recorded references. Now, based on the criteria just discussed, evaluate the reliability of one source of your belief.

Believing and Knowing

Developing beliefs that are as accurate as possible is important to us as critical thinkers because the more accurate our beliefs are, the better we are able to understand the world around us and to make predictions about the future. As the preceding discussion has suggested, however, the accuracy of the beliefs we form can vary tremendously.

We use the word *knowing* to distinguish beliefs supported by strong reasons or evidence (such as the belief that life exists on earth) from beliefs for which there is less support (such as the belief that life exists on other planets) or from beliefs disproved by reasons or evidence to the contrary. This saying expresses another way to understand the difference between believing and knowing:

"You can believe what is not so, but you cannot know what is not so."

In the following essay, an astrophysicist considers a question that would seem to have an obvious answer. In doing so, he analyzes the difference between believing and knowing.

Is the Earth Round or Flat?

BY ALAN LIGHTMAN (b.1948)

A physicist as well as a writer of fiction and nonfiction, Alan Lightman, a professor at the Massachusetts Institute of Technology, has been fascinated by the intersections of science and art since he was a small boy growing up in Tennessee. As an astrophysi-

cist, he has focused his research on gravitation theory, the structure and behavior of ac-
cretion disks, stellar dynamics, radiative processes, and relativistic plasmas. As an ed-
ucator, however, Lightman has been just as fundamentally engaged with how such ar-
cane and technical concepts can be made comprehensible, even entrancing, to a general
audience. "I feel that to most people the scientific culture is like a foreign country,"
Lightman has said. "I take special delight when I can read a good writer from another
culture, bringing me into that world. That's something I would like to do with the sci-
entific culture." Lightman's 1993 novel Einstein's Dreams *has inspired plays and mu-*
sical compositions, and was a runner-up for the 1994 PEN New England/Boston Globe
Winship Award. In 1996 Lightman was elected a fellow of the American Academy of
Arts and Sciences and also won the 1996 American Institue of Physics Andrew Gemant
Award for linking science to the humanities.

I propose that there are few of you who have personally verified that the Earth
is round. The suggestive globe in the den or the Apollo photographs don't
count. These are secondhand pieces of evidence that might be thrown out entirely in court. When you think about it, most of you simply believe what you
hear. Round or flat, whatever. It's not a life-or-death matter, unless you happen
to live near the edge.

A few years ago I suddenly realized, to my dismay, that I didn't know with
certainty if the Earth were round or flat. I have scientific colleagues, geodesists
they are called, whose sole business is determining the detailed shape of the
Earth by fitting mathematical formulae to someone else's measurements of the
precise locations of test stations on the Earth's surface. And I don't think those
people really know either.

Aristotle is the first person in recorded history to have given proof that the
Earth is round. He used several different arguments, most likely because he
wanted to convince others as well as himself. A lot of people believed everything Aristotle said for 19 centuries.

His first proof was that the shadow of the Earth during a lunar eclipse is
always curved, a segment of a circle. If the Earth were any shape but spherical,
the shadow it casts, in some orientations, would not be circular. (That the normal phases of the moon are crescent-shaped reveals the moon is round.) I find
this argument wonderfully appealing. It is simple and direct. What's more, an
inquisitive and untrusting person can knock off the experiment alone, without
special equipment. From any given spot on the Earth, a lunar eclipse can be seen
about once a year. You simply have to look up on the right night and carefully
observe what's happening. I've never done it.

5   Aristotle's second proof was that stars rise and set sooner for people in the
East than in the West. If the Earth were flat from east to west, stars would rise
as soon for Occidentals as for Orientals. With a little scribbling on a piece of
paper, you can see that these observations imply a round Earth, regardless of
whether it is the Earth that spins around or the stars that revolve around the
Earth. Finally, northbound travelers observe previously invisible stars appearing above the northern horizon, showing the Earth is curved from north to

south. Of course, you do have to accept the reports of a number of friends in different places or be willing to do some traveling. Aristotle's last argument was purely theoretical and even philosophical. If the Earth had been formed from smaller pieces at some time in the past (or *could* have been so formed), its pieces would fall toward a common center, thus making a sphere. Furthermore, a sphere is clearly the most perfect solid shape. Interestingly, Aristotle placed as much emphasis on this last argument as on the first two. Those days, before the modern "scientific method," observational check wasn't required for investigating reality. Assuming for the moment that the Earth is round, the first person who measured its circumference accurately was another Greek, Eratosthenes (276–195 B.C.). Eratosthenes noted that on the first day of summer, sunlight struck the bottom of a vertical well in Syene, Egypt, indicating the sun was directly overhead. At the same time in Alexandria, 5,000 stadia distant, the sun made an angle with the vertical equal to 1/50 of a circle. (A stadium equaled about a tenth of a mile.) Since the sun is so far away, its rays arrive almost in parallel. If you draw a circle with two radii extending from the center outward through the perimeter (where they become local verticals), you'll see that a sun ray coming in parallel to one of the radii (at Syene) makes an angle with the other (at Alexandria) equal to the angle between the two radii. Therefore, Eratosthenes concluded that the full circumference of the Earth is 50 x 5,000 stadia, or about 25,000 miles. This calculation is within one percent of the best modern value.

For at least 600 years educated people have believed the Earth is round. At nearly any medieval university, the quadrivium was standard fare, consisting of arithmetic, geometry, music, and astronomy. The astronomy portion was based on the *Tractatus de Sphaera*, a popular textbook first published at Ferrara, Italy, in 1472 and written by a 13th century, Oxford-educated astronomer and mathematician, Johannes de Sacrobosco. The *Sphaera* proves its astronomical assertions, in part, by a set of diagrams with movable parts, a graphical demonstration of Aristotle's second method of proof. The round Earth, being the obvious center of the universe, provides a fixed pivot for the assembly. The cutout figures of the sun, the moon, and the stars revolve about the Earth.

By the year 1500, 24 editions of the *Sphaera* had appeared. There is no question that many people *believed* the Earth was round. I wonder how many *knew* this. You would think that Columbus and Magellan might have wanted to ascertain the facts for themselves before waving good-bye. To protect my honor as a scientist, someone who is supposed to take nothing for granted, I set out with my wife on a sailing voyage in the Greek islands. I reasoned that at sea I would be able to calmly observe landmasses disappear over the curve of the Earth and thus convince myself, firsthand, that the Earth is round.

Greece seemed a particularly satisfying place to conduct my experiment. I could sense those great ancient thinkers looking on approvingly, and the layout of the place is perfect. Hydra rises about 2,000 feet above sea level. If the Earth has a radius of 4,000 miles, as they say, then Hydra should sink down to the horizon at a distance of about 50 miles, somewhat less than the distance you were to sail from Hydra to Kea. The theory was sound and comfortable. At the very least, I thought, you would have a pleasant vacation.

As it turned out, that was all you got. Every single day was hazy. Islands faded from view at a distance of only eight miles, when the land was still a couple of degrees above the horizon. I learned how much water vapor was in the air but nothing about the curvature of the Earth.

10   I suspect that there are quite a few items you take on faith, even important things, even things you could verify without much trouble. Is the gas you exhale the same as the gas you inhale? (Do you indeed burn oxygen in your metabolism, as they say?) What is your blood made of? (Does it indeed have red and white "cells"?) These questions could be answered with a balloon, a candle, and a microscope.

When you finally do the experiment, you relish the knowledge. At one time or another, you have all learned something for yourselves, from the ground floor up, taking no one's word for it. There is a special satisfaction and joy in being able to tell somebody something you have pieced together from scratch, something you really know. I think that exhilaration is a big reason why people do science.

Someday soon, I'm going to catch the Earth's shadow in a lunar eclipse, or go to sea in clear air, and find out for sure if the Earth is round or flat. Actually, the Earth is reported to flatten at the poles, because it rotates. But that's another story.

Questions for Active Reading

1. Using an active reading technique from Chapter 2, read the first and the last paragraphs of this article. Now that you have read the entire article, would you say that technique gave you a good preview?

2. Why is it important to know that Lightman is a scientist? Would an artist or a social worker write about this subject in this way?

3. Where is Lightman using a lighthearted tone? Identify some phrases that show this. Where is he serious? Identify some phrases that show this. What is the effect of these tones?

Questions for Thinking Critically

1. Is it practical for a person to actually conduct a scientific experiment in order to "know" something? Do you think that Lightman is really proposing this? What is he implying?

2. Give one conclusive "proof" for the roundness of the earth that the author identifies and explain why it seems a valid proof.

3. In the next-to-last paragraph, Lightman writes about "a special satisfaction and joy in being able to tell somebody something you have pieced together from scratch. . . . I think that exhilaration is big reason why people do science." Have you experienced satisfaction, joy, and exhilaration after completing a scientific experiment? Have you experienced such emotions after completing some other kind of project? Do you think that satisfaction, joy, and exhilaration are important emotions to experience in one's work?

Thinking ↔ Writing Activity

Weighing Your Beliefs and Knowledge

Look again at the beliefs you have written about for previous activities. Could you say about any of them "I know this" rather than merely "I believe this"? Why? Write answers to these questions.

KNOWLEDGE AND TRUTH

Authorities often disagree about the true nature of a given situation or the best course of action. It is common, for example, for doctors to disagree about a diagnosis, for economists to differ on the state of the economy, or for psychiatrists to disagree on whether a convicted felon is a menace to society or a victim of social forces.

What do we do when experts disagree? As critical thinkers, we must analyze and evaluate all the available information, develop our own well-reasoned beliefs, and recognize when we lack sufficient information to arrive at well-reasoned beliefs. We must realize, too, that such beliefs may evolve over time as we obtain more information or improve our insight.

Although there are compelling reasons to view knowledge and truth as evolving, some people resist doing so. Either they take refuge in a belief in the absolute, unchanging nature of knowledge and truth as presented by the appropriate authorities, or they conclude that there is no such thing as knowledge or truth and that trying to seek either is futile.

UNDERSTANDING RELATIVISM

In this latter view of the world, known as *relativism*, all beliefs are considered "relative" to the person or context in which they arise. For the relativist, all opinions are equal in validity to all others; no one is ever in a position to say with confidence that one view is right and another one wrong. Although a relativistic view is appropriate in some areas of experience—for example, in matters of taste such as fashion—in many other areas it is not. Knowledge, in the form of well-supported beliefs, does exist. Some beliefs are better than others, not because an authority has proclaimed them so but because they can be analyzed in terms of the criteria discussed earlier in this chapter.

UNDERSTANDING FALSIFIABLE BELIEFS

Another important criterion for evaluating certain beliefs is that the beliefs be *falsifiable*. This means that it is possible to state conditions—tests—under which the beliefs could be disproved, and that the beliefs then pass those tests. For example, if you believe that you can create ice cubes by placing water-filled trays in a freezer, you can conduct an experiment to determine whether your belief is accurate. If no ice cubes form after you put the trays in the freezer, your theory is disproved. If, however, you believe that your destiny is related to the positions of the planets and stars (as astrologers do), it is not clear how you can conduct an experiment to determine whether your belief is accurate. Since a belief that is not falsifiable can never be proved, such a belief is questionable.

THE MEDIA AND TRUTH

We are all aware in a general way that the media can shape our beliefs by the information they provide and the interpretations they give to that information. We may not be aware, however, of some of the subtle ways in which this is done or of the profound influences that result. As you read the following essays, consider how your beliefs might be shaped by the sources that these writers discuss.

The following article originally appeared in *Newsweek*. It reports on studies conducted by a University of Pennsylvania professor, concerning the influence of television on people's beliefs.

FROM *Tainted Truth: The Manipulation of Fact in America*

False Truth and the Future of the World
BY CYNTHIA CROSSEN (b. 1951)

Now a senior editor at The Wall Street Journal, *Cynthia Crossen has covered social trends, publishing, education, and financial markets as a reporter and editor at the* Journal *since 1983. In addition to her newspaper work, Crossen has written well-received books.* The Rich and How They Got That Way *was named the WHSmith Business*

Book of the Year in 2001. Included here is a chapter from her book Tainted Truth: The Manipulation of Fact in America, *which was selected as a top book by* Business Week. Tainted Truth *reports on "scientific: studies published under the guise of objectivity that actually are conducted to reflect their sponsors' intentions. This chapter focuses on studies designed to influence beliefs about public policy issues.*

Common sense, common knowledge and the gospels of environmentalism held that disposable diapers were bad for the earth. Yet a study, published to great fanfare in the spring of 1990, found that disposable diapers were actually no worse for the environment than reusable cotton ones.

This was good news for many parents. Cotton diapers may have been ecologically correct, but they were also less efficient and less convenient. Some who bought disposable diapers were guilt-ridden, embarrassed to be seen toting a 26-pack around the neighborhood. Now research exonerated them of a crime against nature. They could love the earth *and* throw away a dozen plastic-and-chemical-gel diapers a day.

The study's sponsor? Procter & Gamble, one of the biggest buyers of research in the United States and, of course, the country's largest maker of disposable diapers. The company controls about half the $3.5-billion-a-year U.S. market with its Pampers and Luvs brands. For several years, it had been fighting a public relations battle against environmentalists and the cloth diaper industry. Although the disposable diaper industry, born in the 1960s, was thriving, the Earth Day mentality had made inroads. Between 1988 and 1990, customers for cloth diapers almost doubled. Even more ominous for the disposable makers, more than a dozen state legislatures were considering various bans, taxes and warning labels on disposable diapers.

A few studies later, the campaign against disposables was all but dead. Researchers paid by the disposable diaper industry had produced a new, improved truth about disposable diapers. Disposables, symbol of the throwaway society, were environmentally correct. In fact, they would no longer even be called disposable; henceforth they would be known as "single-use." The media disseminated the studies' contrarian findings widely. "People Claiming Cloth Diapers Are Clearly Superior May Be All Wet," said the *Louisville* (Kentucky) *Courier-Journal.* "Grass Isn't Greener on Green Side, Environmentally Conscious Choices May Be Doing More Harm," said the *Cincinnati Enquirer.* In statehouses around the country, diaper legislation withered away. By early 1992, Gerber Products, the largest supplier of cloth diapers in the country, said it would close three cloth-weaving operations and lay off 900 workers. "In the past year," Alfred A. Piergallini, Gerber's chairman and chief executive, said at the time, "there was a dramatic change in the cloth diaper market caused by reduced environmental concerns about disposable diapers."

5   Procter & Gamble's diaper study was a landmark example of the public policy study, a form of research that increasingly shapes people's beliefs and decisions on social, political, economic and environmental questions. Political debates of the 1980s and 1990s on issues from homelessness to garbage to the

spotted owl have been driven by research. The industry that generates this research has developed an unspoken but almost inviolable rule: Its numbers will anoint the ideology of whoever commissioned the research. The sponsor is rarely surprised or betrayed.

Studies done for public policy debates rank second only to research done for advertising in their disdain for objectivity and fact. While in other arenas researchers would be embarrassed to admit their study was partisan, in public policy they are not. "Who says it has to be neutral?" challenged an aide to U.S. Representative Fortney H. Stark about a distorted cable television questionnaire his office had sent out. Commenting on the same study, the aide later said, "We're proud that it was biased. Our viewpoint is that cable TV should be re-regulated."

The researchers themselves are not evil. They are devoted to their profession, and they genuinely seek to improve its methods. Yet they have let their ethical habits slip to a level more often seen among lobbyists and public relations executives. A Washington economist, who asked not to be named because his former employer is still a member of the House of Representatives, described two studies he did on a hydroelectric dam project planned for the home district. "My boss says, 'Write me the best justification for this project that you can.' So I did this cost-benefit analysis that made the project look like a gold mine. About a month later, he calls me in and says, 'Give me the most objective, independent, comprehensive analysis of this project you can.' I came back to him and said, 'This project is a dog.' He knew how to use me and that's fine. Researchers are for hire."

Exaggeration, hyperbole, creative projections, wild assumptions and hand-waving are the building blocks of public policy research, where people fight for the ear of the people and the good of the world. Anything goes. Most public policy wars are fought on huge plains, where people are counted in the millions, economic impacts in the billions and the very survival of mankind and the earth may be at stake—the very places it is most tempting to justify means with ends. Public policy studies are seldom challenged by either the press or public because they address mammoth and complex questions about which most people have little if any personal experience or knowledge. Nor has the press, by and large, learned to accord research studies the routine skepticism that reporters bring to more obviously self-serving news releases.

The creative manipulation of public policy studies crosses all political, gender, racial, religious and age lines. Whatever your beliefs and politics, your team does it. Organizations from Procter & Gamble, the country's largest advertiser, to the smallest and poorest social action groups sponsor advocacy research. No result is too absurd or self-evident to be peddled to the press.

- "Rental Housing for Poor Still a Problem, Study Says," announced a newspaper headline about a study sponsored by two nonprofit advocacy groups for the poor.

- "Americans Want to Live to 100 Years, Survey Says; Bar Nursing Homes, Losing Independence," reported the nonprofit Alliance for Aging

Research, which advocates more investment in scientific research about aging.

- "Life on Streets Dangerous for Homeless Youth," concluded a study sponsored by the Chicago Coalition for the Homeless.

10   Public interest groups are masters of the tactical study. Their motives for their creative numbers are less commercial than industry's, but they can be just as self-centered. Public interest groups thrive on attention from the press because that is how they recruit new members. While business may understate hazards, public interest groups tend to exaggerate them. "Each group convinces itself that its worthy goals justify oversimplification to an 'ignorant' public," wrote Daniel E. Koshland, Jr.

Among life-and-death issues, researchers are not quite so fastidious about creating perfectly neutral questions for their surveys. A mail survey for the environmental guerrilla group Greenpeace asked people's attitudes on several issues. Among the leading questions was this: "Depletion of Earth's protective ozone layer leads to skin cancers and numerous other health and environmental problems. Do you support Greenpeace's demand that DuPont, the world's largest producer of ozone-destroying chemicals, stop making unneeded ozone-destroying chemicals immediately?"

But from industry: "Do you favor setting up an additional Consumer Protection Agency over all the others, or do you favor doing what is necessary to make the agencies we now have more effective in protecting the consumer's interests?" asked a survey commissioned by the Business Roundtable, which was opposing the creation of a federal consumer protection agency. Seventy-five percent of those surveyed said they opposed creating such an agency. The survey was released during the height of congressional debate on the subject.

And from a Connecticut representative to Congress, a body that has become addicted to questionnaires: "Would you support universal health care if it would mean the loss of thousands of jobs, particularly in Connecticut?"

Legislators know most studies prepared for policy debates are sponsored by a self-interested industry or lobby. What they may not realize is that such research nevertheless influences the course of events. Occasionally a piece of research has a decisive influence on the outcome of the debate—Procter & Gamble's diaper study, for example. But more often, contradictory studies simply paralyze the decision-making process, shelving the resolution of immediate problems. "Someone will produce a study that statistically demonstrates X or Y," said Ray Sentes, a Canadian political science professor who has studied the effects of asbestos on human health. "So the workers have to rush out and get an epidemiologist to do a study for them. And so it goes. For ten years we flash studies at each other. If the practical outcome of a scientific study ends up being delayed of any activity, shouldn't the scientist say, 'You don't need this study'?" For issues like the health effects of asbestos, Sentes noted, it would take several studies of thousands of people over dozens of years to come up with meaningful results. "They don't have the time or the money or the data," he said. "So they do these slash-and-burn studies that get plonked into the middle of the public policy process."

15   Strategic research has dominated modern debates over abortion, gun control, family leave, recycling, school choice and the speed limit, just to name a few. Each issue has its dueling polls. The timber industry has its polls showing most people wouldn't sacrifice a single job to protect an endangered species; and nature groups have their poll showing that most people support the Endangered Species Act. Proponents of school choice have surveys showing that people want it, and opponents have their surveys showing people do not. Gun control activists have surveys showing that many people want increased regulation of guns; the National Rifle Association has surveys showing the opposite.

The battle over abortion rights has produced hundreds of surveys showing contrary results. In June 1991, the abortion warriors—Planned Parenthood and the National Right to Life Committee—each produced survey results showing people's opinions of a recent Supreme Court ruling that the government could prohibit the discussion of abortion in family planning clinics that received federal funding. Planned Parenthood's survey asked this question: "Do you favor or oppose that Supreme Court decision preventing clinic doctors and medical personnel from discussing abortion . . . ?" Sixty-five percent said they opposed the ruling.

The other survey first asked people if they favored or opposed the Supreme Court ruling. The survey described the ruling as "the federal government is not required to use taxpayer funds for family planning programs to perform, counsel or refer for abortion as a method of family planning." The Supreme Court, of course, had said no such thing: the question was whether the government should be permitted, not required, to finance family planning programs where abortion was discussed. No one was talking about abortion as a method of family planning. And the Supreme Court was ruling on whether such clinics could discuss, not perform, abortions. Even so, only 48 percent said they favored the court's decision. Then the survey asked, "If you knew that any government funds not used for family-planning programs that provide abortion will be given to other family-planning programs that provide contraception and other preventive methods of family-planning, would you then favor or oppose the Supreme Court's ruling?" Here the group got the mandate it was seeking, the one they pitched to the press: 69 percent said they favored the decision. In hearings before the House of Representatives, which was considering an amendment that would prevent the regulation from being enforced, the National Right to Life poll was cited. The amendment was defeated.

Since bigger numbers almost always mean bigger allocations or more attention, most of the numbers flying around policy debates exaggerate on the high side. The National Association for Prenatal Addiction Research and Education says as many as 375,000 babies who may have been affected by drugs are born every year; that is, 375,000 babies whose mothers ingested either alcohol or a drug at one point in their pregnancy. In the late 1970s, the American Cancer Society predicted that cancer would claim the lives of at least 8.5 million

Americans in the 1980s. In fact, between 1980 and 1990, 4.5 million Americans died of cancer. And while it costs only $3,205 to provide disposable cups, forks, plates, etc., for one school for one year, it costs a staggering $12,413 for reusable material—or so argued a Tennessee school district fighting the mandated use of reusable materials. The disposable figure included the price of buying the materials, the labor of handling them and their waste disposal; the figure for reusables included the cost of the materials, the labor to wash them, the cost of the washing equipment and the water. It did not compare the cost of making the reusables and disposables, nor did it take into account environmental costs. Furthermore, if it is so economical to use disposables, why have they not replaced glass, china and stainless steel in every home in America?

"Even if congressmen discount for biases in the material they are given," wrote James Payne, "this does not solve the problem. When you cut a 50-fold exaggeration in half, you are still left believing a 25-fold exaggeration."

20   The size of the homeless population has been the subject of several studies whose estimates range from 230,000 to 3 million. Homeless advocates have estimated 2 million to 3 million people have been homeless at some time during the previous year. (On any particular night, advocates say, the number of homeless may be closer to half a million to one million.) The advocates' number was derived from estimating the percentage of the population that was homeless— 1 percent—and building in a huge margin of error. Martha Burt of the Urban Institute said that the last time 1 percent of the population was homeless was in the heart of the Depression. "Nineteen thirty-three is what 1 percent homeless looks like," she said.

In 1984, the Department of Housing and Urban Development estimated there were between 250,000 and 300,000 homeless. That figure was developed from sixty local experts estimating how many homeless they had in their cities. Their answers were added together and then projected to the nation. In 1987, the Urban Institute estimated 500,000 to 1,000,000 homeless. That number was derived from sampling homeless shelters and soup kitchens in cities with populations of more than 100,000 and then doing elaborate adjustments.

In March 1990, the Census Bureau sent 15,000 census takers out one night— S night, it was called, for streets and shelters—to count the homeless. They found 230,000. Homeless advocates quickly disputed the figure, saying that with a few exceptions the census takers did not go to any city with a population of less than 50,000: they did not count any homeless people they saw in alleyways or streets; and they, like other homeless researchers, had no way of counting the people sleeping on the couch or floor of someone's house who might be looking for shelter the following night. Research built on shelter data is inherently skewed because a huge part of the homeless population—single people who are highly impaired and chronically homeless—tend not to use shelters.

In November 1993, another count of the homeless in two big cities—New York and Philadelphia—was released. This study counted the homeless using computer records of Social Security numbers at city shelters. The study found that 3.3 percent of New York's population had stayed in a shelter sometime over the past five years. The stay could be as short as one day. Should one one-day stay sometime in the past five years define a person as homeless?

It is not possible to count the homeless population precisely; they are transient, wary of authority and sometimes mentally ill or addicted to drugs. Sadly, the issue of counting the homeless long ago overwhelmed the moral debate on what to do about people living in the street, as though without agreeing on the numbers there could be no agreement that homelessness is a problem. A decade after the plight of the homeless appeared on the national agenda, there is still a sizable homeless population. Statistical formulas do not solve our problems any faster or better, and they cannot eliminate politics, as the political scientist Kenneth Prewitt points out. They simply push politics back one stop, to disputes about methods: "Arguments about numerical quotas, availability pools and demographic imbalance become a substitute for democratic discussion of the principles of equity and justice."

25   In public policy debates and deliberations, words like decency, right and wrong, peace, fairness, trust and hope have lost their force. Numbers, which can offer so much illumination and guidance if used professionally and ethically, have become the tools of advocacy. Even if their cause is worthy, people who massage data undermine the power and purity of statistics that may be crucial to future decisions. There are numbers we will never know, and we should admit it. It is essential to understand the homeless before making policy about them. But in this case, as in so many others in public policy, understanding is not the same as counting.

Questions for Active Reading

1. Crossen begins this chapter with three paragraphs about a study on possible environmental effects of disposable diapers. After you have read the entire chapter, consider the effect of this introduction. Does it work well?

2. Crossen gives several examples demonstrating that the way a survey question is worded influences the kinds of responses people make to it. Find one of those examples and identify specific words that might influence responses. How would you respond to those questions?

3. Notice some of the sentences in which Crossen makes general claims. Do these sentences state the main points? Does she provide specific evidence to support the general statements?

Questions for Thinking Critically

1. In the introduction to her book, Crossen states that her own survey found that while 76 percent of her respondents agreed that "you can find a scientific study to prove just about anthing that you want to

prove," 86 percent said that "references to scientific research in a story increased its credibility." How do you explain these apparently contradictory responses?

2. Do you think that a survey can be conducted in a completely objective way? Why or why not?

3. Crossen suggests that competing, contradictory studies can serve to prevent progress toward solving serious social problems such as homelessness. Do you agree with this idea? Can you think of ways that competing beliefs can interact to discover something closer to the "truth"?

Ways of Presenting Beliefs

When you write, you are presenting your beliefs. No matter what its form—letters, college papers, web log, business documents, even stories and poems—your written expression states what you believe. When you write, you present your beliefs in three ways: reports, inferences, and judgments. Your choice of words establishes which of the three you are using:

- Report: My bus was late today.
- Inference: My bus will probably be late tomorrow.
- Judgment: The bus system is unreliable.

Now try to identify which of the three is being used in these statements:

1. Each modern nuclear warhead has over one hundred times the explosive power of the bomb dropped on Hiroshima.

2. With all the billions of planets in the universe, the odds are that there are other forms of life in the cosmos.

3. In the long run, the energy needs of the world will best be met by solar energy technology rather than nuclear energy or fossil fuels.

As you examine these various statements, you can see that they provide readers with different types of information. For example, the first statement in each list reports aspects of the world that can be verified—that is, checked for accuracy. Appropriate investigation can determine whether the bus was actually late today and whether modern nuclear warheads really have the power attributed to them. When you describe the world in ways that can be verified through investigation, you are **reporting factual information**.

Looking at the second statement in each list, you can see that each provides a different sort of information than the first one does. These statements cannot be verified. There is no way to investigate and determine with certainty whether the bus will indeed be late tomorrow or whether there is life on other planets.

Although these conclusions may be based on facts, they go beyond them. When you describe the world in ways based on factual information yet go beyond it to make statements about what is not currently known, you are **inferring** conclusions about the world.

Finally, as you examine the third statement in each list, it is apparent that these statements differ from both factual reports and inferences. In each the speaker is applying certain standards (criteria) to deem the bus service as unreliable and solar energy as more promising than nuclear energy or fossil fuels. You are **judging** when you describe the world in ways that evaluate it on the basis of certain criteria.

You continually use these ways of describing and organizing your world—reporting, inferring, and judging—to make sense of your experience. In most instances, you are not aware that you are actually performing these activities, nor are you usually aware of the differences among them. Yet these three activities work together to help you see the world as a complete picture.

Thinking ↔ Writing Activity

Identifying Reports, Inferences, and Judgments

1. Write three statements that you believe—one as a report, one as an inference, and one as a judgment.
2. Locate a short article from a newspaper or magazine and identify the reports, inferences, and judgments it contains.
3. Share your statements and your findings with classmates.

REPORTING FACTUAL INFORMATION

Statements written as reports express the most accurate beliefs you have about the world. Factual beliefs have earned this distinction because they are verifiable, usually by using one or more of your senses. For example, consider the following factual statement: "That young woman is wearing a brown hat in the rain." This statement about an event in the world is considered factual because you can verify it immediately with sensual experience—what you can (in principle or in theory) see, hear, touch, taste, or smell. It is important to say *in principle or in theory* because often you do not use all of your senses to check out what you are experiencing. Look again at the factual statement: you would normally be satisfied to see this event without insisting on touching the hat or giving the person a physical examination. If necessary, however, you could perform these additional actions.

You use the same reasoning when you believe other people's factual statements that you are not in a position to check immediately. For instance:

- The Great Wall of China is more than fifteen hundred miles long.
- There are large mountains and craters on the moon.
- Your skin is covered with germs.

You consider these factual statements because even though you cannot verify them with your senses at the moment, you could in principle or in theory do so *if* you were flown to China, *if* you were rocketed to the moon, or *if* you were to examine your skin with a powerful microscope. The process of verifying factual statements involves identifying the sources of information on which they are based and evaluating the reliability of these sources.

You communicate factual information to others by means of reports. A **report** is a description of something that has been experienced, then communicated in as accurate and complete a way as possible. Through reports you share your sense experiences with other people, and this mutual sharing enables you to learn much more about the world than if you were confined to knowing only what you experience. The recording (making records) of factual reports has also made it possible to accumulate the knowledge acquired by previous generations.

Because factual reports play such an important role in the exchange and accumulation of information about the world, it is important that they be as accurate and complete as possible. This brings us to a problem. We have already seen in previous chapters that our perceptions and observations often are not accurate or complete. This means that sometimes when we think we are making true factual reports, they actually are inaccurate or incomplete. For instance, consider our earlier factual statement: "That young woman is wearing a brown hat in the rain." Here are questions you could ask concerning the accuracy of the statement:

- Is the woman really young, or does she merely look young?
- Is the person really a woman, or a man disguised as a woman?
- Is that really a hat the woman is wearing, or is it something else (such as a helmet or a paper bag)?

Of course, there are methods you could use to answer these questions. Can you describe some of them?

Besides difficulties with observations, the "facts" that you see in the world actually depend on more *general beliefs* that you have about how the world operates. Consider this question: "Why did the man's body fall from the top of the building to the sidewalk?" Having had some general science courses, you might respond, "The body was simply obeying the law of gravity" and consider that a factual statement. But how did people account for this sort of event before Newton formulated the law of gravity? Some popular responses might have included the following:

- Things always fall down, not up.
- The spirit in the body wanted to join with the spirit of the earth.

In the past, when people made statements like these—such as "Humans can't fly"—they thought they were stating facts. Increased knowledge and understanding have since shown these "factual beliefs" to be inaccurate, so they have been replaced by "better" beliefs. These better beliefs explain the world in a way that is more accurate and predictable. Will many of the beliefs now considered to be factually accurate also be replaced by more precise and predictable beliefs? If history is any indication, this will most certainly happen. Newton's formulations have already been replaced by Einstein's, based on the latter's theory of relativity. Einstein's have been refined and modified as well and may someday be replaced.

Thinking ↔ Writing Activity

Evaluating Factual Information

1. Locate and carefully read, watch, or listen to a report that deals with a major social issue.
2. Identify the main idea and key points of the article.
3. Describe the factual statements used to support the main idea.
4. Evaluate the accuracy of the factual information.
5. Evaluate the reliability of the sources of the factual information.

INFERRING FROM EVIDENCE OR PREMISES

Imagine yourself in the following situations.

1. It is 2:00 A.M. and your roommate comes crashing into the room. He staggers to his bed and falls across it, dropping (and breaking) a nearly empty whiskey bottle. Startled, you gasp, "What's the matter?" With alcohol fumes blasting from his mouth, he mumbles: "I jus' wanna hadda widdel drink!" What do you conclude?

2. Your roommate has just learned that she passed a math exam for which she had done absolutely no studying. Humming the refrain "I did it my way," she comes dancing over to you with a huge grin on her face and says, "Let me buy you dinner to celebrate!" What do you conclude about how she is feeling?

3. It is midnight and the library is about to close. As you head for the door, you spy your roommate shuffling along in an awkward waddle. His coat bulges out in front as if he's pregnant. When you ask, "What's going on?" he gives you a glare and hisses, "Shhh!" Just before he reaches the door, a pile of books slides from under his coat and crashes to the floor. What do you conclude?

In these examples, it would be reasonable to make the following conclusions.

1. Your roommate is drunk.

2. Your roommate is happy.

3. Your roommate is stealing library books.

Although these conclusions are reasonable, they are not factual reports; they are inferences. You have not directly experienced your roommate's "drunkenness," "happiness," or "stealing." Instead, you have inferred it on the basis of your roommate's behavior and the circumstances. What clues in these situations might lead to these conclusions? One way of understanding the inferential nature of these views is to ask yourself the following questions.

1. Have you ever pretended to be drunk when you weren't? Could other people tell?

2. Have you ever pretended to be happy when you weren't? Could other people tell?

3. Have you ever been accused of stealing something when you were perfectly innocent? How did this happen?

From these examples you can see that whereas factual beliefs can in principle be verified by direct observation, *inferential beliefs* go beyond what can be directly observed. For instance, in the previous examples, your observation of some of your roommate's actions led you to infer things that you were not observing directly—"He's drunk," "She's happy," "He's stealing books."

Making such simple inferences is something you do all the time. It is so automatic that usually you are not even aware that you are going beyond your immediate observations or that you may be having trouble distinguishing between what you *observe* and what you *infer*. Making such inferences enables you to see the world as a complete picture, to fill in the blanks and to supplement the fragmentary sensations being presented to your senses. Presenting your inferences along with your beliefs in writing paints a complete picture for your readers.

Your writing may also include *predictions* of what will occur in the near future. Predictions and expectations are also inferences because you attempt to determine what is currently unknown from what is already known.

It is possible that your inferences may be wrong; in fact, they frequently are. You may infer that the woman sitting next to you is wearing two earrings and then discover that she has only one. You may expect the class to end at noon but find that the teacher lets you out early—or late. In the last section, we concluded that not even factual beliefs are ever absolutely certain. Comparatively speaking, inferential beliefs are much more uncertain than factual beliefs, so it is important to distinguish between the two.

The distinction between what is observed and what is inferred is given particular attention in courtroom settings, where defense lawyers usually want witnesses to describe only what they observed—not what they inferred as they observed. When a witness includes an inference such as "I saw him steal it," the lawyer may object that the statement represents a "conclusion of the witness" and move to have the observation struck from the record. For example, imagine that you are a defense attorney listening to the following testimony. At what points would you object by saying, "This is a conclusion of the witness"?

> I saw Harvey running down the street, right after he knocked the old lady down. He had her purse in his hand and was trying to escape as fast as he could. He was really scared. I wasn't surprised because Harvey has always taken advantage of others. It's not the first time that he's stolen, either; I can tell you that. Just last summer he robbed the poor box at St. Anthony's. He was bragging about it for weeks.

Finally, keep in mind that even though in *theory* facts and inferences can be distinguished, in *practice* it is almost impossible to communicate with others in speech or writing by sticking only to factual observations. A reasonable approach is to state your inference along with the observable evidence on which the inference is based (e.g., John seemed happy because . . .). Our language has an entire collection of terms (*seems, appears, is likely,* and so on) that signal when we are making an inference and not expressing an observable fact. Thoughtful writers use these words carefully and deliberately.

Many of the predictions that you make are inferences based on your past experiences and information that you presently have. Even when there appear to be sound reasons supporting them, these inferences are often wrong due to incomplete information or unanticipated events. The fact that even people whom society considers "experts" regularly make inaccurate predictions should encourage you to exercise caution when presenting your beliefs as inferences. Here are some examples:

> "So many centuries after the Creation, it is unlikely that anyone could find hitherto unknown lands of any value." —The Advisory Committee to King Ferdinand and Queen Isabella of Spain, before Columbus's voyage in 1492

> "What will the soldiers and sailors, what will the common people say to 'George Washington, President of the United States'? They will despise him to all eternity." —John Adams, 1789

> "What use could the company make of an electrical toy?" —Western Union's rejection of the telephone in 1878

> "The actual building of roads devoted to motor cars is not for the near future in spite of many rumors to that effect." —a 1902 article in *Harper's Weekly*

"You ain't goin' nowhere, son. You ought to go back to driving a truck." —Jim Denny, Grand Ole Opry manager, firing Elvis Presley after one performance, 1954

Examine the following list of statements, noting which are *factual beliefs* (based on observations) and which are *inferential beliefs* (conclusions that go beyond observations). For each factual statement, describe how you might go about verifying the information. For each inferential statement, describe a factual observation on which the inference could be based. (*Note:* Some statements may contain both factual beliefs and inferential beliefs.)

- When my leg starts to ache, that means snow is on the way.
- The grass is wet—it must have rained last night.
- I think that it's pretty clear from the length of the skid marks that the accident was caused by that person's driving too fast.
- Fifty men lost their lives in the construction of the Queensboro Bridge.
- Nancy said she wasn't feeling well yesterday—I'll bet that she's out sick today.

Now consider the following situations. What inferences might you be inclined to make on the basis of what you are observing? How could you investigate the accuracy of an inference?

- A student in your class is consistently late for class.
- You see a friend driving a new car.
- An instructor asks the same student to stay after class several times.
- You don't receive any birthday cards.

So far, we have been exploring relatively simple inferences. Many of the inferences people make, however, are much more complicated. In fact, much of our knowledge of the world rests on our ability to make complicated inferences in a systematic and logical way. However, just because an inference is more complicated does not mean that it is more accurate; in fact, the opposite is often the case. One of the masters of inference is the legendary Sherlock Holmes. In the following passage, Holmes makes an astonishing number of inferences upon meeting Dr. Watson. Study Holmes's conclusions carefully. Are they reasonable? Can you explain how he reaches them?

"You appeared to be surprised when I told you, on our first meeting, that you had come from Afghanistan."

"You were told, no doubt."

"Nothing of the sort. I knew you came from Afghanistan. From long habit the train of thoughts ran so swiftly through my mind that I arrived at the conclusion without being conscious of intermediate steps. There were such steps, however. The train of reasoning ran, 'Here is a gentleman of a medical type, but with the air of a military man. Clearly an army doctor, then. He is just come from the tropics, for his face is dark, and that is not the natural tint of his skin, for his wrists are fair. He has undergone hardship and sickness, as his haggard face says clearly. His left arm has been injured. He holds it in a stiff and unnatural manner. Where in the tropics could an English army doctor have seen much hardship and got his arm wounded? Clearly in Afghanistan.' The whole train of thought did not occupy a second. I then remarked that you came from Afghanistan, and you were astonished." —Sir Arthur Conan Doyle, *A Study in Scarlet*

Thinking ↔ Writing Activity

Analyzing an Incorrect Inference

Describe an experience in which you made an incorrect inference. For example, it might have been a situation in which you mistakenly accused someone, an accident based on a miscalculation, a poor decision based on an inaccurate prediction, or some other event. Analyze that experience by answering the following questions:

1. What was (were) your mistaken inference(s)?

2. What was the factual evidence on which you based your inference(s)?

3. Looking back, what could you have done to avoid making the erroneous inference(s)?

The following essay illustrates the ongoing process by which natural scientists use inferences to discover factual information and to construct theories explaining the information.

Evolution as Fact and Theory

BY STEPHEN JAY GOULD (1941–2002)

Stephen Jay Gould started his academic career as a professor of geology at Harvard University, but expanded his interests into evolutionary biology. He was curator of invertebrate paleontology at Harvard's Museum of Comparative Zoology and a writer with a gift for translating complex scientific theories into informed, but witty, prose that nonscientists can understand and enjoy. His essays appeared in magazines such as Natural History *and* Discover *and were collected in the books* Ever Since Darwin, The Panda's Thumb, *and* The Flamingo's Smile. *This essay illustrates the ongoing process by which natural scientists use inferences to discover factual information and to construct theories explaining that information.*

Kirtley Mather, who died last year at age 89, was a pillar of both science and the Christian religion in America and one of my dearest friends. The difference of half a century in our ages evaporated before our common interests. The most curious thing we shared was a battle we each fought at the same age. For Kirtley had gone to Tennessee with Clarence Darrow to testify for evolution at the Scopes trial of 1925. When I think that we are enmeshed again in the same struggle for one of the best documented, most compelling and exciting concepts in all of science, I don't know whether to laugh or cry.

According to idealized principles of scientific discourse, the arousal of dormant issues should reflect fresh data that give renewed life to abandoned notions. Those outside the current debate may therefore be excused for suspecting that creationists have come up with something new, or that evolutionists have generated some serious internal trouble. But nothing has changed; the creationists have not a single new fact or argument. Darrow and Bryan were at least more entertaining than we lesser antagonists today. The rise of creationism is politics, pure and simple; it represents one issue (and by no means the major concern) of the resurgent evangelical right. Arguments that seemed kooky just a decade ago have re-entered the mainstream.

Creationism Is Not Science

The basic attack of the creationists falls apart on two general counts before we even reach the supposed factual details of their complaints against evolution. First, they play upon a vernacular misunderstanding of the word "theory" to convey the false impression that we evolutionists are covering up the rotten core of our edifice. Second, they misuse a popular philosophy of science to argue that they are behaving scientifically in attacking evolution. Yet the same philosophy demonstrates that their own belief is not science, and that "scientific creationism" is therefore meaningless and self-contradictory, a superb example of what Orwell called "newspeak."

In the American vernacular, "theory" often means "imperfect fact"—part of a hierarchy of confidence running downhill from fact to theory to hypothesis to guess. Thus the power of the creationist argument: evolution is "only" a theory, and intense debate now rages about many aspects of the theory. If evolution is less than a fact, and scientists can't even make up their minds about the theory, then what confidence can we have in it? Indeed, President Reagan echoed this argument before an evangelical group in Dallas when he said (in what I devoutly hope was campaign rhetoric): "Well, it is a theory. It is a scientific theory only, and it has in recent years been challenged in the world of science—that is, not believed in the scientific community to be as infallible as it once was."

5   Well, evolution *is* a theory. It is also a fact. And facts and theories are different things, not rungs in a hierarchy of increasing certainty. Facts are the world's data. Theories are structures of ideas that explain and interpret facts. Facts do

not go away when scientists debate rival theories to explain them. Einstein's theory of gravitation replaced Newton's, but apples did not suspend themselves in mid-air pending the outcome. And human beings evolved from apelike ancestors whether they did so by Darwin's proposed mechanism or by some other, yet to be discovered.

Moreover, "fact" does not mean "absolute certainty." The final proofs of logic and mathematics flow deductively from stated premises and achieve certainty only because they are *not* about the empirical world. Evolutionists make no claim for perpetual truth, though creationists often do (and then attack us for a style of argument that they themselves favor). In science, "fact" can only mean "confirmed to such a degree that it would be perverse to withhold provisional assent." I suppose that apples might start to rise tomorrow, but possibility does not merit equal time in physics classrooms.

Evolutionists have been clear about this distinction between fact and theory from the very beginning, if only because we have always acknowledged how far we are from completely understanding the mechanisms (theory) by which evolution (fact) occurred. Darwin continually emphasized the difference between his two great and separate accomplishments: establishing the fact of evolution, and proposing a theory—natural selection—to explain the mechanism of evolution. He wrote in *The Descent of Man:* "I had two distinct objects in view; firstly, to show that species had not been separately created, and secondly, that natural selection had been the chief agent of change. . . . Hence if I have erred in . . . having exaggerated its [natural selection's] power . . . I have at least, as I hope, done good service in aiding to overthrow the dogma of separate creations."

Thus Darwin acknowledged the provisional nature of natural selection while affirming the fact of evolution. The fruitful theoretical debate that Darwin initiated has never ceased. From the 1940s through the 1960s, Darwin's own theory of natural selection did achieve a temporary hegemony that it never enjoyed in his lifetime. But renewed debate characterizes our decade, and while no biologist questions the importance of natural selection, many now doubt its ubiquity. In particular, many evolutionists argue that substantial amounts of genetic change may not be subject to natural selection and may spread through populations at random. Others are challenging Darwin's linking of natural selection with gradual, imperceptible change through all intermediary degrees; they are arguing that most evolutionary events may occur far more rapidly than Darwin envisioned.

Scientists regard debates on fundamental issues of theory as a sign of intellectual health and a source of excitement. Science is—and how else can I say it?—most fun when it plays with interesting ideas, examines their implications, and recognizes that old information may be explained in surprisingly new ways. Evolutionary theory is now enjoying this uncommon vigor. Yet amidst all this turmoil no biologist has been led to doubt the fact that evolution occurred; we are debating *how* it happened. We are all trying to explain the same thing: the tree of evolutionary descent linking all organisms by ties of genealogy. Creationists pervert and caricature this debate by conveniently neglecting the common conviction that underlies it, and by falsely suggesting that we now doubt the very phenomenon we are struggling to understand.

10   Using another invalid argument, creationists claim that "the dogma of separate creations," as Darwin characterized it a century ago, is a scientific theory meriting equal time with evolution in high school biology curricula. But a prevailing viewpoint among philosophers of science belies this creationist argument. Philosopher Karl Popper has argued for decades that the primary criterion of science is the falsifiability of its theories. We can never prove absolutely, but we can falsify. A set of ideas that cannot, in principle, be falsified is not science.

The entire creationist argument involves little more than a rhetorical attempt to falsify evolution by presenting supposed contradictions among its supporters. Their brand of creationism, they claim, is "scientific" because it follows the Popperian model in trying to demolish evolution. Yet Popper's argument must apply in both directions. One does not become a scientist by the simple act of trying to falsify another scientific system; one has to present an alternative system that also meets Popper's criterion—it too must be falsifiable in principle.

"Scientific creationism" is a self-contradictory, nonsense phrase precisely because it cannot be falsified. I can envision observations and experiments that would disprove any evolutionary theory I know, but I cannot imagine what potential data could lead creationists to abandon their beliefs. Unbeatable systems are dogma, not science. Lest I seem harsh or rhetorical, I quote creationism's leading intellectual, Duane Gish, Ph.D., from his recent (1978) book *Evolution? The Fossils Say No!* "By creation we mean the bringing into being by a supernatural Creator of the basic kinds of plants and animals by the process of sudden, or flat, creation. We do not know how the Creator created, what processes He used, *for He used processes which are not now operating anywhere in the natural universe* [Gish's italics]. This is why we refer to creation as special creation. We cannot discover by scientific investigations anything about the creative processes used by the Creator." Pray tell, Dr. Gish, in the light of your last sentence, what then is "scientific" creationism?

The Fact of Evolution

Our confidence that evolution occurred centers upon three general arguments. First, we have abundant, direct, observational evidence of evolution in action, from both the field and the laboratory. It ranges from countless experiments on change in nearly everything about fruit flies subjected to artificial selection in the laboratory to the famous British moths that turned black when industrial soot darkened the trees upon which they rest. (The moths gain protection from sharp-sighted bird predators by blending into the background.) Creationists do not deny these observations; how could they? Creationists have tightened their act. They now argue that God only created "basic kinds," and allowed for limited evolutionary meandering within them. Thus toy poodles and Great Danes come from the dog kind and moths can change color, but nature cannot convert a dog to a cat or a monkey to a man.

The second and third arguments for evolution—the case for major changes—do not involve direct observation of evolution in action. They rest upon inference, but are no less secure for that reason. Major evolutionary change requires too much time for direct observation on the scale of recorded human history. All historical sciences rest upon inference, and evolution is no different from geology, cosmology, or human history in this respect. In principle, we cannot observe processes that operated in the past. We must infer them from results that still survive: living and fossil organisms for evolution, documents and artifacts for human history, strata and topography for geology.

15   The second argument—that the imperfection of nature reveals evolution—strikes many people as ironic, for they feel that evolution should be most elegantly displayed in the nearly perfect adaptation expressed by some organisms—the camber of a gull's wing, or butterflies that cannot be seen in ground litter because they mimic leaves so precisely. But perfection could be imposed by a wise creator or evolved by natural selection. Perfection covers the tracks of past history. And past history—the evidence of descent—is our mark of evolution.

Evolution lies exposed in the *imperfections* that record a history of descent. Why should a rat run, a bat fly, or porpoise swim, and I type this essay with structures built of the same bones unless we all inherited them from a common ancestor? An engineer, starting from scratch, could design better limbs in each case. Why should all the large native mammals of Australia be marsupials, unless they descended from a common ancestor isolated on this island continent? Marsupials are not "better," or ideally suited for Australia; many have been wiped out by placental mammals imported by man from other continents. This principle of imperfection extends to all historical sciences. When we recognize the etymology of September, October, November, and December (seventh, eighth, ninth, and tenth, from the Latin), we know that two additional items (January and February) must have been added to an original calendar of ten months.

The third argument is more direct: transitions are often found in the fossil record. Preserved transitions are not common—and should not be, according to our understanding of evolution . . . —but they are not entirely wanting, as creationists often claim. The lower jaw of reptiles contains several bones, that of mammals only one. The nonmammalian jawbones are reduced, step by step, in mammalian ancestors until they become tiny nubbins located at the back of the jaw. The "hammer" and the "anvil" bones of the mammalian ear are descendants of these nubbins. How could such a transition be accomplished?, the creationists ask. Surely a bone is either entirely in the jaw or in the ear. Yet paleontologists have discovered two transitional lineages of therapsids (the so-called mammal-like reptiles) with a double jaw joint—one composed of the old quadrate and articular bones (soon to become the hammer and anvil), the other of the squamosal and dentary bones (as in modern mammals). For that matter, what better transitional form could we desire than the oldest human, *Australopithecus afarensis,* with its apelike palate, its human upright stance, and a cranial capacity larger than any ape's of the same body size but a full 1,000 cubic centimeters below ours? If God made each of the half dozen human species discovered in ancient rocks, why did he create an unbroken temporal sequence of progressively more modern features—increasing cranial capacity, reduced face and teeth, larger body size? Did he create a mimic evolution and test our faith thereby?

Conclusion

I am both angry at and amused by the creationists; but mostly I am deeply sad. Sad for many reasons. Sad because so many people who respond to creationist appeals are troubled for the right reason, but venting their anger at the wrong target. It is true that scientists have often been dogmatic and elitist. It is true that we have often allowed the white-coated, advertising image to represent us— "Scientists say that Brand X cures bunions ten times faster than . . . " We have not fought it adequately because we derive benefits from appearing as a new priesthood. It is also true that faceless bureaucratic state power intrudes more and more into our lives and removes choices that should belong to individuals and communities. I can understand that requiring that evolution be taught in the schools might be seen as one more insult on all these grounds. But the culprit is not, and cannot be, evolution or any other fact of the natural world. Identify and fight your legitimate enemies by all means, but we are not among them.

I am sad because the practical result of this brouhaha will not be expanded coverage to include creationism (that would also make me sad), but the reduction or excision of evolution from high school curricula. Evolution is one of the half dozen "great ideas" developed by science. It speaks to the profound issues of genealogy that fascinate all of us—the "roots" phenomenon writ large. Where did we come from? Where did life arise? How did it develop? How are organisms related? It forces us to think, ponder, and wonder. Shall we deprive millions of this knowledge and once again teach biology as a set of dull and unconnected facts, without the thread that weaves diverse material into a supple unity?

20   But most of all I am saddened by a trend I am just beginning to discern among my colleagues. I sense that some now wish to mute the healthy debate about theory that has brought new life to evolutionary biology. It provides grist for creationist mills, they say, even if only by distortion. Perhaps we should lie low and rally around the flag of strict Darwinism, at least for the moment—a kind of old-time religion on our part.

But we should borrow another metaphor and recognize that we too have to tread a straight and narrow path, surrounded by roads to perdition. For if we ever begin to suppress our search to understand nature, to quench our own intellectual excitement in a misguided effort to present a united front where it does not and should not exist, then we are truly lost.

Questions for Active Reading

1. Gould defines *facts* as the "world's data" and refers to observing an apple fall from the tree as Isaac Newton is alleged to have done. Iden-

tify some of the facts Gould presents as evidence to support the theory of evolution.

2. Gould defines *theories* as "structures of ideas that explain and interpret facts," such as Newton's theory of gravitation, which was introduced to explain facts like falling apples. In addition to facts, Gould states, the theory of evolution is supported by reasonable inferences. Identify some inferences that he cites as evidence.

3. Gould begins this essay with allusions to the Scopes trial of 1925, Darrow, and Bryan. He seems to assume that his readers will know what he is talking about. If you know about this event, how does this reference set the scene for his 1981 essay? If you don't know about it, was your understanding reduced?

Questions for Thinking Critically

1. What does Gould say about creationism? Find specific statements. Is Gould presenting reports, inferences, or judgments about this concept?

2. Gould calls Kirtley Mather a "pillar of both science and the Christian religion in America." Do you know people who are both scientific and spiritual? What do those people say about these two approaches to the world?

3. How can the qualities of a critical reader and thinker be useful in considering the issues involved in discussions of evolution and creationism? In other words, how can being curious, open-minded, knowledgeable, and creative help here?

The comic strip below was probably intended to be funny, but it reflects what Gould says about theories as "structures of ideas that explain and interpret facts." Historical facts are interpreted differently at different times; theories about history change. School textbooks about United States history of fifty years ago usually focused on the Founding Fathers, pioneers moving westward, and military actions. Books published now usually include material on Native Americans, women, slaves, and daily life. You might want to discuss this change with your grandparents or older friends.

© Thaves. Reprinted with permission. Newspaper distributed by NEA, Inc.

JUDGING BY APPLYING CRITERIA

Identify and write a description of a friend, a course you have taken, or the college you attend. Be sure your descriptions are specific and include what you think about the friend, the course, and the college.

1. _____ is a friend I have. He/she is . . .

2. _____ is a course I have taken. It was . . .

3. _____ is the college I attend. It is . . .

Now review your writing. Does it include factual descriptions? Note any facts that can be verified. Your writing may also contain inferences based on factual information. Can you identify any? In addition, your writing may include judgments about the person, the course, and the school—descriptions that express your evaluation based on certain criteria. Facts and inferences help you figure out what is actually happening (or will happen); the purpose of judgments is to express your evaluation about what is happening (or will happen). For example:

- My new car has broken down three times in the first six months. (Factual report)
- My new car will probably continue to have difficulties. (Inference)
- My new car is a lemon. (Judgment)

When you label your new car a "lemon," you are making a judgment based on certain criteria. For instance, a lemon is usually a newly purchased item—often an automobile—with which you have repeated problems. For another example of judging, consider the following statements:

- Carla always does her work thoroughly and completes it on time. (Factual report)
- Carla will probably continue to do her work in this fashion. (Inference)
- Carla is a very responsible person. (Judgment)

By judging Carla to be responsible, you are evaluating her on the basis of the criteria or standards that you believe indicate a responsible person. One such criterion is completing assigned work on time. Can you identify additional criteria for judging someone as being responsible?

Review your previous description of a friend, a course, or your college. Can you identify any judgments in your description? For each judgment you have listed, identify the criteria on which you based the judgment.

Many of our disagreements with others focus on differences in judgments. To write thoughtfully, you need to approach such differences intelligently by following these guidelines:

- Make explicit the criteria or standards used as a basis for the judgment.
- Try to establish the reasons that justify these criteria.

For instance, if you write "Professor Andrews is an excellent teacher," you are basing your judgment on certain criteria of teaching excellence. Once these standards are made explicit, they can be discussed to see whether they make sense and what justifies them. Of course, your idea of what makes an excellent teacher may be different from someone else's, so you can test your conclusion by comparing your criteria with those of your classmates. When disagreements occur, use these two steps for resolution.

In short, not all judgments are equally good or equally poor. The credibility of a judgment depends on the criteria used to make the judgment and on the evidence or reasons that support these criteria. For example, there may be legitimate disagreements about judgments on the following points:

- Who was the greatest United States president?
- Which movie deserves the Oscar this year?
- Which is the best baseball team this year?

However, in these and countless other cases, the quality of judgments depends on presenting the criteria used for the competing judgments and then demonstrating that your candidate best meets the agreed-upon criteria by providing supporting evidence and reasons. With this approach, you can often engage in intelligent discussion and establish which judgments are best supported by the evidence.

Thinking ↔ Writing Activity

Analyzing Judgments

Review the following passages, which illustrate various judgments. For each passage, do the following:

1. Identify the evaluative criteria on which the judgments are based.
2. Describe the reasons or evidence the author uses to support the criteria.
3. Explain whether you agree or disagree with the judgments and give your rationale.

One widely held misconception concerning pizza should be laid to rest. Although it may be characterized as fast food, pizza is not junk food. Especially when it is made with fresh ingredients, pizza fulfills our basic nutritional requirements. The crust provides carbohydrates; from the cheese and meat or fish comes protein; and the tomatoes, herbs, onions, and garlic supply vitamins and minerals. —Louis Philip Salamone, "Pizza: Fast Food, Not Junk Food"

Let us return to the question of food. Responsible agronomists report that before the end of the year millions of people if unaided might starve to death. Half a billion deaths by starvation is not an uncommon estimate. Even though the United States has done more than any other nation to feed the hungry, our relative affluence makes us morally vulnerable in the eyes of other nations and in our own eyes. Garrett Hardin, who has argued for a "lifeboat" ethic of survival (if you take all the passengers aboard, everybody drowns), admits that the decision not to feed all the hungry requires of us "a very hard psychological adjustment." Indeed it would. It has been estimated that the 3.5 million tons of fertilizer spread on American golf courses and lawns could provide up to 30 million tons of food in overseas agricultural production. The nightmarish thought intrudes itself. If we as a nation allow people to starve while we could, through some sacrifice, make more food available to them, what hope can any person have for the future of international relations? If we cannot agree on this most basic of values—feed the hungry—what hopes for the future can we entertain? —James R. Kelly, "The Limits of Reason"

DISTINGUISHING AMONG REPORTS, INFERENCES, AND JUDGMENTS

Although the activities of reporting, inferring, and judging tend to be woven together in your experiences and in your writing, it is important to be able to distinguish these activities. Each plays a different role in helping you make sense of the world for yourself and for your readers, and you should be careful not to confuse these roles. For instance, although writers may appear to be reporting factual information, they may actually be expressing personal evaluations, which are not factual. Consider the statement "Los Angeles is a smog-ridden city drowning in automobiles." Although seeming to be reporting factual information, the writer really is expressing his or her personal judgment. Of course, writers can identify their judgments with such phrases as "in my opinion," "my evaluation is," and so forth.

Sometimes, however, writers do not identify their judgments. In some cases they do not do so because the context within which they are writing (such as a newspaper editorial) makes it clear that the information is judgment rather than fact. In other cases, however, they want their judgments to be treated as factual information. Confusing the activities of reporting, inferring, and judging, whether accidental or deliberate, can be misleading and even dangerous.

Confusing factual information with judgments can be personally damaging as well. For example, there is a big difference between these two statements:

- I failed my exam today. (Factual report)
- I am a failure. (Judgment)

Stating the fact "I failed my exam today" describes your situation in a concrete way, enabling you to evaluate (judge) it as a problem you can hope to solve through reflection and hard work. If, however, the situation causes you to make the judgment "I am a failure," this sort of general evaluation will not encourage you to explore solutions to the problem or improve your situation.

Finally, another main reason for distinguishing among the activities of reporting, inferring, and judging concerns the accuracy of statements. We noted, for instance, that factual statements tend to be reasonably accurate because they are by nature verifiable whereas inferences are usually much less certain. As a result, it is crucial to be aware of whether you are presenting a belief as a report, an inference, or a judgment. If you write the superintendent of your apartment building a note saying "My thermostat is broken," an inference on your part based on the fact that you feel uncomfortably hot, you will feel foolish if you later discover that you have a fever and that the thermostat is functioning well.

Presenting Beliefs in Your Writing

Understanding and evaluating beliefs pertains in three particular ways to your college papers as well as to the writing you will do in other settings. First, as you are better able to distinguish among reports, inferences, and judgments, you will be able to present different types of beliefs more accurately. Although you may not often use the term *report, inference,* or *judgment,* you will word your beliefs in precise ways that indicate the level of speculation behind your statements.

Second, a strong relationship exists between the thesis of a paper and your beliefs about the topic. The thesis, most of all, expresses what you believe is the main point of your paper. As you work to clarify your thesis statement, you also clarify your beliefs about the issue you are addressing. And when you state the thesis clearly in your paper, you are making your beliefs clear to your readers.

Third, as a college writer and quite possibly as a working professional, you will regularly use source material in your papers. The techniques for evaluating beliefs will help you evaluate sources of information. Then, as you present in your researched writing what others have said, you can comment on their beliefs as you integrate the material into your papers. (See Chapter 14 on research.)

Writing Project: Analyzing Influences on Your Beliefs About a Social or Academic Issue

This chapter has included both readings and Thinking-Writing Activities that encourage you to think about the sources of your beliefs. Be sure to reread what you wrote for the activities as you may be able to use some of it in completing this project.

Write an essay in which you consider some influences on the development of your beliefs about a social issue or an idea related to an academic field. As much as possible, apply the concepts discussed in this chapter.

As a college student, you receive much of your information about social or academic issues from print and electronic sources. Therefore, you should analyze at least two media sources such as newspaper, magazine, or journal articles; material from a web site; a film or a video; a book or book chapter. In addition, think about what your teachers and other people have told you and, perhaps, about personal experiences.

Begin by considering the key elements of the Thinking-Writing Model.

THE WRITING SITUATION

Purpose   Your primary purpose here is to further your own development as a capable college student. You will be exploring some of the ways in which you come to accept concepts. In addition, you will be sharing your insights with your audience, which always provides another purpose: to write an effective paper.

On a technical level, you are required to take different kinds of information and pull them together. Such *synthesis* is the central purpose of many kinds of academic and professional writing. Most research papers, case studies, field reports, project summaries, product proposals, and business plans use information which must be analyzed and synthesized.

You also have an intellectual purpose. You will look closely at your own ways of defining what you believe and what you consider true as well as what you do not believe and what you consider false.

Audience   As usual, your classmates are a good audience for this paper, both in draft and finished versions, since they are doing the same assignment and will want to see how you handle it. In addition, people interested in the social issue or academic field will naturally be potential readers. If you are taking a class pertaining to your subject, you could share your paper with those students. If you are writing about a social issue relevant to your community, you could share your work in a newsletter or on a web site.

Of course, your instructor remains the audience who will judge how well you have articulated your beliefs, how you have selected the influences on your beliefs, how you have handled the sources, and how you have planned, drafted, revised, and edited your essay.

Subject Examining the sources of beliefs and evaluating evidence are among the most challenging of activities. If you are just beginning to learn about the issue on which you are writing, you may not have enough background to be very inquisitive or judgmental. However, you should be aware of criteria that any thoughtful student can detect: specific support for a claim, whether information is current, appropriateness of examples and authorities, and responsible attribution. Also, you have some understanding of reports, inferences, predictions, and judgments to apply to your analysis.

Writer For this Writing Project, you should be as open as possible to new ways of thinking about your beliefs. After such critical analysis, some writers find that their beliefs have been strengthened; others may realize that some of their beliefs were based on unreliable information and need to be reevaluated.

As with the Writing Projects in Part One, you are in a position of authority here when you are writing about your own reactions and realizations. At the same time, since you are writing about a social issue or an academic field instead of about your personal life, you are a writer who is dealing with other people's beliefs in addition to your own. After writing the paper, you may want to consider whether you are a more accepting or more skeptical person.

THE WRITING PROCESS

The following sections will guide you through the stages of planning, drafting, and revising your essay analyzing the sources of your beliefs.

Generating Ideas

- Identify some ideas in the Thinking-Writing Activities that you may be able to use. Then write informally about them.
- Think about teachers, books, films, articles, the Internet, and other sources of information in your field that have provided you with information that you believe. Why have they had this effect?
- Think about any sources that you are reluctant to trust or believe. Why have they had this effect?
- What concepts in this field do you believe most firmly?
- Are there some that you question?
- Freewrite for five minutes about your ideas for this project.
- Look at the list of questions for exploring topics in Chapter 4. Which of them can help you generate ideas for this project?

Defining a Focus

- The Writing Project itself provides a wide-angle focus, but you must sharpen it in order to produce an understandable paper.

- Notice if your issue or idea has several components. For example, the issue of high-stakes testing in public schools raises questions about the kind of tests used, the effects on students' passing to the next level, the effects on school funding or ratings, and the effects on curriculum. You may want to focus only on one aspect. Perhaps your beliefs about evolution in biology or parallel processing in computer science are really beliefs about several components of the general idea.

- Write down your belief to be sure that you can state it well. If you haven't decided on one belief, write several. Are they interpretations, evaluations, conclusions, or predictions in your statement? Do these terms help you find a focus?

- Consider your level of belief. Are you strongly convinced that your belief is plausible? Do you have questions about it? Why?

- Focus on differences. Does a popular press, TV, or web site account differ from what a book says or what a professor has taught you?

- Draft a thesis statement that gives direction to the essay.

- Create a map, web, or rough outline so that you can see how ideas might cluster or separate.

Organizing Ideas If you created a map or rough outline while you were looking for a focus, review it and try to be more specific about how to arrange the ideas for your paper.

- Have you drafted a tentative thesis that states your belief, one that says something about the sources of the belief, or one that includes both? What kind would be most effective?

- If you have several sources for your belief, does each one deserve a paragraph?

- If your beliefs have changed, have you discussed this in an effective place?

- If you are contrasting two differing perspectives, have you structured the contrast logically?

- If you are presenting similar perspectives, have you structured the comparison logically?

- Have you planned a conclusion? Does it refer to the influences on your beliefs?

- Remember that you may modify your plan or outline as you draft.

Drafting

- Begin with the part easiest to draft. Is it writing about your teachers or dealing with your print or electronic sources?

- Perhaps you should then shift to a part that is hard to draft and at least make some notes or write questions.

- Draft a new outline or map, if necessary, as you rethink what you want to say. Look at the preliminary thesis statement that you drafted. Do you need to rework it now, or should you wait until you have drafted more?

- Shape the paragraphs that will make up the body of your essay. Draft clear topic sentences; think about where the topic sentence should be placed in each paragraph.

- Draft an opening paragraph and a concluding paragraph, understanding that you may want to revise them substantially later.

Revising, Editing, and Proofreading Use the Step-by-Step method on pages 160–161, to revise your essay and prepare a final draft.

STUDENT WRITING

JESSIE LANGE'S WRITING PROCESS

The following essay was written for a criminal justice course. Jessie's professor asked students to demonstrate how media treatments of a current criminal justice issue helped to shape the beliefs they hold about that issue. For students in a criminal justice course, who might someday be dealing with offenders or victims of a particular kind of crime, the ability to distinguish between personal beliefs and objective evidence (and to make a distinction between how they might personally feel about an issue and what the law says about that issue) is of critical importance. But Jessie realized that as a concerned citizen, it was also her responsibility to be informed about criminal justice issues that might impact her as a woman, a voter, and a future parent. Jessie used the Thinking-Writing Activity entitled Evaluating Factual Information on page 415 to discuss her two key sources.

Dealing with Sex Offenders
BY JESSIE LANGE

In the past few years we have heard much about Megan's Law, which states that people should be made aware of charged sex offenders in their community. While I wholeheartedly believe that people, for the protection of themselves and their children, have the right to know, there is another twist on the issue I hadn't thought about until I heard a story recently on "60 Minutes." The story involved Stephanie's Law—a new law in place in some states under which sex offenders are kept *after* they have served their time to go through a therapy program in an attempt to "cure" them. The question that this provoked in me was not whether the state should have the right to hold sexual criminals beyond their sentence, but whether they can be cured at all. If not, should they ever be released back into a world where they are likely to do more damage, destroy more lives?

A recent *New York Times* article described a rehabilitation program in Texas whereby prisoners are immersed in religion—taking classes, having discussions, and owning up to their "sins." Interestingly, while there are 79 men convicted of "robbery, drug possession, and murder" participating, those convicted of sexual crimes are not accepted into the program. This is partly because they are "looked down on by other prisoners" and partly because, according to criminologists, "sexual criminals are the most difficult to rehabilitate."

In fact, there is a question as to whether this rehabilitation is even possible. Sexual criminals in particular seem to be under the influence of urges which are out of their control. The "60 Minutes" report said that, while many may have good intentions in being treated through therapy and returning to society, it may be out of their hands. They may say they understand their wrongs, they may feel cured, but if they are released it seems impossible for even the offenders to know if they will be able to control their impulses. If there is such a question, do they deserve a chance at freedom when it means potentially committing another crime?

There is no question in my mind that, while many sex offenders do not repent for what they have done and have no real interest in being cured, there are also many for whom their crimes are almost out of their hands—as disgusting to them as to anyone else. The *New York Times* ran an article entitled "Sex Offender Agrees To Be Castrated." In Illinois, a convicted child sex offender is having himself castrated "in an effort to win a lighter sentence." The offender, in fact, "volunteered to be castrated even before he was convicted" previously of an attack on a young girl. It seems as though the man is making an attempt to control his urges but, according to the article, "experts disagree on whether castration helps" in controlling these urges.

Both the *New York Times* and "60 Minutes" have good reputations as reliable media sources. I read this paper and watch this show regularly. (I'm pleased that my parents introduced me to them.) I think that these reports are as reliable as the popular press can be. If I decide to do research on this subject and write a substantial paper, I will have to use criminal justice and sociology journals and try to interview one or two experts, as well.

I have not had any personal experience with sex offenders, but I have read and heard enough to know that their crimes destroy not only the lives of victims but also the lives of families and friends of the victims and that their crimes can so haunt victims that these fears are never resolved. In addition, victims of sexual crimes may grow up to inflict these crimes on others, continuing the cycle. In my opinion, the damage done by sex offenders and the risk of untreatable urges to commit these crimes, a risk illustrated by the high percentage of repeat offenders, is too great to justify their release. At least not until there is a proven "cure," a sure-fire way to *know* that they are treatable, have been treated, and will not continue to make victims of others.

Through the media, I have come to understand that many may be operating on urges not within their control, but this does not justify their release. At some point the blame has to fall on the individual. If they were to learn that their rehabilitation was an impossibility, I think that those who are truly disgusted by their crimes might even agree that they are too dangerous to be returned to a society where they have already done so much damage.

Works Cited

60 Minutes, January 11, 1998.

The *New York Times*, June 24, 1997.

ALTERNATIVE WRITING PROJECT: EVOLVING BELIEFS IN AN ACADEMIC FIELD

Locate a college or high school science, history, or literature textbook from forty or fifty years ago. Compare several specific points made in the decades-old book with points made in one of your textbooks in the same field.

In order to establish a context for what you observe, ask your instructor or a librarian to guide you to sources that discuss changes in theories in the field that your material is about. For example, in history, you could examine material about multicultural or gender-based approaches; in literature, material about "the canon"; in science, material about a specific discovery in genetics or physics.

Write an essay presenting the differences and similarities that you have found and comment on what beliefs they seem to reflect. Follow your instructor's directions for topic limitation, length, format, and citation methods.

12

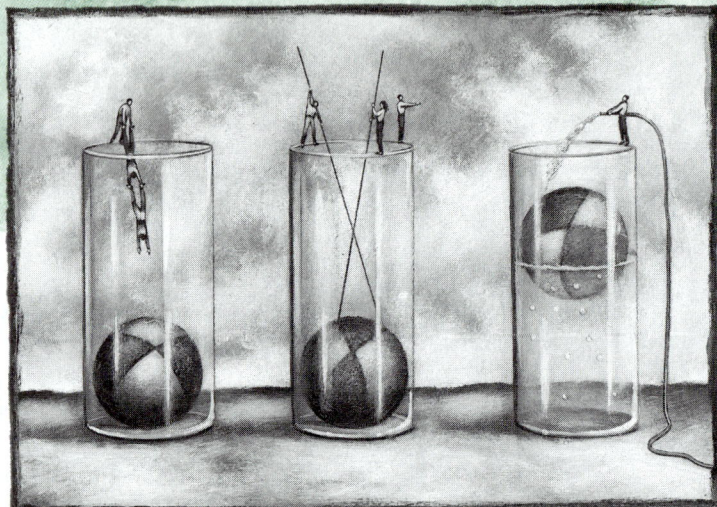

Solving Problems

Writing to Propose Solutions

"Problems call forth our courage and our wisdom. . . . It is only because of problems that we grow mentally and spiritually."
—M. Scott Peck

Critical Thinking Focus: The problem-solving model

Writing Focus: Applying the problem-solving model

Reading Theme: Solving a social problem

Writing Project: Proposing a solution to a problem

P roblem solving is one of the most powerful thinking patterns we possess, and writing is the main vehicle we use to analyze challenging problems and propose solutions. On a personal level, you have probably written a letter or email about a problem you were dealing with. You may have been trying to sustain a romantic relationship with someone while geographically separated, helping a friend resolve a personal crisis, or writing to family members to co-ordinate a holiday reunion. To address civic problems, you or family members may have written letters to newspapers or petitioned your local government. Writing memos and position papers to solve problems is an integral part of most careers, from finance to filmmaking.

Although proposing solutions is a common form of writing, it is challenging. In order to compose an insightful document, you need to do the following.

- *Define the problem clearly.* Your audience needs to understand that there *is* a problem and know exactly what it is.

- *Analyze the problem systematically.* Complex problems are often a confusing tangle of needs, ideas, frustrations, goals, and pieces of information. You need to disentangle the issues so that your audience can understand the core of the problem and what alternatives are possible.

- *Propose a well-reasoned solution.* After presenting a lucid analysis of the problem, along with feasible alternatives, you need to reach a conclusion that you support with thoughtful reasoning and solid evidence. As part of your proposed solution, you should explain why other alternative solutions are less desirable than yours. You should also address anticipated objections to your solution and explain how these difficulties can be overcome.

You will notice that the problem-solving method is similar to the decision-making method discussed in Chapter 5. However, this chapter presents the process in more detail; the focus is on problems instead of on decisions, and you will be considering social issues as well as personal ones. The chapter readings address societal problems. This chapter asks you to work with a powerful problem-solving method, and the Writing Project involves analyzing a social or personal problem that needs a solution.

Problems in Personal and Civic Life

Throughout your life, you will continually be solving problems. As a student, for example, you deal with a steady stream of academic assignments—quizzes, exams, papers, homework projects, and oral presentations. In order to solve these academic problems effectively—how to do well on an exam, for example—you need to define the problem (what areas will the exam cover, and what will its format be?), identify and evaluate various alternatives (what are possible study approaches?), and then combine all these factors to reach a solution (what will your study plan and schedule be?). Relatively simple problems like preparing for an exam do not require a systematic or complex analysis. You can solve them with a little effort and concentration. However, the difficult and complicated problems in your personal life, such as choosing a college major or ending a relationship, may be a different story. Because these are such crucial situations, you will need to to solve such problems in the best possible way by using all your creative and critical thinking skills.

The problems that exist in society also need the very best thinking of all citizens. Violent crime is far too common, parents feel stressed about their children's safety, drugs and alcohol continue to destroy lives, and both racism and sexism create conflicts. These problems may seem overwhelming, and it is true that you cannot control them in the same way that you can control your own life situations. Still, by thinking creatively and critically about such issues, and by gathering information, you can at least develop your own views about contending with them. Then you will be in a position to act on such problems and to vote for candidates whose positions are similar to yours.

Basics of the Problem-Solving Method

Consider the following problem:

My best friend is addicted to drugs, but he won't admit it. Jack always liked to drink, but I never thought too much about it. After all, a lot of people like to drink socially, get relaxed, and have a good time. But over the last few years, he's started using other drugs as well as alcohol, and it's ruining his life. He's stopped taking classes at the college and will soon lose his job if he doesn't change. Last week I told him that I was really worried about him, but he told me that he has no drug problem and that in any case it really isn't any of my business. I don't know what to do. I've known Jack since we were in elementary school together, and he's a wonderful person. It's as if he's in the grip of some terrible force and I'm powerless to help him.

In working through this problem, the writer of this description could only think of one possible course of action to try. But if he or she chose instead to approach the problem as a critical thinker, the writer would have to think carefully and systematically in order to reach a solution.

In order to think effectively in situations like this, we usually ask ourselves a series of questions, although we may not be aware of this mental process. These are the questions to ask in a five-step problem-solving method:

1. What is the *problem*?
2. What are the *alternatives*?
3. What are the *advantages* and/or *disadvantages* of each alternative?
4. What is the *solution*?
5. How well is the solution *working*?

Put yourself in the position of the student whose friend seems to have a serious addiction and apply the questions to that problem.

1. WHAT IS THE PROBLEM?

There are a variety of ways to define the problem. For instance, you might define it simply as "Jack has a drug dependency." You might view the problem as "Jack has a drug dependency, but he won't admit it." You might even define the problem as "Jack has a drug dependency, but he won't admit it—and I want to help him solve this problem." Notice that each redefinition of the problem results in a more specific definition, which in turn helps you better understand the essence of the problem and your responsibility with respect to it.

2. WHAT ARE THE ALTERNATIVES?

In dealing with this problem, you can consider a wide variety of possible actions before selecting the best ones. Identify some of the alternatives.

(example): Speak to my friend in a candid and forceful way to convince him that he has a serious drug dependency.

3. WHAT ARE THE ADVANTAGES AND DISADVANTAGES OF EACH ALTERNATIVE?

Evaluate the strengths and weaknesses of each alternative you have identified so that you can weigh your choices and determine the best course of action.

Speak to my friend in a candid and forceful way to convince him that he has a serious problem.

Advantage: He may respond to my direct emotional appeal, acknowledge that he has a problem, and seek help.

Disadvantage: He may react angrily, further alienating me from him and making it more difficult for me to have any influence on him.

4. WHAT IS THE SOLUTION?

After evaluating the various alternatives, select the one you think would be most effective for solving the problem and describe the sequence of steps you would take to act on that alternative.

5. HOW WELL IS THE SOLUTION WORKING?

The final step in the process comes after you have begun to implement your choice of action. You review the solution and decide whether it is working well. If it is not, you must modify your solution or perhaps try an alternate solution you disregarded earlier. In this situation, trying to figure out the best way to help your friend recognize his dependency and seek treatment leads to a series of decisions. This is what the thinking process is all about—trying to make sense of what is going on in the world and acting appropriately in response. When we solve problems effectively, our thinking process exhibits a coherent organization, following the general approach just outlined.

If we can understand the way the mind operates when we are thinking effectively, we can apply this understanding to improve our thinking in new, challenging situations. In the remainder of this chapter, we will explore a more sophisticated version of this problem-solving approach and apply it to a variety of complex, difficult problems.

Thinking ↔ Writing Activity

Analyzing a Problem Solved Previously

1. Write a description of a problem you have recently solved.
2. Explain how you went about solving the problem. What were the steps, strategies, and approaches you used to understand the problem and to make an informed decision?
3. Analyze your thinking process by applying the five-step problem-solving method we have been exploring.
4. Share your problem with classmates and have them try to analyze and solve it. Then explain the solution you arrived at.

The Problem-Solving Method in Detail

Imagine yourself in the following situation. What would be your next move, and what are your reasons for deciding on it?

You are about to begin your second year of college, following a very successful first year. Until now, you have financed your education through a combination of savings, financial aid, and a part-time job (sixteen hours a week) at a local store. However, you just received a letter from your college saying that your financial aid package has been reduced by half due to budgetary problems. The letter concludes, "We hope this aid reduction will not prove to be too great an inconvenience." From your perspective, the loss of aid isn't an inconvenience—it's a disaster! Your budget last year was already tight, and with your job, you barely had enough time to study, participate in a few college activities, and have a modest (but essential) social life. To make matters worse, your mother has been ill, reducing her income and creating financial problems at home. You're panicking—what in the world are you going to do?

As noted earlier, at first a difficult problem often seems like a confused tangle of information, feelings, alternatives, opinions, considerations, and risks. The problem just described is a complicated situation that does not seem to have a single simple solution. Without applying a systematic approach, your thoughts might wander through the tangle of issues in this manner:

I want to stay in school, . . . but I'm not going to have enough money. . . . I could work more hours at my job, . . . but I might not have enough time to study and get top grades . . . and if all I'm doing is working and studying, what about my social life? . . . and what about Mom and the kids? They might need my help. . . . I could drop out of school for a while, . . . but if I don't stay in school, what kind of future do I have?

Very often, when faced with difficult problems like this one, you simply may not know where to begin to try to solve them. Every issue is connected to many others. Frustrated by not knowing where to take the first step, you may give up trying to understand the problem. Or you may behave in one of the following ways:

1. Act impulsively without thought or consideration (e.g., "I'll just quit school").
2. Follow someone else's advice without seriously evaluating the suggestion (e.g., "Tell me what I should do—I'm tired of thinking about this").
3. Do nothing as you wait for events to make the decision for you (e.g., "I'll just wait and see what happens").

None of these approaches is likely to succeed in the long run, and each can gradually reduce your confidence in dealing with complex problems. An alternative to these reactions is to *think critically* about the problem, analyzing it with an organized approach based on the following five-step method.

Detailed Method for Solving Problems

Step 1: What is the problem?

    a. What do I know about the situation?

    b. What results am I seeking in this situation?

    c. How can I define the problem?

Step 2: What are the alternatives?

  a. What are the boundaries of the problem situation?

  b. What alternatives are possible within these boundaries?

Step 3: What are the advantages and disadvantages of each alternative?

  a. What are the advantages?

  b. What are the disadvantages?

  c. What additional information do I need in order to evaluate this alternative?

Step 4: What is the solution?

  a. Which alternative(s) will I pursue?

  b. What steps can I take to act on this/these alternative(s)?

Step 5: How well is the solution working?

  a. What is my evaluation?

  b. What adjustments are necessary?

Even when we are using an organized method for working through difficult problems and arriving at thoughtful conclusions, our minds may not always work in a logical, step-by-step fashion. Effective problem solvers typically pass through all the steps we will be examining, but not always in sequence.

Instead, the best problem solvers take a flexible approach to the process, one in which they utilize a repertoire of problem-solving strategies as needed. Sometimes, exploring the various alternatives helps them to go back and redefine the original problem. Similarly, seeking to implement the solution can often suggest a new alternative or alternatives that combine the best points of previous ones. This approach is shown in Figure 12.1.

The key point is that although the problem-solving steps are presented in a logical sequence here, you need not follow them in a mechanical and unimaginative fashion. At the same time, in learning a problem-solving method like this, it is generally not wise to skip steps because each one deals with an important aspect of the problem. As you become more proficient in using the method, you will find that you can apply its concepts and strategies to problem solving in an increasingly flexible and natural fashion, just as learning the basics of an activity like driving a car gradually results in a more integrated performance of the skills involved.

BEFORE YOU BEGIN: ACCEPTING THE PROBLEM

To solve a problem, you must first be willing to *accept* the problem by acknowledging that it exists and committing yourself to trying to solve it. Sometimes you may have difficulty recognizing there is a problem unless it is pointed out

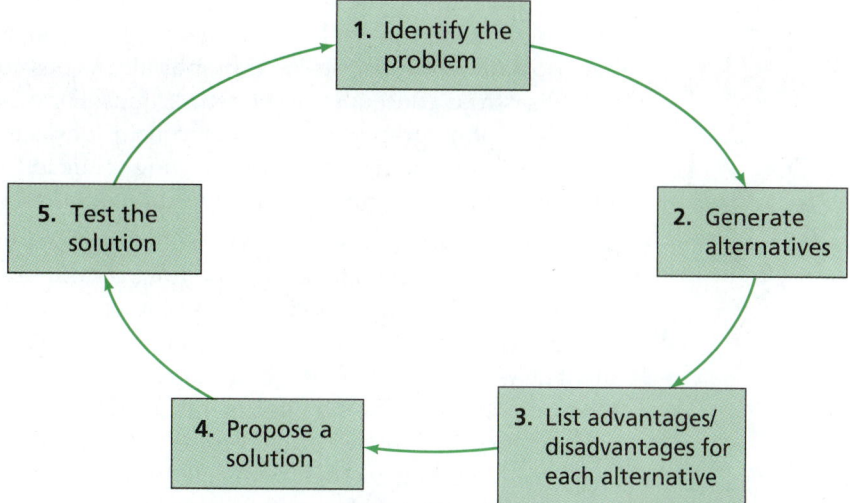

Figure 12.1 A Flexible Approach to Problem Solving

to you. At other times, you may actively resist acknowledging a problem, even when it is pointed out to you. The person who confidently states, "I don't really have any problems," sometimes has very serious problems—but is simply unwilling to acknowledge them.

However, mere acknowledgment is not enough to solve a problem. Once you have identified a problem, you must commit yourself to solving it. Successful problem solvers are highly motivated and willing to persevere through the many challenges and frustrations of the problem-solving process. How do you find this motivation and commitment? There are not simple answers, but the following strategies may help:

- *List the benefits.* Making a detailed list of the benefits you will derive from successfully dealing with the problem is a good place to begin. Such a process helps you clarify why you might want to tackle the problem, motivates you to get started, and serves as a source of encouragement when you encounter difficulties or lose momentum.

- *Formalize your acceptance.* You can formalize your acceptance of a problem by "going on record," either by preparing a signed declaration or by signing a "contract" with someone else. This formal commitment can serve as an explicit statement of original intentions to which you can refer if your resolve weakens.

- *Accept responsibility for your life.* Former U.S. Attorney General Robert F. Kennedy, who was assassinated in 1968, once said, "Some people see things as they are, and ask, 'Why?' I see things as they could be, and ask, 'Why not?'" You have the potential to control the direction of your own life, but to do so, you must accept your freedom to choose and the responsibility that goes with it.

- *Create a "worst case" scenario.* Some problems persist because people are able to ignore their possible implications. When you create a worst-case scenario, you remind yourself, as graphically as possible, of the potentially disastrous consequences of your actions. For example, looking at vivid color photographs and research conclusions can remind a person that excessive smoking, drinking, or eating can lead to myriad health problems and social and psychological difficulties as well as death.

- *Identify the constraints.* If you are having trouble accepting a problem, it is usually because something is holding you back. For example, you might be concerned about the amount of time and effort involved, you might be reluctant to confront the underlying issues the problem represents, you might be worried about finding out unpleasant things about yourself or others, or you might be inhibited by other problems in your life, such as a tendency to procrastinate. Whatever the constraints, using this strategy involves identifying and describing all the factors that are preventing you from attacking the problem and then addressing them one at a time.

STEP 1: WHAT IS THE PROBLEM?

The problem-solving process begins by determining exactly what the central issues of the problem are. Otherwise, your chances of solving it are considerably reduced. You may even spend time trying to solve the wrong problem. For instance, consider the different formulations of the following problems. How might they lead a person in different directions when trying to solve it?

"School is boring" versus "I am bored in accounting class."

"I'm unloveable" versus "I was just turned down for a date."

In each of these cases, a very general conclusion (first formulation) has been replaced by a more specific characterization of the problem (second formulation). The general conclusions ("I'm a failure") do not suggest productive ways of resolving the difficulties. They are too absolute, too all-encompassing. On the other hand, the more specific descriptions of the problem situation ("I just failed an exam") do permit you to attack problems with useful strategies. In short, the way you define a problem determines not only how you will go about solving it, but whether you feel that the problem can be solved at all. Correct identification of a problem is essential if you are going to be able to successfully analyze it and reach an appropriate conclusion. Incorrectly identifying the problem can lead to pursuing an unproductive, even destructive, course of action.

Consider the problem of the college student whose financial aid package was cut in half (pages 440–441) and analyze it using this problem-solving method. Ask:

1. What do I know about the situation?
2. What results am I aiming for in this situation?
3. How can I define the problem?

Step 1A: What do I know about the situation? Solving a problem begins with determining what you *know* to be the case and what you *think* may be the case. To explore the problem successfully, you need to have a clear idea of the details of your beginning circumstances. Sometimes a situation may appear to be a problem when it really isn't, simply because your information isn't accurate. Suppose you are convinced that someone you are attracted to doesn't reciprocate your interest. If this belief is inaccurate, your "problem" doesn't really exist.

You can identify and organize what you know about the problem situation by posing key questions. By asking—and trying to answer—questions of fact, you are establishing a sound foundation for exploring your problem. Imagine that you are the student described earlier who is facing a reduction in financial aid. Answer the following questions of fact—who? what? where? when? how? why?—about your problem.

- *Who* are the people involved in this situation?

   Who will benefit from my solving this problem?

   Who can help me solve this problem?

- *What* are the various parts or dimensions of the problem?

   What are my strengths and resources for solving this problem?

- *When* did the problem begin?

   When should the problem be resolved?

- *How* did the problem arise or develop?

- *Why* is solving this problem important to me?

   Why is this problem difficult to solve?

- Additional questions: _____

Step 1B: What results am I aiming for in this situation? The second part of answering the question "What is the problem?" consists of identifying the specific results or objectives you are trying to achieve. The results will eliminate the problem if you are able to achieve them. Whereas the first part of step 1 oriented you in terms of the history of the problem and the current situation, this part encourages you to look to the future. To identify results, you need to ask yourself the question "What are the objectives that, once achieved, will solve this problem?" For instance, one of the results or objectives in the sample problem might be having enough money to pay for college. Describe additional results you might be trying to achieve in this situation.

1. Having enough money to pay for college.

2. _____

3. _____

4. _____

Step 1C: How can I define the problem? After exploring what you know about the problem and the results you want to achieve, you need to conclude step 1 by defining the problem as clearly and specifically as possible. This is a crucial task in the problem-solving process because this definition will determine the direction of your analysis. To define the problem, you need to identify its central issue(s). Sometimes defining the problem is relatively straightforward, such as "trying to find enough time to exercise."

Often, however, identifying the central issue of a problem is a much more complex process. For example, the statement "My problem is relating to other people" suggests a complicated situation with many interacting variables that resists simple definition. In fact, you may not even begin to develop a clear idea of the problem until you engage in the process of trying to solve it. Or you might begin by believing that your problem is, say, not having the ability to succeed but end by concluding that the problem is really a fear of success.

As you will see, the same insights also apply to societal problems. For example, the problem of high school dropouts might initially be defined in terms of problems in the school system whereas later formulations might identify drug use or social pressure as the core of the problem.

Although there are no simple formulas for defining challenging problems, you can try several strategies to identify the central issue most effectively:

- *View the problem from different perspectives.* As you saw in Chapters 3, 7, and 8, perspective taking is a key ingredient of thinking critically; it can also help you to zero in on many problems. When you describe how various individuals might view a given problem—such as the high school dropout rate—the essential ingredients of the problems begin to emerge. In the student financial-aid problem, how would you describe the student's perspective? the college's perspective? the student's mother's perspective?

- *Identify component problems.* Larger problems are often composed of component problems. To define a larger problem, it is often necessary to identify and describe the subproblems that comprise it. A student's poor school performance, for instance, might result from a number of factors like ineffective study habits, inefficient time management, and preoccupation with a personal problem. Defining, and dealing effectively with, a larger problem means defining and dealing with the subproblems first. Can you identify two possible subproblems in the financial-aid problem?

- *State the problem clearly and specifically.* A third defining strategy is to state the problem as clearly and specifically as possible as you examine your objectives for solving it. Stating this sort of precise description of the problem is an important step toward solving it. If you state the problem in very general terms, you won't have a clear idea of how best to proceed in dealing with it. However, if you can describe it in specific terms, your description will begin to suggest actions you can take to solve the problem. Examine the differences between the statements of the following problem:

  General: "My problem is money."

  More specific: "My problem is needing to budget my money so that I won't always run out of it near the end of the month."

  Most specific: "My problem is my need to develop the habits and discipline to budget my money so that I won't always run out of it near the end of the month."

Review your analysis of the student's financial-aid problem; then state the problem in writing as clearly and specifically as you can.

STEP 2: WHAT ARE THE ALTERNATIVES?

Once you have identified a problem clearly and specifically, your next move is to examine each possible action that might help you to solve it. Before you list the alternatives, however, it makes sense to explore the situation's boundaries to determine which actions are possible and which are not.

Step 2A: What are the boundaries of the problem situation? Boundaries are limits that you simply cannot change. They are part of the problem, and they must be accepted and dealt with. For example, in the case involving the loss of financial aid, the fact that a day has only twenty-four hours must be accepted as part of the problem situation. There is no point in developing alternatives that ignore this fact. At the same time, you must be careful not to identify as boundaries circumstances that *can* be changed. For instance, again imagining yourself as the student with the financial-aid problem, you might assume that your problem must be solved in your current location, without realizing that transferring to a less expensive college is one of your options. Identify additional boundaries that might be part of this sample situation and list some of the questions you should answer about these boundaries.

Step 2B: What alternatives are possible within these boundaries? After you have established a general notion of the boundaries of the problem situation, you can proceed to identify the possible courses of action that can occur within them. Of course, identifying all the possible alternatives is not always easy; in fact, that may be part of your problem. Often we cannot see a way out of a problem because our thinking is set in certain ruts, fixed in certain perspectives. We may be blind to other approaches, either because we reject them without seriously considering them ("That will never work!") or because they simply do not occur to us. You can use several strategies to overcome these obstacles:

- *Discuss the problem with other people.* Discussing possible alternatives with others uses a number of the aspects of critical thinking we explored in Chapter 1. Thinking critically involves being open to seeing situations from different viewpoints and discussing ideas with others in an organized way. Both of these abilities are important in solving problems. As critical thinkers we live—and solve problems—in a community, not simply by ourselves. Other people can often suggest alternatives we haven't thought of since they are outside the situation and thus have a more objective perspective, and since they naturally view the world differently than we do because of their past experiences and their personalities. In addition, discussions are often creative experiences that generate ideas participants would not have come up with on their own. The dynamics of these interactions lead to products that are greater than the individual "sum" of the ideas of those involved.

- *Brainstorm ideas.* Group brainstorming, a method introduced by Alex Osborn, builds on the strengths of working with other people to generate ideas and solve problems. In a typical brainstorming session, a group of people work together to propose as many ideas as possible in a specific time period. As ideas are produced, they are not judged or evaluated, as this tends to inhibit the free flow of ideas and discourage people from making suggestions. Evaluation is deferred until a later stage. People are encouraged to build on the ideas of others since the most creative ideas are often generated through the constructive interplay of various minds.

- *Change your location.* Your perspectives on a problem are often tied to the circumstances in which the problem exists. For example, a problem you may be having in school is connected with your daily experiences and your habitual reactions to them. Sometimes you need a fresh perspective, which you can gain by getting away from the problem situation so that you can view it more clearly in a different light. Perhaps spending a day or two out of town will help, or even taking a long walk in a different neighborhood.

Using these strategies, as well as your own reflections, identify as many alternatives to help solve the financial-aid problem that you can think of.

1. Attend school part-time

2. _____

3. _____

4. _____

STEP 3: WHAT ARE THE ADVANTAGES AND DISADVANTAGES OF EACH ALTERNATIVE?

Once you have identified the various alternatives, your next step is to evaluate them. Each possible course of action offers certain advantages in the sense that if you were to select that alternative, there would be some positive results. At the same time, each possible course of action probably also has disadvantages in the sense that if you were to select that alternative, you may incur a cost or risk some negative results. Determine how helpful each course of action would or would not be in solving the problem.

Step 3A: What are the advantages of each alternative? The alternative we listed in step 2 for the sample problem ("Attend college part-time") might include the following advantages.

Alternative	Advantages
Attend college part-time	1. Doing this would remove some of the immediate time and money pressures I am experiencing while still allowing me to prepare for the future.
	2. I would have more time to focus on the courses that I would be taking and to work additional hours.

Identify the advantages of each of the alternatives that you listed in step 2. Be sure that your responses are thoughtful and specific. For example, how many additional hours could you work? How much additional income would doing that generate?

Step 3B: What are the disadvantages of each alternative? The alternative we listed in step 2 for the sample problem might include the following disadvantages.

Alternative	Disadvantages
Attend college part-time	1. It would take me much longer to complete my schooling, thus delaying my progress toward my goals.
	2. I might lose motivation and drop out before completing school because the process would be taking so long.
	3. Being a part-time student might threaten my eligibility for financial aid.

Now identify the disadvantages of each of the alternatives that you listed for step 2. Make sure that your responses are thoughtful and specific. For example, how much longer would it take you to get your degree?

Step 3C: What additional information do I need to evaluate each alternative?
The next part of step 3 consists of determining what you must know (information needed) to best evaluate and compare the alternatives. For each alternative there are questions that you must answer in order to establish which alternatives make sense and which do not. In addition, you need to figure out where to get this information (sources).

The information—and the sources of it—that must be located for the first alternative in the sample problem might include the following.

Information Needed

1. How long will it take me to complete my schooling?
2. How long can I continue in school without losing interest and dropping out?
3. Will I threaten my eligibility for financial aid if I become a part-time student?

   Sources: Myself, other part-time students, school counselors, financial aid office

Identify the information needed and the sources of this information for each of the alternatives that you identified on pages 447–448. Be sure that your responses are thoughtful and specific.

STEP 4: WHAT IS THE SOLUTION?

The purpose of steps 1 through 3 is to analyze your problem in a systematic and detailed fashion—to work through the problem in order to become thoroughly familiar with it and with possible solutions. After breaking down the problem in this way, your final step should be to try to put the pieces back together—that is, to decide on a thoughtful course of action based on your increased understanding. Even though conducting this sort of problem analysis does not guarantee finding a specific solution to the problem, it should deepen your understanding of exactly what the problem is. And in locating and evaluating the alternatives, it should give you some very good ideas about the general direction in which you should move and the immediate steps you should take.

Step 4A: Which alternative(s) will I pursue? There is no simple formula to tell you which alternatives to select. As you work through the different courses of action that are possible, you may find that you can immediately rule some out. In the sample problem, for example, you may know with certainty that you do not want to attend college part-time (alternative 1) because you will forfeit your remaining financial aid. However, it may not be as simple to select which of the other alternatives you wish to pursue. How do you decide?

The decisions we make usually depend on what we believe is most important to us. These beliefs are known as **values.** Our values are the starting points of our actions and strongly influence our decisions. For example, if we value staying alive (as most of us do), we will make many decisions each day that express this value—eating proper meals, not walking in front of moving traffic, and so on.

Our values help us set priorities in life—that is, decide what aspects of our lives are most important to us. We might decide that for the present, going to school is more important than having an active social life. In this case, going to school has higher priority than having an active social life. Unfortunately, our values are not always consistent with each other—we may have to choose either going to school or having an active social life. Both activities may be important to us; they are simply not compatible with each other. Very often the *conflicts* between our values constitute the problem. Let's examine some strategies for selecting alternatives that might help to solve the sample problem.

- *Evaluate and compare alternatives.* Although each alternative may have certain advantages and disadvantages, not all advantages are equally desirable or potentially effective. For example, giving up college entirely would certainly solve some aspects of the sample problem, but its obvious disadvantages would rule out this solution for most people. Thus, it makes sense to try to evaluate and rank the various alternatives on the basis of how effective they are likely to be and how they match up with your value system. A good place to begin is at the "Results" stage, step 1B. Examine each of your alternatives and evaluate how well it will contribute to achieving the results you are aiming for in the situation. You may want to rank the alternatives or develop your own rating system to assess their relative effectiveness.

    After evaluating the alternatives in terms of their anticipated *effectiveness,* the next step is to evaluate them in terms of their *desirability* relative to your needs, interests, and value system. Again, you can use either a ranking or a rating system to assess their relative desirability. After completing these two separate evaluations, you can select whatever alternatives seem most appropriate. Review the alternatives you identified in the sample problem; then rank or rate them according to their potential effectiveness and desirability.

- *Synthesize a new alternative.* After reviewing and evaluating the alternatives you have generated, you may develop a new alternative that combines the best qualities of several options while avoiding the disadvantages some of them would have if implemented exclusively. In the sample problem, you might combine attending college part-time during the academic year with attending school during summer session so that progress toward your degree wouldn't be impeded. Examine the alternatives you identified and develop a new option that combines the best elements of several of them.

- *Try out each alternative—in your imagination.* Focus on each alternative and try to imagine, as concretely as possible, what it would be like if you actually selected it. Visualize what impact your choice would have on your problem and what the implications would be for your life as a whole. By trying out the alternative in your imagination, you can sometimes avoid unpleasant results or unexpected consequences. As a variation of this strategy, you can sometimes test alternatives on a very limited basis in a practice situation. Suppose you are trying to overcome your fear of speaking out in groups. You can practice various speaking techniques with your friends or family until you find an approach that works for you.

Step 4B: What steps can I take to act on the alternative(s) chosen? Once you have decided on an alternative to pursue, your next move is to plan what steps to take in acting on it. Planning the specific steps you will take is extremely important. Although thinking carefully about your problem is necessary, it is not enough if you hope to solve the problem. You have to take action. In the sample problem, for example, imagine that one of the alternatives you have selected is "find additional sources of income that will enable me to work part-time and attend school full-time." The specific steps you would take might include these:

- Contact the financial-aid office to learn what other forms of monetary aid are available and how to apply for them.
- Contact some local banks to find out what sort of student loans they offer.
- Look for a higher-paying job to earn more money without working additional hours.
- Discuss your problem with students in similar circumstances in order to generate new ideas.

Identify the steps you would have to take to pursue the alternative(s) you identified on pages 447–448.

Plans, of course, do not implement themselves. Once you know what actions are needed, you have to make a commitment to taking the necessary steps. This is where many people stumble in the problem-solving process; they remain paralyzed by inertia or fear. To overcome such blocks and inhibitions, you sometimes need to re-examine your original acceptance of the problem, perhaps making use of some of the strategies you explored on pages 443–444. Once you get started, the rewards of actively attacking your problem are often enough incentive to keep you focused and motivated.

STEP 5: HOW WELL IS THE SOLUTION WORKING?

As you work toward reaching a reasonable and informed conclusion, be wary of falling into the trap of thinking that there is only one "right" solution and that if you don't figure out what it is and implement it, all is lost. You should remind yourself that any analysis of problem situations, no matter how careful and systematic, is ultimately limited. You simply cannot anticipate or predict everything that will happen in the future. Consequently, every decision you make is provisional in the sense that your ongoing experience will inform you whether it is working out or needs to be modified.

Maintaining this perspective is precisely the attitude of the critical thinker—someone who is receptive to new ideas and experiences and flexible enough to change or modify beliefs on the basis of new information. Critical thinking is not a compulsion to find the "right" answer or make the "correct" decision; it is a continuing process of exploration and discovery.

Step 5A: What is my evaluation? In many cases the relative effectiveness of your efforts will be apparent. In other cases you will find it helpful to pursue a more systematic evaluation along the lines suggested in the following strategies.

- *Compare the results with the goals.* The essence of evaluation is comparing the results of your efforts with your initial goals. For example, the goals of the sample problem are embodied in the results you specified on pages 445–446. Compare the anticipated results of the alternative(s) you selected. To what extent will your choice(s) meet these goals? Are any goals not likely to be met by your alternative(s)? If so, which ones? Could they be addressed by other alternatives? Asking these questions and others will help you to assess the success of your efforts and will provide a foundation for future decisions.

- *Get other perspectives.* As you have seen throughout the problem-solving process, getting the opinions of others is a productive strategy at virtually every stage, and this is certainly true of evaluation. Other people often can provide perspectives that are both different and more objective than your own. Naturally, the evaluations of others are not always better or more accurate than yours, but even when they are not, reflecting on these different views usually deepens your understanding of the situation. It is not always easy to accept the evaluations of others, but keeping an open mind about outside opinions is a very valuable attitude to cultivate, because it will stimulate and guide you to produce your best efforts.

    To receive specific, practical feedback, you need to ask specific, practical questions that will elicit such information. General questions ("What do you think of this?") typically receive overly general, unhelpful answers ("It sounds okay to me"). Be focused when soliciting feedback and remember that you do have the right to ask people for *constructive* comments—that is, to provide suggestions for improvement rather than just to tell you what they think is wrong. For example, you could say, "What do you know about me that you think will help me maintain my motivation to stay in school—even if it takes two years longer than I had planned?" Or you can ask, "Do you have any ideas about how I can cut my expenses by 10 percent each month?"

Step 5B: What adjustments are necessary? As a result of your review, you may discover that the alternative you selected is not feasible or is not producing satisfactory results. Suppose that in the sample problem, you cannot find additional sources of income that will allow you to work part-time instead of full-time. In that case, you simply have to go back and review the other alternatives to identify another possible course of action. At other times, you may find that the alternative you selected is succeeding fairly well but requires some adjustments as you continue to work toward your goals. In fact, this is a typical situation that you should expect to occur. Even when things initially appear to be working reasonably well, an active thinker continues to ask questions such as "What might I have overlooked?" and "How could I have done this differently?" Of course, asking—and trying to answer—questions like this is even more essential if solutions are hard to come by (as they usually are in real-world problems) and if you are to retain the flexibility and optimism you will need to tackle a new option.

Thinking ↔ Writing Activity

Analyzing a Problem in Your Life

This Thinking-Writing Activity provides you with the opportunity to apply the problem-solving method to an important *un*solved problem in your own life. First, select from your own life a problem that you are currently grappling with and have not been able to solve. Next, strengthen your acceptance of the problem by using several strategies described on pages 443–444. Finally, work your way through each of the problem-solving steps outlined on pages 441–442. Write out responses to the questions in each step, and be sure to discuss your problem with other class members to generate fresh perspectives and unusual alternatives that might not have occurred to you. Your ultimate goal is to decide on a provisional solution to your problem and establish a plan of action that will help you move in the right direction.

The following are some common problems other students have described. Your instructor may have you work in a group with other class members to analyze one of these problems as a way of preparing you to analyze one of your own.

Problem 1: Taking Tests. One of my problems is that I have trouble taking tests. It's not that I don't study. What happens is that when I get the test, I panic and forget what I have studied. For example, in my social science class, the teacher told the class on Tuesday that there would be a test on Thursday. That afternoon I went home and began studying for the test. By Thursday I knew most of the material, but when the test was handed out, I got nervous and my mind went blank. For a long time I just stared at the test, and I ended up failing it.

"As soon as one problem is solved, another rears its ugly head."

Problem 2: Smoking. My problem is tobacco use. I have been smoking cigarettes for over five years. At first I did it because I liked the image, and most of my friends were also smoking. Gradually, I got hooked. It's such a part of my life now that I don't know if I can quit. Having a cup of coffee, studying, talking to people—it just also seems natural to have a cigarette in my hand. I know there are a lot of good reasons for me to stop. I've even tried a few times, but I always end up bumming cigarettes from friends and then giving up on quitting. I don't want my health to go up in smoke, but I don't know what to do.

Problem 3: Learning English. One of the serious problems in my life is learning English. It is not easy to learn a new language, especially when you live in an environment where only your native language is spoken. When I came to this country three years ago, I could speak almost no English. I have learned a lot, but my lack of fluency is causing problems with my studies and my social relationships.

Solving Social Problems

The problems we have analyzed up to this point are "personal" problems in the sense that they represent individual challenges we encounter as we live our lives. Problems are not only of a personal nature, however. We also face problems as members of a community, the larger society, and the world.

As with personal problems, we need to approach these kinds of problems in an organized and thoughtful way in order to explore the issues, develop a clear understanding, and decide on an informed plan of action. For example, racism and prejudice directed toward African Americans, Hispanics, Asians, Jews, homosexuals, and other groups seem to be on the rise at many college campuses. There has been an increase of overt racist incidents at colleges and universities during the past several years, which is particularly disturbing given the lofty egalitarian ideals of higher education. Experts from different fields have offered a variety of explanations to account for this behavior. Think about why you believe these racial and ethnic incidents are occurring.

Making sense of this kind of complex, challenging situation is not a simple process. Although the problem-solving method we have been using in this chapter is a powerful approach, its successful application depends on having sufficient information about the situation to be solved. Therefore, it is often necessary for us to find articles and other sources of information to develop informed opinions about the problem we are investigating.

The famous newspaperman H. L. Mencken once said, "To every complex question there is a simple answer—and it's wrong!" In this chapter we have seen that complex problems do not have simple solutions, whether they are personal problems or larger social problems like racial prejudice or world hunger. We have also learned that by working through these complex problems thoughtfully and systematically, we can achieve a deeper understanding of their many interacting elements as well as develop and implement strategies for solving them.

A thoughtful problem solver employs all the critical thinking abilities we have examined in this book. And although we might agree with Mencken's evaluation of simple answers to complex questions, we would expand upon it: "To many complex questions there are complex answers—and these are well worth pursuing."

The following reading selections deal with significant social problems. The information that they present provides a framework for thoughtful analysis and productive solutions. The *Washington Post* article "Public Backs Uniform U.S. Voting Rules" tells of solutions suggested by the general public in a poll addressing the problem of varied voting procedures. "Young Hate" examines the insidious problem of intolerance on college campuses while "When Is It Rape?" explores the issues related to the problem of "date rape."

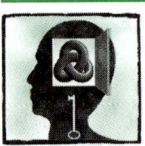

Thinking ↔ Writing Activity

Analyzing a Social Problem

Work with one of the following articles. After reading the article carefully, identify and analyze the problem being discussed by using the problem-solving method explained in this chapter.

FROM

Public Backs Uniform U.S. Voting Rules

Poll Finds Wide Support for Guidelines on Ballots, Closing Times, Recounts

Washington Post, December 18, 2000

BY RICHARD MORIN AND CLAUDIA DEANE

Journalists Richard Morin and Claudia Deane both write for the Washington Post, *where this article was published in December 2000. Morin covers new research in the social sciences in his column "Unconventional Wisdom," which appears every Sunday in the* Post's *Outlook section. His recent topics have included "Psychopaths at Work," "The GOP Problem with Women," and "Political Ads and the Voters They Attract." Deane also writes about the social sciences and is co-author of a book about the controversial 2000 presidential election,* Deadlock: The Inside Story of America's Closest Election.

Overwhelming majorities of Americans support a major overhaul of election rules and procedures, including a uniform poll-closing time across the nation, a standard ballot design and consistent rules for conducting recounts, according to a *Washington Post*–ABC News poll.*

The survey also found that most Americans want to strip authority for setting election rules from local and state officials and give the federal government the task of imposing order on election laws and practices that currently vary widely from state to state and county to county.

On question after question, the survey suggests that the public, sharply divided at virtually every bizarre twist and turn of the [2000] post-election drama, has finally found common ground: Nearly everyone agrees that America must change the way it elects its president.

Some reform-minded voters were startled by the variety and the vagaries of voting procedures revealed since Election Day. "I just always assumed it was standardized. Wasn't that stupid of me?" laughed Karin Cabell, 36, a customer service representative who lives in Hazleton, PA, and voted to elect Texas Gov[ernor] George W. Bush. "I thought everyone voted in the same manner everywhere. It just blew my mind."

5   Despite the broad call to change the way Americans vote, the *Post*–ABC News poll found the post-election struggle has done little immediate damage to

---

*This *Washington Post*–ABC News poll is based on telephone interviews with 807 randomly selected adults nationwide, conducted December 14–15. The margin of error for overall results is plus or minus 3.5 percentage points. Sampling error is only one of many potential sources of error in this or any other public opinion poll. Interviewing was conducted by TNS Intersearch of Horsham, PA.

public confidence in the political system or major political institutions, including the U.S. Supreme Court, the Congress and the presidency. Nine in 10 Americans still remain confident that, despite all its problems, this country still has "the best system of government in the world." . . .

But most voters agreed that the election revealed problems. . . . Fifty-three percent of those interviewed said the post-election controversies have revealed "serious problems in this country's system of electing the president"—up 21 percentage points from a *Post*–ABC News poll conducted five days after the Nov[ember] 7 election.

Most voters agree it's a mess, and 61 percent said they want the federal government to clean it up. Barely a third said they wanted to allow local and state governments to continue to set election law.

"I think they need to get a system that everybody votes the same in the United States," said Nancy Jackson, 74, a retiree living in Detroit who voted for Gore. "It partially made me sick, it was so unfair. I'm African American. There are so many young black people we got out to vote, and then their vote wasn't counted."

Nine in 10 said they want a federal law that requires the same design and layout for all presidential election ballots, retiring forever Palm Beach County's confusing "butterfly ballot."

10 About two in three say they want the federal government to outlaw punch-card ballots, ending the possibility of future debates over whether to count or ignore dimpled, pregnant or hanging chads.

Nearly nine in 10 want a federal rule that requires all jurisdictions in the country to use one kind of voting machine, effectively eliminating current claims that some voters, including many African Americans and other minorities, were discriminated against because they live in areas that use older, more error-prone voting machines.

And a similar percentage—86 percent—said they want standard rules for how and when recounts are done, issues that were at the heart of the vote-counting controversy in South Florida that ultimately was decided by the U.S. Supreme Court.

Two in three support a single poll-closing time across the country, which would eliminate the possibility that news reports of election results from states in the East would affect voter turnout in the West.

"I don't have a chance to get to the voting booth until 6 or 6:30 at night, and I'm intending to vote for Bush, and they're telling me Gore already won," said Rachel Glidden, 44, an operating room technician from La Luz, NM. "That's not fair. I haven't even had a chance to voice my say, and I already know what the result is."

15 Overall, the survey suggests Americans want uniformity and simplicity in their election laws as well as in the way people vote.

"I never thought we still used punch machines," said Yvonne Martin, 55, a retiree who voted for Gore and lives in Rome, NY. "That's primitive."

Martin said it's critical that the federal government and not the states or counties establish the rules and decide which type of voting machine is used—

with no exceptions granted. "One state can really mess it up if they don't do it right," she said. "I mean, Mickey Mouse could have done a better job than the election officials in Florida."

About six in 10 Americans say they want to amend the U.S. Constitution to select the president by direct popular vote and do away with the electoral college. If this system had been in place this year, Gore would have won because he received approximately 300,000 more votes nationwide than Bush.

"The electoral college is completely outdated," said Ed Evans, 29, a computer analyst in Beaverton, OR, who voted for Gore. "It may have made sense 120 years ago. But we have the technology now that we can get an accurate popular vote. This is the country that invented democracy. Al Gore won the popular vote. It was the will of the people to elect him as president, but because of the electoral college, George Bush will be the president."

20   But most political observers say lawmakers and residents of less-populated states fear that presidential candidates would ignore them in favor of the larger states, and would effectively block any constitutional amendment.

That argument clearly resonates with the public, the *Post*–ABC News poll found. When those who supported direct election of a president were asked, "What if it meant presidential candidates paid less attention to the smaller states," the proportion favoring direct election dropped from 62 percent to 42 percent.

"I have mixed feelings," Martin said. "I realize that some of the states are smaller and they're helped [by the electoral college]. But in many ways, the public really feels the vote has been taken out of our hands in this election. It needs to be looked at but maybe not changed."

Questions for Active Reading

1. Using information from the article, define the problem that prompted this poll as clearly as you can.

2. Identify the sentence that functions as the thesis by stating the overall finding of the poll.

3. How did the respondents to the poll suggest that the problem be corrected? What are the advantages and/or disadvantages of each proposed solution?

4. What effect do the quotations from the respondents have on you as a reader?

Questions for Thinking Critically

1. Are you comfortable accepting a poll based on 807 respondents that generalizes about "overwhelming majorities of Americans"? Does the announced margin for error make you feel more or less comfortable accepting the poll's findings?

2. In your own opinion, what were the three biggest problems responsible for the 2000 post-election confusion?

3. Imagine that you have been appointed U. S. Commissioner of Elections. What steps would you take to solve the problems that you identified in the previous question?

If you can, discuss your answers to all these questions with classmates.

Young Hate

BY DAVID SHENK (b. 1966)

David Shenk, a graduate of Brown University, is an award-winning author of four books and a contributor to numerous magazines, including National Geographic, The New Yorker, Harper's, The New Republic, Wired, Technology Review, *and* The American Scholar. *His book* The Forgetting, *which is about Alzheimer's disease, won first prize in the British Medical Association's Popular Medical Book Awards and was the basis for a PBS film in January 2004. Shenk's other books are* The End of Patience, *about the current Information Age;* Data Smog, *also about information and technology; and* Skeleton Key: A Dictionary for Deadheads. *Shenk lives in Brooklyn.*

"Young Hate" was first published in 1989 in Career Vision, *a magazine distributed on college campuses.*

Death to gays. Here is the relevant sequence of events: On Monday night Jerry Mattioli leads a candlelight vigil for lesbian and gay rights. *Gays are trash.* On Tuesday his name is in the school paper and he can hear whispers and feel more, colder stares than usual. On Wednesday morning a walking bridge in the middle of the Michigan State campus is found to be covered with violent epithets warning campus homosexuals to *be afraid, very afraid,* promising to *abolish faggots from existence,* and including messages specifically directed at Mattioli. Beginning Friday morning fifteen of the perpetrators, all known to Mattioli by name and face, are rounded up and quietly disciplined by the university. *Go home faggots.* On Friday afternoon Mattioli is asked by university officials to leave campus for the weekend, for his own safety. He does, and a few hours later receives a phone call from a friend who tells him that his dormitory room has been torched. MSU's second annual "Cross-Cultural Week" is over.

"Everything was ruined," Mattioli says. "What wasn't burned was ruined by smoke and heat and by the water. On Saturday I sat with the fire investigator all day, and we went through the room, literally ash by ash. . . . The answering machine had melted. The receiver of the telephone on the wall had stretched to about three feet long. That's how intense the heat was."

"Good news!" says Peter Jennings. A recent *Washington Post*–ABC News poll shows that integration is up and racial tension is down in America, as compared with eight years ago. Of course, in any trend there are fluctuations, exceptions. At the University of Massachusetts at Amherst, an estimated two

What is the best way to deal with people espousing racist views? How can we best encourage such people to develop more open-minded ideas? © John S. Zeedick/Liaison.

What do you think motivates people to join an organization like the KKK? What is the source of their ideas regarding other races? © Corbis Sygma.

thousand whites chase twenty blacks in a clash after a 1986 World Series game, race riots break out in Miami in 1988 and in Virginia Beach in 1989; and on college campuses across the country, our nation's young elite experience an entire decade's aberration from the poll's findings: incidents of ethnic, religious, and gender-related harassment surge throughout the eighties.

Greatest hits include Randy Bowman, a black student at the University of Texas, having to respectfully decline a request by two young men wearing Ronald Reagan masks and wielding a pistol to exit his eighth-floor dorm room through the window; homemade T-shirts, *Thank God for AIDS* and *Aryan by the Grace of God*, among others, worn proudly on campus; Jewish student centers shot at, stoned, and defaced at Memphis State, University of Kansas, Rutgers (*Six million, why not*), and elsewhere; the black chairperson of United Minorities Council at U Penn getting a dose of hi-tech hate via answering machine: *We're going to lynch you, nigger shit. We are going to lynch you.*

5   The big picture is less graphic, but just as dreadful: reports of campus harassment have increased as much as 400 percent since 1985. Dropout rates for black students in predominantly white colleges are as much as five times higher than white dropout rates at the same schools and black dropout rates at black schools. The Anti-Defamation League reports a sixfold increase in anti-Semitic episodes on campuses between 1985 and 1988. Meanwhile, Howard J. Ehrlich of the National Institute Against Prejudice and Violence reminds us that "up to 80 percent of harassed students don't report the harassment." Clearly, the barrage of news reports reveals only the tip of a thoroughly sour iceberg.

Colleges have responded to incidents of intolerance—and the subsequent demands of minority rights groups—with the mandatory ethnic culture classes and restrictions on verbal harassment. But what price tranquility? Libertarian and conservative student groups, faculty, and political advisors lash out over limitations on free speech and the improper embrace of liberal political agendas. "Progressive academic administrations," writes University of Pennsylvania professor Alan Charles Kors in the *Wall Street Journal*, "are determined to enlighten their morally benighted students and protect the community from political sin."

Kors and kind bristle at the language of compromise being attached to official university policy. The preamble to the University of Michigan's new policy on discriminatory behavior reads, in part, "Because there is tension between freedom of speech, the right of individuals to be free from injury caused by discrimination, and the University's duty to protect the educational process . . . it may be necessary to have varying standards depending on the locus of regulated conduct." The policy tried to "strike a balance" by applying different sets of restrictions to academic centers, open areas, and living quarters, but in so doing, hit a wall. Before the policy could go into effect, it was struck down in a Michigan court as being too vague. At least a dozen schools in the process of formulating their own policies scurried in retreat as buoyant free-speech advocates went on the offensive. Tufts University president Jean Mayer voluntarily dismissed his school's "Freedom of Speech versus Freedom from Harassment" policy after a particularly inventive demonstration by late-night protesters who used chalk, tape, and poster board to divide the campus into designated free speech, limited speech, and non-free speech zones. "We're not working for a right to offensive speech," says admitted chalker Andrew Zappia, co-editor of the conservative campus paper, *The Primary Source.* "This is about protecting free speech, in general, and allowing the community to set its own standards about what is appropriate. . . .

"The purpose of the Tufts policy was to prosecute people for what the university described as 'gray area'—meaning unintentional—harassment." Zappia gives a hypothetical example: "I'm a Catholic living in a dorm, and I put up a poster in my room [consistent with my faith] saying that homosexuality is bad. If I have a gay roommate or one who doesn't agree with me, he could have me prosecuted, not because I hung it there to offend him, but because it's gray area harassment. . . . The policy was well intended, but it was dangerously vague. They used words like *stigmatizing, offensive, harassing*—words that are very difficult to define."

Detroit lawyer Walter B. Connolly, Jr., disagrees. He insists that it's quite proper for schools to act to protect the victims of discrimination as long as the restrictions stay out of the classroom. "Defamation, child pornography, fighting words, inappropriate comments on the radio—there are all sorts of areas where the First Amendment isn't the preeminent burning omnipotence in the sky. . . . Whenever you have competing interests of a federal statute [and] the Constitution, you end up balancing."

10   If you want to see a liberal who follows this issue flinch, whisper into his or her ear the name Shelby Steele. Liberals don't like Steele, an (African American) English professor at California's San Jose State; they try to dismiss him as having no professional experience in the study of racial discrimination. But he's heavily into the subject, and his analyses are both lucid and disturbing. Steele doesn't favor restrictions on speech, largely because they don't deal with what he sees as the problem. "You don't gain very much by trying to legislate the problem away, curtailing everyone's rights in the process," he says. In a forum in which almost everyone roars against a shadowy, usually nameless contingent of racist thugs, Steele deviates, choosing instead to accuse the accusers. He blames not the racists, but the weak-kneed liberal administrators and power-hungry victims' advocates for the mess on campuses today.

"Racial tension on campus is the result more of racial equality than inequality," says Steele. "On campuses today, as throughout society, blacks enjoy equality under the law—a profound social advancement. . . . What has emerged in recent years . . . in a sense as a result of progress . . . is *a politics of difference,* a troubling, volatile politics in which each group justifies itself, its sense of worth and its pursuit of power, through difference alone." On nearly every campus, says Steele, groups representing blacks, Hispanics, Asians, gays, women, Jews, and any combinations therein solicit special resources. Asked for—often demanded, in intense demonstrations—are funds for African-American (Hispanic . . .) cultural centers, separate (face it, segregated) housing, ethnic studies programs, and even individual academic incentives—at Penn State, minority students are given $275 per semester if they earn a C average, twice that if they do better than 2.75.

These entitlements, however, do not just appear *deus ex machina*. Part two of Steele's thesis addresses what he calls the "capitulation" of campus presidents. To avoid feelings of guilt stemming from past discrimination against minority groups, Steele says, "[campus administrators have] tended to go along with whatever blacks put on the table, rather than work with them to assess their real needs. . . . Administrators would never give white students a theme house where they could be 'more comfortable with people of their own kind,' yet more and more universities are doing this for black students." Steele sees white frustration as the inevitable result.

"White students are not invited to the negotiating table from which they see blacks and others walk away with concessions," he says. "The presumption is that they do not deserve to be there, because they are white. So they can only be defensive, and the less mature among them will be aggressive."

Course, some folks see it another way. The students fighting for minority rights aren't wicked political corrupters, but champions of a cause far too long suppressed by the white male hegemony. Responsive administrators are engaged not in capitulation, but in progress. And one shouldn't look for the cause of this mess on any campus, because he doesn't live on one. His address used to be the White House, but then he moved to 666 St. Cloud Road. Ronald Reagan, come on down.

15   *Dr. Manning Marble, University of Colorado:* "The shattering assault against the economic, social, and political status of the black American community as a whole [is symbolized by] the Reagan Administration in the 1980s. The Civil Rights Commission was gutted; affirmative action became a 'dead letter'; social welfare, health care, employment training, and educational loans were all severely reduced. This had a disproportionately more negative impact upon black youth."

The "perception is already widespread that the society at large is more permissive toward discriminatory attitudes and behaviors, and less committed to equal opportunity and affirmative action," concluded a 1988 conference at Northern Illinois University. John Wiener, writing in *The Nation*, attacks longstanding institutions of bigotry, asserting, for example, that "racism is endemic to the fraternity subculture," and praises the efforts of some schools to double the number of minority faculty and increase minority fellowships. On behalf of progressives across the land, Wiener writes off Shelby Steele as someone who is content to "blame the victim."

So the machine has melted, the phone has stretched to where it is useless. This is how intense the heat is. Liberals, who largely control the administration, faculty, and students' rights groups of leading academic institutions, have, with virtually no intensive intellectual debate, inculcated schools with their answers to the problem of bigotry. Conservatives, with a long history of insensitivity to minority concerns, have been all but shut out of the debate, and now want back in. Their intensive pursuit of the true nature of bigotry and the proper response to it—working to assess the "real needs" of campuses rather than simply bowing to pressure—deserves to be embraced by all concerned parties, and probably would have been by now but for two small items: (a) Reagan, their fearless leader, clearly *was* insensitive to ethnic/feminist concerns (even Steele agrees with this); and (b) some of the more coherent conservative pundits *still* show a blatant apathy to the problems of bigotry in this country. This has been sufficient ammunition for liberals who are continually looking for an excuse to keep conservatives out of the dialogue. So now we have clashes rather than debates: on how much one can say, on how much one should have to hear. Two negatives: one side wants to crack down on expression, the other on awareness. The machine has melted, and it's going to take some consensus to build a new one. Intellectual provincialism will have to end before young hate ever will.

A Month in the Life of Campus Bigotry

April 1 Vandals spray-paint "Jewhaters will pay" and other slogans on the office walls of *The Michigan Daily* (University of Michigan) in response to editorials condemning Israel for policies regarding the Palestinians. Pro-Israeli and pro-Palestinian shanties defaced; one is burned.

U of M: Fliers circulated over the weekend announce "White Pride Month."

Southern Connecticut State University reportedly suspends five fraternity officers after racial brawl.

April 2 Several gay men of the University of Connecticut are taunted by two students, who yell "faggot" at them.

April 3 The University of Michigan faculty meet to discuss a proposal to require students to take a course on ethnicity and racism.

April 4 Students at the University of California at Santa Barbara suspend hunger strike after university agrees to negotiate on demands for minority faculty hiring and the changed status of certain required courses.

April 5 The NCAA releases results of survey on black student athletes, reporting that 51 percent of black football and basketball players at predominantly white schools express feelings of being different; 51 percent report feelings of racial isolation; 33 percent report having experienced at least six incidents of individual racial discrimination.

The *New York Times* prints three op-ed pieces by students on the subject of racial tension on campus.

Charges filed against a former student of Penn State for racial harassment of a black woman.

April 6 University of Michigan: Hundreds of law students wear arm bands, boycott classes to protest lack of women and minority professors.

Michigan State University announces broad plan for increasing the number of minority students, faculty, and staff; the appointment of a senior advisor for minority affairs; and the expansion of multicultural conferences. "It's not our responsibility just to mirror society or respond to mandates," President John DiBioggio tells reporters, "but to set the tone."

April 7 Wayne State University (Detroit, Michigan) student newspaper runs retraction of cartoon considered offensive following protest earlier in the week.

30   Controversy develops at the State University of New York at Stony Brook, where a white woman charges a popular black basketball player with rape. Player denies charges. Charges are dismissed. Protests of racial and sexual assault commence.

April 12 Twelve-day sit-in begins at Wayne State University (Michigan) over conditions for black students on campus.

April 14 Racial brawl at Arizona State.

April 20 Demonstrations at several universities across the country (Harvard, Duke, Wayne State, Wooster College, Penn State, and so on) for improvements in black student life.

    Separate escort service for blacks started at Penn State out of distrust of the regular service.

35   **April 21** 200-student sit-in ends at Arizona State University when administrators agree to all thirteen demands.

April 24 Proposed tuition increase at City Universities of New York turns into racial controversy.

April 25 After eighteen months in office, Robert Collin, Florida Atlantic University's first black dean, reveals he has filed a federal discrimination complaint against the school.

    Two leaders of Columbia University's Gay and Lesbian Alliance receive death threat. "Dear Jeff, I will kill you butt fucking faggots. Death to COLA!"

April 26 A black Smith College (Massachusetts) student finds note slipped under door, ". . . African monkey do you want some bananas? Go back to the jungle. . . ."

40   "I don't think we should have to constantly relive our ancestors' mistakes," a white student at the University of North Carolina at Greensboro tells a reporter. "I didn't oppress anybody. Blacks are now equal. You don't see any racial problems anymore."

    White Student Union is reported to have been formed at Temple University in Philadelphia, "City of Brotherly Love."

April 28 Note found in Brown University (Rhode Island) dorm. "Once upon a time, Brown was a place where a white man could go to class without having to look at little black faces, or little yellow faces or little brown faces, except when he went to take his meals. Things have been going downhill since the kitchen help moved into the classroom. Keep white supremecy [sic] alive!!! Join the Brown chapter of the KKK today." Note is part of series that began in the middle of the month with "Die Homos." University officials beef up security, hold forum.

April 29 Controversy reported over proposed ban on verbal harassment at Arizona State.

April 30 Anti-apartheid shanty at University of Maryland, Baltimore County, is defaced. Signs read "Apartheid now," and "Trump Plaza."

45   University of California at Berkeley: Resolution is passed requiring an ethnic studies course for all students.

University of Connecticut: Code is revised to provide specific penalties for acts of racial intolerance.

Questions for Active Reading

1. What is your reaction to Shenk's opening phrase, *"Death to gays"*? Why do you think that he began his article this way?

2. What evidence does Shenk offer for his claim: "So now we have clashes rather than debates: on how much one can say, on how much one should have to hear. Two negatives: one side wants to crack down on expression, the other on awareness." Who are the "sides" to which he refers? What are their positions, according to Shenk?

3. How do you react to Shenk's list of items in "A Month in the Life of Campus Bigotry"? How does this list function as a conclusion to the Article?

Questions for Thinking Critically

1. Has your own campus experienced incidents of bigotry directed at people because of their race, sexual orientation, religion, or some other quality? If so, describe one such incident and analyze its probable causes. If your campus has not seen "young hate," explain why.

2. Have you ever been the victim of prejudice or discrimination? If so, describe your experience and explain how the incident made you feel about yourself and the people victimizing you.

3. Using the problem-solving method in this chapter, analyze the problem of bigotry on college campuses—yours or others. Develop some practical solutions for dealing with this troubling issue.

When Is It Rape?

BY NANCY GIBBS

Nancy Gibbs is an editor-at large for Time *magazine. She has written nearly one hundred stories and also was a major contributor to the issue commemorating September 11. She won the Luce Award and the Society of Professional Journalists' Sigma Delta Chi Magazine Writing Award. Gibbs, who holds degrees from Yale and Oxford universities, has taught journalism at Princeton. She joined* Time *in 1985.*

Be careful of strangers and hurry home, says a mother to her daughter, knowing that the world is a frightful place but not wishing to swaddle a child in fear. Girls grow up scarred by caution and enter adulthood eager to shake free of their parents' worst nightmares. They still know to be wary of strangers. What they don't know is whether they have more to fear from their friends.

Most women who get raped are raped by people they already know—like the boy in biology class, or the guy in the office down the hall, or their friend's brother. The familiarity is enough to make them let down their guard, sometimes even enough to make them wonder afterward whether they were "really raped." What people think of as "real rape"—the assault by a monstrous stranger in the shadows—accounts for only one out of five attacks.

So the phrase "acquaintance rape" was coined to describe the rest, all the cases of forced sex between people who already knew each other, however casually. But that was too clinical for headline writers, and so the popular term is the narrower "date rape," which suggests an ugly ending to a raucous night on the town.

These are not idle distinctions. Behind the search for labels is the central mythology about rape; that rapists are always strangers, and victims are women who ask for it. The mythology is hard to dispel because the crime is so rarely exposed. The experts guess—that's all they can do under the circumstances—that while one in four women will be raped in her lifetime, less than 10 percent will report the assault, and less than 5 percent of the rapists will go to jail.

5   Women charge that date rape is the hidden crime; men complain it is hard to prevent a crime they can't define. Women say it isn't taken seriously; men say it is a concept invented by women who like to tease but not take the consequences. Women say the date-rape debate is the first time the nation has talked frankly about sex; men say it is women's unconscious reaction to the excesses of the sexual revolution. Meanwhile, men and women argue among themselves about the "gray area" that surrounds the whole murky arena of sexual relations, and there is no consensus in sight.

In court, on campus, in conversation, the issue turns on the elasticity of the word *rape,* one of the few words in the language with the power to summon a shared image of a horrible crime.

At one extreme are those who argue that for the word to retain its impact, it must be strictly defined as forced sexual intercourse: a gang of thugs jumping a jogger in Central Park, a psychopath preying on old women in a housing complex, a man with an ice pick in a side street. To stretch the definition of the word risks stripping away its power. In this view, if it happened on a date, it wasn't rape. A romantic encounter is a context in which sex *could* occur, and so what omniscient judge will decide whether there was genuine mutual consent?

Others are willing to concede that date rape sometimes occurs, that sometimes a man goes too far on a date without a woman's consent. But this infraction, they say, is not as ghastly a crime as street rape, and it should not be taken as seriously. The New York *Post,* alarmed by the Willy Smith case, wrote in a recent editorial, "if the sexual encounter, *forced or not,* has been preceded by a series of consensual activities—drinking, a trip to the man's home, a walk on a deserted beach at three in the morning—the charge that's leveled against the alleged offender should, it seems to us, be different than the one filed against, say, the youths who raped and beat the jogger."

This attitude sparks rage among women who carry scars received at the hands of men they knew. It makes no difference if the victim shared a drink or a moonlit walk or even a passionate kiss, they protest, if the encounter ended with her being thrown to the ground and forcibly violated. Date rape is not about a misunderstanding, they say. It is not a communications problem. It is not about a woman's having regrets in the morning for a decision she made the night before. It is not about a "decision" at all. Rape is rape, and any form of forced sex—even between neighbors, coworkers, classmates and casual friends—is a crime.

10   A more extreme form of that view comes from activists who see rape as a metaphor, its definition swelling to cover any kind of oppression of women. Rape, seen in this light, can occur not only on a date but also in a marriage, not only by violent assault but also by psychological pressure. A Swarthmore College training pamphlet once explained that acquaintance rape "spans a spectrum of incidents and behaviors, ranging from crimes legally defined as rape to verbal harassment and inappropriate innuendo." No wonder, then, that the battles become so heated. When innuendo qualifies as rape, the definitions have become so slippery that the entire subject sinks into a political swamp. The only way to capture the hard reality is to tell the story.

A 32-year-old woman was on business in Tampa last year for the Florida supreme court. Stranded at the courthouse, she accepted a lift from a lawyer involved in her project. As they chatted on the ride home, she recalls, "he was saying all the right things, so I started to trust him." She agreed to have dinner, and afterward, at her hotel door, he convinced her to let him come in to talk. "I went through the whole thing about being old-fashioned," she says. "I was a virgin until I was twenty-one. So I told him talk was all we were going to do."

But as they sat on the couch, she found herself falling asleep. "By now, I'm comfortable with him, and I put my head on his shoulder. He's not tried anything all evening, after all." Which is when the rape came. "I woke up to find him on top of me, forcing himself on me. I didn't scream or run. All I could think about was my business contacts and what if they saw me run out of my room screaming rape.

"I thought it was my fault. I felt so filthy, I washed myself over and over in hot water. Did he rape me? I kept asking myself. I didn't consent. But who's gonna believe me? I had a man in my hotel room after midnight." More than a year later, she still can't tell the story without a visible struggle to maintain her composure. Police referred the case to the state attorney's office in Tampa, but without more evidence it decided not to prosecute. Although her attacker has admitted that he heard her say no, maintains the woman, "he says he didn't know that I meant no. He didn't feel he'd raped me, and he wanted to see me again."

Her story is typical in many ways. The victim herself may not be sure right away that she has been raped, that she had said no and been physically forced into having sex anyway. And the rapist commonly hears but does not heed the protest. "A date rapist will follow through no matter what the woman wants because his agenda is to get laid," says Claire Walsh, a Florida-based consultant on sexual assaults. "First comes the dinner, then a dance, then a drink, then the coercion begins." Gentle persuasion gives way to physical intimidation with alcohol as the ubiquitous lubricant. "When that fails, force is used," she says. "Real men don't take no for an answer."

15   The Palm Beach case serves to remind women that if they go ahead and press charges, they can expect to go on trial along with their attacker, if not in a courtroom then in the court of public opinion. The New York *Times* caused an uproar on its own staff not only for publishing the victim's name but also for laying out in detail her background, her high-school grades, her driving record, along with an unattributed quote from a school official about her "little wild streak." A freshman at Carleton College in Minnesota, who says she was repeatedly raped for four hours by a fellow student, claims that she was asked at an administrative hearing if she performed oral sex on dates. In 1989 a man charged with raping at knife point a woman he knew was acquitted in Florida because his victim had been wearing lace shorts and no underwear.

From a purely legal point of view, if she wants to put her attacker in jail, the survivor had better be beaten as well as raped, since bruises become a badge of credibility. She had better have reported the crime right away, before taking the hours-long shower that she craves, before burning her clothes, before curling up with the blinds down. And she would do well to be a woman of shining character. Otherwise the strict constructionist definitions of rape will prevail in court. "Juries don't have a great deal of sympathy for the victim if she's a willing participant up to the nonconsensual sexual intercourse," says Norman Kinne, a prosecutor in Dallas. "They feel that many times the victim has placed herself in the situation." Absent eyewitnesses or broken bones, a case comes down to her word against his, and the mythology of rape rarely lends her the benefit of the doubt.

She should also hope for an all-male jury, preferably composed of fathers with daughters. Prosecutors have found that women tend to be harsh judges of one another—perhaps because to find a defendant guilty is to entertain two grim realities: that anyone might be a rapist, and that every woman could find herself a victim. It may be easier to believe, the experts muse, that at some level the victim asked for it. "But just because a woman makes a bad judgment, does that give the guy a moral right to rape her?" asks Dean Kilpatrick, director of the Crime Victim Research and Treatment Center at the Medical University of South Carolina. "The bottom line is, Why does a woman's having a drink give a man the right to rape her?"

Last week the Supreme Court waded into the debate with a 7-to-2 ruling that protects victims from being harassed on the witness stand with questions about their sexual history. The Justices, in their first decision on "rape shield laws," said an accused rapist could not present evidence about a previous sexual relationship with the victim unless he notified the court ahead of time. In her decision, Justice Sandra Day O'Connor wrote that "rape victims deserve heightened protection against surprise, harassment, and unnecessary invasions of privacy."

That was welcome news to prosecutors who understand the reluctance of victims to come forward. But there are other impediments to justice as well. An internal investigation of the Oakland police department found that officers ignored a quarter of all reports of sexual assaults or attempts, though 90 percent actually warranted investigation. Departments are getting better at educating officers in handling rape cases, but the courts remain behind. A New York City task force on women in the courts charged that judges and lawyers were routinely less inclined to believe a woman's testimony than a man's.

20   The present debate over degrees of rape is nothing new; all through history, rapes have been divided between those that mattered and those that did not. For the first few thousand years, the only rape that was punished was the defiling of a virgin, and that was viewed as a property crime. A girl's virtue was a marketable asset, and so a rapist was often ordered to pay the victim's father the equivalent of her price on the marriage market. In early Babylonian and Hebrew societies, a married woman who was raped suffered the same fate as an adulteress—death by stoning or drowning. Under William the Conqueror, the penalty for raping a virgin was castration and loss of both eyes—unless the violated woman agreed to marry her attacker, as she was often pressured to do. "Stealing an heiress" became a perfectly conventional means of taking—literally—a wife.

It may be easier to prove a rape case now, but not much. Until the 1960s it was virtually impossible without an eyewitness; judges were often required to instruct jurors that "rape is a charge easily made and hard to defend against; so examine the testimony of this witness with caution." But sometimes a rape was taken very seriously, particularly if it involved a black man attacking a white woman—a crime for which black men were often executed or lynched.

Susan Estrich, author of *Real Rape*, considers herself a lucky victim. This is not just because she survived an attack 17 years ago by a stranger with an ice pick, one day before her graduation from Wellesley. It's because police, and her friends, believed her. "The first thing the Boston police asked was whether it was a black guy," recalls Estrich, now a University of Southern California law professor. When she said yes and gave the details of the attack, their reaction was, "So you were really raped." It was an instructive lesson, she says, in understanding how racism and sexism are factored into perceptions of the crime.

A new twist in society's perception came in 1975, when Susan Brownmiller published her book *Against Our Will: Men, Women and Rape*. In it she attacked the concept that rape was a sex crime, arguing instead that it was a crime of violence and power over women. Throughout history, she wrote, rape has played a critical function. "It is nothing more or less than a conscious process of intimidation, by which *all men* keep *all women* in a state of fear."

Out of this contention was born a set of arguments that have become politically correct wisdom on campus and in academic circles. This view holds that rape is a symbol of women's vulnerability to male institutions and attitudes. "It's sociopolitical," insists Gina Rayfield, a New Jersey psychologist. "In our culture men hold the power, politically, economically. They're socialized not to see women as equals."

25   This line of reasoning has led some women, especially radicalized victims, to justify flinging around the term *rape* as a political weapon, referring to everything from violent sexual assaults to inappropriate innuendoes. Ginny, a college senior who was really raped when she was sixteen, suggests that false accusations of rape can serve a useful purpose. "Penetration is not the only form of violation," she explains. In her view, *rape* is a subjective term, one that women must use to draw attention to other, nonviolent, even nonsexual forms of oppression. "If a woman did falsely accuse a man of rape, she may have had reasons to," Ginny says. "Maybe she wasn't raped, but he clearly violated her in some way."

Catherine Comins, assistant dean of student life at Vassar, also sees some value in this loose use of "rape." She says angry victims of various forms of sexual intimidation cry rape to regain their sense of power. "To use the word carefully would be to be careful for the sake of the violator, and the survivors don't care a hoot about him." Comins argues that men who are unjustly accused can sometimes gain from the experience. "They have a lot of pain, but it is not a pain that I would necessarily have spared them. I think it ideally initiates a process of self-exploration. 'How do I see women?' 'If I didn't violate her, could I have?' 'Do I have the potential to do to her what they say I did?' Those are good questions."

Taken to extremes, there is an ugly element of vengeance at work here. Rape is an abuse of power. But so are false accusations of rape, and to suggest that men whose reputations are destroyed might benefit because it will make them more sensitive is an attitude that is sure to backfire on women who are seeking justice for all victims. On campuses where the issue is most inflamed, male students are outraged that their names can be scrawled on a bathroom-wall list of rapists and they have no chance to tell their side of the story.

"Rape is what you read about in the New York *Post* about seventeen little boys raping a jogger in Central Park," says a male freshman at a liberal-arts college, who learned that he had been branded a rapist after a one-night stand with a friend. He acknowledges that they were both very drunk when she started kissing him at a party and ended up back in his room. Even through his haze, he had some qualms about sleeping with her: "I'm fighting against my hormonal instincts, and my moral instincts are saying, 'This is my friend and if I were sober, I wouldn't be doing this.'" But he went ahead anyway. "When you're drunk, and there are all sorts of ambiguity, and the woman says 'Please, please' and then she says no sometime later, even in the middle of the act, there still may very well be some kind of violation, but it's not the same thing. It's not rape. If you don't hear her say no, if she doesn't say it, if she's playing around with you—oh, I could get squashed for saying it—there is an element of say no, mean yes."

The morning after their encounter, he recalls, both students woke up hung over and eager to put the memory behind them. Only months later did he learn that she had told a friend that he had torn her clothing and raped her. At this point in the story, the accused man starts using the language of rape. "I felt violated," he says, "I felt like she was taking advantage of me when she was very drunk. I never heard her say 'No!,' 'Stop!,' anything." He is angry and hurt at the charges, worried that they will get around, shatter his reputation and force him to leave the small campus.

30   So here, of course, is the heart of the debate. If rape is sex without consent, how exactly should consent be defined and communicated, when and by whom? Those who view rape through a political lens tend to place all responsibility on men to make sure that their partners are consenting at every point of a sexual encounter. At the extreme, sexual relations come to resemble major surgery, requiring a signed consent form. Clinical psychologist Mary P. Koss of the University of Arizona in Tucson, who is a leading scholar on the issue, puts it rather bluntly: "It's the man's penis that is doing the raping, and ultimately he's responsible for where he puts it."

Historically, of course, this has never been the case, and there are some who argue that it shouldn't be—that women too must take responsibility for their behavior, and that the whole realm of intimate encounters defies regulation from on high. Anthropologist Lionel Tiger has little patience for trendy sexual politics that make no reference to biology. Since the dawn of time, he argues, men and women have always gone to bed with different goals. In the effort to keep one's genes in the gene pool, "it is to the male advantage to fertilize as many females as possible, as quickly as possible and as efficiently as possible." For the female, however, who looks at the large investment she will have to make in the offspring, the opposite is true. Her concern is to "select" who "will provide the best set-up for their offspring." So, in general, "the pressure is on the male to be aggressive and on the female to be coy."

No one defends the use of physical force, but when the coercion involved is purely psychological, it becomes hard to assign blame after the fact. Journalist Stephanie Gutmann is an ardent foe of what she calls the date-rape dogmatists. "How can you make sex completely politically correct and completely safe?" she asks. "What a horribly bland, unerotic thing that would be! Sex is, by nature, a risky endeavor, emotionally. And desire is a violent emotion. These people in the date-rape movement have erected so many rules and regulations that I don't know how people can have erotic or desire-driven sex."

Nonsense, retorts Cornell professor Andrea Parrot, co-author of *Acquaintance Rape: The Hidden Crime*. Seduction should not be about lies, manipulation, game playing or coercion of any kind, she says. "Too bad that people think that the only way you can have passion and excitement and sex is if there are miscommunications, and one person is forced to do something he or she doesn't want to do." The very pleasures of sexual encounters should lie in the fact of mutual comfort and consent: "You can hang from the ceiling, you can use fruit, you can go crazy and have really wonderful sensual erotic sex, if both parties are consenting."

It would be easy to accuse feminists of being too quick to classify sex as rape, but feminists are to be found on all sides of the debate, and many protest the idea that all the onus is on the man. It demeans women to suggest that they are so vulnerable to coercion or emotional manipulation that they must always be escorted by the strong arm of the law. "You can't solve society's ills by making everything a crime," says Albuquerque attorney Nancy Hollander. "That comes out of the sense of overprotection of women, and in the long run that is going to be harmful to us."

35   What is lost in the ideological debate over date rape is the fact that men and women, especially when they are young, and drunk, and aroused, are not very good at communicating. "In many cases," says Estrich, "the man thought it was sex, and the woman thought it was rape, and they are both telling the truth." The man may envision a celluloid seduction, in which he is being commanding, she is being coy. A woman may experience the same event as a degrading violation of her will. That some men do not believe a woman's protests is scarcely surprising in a society so drenched with messages that women have rape fantasies and a desire to be overpowered.

By the time they reach college, men and women are loaded with cultural baggage, drawn from movies, television, music videos and "bodice ripper" romance novels. Over the years they have watched Rhett sweep Scarlett up the stairs in *Gone With the Wind*; or Errol Flynn, who was charged twice with statutory rape, overpower a protesting heroine who then melts in his arms; or Stanley rape his sister-in-law Blanche du Bois while his wife is in the hospital giving birth to a child in *A Streetcar Named Desire*. Higher up the cultural food chain, young people can read of date rape in Homer or Jane Austen, watch it in *Don Giovanni* or *Rigoletto*.

The messages come early and often, and nothing in the feminist revolution has been able to counter them. A recent survey of sixth- to ninth-graders in Rhode Island found that a fourth of the boys and a sixth of the girls said it was acceptable for a man to force a woman to kiss him or have sex if he has spent money on her. A third of the children said it would not be wrong for a man to rape a woman who had had previous sexual experiences.

Certainly cases like Palm Beach, movies like *The Accused* and novels like Avery Corman's *Prized Possessions* may force young people to reexamine assumptions they have inherited. The use of new terms, like *acquaintance rape* and *date rape*, while controversial, has given men and women the vocabulary they need to express their experiences with both force and precision. This dialogue would be useful if it helps strip away some of the dogmas, old and new, surrounding the issue. Those who hope to raise society's sensitivity to the problem of date rape would do well to concede that it is not precisely the same sort of crime as street rape, that there may be very murky issues of intent and degree involved.

On the other hand, those who downplay the problem should come to realize that date rape is a crime of uniquely intimate cruelty. While the body is violated, the spirit is maimed. How long will it take, once the wounds have healed, before it is possible to share a walk on a beach, a drive home from work or an evening's conversation without always listening for a quiet alarm to start ringing deep in the back of the memory of a terrible crime?

Questions for Active Reading

1. What are some of the definitions of rape that Gibbs presents? Why does she begin her article with nine paragraphs devoted to definitions?

2. Why do you think that she then writes, "The only way to capture the hard reality is to tell the story"? What effect do the narratives in the article have?

3. Find places where Gibbs discusses racism, sexism, anthropology, and psychology. How do these references to social, political, and scientific ideas contribute to the article?

Questions for Thinking Critically

1. Do you know someone who has been involved in a date rape situation? If so, describe this person's experience (without divulging his or her identity).

2. How can society protect the rights of both the accuser and the accused in rape cases to ensure that justice is served?

3. Imagine that you are the dean of students at your college. What actions would you take to address the problem of date rape? Explain your reasons for considering these actions.

If you can, discuss your responses to all these questions with classmates.

Taking a Problem-Solving Approach to Writing

Problem solving provides you with a framework that you can use in much of your writing. A problem-solving approach can assist you in generating ideas and organizing information for most subjects. For example, you can look at a writing assignment as a problem and use a modification of the five-step method as a way to work on it:

1. What exactly is the assignment?

2. What are some alternative ways to complete it?

3. What are the advantages and disadvantages of the alternatives?

4. What is the best way for me to complete this assignment?

5. After some drafting ask: How is my solution to the problem of the assignment working out?

Then, as you write any paper, you can use modifications of the problem-solving steps at any stage. Look at the thesis as a problem and ask the preceding questions about it. Look at any part of the paper and ask the questions. Actually, effective writers do this to some extent—perhaps less systematically—as they draft, plan, and revise. As you recall, Chapter 5 sets forth a similar pattern for approaching revision.

Also, research projects are often seen and approached as problems. Just as you can apply a problem-solving approach to any writing assignment, so can you apply it to most research projects (see Chapter 14).

When you are asked to write a proposal or a paper about solving a problem, as this chapter's Writing Project does, you can use the problem-solving method as a system of organization. The following principles for writing about problem solving may not apply to every instance, but they should help you convert answers to the questions in the problem-solving model into an effective essay.

1. Be aware of the needs of your audience. You may have lived with the problem for so long, or researched it so thoroughly, that you almost cannot remember a time when the details were not familiar to you. However, your readers need specific details about background, history, special circumstances, and so forth, and they need to have this information presented in an order that they can understand. So unless you have some pressing reason not to do so, begin by presenting this information in the clearest order you can devise. As you write your essay, continually ask yourself, "Does my audience have all the information necessary to understand the point I am trying to make?"

2. Present all the information your audience needs in order to understand the problem before you begin to discuss alternative solutions.

3. Include a thesis statement indicating that you are going to discuss alternative solutions. You may also want to mention your proposed solution.

4. Discuss each alternative solution by explaining what it would involve and by presenting its advantages and disadvantages. Provide enough specific information to allow your audience to see these advantages and disadvantages. Don't just say, "A program could be developed to help students see how to avoid date rape." Instead, begin a paragraph by saying: "Respected student leaders from honor societies and athletic teams could participate in a forum explaining how excessive drinking, certain drugs, and certain behaviors can lead to situations in which date rape might occur."

5. Present the alternative solutions in the order that will most help your audience comprehend them and understand why you would select the one you did.

6. Conclude your essay by stating one solution, or some combination of solutions, and explain clearly why you chose it. If you have had time

to implement the solution, tell whether or not it is working. If you have not yet implemented it, explain how you will determine whether or not it is working.

Writing Project: Proposing a Solution to a Problem

This chapter includes both readings and Thinking-Writing Activities that encourage you to familiarize yourself with the problem-solving model and the steps required for implementing it. Be sure to reread what you wrote for those activities, as you may be able to use some of that material when completing this project.

> Write an essay in which you apply the five-step problem-solving method to a local, national, or international problem or to a personal problem. If you are analyzing a social problem, you will have to do some research and locate several articles that provide background information about and discussion of the problem. If you are analyzing a personal problem, you will enrich your paper by consulting some sources that pertain to it. Be sure to document all sources honestly and correctly in the format required by your instructor.
>
> After you have drafted your essay, revise it to the best of your ability. Follow your instructor's directions about focus, length, scope, format, and so on.

Begin by considering the key elements in the Thinking-Writing Model.

THE WRITING SITUATION

Purpose You have a variety of purposes here. You can use this opportunity to learn about a major problem in order to arrive at the best possible solution—and thus become a better-informed citizen. You might be able to help solve the problem if you are involved in the situation. Also, you will be practicing the creative and critical thinking involved in the problem-solving model.

Audience As usual, you will have several audiences for your paper. While working through the problem-solving model, you will be your own audience since in describing the problem and working through the alternative solutions, you will be determining the solution to the problem. As you begin to shape the answers to the model's questions into an essay, your audience will include readers other than yourself, so their needs should now occupy your attention.

Your classmates can be a valuable audience for peer review of a draft. They can react as intelligent readers who are not as knowledgeable as you are about the problem and its possible solutions but who can become interested as they read your description of it and your evaluation of the possible solutions. Finally, your instructor remains the audience who will judge how well you have analyzed the problem. As a writing teacher, he or she cares about a clear focus, logical organization, relevant details and examples, and accepted usage. Keep these factors in mind as you revise, edit, and proofread.

Subject Problems are problems precisely because they are difficult to think about and to solve. Often this is true because we don't have enough accurate information to arrive at an intelligent solution. Working on this paper will encourage you to find good information and to think about viable alternative solutions. Since you will be deeply involved in the subject, select a problem that you care about, one that is challenging—but compelling—to write about.

Writer This assignment provides you an opportunity to learn more about a problem that you care about but perhaps do not know enough about to propose a solid solution. You will have the chance to use the Internet or your library's holdings to find articles that will increase your knowledge of the problem and give you the pleasure of having additional expertise about something significant. If your instructor asks or allows you to write about a personal problem, you might not have to do as much research, but you will have the opportunity to work out something that is of immediate concern. Equipped with the problem-solving model and the direction it provides, you should work as a confident writer as you complete this assignment.

THE WRITING PROCESS

The following sections will guide you through the stages of generating, planning, drafting, and revising as you work on an essay about solving an important problem. Try to be particularly conscious of both the critical thinking you do while working through the problem-solving model and the critical thinking and decision making you do as you revise.

Generating Ideas You may find yourself in one of three situations:

1. If your instructor's directions specify that you must write about a particular local, national, or international problem, you must begin there. You might start by working through the problem-solving model and answering each question on the basis of your current knowledge. Then

you will be able to see what additional information you need to know and thus will be aware of what to look for as you research the problem.

2. If your instructor's directions allow you to choose any important local, national, or international problem, you might begin by brainstorming a list of each of these types of problems. Then you can select the one that seems most important, the one that interests you most, or the one about which you are most informed.

3. If your instructor's directions allow you to write about a personal problem, you might begin by brainstorming a list of problems you now face. It might help to make three columns: school problems, work problems, and personal problems. Then you can pick one, preferably one that you have to solve soon and for which you would need to gather information to write about.

Whichever situation describes yours, once you have worked through the problem-solving model, you will almost certainly spot gaps in your information. Think about how much additional information you will need in order to evaluate each of the alternative solutions. Then locate that information, asking a librarian for assistance if necessary.

Once you have filled in all the gaps and selected a solution—and a means to determine whether it is working—you are ready to turn your attention to presenting your information to your audience.

Defining a Focus   Write a thesis statement that will make clear to your audience that you are going to explore a problem-solving situation. You might decide to write something like "After thinking about the problem carefully, I realize that I have only two possible choices." Or you might decide to name the possible choices: "Newton's possible solutions to its budget problem include raising more revenue, cutting the budget, or some combination of the two." You may even decide to announce your chosen solution in your thesis statement: "After carefully weighing the alternatives, raising more revenue while continuing to cut the budget appears to be the best choice."

Organizing Ideas   The five-step method for solving problems fits well with essay structure. Your description of the problem together with its necessary history and other background information will give you a working introduction which can end with your thesis statement. Each of the alternative solutions, explained in as much detail as possible, along with its advantages and disadvantages, will provide one section of the body (one or more paragraphs). Your determination of the best solution and how it could be monitored will provide a conclusion.

Drafting   Begin with the easiest paragraph to draft. Keep your written answers to each part of the problem-solving model in front of you.

Remember to begin each section of the body with a topic sentence that names the alternative solution being discussed. If you are discussing advantages or disadvantages in separate paragraphs, draft topic sentences that prepare your readers for that information—such as "Unfortunately, cutting the budget further will create serious disadvantages for many citizens." Then provide specific information.

You will, of course, have to determine the best order in which to arrange the sections. Experiment until you find the one that seems most helpful to your audience. Switch the sections around on your word processor. You could even cut up a printout and tape the sections together in different arrangements until you discover one that seems smooth and logical.

Be sure to indicate the sources of your information. You do not have to use the correct citation format in a draft, but you do have to remind yourself exactly where you obtained the material so that you won't forget to cite it as you finish the paper.

In your conclusion, name the solution you have chosen. You may want to explain why you selected it if you think that will not be obvious to your audience. Remember to explain how you will evaluate the effectiveness of your solution.

Revising, Editing, and Proofreading   Use the step-by-step method on pages 160–161 to revise your essay and prepare a final draft.

The following essay shows how a student responded to this assignment—by writing about a social problem and citing according to Modern Language Association (MLA) format.

STUDENT WRITING
JOSHUA BARTLETT'S WRITING PROCESS

As a first-year college student, Joshua witnessed firsthand the impact of irresponsible attitudes toward alcohol among his peers. Even though he and his classmates were required to participate in various "alcohol awareness" education programs as part of freshman orientation at their campus, Joshua knew that the programs were not engaging, urgent, or serious enough to get the attention of young people like himself. Because Joshua was writing a formal argument, and because he was required to use sources to provide information, Joshua did not include anecdotes from his own personal experience. Had he been writing an opinion piece for his campus newspaper, he might well have described a campus party in which a fellow student was seriously hurt in an alcohol-related incident; he might even have described his own experiences with binge drinking. Although that evidence would certainly be compelling, it might not be adequately objective for an academic audience—and you can imagine how it might undermine his credibility with his professor! Instead, Joshua provides objective evidence from a range of sources to support his well-thought-out approach to the problem of alcohol abuse on college campuses.

To structure his draft, Joshua used the Detailed Method for Solving Problems (pages 441–442)

Critical Thinking About Uncritical Drinking

BY JOSHUA BARTLETT

There is widespread agreement that excessive student drinking is a serious problem on many college campuses. However, there are different views on the causes of this problem and on the best solutions for it. In this paper I will present some perspectives on the problem of student drinking and conclude with suggestions on how to deal with this serious threat to student health and success.

Why do college students drink to excess? According to many experts, it is mainly due to the influence of the people around them. When most students enter college, they do not have a drinking problem. However, although few realize it, they are entering a culture in which alcohol is often the drug of choice, one that can easily destroy their lives. According to some estimates, 80 to 90 percent of the students on many campuses drink alcohol, and many of them are heavy drinkers (Engs 543). One study found that nearly 30 percent of university students consume more than 15 alcoholic drinks a week (Gerson A43). An additional study found that among those who drink at least once a week, 92 percent of the men and 82 percent of the women consume at least five drinks in a row, and half said they wanted to get drunk (Rosenberg 81).

The results of all this drinking are predictably deadly. Virtually all college administrators agree that alcohol is the most widely used drug among college students and that its abuse is directly related to emotional problems and violent behavior, ranging from date rape to death (Dodge, "Campus Crime" A33+; Leatherman A33). For example, at one university, a 20-year-old woman became drunk at a fraternity party and fell to her death from the third floor ("Clemson" A3). At another university, two students were killed in a drunk-driving accident after drinking alcohol at an off-campus fraternity house; the families of both students have filed lawsuits against the fraternity (Dodge, "Beer Kegs Banned" A28). When students enter a college or university, they often become socialized into the alcohol-sodden culture of "higher education," at both formal and informal parties. The influence of peer pressure is enormous. Students often find it difficult to resist the pressures from their friends and fellow students to drink.

However, some observers of young people believe that, although peer pressure is certainly a factor in excessive college drinking, it is only one of a number of factors. They point out that the misuse of alcohol is a problem for all youth in our society, not just college students. For example, a recent study by the surgeon general's office shows that 1 in 3 teenagers consumes alcohol every week. This abuse leads to traffic deaths, academic difficulties, and acts of violence (Elson 64). Another study based on a large, nationally representative sample indicates that although college students are more likely to use alcohol, they tend to drink less per drinking day than nonstudents of the same age (Crowley 14); in other words, most college students who drink are more social drinkers than problem drinkers. One survey of undergraduate students found that college drinking is not as widespread as many people think (O'Hare 540). The conclusion from this data is that even though drinking certainly takes place on college campuses, it is no greater a problem than in the population at large.

Whatever the extent, the misuse of alcohol by college students is a serious situation with a number of probable causes. Certainly the influence of friends, whether in college or out, plays a role, as I've already discussed. But it is not the only factor. To begin with, there is evidence that family history is related to alcohol abuse. For example, one survey of college students found more problem drinking among students whose parents or grandparents had been diagnosed with alcoholism (Perkins and Berkowitz 237–240). Another study found that college students who come from families with high degrees of conflict display a greater potential for alcoholism (Pardeck 342–343).

Another important factor to consider in the misuse of alcohol by young people is advertising. A recent article entitled "It Isn't Miller Time Yet, and This Bud's Not for You" underscores the influence advertisers exert on the behavior of youth (Siler 52). By portraying beer drinkers as healthy, fun-loving, attractive young people, they create role models that many youths imitate. In the same way that cigarette advertisers used to encourage smoking among our youth—without regard for the health hazards—so alcohol advertisers try to sell as much booze as they can to whoever will buy it—no matter what the consequences.

A final factor in the abuse of alcohol is the people themselves. Although young people are subject to a huge number of influences, in the final analysis, they are free to choose what they want to do. They don't have to drink, no matter what the social pressures. In fact, many students resist these pressures and choose not to drink excessively or at all. In short, some students choose to think critically, while others choose to drink uncritically.

In order to encourage good judgment by more students and to minimize the causes of excessive drinking, I think that the following strategies could help solve the college alcohol problem. Only the last one has any disadvantages to be considered.

1. Colleges should have orientation and educational programs aimed at preventing alcohol abuse, and colleges should give top priority to campaigns against underage and excessive drinking.

2. Advertising and promotion of alcoholic beverages on college campuses and in college publications should be banned. Liquor distributors should not sponsor campus events. In addition, alcoholic beverage companies should be petitioned not to target young people in their ads.

3. Depending on the campus culture, colleges should ban or restrict alcohol use on campus and include stiff penalties for students who violate the rules.

4. Students at residential colleges should be able to live in substance-free housing, offering them a voluntary haven from alcohol, other drugs, tobacco, and peer pressure.

5. Colleges should create attractive alcohol-free clubs or pubs.

6. Colleges should ban the use of beer kegs, a symbol of cheap and easy availability of alcohol.

7. Fraternities should eliminate all alcohol-based contests or hazing torments.

8. Where possible, the on-campus drinking age should be reduced to 18, so that students won't be forced to move parties off-campus. At off-campus parties, there is no college control, and as a result, students tend to drink greater quantities and more dangerous concoctions.

Of course, this suggestion has the disadvantages of being in conflict with laws in many states or counties and also of seeming to encourage drinking by connecting it even more extensively with social events. But it has the advantages of control and of eliminating the attraction of what's forbidden.

In conclusion, alcohol abuse on college campuses is an extremely serious problem that is threatening the health and college careers of many students. As challenging as this problem is, I believe that it can be solved if students, teachers, and college officials work together in harmony and with determination to implement the suggestions made in this paper.

Works Cited

"Clemson Issues Ban on Parties Using Alcohol." <u>Chronicle of Higher Education</u> 31 Jan. 1990: A3.

Crowley, Joan E. "Educational Status and Drinking Patterns: How Representative Are College Students?" <u>Journal of Studies on Alcohol</u> 52.1 (1991) : 10–16.

Dodge, Susan. "Campus Crime Linked to Students' Use of Drugs and Alcohol." <u>Chronicle of Higher Education</u> 17 Jan. 1990 : A33+.

––– ."Use of Beer Kegs Banned by Some Colleges and National Fraternities." <u>Chronicle of Higher Education</u> 12 June 1991 : A27–28.

Elson, John. "Drink Until You Finally Drop." <u>Time</u> 16 Dec. 1991 : 64.

Engs, Ruth C. "Family Background of Alcohol Abuse and Its Relationship to Alcohol Consumption Among College Students: An Unexpected Finding." <u>Journal of Studies on Alcohol</u> 51.6 (1990) : 542–547.

Gerson, Mark. "30 Pct. of Ontario's Students Called 'Heavy Drinkers.'" <u>Chronicle of Higher Education</u> 12 April 1989 : A43.

Leatherman, Courtney. "College Officials Are Split on Alcohol Policies; Some Seek to End Underage Drinking; Others Try to Encourage 'Responsible' Use." <u>Chronicle of Higher Education</u> 31 Jan. 1990 : A33–35.

O'Hare, Thomas M. "Drinking in College: Consumption Patterns, Problems, Sex Differences and Legal Drinking Age." <u>Journal of Studies on Alcohol</u> 51.6 (1990) : 536–541.

Pardeck, John T. "A Multiple Regression Analysis of Family Factors Affecting the Potential for Alcoholism in College Students." <u>Adolescence</u> 26.102 (1991) : 341–347.

Perkins, H. Wesley, and Alan D. Berkowitz. "Collegiate COAs and Alcohol Abuse: Problem Drinking in Relation to Assessment of Parent and Grandparent Alcoholism." <u>Journal of Counseling and Development</u> 69.3 (1991) : 237–240.

Rosenberg, Debra. "Bad Times at Hangover U." <u>Newsweek</u> 19 Nov. 1990 : 81.

Siler, Julie Flynn. "It Isn't Miller Time Yet, and This Bud's Not for You." <u>Business Week</u> 24 June 1991 : 52.

13

Constructing Arguments

Writing to Persuade

"Give me the liberty to know, to utter, and to argue freely according to conscience, above all liberties." —John Milton

Critical Thinking Focus: Using reasons, evidence, and logic

Writing Focus: Convincing an audience

Reading Theme: Arguments about important issues

Writing Project: Arguing a position on a significant issue

Principles of Argument

People who study communication, argument, and rhetoric believe that much of what we say and write can be defined as argument because most statements seek listeners' or readers' agreement with the ideas being presented. Unless someone is just saying "Hmmmm" or "Hello" or is asking a question only to obtain information, the purpose of his or her statement usually is to make a point, to convince the audience of its validity, and often to bring about change or action. Essays, letters, stories, poems, movies, web sites—and even paintings and clothes—can be considered arguments or have argumentative purposes.

This chapter is devoted to argument, even though most of your previous writing has had argumentative characteristics. Some writing is supposed to be predominantly argumentative, and you need to know how to produce it and how to analyze it. Arguing effectively is essential to academic and professional success. In addition, because both politicians and advertisers use argumentative techniques, you need to understand both valid and fallacious arguments in order to evaluate claims that people want you to accept.

Thinking ↔ Writing Activity

Analyzing Argumentative Writing

1. Select an essay that you have written for this course that you believe has an argumentative purpose. What is your thesis or claim? What specific evidence do you present? Who are your audiences? Does the paper advocate for any change or action? What is it?

2. Select a reading from a previous chapter that you consider argumentative. What is its claim? What evidence does it present? Who are its audiences? What change or action does it seek?

This chapter will introduce concepts related to argument, provide readings and Thinking-Writing Activities to help you grasp them, and conclude with a Writing Project that asks you to write a logical, well-organized argument for a position that is important to you. The chapter will also explore ways to construct effective arguments and to evaluate arguments.

CLASSICAL CONCEPTS OF ARGUMENT

The concepts that guide logical argument are central to Western culture. Articulated by the philosophers and rhetoricians of ancient Greece and Rome, they have been studied and applied for more than two thousand years. Even though emotions, gut reactions, and intuition cannot be brushed aside—because they are so human—logical thinking and the resulting structured arguments are expected in business, government, and scholarship. Therefore, as a college composition student, you have both practical and historical reasons for giving attention to principles of argument or rhetoric.

The Greek philosopher Aristotle, in his famous work the *Rhetoric* and in other writings on logic, is the source of many concepts basic to our ideas of argument. But even Aristotle, more than three hundred years B.C.E., was responding to earlier works on rhetoric; and to this day, those who have followed him have modified and redefined his ideas and those of other classical rhetoricians. Those concepts include *ethos,* the character of the speaker or writer; *pathos,* the effect on the audience; and *logos,* the logic and substance of an argument. Some other centuries-old concepts are the techniques for generation or discovery of ideas, the arrangement of sections of an argument, the thinking methods of deduction and induction, techniques for refutation, and moral concerns about the use of rhetorical power for honorable ends.

Links to the Thinking-Writing Model   The classical rhetoricians were concerned with speech; literacy for all, print, and electronics were yet to come. Speech is, of course, still essential to communication, both face to face and via electronic media. This book concentrates on writing, but the ancient concepts have never gone out of use, and they function well to promote effective writing. The topics in the Thinking-Writing Model that is the foundation of this book demonstrate contemporary applications of many classical principles.

Notice how subject, purpose, audience, and writer connect in multiple ways with the concepts of *logos, pathos,* and *ethos.* If *logos* means both content and the logic of its presentation, *logos* connects with the Model's topics of subject, defining a thesis, and organizing ideas as well as with thinking critically. *Pathos* connects, of course, with the Model's audience and purpose; *ethos,* with the writer and also with the editing and proofreading stages of revising since a well-finished paper gives a good impression of its writer.

The classical concepts of *discovery* and *arrangement* are clearly connected to the Model's notions of thinking creatively, generating ideas, organizing ideas, and drafting.

Good Rhetoric   Today, the words *argument* and *rhetoric* are regularly used in conversation and in the media differently from the ways in which they are used in this chapter. Popularly, *argument* often means "a quarrel," and *rhetoric* is often used to mean "insubstantial or misleading language" (which is connected to the classical concerns about the use of rhetorical power for honorable ends). In this chapter, **rhetoric** means "the use of the best means of persuasion." We will discuss argument throughout the chapter and define the term on page 497.

MODERN CONCEPTS OF ARGUMENT

In the twentieth and twenty-first centuries, much attention has been paid to argument, at least partly because both mass media and education have extended their reaches. More communication and analyses of it from different points of view continue to provide new ways of thinking about arguments. Three important modern approaches are the **Toulmin method,** analyzing the effects of electronic communication, and various consensus-building strategies.

Toulmin's Method   College composition students are often introduced to some concepts that have developed from the work of the British professor of philosophy Stephen Toulmin. Professor Toulmin's ideas about argument can be applied to almost any argument, no matter how it is constructed. Concepts important to the Toulmin method are *claim* and *qualified claim, grounds, warrants,* and *backings.*

You already understand **claim** because *thesis, main point,* and *conclusion* are other ways to say it. You already understand **grounds** because it means *reasons, evidence, support, examples,* and *data.* You have established a thesis and provided support for it in most papers that you have written for this course.

As you improved your ability to develop a good thesis and studied Chapter 8's material on definition and classification, you were learning about qualified claims or qualifiers. A **qualified claim** is an accurately worded claim, one that establishes the category to be discussed. A qualified claim is not exaggerated or overly general. For example, you might not want to claim that *"Teenagers* should not be allowed to drive after midnight." Instead, you might claim that "People *under eighteen years* of age should not be allowed to drive after midnight." That way you would be acknowledging the probable differences in experience and maturity between a sixteen-year-old and an eighteen- or nineteen-year-old and showing that the overly general word *teenager* needs qualification. Properly qualified claims produce effective arguments.

Warrants are the assumptions, principles, premises, and beliefs that are the foundations of most arguments. This is an important concept to understand because warrants are not always stated. However, warrants provide the connection between a claim and its grounds, and they enable the acceptance or rejection of an argument. Here's a simple example:

Claim: People should brush and floss their teeth regularly.

Grounds: Dentists tell us that brushing and flossing will help prevent tooth decay and gum disease.

Warrants: People do not want their teeth to fall out. They do not want to have toothaches or ugly decayed teeth. People do not want drilling, fillings, and dentists' bills.

Backings are larger principles that support warrants. They are the foundations of the foundations. A backing for the warrants about brushing and flossing is the generally accepted principle of self-interest. People are concerned about their own health, appearance, and finances; people are concerned about situations that affect them. Therefore, the backing of the principle of self-interest supports the warrants about what people don't want, which support and connect the claim and grounds about dental hygiene.

This use of the word *warrant* is related to its use in law enforcement—a warrant for an arrest or a search warrant, which authorizes actions. The warrants of an argument are also related to the sources of beliefs (see Chapters 3 and 11). In addition, warrants are related to the premises used in deductive reasoning, which you will study later in this chapter.

Just as you need to understand the sources of your beliefs and those of others, you need to understand the warrants behind the arguments that you make and that people present to you. You need to recognize them when they are stated as part of an argument and search for them if they are not stated.

Looking at these U.S. Army recruitment materials should help you understand warrants. Can you see some assumptions, principles, beliefs—or warrants—that are behind the approaches taken by the poster and by the web site as they try to convice young people to enlist?

I Want **You** *for U.S. Army*

BY JAMES MONTGOMERY FLAGG (1877–1960)

Born in New York in 1877, James Montgomery Flagg had an illustrious career as an illustrator for both books and magazines, but he is especially remembered today as the creator of the famous Uncle Sam recruiting poster. Flagg made his first sale to a well-known magazine at the age of twelve, and by fifteen had joined the staffs of Life *and* Judge *magazines. Among his best-known illustrations were those for the* Jeeves *novels of P. G. Wodehouse.* Leslie's *magazine asked him to paint "Uncle Sam" for their July 4, 1916, issue. When World War I broke out, the U.S. government asked him to create a recruiting poster featuring that figure. Flagg created forty-five other posters for the government during that war. In 1980, Flagg was elected to the Society of Illustrators Hall of Fame.*

Questions for Active Reading

1. What is your reaction to the figure of Uncle Sam? How do you read the gesture he is making? At whom is he pointing?

2. What is your reaction to the verbal text of the poster? Is it intimidating? Commanding?

3. Who was the "you" he wanted? In 1917, who would Uncle Sam not have been recruiting?

Questions for Thinking Critically

1. What are some assumptions, principles, beliefs—or warrants—that provide a foundation for the argument presented by this poster?

2. Why are warrants about service and patriotism powerful?

3. What is the meaning or symbolism of the fact that Uncle Sam appears to be an older white man?

www.goarmy.com

U.S. ARMY

The United States Army, the oldest branch of the U.S. Military, has its origins in the Continental Army commanded by George Washington during the Revolutionary War. During the 1800s, administration was centralized and the army became more professional, with career officers and standard operating procedures. The army has been responsible, together with the other branches of the armed services, for national defense as well as for certain policing functions withing the country. Today the army is staffed with volunteers, so recruitment efforts are extremely important in order to maintain a force large enough for any contingency.

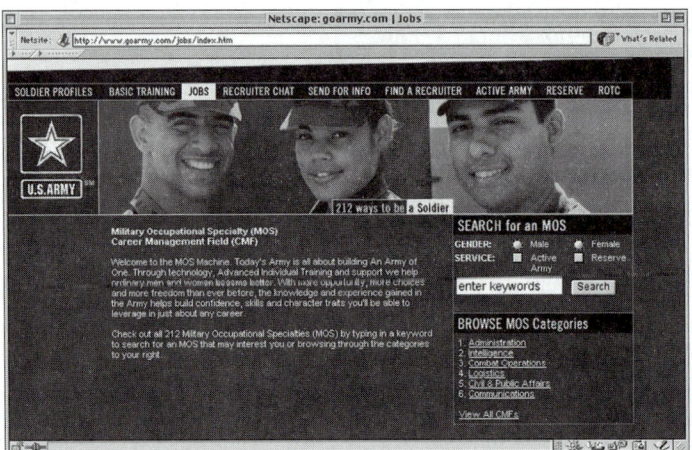

Questions for Active Reading

1. What are the demographics in the two images shown on the web site? How do they compare to the 1917 poster?

2. What does the idea of an "Army of One" suggest to you?

3. While both this and the 1917 poster are recruitment devices, what different appeals do they make to potential enlistees? Consider the web site's use of "leverage" and "skills."

Questions for Thinking Critically

1. What are some assumptions, principles, beliefs—or warrants—that provide a foundation for the argument presented by this web site? Visit the U. S. Army web site at www.goarmy.com to gather additional information for your analysis.

2. Why are warrants for self-development powerful? Can you identify any backings for the warrants you found?

3. List the warrants you found for the poster and the web site. See if you and your classmates found the same ones.

Argument and Electronic Media   There is currently much speculation about the effects of electronic communication on arguments. Of course, different kinds of electronic technologies raise different questions. Obviously, radio transmits spoken arguments, and television uses both sound and visuals to produce its well-known impact on audiences. Computers do so many things that analysis is difficult—but exciting. Visuals, sounds, and texts can be combined in countless ways, so distinctions among written, pictorial, and spoken arguments are blurred.

Many characteristics of computerized communication can affect arguments. The movement of linking means that logical connections are not always made. The speed at which ideas are transmitted and the rapidity with which some information can change can cause confusion and raise questions about credibility. Many people tend to write more informally in email than on paper, and such informality can change the tone of an argument for better or for worse. The rapid transmission of email can quickly conclude an argument or cause it to go on longer.

On the other hand, many Internet texts are simply posted versions of printed material or have been composed in a traditional manner. We need to be aware of the ways in which electronic and written communications differ as well as the ways in which argumentative concepts operate similarly in various media.

More Links to the Thinking-Writing Model Just as the concepts of classical rhetoric connect with components in the Thinking-Writing Model, so do the modern concepts. A claim, especially a qualified claim, clearly relates to defining a thesis. Grounds are important for generating and organizing ideas. Warrants and backing connect significantly with audience, purpose, and the writer. Writers need to understand their own assumptions and basic beliefs as they develop arguments in order to think critically about what they are presenting. Also, since assumptions and basic beliefs can differ in various communities, writers need to consider how the warrants beneath an argument might affect their audiences. Consensus-building approaches relate most obviously to reaching an audience but also pertain to purposes and to organizing ideas.

Achieving Mutual Understanding Some people believe that the purpose of argument is to coerce or to "win." As we have seen in this book, though, critical thinkers strive to develop the most informed understanding, which involves trying to fully appreciate other perspectives. Instead of attempting to prove others wrong, a more desirable purpose is to arrive at a clear and mutual understanding about the issue being discussed. Sometimes people are so far apart in their convictions that agreement cannot be reached and an impasse (or worse) occurs. At other times people "agree to disagree" and work around their differences; but if agreement does come, good feelings can result in progress, problem solving, or other desired achievements. By thinking critically, you can inspire others to think critically as well so that all parties are working together to achieve the clearest understanding rather than splintering into adversarial factions. In the cartoon on the next page , the man on the right seems to be pursuing conflict rather than mutual understanding. What are the disadvantages of such an approach? Can you think of some more constructive strategies that he could use?

"I shall now punch a huge hole in your argument."

Considering Other Points of View People do not argue about things on which they agree, nor do they argue about concepts that are accepted as facts. For example, it's not likely that an argument would arise over the relative lengths of a meter and a yard. A measuring tape takes care of the question. However, people do argue about whether the United States should adopt the metric system. Arguments develop because people have different opinions about issues.

You should not ignore opposing points of view when you are making an argument. Sometimes, people will ignore other ideas and present one-sided cases—as in most advertisements, some sermons, many political statements, and attempts at pushing proposals through. But in reasoned arguments, you should address varying ideas in order to demonstrate your grasp of the issue and also to try to achieve mutual understanding and, if possible, consensus or agreement.

Guidelines for Addressing Other Points of View

1. *Restate the other claim to show that you understand it.* This is often easier to do in a face-to-face discussion than in writing, but it is important in any argument. Sometimes misunderstandings can be uncovered by this technique. Restatements can also lead to finding common ground. A restatement should be made in a nonjudgmental, respectful tone.

2. *Find areas of agreement, or common ground, at the outset of the argument.* This, too, is sometimes easier to do in a face-to-face discussion than in writing. It is a technique often used in negotiations and mediation.

However, in a written argument, you should try whenever you can to establish common ground with those who have other beliefs about the issue that you are addressing. Often identifying warrants can lead parties to find areas of agreement. When people see that they agree about some parts of an issue, they can establish mutual respect and then examine their differing opinions carefully.

3. *Identify which differences are important and which are trivial.* This, too, is more easily done when people talk with each other, but it is also something that can be attempted in written argument. Here, too, identifying warrants sometimes clarifies the significance of some parts of an argument.

4. *Concede points that you cannot uphold.* Sometimes you will have to concede that some of your opponents' ideas are so strong that you cannot counter them, even if you do not agree with them.

5. *Compromise.* At times, accepting a middle position or a partial achievement of your purpose is better than arguing for its complete achievement.

6. *Rebut.* This means to refute or to present opposing evidence. Rebuttal often seems necessary. It is part of the debate tradition and is important in legal arguments, but it maintains adversarial positions. If you have to rebut an opposing point, do so courteously.

7. *Be sensitive to different argumentative philosophies.* Some cultures, some groups, and some individuals prefer indirect methods of argumentation while others want to get to the point quickly. Sometimes a direct approach is seen as rude or overly aggressive; sometimes an indirect approach is seen as weak, sneaky, or confusing. In the United States, directness is often considered as the best approach. If your audience is from a different culture, however, be sure that you understand that culture's argumentative style.

Thinking ↔ Writing Activity

Establishing Agreement

1. Find a classmate who disagrees with you about something—for example, the quality of a specific television show, a political principle, or a controversy at your college. Each of you should then write a brief statement about your position. Next, read each other's statements.

2. See if you can establish some areas of agreement. Can you identify warrants for your position and for your classmate's? Where might you compromise? Determine whether any differences are not important. Do either of you have to concede a point?

Analyzing the Audience You learned long ago that you should speak and write differently to different audiences. You use one kind of vocabulary and tone with your friends and another with your grandparents. You write formally in a job application letter and informally in an email to your sister telling what you did last weekend.

The suggestions for completing every Writing Project in this book include some discussion of your audience because it is one of the major components of any writing situation and therefore is prominently featured in the Thinking-Writing Model. However, consideration of audience is especially important when you are writing an argumentative paper, particularly if you hope to ef-fect some change or action. Also, remember that you may have more than one audience. Here are some questions to ask yourself about the audiences for any argument you write:

- Who is interested in this issue?
- What concerns do these interested people have?
- What is their level of education or expertise?
- What related issues interest them?
- How much time might they give to reading my argument?
- Who can do something about the situation?
- Who is opposed to my point of view?
- What are the opposing claims?
- What format, tone, or method of presentation will be effective with this audience?

Can you think of other questions to ask about audiences?

Going Too Far Paying attention to audiences does not mean telling an audience only what it wants to hear or manipulating ideas just to reach a certain audi-ence. Some advertisers and politicians mislead audiences in such ways. Pan-dering to an audience is one of the ways in which rhetoric can be misused. Responsible writers and speakers accommodate their audiences honestly.

Recognizing Arguments

TWO FRIENDS ARGUE: SHOULD MARIJUANA BE LEGALIZED?

Consider the following dialogue about whether marijuana should be legalized. Have you participated in such exchanges? In what ways do dialogues like this differ from written argument? How do such dialogues provide a starting point for written arguments?

Dennis: Have you read about the medical uses of marijuana—that people who have cancer, AIDS, and some other diseases might be helped by smoking? I think some doctors are prescribing it, and some states may be changing their laws. This might change people's thinking more than all those discussions about unenforced laws, unjust punishments, and victimless crimes that have been going on since my uncles were in college.

Caroline: Well, I agree that we need to think about drug laws. But I hope you agree that we have to be careful. Drugs pose a serious threat to the young people of our country. Look at all the people who are addicted to drugs, who have their lives ruined, and who often die at an early age of overdoses. And think of all the crimes people commit to support their drug habits. So I don't know if anything that's illegal now should be legalized, . . . and the laws should be enforced.

Dennis: That's ridiculous. Smoking marijuana is nothing like using drugs such as heroin or even cocaine. It follows that smoking marijuana should not be against the law if it's harmless and maybe even helpful to some sick people.

Caroline: I don't agree. Although marijuana may not be as dangerous as some other drugs, it does affect things like a driver's ability to judge distances. And smoking it surely isn't good for you. And I don't think that anything that is a threat to your health should be legal.

Dennis: What about cigarettes and alcohol? We know that they are dangerous. Medical research has linked smoking cigarettes to lung cancer, emphysema, and heart disease. Alcohol damages the liver and also the brain. Has anyone ever proved that marijuana is a threat to our health? And even if it does turn out to be somewhat unhealthy, it's certainly not as dangerous as cigarettes and alcohol.

Caroline: That's a good point. But to tell you the truth, I'm not so sure that cigarettes and alcohol should be legal. And in any case, they are legal. The fact that cigarettes and alcohol are bad for your health is not reason to legalize another drug that can cause health problems.

Dennis: Look—life is full of risks. We take chances every time we cross the street or climb into our cars. In fact, with all the irresponsible drivers on the road, driving could be a lot more hazardous to our health than any of the drugs around. Many of the foods we eat can kill. For example, red meat contributes to heart disease, and artificial sweeteners can cause cancer. The point is, if people want to take chances with their health, that's up to them. And many people in our society like to mellow out with marijuana. I read somewhere that over 70 percent of the people in the United States think that marijuana should be legalized.

Caroline: There's a big difference between letting people drive cars and letting them use dangerous drugs. Society has a responsibility to protect people from themselves. People often do things that are foolish if they are encouraged to or given the opportunity. Legalizing something like marijuana encourages people to use it, especially young people. It follows that many more people would use marijuana if it were legalized. It's like society saying "This is all right—go ahead and use it."

Dennis: I still maintain that marijuana isn't dangerous. It's not addictive—like heroin is—and there is no evidence that it harms you. Consequently, anything that is harmless should be legal.

Caroline: Marijuana may not be physically addictive like heroin, but I think that it can be psychologically addictive because people tend to use more and more of it over time. I know a number of people who spend a lot of their time getting high. What about Carl? All he does is lie around and get high. This shows that smoking it over a period of time definitely affects your mind. Think about the people you know who smoke a lot—don't they seem to be floating in a dream world? How are they ever going to make anything of their lives? As far as I'm concerned, a pot-head is like a zombie—living but dead.

Dennis: Since you have had so little experience with marijuana, I don't think that you can offer an informed opinion on the subject. And anyway, if you do too much of anything, it can hurt you. Even something as healthy as exercise can cause problems if you do too much of it. But I sure don't see anything wrong with toking up with some friends at a party or even getting into a relaxed state by yourself. In fact, I find that I can even concentrate better on my school work after taking a little smoke.

Caroline: If you believe that, then marijuana really has damaged your brain. You're just trying to rationalize your drug habit. Smoking marijuana doesn't help you concentrate—it takes you away from reality. And I don't think that people can control it. Either you smoke and surrender control of your life, or you don't smoke because you want to retain control. There's nothing in between.

Dennis: Let me point out something to you. Because marijuana is illegal, organized crime controls its distribution and makes all the money from it. If marijuana were legalized, the government could tax the sale of it—like cigarettes and alcohol—and use the money for some worthwhile purpose. For example, many states have legalized gambling and use the money to support education. In fact, the major tobacco companies have already copyrighted names for different marijuana brands—like "Acapulco Gold." Obviously they believe that marijuana will soon become legal.

Caroline: The fact that the government can make money out of something doesn't mean that they should legalize it. We could also legalize prostitution or muggings and then tax the proceeds. Also, even if the cigarette companies are prepared to sell marijuana, that doesn't mean that selling it makes sense. After all, they're the ones who are selling us cigarettes. . . .

Can you think of other views on the subject of legalizing marijuana? Can you think of other subjects about which such dialogues are taking place now?

The previous discussion illustrates two people's engaging in dialogue, the systematic exchange of ideas. Discussing issues with others encourages you to be mentally active, to ask questions, to view issues from different perspectives, to develop reasons that support conclusions, and to write convincingly.

This chapter focuses on the last quality of thinking critically—supporting claims with reasons—because when we offer reasons to support a conclusion, we are presenting an argument, the essence of most college and business writing. An **argument** is a form of thinking in which certain statements (reasons or evidence) are offered to support another statement (a conclusion or a claim).

In the dialogue, Dennis presents the following argument for legalizing marijuana:

Reason: Marijuana might help some people who have serious diseases.

Reason: Marijuana isn't dangerous like heroin and cocaine.

Reason: Governments could tax the sale of marijuana as they do cigarettes and alcohol.

Claim: Marijuana should be legalized.

Expanding the definition of *argument*, we can define the main ideas that make up an argument. **Reasons, evidence,** or **grounds** are statements that support another statement (a conclusion, claim, or thesis), justify it, or make it more probable. The **claim, thesis,** or **conclusion** is a statement that explains, asserts, or predicts on the basis of statements (known as reasons) that are offered as evidence to support it.

The type of thinking that uses argument—presenting reasons to support conclusions—is known as **reasoning,** and it is a type of thinking explained throughout this book. We are continually trying to explain, justify, and predict through the process of reasoning, and often we must present such thinking in writing.

Of course, our reasoning—and that of others—is not always correct. The reasons someone offers may not really support the claim they are intended to, a conclusion may not really follow from the reasons stated, or the reasons may be questionable or wrong. These difficulties are illustrated in a number of the arguments contained in the previous discussion on marijuana.

Nevertheless, whenever we accept a conclusion as likely or true on the basis of certain reasons, or whenever we offer reasons to support a conclusion, we are using arguments—even if our reasoning is weak or faulty and needs improvement.

Let's return to the discussion about marijuana. After Dennis presents one argument, Caroline presents another, giving reasons that lead to a conclusion that conflicts with the one Dennis has offered.

Reason: Drugs pose a very serious threat to the young people of our country.

Reason: Many crimes are committed to support drug habits.

Claim: As a result, society has to have drug laws and enforce them to convince people of the seriousness of the situation.

Which of Dennis's or Caroline's arguments do you see as reasonable? Which seem weak or faulty?

English, like other languages, provides guidance in our efforts to identify reasons and conclusions. Certain key words, or cue words, signal that a reason is being offered to support a conclusion or that a conclusion is being drawn on the basis of certain reasons. After you read the following list, go back to the dialogue and see how and when Dennis and Caroline use these words.

Below are some commonly used cue words for reasons and conclusions.

Useful Words for Recognizing and Writing Arguments

Cue Words Signaling Reasons

since	in view of
for	first, second
because	in the first (second) place
as shown by	may be inferred from
as indicated by	may be deduced from
given that	may be derived from
assuming that	for the reason that

Cue Words Signaling Conclusions

therefore	then
thus	it follows that
hence	thereby showing
so	demonstrates that
(which) shows that	allows us to infer that
(which) proves that	suggests very strongly that
implies that	you see that
points to	leads me to believe that
as a result	allows us to deduce that
consequently	

Of course, identifying reasons, claims, and conclusions involves more than looking for cue words. The words and phrases just listed do not always signal reasons and conclusions, and in many cases people present arguments without using cue words. Cue words, however, do alert us that an argument is being offered. Careful use of cue words helps us to write effective arguments.

Thinking ↔ Writing Activity

Analyzing a Dialogue

Write responses to the previous dialogue. Then share your responses with classmates and note where you agree and disagree.

1. Review the discussion and underline cue words that signal when Dennis and Caroline are giving reasons or announcing conclusions.

2. Identify one argument in the dialogue that you find convincing and one that seems unconvincing. Write your reasons for your opinions, referring to specific places in the dialogue.

The following two essays discuss the issue of whether drugs should be legalized. The first passage is by essayist and novelist Gore Vidal. The second is by *New York Times* editor and columnist A. M. Rosenthal.

Drugs

BY GORE VIDAL (b.1925)

An amazingly prolific writer of novels, short stories, plays, and essays, Gore Vidal holds a unique place in American life and letters. Among his many publications are the satiric novels Myra Breckinridge *and* Live from Golgotha, *the play* Visit to a Small Planet, *and the screenplays for* The Catered Affair *and* Suddenly Last Summer. *He won the National Book Award in 1993 for* United States: Essays, 1952–1992. *Often compared to both Henry James and Mark Twain, two vastly different writers, Vidal is known for his satiric wit, his humor, and his willingness to say what he thinks without worrying about the consequences.*

It is possible to stop most drug addiction in the United States within a very short time. Simply make all drugs available and sell them at cost. Label each drug with a precise description of what effect—good and bad—the drug will have on the taker. This will require heroic honesty. Don't say that marijuana is addictive or dangerous when it is neither, as millions of people know—unlike "speed," which kills most unpleasantly, or heroin, which is addictive and difficult to kick.

For the record, I have tried—once—almost every drug and liked none, disproving the popular Fu Manchu theory that a single whiff of opium will enslave the mind. Nevertheless many drugs are bad for certain people to take and they should be told why in a sensible way.

Along with exhortation and warning, it might be good for our citizens to recall (or learn for the first time) that the United States was the creation of men who believed that each man has the right to do what he wants with his own life as long as he does not interfere with his neighbor's pursuit of happiness. (That his neighbor's idea of happiness is persecuting others does confuse matters a bit.)

This is a startling notion to the current generation of Americans. They reflect a system of public education which has made the Bill of Rights, literally, unacceptable to a majority of high school graduates who now form the "silent majority"—a phrase which that underestimated wit Richard Nixon took from Homer who used it to describe the dead.

5   Now one can hear the warning rumble begin: If everyone is allowed to take drugs, everyone will and the GNP will decrease, the Commies will stop us from making everyone free, and we shall end up a race of zombies, passively murmuring "groovy" to one another. Alarming thought. Yet it seems most unlikely that any reasonably sane person will become a drug addict if he knows in advance what addiction is going to be like.

Is everyone reasonably sane? No. Some people will always become drug addicts just as some people will always become alcoholics, and it is just too bad. Every man, however, has the power (and should have the legal right) to kill himself if he chooses. But since most men don't, they won't be mainliners either. Nevertheless, forbidding people things they like or think they might enjoy only makes them want those things all the more. This psychological insight is, for some mysterious reason, perennially denied by our governors.

It is a lucky thing for the American moralist that our country has always existed in a kind of time-vacuum: We have no public memory of anything that happened before last Tuesday. No one in Washington today recalls what happened during the years alcohol was forbidden to the people by a Congress that thought it had a divine mission to stamp out Demon Rum—launching, in the process, the greatest crime wave in the country's history, causing thousands of deaths from bad alcohol, and creating a general (and persisting) contempt among the citizenry for the laws of the United States.

The same thing is happening today. But the government has learned nothing from past attempts at prohibition, not to mention repression.

Last year when the supply of Mexican marijuana was slightly curtailed by the Feds, the pushers got the kids hooked on heroin and deaths increased dramatically, particularly in New York. Whose fault? Evil men like the Mafiosi? Permissive Dr. Spock? Wild-eyed Dr. Leary? No.

10   The Government of the United States was responsible for those deaths. The bureaucratic machine has a vested interest in playing cops and robbers. Both the

Bureau of Narcotics and the Mafia want strong laws against the sale and use of drugs because if drugs are sold at cost, there would be no money in it for anyone.

If there was no money in it for the Mafia, there would be no friendly playground pushers, and addicts would not commit crimes to pay for the next fix. Finally, if there was no money in it, the Bureau of Narcotics would wither away, something they are not about to do without a struggle.

Will anything sensible be done? Of course not. The American people are as devoted to the idea of sin and its punishment as they are to making money—and fighting drugs is nearly as big a business as pushing them. Since the combination of sin and money is irresistible (particularly to the professional politician), the situation will only grow worse.

Questions for Active Reading

1. State Vidal's thesis or claim in one sentence. Where did he place it? Is this placement effective?

2. Identify at least two specific reasons that he gives to support his thesis.

3. Can you identify any warrants and backings for his arguments?

4. Vidal is known for his satire. Which, if any, sentences do you think are not intended to be taken literally? Why do you think so?

Questions for Thinking Critically

1. Do you agree with Vidal's argument that drugs should be legalized? Why or why not?

2. Do you agree with Vidal's comparison of the Bureau of Narcotics and the Mafia? How do you think agents for the Bureau would react to this comparison? How might members of the Mafia react?

3. What can you infer about Vidal's attitude toward American politics?

The Case for Slavery

BY A. M. ROSENTHAL (b. 1922)

Born in Sault Ste. Marie, Ontario, A. M. Rosenthal came to New York as a small child and became a reporter for the New York Times *while still in college. After covering the then-new United Nations, he served as a foreign correspondent in India, Switzerland, Japan, and Poland. He received the Pulitzer Prize for his reporting from Poland in 1960. He has also won several Overseas Press Club awards, Front Page prizes, and a variety of other awards for his books and magazine articles. He is the author of "On*

My Mind," a column for the New York Times, *and a contributing writer for several news and political periodicals.*

Across the country, a scattered but influential collection of intellectuals is intensely engaged in making the case for slavery.

With considerable passion, these Americans are repeatedly expounding the benefits of not only tolerating slavery but legalizing it:

It would make life less dangerous for the free. It would save a great deal of money. And since the economies could be used to improve the lot of the slaves, in the end they would be better off.

The new antiabolitionists, like their predecessors in the nineteenth century, concede that those now in bondage do not themselves see the benefits of legalizing their status.

5   But in time they will, we are assured, because the beautiful part of legalization is that slavery would be designed so as to keep slaves pacified with the very thing that enslaves them!

The form of slavery under discussion is drug addiction. It does not have every characteristic of more traditional forms of bondage. But they have enough in common to make the comparison morally valid—and the campaign for drug legalization morally disgusting.

Like the plantation slavery that was a foundation of American society for so long, drug addiction largely involves specifiable groups of people. Most of the enchained are children and adolescents of all colors and black and Hispanic adults.

Like plantation slavery, drug addiction is passed on from generation to generation. And this may be the most important similarity: Like plantation slavery, addiction can destroy among its victims the social resources most valuable to free people for their own betterment—family life, family traditions, family values.

In plantation-time America, mothers were taken from their children. In drug-time America, mothers abandon their children. Do the children suffer less, or the mothers?

10   Antiabolitionists argue that legalization would make drugs so cheap and available that the profit for crime would be removed. Well-supplied addicts would be peaceful addicts. We would not waste billions for jails and could spend some of the savings helping the addicted become drug-free.

That would happen at the very time that new millions of Americans were being enticed into addiction by legalization—somehow.

Are we really foolish enough to believe that tens of thousands of drug gang members would meekly steal away, foiled by the marvels of the free market?

Not likely. The pushers would cut prices, making more money than ever from the ever-growing mass market. They would immediately increase the potency and variety beyond anything available at any Government-approved narcotics counters.

Crime would increase. Crack produces paranoid violence. More permissiveness equals more use equals more violence.

15   And what will legalization do to the brains of Americans drawn into drug slavery by easy availability?

Earlier this year, an expert drug pediatrician told me that after only a few months babies born with crack addiction seemed to recover. Now we learn that stultifying behavioral effects last at least through early childhood. Will they last forever?

How long will crack affect neurological patterns in the brain of adult crack users? Dr. Gabriel G. Nahas of Columbia University argues in his new book, *Cocaine: The Great White Plague*, that the damage may be irreversible. Would it not be an act of simple intelligence to drop the legalization campaign until we find out?

Then why do a number of writers and academicians, left to right, support it? I have discussed this with antidrug leaders like Jesse Jackson, Dr. Mitchell Rosenthal of Phoenix House, and William J. Bennett, who search for answers themselves.

Perhaps the answer is that the legalizers are not dealing with reality in America. I think the reason has to do with class.

20   Crack is beginning to move into the white middle and upper classes. That is a tragedy for those addicted.

However, it has not yet destroyed the communities around which their lives revolve, not taken over every street and doorway. It has not passed generation to generation among them, killing the continuity of family.

But in ghetto communities poverty and drugs come together in a catalytic reaction that is reducing them to social rubble.

The antiabolitionists, virtually all white and well-to-do, do not see or do not care. Either way they show symptoms of the callousness of class. That can be a particularly dangerous social disorder.

Questions for Active Reading

1. State Rosenthal's thesis or claim in one sentence. Where did he place it? Is this placement effective?

2. Identify at least two specific reasons that he gives to support his thesis.

3. Can you identify any warrants and backings for his argument?

4. What impression does Rosenthal convey of himself? How is this similar or different from the impression conveyed by Vidal?

Questions for Thinking Critically

1. Do you agree with Rosenthal's argument that drugs should not be legalized? Why or why not?

2. Do you agree with Rosenthal's point that differences of opinion on this topic have to do with class? How might someone counter that point?

Arguments as Inferences

When you construct arguments, you are constructing views of the world by means of your ability to infer. As you saw in Chapter 11, inferring is a thinking process used to reason from what one already knows (or believes to be the case) to acquire new knowledge or beliefs. This is usually what you do when you construct arguments: work from reasons you know or believe to draw conclusions based on them.

Just as you can use inferences to make sense of different types of situations, you can also construct arguments for different purposes. As already noted, some people believe in using arguments to coerce or to "win." A more desirable goal is to use arguments to clarify issues, develop mutual understanding, and if possible, bring about agreement or consensus on the issue being discussed. Notice how you can work toward agreement when you construct arguments to do any of the following: decide, explain, predict, persuade.

CONSTRUCTING ARGUMENTS TO DECIDE

Reason: Throughout my life, I've always been interested in all kinds of electricity.

Reason: There are many attractive job opportunities in the field of electrical engineering.

Claim: Electrical engineering would be a good major for me.

Audience: Myself, my parents, my academic adviser, the scholarship office

CONSTRUCTING ARGUMENTS TO EXPLAIN

Reason: I was delayed leaving my house because my dog needed emergency walking.

Reason: There was an unexpected traffic jam caused by motorists slowing down to view an overturned chicken truck.

Claim: Therefore, I couldn't help being late for our appointment.

Audience: The person waiting for me

CONSTRUCTING ARGUMENTS TO PREDICT

Reason: Some people will always drive faster than the speed limit allows, no matter whether the limit is 55 or 65 mph.

Reason: Car accidents are more likely to occur at higher speeds.

Claim: A reinstated 65 mph speed limit will result in more accidents.

Audience: Legislators, voters, drivers

CONSTRUCTING ARGUMENTS TO PERSUADE

Reason: Chewing tobacco can lead to cancer of the mouth and throat.

Reason: Young people sometimes begin chewing tobacco because they see ads that feature sports heroes they admire doing it.

Claim: Ads for chewing tobacco should be banned.

Audience: Parents, voters, legislators, advertising agencies, media executives

Evaluating Arguments

To construct good arguments, you must be skilled at evaluating the effectiveness, or soundness, of arguments already constructed. You must investigate the components of an argument to determine the soundness of the argument as a whole.

1. How true are the reasons being offered to support the conclusion?

2. To what extent do the reasons support the conclusion, claim, or thesis—or to what extent does the conclusion follow from the reasons offered?

TRUTH: HOW TRUE ARE THE SUPPORTING REASONS?

The first aspect of an argument that you must evaluate is the truth of the reasons being used to support a conclusion. Ask yourself these questions:

- What specific evidence is the writer offering to illustrate each reason?
- Are any reasons consistent with my own experience?
- Are the reasons based on reliable sources?
- Are the reasons relevant to the subject of the argument?

You use these questions and others like them to analyze the reasons offered and to determine how true they seem to be. As you saw in Chapter 11, evaluating the kinds of beliefs used as reasons in arguments is a complex challenge.

VALIDITY: DO THE REASONS SUPPORT THE CLAIM OR CONCLUSION?

In addition to determining whether the reasons are true, evaluating arguments involves investigating the relationship between the reasons and the claim or the conclusion (which becomes the thesis of a piece of writing that argues a position on an issue).

When the reasons support the conclusion in such a way that the conclusion follows from them, you have a **valid argument.** If, however, the reasons do not support the conclusion—that is, if the conclusion does not follow from the reasons being offered—you have an **invalid argument.** Remember that the words *valid* and *true* do not have the same meaning. You must first evaluate the truth of a reason, then determine its validity.

One way to focus on the concept of *validity* is to assume that all the reasons in an argument are true, then try to determine how probable they make the conclusion. The following is an example of one type of valid argument.

Reason: Anything that is a threat to our health should not be legal.

Reason: Marijuana is a threat to our health.

Conclusion: Therefore, marijuana should not be legal.

This is a valid argument because if we assume that the reasons are true, its conclusion does necessarily follow from them.

Of course, we may not agree that either or both of the reasons are true; in that case, we would not agree with the conclusion. Nevertheless, the structure of the argument is valid. This particular form of thinking is known as *deduction.*

Here is a different type of argument:

Reason: As part of a project in my social science class, we selected one hundred students in the school to be interviewed. We took special steps to ensure that these students were representative of the student body as a whole (total students: 4,386). We asked the students whether they thought that the United States should actively try to overthrow foreign governments that it disapproves of. Of the one hundred students interviewed, eighty-eight said that the United States should definitely not be involved in such activities.

Conclusion: We can conclude that most students in this school believe that the United States should not be engaged in attempts to actively overthrow foreign governments that it disapproves of.

This is a persuasive argument because if we assume that the reason is true, that reason provides strong support for the conclusion. In this case, the key part of the reason is the statement that the one hundred students selected were representative of the entire student population at the school. To evaluate the truth of the reason, we might want to investigate the procedure used to select the one hundred students in order to determine whether this sample was in fact representative of all the students. (Notice that the conclusion carefully said "in this school." It did not imprecisely say "most students.")

This particular form of thinking is an example of *induction*.

SOUNDNESS: IS THE ARGUMENT BOTH TRUE AND VALID?

When an argument includes both true reasons and a valid structure, the argument is considered sound. When an argument has either false reasons or an invalid structure, however, the argument is considered unsound.

Figure 13.1 reminds us that in terms of arguments, *truth* and *validity* are not identical concepts. An argument can have true reasons and an invalid structure or have false reasons and a valid structure. In both cases the argument is unsound. Consider the following argument:

Reason: Professor Davis believes that megadoses of vitamins can cure colds.

Reason: Davis is a professor of computer science.

Conclusion: Megadoses of vitamins can cure colds.

This argument is obviously not valid: even if we assume that the reasons are true, the conclusion does not follow. Professor Davis's expertise with computers does not provide her with special knowledge about nutrition and medicine. This invalid thinking is neither structurally nor factually acceptable. It is clearly not a sound argument. Now, consider this argument:

Reason: For a democracy to function most effectively, the citizens should be able to think critically about the major social and political issues.

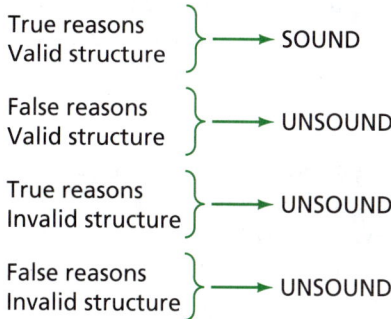

Figure 13.1 Sound and Unsound Arguments

Reason: Education plays a key role in developing critical thinking abilities.

Conclusion: Therefore, education plays a key role in ensuring that a democracy is functioning most effectively.

A good case could be made for the soundness of this argument because the reasons are persuasive and the argument structure is valid. Of course, someone might counter that one or both of the reasons are not completely true, which illustrates an important point about the arguments we construct and evaluate. Many of the arguments we encounter in life fall somewhere between complete soundness and complete unsoundness because often we are not sure if our reasons are completely true. Throughout this book, we have found that developing accurate beliefs is an ongoing process and that our beliefs are subject to clarification and revision. As a result, the conclusion of any argument can be only as certain as the reasons supporting the conclusion.

The following two articles present different points of view about "end of life" issues. A variety of topics are now receiving attention: passive euthanasia, or nontreatment; active euthanasia or mercy killing; assisted suicide; the work of Dr. Kevorkian (nicknamed "Dr. Death"); the hospice movement (termed "Dr. Dignity"); the "right to die" laws of the state of Oregon and of the Netherlands.

These articles use different argumentative approaches. The first gives a human example, uses description, and employs *pathos*. The second, taken from the web site of the Hemlock Society, emphasizes logical argument, using many thinking patterns discussed in this book: contrast, comparison, definition, and causal analysis. It also refers to the fallacies *false dichotomy* and *slippery slope*.

In No Hurry for Next Leg of the Journey
BY DAVID GONZALEZ

Before joining the New York Times *in 1990, David Gonzalez wrote for* Newsweek *from 1983 to 1990. A native of the Bronx, he often featured locations there in the "About New York" column he wrote in the* Times *from 1995 to 1999. He then became Caribbean and Central American bureau chief for the* Times *and, while based in Miami, reported on the political and social struggles in Haiti and the changes in Cuba after the fall of the Soviet Union, as well as other issues throughout Central America. He returned to New York and writes the "Citywide" column for the paper as well as other news and feature articles. He has received numerous awards, including Columbia University's Mike Berger Award in 1992.*

The waning afternoon sunlight slipped into the rooms of Calvary Hospital in the Bronx. Outside, the trees looked like propped-up sticks, gray, crooked and ready for winter. Inside, it was warm and quiet, in anticipation of a bigger chill. Michael Burke lay in his bed, the latest stop in a medical journey that started in September with treatment at another hospital for a cancer that spread from his colon to his lung and brain.

"The doctors think I'm terminal," he said. "I think I'm terminal."

Calvary Hospital bills itself as the country's only specialty hospital for adults in the final stages of advanced cancer. It is not a hospice, since its patients require constant medical attention to stabilize them and ease their pain. Doctors tend to nearly every aspect of a patient's physical and emotional comfort as well as helping families that are emotionally battered by the disease.

Doctors at Calvary, which started almost 100 years ago in a Greenwich Village house, see their work as a counterpoint to those who advocate "a definitive medical response" to terminal illness. In plain English, they offer the dying patient an alternative to assisted suicide. It's not a place that Dr. Jack Kevorkian, who was ordered this week to stand trial on murder charges for his role in a suicide shown on television, has ever visited.

5   Mr. Burke, 45, a mechanical contractor, understands how frustration and despair drive some people to suicide, even if they have received the best care. But he does not consider that an option, and he is alarmed by Dr. Kevorkian's increasingly brazen attempts to force the issue.

"He seems seriously aggressive about it," Mr. Burke said. "But what constitutes the envelope of what he considers candidates for euthanasia would become bigger and bigger. I think people need to make it difficult for guys like that."

Calvary operates under the auspices of the Roman Catholic Archdiocese of New York, so its opposition to suicide hews to church teaching. Its patients—200 on any given day—represent many faiths. In rare cases, critically ill patients arrive at the hospital asking for a quick end. More common are feelings of depression or emotional suffering, which, if not addressed by doctors, psychiatrists and social workers, could lead to desperate yearnings.

"Depression is more painful than physical pain," said Dr. Michael Brescia, the hospital's medical director. "Emotional suffering is the absence of love. This is a time when people have to say final farewells to their children. There are no more holidays. No future. You're not in this life, you're on the outside looking in. Everybody else has a life and you don't have one. Most people, if they ask for suicide, it's from the emotional aspects of this disease."

Those emotional hardships, doctors said, aren't made any easier by the difficulties patients have in persuading their health maintenance organizations to allow them to seek appropriate care in other hospitals, or at least let them check into Calvary when death is near. Dr. James Cimino, director of Calvary's palliative care institute, said the medical run-around has been exploited by proponents of assisted suicide, who present euthanasia as a dignified response to the indignities of the health care bureaucracy.

10   "Kevorkian forced us as a society to ask why people want to die prematurely," Dr. Cimino said. "But we should have confronted it before."

He knows that other doctors—good, well-meaning ones—also support euthanasia. But each day he sees patients who resist an early demise. "Maybe it's something about the nature of the person that they have this suffering, yet they don't request suicide," he said. "I don't want to get into the philosophy of that."

But Michael Burke does.

"Kevorkian is assuming there's nothing out there after this," he said. "I assume there is. I think that's where we part company."

He said that as long as he was comfortable—and he was—he had no problem. Suicide, he said, would be unfair to his wife and two children.

15   "I wouldn't want them to believe Daddy had the option of pushing this button and leaving," he said. "I'm not trying to squeeze every last moment. But if I can live for a week and see my son one more time, I would. As opposed to seeing Kevorkian this afternoon. Not that I think they would let him in the door here."

He gave a small smile and a thumbs-up sign. The gesture was his own definitive response.

Questions for Active Reading

1. What is the central claim or thesis of Gonzalez's argument? Where did he place it? Is this placement effective?
2. How does he develop his thesis? What kind of evidence does he use?
3. What warrants and backings underlie his argument?

Questions for Thinking Critically

1. Although Calvary Hospital is not a hospice, its philosophy of easing the pain of dying patients and the families is practiced by hospices. Have you ever known anyone who entered into hospice care? What was that person's experience with hospice?
2. If given a terminal diagnosis, would you seek hospice care for yourself or for a loved one? Why or why not?

Hospice Care or Assisted Suicide: A False Dichotomy
BY JOHN L. MILLER

John L. Miller believes in the value of hospice care but also believes that it may not be for everyone. In the following article, reprinted from American Journal of Hospice and Palliative Care *and later available on the Hemlock Society's web site (www .hemlock.org), Miller argues for certain forms of physician-assisted suicide. He refers both to Dr. Kevorkian, nicknamed "Dr. Death" because he has assisted in patient suicides, and to the hospice program, nicknamed "Dr. Dignity."*

For the past few months, I have been reading, with great interest, the editorials and updates regarding the "Dr. Dignity" program. I would like to offer a different perspective. The view expressed here is one which comes from within the hospice movement, but which supports legal reforms to allow physician-assisted suicide.

Specifically, the legal reforms I am referring to would require many important safeguards which Dr. Kevorkian does not implement. A responsible assisted suicide would require free and repeated requests by the patient, with a substantial interval between requests. The involvement of a third party in a suicide ethically requires us to make sure the suffering is not temporary, or due to lack of information or obtainable (and desired) treatment. Informed consent, confirmed by two independent medical practitioners, would be required only after all available alternatives have been offered and explored. The fine details of these conditions are, of course, much debated. This article, however, looks not at these details, but at the ethical justification for such a position.

To begin, I applaud the promotion of hospice care in the media. Promoting compassionate palliative care to the general public is essential, especially if one believes that physician-assisted suicide should be made available in the context of offering choices.

But the "Dr. Dignity" program does not promote hospice care as just a choice. It promotes it as the only moral choice and, in doing so, sets up a false dichotomy. If one were to believe the editorials in this journal, one might mistakenly conclude that all proponents of legal reform were either historically naive, ignorant of hospice and palliative care, or both. And while some people may be guilty of this lack of information, many others are not.

5   Many people who have devoted their lives to the care of the dying are not opposed to physician-assisted suicide. Such people believe it should be available as one of several options, and, therefore, do not believe that promoting hospice[s] and advocating for the availability of regulated physician-assisted suicide are contradictory goals.

Understanding this position begins with an understanding of how and why assisted suicide and euthanasia differ. Not surprisingly, most people in the general public do not know the difference between the two terms; opponents of assisted suicide often deliberately obscure these differences by using the terms interchangeably.

But, many people support legalized assisted suicide for the same reason that they oppose euthanasia: the first offers us life choices and power over our own bodies, while the second takes control and choices away from us. Hospice care also offers people an essential choice, and so, on we campaign to make it available, and to make it better.

The problem with hospice care, however, is that in spite of our best public relations efforts, it doesn't always take away people's pain, and it isn't always wanted.

Parallels are often drawn between this debate and the one on abortion rights. These parallels are indeed apt. And since the war of words is as confusing there as it is here, let's blow away the fog: Mainstream proponents of legalized, assisted suicide advocate for its availability not because they are pro death, but because they believe in a person's right to control his/her life, and the right of a person to a death which s/he feels is dignified (even if we don't agree that it is).

10   In the assisted suicide debate, opponents sometimes use logical fallacies and historical misinformation to point fear at the wrong menace. It is easy to quell dissent in this way.

Take the argument, for instance, that assisted suicide will lead to euthanasia, eugenics, or even genocide. For a "slippery slope" argument to be valid, there must be a connection between an initial minor social ill and a potentially more serious one—an ill which, when amplified incrementally, creeps up on us and finally, has catastrophic, societal results. This connection usually exists because the minor social ill is of the same kind as the more serious one, and because taking one step makes the next one easier.

In this case, it is not valid to link assisted suicide to the more serious threat of euthanasia, eugenics, and genocide simply because they all involve third parties in the death of another person. One of these things is not like the others. To link them in this way is as ridiculous as saying that electing a government to make state decisions leads to fascism. Just because both involve state rule doesn't mean that giving a government power inevitably leads to its absolute power. A slippery slope to fascism happens when the checks which make governments representative and accountable are subtly removed, one by one.

Fear of a societal erosion of personal autonomy is a valid concern. The response must be to give people more choices, not fewer; more autonomy, not less. The legal reforms I offer for debate move us further away from fascism, not towards it.

If assisted suicide were an act, which in some small way diminished a person's power of self-determination, then one might make an argument that allowing such an act pushes us down a slippery slope towards more serious violations of this kind. The slow whittling away of self-determination can creep up on us, if we don't watch out.

15   And so, concerns should be expressed when laws which erode people's rights are created, or when existing rights legislation is revoked. Concern should be expressed when states give power to medical practitioners to override informed consent.

In remembering history, let's remember that this is exactly what occurred in Nazi-occupied Europe. Under the Nazis, "physician-assisted suicide" was never any such thing. It was always murder, the taking of someone's life against his/her will. Doctors assisted in these murders in a context where Jews and other minorities had no rights of any kind, and where neither quality of life, nor life itself were valued.

It is indeed conceivable that personal freedoms may be eroded in North America. But the top of the slippery slope is not assisted suicide. If anything, the "slope" is the loss of personal autonomy, and it exists already. We are teetering on the edge, and proponents of assisted suicide are reaching out to help pull us back up, not to push us down.

If, in North America, the right to control our bodies and our lives is further eroded in any significant way, physician-assisted suicide would certainly never become available. Women's reproductive rights would also be targets (they already are), as would informed consent in any medical decision, including one involving hospice care.

Dressing up hospice care is a panacea, and the only moral alternative to physician-assisted suicide is unhelpful, and inaccurate.

20   This issue is not simplistic. Reforms must happen in a context where we continue to promote alternatives, where we understand that several things can be true at the same time. Hospice care is wonderful for some. Physician-assisted suicide is a valid choice for others. People will always seek to influence the vulnerable and the sick. With freedoms come responsibilities.

Disabled rights activists, and indeed those of us in the hospice movement, know that it is not just the state which can coerce people to make unwanted or unnecessary choices. Family members, friends, [and] peers can also put subtle pressures on loved ones to choose a path which is better for the well person than for the sick.

But these pressures work both ways, unfortunately. Just as there are those who pressure people they love to end it all, there are also those who push people unduly to "hang on until the end." Knowing when to step back, knowing when to move forward, finding this balance in supporting the dignity of those we care for—this is the precious challenge with which we are all entrusted in hospice care.

We must be wary of the danger of falling to the extremes. At one end, are those who value life at all cost—even at the expense of quality. At this end, preventing another person from ending his/her life regardless of the circumstances is seen as acceptable. At the other end are those who put quality of life first, but who also believe that they can know how good or bad someone else's life is. People who think this way can be equally dangerous, because they feel no qualms about either pressuring us to end our life if they feel we are too miserable, or pressuring us to hang on, if they decide for us that our life is still worth living.

When we fall to the extremes, we take choices away from those who[m] we believe we are helping. But, there is a middle ground. When we aim for that middle ground, we all win.

Questions for Active Reading

1. What is the central claim or thesis of Miller's argument? Where did he place it? Is this placement effective?

2. How does he develop his thesis? What kind of evidence does he use?

3. What warrants and backings underlie his argument?

Questions for Thinking Critically

1. Have you ever known anyone who chose physician-assisted suicide? How would you feel if a loved one chose it?

2. Miller refers to the fallacies *false dichotomy* and *slippery slope.* What do these terms mean? Do you think he uses them correctly here?

3. Gonzalez focused on a particular patient while Miller argued historical, political, and ethical issues. Which technique is more effective? Why?

Forms of Argument

Arguments occur in many forms, but two major thinking methods—deduction and induction—provide the foundations for most arguments and also influence the organizational structure of arguments. They can be seen as (1) moving from general principles to specific applications and (2) moving from specific examples to general conclusions. Deduction and induction are seldom applied in "pure" or textbook ways in real-life arguments. Instead, they often are compressed or combined, so recognizing and analyzing their uses can sometimes be difficult. In fact, some teachers and students feel that studying them separately is more a mental exercise than a practical activity. However, as a critical thinker, a writer of arguments, and an analyst of arguments, you need to understand these principles.

DEDUCTIVE REASONING

The deductive argument is the one most commonly associated with the study of logic. Though it has a variety of valid forms, they all share one characteristic: if you accept the supporting reasons (also called **premises**) as true, you must also accept the conclusion as true. A **deductive argument** is an argument form in which one reasons from premises that are known or assumed to be true to a conclusion that necessarily follows from these premises. For example, consider the following famous deductive argument:

Reason/Premise: All persons are mortal.

Reason/Premise: Socrates is a person.

Conclusion: Therefore, Socrates is mortal.

In this example of **deductive reasoning,** accepting the premises of the argument as true means that the conclusion necessarily follows; it cannot be false. Many deductive arguments, like this one, are structured as **syllogisms,** an argument form that consists of two supporting premises and a conclusion. There are also, however, a large number of invalid deductive forms, one of which is illustrated in the following defective syllogism:

Reason/Premise: All persons are mortal.

Reason/Premise: Socrates is a person.

Conclusion: Therefore, all persons are Socrates.

This example is deliberately absurd, but people do shift terms in these ways and think things such as "all tall people should play basketball" just because basketball players are usually tall. Despite the variety of invalid deductive structures, once you become aware of the concept of *validity,* you should be able to detect invalidity.

One way to do this is through the application of a general rule. Whenever we reason by using the form illustrated by the valid Socrates syllogism, we are using the following argument structure:

Premise: All A (people) are B (mortal).

Premise: S is an A (Socrates is a person).

Conclusion: Therefore, S is B (Socrates is mortal).

This basic argument form is valid no matter what terms are included. For example:

Premise: All politicians are untrustworthy.

Premise: Bill White is a politician.

Conclusion: Therefore, Bill White is untrustworthy.

Notice again that with any valid deductive form, if we assume that the premises are true, we must accept the conclusion. Of course, in this case it is unlikely that the first premise is true.

Although we are not always aware of doing so, we use this basic type of reasoning whenever we apply a general rule. For instance:

Premise: All eight-year-old children should be in bed by 9:30 P.M.

Premise: You are an eight-year-old child.

Conclusion: Therefore, you should be in bed by 9:30 P.M.

Often we present this kind of reasoning in an abbreviated form called an *enthymeme,* which assumes the first premise: You should be in bed by 9:30 because you're an eight-year-old child; Bill White is a politician, so he's untrustworthy.

Describe an example from your own experience in which you use this deductive form, both as a syllogism and as an enthymeme.

OTHER DEDUCTIVE FORMS

Deductive arguments, or syllogisms and enthymemes, come in many other forms, most of which have been named by logicians. At some point in your college education, you should consider taking a course in critical thinking or logic to learn about as many kinds of reasoning as you can. This chapter provides only an introduction.

Affirming the antecedent

Premise: If I have prepared thoroughly for the final exam, I will do well.

Premise: I prepared thoroughly for the exam.

Conclusion: Therefore, I will do well on the exam.

When we reason like this, we are using the following argument structure:

Premise: If A (I have prepared thoroughly), then B (I will do well).

Premise: A (I have prepared thoroughly).

Conclusion: Therefore, B (I will do well).

Like all valid deductive forms, this form is valid no matter what specific terms are included. For example:

Premise: If the Democrats register 20 million new voters, they will win the presidential election.

Premise: The Democrats have registered more than 20 million new voters.

Conclusion: Therefore, the Democrats will win the presidential election.

As with other valid argument forms, the conclusion will be true if the reasons are true. Although the second premise in this argument expresses information that can be verified, the first premise would be more difficult to establish.

Denying the consequent

Premise: If Michael were a really good friend, he would lend me his car for the weekend.

Premise: Michael refuses to lend me his car for the weekend.

Conclusion: Therefore, Michael is not a really good friend.

When we reason in this fashion, we are using the following argument structure:

Premise: If A (Michael is a really good friend), then B (He will lend me his car).

Premise: Not B (He won't lend me his car).

Conclusion: Therefore, not A (He's not a really good friend).

Again, like other valid reasoning forms, this form is valid no matter what subject is being considered. As always, the truth of the premises must be evaluated.

Disjunctive syllogism

Premise: Either I left my wallet on my dresser, or I have lost it.

Premise: The wallet is not on my dresser.

Conclusion: Therefore, I must have lost it.

When we reason in this way, we are using the following argument structure:

> *Premise:* Either A (I left my wallet on my dresser) or B (I have lost it).
>
> *Premise:* Not A (I didn't leave it on my dresser).
>
> *Conclusion:* Therefore, B (I have lost it).

This valid reasoning form can be applied to any number of situations and still yield accurate results. For example:

> *Premise:* Either your stomach trouble is caused by what you are eating, or it is caused by nervous tension.
>
> *Premise:* You tell me that you have been very careful about your diet.
>
> *Conclusion:* Therefore, your stomach trouble is caused by nervous tension.

To determine the accuracy of the conclusion, we must determine the accuracy of the premises. If they are true, then the conclusion must also be true.

All of the preceding basic argument forms can be found not only in informal daily conversations but also at more formal levels of thinking. They appear in academic disciplines, in scientific inquiry, in debates on social issues, and so on. Many other argument forms—both deductive and inductive—also constitute human reasoning. By sharpening your understanding of these ways of thinking, you will be better able to make sense of the world by constructing and evaluating effective arguments.

Thinking ↔ Writing Activity

Evaluating Deductive Arguments

Analyze the following arguments by completing these steps.

1. Summarize the reasons and conclusions given.
2. Identify which, if any, deductive argument forms are being used.
3. Evaluate the truth of the reasons that support the conclusion.

For if the brain is a machine of ten billion nerve cells and the mind can somehow be explained as the summed activity of a finite number of chemical and electrical reactions, [then] boundaries limit the human prospect—we are biological and our souls cannot fly free. —Edward O. Wilson, *On Human Nature*

The extreme vulnerability of a complex industrial society to intelligent, targeted terrorism by a very small number of people may prove the fatal challenge to which Western states have no adequate response. Counterforce alone will never suffice. The real challenge of the true terrorist is to the basic values of a society. If there is no commitment to shared values in Western society—and if none are imparted in our amoral institutions of higher learning—no increase in police and burglar alarms will suffice to preserve our society from the specter that haunts us—not a bomb from above but a gun from within. —James Billington, "The Gun Within"

To fully believe in something, to truly understand something, one must be intimately acquainted with its opposite. One should not adopt a creed by default, because no alternative is known. Education should prepare students for the "real world" not by segregating them from evil but by urging full confrontation to test and modify the validity of the good. —Robert Baron, "In Defense of Teaching Racism, Sexism, and Fascism"

The inescapable conclusion is that society secretly wants crime, needs crime, and gains definite satisfactions from the present mishandling of it! We condemn crime; we punish offenders for it; but we need it. The crime and punishment ritual is a part of our lives. We need crimes to wonder at, to enjoy vicariously, to discuss and speculate about, and to publicly deplore. We need criminals to identify ourselves with, to envy secretly, and to punish stoutly. They do for us the forbidden, illegal things we wish to do and, like scapegoats of old, they bear the burdens of our displaced guilt and punishment—"the iniquities of us all." —Karl Menninger, "The Crime of Punishment"

INDUCTIVE REASONING

The preceding section focused on deductive reasoning, an argument form in which one reasons from premises that are known or assumed to be true to a conclusion that follows necessarily from the premises. This section introduces **inductive reasoning,** an argument form in which one reasons from premises or instances that are known or assumed to be true to a conclusion that is supported by the premises but does not necessarily follow from them.

When you reason inductively, your premises, instances, or data provide evidence that makes it more or less probable (but not certain) that the conclusion is true. The following statements are examples of conclusions reached through inductive reasoning. As you read them, think about how the data might have been obtained and what arguments could be based on each statement.

1. A recent Gallup poll reported that 74 percent of the American public believes that abortion should remain legal.

2. On the average, a person with a college degree will earn over $830,000 more in his or her lifetime than a person with just a high school diploma.

3. The outbreak of food poisoning at the end-of-year school party was probably caused by the squid salad.

4. The devastating disease AIDS is caused by a particularly complex virus that may not be curable.

5. The solar system is probably the result of an enormous explosion—a "big bang"—that occurred billions of years ago.

Each of the first two statements is an example of inductive reasoning known as **empirical generalization**—a general statement about an entire group made on the basis of observing some members of the group. The final three statements are examples of **causal reasoning**—a form of inductive reasoning which claims that an event (or events) is the result of the occurrence of another event (or events).

CAUSAL REASONING

You were introduced to causal analysis in Chapter 10 and also to the fallacies that can result if causes are not analyzed logically. Review pages 356–357 to recall the characteristics of this pattern of induction.

Causal reasoning is the backbone of the natural and the social sciences. It is also central to the *scientific method,* which operates on the assumption that the world is constructed in a complex web of causal relationships that can be discovered through systematic investigation. You apply the scientific method in your science courses.

EMPIRICAL GENERALIZATION

An important tool used by both natural and social scientists is empirical generalization. Have you ever wondered how the major television and radio networks can predict election results hours before the polls close? These predictions are made possible by using **empirical generalization,** a form of inductive reasoning which is defined as "reasoning by examining a limited sample to reach a general conclusion based on that sample."

Network election predictions, as well as public opinion polls that are conducted throughout a political campaign, are based on interviews with a select number of people. Ideally, pollsters would interview everyone in the "target population" (in this case, voters), but doing this, of course, is hardly practical. Instead, they select a relatively small group of individuals from the target population, known as a "sample," who they have determined will adequately represent the group as a whole. Pollsters believe that they can then generalize the opinions of this smaller group to the target population. The results are often accurate—with a few notable exceptions (such as the 2000 presidential election in which Al Gore withdrew his concession to George W. Bush on election night, following a changed projection in the state of Florida).

There are three key criteria for evaluating inductive arguments:

- Is the sample known?
- Is the sample sufficient?
- Is the sample representative?

Is the Sample Known?   An inductive argument is only as strong as the sample on which it is based. For example, sample populations described in vague terms—such as "highly placed sources" or "many young people interviewed"—provide a treacherously weak foundation for generalizing to larger populations. In order for an inductive argument to be persuasive, the sample population should be explicitly known and clearly identified. Natural and social scientists take great care when selecting members of sample groups. They also make information on members of the sample groups available to outside investigators who may wish to evaluate and verify the results.

Is the Sample Sufficient?   The second criterion for evaluating inductive reasoning is to consider the size of the sample. It should be large enough to provide an accurate sense of the group as a whole. In the polling example discussed earlier, we would be concerned if only a few registered voters had been interviewed, and the results of the interviews were then generalized to a much larger population. Overall, the larger the sample, the more reliable the inductive conclusions. Natural and social scientists have developed precise guidelines for determining the size of the sample needed to achieve reliable results. For example, poll results are often accompanied by a qualification such as "These results are subject to an error factor of ± 3 percentage points." This means that if the sample reveals that 47 percent of those interviewed prefer candidate X, we can reliably state that 44 to 50 percent of the target population prefers candidate X. Because a sample is usually a small portion of the target population, we can rarely state that the two match each other exactly—there must always be some room for variation. The exceptions to this are situations in which the target population is completely homogeneous. For instance, tasting one cookie from a bag of cookies is usually enough to tell us whether or not the contents of the entire bag are stale.

Is the Sample Representative?   The third crucial element in effective inductive reasoning is the representativeness of the sample. If we are to generalize with confidence from the sample to the target population, we have to be sure the sample is similar in all relevant aspects to the larger group from which it is drawn. For instance, in the polling example, the sample population should reflect the same percentage of men and women, of Democrats and Republicans, of young and old, and so on, as exists in the target population. It is obvious that many characteristics—such as hair color, favorite food, and shoe size—are not relevant to the comparison. The better the sample reflects the target population in terms of relevant qualities, however, the better the accuracy of the generalizations. On the other hand, when the sample does not represent the target population—for example, if the election pollsters interviewed only females between the ages of thirty and thirty-five—the sample is termed *biased,* and any generalizations about the target population will be highly suspect.

How do we ensure that the sample is representative of the target population? One important device is *random selection,* a selection strategy in which every member of the target population has an equal chance of being included in the sample. For example, the various techniques used to select winning lottery tickets are supposed to be random—each ticket is supposed to have an equal chance of winning. In complex cases of inductive reasoning—such as polling—random selection is often combined with the confirmation that all the important categories in the population are adequately represented. For example, an election pollster would want to ensure that all significant geographical areas are included and then would randomly select individuals from within those areas to compose the sample.

Understanding the principles of empirical generalization is crucial to effective thinking because we are continually challenged to evaluate this form of inductive thinking in our lives. In addition, when writing about political or social issues, we often use the results of inductive investigations, so we should be able to determine their accuracy and relevance.

Thinking ↔ Writing Activity

Analyzing Empirical Generalization

Review the following examples of empirical generalizing. Select two and then evaluate the quality of the thinking by answering the following questions.

1. Is the sample known?
2. Is the sample sufficient?
3. Is the sample representative?
4. Do you believe that the conclusions are likely to be accurate? Why or why not?
5. What are some arguments that might be based on your answers?

In a study of a possible relationship between pornography and antisocial behavior, questionnaires went out to 7,500 psychiatrists and psychoanalysts whose listing in the directory of the American Psychological Association indicated clinical experience. Over 3,400 of these professionals responded. The result: 7.4 percent of the psychiatrists and psychologists had cases in which they were convinced that pornography was a causal factor in antisocial behavior, an additional 9.4 percent were suspicious, 3.2 percent did not commit themselves, and 80 percent said they had no cases in which a causal connection was suspected.

A survey by the Sleep Disorder Clinic of the VA hospital in La Jolla, California (involving more than one million people), revealed that people who sleep more than ten hours a night have a death rate 80 percent higher than those who sleep only seven or eight hours. Men who sleep fewer than four hours a night have a death rate 180 percent higher, and women with less [than four hours'] sleep have a rate 40 percent higher. This might be taken as indicating that too much and too little sleep cause death.

In a recent survey, twice as many doctors interviewed stated that if they were stranded on a desert island, they would prefer X Aspirin to Extra Strength Y.

Being a general practitioner in a rural area has tremendous drawbacks—being on virtual 24-hour call 365 days a year, patients without financial means or insurance, low fees in the first place, inadequate facilities and assistance. Nevertheless, America's small-town G.P.s seem fairly content with their lot. According to a survey taken by *Country Doctor,* fully 50 percent wrote back that they "basically like being a rural G.P." Only 1 in 15 regretted that he or she had not specialized. Only 2 out of 20 rural general practitioners would trade places with their urban counterparts, given the chance. And only 1 in 30 would "choose some other line of work altogether."

More Fallacies: Forms of False Reasoning

As we pointed out in Chapter 10, certain forms of reasoning are not logical. These types of pseudoreasoning (false reasoning) are often termed *fallacies:* arguments that are not sound because of various errors in reasoning. Fallacious reasoning is sometimes used to influence others. It seeks to persuade not on the basis of sound arguments and critical thinking but rather on the basis of emotional and illogical factors. Sometimes fallacious reasoning is used inadvertently. However, it is always dangerous, so it is important to recognize it as well as to avoid using it. Detecting fallacious reasoning is a significant factor in evaluating sources of beliefs, the concept discussed in Chapter 11.

In Chapter 8, we explored the way in which we form concepts through the interactive process of generalizing (identifying the common qualities that define the boundaries of the concept) and interpreting (identifying examples of the concept). This process is similar to the process involved in constructing empirical generalizations as we seek to reach a general conclusion based on a limited number of examples and then apply this conclusion to other examples. Although generalizing and interpreting are useful in forming concepts, they also can lead to fallacious ways of thinking, including hasty generalization, sweeping generalization, and false dilemma.

HASTY GENERALIZATION

Consider the following examples of reasoning. Do you think the arguments are sound? Why or why not?

- My boyfriends have never shown any real concern for my feelings. My conclusion is that men are insensitive, selfish, and emotionally superficial.
- My mother always gets upset over insignificant things. This leads me to believe that women are very emotional.

In both of these cases, a general conclusion has been reached that is based on a very small sample. As a result, the reasons provide very weak support for the conclusions. It does not make good sense to generalize from one or a few individuals to all men or all women. The conclusion is *hasty* because the information is not adequate enough to justify the generalization.

SWEEPING GENERALIZATION

Whereas the fallacy of hasty generalization deals with errors in the process of generalizing, the fallacy of *sweeping generalization* stems from difficulties in the process of interpreting. Consider the following examples of reasoning. Do you consider the arguments sound? Why or why not?

- Vigorous exercise contributes to overall good health. Therefore, vigorous exercise should be practiced by recent heart-attack victims, people who are out of shape, and women in the last month of pregnancy.
- People should be allowed to make their own decisions, providing that their actions do not harm other people. Therefore, people who are trying to commit suicide should be left alone to do as they please.

In both of these cases, generalizations that are true in most cases have been deliberately applied to examples that are clearly intended to be exceptions to the generalizations because of their special features. Of course, the use of a sweeping generalization motivates us to clarify the generalization, rephrasing it to exclude examples, like those given here, that have special features. For example, the first generalization could be reformulated as "Vigorous exercise contributes to the overall good health of most people *except* recent heart-attack victims, people who are out of shape, and women who are about to give birth." Sweeping generalizations become dangerous when they are accepted without critical analysis.

Examine the following examples of sweeping generalizations. In each case (a) explain why it is a sweeping generalization and (b) reformulate the statement to make it a legitimate generalization.

1. A college education stimulates you to develop as a person and prepares you for many professions. Therefore, all people should attend college, no matter what career interests them.

2. Drugs such as heroin and morphine are addictive and therefore qualify as dangerous drugs. This means that they should never be used, even as painkillers in medical situations.

3. Once criminals have served time for the crimes they have committed, they have paid their debt to society and should be permitted to work at any job they choose.

FALSE DILEMMA

The fallacy of the *false dilemma*—also known as the *either/or* fallacy and the *false dichotomy* fallacy—occurs when one is asked to choose between two extreme alternatives without being able to consider additional options. For example, we may say, "You're either for me or against me." Sometimes giving people only two choices on an issue makes sense ("If you decide to swim the English Channel, you'll either make it or you won't"). At other times, however, viewing a complicated situation in such extreme terms can result in a serious oversimplification.

The following statements are examples of false dilemmas. After analyzing the fallacy in each case, suggest different alternatives than those being presented.

> *Example:* "Everyone in Germany is a National Socialist—the few outside the party are either lunatics or idiots." (Adolf Hitler, quoted by the *New York Times,* April 5, 1938)

> *Analysis:* Hitler was saying that Germans who were not Nazis were lunatics or idiots. By limiting the classification of the population to these three categories, Hitler was simply ignoring all the people who did not qualify as Nazis, lunatics, or idiots.

1. "America—love it or leave it!"
2. "She loves me; she loves me not."
3. "Live free or die."
4. "If you're not part of the solution, you're part of the problem."
5. "If you know about a BMW, you either own one or you want to."

FALLACIES OF RELEVANCE

Many fallacious arguments try to gain support by appealing to factors that have little or nothing to do with the arguments. In these cases, false appeals substitute for sound reasoning and a critical examination of the issues. Such appeals are known as fallacies of *relevance*.

Appeal to Authority In Chapters 3 and 8, we explored the ways in which we sometimes use various authorities to establish our beliefs or to prove our points. At that time, we noted that to serve as a basis for beliefs, authorities must have legitimate expertise in the area in which they are advising—for example, an experienced mechanic could diagnose your car's problem. However, people occasionally appeal to authorities who are not qualified to give an expert opinion. Consider the reasoning in the following advertisements. Do you think the arguments are sound? Why or why not?

- Hi. You've probably seen me out on the football field. After a hard day's work crushing halfbacks and sacking quarterbacks, I like to settle down with a cold, smooth Maltz beer.
- SONY. Ask anyone.
- Over 11 million women will read this ad. Only 16 will own the coat.

Each of these arguments is intended to persuade us of the value of a product through the appeal to various authorities. In the first case, the authority is a well-known sports figure; in the second, the authority is large numbers of people; in the third, the authority is a select few, so the appeal is to our desire to be exclusive ("snob appeal"). Unfortunately, none of these authorities offers legitimate expertise about the product. Football players are not beer experts, large numbers of people are often misled, and exclusive groups of people are frequently mistaken in their beliefs. To evaluate authorities properly, we have to ask:

What are the professional credentials on which the authorities' expertise is based?
Is their expertise in the area on which they are commenting?

Appeal to Pity Consider the reasoning in the following arguments. Do you think the arguments are sound? Why or why not?

- I know that I haven't completed my term paper, but I really think that I should be excused. This has been a very difficult semester for me. I caught every kind of flu that came around. In addition, my brother has a drinking problem, and this has been very upsetting for me. Also, my dog died.
- I admit that my client embezzled money from the company, Your Honor. However, I would like to bring several facts to your attention. He is a family man with a wonderful wife and two terrific children. He is an important member of the community. He is active in his church, coaches a Little League baseball team, and has worked very hard to be a good person who cares about people. I think that you should take these things into consideration when handing down your sentence.

In each of these arguments, the reasons offered to support the conclusions may indeed be true, yet they are not relevant to the conclusion. Instead of providing evidence that supports the conclusion, the reasons are designed to make us feel sorry for the person involved and therefore to agree with the conclusion out of sympathy. Although these appeals can often be effective, the arguments are not sound. The validity of a conclusion can only be established by reasons that support and are relevant to the conclusion.

Appeal to Fear   Consider the reasoning in the following arguments. Do you consider the arguments sound? Why or why not?

- I don't think you deserve a raise. After all, there are many people who would be happy to have your job at the salary you are currently receiving. I would be happy to interview some of these people if you really think that you are underpaid.

- If you continue to disagree with my interpretation of *The Catcher in the Rye*, I'm afraid it may affect the grade on your paper.

In both of these arguments, the conclusions being suggested are supported by an appeal to fear, not by reasons that provide evidence for the conclusions. In the first case, the threat is that if you do not forgo your salary demands, your job may be in jeopardy. In the second case, the threat is that if you do not agree with the teacher's interpretation, you may receive a low grade. In neither instance are the real issues—Is a salary increase deserved? Is the student's interpretation legitimate?—being discussed. People who appeal to fear to support their conclusions are interested only in prevailing, regardless of which position might be more justified.

Appeal to Ignorance   Consider the reasoning in the following arguments. Do you find the arguments sound? Why or why not?

- You say that you don't believe in God. But can you prove that an omnipotent spirit doesn't exist? If not, then you have to accept the conclusion that it does in fact exist.

- Greco Tires are the best. No others have been proved better.

When this argument form is used, the person offering the conclusion is asking his or her opponent to *disprove* the conclusion. If the opponent is unable to do so, the conclusion is asserted to be true. This argument form is not valid because it is the task of the person proposing the argument to prove the conclusion. The fact that an opponent cannot disprove it offers no evidence that the conclusion is justified.

Appeal to Personal Attack   Consider the reasoning in the following arguments. Do you think the arguments are valid? Why or why not?

- Senator Smith's opinion about a tax cut is wrong. It's impossible to believe anything he says since he left his wife for that model.

- How can you have an intelligent opinion about abortion? You're not a woman, so this is a decision that you'll never have to make.

This argument form has been one of the fallacies most frequently used through the ages. Its effectiveness results from ignoring the issues of the argument and focusing instead on the qualities of the person presenting it. Trying to discredit the other person is an effort to discredit the argument—no matter what reasons are offered. This fallacy is also referred to as the *ad hominem* argument (which means drawing attention "to the man" rather than to the issue) and as *poisoning the well* (since the speaker is trying to ensure that any water drawn from the opponent's well will be regarded as undrinkable).

The effort to discredit can take two forms, as illustrated in the preceding examples. The fallacy can be *abusive* by directly attacking the credibility of an opponent. In addition, the fallacy can be *circumstantial* by claiming that a person's circumstances, not character, render his or her opinion so biased or uninformed that it cannot be treated seriously. Another example of the circumstantial form would be disregarding the views on nuclear-plant safety that were presented by an owner of a nuclear plant.

Thinking ↔ Writing Activity

Analyzing Fallacies

1. Find in advertisements, political statements, or other arguments that you have encountered, examples of two or three false appeals. Write a brief explanation of why you think the appeal is not warranted. Look for the following fallacies:

   - Appeal to authority
   - Appeal to pity
   - Appeal to fear
   - Appeal to ignorance
   - Appeal to personal attack

2. Share the fallacies you have found with classmates and also examine the ones they have identified.

3. Write a few sentences explaining how you can avoid using fallacies in your own writing.

Analyzing well-known arguments to see how they use deduction, induction, evidence *(logos), ethos, pathos,* appeals—and perhaps fallacious reasoning—is a challenging activity and one that can help you with your own arguments. Read the Declaration of Independence and the Declaration of Sentiments and Resolutions, which follow, and Martin Luther King Jr.'s speech, "I Have a Dream" (page 181 in Chapter 6). Then answer the questions that follow the readings.

The Declaration of Independence

In Congress, July 4, 1776
The unanimous declaration of the thirteen
United States of America

When in the course of human events, it becomes necessary for one people to dissolve the political bands which have connected them with another, and to assume among the powers of the earth, the separate and equal station to which the Laws of Nature and of Nature's God entitle them, a decent respect to the opinions of mankind requires that they should declare the causes which impel them to the separation.

We hold these truths to be self-evident, that all men are created equal, that they are endowed by their Creator with certain unalienable rights, that among these are life, liberty and the pursuit of happiness. That to secure these rights, governments are instituted among men, deriving their just powers from the consent of the governed. That whenever any form of government becomes destructive of these ends, it is the right of the people to alter or to abolish it, and to institute new government, laying its foundation on such principles and organizing its powers in such form, as to them shall seem most likely to effect their safety and happiness. Prudence, indeed, will dictate that governments long established should not be changed for light and transient causes; and accordingly all experience hath shown, that mankind are more disposed to suffer, while evils are sufferable, than to right themselves by abolishing the forms to which they are accustomed. But when a long train of abuses and usurpations, pursuing invariably the same object evinces a design to reduce them under absolute despotism, it is their right, it is their duty, to throw off such government, and to provide new guards for their future security. Such has been the patient sufferance of these Colonies; and such is now the necessity which constrains them to alter their former systems of government. The history of the present King of Great Britain is a history of repeated injuries and usurpations, all having in direct object the establishment of an absolute tyranny over these States. To prove this, let facts be submitted to a candid world.

He has refused his assent to laws, the most wholesome and necessary for the public good.

He has forbidden his Governors to pass laws of immediate and pressing importance, unless suspended in their operation till his assent should be obtained; and when so suspended, he has utterly neglected to attend to them.

5   He has refused to pass other laws for the accommodation of large districts of people, unless those people would relinquish the right of representation in the Legislature, a right inestimable to them and formidable to tyrants only.

He has called together legislative bodies at places unusual, uncomfortable, and distant from the depository of their public records, for the sole purpose of fatiguing them into compliance with his measures.

He has dissolved representative houses repeatedly, for opposing with manly firmness his invasions on the rights of the people.

He has refused for a long time, after such dissolutions, to cause others to be elected; whereby the legislative powers, incapable of annihilation, have returned to the people at large for their exercise; the State remaining in the meantime exposed to all the dangers of invasion from without and convulsions within.

He has endeavoured to prevent the population of these States; for that purpose obstructing the laws of naturalization of foreigners; refusing to pass others to encourage their migration hither, and raising the conditions of new appropriations of lands.

He has obstructed the administration of justice, by refusing his assent to laws for establishing judiciary powers.

He has made judges dependent on his will alone, for the tenure of their offices, and the amount and payment of their salaries.

He has erected a multitude of new offices, and sent hither swarms of officers to harass our people, and eat out their substance.

He has kept among us, in times of peace, standing armies without the consent of our legislatures.

He has affected to render the military independent of and superior to the civil power.

He has combined with others to subject us to a jurisdiction foreign to our constitution, and unacknowledged by our laws; giving his assent to their acts of pretended legislation:

For quartering large bodies of armed troops among us:

For protecting them, by a mock trial, from punishment for any murders which they should commit on the inhabitants of these States:

For cutting off our trade with all parts of the world:

For imposing taxes on us without our consent:

For depriving us, in many cases, of the benefits of trial by jury:

For transporting us beyond seas to be tried for pretended offences:

For abolishing the free system of English laws in a neighbouring Province, establishing therein an arbitrary government, and enlarging its boundaries so as to render it at once an example and fit instrument for introducing the same absolute rule into these Colonies:

For taking away our Charters, abolishing our most valuable laws, and altering fundamentally the forms of our governments:

For suspending our own Legislatures, and declaring themselves invested with power to legislate for us in all cases whatsoever.

He has abdicated government here, by declaring us out of his protection and waging war against us.

He has plundered our seas, ravaged our coasts, burnt our towns, and destroyed the lives of our people.

He is at this time transporting large armies of foreign mercenaries to complete the works of death, desolation and tyranny, already begun with circumstances of cruelty and perfidy scarcely paralleled in the most barbarous ages, and totally unworthy the head of a civilized nation.

He has constrained our fellow citizens taken captive on the high seas to bear arms against their country, to become the executioners of their friends and brethren, or to fall themselves by their hands.

He has excited domestic insurrections amongst us, and has endeavoured to bring on the inhabitants of our frontiers, the merciless Indian savages, whose known rule of warfare, is an undistinguished destruction of all ages, sexes, and conditions.

30   In every stage of these oppressions we have petitioned for redress in the most humble terms: our repeated petitions have been answered only by repeated injury. A prince whose character is thus marked by every act which may define a tyrant is unfit to be the ruler of a free people.

Nor have we been wanting in attention to our British brethren. We have warned them from time to time of attempts by their legislature to extend an unwarrantable jurisdiction over us. We have reminded them of the circumstances of our emigration and settlement here. We have appealed to their native justice and magnanimity, and we have conjured them by the ties of our common kindred to disavow these usurpations, which would inevitably interrupt our connections and correspondence. They too have been deaf to the voice of justice and of consanguinity. We must, therefore, acquiesce in the necessity, which denounces our separation, and hold them, as we hold the rest of mankind, enemies in war, in peace friends.

We, therefore, the Representatives of the United States of America, in General Congress assembled, appealing to the Supreme Judge of the world for the rectitude of our intentions, do, in the name, and by the authority of the good people of these Colonies, solemnly publish and declare, That these United Colonies are, and of right ought to be Free and Independent States; that they are absolved from all allegiance to the British Crown, and that all political connection between them and the State of Great Britain, is and ought to be totally dissolved; and that as Free and Independent States, they have full power to levy war, conclude peace, contract alliances, establish commerce, and to do all other acts and things which Independent States may of right do. And for the support of this declaration, with a firm reliance on the protection of Divine Providence, we mutually pledge to each other our lives, our fortunes, and our sacred honor.

Declaration of Sentiments and Resolutions

BY ELIZABETH CADY STANTON (1815–1902)

A leading suffragist of the nineteenth century, Elizabeth Cady Stanton was born in Jamestown, New York. Her father was a judge, and while working as his assistant, Stanton became aware of the extent of male dominance in the eyes of the law. She married an abolitionist, in spite of her parents' concerns, and together they crusaded to change racial and gender inequities. She organized the first Women's Rights Convention in Seneca Falls, New York, in 1848. In 1851, she formed a working relationship with Susan B. Anthony that united them for the rest of their lives. Stanton ran for Congress in 1866 and cofounded The Revolution, *a suffragist newspaper, in 1868. Today, she is revered by feminists as an early leader in the fight for equality.*

When, in the course of human events, it becomes necessary for one person of the family of man to assume among the people of the earth a position different from that which they have hitherto occupied, but one to which the laws of nature and nature's God entitle them, a decent respect to the opinions of mankind requires that they should declare the causes that impel them to such a course.

We hold these truths to be self-evident: that all men and women are created equal; that they are endowed by their Creator with certain inalienable rights; that among these are life, liberty, and the pursuit of happiness; that to secure these rights governments are instituted, deriving their just powers from the consent of the governed. Whenever any form of government becomes destructive of these ends, it is the right of those who suffer from it to refuse allegiance to it, and to insist upon the institution of a new government, laying its foundation on such principles, and organizing its powers in such form, as to them shall seem most likely to effect their safety and happiness. Prudence, indeed, will dictate that governments long established should not be changed for light and transient causes; and accordingly all experience hath shown that mankind are more disposed to suffer, while evils are sufferable, than to right themselves by abolishing the forms to which they were accustomed. But when a long train of abuses and usurpations, pursuing invariably the same object evinces a design to reduce them under absolute despotism, it is their duty to throw off such government, and to provide new guards for their future security. Such has been the patient sufferance of the women under this government, and such is now the necessity which constrains them to demand the equal station to which they are entitled.

The history of mankind is a history of repeated injuries and usurpations on the part of man toward woman, having in direct object the establishment of an absolute tyranny over her. To prove this, let facts be submitted to a candid world.

He has never permitted her to exercise her inalienable right to the elective franchise.

5   He has compelled her to submit to laws, in the formation of which she had no voice.

He has withheld from her rights which are given to the most ignorant and degraded men—both natives and foreigners.

Having deprived her of this first right of a citizen, the elective franchise, thereby leaving her without representation in the halls of legislation, he has oppressed her on all sides.

He has made her, if married, in the eye of the law, civilly dead.

He has taken from her all right in property, even to the wages she earns.

10   He has made her, morally, an irresponsible being, as she can commit many crimes with impunity, provided they be done in the presence of her husband. In the covenant of marriage, she is compelled to promise obedience to her husband, he becoming, to all intents and purposes, her master—the law giving him power to deprive her of her liberty, and to administer chastisement.

He has so framed the laws of divorce, as to what shall be the proper causes, and in case of separation, to whom the guardianship of the children shall be given, as to be wholly regardless of the happiness of women—the law, in all cases, going upon a false supposition of the supremacy of man, and giving all power into his hands.

After depriving her of all rights as a married woman, if single, and the owner of property, he has taxed her to support a government which recognizes her only when her property can be made profitable to it.

He has monopolized nearly all the profitable employments, and from those she is permitted to follow, she receives but a scanty remuneration. He closes against her all the avenues to wealth and distinction which he considers most honorable to himself. As a teacher of theology, medicine, or law, she is not known.

He has denied her the facilities for obtaining a thorough education, all colleges being closed against her.

15   He allows her in Church, as well as State, but a subordinate position, claiming Apostolic authority for her exclusion from the ministry, and, with some exceptions, from any public participation in the affairs of the Church.

He has created a false public sentiment by giving to the world a different code of morals for men and women, by which moral delinquencies which exclude women from society are not only tolerated, but deemed of little account in man.

He has usurped the prerogative of Jehovah himself, claiming it as his right to assign for her a sphere of action, when that belongs to her conscience and to her God.

He has endeavored, in every way that he could, to destroy her confidence in her own powers, to lessen her self-respect, and to make her willing to lead a dependent and abject life.

Now, in view of this entire disfranchisement of one-half the people of this country, their social and religious degradation—in view of the unjust laws above mentioned, and because women do feel themselves aggrieved, oppressed, and fraudulently deprived of their most sacred rights, we insist that they have immediate admission to all the rights and privileges which belong to them as citizens of the United States.

20   In entering upon the great work before us, we anticipate no small amount of misconception, misrepresentation, and ridicule; but we shall use every instrumentality within our power to effect our object. We shall employ agents, circulate tracts, petition the State and National legislatures, and endeavor to enlist the pulpit and the press in our behalf. We hope this Convention will be followed by a series of Conventions embracing every part of the country.

Resolutions

WHEREAS, The great precept of nature is conceded to be, that "man shall pursue his own true and substantial happiness." Blackstone in his Commentaries remarks, that this law of Nature being coeval with mankind, and dictated by God himself, is of course superior in obligation to any other. It is binding over all the globe, in all countries and at all times; no human laws are of any validity if contrary to this, and such of them as are valid, derive all their force and all their validity, and all their authority, mediately and immediately, from this original; therefore,

Resolved, That such laws as conflict, in any way, with the true and substantial happiness of woman, are contrary to the great precept of nature and of no validity, for this is "superior in obligation to any other."

Resolved, That all laws which prevent woman from occupying such a station in society as her conscience shall dictate, or which place her in a position inferior to that of man, are contrary to the great precept of nature, and therefore of no force or authority.

Resolved, That woman is man's equal—was intended to be so by the Creator, and the highest good of the race demands that she should be recognized as such.

25　*Resolved,* That the women of this country ought to be enlightened in regard to the laws under which they live, that they may no longer publish their degradation by declaring themselves satisfied with their present position, nor their ignorance, by asserting that they have all the rights they want.

Resolved, That inasmuch as man, while claiming for himself intellectual superiority, does accord to woman moral superiority for it is preeminently his duty to encourage her to speak and teach, as she has an opportunity, in all religious assemblies.

Resolved, That the same amount of virtue, delicacy, and refinement of behavior that is required of woman in the social state, should also be required of man, and the same transgressions should be visited with equal severity on both man and woman.

Resolved, That the objection of indelicacy and impropriety, which is so often brought against woman when she addresses a public audience, comes with a very ill-grace from those who encourage, by their attendance, her appearance on the stage, in the concert, or in feats of the circus.

Resolved, That woman has too long rested satisfied in the circumscribed limits which corrupt customs and a perverted application of the Scriptures have marked out for her, and that it is time she should move in the enlarged sphere which her great Creator has assigned her.

30　*Resolved,* That it is the duty of the women of this country to secure to themselves their sacred right to the elective franchise.

Resolved, That the equality of human rights results necessarily from the fact of the identity of the race in capabilities and responsibilities.

Resolved, therefore, That, being invested by the Creator with the same capabilities, and the same consciousness of responsibility for their exercise, it is demonstrably the right and duty of woman, equally with man, to promote every righteous cause by every righteous means; and especially in regard to the great subjects of morals and religion, it is self-evidently her right to participate with her brother in teaching them, both in private and in public, by writing and by speaking, by any instrumentalities proper to be used, and in any assemblies proper to be held; and this being a self-evident truth growing out of the divinely implanted principles of human nature, any custom or authority adverse to it, whether modern or wearing the hoary sanction of antiquity, is to be regarded as a self-evident falsehood, and at war with mankind.

[At the last session Lucretia Mott offered and spoke to the following resolution:]

Resolved, That the speedy success of our cause depends upon the zealous and untiring efforts of both men and women, for the overthrow of the monopoly of the pulpit, and for the securing to women an equal participation with men in the various trades, professions and commerce.

Questions for Active Reading

1. What is the thesis of each of these arguments? Where is it stated in each of these arguments?

2. How does the Declaration of Independence use deduction and induction? Identify the premises and the conclusion in the second paragraph. Comment on the effectiveness of this deliberate use of these basic reasoning methods.

3. How does the Declaration of Sentiments and Resolutions use induction to support the central claim? What are the effects of its parallels with the Declaration of Independence?

Questions for Thinking Critically

1. In your library or on the Internet, locate a copy of Martin Luther King Jr.'s "Letter from Birmingham Jail." What differences in approach do you see between it and "I Have a Dream" page 161? What about the tone or *ethos?* Can you identify the warrants and qualifiers in King's arguments?

2. These political arguments address profound questions about human rights. What in these arguments could be applicable to arguments that you might write about academic or business issues? What might not be applicable?

3. How would you define "liberty" and "the pursuit of happiness"? Is it possible, in your current circumstances, to achieve either liberty or happiness? To what extent is the state responsible for guaranteeing

"liberty" and "the pursuit of happiness," according to your definition of both terms?

Deductive and Inductive Reasoning in Writing

As pointed out earlier in this chapter, writers and speakers seldom use deductive or inductive reasoning solely or purely. In their arguments, conclusions reached by induction become premises for deductions; statements that are premises are asserted but not demonstrated, as in the opening sentences of the Declaration of Independence. Deductively developed paragraphs interact with inductively developed ones, as in Gould's "Evolution as Fact and Theory" in Chapter 11.

However, deduction is used obviously when a definition or principle is established by the writer and the point of the paper or paragraph is to claim that the subject being discussed fits the definition or demonstrates the principle. If the readers agree with the definition and also agree that the subject fits it, the claim is proved for whatever purpose the writer has. Political science, literature, philosophy, theology, psychology, and law are among the many fields that employ deductive arguments in this way.

Inductive reasoning is reflected in two ways in writing. One is structural. When a writer chooses to present instances of evidence first, leading readers to the claim presented as a conclusion, the paragraph or paper is organized inductively. Composition instructors tend to steer students away from using this technique to structure entire papers since great skill is needed to keep readers with the argument. The sections Organizing Ideas and Revising in the Writing Projects have asked you to think carefully about where you state your thesis or claim for this reason. It is usually more effective to use a deductively based structure.

A reflection of inductive reasoning that is often used in writing occurs when the writer makes a claim in a topic sentence or thesis statement, then simply exemplifies it. The writer is asking the readers to re-enact the inductive process that led him or her to make the claim. Notice how the list of evils alleged to have been committed by the British government functions this way in the Declaration of Independence. Notice how regularly you use this technique, and how often much of what you read uses it, too.

In addition, deduction often appears in the abbreviated form of the enthymeme (see page 515), and induction is commonly presented through the small sample of the example, the inference, and the anecdote. These practices are neither wrong nor fallacious. Writers cannot take the time or space to state all the premises of every deduction or to give multiple instances to support each idea. However, critical thinkers need to understand these reductions so that claims and evidence can be evaluated. Deduction and induction, the basic reasoning methods, are at work in various ways in what we write and read.

Principles for Writing Responsible Arguments

The following principles for writing responsible arguments are fundamental to the Western tradition of logical, structured argument. Always be sure to follow them as well as you can.

Principles for Writing Responsible Arguments

1. Formulate and qualify the thesis statement carefully. Place it purposefully. Use deductive and inductive approaches as appropriate to develop and support the thesis.

2. Provide a context for the thesis; give reasons for its importance. These might be warrants.

3. Provide sound evidence, or grounds, presented clearly and specifically.

4. Acknowledge and demonstrate understanding of other points of view. Grant validity to any point when it is justified. To strengthen your argument, refute courteously points with which you disagree.

5. Use the thinking/organizing patterns in Part Two. Arguments often rely on definitions. Causes of a situation and the effects of a proposal are often vital to an argument. Narratives and chronologies are often effective. Contrasts, comparisons, and analogies illuminate your points.

6. Don't use fallacious reasoning.

7. Be aware of your tone. You want to sound reasonable, thoughtful, and polite as you argue your points.

8. Remember that the conclusion to an argument is extremely important. Restate the thesis or claim with a suggestion, a call for action, a decision, or further thought.

Writing Project: Arguing a Position on a Significant Issue

This chapter has emphasized the importance of the basic concepts and terminology connected with argument because reasoned argument leading to mutual understanding, concensus, or agreement is the foundation of a democratic society and also is often the key to success in personal, academic, and business activities.

Because so much college and professional writing is argumentative, this Writing Project asks you to concentrate on the two central elements of argument: establishing a clear thesis and providing sound evidence for it. In addition, you should be particularly careful to be logical, to avoid fallacious statements, to consider your audience, and to present yourself as a reasonable, well-informed proponent of your claims.

Write an essay in which you argue logically for a position on an issue that you consider significant. Use print sources, electronic sources, and—if possible—an interview with an informed individual to support your claims. Follow your instructor's directions regarding the number and range of sources, length of the paper, and academic format for citation of sources. Be sure to follow exactly the model in your handbook when you complete your paper in MLA, APA, or other appropriate format. Consult Chapter 14 in this book.

On a page separate from your paper, identify the audience to whom you are addressing your argument and explain why it will benefit from understanding your position. Also, either within the paper or in an accompanying note, explain why this issue is important to you so that your classmates and instructor, as they help you revise your drafts, can be aware of the nature of your expertise and any possible biases.

This chapter has included both readings and Thinking-Writing Activities that encourage you to think about argument. Be sure to reread what you wrote for those activities; you may be able to use some of the material for this Writing Project.

Begin by considering the key elements in the Thinking-Writing Model on page 6.

THE WRITING SITUATION

Purpose Your primary purpose is to write an argument that will persuade your intended audience to agree with your claim or thesis. As you work toward that goal, you will have to think critically about a subject that you care about and clarify or modify your view of it, which is another useful purpose.

Audience The audience is a major concern in any argument. A successful writer understands the characteristics and attitudes of his or her audience. When you develop an argument, you must have a specific audience in mind. Although pandering dishonorably to the audience by distorting evidence or by using flattery is bad rhetoric, an arguer still should be aware of the makeup of the audience and accommodate its needs. Some factors to consider are knowledge (an expert audience needs less background than an uninformed one does), age (younger and older people often have different points of view), roles (people have various roles and respond differently as those roles change), relationships (an audience of peers can be approached differently than another kind of audience), and the emotional level of the issue and situation (a highly charged situation should be approached differently than a calm one would be).

Subject Whenever you argue for a position about which you are concerned, you are addressing an important subject. In addition, the techniques of argument themselves constitute a subject that merits much attention because argument has such importance in people's lives.

Writer If you have been using sources for other projects, you should be comfortable incorporating other people's ideas into your writing and documenting them appropriately. A new role for you may be that of the good rhetorician, the responsible arguer; if you use your developing critical thinking abilities, you will manage that role well.

THE WRITING PROCESS

The following sections will guide you through the stages of generating, planning, drafting, and revising as you develop your argument.

Generating Ideas

- You may be involved with an issue because of your sex, ethnicity, or field of study or through some organization in which you participate. Or you may be concerned about a problem at your college, in your community, in your country, or elsewhere in the world. If so, you should have no problem deciding what to write about.
- If no issue comes quickly to mind, look around your campus and community to see what problems exist or what changes could be made.
- Watch the news and read the local paper and national publications such as the *New York Times*, the *Wall Street Journal*, *Newsweek*, and *Time*. Talk with friends, family members, and professors about significant issues.
- Think about questions in your areas of interest: your favorite college subjects, sports, entertainment, food, cars, the environment, architecture. Some of these questions may pertain to serious issues; some might be more lighthearted; many will merit a reasoned argument.
- Freewrite about one or two of your concerns. See how many issues or positions you can come up with in five minutes.

Defining a Focus After selecting an issue to write about, draft a thesis statement that describes the position that you will argue. Be sure that the statement states your points accurately; it may be a complex sentence. Then share it with classmates to profit from their responses. Revise it on the basis of their feedback.

Organizing Ideas Your argument should probably be set up in the traditional "no-fail" structure: introduction, thesis, evidence, handling of other views, summing up, conclusion/recommendation for action. However, you may be able to use some other arrangement effectively.

Notice how your material adapts itself to various thinking patterns. Use them firmly to clarify your points.

Select and place material from your sources carefully. Connect source material smoothly with your ideas by introducing and commenting on it.

Drafting Begin with the easiest part to write, which for this paper might be the beginning since you have been thinking so much about your thesis and its context.

However, never get stymied by trying to compose a beginning. Draft sections in any order that works for you. You might want to draft the paragraphs that present your evidence, then consider what inductive or deductive methods you should use.

- Sometimes copying a draft or parts of it and revising one version while retaining another is productive. That way, if a revision is not satisfactory, you have preserved the earlier version.

- Sometimes writers need to start over by making a new file for a revised version.

- Sometimes it helps to scroll down or up and to rewrite a paragraph or section. Then you can use the better version and delete the weaker one.

Be sure to keep track of publication information for all sources. Note abbreviated titles, authors, and pages in your draft. Then, when you revise, you can cite the sources in the required format. Be sure to use quotation marks or indenting in your draft whenever you quote.

Revising, Editing, and Proofreading Use the Step-by-Step method on pages 160–162 to revise your essay and prepare a final draft.

Guidelines for Revising an Argument

❏ Is my claim clearly stated and adequately qualified?

❏ Do I provide adequate evidence to support the validity of my claim? Have I correctly cited and documented the sources of that evidence?

❏ Are any of my statements fallacious? Have I double-checked my argument for fallacies?

❏ Should I clearly state the warrants for my argument, or should I leave them unstated?

❏ Have I appropriately established my *ethos* (the impression my audience will have of me) and *pathos* (the effect my argument will have on my audience)?

❏ Have I considered, and included, other points of view? Does my argument clearly prove why my claims are more logical, sensible, useful, or appealing than the opposition's viewpoints?

STUDENT WRITING
JOSEPHINE CIMINO'S WRITING PROCESS

Part-time student Josephine Cimino makes use every day of critical thinking and problem-solving strategies. As a mother of two who also holds a full-time job, Cimino has multiple responsibilities that require her to make thoughtful decisions no matter how difficult or pressing the circumstances. Her reasoning abilities and careful, logical thinking are evident in the following argument. Although she recognized that the issue of cell phones in schools is not as obviously urgent as the human rights issues addressed by Elizabeth Cady Stanton and Martin Luther King Jr.—or as difficult and problematic as the issues of rape and alcohol abuse discussed in Chapter 12—Cimino chose an issue that was of close personal interest. This allows her to clearly establish her *ethos* (as a working parent) and to visualize a specific audience (other parents of school-age children). Josephine began with the exercise on page 505, Constructing Arguments to Persuade, as a way of structuring her thinking about this issue.

> *Reason:* For many working parents, cell phones allow them to keep track of their children's whereabouts and safety.
>
> *Reason:* Because of the increasing use of cell phones, there are very few public pay telephones available either on school grounds or at places like athletic fields where students go after school.
>
> *Claim:* Students should be allowed to carry cell phones on school grounds and during after-school activities.
>
> *Audience:* Other parents who might not be aware of current efforts to make cell phones illegal on school grounds.

Cellular Phones in Public Schools
BY JOSEPHINE R. CIMINO

As one half of a two-income domestic partnership, I find it very difficult to keep track of my son's, my husband's and my own activities. I can only imagine how much harder it is for families with more children. My husband's job requires him to travel, often out of state. As a very concerned and involved parent, I am left with the task of keeping track and assuring the safety of our child. My son is now in high school, and his day is filled with school, sports, and other extracurricular activities.

He went to a high school football game not too long ago, and I did not have to worry about him because one of his friend's parents was going to give him a ride home. When he got home, he said one of his other friends was caught using a cellular phone to call his parents to pick him up. Unfortunately, the assistant principal saw and confiscated the phone. The student was automatically suspended for ten days for violating Maryland law and school policy. I was so perturbed by this incident that I spoke with a school administrator, Mrs. Shenk, who stated she agreed that the law should be changed. In fact, she had given her daughter, a senior in high school, a cell phone to keep in her car. The administrator admitted that her daughter kept the cellular phone hidden at all times to avoid detection by other school administrators or teachers.

A law was enacted in Maryland in 1989 banning cellular phones and pagers from school grounds and school-related activities (Shen M3). According to a Montgomery County Public Schools regulation, if a student is caught using a cellular phone, the phone is confiscated, and the student is automatically suspended for ten days. In addition, for a second offense, the school is obliged to notify the police. Further, the student can also be expelled if the use of the cell phone was related to any criminal activity (Regulation). According to Shen, violation of the law is a misdemeanor, punishable by a fine of as much as $2500, and a maximum six-month imprisonment (M1).

Various news reports state that some educators and lawmakers have been opposed to the use of cellular phones on school grounds and at school-related activities due to the perception in the late 1980's and early 1990's that cellular phones were used for drug and other illegal activities. According to Mrs. Shenk, some educators and opponents of cellular phones think that cell phones will cause undue disruption in the schools because of the ringing of phones and kids talking on the phones inappropriately. She further states that another argument against cell phones is the possible loss or theft of cell phones by other students. Further, she states, cell phones can also distract students from their school-related activities and their studies.

I do not agree with the current Maryland law. I believe that this law has been surpassed by the electronic age and the availability of cellular phones. I believe that students in the middle schools and high schools should be allowed to carry cellular phones on school grounds and be allowed to use them before and after classes. Further, I believe that students should be allowed to carry and use cellular phones at school-related activities as long as the use is not related to something illegal.

The reasons for having cell phones available to students in schools are compelling. First of all, cell phones are a real time-saver for busy working parents with several children who need to be in several places. Parents do not have to wait around for activities to finish. The children can call when they are ready to be picked up, or to say that they are staying longer and need to be picked up later. Parents still spend an inordinate amount of time in their cars waiting for their children to finish their activities. If children are allowed to have cell phones, parents can use their time more productively. An example is my son's friend at the football game. His parents were probably doing errands or eating dinner, rather than waiting in the parking lot. They probably used their time for something they wanted or needed to do, other than just waiting for their son.

The availability and accessibility of regular pay phones in schools and on school grounds are sadly lacking. There is only one pay phone outside of my son's high school building, and there are no pay phones available near the football field, the basketball courts, or the soccer field. The school is often closed when games are played during the evening hours; therefore, the pay phones inside cannot be accessed. The students often have to wait in long lines to use the one pay phone available on school grounds to call their parents.

Another reason why students should be allowed to have cell phones is so parents can keep track of their children. Parents like me want to know what their children are doing at all times. I, for one, want to know where my son is so that I can be assured that everything is going the way it should. If he tells me he is going home with another child, I want to know for sure that this is what he is doing and that there are no hitches in the plans. I do not want him to be stranded somewhere because his plans fell apart. Parents should be able to call their children after school is over to confirm their schedules and activities.

Finally, students should be allowed to have cellular phones for safety reasons. With the current prevalence of abductions, kidnappings, and school violence, students should be allowed the safety net of having a cellular phone. It would be easy to dial 911 in case of an accident, or if the safety of the child was in question. Students should be able to call parents in case of a dead car battery after a school activity, or if a ride home fell through, or they are separated from friends during a football game. Numerous news reports said that some students were able to call their parents during the Columbine shooting in Colorado. Parents were assured that their children were still alive and able to talk to them about what was happening.

Incidents like the Columbine shooting and other reports of abductions and kidnappings on the way to and from school force parents to think of safety first and to minimize the consequences if a child is caught using the cell phone during school-related activities. Most parents would rather have their kids safe than take the risk of their being harmed.

Earlier this year, a bill was introduced unsuccessfully to change the current laws regulating cellular phones in public schools (Shen M1). However, on April 26, 2000, the School Board of Montgomery County gave the principals in all Montgomery County public schools the discretion of suspending students from one to ten days, instead of the previous automatic ten-day suspension (MCPS–Board). Obviously educators and school administrators agreed that the law needed changing by this revision of county policy. This is a good start, but is not enough to keep our children safe.

Parents, as advocates for the safety of children, should continue efforts to convince lawmakers to change the current law. Students should be allowed to use and carry cell phones in schools and during school activities under strict guidelines. If these guidelines are not followed, then those students should suffer the consequences. Students should not be punished for wanting to be safe and to be in contact with their parents. The safety of our children should be our foremost priority.

Works Cited

Montgomery County Public Schools. "Board Endorses Reduced Penalty for Use of Cellular Phones, Approves Non-Recommended Reductions to FY2001 Operating Budget Request." MCPS Media Announcement. 26 April 2000 <http/filemaker.mcps.k12.md.us>.

———. "Regulation—Portable Communication Devices COG-RA." 26 April 2000 <http/www.mcps.k12.md.us>.

Shen, Fern. "Rules on Cell Phones Decried." <u>Washington Post</u> 17 February 2000: M1+.

Shenk, Susan. Personal interview. 2 January 2000.

14

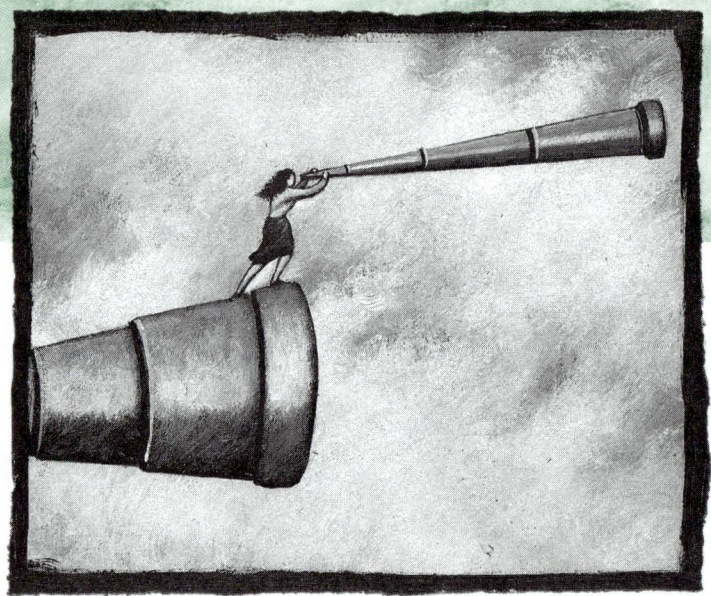

"If we would have new knowledge, we must get a whole world of new questions." —Susanne K. Langer

Thinking About Research

Writing About Investigations

Critical Thinking Focus: Deciding what information to look for, what to use, and how to present it

Writing Focus: Completing a researched paper

Writing Project: A research project

Rewards of Research

The *Oxford English Dictionary* gives the year 1593 as the earliest written use of the word *research* to mean "to investigate or study closely." Of course, men and women all over the world had investigated and studied for thousands of years before that word came into use. Thus, when you work on your college research projects, you are participating in one of humanity's oldest and most productive efforts.

You can easily come up with an endless list of scientific, technical, historical, and social investigations that have made our lives richer and safer. Then, thinking personally, you can come up with a shorter list of the ways in which doing good research can be rewarding for you. It can contribute to your success in college and, often, to your progress in a career. And although research can be hard work and can be frustrating when answers don't come, completing a project will usually give you much satisfaction.

As you continue your studies, you will do several kinds of research, including retrieving and understanding what others have discovered, synthesizing and connecting others' discoveries, connecting others' discoveries with your own ideas, and formulating new concepts and theories yourself. Each of these activities is rewarding in itself, and each is also an important component in research as an extensive human activity.

Critical and creative thinking are parts of all aspects of research. The concepts discussed in every chapter of this book also pertain to research. As people seek information, they constantly deal with *perceptions, beliefs, perspectives, processes, causes, comparisons, contrasts, analogies, definitions,* and *arguments.* Research often involves *making decisions* and *problem solving.* Researchers present *reports, inferences,* and *judgments.*

In addition, like writing, research is often a recursive process rather than a linear one. One source will lead to another, new questions will arise, a creative insight will illuminate a topic, or a critical analysis will change the direction of a project.

This chapter emphasizes some of the logic behind using researched information in academic papers. Your handbook will give you full explanations of various formats and techniques, as will guides to writing research papers that you can find in your college bookstore. Your bookstore will also have publications that provide detailed instructions for using the Internet.

An appendix to this book provides guidelines for using the Modern Language Association (MLA) documentation style and the American Psychological Association (APA) documentation style.

Starting with Questions

The starting point in research is usually a question. When people do research, they are looking for answers. Even when an instructor assigns a topic, asking questions about it is usually an effective approach because questions can help you find a focus and can stimulate inquiry. Questions can help you in various ways.

QUESTIONS THAT IDENTIFY YOUR TOPIC

If you are choosing your own topic, you can ask questions like these:

- What interests me most within the guidelines for this project?
- What within the guidelines pertains to my college major or my future career?

- What affects my life or the lives of people close to me?
- What affects my community?
- What topics can I find material about in my college library and on the Internet?

QUESTIONS THAT NARROW YOUR TOPIC

After you have selected a broad topic, or if your instructor has assigned a topic, you can use questions to narrow it into a manageable and interesting focus. Ask questions like the following. (Notice how many of these questions use the thinking patterns discussed in previous chapters of this book.)

- What are the issues involved in a topic? How are they defined? (Chapter 8)
- What are some different perspectives on the issues? (Chapter 9)
- What did people believe about it in previous historical periods? (Chapter 11)
- How have theories about it changed? (Chapter 11)
- What caused it? (Chapter 10)
- What problems are connected with it? How might they be solved? (Chapter 12)
- What are future concerns about it likely to be?

The specific question that you want to investigate can be called a **research question.**

Can you formulate the questions that might have inspired some of the student papers in this book? Perhaps they were the following:

What caused the congregating of birds in a mall's parking lot? (Chapter 10)

How can college drinking be reduced? (Chapter 11)

What influences youth violence? (Chapter 14)

Most major discoveries have begun with a question. Do you think that some famous people might have asked these?

How can a European find a short ocean route to India?

Why do birds on the Galapagos Islands look different than those on the mainland?

How can large numbers of automobiles be produced and sold at affordable prices?

Thinking ↔ Writing Activity

Developing Research Questions

1. Identify a field of study which interests you. Then write two or three questions about specific issues in that field.

2. If you can, show your questions to a professor or graduate student in the field. Ask her or him if these questions have been answered or if researchers are still working on them.

3. Share your questions with classmates. See if they have additional questions that pertain to this field of study.

Searching for Information

FINDING ELECTRONIC AND PRINT SOURCES IN THE LIBRARY

Finding information is easier now than it was in the past simply because of computers. Indeed, it sometimes seems as if too much data is available when the entry of a key word brings up a hundred (or more) possible matches! You are probably accustomed to asking an online service or a search engine to connect

you with all kinds of information. However, if you are not yet comfortable online, you should take a class, find some up-to-date instructional books, have a skilled friend teach you, or get help at your college's computer center or library.

Your college library is designed to assist you, your classmates, and your professors. Your library has a collection of books, magazines, journals, newspapers, pamphlets, and other print material that has been assembled for you and your fellow students. The librarians are specially trained to guide students and faculty to material for their work.

Also, your library uses computers in at least four ways to direct you to source material:

1. The library's holdings are *cataloged* via a computer program, so the best way for you to find books, articles, and videos is to learn to use the terminals in your library.

2. Most college libraries subscribe to *databases* such as Expanded Academic ASAP and National Newspapers that contain whole texts of articles from newspapers, magazines, and specialized journals, so a good way for you to find solid information is to learn to use whatever service your library has. The library provides databases that cannot be accessed on most home computers.

3. Your library probably has a *collection of CD-ROMs* containing encyclopedias, books, poems, and visuals.

4. Your library probably has computer terminals through which you can access the Internet and use various search engines to find an infinite variety of material.

Most college libraries provide guides to their resources. Some instructors or departments require completion of a workbook or physical or online attendance at library orientation sessions. You should take every opportunity to improve your ability to use your college library and the Internet.

Thinking ↔ Writing Activity

Learning About Your Library

1. Go to your college library. Find out how to access its holdings and learn what Internet services it provides.

2. Write a paragraph explaining what your library can do for you and how to use its computers. Also, explain how you would go about obtaining print sources.

COLLECTING INFORMATION FROM PEOPLE AND FROM THE FIELD

In addition to obtaining material from print and electronic sources, you can get information from people who have expertise on your subject. Also, you can go to places or events that are important to your research questions and observe what goes on.

Interviews Conducting an interview can be a valuable way to obtain information. Your creativity and critical abilities will be well used in an interview. Here are some guidelines for interviewing:

1. Identify the person with whom you wish to talk and then make an appointment with that person.

2. Carefully develop—and write out—the questions you will ask. You might want to email them to the interviewee ahead of time so that he or she will be able to prepare thorough responses.

3. Be careful as you record the interview. If you want to tape the interview, you must ask permission. If you are writing down the responses or keying them into a laptop computer, you must be sure to be accurate.

4. Do not take up too much of your interviewee's time, and—of course—give appropriate thanks.

5. Use and cite the material from an interview as you would any other source (see the MLA appendix, page 610, for guidelines). It should be effectively integrated into your paper where it works best to develop the points that you are making. Often information from an interview can be used in several sections of a paper; occasionally, the interview can be presented as a feature.

6. If you can, give your interviewee a draft of your paper to show how you have presented the material and be willing to heed suggestions if any are offered.

7. Provide the person interviewed with a copy of the completed paper and thank him or her again.

Questionnaires Using questionnaires is another way to obtain information from people, but they are difficult to design well. If you want to gather information with a questionnaire, you should review the material on inductive reasoning and empirical generalization in Chapter 13 on pages 518–521. As a beginning researcher, you should only ask a few questions, perhaps no more than three or four.

Also, think about these concerns:

1. What exactly is the issue about which you want people's opinions? Define it very clearly.

2. How can you state questions to obtain unambiguous information? Sometimes "yes-no" or "two-way" questions are best since they elicit

specific responses. However, sometimes yes-no questions are frustrating because people do not want to respond in such a limited way.

3. If you do not ask yes-no questions, how can you obtain possible responses in a small number of consistent categories that pertain to the information you want? Do you want choices? Do you want to construct a scale?

4. Can the responses be easily tabulated?

5. How many people can you poll in the time that you have and with the methods that you want to use? Will that group provide a representative sample appropriate for the scope of your project?

6. How will you use the results? How can you report them accurately, clearly identifying the characteristics and numbers of those who responded?

7. How can you use caution when drawing conclusions?

Questionnaires can be administered in several ways: by face-to-face polling; by mailing forms with a stamped, addressed return envelope; or by email. Practically speaking, a first attempt should focus on a small group—for example, asking the people on your block about a community issue or asking the students in one of your classes about a campus or political issue.

If you know someone experienced in questionnaire use—such as a social science professor, a public health researcher, or a journalism major—you might ask that person to help you craft your instrument. Also, test your questions on a few close friends or family members to see what kinds of answers you get. Then, after revising any questions that need adjusting, pose them to your selected group.

Observations, or Field Research   Observations provide firsthand data and are often used in art history, sociology, education, environmental studies, medicine, and other branches of science. If you want to conduct an observation, you should review Chapter 7 to remind yourself about factors that might affect your perceptions and Chapter 9 to recall different perspectives that you might take as an observer, either consciously or unconsciously. You should consider the following principles when you conduct an observation.

1. Identify a place, situation, or object that pertains to your research question.

2. Ask permission from an appropriate person if the site is reserved for use by a specific group such as a class, a club, or a religious assembly.

3. Select a good time to go to your observation site.

4. Do not become involved in any of the activities that you have come to observe.

5. Be as unobtrusive as possible. The presence of an observer often alters the dynamics of a situation.

6. If you are observing an object such as a painting, statue, building, or element of nature, try to study it at different times of day or under varying circumstances. In your write-up, accurately report the circumstances under which you made your observations.

7. Note your observations carefully.

8. Present your observations as objectively as possible. State any inferences and judgments carefully and separate them from your reporting of information obtained through your senses.

Thinking ↔ Writing Activity

Interviews, Questionnaires, and Observations

1. Interview one of your instructors about using firsthand sources of information. Ask him or her about how observations, questionnaires, and interviews are used in his or her field. Ask how these instruments should be designed and what pitfalls to avoid.

2. Write a paragraph or two about what you have learned from the interview.

Using Information

Finding material is relatively easy. Dealing with it is the challenging part. You must evaluate the information that you have found, which involves active and critical reading. You must select what you will use, which involves critical thinking, and then save, copy, or take notes from it carefully. Eventually, you must write your paper, which involves all the interrelated elements of the Thinking-Writing Model. In addition, you must integrate and cite source material in a prescribed academic format, which may at first seem difficult. Most important, you must present information accurately and honestly. A goal of this chapter is to help you do all these things by showing you some of the thinking that directs research itself and the writing of academic papers.

EVALUATING SOURCES FOR A RESEARCH PROJECT

All material found during research has to be evaluated. Sometimes evaluation is easy—a source may be so obviously good that you know you will use it, or it may be so clearly weak or irrelevant to your inquiry that you know you will not need it.

Here are some guidelines for deciding whether material will be useful to you. These guidelines are an abbreviated version of the material on pages 398–400. You may want to review those pages. Also, you may want to consult Chapters 3 and 11 to think again about some of the ways in which your beliefs have been formed since beliefs have a strong influence on evaluation.

These basic questions can help to judge information and sources:

1. *How reliable is the source?* Some sources, such as advertising, can be unreliable. Some that are clearly presenting a particular point of view, such as political campaign material or a newspaper editorial, can be one-sided. Some might be outdated. In order to identify solid, well-informed, current, and balanced material, ask yourself:

   - What kind of text is this? an editorial, a report, an advertisement?
   - Who is its intended audience? Is this audience important to the text's point of view?
   - When was it written? Is the date relevant to my research question?

2. *How knowledgeable or experienced is the author?* Some people of authority or recorded references offer stronger information than others. Scholars, scientists, and people whose lives have been devoted to any field can usually give broad and deep coverage of their areas of expertise. On the other hand, personal experience can often provide intense accounts of a situation, so sometimes an inexperienced observer can present a fresh point of view. Ask yourself:

   - What credentials does the person who provided this information have?
   - If the person is not an expert, under what circumstances did she or he provide the information?

3. *What specific ideas are being presented?* Ask yourself these questions about any material that you find:

   - What is the main point, claim, or thesis?
   - What reasons or evidence support the information? Does anything about it seem false?
   - Does anything seem to have been left out?
   - Are interests, purposes, and intended audiences apparent?
   - If an argument is presented, can you identify its warrants?

Material found on the Internet needs to be carefully evaluated. Online texts of articles from well-known publications have some built-in reputation since they have undergone a review process before being printed and posted online. If a newspaper, magazine, or journal is known for publishing sound material, then an article from it is probably reliable. However, if the publication is considered biased or shallow, then you must examine the article more carefully.

Material from individual web sites needs special scrutiny. The following checklist will help you develop a healthy skepticism.

Guidelines for Evaluating the Reliability of a Web Site

Criterion 1: Authority

❑ Is it clear who sponsors the site and what the sponsor's purpose is in maintaining it?

❑ Is it evident who wrote the material and what the author's qualifications for writing on this topic are?

❑ If the material is protected by copyright, is the name of the copyright holder given?

❑ Is there a way to verify the legitimacy of the page's sponsor; that is, is there a phone number or postal address to contact for more information? If there is, don't hesitate to send a letter or email or to phone. You may even end up with more information for your project.

❑ If you recognize the source and are sure that it is operating the site, you are likely to be on solid ground. But don't forget that some of the people running sites are trying to confuse you, that sites on a particular topic often carry opposing messages, and that hackers can sometimes commandeer legitimate sites.

❑ A *tilde* in the web site's address (as in ~jdoe) often indicates a personal home page, not one sponsored by an organization or institution. Another clue that a site is a personal page is when the address includes the name of a common Internet service provider—such as *geocities*, *tripod*, or *members.aol.com*.

❑ If you come across unfamiliar topics or web site authors, run their names through a search engine to see what other people have said about them.

Criterion 2: Accuracy

❑ Are the sources of any factual information clearly listed so that they can be verified in another source?

❑ Has the sponsor provided a link to other sites and sources—such as product reviews or reports filed with government organizations— that can be used to verify the sponsor's claims? Even better, does the site contain some references to print and other offline sources?

❑ Is statistical data in graphs and charts well labeled and easy to read?

❑ Is the information free of grammatical, spelling, and typographical errors? These kinds of errors sometimes indicate a lack of quality control and can also produce inaccuracies in the information.

Criterion 3: Objectivity

❏ For any given piece of information, is the sponsor's motivation for providing it evident?

❏ Is the information content obviously separated from any advertising or opinion content?

❏ Is the sponsor's point of view presented in a clear manner with well-supported arguments?

❏ If the site is not objective, does it at least take opposing points of view into account?

Criterion 4: Currency

❏ Is the material recent enough to be relevant to your project?

❏ Are there any indications that the material is kept up-to-date? On a browser such as Netscape Navigator, you can click on View and Page Info to see when the site was last revised.

❏ If the site contains charts and graphs, do you see statements indicating when the data were gathered?

❏ Is there an indication that the site has been completed and is not still being developed?

Thinking ↔ Writing Activity

Evaluating Print and Web Sources

1. After you have found a print source, ask the evaluative questions above and then write your answers.

2. Go to an Internet site and evaluate it according to the web guidelines. Then write your answers.

3. Examine your answers to the previous two questions. How will they influence your possible use of these sources?

MOVING FROM QUESTIONS TO FOCUS

At some point, you will move from your research questions to a focus for the paper in which you will write about your findings. Sometimes this happens very quickly; at other times, it takes a while. The guidelines for all of this book's Writing Projects include suggestions for identifying a focus and defining a thesis. Reviewing these suggestions will help you when you are writing a research paper.

Some research papers take an informative position; others are strongly argumentative. This distinction will depend on your purpose, the traditions of the discipline in which you are writing the paper, and your instructor's goals for the assignment. Be sure that you understand whether your instructor wants your paper to be informative or argumentative.

Thinking ↔ Writing Activity

Going from Questions to Thesis

1. Select one of the questions that you wrote for the Thinking-Writing Activity: Developing Research Questions on page 547. Then find or imagine some answers to it. Next, write at least one thesis statement that answers it or makes a claim about an answer to it.

2. Look at the questions and statements that two or three of your classmates created for this Thinking-Writing Activity. Identify the statements that seem clearest and have the most potential to be developed into solid papers.

Using Information Ethically and Understanding Plagiarism

It should not be necessary to discuss honesty and accuracy in your research. You and your fellow students should never consider using ideas any other way. However, enough ethical lapses occur, both at colleges and in publications, to make this discussion necessary. You must resolve to avoid two serious ethical lapses: *plagiarism* and *fabrication.* Therefore, you need to understand how to avoid them.

Plagiarism is presenting another person's ideas or words as your own. There are two good reasons not to plagiarize. The first is honesty. Most people do not want to be fakes; they want to be honest, and so they do not want to use others' ideas without giving credit. The second is that plagiarism can bring penalties, both in college and at work.

In college studies, two kinds of plagiarism are possible. One is deliberate and dishonorable—the willful copying of all or part of another student's paper or all or part of a source. Buying a paper from a service is a form of plagiarism because a student who does this is taking credit for someone else's words, ideas, and effort. Unfortunately, the easy accessibility of all kinds of texts on the Internet makes plagiarism technically easy.

The other kind of plagiarism is accidental and happens when a student does not know how to document properly. Once you understand that you must always signal where any material from a source begins and ends, and that you must always make clear who said something and where it was said, you should be able to avoid accidental plagiarism. The sections in this chapter on Taking Notes, The Logic Behind Documentation Formats, and Tips on Avoiding Plagiarism will help.

A *fabrication* is a deliberately false or invented statement. It presents as true something that is made up or distorted, such as an event that did not happen, a statement that was not made, a misleading addition or omission of words or data, listing a source that was not used. Some writers are tempted to fabricate or falsify if they do not have real information that they need in order to make a point or create a desired effect. Yet readers must be able to trust the material that is presented in academic work and in responsible media.

Fabrication is different from making a mistake, which unfortunately almost everyone does occasionally, but not deliberately. A fabrication is different from a hypothesis or hypothetical example, which should be identified as such.

Thinking ↔ Writing Activity

Plagiarism in the News

1. Read carefully your college's statements about plagiarism. Does your college have an honor code? If so, what does it say about plagiarism? Write a few sentences giving your responses to these statements.

2. Search for information about Stephen Glass, Jayson Blair, Janet Cook, Stephen Ambrose, or Doris Goodwin. Find out what any of these writers are reported to have done, what they said about their situations, and what happened to them.

3. What can college students learn from the experiences of these professionals?

If you can, share your responses to these questions with classmates and see how your ideas are similar or different.

Taking Notes

Although photocopying and downloading have made note taking less necessary than it was in previous eras, researchers still need to have methods for deciding what to note, highlight, or underline; for accurately recording content and bibliographic information; and for placing source material into the parts of a paper where it belongs.

DECIDING WHAT TO NOTE

Sometimes you can easily see that certain parts of an article, book, or web site relate to your research question or working thesis. Naturally, in such cases, you will then note the material or photocopy, highlight, or download it. However, at other times, you may not be sure what to select from a source. Of course, one way to avoid making selections for a while is to photocopy the entire article or to check the book out of the library for the longest time possible. But eventually you will have to decide what material you want to use in your paper in order to answer your research question or to support your thesis.

Your critical reading abilities will come into play here. Before you even think about taking notes, you should read an entire article. If you are consulting a book, read the whole book—if possible—or skim it, consult the index, and read the chapters that contain information related to your topic. Look for headings, topic sentences, chapter titles—all the elements that point out what the writer is discussing. As you read through, jot down page numbers or mark passages that strike you in some way, but you really should not take notes until you have a grasp of the entire piece.

After getting an overview of the work, you need to go back and select specific points that pertain to your question or thesis. If you're not sure how the material relates, note it! You want too much information instead of too little. Highlighting and underlining are forms of note taking because you are choosing information.

QUOTING OR PARAPHRASING

Another decision that you have to make while taking notes is whether to quote (using exact words) or to paraphrase (restating). Highlighting and underlining are forms of quoting. There are only two rules:

1. When you quote, put all of the quoted material inside quotation marks in your notes so that you will never forget that these are the author's exact words. Then you will know that anything else in your notes that is not in quotation marks is paraphrased.

2. Be accurate.

The following are some guidelines.

- If the author has said something in a distinctive way, quote or highlight it.
- If the author has said something complicated and/or technical, quote or highlight it.
- If the author has said something controversial, quote or highlight it.

- When in doubt, quote the author's words in your notes. You can decide if you would rather paraphrase them later when you are writing your paper.
- If you know that you only want a summary of a source or an indication of what it says, paraphrase it.

Here are examples of a full note and the paraphrased version:

Quoted note: "A Kampala journalist named Michael Wakabi told me that Kampala has become a 'used culture.' The cars are used—they arrive from Japan with broken power windows and air conditiong, so Ugandan drivers bake in the sun. Used furniture from Europe lines the streets in Kampala. The Ugandan Army occupies part of neighboring Congo with used tanks and aircraft from Ukraine. And the traditional Ugandan dress made from local cotton, called gomesi, is as rare as the mountain gorilla. To dress African, Ugandans have to have money." (Packer 58)

Paraphrased note: The economy of Uganda is ruined by exploitation—local industries and culture are almost extinct. Nothing is fabricated or produced in Uganda anymore; most consumer goods are rejects from Western countries. Because native Ugandan products are so rare, only wealthy Ugandans can have them. (Packer 58)

The author's full name and all publication information will be on a bibliography card or list. See pages 559–560.

CHARACTERISTICS OF EFFECTIVE NOTE-TAKING SYSTEMS

Good note-taking systems include

- accuracy in recording material
- accuracy in recording full bibliographic information
- differentiation between quoted and paraphrased material
- indication of the source from which a specific note is taken
- indication of the section of a paper to which a specific note pertains
- capacity to rearrange notes to put material into the appropriate sections of a paper

The old-fashioned technique of using note cards has all of these characteristics. Other methods can accomplish the same tasks, but researchers need to use care to separate noted items and to find a way to sort information in order to insert it in its logical place in the paper. If, like many students today, you only use note cards when you cannot photocopy or download a source, you need to think carefully about ways to develop a method that will provide you with the benefits of the note-card system.

The old system has two parts: a note card for each piece of information and a bibliographic card for every source.

Note Cards A note card contains only one item of information. The act of selecting specific items motivates you to think carefully about what *you* are looking for in order to present your ideas in the paper. Figure 14.1 shows an example of a note card.

You indicate clearly on the card whether the material is quoted by using quotation marks or whether it is paraphrased by not using the marks. You also briefly identify the source on the card and note the section or subtopic of your paper to which the information pertains. As you begin drafting, arrange the cards in groups according to the places in the paper where that information will be used. Citation of sources is easy because each card records its source.

Think about these questions as you look at Figure 14.1: Did this student quote or paraphrase from her source? How do you know? Did she omit some words that were in the original? Who are the authors? To what section of her paper does this material pertain? What pages did this information come from? Why will this material be easy for this student to use when she writes her paper?

Bibliographic Cards A good note-taking system includes a set of bibliography cards (or a list) which provides the full publication information for each source. You arrange the cards alphabetically by author or title when preparing your Works Cited list.

Figure 14.2 shows the bibliography card for the source of the quotation illustrated in Figure 14.1.

Look at the Works Cited list for one of the documented student papers in this book or consult your handbook. Then ask yourself: Is this source recorded in the MLA Works Cited–list format? Is it a book, a periodical, or an Internet source? Why will it be easy for this student to insert this source into her Works Cited list?

Using Your Computer to Take Notes Computers can be used in many ways for note taking. Simply by using a word-processing program, you can enter notes in appropriate files or under specific headings, and by pasting, copying, or using other combining methods, you can put the information into the part of your paper where you want it. You should double- or triple-space so that you can

Figure 14.1
Note Card

Kosmin, Lachman   history

"America's religious history began on October 12, 1492, when Christopher Columbus… took possession of an island in the New World, which he names San Salvador (Holy Saviour)… and his mission was to convert the Native Americans who inhabited the island to Christianity… and many of them adopted the Christian faith as their own."

pp. 18–19

Kosmin, A. Barry, and Seymour P. Lackman. One Nation Under God: Religion in Contemporary American Society. New York: Harmony, 1993.

Figure 14.2
Bibliography
Card

see items clearly, write changes interlinearly on printouts, and cut pages up to rearrange material. You can compile a Works Cited list by using an alphabetizing program or simply by copying or pasting.

Computer programs have been developed that produce virtual note cards, sort material into outlines, and print Works Cited, Reference, or Bibliography lists. In addition, database programs, scanners, and other electronic tools can help you to record information and incorporate it wherever you want it.

Printouts and photocopies can be cut up (always note the source on each piece) so that you can sort highlighted material as you would note cards.

Most students today are likely to use combinations of note taking and recording methods—card- or paper-based systems when necessary, electronic-based ones when possible. Probably the most unwieldy system—and one to avoid—is writing page after page of notes in a notebook, on both sides of the paper, without leaving spaces for notes to be annotated or cut apart and rearranged. You should avoid using any technique that does not allow you to review and organize material easily.

Thinking ↔ Writing Activity

Learning About the Methods of Experienced Note Takers

1. Ask one of your instructors or a successful upper-division student how he or she takes notes, keeps records of sources, and arranges source material for use in a paper. Ask her or him about the advantages and disadvantages of the system.

2. Write a paragraph summarizing what you have learned. Then share what you have written with classmates and see what systems they have learned about.

Thinking ↔ Writing Activity

Creating Your Own Methods

1. If you have previously worked on research projects, write an explanation of your own note-taking and record-keeping processes. How do you use your computer to complete tasks? What do you do that is effective? What do you need to improve?

2. Share your system with your classmates and learn about their systems. Does a classmate have a technique that you would like to adopt?

SUMMARIZING

You will often need to summarize what a source says, either as a way of taking notes or as a way of inserting information into your paper. Your critical reading abilities will serve you well when you write a summary. Here are some guidelines:

- A summary is by definition short. An article or book chapter might be summarized in five or six sentences.

- A summary presents major points, not introductory material or multiple examples. It might give one necessary example.

- A summary should state the main point or the thesis clearly, probably at the beginning.

- A summary does not include your commentary on or evaluation of the material. You can comment later as you introduce summarized material into your paper or after you have included it.

  Comment or evaluation: "This article discussed a major breakthrough. . . ."

  Summary: "It says . . ."

  Comment or evaluation: "This book takes a stand that is no longer accepted. . . ."

  Summary: "It claims . . ."

- Signal that you are presenting summarized material. One way to begin a summary is to state the main point. Signal words such as "The article says . . ." "He points out . . ." or "She concludes . . ." are helpful throughout a summary.

- Usually a summary paraphrases a source, but if you quote special words, graceful phrases, or entire sentences, be sure to use quotation marks.

- A summary is accurate.

The following is a professionally written summary of the article "Hospice Care or Assisted Suicide: A False Dichotomy" that appears in Chapter 13 on pages 510–513.

> In this paper, the author argues that making assisted suicide available is not a contradictory position to espousing hospice care. He draws on historical and political examples to explain the ethical basis for this assertion. By defining the issue at stake as one of personal autonomy (the loss or gain thereof), the author challenges the argument that making assisted suicide available leads to a slippery slope toward euthanasia, eugenics, or genocide. He asserts that narrowing choices by preventing people from seeking assistance in suicide is more likely to lead us down the slippery slope toward coercive medical and state intervention in our lives.

Thinking ↔ Writing Activity

Learning to Summarize

1. Write a four- or five-sentence summary of one of the sources that you evaluated for the Thinking-Writing Activity: Evaluating Print and Web Sources on page 554.
2. If you can, ask a classmate to read the source and then comment on whether your summary seems accurate.

Preparing an Annotated Bibliography

One technique that can help you evaluate your sources is writing an annotated bibliography. Annotated bibliographies have been printed about many subjects, either as books or as indexes. Perhaps one of the librarians can direct you to such a bibliography so that you can see how useful annotation can be.

Sometimes instructors will ask students to create such a bibliography as a part of a research project. An **annotated bibliography** is simply a list of sources with a brief summary of and some evaluative comments about each one. An instructor might ask you to write one or two sentences about each source's potential value in a paper.

A student who was researching the role of religion in United States politics made the entries shown in the example in Figure 14.3 on page 563. Her instructor had required students to prepare an annotated bibliography of several sources before drafting their research papers.

Thinking ↔ Writing Activity

Creating an Annotated Bibliography

1. Find three sources that pertain to one of the questions that you used in a previous Thinking-Writing Activity or to a paper that you are writing.

2. After you have read the sources carefully, create an annotated bibliography in which you list full bibliographic information. Also, summarize each source in one or two sentences and comment in one or two sentences about what each source's value would be in a paper about the subject.

Figure 14.3 Annotated Bibliography

Lessner, Lori. "A Passionate Political Embrace of Faith." Philadelphia Enquirer 8 Nov 1999: A1+.

This article says that many of the current presidential candidates have been vociferous in talking about their religious beliefs. Lessner explains that this religious openness could affect these candidates' campaigns because some analysts say that candidates could lose votes from differing religious groups.

I will use this article to show how religion can help or harm a candidate's campaign.

Rosen, Jeffery. "Is Nothing Secular?" New York Times Magazine 30 Jan 2000: 40–45.

This article explains how religion is playing an important part in the 2000 presidential primary campaign. Rosen says that most of the religiously outspoken candidates of the past have been from the South. He also explains how religion has been a part of American politics since the Revolutionary War.

I will use this article to provide some historical background.

Integrating Source Material: Being a Good Host

The most important part of any research project is writing up the findings. Of course, there are many forms for presenting research findings, such as laboratory reports and government documents. However, since this book focuses on undergraduate-level research essays, especially those written for English classes and courses in other disciplines, we will examine formats appropriate for such writing.

Research has often been described as an endless conversation. The formats in which academic work is presented reflect the metaphor of research as conversation by indicating who is saying what.

The most important point to remember is that *you* are the person presenting the information in your paper. You are, in effect, participating in a conversation with your sources and your readers. Your paper is not just a series of quotations and paraphrases from sources; instead, it is a presentation of your ideas about the issue and your thinking about what your sources have said.

SEEING YOUR PROJECT AS A TALK SHOW

An extension of the notion of research as conversation is seeing a research paper as analogous to a dignified television or radio talk show or a panel discussion about a current issue. Think of yourself as a talk-show host as you write a paper that uses source material. Just as the host sets up the discussion, you will provide a context and purpose for presenting the material that you have found. Just as the host introduces each guest to the audience, you will introduce each source into your paper. Just as the host helps the guests interact, you will point out the connections and oppositions between and among your sources. And just as the host wraps the show up, you will conclude your paper in an effective manner.

To be a good host, you will need to know how academic writers signal that a source is coming into a paper. Here are some techniques:

- *Use the name of the author, especially a significant writer or scholar:*
  "Elizabeth Cady Stanton wrote that 'it is the duty of the women of this country to secure to themselves their sacred right to the elective franchise.'"

- *Use the name of the publication:*
  "A *New York Times* article provides guidelines for evaluating information found on the Web. It says . . ."

- *Establish a context:*
  "Students now receive much advice about how to decide whether information found on the Internet is likely to be good or useless. For example, an article in the *New York Times* provides a list of hints and warnings. This article says . . ."

- *Indicate why you are presenting the information.* This is part of the research conversation. You are talking about the source. In the following passage, a student has commented in his own voice both before and after paraphrasing from a source.

Student {
Clearly, the political events of the past century, as well as current events,

show a need for real and comprehensive reform in the campaign finance system.

Source {
Sabato and Simpson say that influence peddling and other forms of corruption

are now worse than they ever have been because they are part of a political

tradition that has been institutionalized (7).

Student {
The question remains: What is the best approach for achieving meaningful

reform, given the realities of the American political and electoral system?

ESTABLISHING YOUR VOICE

You will use your own voice in your research writing to fulfill several purposes. First, as just explained, you will always signal in some way that you are introducing source material into your paper. In addition, as the author of a paper, not just a compiler of other people's ideas, you might

- *Comment on what sources say.* You should indicate why you have included the source material in the paper. You could express agreement or disagreement with particular sources. You might explain which sources you consider most important to the points you are making in the paper. Providing such commentary is an important part of your role as "host."

- *Synthesize what sources say.* You should discuss ways in which sources relate to each other. You might point out a chronological sequence of concepts or explain how theories differ from each other. You could show how sources agree.

- *Present your own thinking.* You have established a thesis for your paper, and, of course, you will present ideas to support it. You might explain why you agree with one source or a group of sources or why you differ from them all and have your own claim to put forth. You might present ideas that have come from your experiences, your observations, your interpretations, or your creative thinking.

You need to clarify when you are speaking in order to be credited for your ideas and comments, just as you must indicate when your sources are speaking so that proper credit is given to them.

Your voice should be easily identifiable as long as you have indicated where all source material begins and ends. Then everything else is either your commentary, your synthesis, or your own thinking. Often, you will want to use words or phrases to show that you are commenting—such as "Therefore," "A consideration of these concepts shows . . . ," or "Another significant idea is . . ."

CHOOSING PRONOUNS

If your instructor agrees, you could simply present some of your comments and ideas as first-person statements: "I want to suggest . . ."; "After analyzing these reports, I decided . . ."; "I believe . . ." However, some instructors are not comfortable with the use of *I*. There is an academic tradition that discourages the use of the first person singular pronoun (*I*) in order to suggest an objective and impersonal point of view. This tradition is stronger in some disciplines than in others. You should ask your instructors about the preferred pronoun use in research papers and also look at pronoun use in academic journals in the fields in which you are studying.

Also be careful about using *we*. Be sure you identify who "we" is—people sometimes use the word to mean society at large, the citizens of a particular country, or the readers of a particular newspaper or magazine. However, your readers should never have to assume. In addition, *you* is rarely used in academic writing.

Thinking ↔ Writing Activity

Clarifying Who Is Talking

1. Look at the student paper at the end of this chapter, at other documented papers in this book, or at a research paper in your handbook. Notice how the student writers introduce other people's ideas into their papers. Then write a paragraph about what you have observed. Quote some different ways in which these student writers bring sources into their papers.

2. Notice how the writers clarify what their own thinking is about the source material or about the point that the source is being used to support. Identify two specific places where student writers are speaking in their own voices.

Think about how this activity might help you to write your next documented paper and to avoid creating a paper that is just a string of quotations and paraphrases of others' ideas.

The Logic Behind Documentation Formats

REASONS FOR DOCUMENTATION

Two principles underlie academic documentation formats:

- Readers have to know *who* says something.
- Readers have to know *where* something is said.

All academic formats provide this information in logical systems whether they use parentheses, endnotes, or footnotes. Different disciplines use different formats, but they are all based on these two principles. Your handbook or guide to research will explain most of the formats, such as those adopted by the American Psychological Association (APA), the Council of Biology Editors (CBE), and the Modern Language Association (MLA). Also, these associations maintain web sites on which you can find the most current format models. Guidelines to the MLA and APA styles are in this book's appendix.

Researchers clarify who said something and where it was said for a number of reasons:

- *To give credibility to a paper.* The strength or weakness of source materials helps readers judge the strength or weakness of a research project and its presentation.

- *To help readers and other researchers learn more.* Proper documentation can direct readers to sources so that they can find out more about a subject than what is presented in a paper.

- *To give credit where credit is due.* Research papers combine many people's ideas. Democracy tells us that each person is important. Giving appropriate credit shows respect for the human being who expressed the idea being used. Further, out of self-respect, researchers and writers want their own ideas to be credited to them just as much as they want to acknowledge others' ideas.

- *To observe the courtesies of conversation.* If research is a millennia-long conversation, the courtesies of conversation are in order. People take turns speaking during a conversation; sometimes points are recapped; often questions are asked and answered. It is usually important to know who is speaking in a conversation.

- *To avoid plagiarism.*

Guidelines for Avoiding Plagiarism

- ❑ Remember that all material from any source must be documented in some way. Downloaded items, web sites, email, interviews, illustrations, DVDs, videos, films, broadcasts, lectures, books, articles—

anything that is not drawn from your own experience, observation, or creativity—must be cited appropriately.

❑ Learn the different methods of citation used in various writing situations. In college, you may need to use different formats in papers written for different classes. These disciplinary formats are explained in guides to research and handbooks. At work, you will give credit to others as expected in your occupation. In writing done for community activities, you will probably cite information informally, just stating that a person, article, or report said something.

❑ Be sure to present quoted material (exact words) in quotation marks, indented, or in some other indicative way, depending on the format that you are using.

❑ Remember that copied-and-pasted material, paraphrases, summaries, and short extracts, even of less than a sentence, all must be cited. Other people's ideas must be documented as well as their exact words.

❑ Signal where material from others begins and where it ends. Learn to do this in a variety of ways, as appropriate to the writing situation.

❑ Take pride in presenting your own thinking and distinguish your ideas clearly from those of your sources.

❑ Be careful to capture all bibliographic material as you download, photocopy, and take notes so that you can easily provide documentation. Be sure to record authors' full names, exact titles, publication information, dates, page numbers, URLs, and other access items.

❑ Consult with your instructors and writing center tutors about citing sources when you are drafting your researched writing.

❑ When in doubt, cite.

Thinking ↔ Writing Activity

Citing and Paraphrasing

Students usually know that quoted material of a sentence or more must be documented. However, students sometimes have difficulty understanding that paraphrases and quotations of short, "apt phrases" must also be cited. Read the passage below that was written by Lynn Z. Bloom and appears on page 121 of the seventh edition of *The Essay Connection,* published by Houghton Mifflin in 2004.

> Original passage: "Narratives have as many purposes, as many plots, as many characters as there are people to write them. You have but to examine your life, your thoughts, your experiences, to find an unwritten library of narratives yet to tell."

Why is this use acceptable?

1. Lynn Bloom points out that all people have stories worth telling if they will just look into their lives and experiences where they will "find an unwritten library of narratives." (121)

Why could this use be seen as plagiarism by some or as an error in punctuation by others. What do you think?

2. Each person's life can be seen as holding an unwritten library of narratives. (Bloom 121)

Where do you see plagiarism here?

3. Story-telling may be one of the defining characteristics of the human species. Stories come in countless forms, and have been told in various ways by almost everybody who has ever lived. Indeed, narratives have as many purposes, as many plots, as many characters as there are people to tell them.

USING COMMON KNOWLEDGE

It is usually not necessary to document information that is considered "common knowledge," or things that "everybody" knows. Common knowledge is often factual, such as the fact that hijacked planes piloted by terrorists crashed into the World Trade Center on September 11, 2001. Well-known sayings like "Haste makes waste" are usually not documented, nor are accepted concepts like consuming large amounts of high-calorie food will cause most people to gain weight. However, discussions of facts or well-known ideas are not common; they are produced by individuals and must be documented.

In addition, common knowledge is not universally common. Different cultures, different time periods, different academic disciplines, different occupations all have their own common knowledge and often do not see ideas from other groups or eras as well known. Therefore, you need to be cautious about presenting something as common knowledge, and perhaps consult with your instructor. If in doubt, document. It is better to overcite than to plagiarize.

THE LOGIC OF MLA STYLE

The MLA system is used in this book because it is widely used in English classes. To understand how it works, look at the paper at the end of this chapter or at a model in your handbook or guide to research.

1. First, note that at the end of a paper, there is a list of Works Cited, with the sources listed alphabetically according to *author*, or if no author is given, according to the *title* of the source. Full bibliographic information is given in this list so that it does not have to be provided in the parenthetical citations within the body of the paper.

2. Next, look at the places within the paper where sources are cited. Note that when material has been taken from a source, the last name or an abbreviated title under which it is listed in Works Cited is given— either when the material is introduced or in parentheses at the end of its use. The number of the page on which the material can be found is given in parentheses at the end of the quotation or paraphrase. The parentheses signal the end of the source material.

3. If a source does not have a page number, then a number cannot be given, so you must otherwise signal that use of the source has ended. Many documents downloaded from the Internet do not show page numbers, so you must be careful to indicate where your use of such a source ends. One way to do this is to end a paragraph. You must clearly signal the place at which the next source comes into the paper or comment so that readers know that you or another source is now contributing information and that the use of the unpaginated source has ended. You need to signal the end of material from an interview in the same manner.

Thinking ↔ Writing Activity

Explaining the MLA System

1. Look again at the documented paper in this chapter or in your handbook. Then write an explanation of how the MLA system works as illustrated in that paper. Explain the relationship between the Works Cited list and the parenthetical citations.

2. Next, explain the MLA system to a classmate. Then tell your classmate why you believe the reasons for documentation are important. See if she or he agrees.

Working Thoughtfully on Research Projects

Much of the work you do to produce a research paper is similar to what you do when you write from your own resources. However, research projects often involve some special steps and concerns, including scheduling a significant amount of time, planning your paper carefully, using a specified academic format, and, often, consulting with librarians and with your instructor.

TIME

No one needs to tell you that you cannot just sit down and write up the results of a research project in a short hour spent at your keyboard. Indeed, you know from experience, from this book's advice, and from your writing instructors that you seldom can write a personal piece without spending time thinking, drafting, and revising. However, a researched piece of writing demands a great deal of time.

Doing the research itself is time-consuming. The Internet has made it easy to locate some sources, and the miracle of electronics can quickly bring sources to computer screens. Yet reading, evaluating, selecting, noting, commenting on, and arranging material demands the use of critical and creative thinking processes that usually cannot be hurried.

Using a library can involve waiting for help from a librarian, learning to use the computerized catalog, searching the shelves for material, seeing interesting material that doesn't pertain to your paper, and, of course, having to read, evaluate, copy, take notes, and think about what you've found. College libraries are pleasant places where time is usually well spent—and where you will spend much time while working on a research project.

Deciding on the scope of a project, working though research questions, narrowing a topic, interviewing knowledgeable persons, and revising and qualifying a thesis all take time.

Therefore, you should make a schedule when you begin a research project. You must complete the project within the time frame that your instructor allows. Instructors usually give weeks or months for research projects, but it is amazing how quickly that time evaporates and how suddenly deadlines are staring you in the face. Start as soon as you are given the assignment. Block out time to work on it regularly. Be sure to follow any time line that your instructor establishes for topic selection, working on drafts, and conferences.

PLANNING AND OUTLINING

Since research papers are often longer than essays or reports, planning and outlining are important steps. You will probably have to gather information before you can see what shape your paper will take, but as soon as you can, you will want to block out the sections of the paper and make a working outline (to be changed as the paper develops). If your instructor requires that a formal outline be submitted with your finished paper, look at the paper at the end of this chapter or consult your handbook for a model. Some word-processing programs include formal outlines in their formatting options, so your computer might help you with an outline.

FORMATS AND MODELS

You must use an accepted academic documentation format when you write a research paper for a college class. You cannot be creative about documentation. You must follow the models exactly.

COLLABORATION

 The research conducted in business, at large laboratories, and by think tanks and professional organizations is often done by teams. Therefore, to give students this experience, some instructors may assign team projects in college classes. But even if the project that you will be working on will be an individual effort, other people can provide much help. You will want to work with your instructor, the librarians, computer experts, and your classmates as much as you can as you complete your research.

Writing Project: A Research Paper

This chapter emphasizes the reasoning behind many of the activities that occur while you are engaged in research. The Thinking-Writing Activities should help you find and use information. Be sure to reread what you wrote for those activities.

> Following all instructions given by your instructor, complete a research project and write a well-documented paper in which you report and discuss your findings.

Begin by considering the key elements in the Thinking-Writing Model on page 6.

As tempting as this "mental blender" approach to research might appear, there is at this time no substitute for research based on thoughtful exploration, effective planning, productive collaboration, and above all, critical thinking. © Reprinted with special permission of King Features Syndicate.

THE WRITING SITUATION

Purpose Of course, your two major purposes here are to learn as much as you can about the issue that you are researching and then to present your thinking about your findings in an effective paper. Also, you can improve your ability to use your college library and the Internet. You can also become more skilled at using and better understanding academic formats. In addition, you will further develop your critical and creative thinking abilities as you apply almost every concept presented in this book to your research project.

Audience If your classmates are working on similar projects, they will be an excellent audience for your finished paper as well as for drafts. If your research topic is about a social or political issue, your audience might include people beyond your college. Perhaps you can find a way to share what you've learned at a community forum; in a newspaper, newsletter, or listserv; or on a web site. Naturally, your instructor remains the audience who will judge how well you have shaped your research question, investigated possible answers, discussed what you have found, and documented your paper in the required academic format.

Subject Obviously, you should be interested in the subject of your research so that your work will be a pleasure rather than a chore. If the subject is significant in your life or connected with one of your favorite academic fields, you should be able to think of a stimulating research question. If the subject has been assigned and, perhaps, is not among your interests, do everything you can to connect it to your interests. Ask questions about it, read as widely as you can, and consult web sites. You will almost surely find issues within any subject that you can relate to your own concerns.

Writer   If you've already worked on research projects in previous classes, you should feel confident as you undertake this one, but you should be willing to improve your abilities throughout the entire process. If you have not done research before, jump in and swim as well as you can. Be your most efficient self by setting up a schedule, working steadily, and meeting all deadlines. Don't hesitate to ask for help from librarians, computer room staff, and your instructor.

Remember the talk-show analogy presented in this chapter: you are the host, in charge of the paper. Comment on what you discover during your investigation; present your own thinking and keep yourself in the paper as much as is appropriate to the subject, to the traditions of the discipline in which you are working, and to your assignment.

THE WRITING PROCESS

Much of the material already presented in this chapter relates to generating ideas, finding a focus, and defining a thesis as you work on a research project. You should review it before you begin your paper.

Generating Ideas

- As you use the technique of asking questions about your subject, look again at the questions presented in Chapter 4 (pages 97–99). Apply as many of those questions as you can.

- Brainstorm and freewrite as you begin your research project, just as you would do when writing a paper from your own experience. "Talk to yourself" on paper about what you want to investigate and what you want to say about the topic.

- Use the thinking patterns discussed in Chapters 7 to 10 as ways to find ideas. Ask yourself about any processes involved in your subject. Describe important objects connected with it. Think about similarities and differences within it. Identify causal relationships. Define important terms. And be sure to write down what the thinking patterns show you.

- Before you decide on a limited focus, read widely about your subject. Consult encyclopedias and web sites to get background information and ideas.

Defining a Thesis   As you turn your research question (or questions) into a tentative thesis statement, you need to be sure that your thesis reflects the rhetorical purpose of your paper. Are you explaining, presenting different points of views, or arguing for a specific position?

Notice how the documented student papers in Chapters 8 and 10 explain their topics. Notice how Joshua Bartlett's paper in Chapter 12 and the paper in Chapter 13 argue for specific changes. Notice how the paper in this chapter argues for a claim.

Draft more than one possible thesis statement and then decide which one best serves your purposes. Remember that you may refocus your paper as you draft and revise it, so you should be open to reshaping your thesis statement as you rework the paper.

Organizing Ideas Research papers, especially those longer than three or four pages, are usually divided into logically distinguished sections. As you organize your paper, you need to think about how the material that you have found pertains to different aspects of the topic. And in an interactive process, as your research develops, the material you find will suggest different points that you may want to develop.

For example, if you are researching changes in beliefs about healthy diets, you might divide your paper chronologically or according to food groups, depending on what you decide to emphasize. If you are researching homelessness in a community in order to present an overview of it to an audience of relatively affluent young people, your paper might include almost equally developed sections on the estimated numbers of homeless people, the causes of homelessness, and the programs to help the homeless. If your purpose is to argue for improved programs, your paper might have a short introductory section on the numbers and causes and well-developed sections on various options for helping the homeless.

If you have used note cards and classified them according to the aspect of your topic to which they contribute, you can easily arrange and rearrange them as you incorporate information into your draft. If you have taken notes on paper, you can cut up the pages to arrange information. If you have taken notes on your computer, you can print files and/or copy and organize. If you have assembled printouts and photocopies of articles and pages, you'll need to identify the parts of your paper where this information belongs and sort it appropriately. If you have a combination of downloaded material, photocopies, and written notes—which is likely—you will need to put them in logical piles or arrange them near your keyboard in a way that will help you to incorporate information and keep track of where every item came from.

Outlines are usually necessary planning tools for long research papers. You should create rough, working outlines several times during your research process. If your instructor requires a formal outline, you can write one at the end of your planning, after you have completed a good draft, or after you finish the paper. A formal outline will provide a good measure of the organization of your paper. See your handbook or your word processor's outline format option or consult with your instructor.

Drafting   Drafting a research paper differs from drafting a personal paper in one important way: you must remember to indicate within the draft where source material begins, where it ends, where it is from, and whether it is quoted or paraphrased. In a draft, citation formats and wordings of the signals that indicate a source do not have to be perfect. You can polish these up when you revise and edit, but you must keep track of this material as you draft.

One decision you will have to make during drafting is whether to quote, paraphrase, or summarize source material. This is not always an easy choice. You do not want to quote too much, yet you do need to report what sources say. You should read documented papers and articles in your fields of interest in order to develop a sense of how experienced academic writers use their sources. Notice how these writers use short quotations, long quotations, paraphrases, and summaries.

The following are some guidelines for deciding what to quote, paraphrase, or summarize.

- You probably should quote if what a source has said is worded in a special way, is complicated or technical, or is controversial.

- If you are still learning about the field that your sources are discussing, you might need to quote more than an expert would.

- You should not use many long quoted passages. If you include a lot of lengthy quotations, you may end up compiling a small anthology instead of writing a paper.

- Remember that you do not have to quote whole sentences; often a few words will suffice. Example: In contrasting facts and theories, Stephen Jay Gould calls facts "the world's data," and theories "structures of ideas that explain and interpret facts" (420).

- You might want to quote fairly extensively in an early draft and then ask your classmates, writing center tutors, or instructor for help with shortening quotations and paraphrasing.

- **Paraphrasing,** or restating another's ideas in your own words, requires a good vocabulary and well-developed critical reading skills. Ask yourself as you are drafting: "Let's see. What is this source saying? How do these ideas help develop my paper?" Then write your answers and see how they might help you to incorporate the source into your paper.

- You use **summaries** to show the main points of an article, section, chapter, book, or Internet source. Remember to explain the significance of the summarized material.

Remember that you must always signal the beginning and end of source use and cite appropriately, whether you are quoting, paraphrasing, or summarizing.

You should remain aware of your talk-show host role as you comment on what you have used from your sources. You will probably need to draft your statements several times as you reread your notes and sources and rethink what you want to say.

Revising, Editing, and Proofreading   Use the Step-by-Step Method on pages 160–161 to revise your essay and prepare a final draft.

Annotated Student Research Paper with Outline and Drafts

The paper on pages 583–593 was written for an English composition course that emphasizes argument and research. Dr. Michael Eckert taught the course; Reuben Smith is the student author. A sequence of reading and writing assignments led up to the paper assignment. Students wrote short papers exploring the issue that they had selected and papers analyzing arguments about various aspects of violence. Students responded to each other's drafts during two Writers' Circle Workshops (peer review sessions) held two weeks and one week before the paper was due. Reuben Smith discussed his work on this paper in an interview with one of this book's authors.

REUBEN'S WRITING SITUATION

Purpose   The course concluded with this paper in which the students were to apply what they had learned about argument and research. The paper had to be based on research, and it had to argue for a position on an issue concerning violence, a reading theme for the semester. Students had to decide whether to use an adversarial or consensus-building approach. Reuben chose consensus building.

Audience   Reuben identified his classmates as his primary audience, although he realized that parents of young children would be a good audience, too. He described his classmates as "a small group of college students from various ethnic and cultural backgrounds. The readers are all under the age of 25 and not yet parents. Some may have come from broken, neglectful, or abusive homes and may know the effects of such an atmosphere firsthand." Dr. Eckert advised the students to consider their classmates and him as their audience. Reuben said that Dr. Eckert reassured them by saying that they weren't writing for publication, so they shouldn't have stage fright. (Now Reuben laughs: "And here my paper is—in a book!")

Subject Reuben said that at first he was not enthusiastic about the assigned subject. He said, "Sure, violence is bad, but I didn't have any other strong opinions about it. So I had to connect it with things that I am interested in. I'm a young person, and I really care about children. It pains me to think about children being abused and young people in big trouble. So I decided to focus on youth violence. And I got more interested as I got into it." Reuben said that he came to be "appreciative of the focus" that Dr. Eckert had established because it provided direction for the entire class.

Writer Reuben described himself as "an 18-year-old college freshman who has explored the issue of youth violence in considerable detail over the semester." He said that he "writes from the position of having been raised in a loving and supportive family environment." Reuben likes to write, can use a word processor pretty well, and has a good computer and printer at home.

REUBEN'S WRITING PROCESS

As he thought about drafting, organizing, revising, and collaborating, Reuben made the following observations.

- Dr. Eckert's clear instructions and the sequence of assignments made drafting easy. Much of what was in the preliminary exploratory and analytical writings could fit into the paper (and was supposed to). Working "piece by piece" helps, Reuben said.

- Reuben liked the Writers' Workshops (peer review sessions), which were similar to those in which he had participated in high school. His classmates' responses helped him to see where his drafts needed more work. He also regarded these sessions as establishing "three due dates," which forced him to finish his drafts promptly instead of writing them at the last minute.

- Reuben's sources were books from the college library, an anthology of essays that was assigned for the course, downloaded Internet articles, and interview notes. He likes to spread his material around him on a table and go from source to source to find useful information to put into his word-processed drafts. He said that he handwrote some notes from the books on pieces of paper in order "to see what I had." Using bookmarks confused him, so he found that he needed to take notes.

- Reuben knew that he had to identify sources carefully as he inserted material from them into a draft. He said, "I don't trust myself to put in names and pages later. If you mess up, it shoots the paper!"

- Reuben was surprised that some of his classmates seemed "scared of sources." He wanted to tell them, "Sources are our friends. They'll write the paper for you, just about. They are the experienced voices."

- Reuben writes on his computer. He made rough outlines of his paper on the computer several times. He said that he's not much of a freewriter. He likes to try to get drafts on the screen in fairly good shape, but he rewrites sentences and paragraphs as he goes. He prints out drafts in order to revise. He explained that he "has to see the whole thing on paper" because he's "big on flow." Moving readers from source to source with comments helps a research paper flow, he said.

One version of his outline follows.

Addressing the Issue of Violence by Young People

<u>Claim:</u> In an aggressive world of broken families, media violence, and school shootings, it is crucial that a child has the guidance of an involved parent to help him or her sort out these influences and respond to them in a healthy way.

  I. Youth violence—a disturbing fact of life

 II. Debate over causes

    A. Breakdown of the two-parent family

    B. The individual

    C. The media

    D. Child abuse

    E. Strongest influence—family life

 III. Breakdown of the two-parent family

    A. Divorce rate

    B. Violent teenage crime and absent fathers

    C. Single-parent pressures

    D. Unsupervised children

 IV. Violence in the Media

    A. Extent

    B. Possible influence

  V. Many factors—role of parenting

 VI. Dysfunctional families

    A. Definitions

    B. Abuse

1. Crawford example
2. Thornberry study

C. Parental neglect

VII. Parents' responsibilities

A. Fulfilling needs
B. Constructive discipline

VIII. Steps to reduce juvenile violence

A. Reclaiming the children
B. Programs

<u>Conclusion:</u> Full statement of claim, thesis, conclusion

Reuben made three drafts of his paper before writing the final draft. He participated in a peer review session and a meeting with a writing center tutor, and he conducted an additional interview that reminded him of the recent decrease in crime rates. After getting all this input, Reuben felt that he should rethink the beginning of his paper.

The following is the third draft of his beginning, marked with his notes about what he decided to change.

One event not enough

On April 20, 1999, eighteen-year-old Eric Harris and his friend and cohort, seventeen-year-old Dylan Klebold, opened fire on their fellow classmates and teachers in Littleton, Colorado. For nearly five hours, the two teenaged gunmen methodically killed or wounded thirty-five students and one teacher before ultimately taking their own lives (Breggin 1).

Change this

repeat

The debate over what causes youth violence has escalated in recent years, perhaps reaching an apex after the ~~recent~~ shootings at Columbine High School.

Toll and effect not discussed in paper

~~Those who feel youth violence is a serious issue that~~

~~must be addressed point to such instances as devastat-~~

~~ing testimonies to the toll youth violence can take on~~

~~a nation.~~ The issues surrounding the cause and effect ^s^   *many causes*

of violence in this country are vast and numerous. As

more and more people become aware of the rising   *Not rising now*

problem of youth violence, many are scrambling to

find some institution on which to place the blame.

Some point to the breakdown of two-parent families

as the root cause of juvenile aggression, while others

blame the individual who committed the crime. There

are those who hold the media responsible, while still

others link youth violence to child abuse within the

Not clear: family. There may indeed be many factors that con-
factors?
traced?   tribute to the development of violence in a person, but

nearly each one can be traced back to what a child is   *Qualify more*

exposed to in the home.

This final draft of Reuben's beginning is annotated to point out the improvements he made:

Television newscasts, web sites, and newspapers regularly give reports of

violent actions committed by young people. A headline says "Teen Convicted

of First-Degree Murder." An Internet search produces many items, including a

"fact sheet" titled "Youth Violence: A Public Health Concern." The murderous

Revised paragraph

assault by two teenaged gunmen at Columbine High School in Colorado horrified the nation in April 1999. Even though there has been a recent decrease in

crime, including juvenile crime, youth violence is widely considered to be one

of the most disturbing facts of life in the United States today.

The debate over what causes youth violence has escalated in recent years,

perhaps reaching an apex after the shootings at Columbine. The issues sur-

rounding the causes of violence in this country are vast and numerous. As

More accurate wordings   more and more people become aware of the problem of youth violence, many

are looking for some institution on which to place the blame. Some point to

the breakdown of two-parent families as the root cause of juvenile aggression,

while others blame the individual who committed the crime. There are those

who hold the media responsible, while still others link youth violence to child

abuse within the family. There may indeed be many factors that contribute to

Clearer statement;
better qualification   the development of violence in a person, but probably the strongest influence
of partial thesis

is a child's family life.

Here is Reuben's complete, final paper. The annotations indicate format
requirements and point out Reuben's opening and closing strategies as well as
the ways in which he introduces and cites sources.

As you read this paper, observe how topic sentences and transitional words
help the flow. Notice where the student writer is speaking and think about his
abilities as a host. Consider the support or grounds that he offers for his claim.
Also, decide whether the tone and approach encourage agreement.

1"

½"

Smith 1

Reuben Smith

English 102

Double space

Dr. Michael Eckert

December 1, 2003

Addressing the Issue of

Violence by Young People

center title

Indent five spaces Television newscasts, web sites and newspapers regu-

larly give reports of violent actions committed by young

people. A headline says "Teen Convicted of First-Degree

Murder." An Internet search produces many items, includ-

ing a "fact sheet" titled "Youth Violence: A Public Health

Concern." The murderous assault by two teenaged gunmen

at Columbine High School in Colorado horrified the nation

1" in April 1999. Even though there has been a recent   1"

decrease in crime, including juvenile crime, youth violence

is widely considered to be one of the most disturbing facts

of life in the United States today.

The debate over what causes youth violence has escalated

in recent years, perhaps reaching an apex after the shootings

at Columbine. The issues surrounding the causes of violence

in this country are vast and numerous. As more and more peo-

ple become aware of the problem of youth violence, many are

looking for some institution on which to place the blame.

Some point to the breakdown of two-parent families as the

root cause of juvenile aggression, while others blame the indi-

vidual who committed the crime. There are those who hold the

media responsible, while still others link youth violence to child

abuse within the family. There may indeed be many factors

1"

Introduction of the subject; warrants for the argument

Preview of specific topics; more warrants

Partial statement of thesis or claim

that contribute to the development of violence in a person, but probably the strongest influence is a child's family life.

Some argue that the breakdown of stable, two-parent families is directly responsible for youth violence. They claim that without the dual influence and provision of two parents during a child's early years, youngsters are more likely to turn to destructive substitutes such as gangs, drugs, and violent crime. In the U.S. today the divorce rate continues to mount. In his book <u>Coping in a Dysfunctional Family,</u> Raymond Jamiolkowski reports that "[56] percent of all children in America live or will live in a family that has gone through a divorce. This is more than 10 million people. Sixty percent of all single-parent families are created through divorce" (124). Patrick F. Fagan, a senior policy analyst at the Heritage Foundation in Washington, D.C., points to social science studies that show how "over the past thirty years, the rise in violent teenage crime has paralleled the number of homes abandoned by fathers" (86).

While Jamiolkowski concedes that "a family is not dysfunctional simply because it is headed by a single parent," he observes that single parents face unique pressures and greater demands that might otherwise be shared (120). For example, without the additional support of a husband, a single mother must often juggle multiple jobs on top of rearing her children. This leaves less time to spend with her children and puts a strain on the family. As a result, Fagan concludes, children are left in the care of others or merely left to themselves with weaker feelings of connection to their parents (90). Making a similar point in an interview, a professor of criminal justice at Montgomery College, Vicky Dorworth, said that a major source of serious problems is that too many children are unsupervised.

Still others argue that regardless of the situation at home, the family is being attacked by a barrage of violence in the media. Gruesome acts of hostility that a child may never be exposed to in the home or the community can be vividly

Book title and author introduce quoted material; page number in parentheses before period

Interview

Smith 3

portrayed on the TV screen. In many families today, according to Mortimer B. Zuckerman, the editor-in-chief of U.S. News and World Report, children are spending far too much time in front of the television. Zuckerman explains, "It has become the nation's mom and pop, storyteller, baby sitter, preacher and teacher. Our children watch an astonishing 5,000 hours by the first grade and 19,000 hours by the end of high school—more time than they spend in class" (53). With all the time children spend in front of the tube, many have questioned just how much violence they are being exposed to. Zuckerman says that TV Guide did a study on this in which it looked at ten channels during a regular 18-hour day and was able to identify 1,846 individual acts of violence (53). Whether or not children are becoming more aggressive by viewing violence on TV, it is difficult to dispute that a considerable amount of violence is indeed being portrayed on TV daily.

Holding that children are imitative by nature, many claim that by viewing violent acts played out on television, youngsters could respond to what they see by mimicking it and perceiving it as acceptable behavior. Barbara Hattemer, the president of the National Family Foundation, observes that "two- to six-year-old children cannot evaluate the messages they receive from the media they watch. . . . Six- to twelve-year-olds imitate what they see and hear without fully understanding the consequences of what they are doing" (63). While children may not immediately put what they see into action, what they are exposed to may resurface again down the road. An article from the Ann Arbor News reports that experts have found that "children who are exposed to significant amounts of TV violence at the age of 8 are consistently more likely to commit violent crimes, abuse their spouses, or abuse their children later in life" (Disher).

After observing these statistics, it seems fair to conclude that children growing up in single-parent households and

those exposed to significant amounts of violence are in fact
more likely to turn to destructive crime. However, these factors
alone are not necessary requisites for juvenile violence.
Experts agree that there are many facets to this complex
problem. Writes Madeline Levine in her book <u>Viewing Violence:</u>

> The fact remains that no one theory of aggression
> is able to make sense of all acts of aggression.
> Furthermore, no individual factor, by itself, is a
> good predictor of aggressive behavior. When look-
> ing at the factors that contribute to aggression we
> would do well to think in terms of "all the above"
> rather than "either/or." (53)

The question then might be asked: How many of these contributing factors are strengthened or nullified by the influence of a child's parents? How pivotal is the role of
parenting in the development of juvenile violence? Might the
example set by parents in the home be either one of the
greatest weapons against violence or one of the strongest
enforcements of it?

Before moving on, it is important to define a couple of
key terms. In <u>Coping in a Dysfunctional Family,</u> Raymond
Jamiolkowski provides a definition: "A dysfunctional family
is one that fails to meet the basic needs of its members.
These basic needs are survival, safety and security, love and
belonging, self-esteem, growth, and development of skills
needed for independent living" (120). He goes on to say
that the structure of a family does not determine dysfunc-
tion. Regardless of the family dynamics, Jamiolkowski
claims that most obstacles can be overcome in a functional
family where each member's needs are being met (123). In
this respect, dysfunctional or poor parenting will be defined
as parental behavior that hinders a child's basic needs.
Whether it manifests itself in the form of neglect, physical

*Four lines or more
quoted; indented; no
quotation marks; page
number in parentheses
after period*

*Source quoted and
cited; then paraphrased
and cited*

or emotional abuse, brutal discipline or no discipline at all, poor parenting can greatly intensify the effects of violent influences from the outside.

Christina Crawford, who wrote the poignant autobiography Mommie Dearest in 1978, knows firsthand the pain caused by an abusive parent. In her recent book entitled No Safe Place, Crawford speaks of her own childhood experience:

> My body was physically hurt, punished, and
> ridiculed. My mind was programmed for servitude
> and made susceptible to manipulation. . . .
> Instead of being protected, guided, and loved, I
> was taught to be ashamed, alone, frightened, sus-
> picious, enraged, and empty, that I didn't belong
> anywhere and that nothing belonged to me. . . . As
> a small child, I was beaten with objects, threat-
> ened, deprived of basic necessities such as food
> and sleep, ignored, abandoned, disrespected, sex-
> ualized, and manipulated . . . convinced that I was
> a fundamentally flawed human being and that
> probably nothing would set me right. (12)

Crawford explains how she would regularly engage in violent activities such as schoolyard fistfights and verbal shouting matches as a child. Because physical and emotional abuse was the only life she knew at home, her behavior became a reflection of this (3). Asserting that violence begets vio-lence, Crawford predicts that the epidemic of violence in this country will continue to surge out of control: "If vio-lence within the family is not addressed, we as a society will never be able to stop the violence in streets [and] between races, nations, and religions, which creates the feeling that there is no safe place for anyone, anywhere, anytime" (10).

Extensive research has been conducted in order to confirm the correlation between parental violence and youth violence. In his essay "Family Violence Causes Youth Violence," Terence P. Thornberry, a professor, highlights the results of an ongoing study of delinquency called The Rochester Youth Development Study. In this study, young students from seventh to twelfth grade were interviewed along with their primary caretakers every six months. They were asked to personally report any involvement in delin-quent behavior defined under six categories ranging from simple assault to armed robbery. Thornberry explains that information from schools, police, social services, and other relevant agencies was also taken into account during the study (109). According to the results, children who had experienced multiple forms of family violence—ranging from violence between parents to violence against the child or another sibling—were much more likely to turn to violent crime:

> While 38 percent of the youngsters from non-vio-lent families reported involvement in violent youth delinquency, this rate increased to 60 percent for youngsters whose family engaged in one of these forms of violence, to 73 percent for those exposed to two forms of family violence, and further increased to 78 percent for adolescents exposed to all three forms of family violence. (Thornberry 111)

Drastic instances of physical and verbal abuse are not the only sort of harm parents can inflict upon their chil-dren. Many claim that the act of neglecting children is far more common than overt abuse and can have just as destructive results. John J. Dilulio Jr., a professor of politics and public affairs at Princeton University, claims that many children live in a state of moral poverty without the pres-ence of positive adult influence. Dilulio says, "Moral poverty is the poverty of being without loving, capable, responsible

Smith 7

Material omitted;
pages given

adults who teach you right from wrong. . . . It is the poverty of growing up in the virtual absence of people who teach morality by their everyday example . . ." (111–112).

As has already been stated, parental neglect can do much to push children toward violent activity. A family does not need to be broken to be neglectful. Two-parent families can be just as neglectful to children. Delbert S. Elliott is the director of the Institute of Behavioral Science's Center for the Study and Prevention of Violence at the University of Colorado in Boulder. Writes Elliott:

> Even if violence is not modeled in the home, research suggests that the absence of effective social bonds and control, together with failure of parents to teach (and children to internalize) conventional norms and values, puts children at risk of later violence. In fact, parental neglect may have an even stronger effect than the physical abuse on later violence, as it appears to be more damaging to the subsequent course of youth development and involves three times as many youth. (85)

Considering all this, it is important to keep in mind that parents have a far greater responsibility than simply paying attention to their children and avoiding maltreatment. A loving, healthy, and functional family environment is one in which each child's primary needs are met within the home. "Needs, however," writes Jamiolkowski on the subject, "are not the same as wants, wishes, or desires. Being a part of a family means cooperating so that every member is able to have his needs fulfilled" (3). Jamiolkowski stresses the importance of active, loving parenting in developing healthy children (3–4).

Even though the harmful effects of physical abuse have been clearly demonstrated, experts agree that functional parenting requires enforcing some form of constructive

Smith 8

discipline. While there is considerable disagreement as to what this discipline ought to look like specifically, experts in child development emphasize the need for caring, rational discipline that is bathed in communication, respect, and love. James Dobson, who holds a Ph.D. in child development and wrote the best-selling book <u>The New Dare to Discipline,</u> comments on the need for active parents who will love their children enough to train them:

> Children thrive best in an atmosphere of genuine love undergirded by reasonable, consistent discipline. In a day of widespread drug usage, immorality, sexually transmitted diseases, vandalism, and violence, we must not depend on hope and luck to fashion the critical attitudes we value in our children. (7)

First statement of conclusion and claim

Parents who do not lovingly work to foster their child's physical, emotional, and moral well-being will only worsen the ever-growing problem of youth delinquency in this nation. If in fact parents do have a lasting impact on their children's lives for the better or for the worse, it seems the logical first step in undermining the potency of juvenile violence would be to strengthen and improve the family. This calls for a change in how seriously a person views the role of parenting. In his book <u>Reclaiming Our Children,</u> Peter R. Breggin writes: "Reclaiming our children and rescuing them from violence and despair requires a change of heart not in our children but in ourselves. Our children will then manifest the effect of our good efforts in their own improved lives" (282). Breggin drives home the point that parents must place a higher priority on nurturing the children they bring into this world:

> Our children need more of us—our unconditional love and unambiguous caring, our serious attention,

Smith 9

our moral leadership, our precious time, our economic resources. Whether we are parents, teachers,
counselors, ministers, police officers, mentors,
politicians, government administrators, or leaders of
great corporations and universities, we must make
children a higher priority in our personal lives and in
our social and economic policies. (283)

These arguments are based on the warrant that children
learn primarily by example; the qualities to which children
are exposed during their early years of development will
usually be reflected in their lives later on.

On the positive side, Criminal Justice Professor Dorworth
said that she believes youth violence has been reduced as
the result of programs that she hopes will continue. She
points to an increase in after-school activities for unsupervised children. She also said that many agencies and
groups are doing more to encourage good parenting.

Conclusion; claim; thesis

If poor parenting marked by physical, emotional, and neglectful maltreatment is a compelling factor of youth violence,
then it stands to reason that good parenting marked by loving
and supportive nourishment can do much to prevent it. This
world into which children are born is not a perfect one, and no
parents can hope to protect their children from every violent
influence to which they may be exposed. No matter how nourishing and active parents may be in the lives of their children,
they will never be able to keep their lives entirely untouched by
the scope of violence. In an aggressive world of broken families, media violence, and school shootings, it is crucial that a

Conclusion

child has the guidance of an involved parent to help him or
her sort out these influences and respond to them in a
healthy way. Though the negative effects of these factors can
be strong, a stronger bond of family love can greatly reduce
the destructive forces of violence.

Smith 10

Works Cited

book

Breggin, Peter R. <u>Reclaiming Our Children</u>. Cambridge, MA:
    Perseus Books, 2000.

Crawford, Christina. <u>No Safe Place</u>. New York: Station Hill,
    1994.

work in a collection

Dilulio, John J., Jr. "A Lack of Moral Guidance Causes Juve-
    nile Crime and Violence." <u>Juvenile Crime: Opposing</u>
    <u>Viewpoints</u>. Ed. A. E. Sadler and Scott Barbour. San
    Diego: Greenhaven, 1997. 107–116.

article in a database

Disher, Michael J. "Opinion: Other Voices: Effect of TV Violence
    Has Been Clearly Demonstrated." <u>Ann Arbor News</u> 29
    Dec. 1995: A8. 25 Oct. 2000 <http://www.pierian-
    press.net/databases/cgi-bin/srvdoc.asp?doc>.

Dobson, James. <u>The New Dare to Discipline</u>. Wheaton, IL:
    Tyndale House Publishers, Inc., 1992.

interview

Dorworth, Vicky. Telephone interview. 20 Nov. 2000.

Elliott, Delbert S. "Environmental Factors Contribute to
    Juvenile Crime and Violence." <u>Juvenile Crime: Oppos-
    ing Viewpoints</u>. Ed. A. E. Sadler and Scott Barbour. San
    Diego: Greenhaven, 1997. 83–89.

Fagan, Patrick F. "The Breakdown of Families Causes Vio-
    lence." <u>Violence: Opposing Viewpoints</u>. Ed. Scott Bar-
    bour and Karen Swisher. San Diego: Greenhaven, 1996.
    85–95.

One space

Hattemer, Barbara. "Violence in the Media Causes Youth
    Violence." <u>Violence: Opposing Viewpoints</u>. Ed. Scott
    Barbour and Karen Swisher. San Diego: Greenhaven,
    1996. 62–69.

Indent five spaces

Jamiolkowski, Raymond M. <u>Coping in a Dysfunctional Family</u>.
    New York: Rosen, 1998.

Levine, Madeline. <u>Viewing Violence</u>. New York: Doubleday,
    1996.

Smith 11

Thornberry, Terence P. "Family Violence Causes Youth Violence." <u>Violence: Opposing Viewpoints</u>. Ed. Scott Barbour and Karen Swisher. San Diego: Greenhaven, 1996.
108–112.

"Youth Violence: A Public Health Concern." CSVP Fact Sheet
No. 9. <u>Center for the Study and Prevention of Violence</u>.
1998. 30 Nov. 2000 <http://www.colorado.edu/cspv/
factsheets/factsheet9.html>.

Zuckerman, Mortimer B. "Television Violence Contributes to
Juvenile Crime." <u>Juvenile Crime: Opposing Viewpoints</u>.
Ed. A. E. Sadler and Scott Barbour. San Diego: Green-
haven, 1997. 52–55.

MLA and APA Documentation Styles

Modern Language Association Style

Careful documentation and a complete works-cited list provide readers with full information on sources cited in the paper. (See The Logic of MLA Style, Chapter 14, page 570 for information on in-text citations.)

To be useful to readers, citations must be clear and consistent. Therefore, very specific rules of documentation have been devised and must be applied.

Quick Reference

Using the following formats, begin preparing your works-cited entries as soon as you begin taking notes. Use a new 3- by 5-inch card for each entry or create a works-cited file on your computer.

❑ A book by one author

Author's last name, first name. *Book title.* Additional information.
City of publication: Publishing company, publication date.

❑ An article by one author

Author's last name, first name. "Article title." *Periodical title* Date: inclusive pages.

Guidelines for preparing entries for other types of sources appear on the pages that follow.

Citation Format

Most researched writing in English and other humanities courses uses the documentation format described in Joseph Gibaldi's *MLA [Modern Language Association] Handbook for Writers of Research Papers,* sixth edition (New York: MLA, 2003). This documentation format, known as MLA style, is simple, clear, and widely accepted.

Other subjects, however, may require other styles of documentation, so always ask instructors, especially in nonhumanities courses, whether MLA style is acceptable. In addition to the *MLA Handbook,* a number of other style guides are frequently used.

FREQUENTLY USED STYLE GUIDES

The Chicago Manual of Style. 14th ed. Chicago: U of Chicago P, 1993.

Publication Manual of the American Psychological Association. 5th ed. Washington: APA, 2001.

Scientific Style and Format: The CBE [Council of Biology Editors] Manual for Authors, Editors, and Publishers. 6th ed. Chicago: Cambridge UP, 1994.

Turabian, Kate L. *A Manual for Writers of Term Papers, Theses, and Dissertations.* Rev. John Grossman and Alice Bennett. 6th ed. Chicago: U of Chicago P, 1996.

The most widely used of these alternate styles is that of the American Psychological Association (APA), often the preferred style for writing in the social sciences. Guidelines for using APA style appear later in the appendix.

Accuracy and Completeness

Because works-cited entries direct readers to sources used in researched writing, they must be as complete as possible and presented in a consistent and recognizable format. If the following guidelines do not cover a source you want to use, consult the *MLA Handbook.*

To complete a citation, leaf through the following samples until you find the one that most closely corresponds to your source; be aware that some sources will require you to combine information from several samples according to the guidelines that follow. Prepare your citations using 3- by 5-inch index cards (one citation per card), sheets of paper, or a computer.

If you prepare citations on a computer, use a separate file with an easily recognizable name (for example, *paper2.cit, research.cit,* or *aviation.cit*). Since a citation file will remain comparatively small, you can retrieve it quickly, add to it and delete from it, and then append the complete works-cited file to the final draft of your paper.

Whichever pattern you choose—index card, paper, or computer—record complete and accurate citations. If you do not record full information when you first use a source, you will have to return to it at a later—and potentially less convenient—time to supply the missing information.

INFORMATION FOR MLA CITATIONS

MLA citations present information in an established order. When combining forms (to list a translation of a second edition, for example), follow these guidelines to determine the order of information:

1. *Author(s).* Use the name or names with the spelling and order shown on the title page of a book or on the first page of an article, without degrees, titles, or affiliations. If no author (individual or organization) is named, list the work by title in the works-cited entry.

2. *Title.* List titles from part to whole: the title of an essay (the part) before the book (the whole), the title of an article before the periodical title, an episode before the program, or a song before the compact disc. Use complete titles, including subtitles, no matter how long they are.

3. *Additional information.* In the order noted next, include any of the following information listed on the title page of the book or on the first page of an article: editor, translator, compiler, edition number, volume number, or name of series.

4. *Facts of publication.* For a book, find the publisher's name and the place of publication on the title page and the date of publication on the copyright page (immediately following the title page). Use the publisher's name in abbreviated form (numerous samples are present throughout the appendix), use the first city listed if more than one is given, and use the most recent date shown. When a city is outside the United States, include an abbreviation for the country, if necessary for clarity. For a periodical, find the volume number, issue number, and date on the masthead (at the top of the first page of a newspaper or within the first few pages in a journal or magazine, often in combination with the table of contents).

5. *Page numbers.* When citing a part of a book or an article, provide inclusive page numbers without page abbreviations. Record inclusive page numbers from one to ninety-nine in full form (8–12, 33–39, 68–73); in-

MLA STYLE

clusive numbers of one hundred or higher require at least the last two digits and any other digits needed for clarity (100–02, 120–36, 193–206).

FORMAT FOR MLA CITATIONS

MLA citations follow these general formatting guidelines:

- Begin the first line of each entry at the left margin and indent subsequent lines one-half inch (five spaces).
- Invert the author's name so that it appears with the last name first (to alphabetize easily). If sources are coauthored, list additional authors' names in normal, first-last order.
- Italicize or underline titles of full-length works (the meaning is the same), but do not underline the period that follows the title. Be consistent throughout the paper.
- Separate major sections of entries (author, title, and publication information) with periods and one space, not two. When other forms of end punctuation are used (when titles end with question marks or exclamation points, for example), the period may be omitted.
- Double-space all entries; do not insert additional space between entries.

ANNOTATIONS

Annotations are sometimes used to clarify for readers the value of sources or to provide additional information. Typically, these comments assess the quality of the source, describe the source's condition or availability, or provide additional clarification. In most student writing, annotations usually evaluate a source's value for the research project by highlighting its special features.

Present an annotation in one or more complete sentences. It follows the citation's closing period and retains the citation's indention pattern and line spacing, as in this sample.

> National Commission on Excellence in Education. *A Nation at Risk: The Imperative for Educational Reform.* Washington: GPO, 1983. With its aggressively critical tone, this small publication by the NCEE launched the educational reform movement that is affecting our schools today.

Books

Book by one author   Monmonier, Mark. *Air Apparent: How Meteorologists Learned to Map, Predict, and Dramatize Weather.* Chicago: U of Chicago P, 1999.

MLA STYLE

(The letters *U* and *P*, without periods, abbreviate *University* and *Press*.)

Book by two or more authors Authors' names appear in the order in which they are presented on the title page, which may or may not be alphabetical. A comma follows the initial author's first name; second and third authors' names appear in normal order.

Kegley, Charles W., and Gregory A. Raymond. *How Nations Make Peace.* New York: St. Martin's, 1999.

When a book has four or more authors, include only the first author's name in full form; substitute *et al.* (meaning "and others," not italicized), for the names of additional authors.

Tucker, Susan Martin, et al. *Patient Care Standards: Collaborative Planning and Nursing Interventions.* 7th ed. St. Louis: Mosby, 2000.

Book with no author When no author is named, list the work by title. Alphabetize books listed by title using the first important word of the title, not the articles *a, an,* or *the.*

United Press International Stylebook: The Authoritative Handbook for Writers, Editors, and News Directors. 3rd ed. Lincolnwood: Natl. Textbook, 1992.

(Note that *national* is abbreviated when it is part of a publisher's name.)

Multiple works by the same author When citing multiple works by the same author, present the first citation completely. Subsequent entries, alphabetized by title, are introduced by three hyphens and a period. Coauthored works require full names and are alphabetized after those with single authors.

Ehrenreich, Barbara. "Barefoot, Pregnant, and Ready to Fight." *Time* 8 May 2000: 62.

---. "Who Needs Men? Addressing the Prospect of a Matrilinear Millennium." Interview. With Lionel Tiger. *Harper's* June 1999: 33–46.

Ehrenreich, Barbara, Elizabeth Hess, and Gloria Jacobs. *Re-Making Love: The Feminization of Sex.* Garden City: Anchor-Doubleday, 1986.

(Notice that the publisher of the last selection includes a two-part name: the imprint and the major publisher; see An Imprint, page 602, for an additional sample).

Book with an organization as author   When an organization is both the author and the publisher, present the name completely in the author position and use an abbreviation in the publisher position.

> American Psychological Association. *Publication Manual of the American Psychological Association.* 5th ed. Washington: APA, 2001.

Edition other than the first   The edition number, noted on the title page, follows the title of the book. When a book also has an editor, translator, or compiler, the edition number follows that information. Edition numbers are presented in numeral-abbreviation form (2nd, 3rd, 4th).

> Terril, Richard J. *World Criminal Justice Systems: A Survey.* 4th ed. Cincinnati: Anderson, 1999.

Reprint   A reprint, a newly printed but unaltered version of a book, is identified as such on the title page or copyright page. The original publication date precedes the facts of publication, and the date of the reprinted edition follows the publisher's name.

> Beck, Theodric Romeyo. *Elements of Medical Jurisprudence.* 1823. Union: Lawbook Exchange, 1997.

Multivolume work   A multivolume work may have one title, or it may have a comprehensive title for the complete work and separate titles for each volume. When you use the entire set of volumes, use the collective title and note the number of volumes. If volumes are published over several years, provide inclusive dates (2000–02); if the work is still in progress, include the earliest date, a hyphen, one space, and the closing period (1999–.).

> *Perspectives on Western Art: Source Documents and Readings from the Renaissance to the 1970s.* Ed. Linnea H. Wren. 2 vols. New York: Icon-Harper, 1994.

To emphasize a single volume, first cite the volume as a separate book. Then add the volume number, the collection title, and the total number of volumes.

> Roberts, J. M. *The Age of Revolution.* New York: Oxford UP, 1999. Vol. 7 of *The Illustrated History of the World.* 10 vols.

Work in a collection   To cite a work in a collection, include the name of the selection's author, the title of the specific selection (appropriately punctuated), the collection title, publication facts, and the inclusive page numbers for the selection (without page abbreviations). To cite more than one selection from the collection, prepare separate citations (see Multiple Selections from the Same Collection, below).

> McKnight, Richard. "Spirituality in the Workplace." *Transforming Work.* Ed. John D. Adams. 2nd ed. New York: Miles River, 1998. 160–78.

Previously published work in a collection   To indicate that a selection has been previously published, begin the citation with original facts of publication. *Rpt.,* meaning "reprinted," begins the second part of the citation, which includes information about the source you have used.

> Wallace, Mike. "Mickey Mouse History: Portraying the Past at Disney World." *Radical History Review* 32 (1985): 33–55. Rpt. in *Customs in Conflict: The Anthology of a Changing World.* Ed. Frank Manning and Jean-Marc Philbert. Peterborough, ON: Broadview, 1990. 304–32.

Multiple selections from the same collection   To cite several selections from the same collection, prepare a citation for the complete work—beginning either with the editor's name or with the collection title. Additional references begin with the author of the individual selection and its title. However, instead of providing full publication information, include the editor's name or a shortened version of the title; provide inclusive page numbers for the selection. Notice that all citations are alphabetized.

> Colton, Catherine A. "Alice Walker's Womanist Magic: The Conjure Woman as Rhetor." Dieke 33–44.
>
> Dieke, Ikenna, ed. *Critical Essays on Alice Walker.* Westport: Greenwood, 1999.
>
> Kelly, Erna. "A Matter of Focus: Men in the Margins of Alice Walker's Fiction." Dieke 171–83.

Article in an encyclopedia or other reference work   Use an author's name when it is available. If only initials are listed with the article, match them with the name from the list of contributors. Well-known reference books require no information other than the title, edition number (if any), and date. Citations for less well-known or recently published reference works include full publication information. Page numbers are not needed when a reference work is arranged alphabetically.

> Abrams, Richard M. "Theodore Roosevelt." *The Presidents: A Reference History.* Ed. Henry F. Graff. 2nd ed. New York: Scribner's, 1996. 325–46.

(Because the articles on presidents are arranged chronologically, not alphabetically, page numbers are required.)

> Angermüller, Rudolph. "Salieri, Antonio." *The New Grove Dictionary of Music and Musicians.* 1980 ed.

(This twenty-volume set is extremely well known and consequently needs no publication information.)

When no author's name or initials appear with an article, begin with the title, reproduced to match the pattern in the reference book. Other principles remain the same.

> "Flatbed Scanner." *The GATF [Graphic Arts Technology Foundation] Encyclopedia of Graphic Communication.* Ed. Frank J. Romano. Upper Saddle River: Prentice, 1998.

(Brackets are used to enclose the full name of the organization.)

Work in a series The name of a series (a collection of books related to the same subject, genre, time period, and so on) is typically found on a book's title page and should be included just before the publishing information. Abbreviate the word *Series* (Ser.) if it is part of the series title.

> Morley, Carolyn. *Transformation, Miracles, and Mischief: The Mountain Priest Plays of Kyogen.* Cornell East Asia Ser. Ithaca: Cornell UP, 1993.

When a volume in a series is numbered, include both the series name and the number, followed by a period.

> Cather, Willa. *My Antonia.* Everyman's Library 228. New York: Knopf, 1996.

Imprint An imprint is a specialized division of a larger publishing company. When an imprint name and a publisher name both appear on the title page, list them together (imprint name first), separated by a hyphen and no additional spaces.

> Jardine, Lisa. *Ingenious Pursuits: Building the Scientific Revolution.* New York: Talese-Doubleday, 1999.

(Nan A. Talese is the imprint, which is shortened to *Talese*; Doubleday is the publisher.)

Translation A translator's name must always be included in a citation for a translated work because he or she prepared the version that you read. To emphasize the original work (the most common pattern), place the abbreviation *Trans.* (for "translated by," not italicized) and the translator's name after the title (but following editors' names, if the translator translated the entire work).

> Esquivel, Laura. *Like Water for Chocolate: A Novel in Monthly Installments, with Recipes, Romances, and Home Remedies.* Trans. Carol Christensen and Thomas Christensen. New York: Doubleday, 1992.

If selections within a collection are translated by different people, then each translator's name should follow the appropriate selection.

Kiš, Danilo. "Dogs and Books." Trans. Duška Mikic-Mitchell. *The Oxford Book of Jewish Stories.* Ed. Ilan Stavans. New York: Oxford UP, 1998. 325–35.

(This citation indicates that Duška Mikic-Mitchell translated only "Dogs and Books"; other selections in the collection were, by implication, translated by other people.)

CONGRESSIONAL RECORD

Government Document   A citation for *Congressional Record* is exceedingly brief: the italicized and abbreviated title, *Cong. Rec.,* the date (presented in day-month-year order), and the page number. Page numbers used alone indicate Senate records; page numbers preceded by an *H* indicate records from the House of Representatives.

Cong. Rec. 18 May 1995: 6931.

(This simple citation for a Senate record describes the introduction of the Telecommunication and Deregulation Act of 1995.)

Cong. Rec. 7 Oct. 1994: H11251.

(Note the page reference, with the H indicating that the cited summary, titled "Appropriations for the Bureau of Land Management [State by State]," was part of House records.)

COMMITTEE, COMMISSION, DEPARTMENT

Information to describe a government document is generally presented in this order: (1) country, state, province, or county; (2) government official, governing body, sponsoring department, commission, center, ministry, or agency; (3) office, bureau, or committee; (4) the title of the publication, italicized; (5) if appropriate, the author of the document, the number and session of Congress, the kind and number of the document; (6) the city of publication, the publisher, and the date.

When citing more than one work from the same government or agency, use three hyphens and a period to substitute for identical elements.

United States. Cong. Senate. Committee on Aging. *Hearing.* 101st Cong., 1st sess. 1989. Washington: GPO, 1990.

---. Dept. of Education. *Alcohol, Other Drugs, and College: A Parent's Guide.* Washington: GPO, 2000.

---. ---. *School Involvement in Early Childhood.* By Donna Hinkle. Washington: GPO, 2000.

(The Government Printing Office, the publisher of most federal documents, is abbreviated to save space. The two sets of hyphens in the last citation indicate that it was also prepared by the United States Department of Education.)

Preface, introduction, foreword, epilogue, or afterword To cite material that is separate from the primary text of a book, begin with the name of the person who wrote the separate material, an assigned title (if applicable) in quotation marks, a descriptive title for the part used (capitalized but not punctuated), the title of the book, the name of the book's author (introduced with *By*, not italicized), publication facts, and inclusive page numbers for the separate material. Note that most prefatory or introductory material is paged using lowercase roman numerals.

Dabney, Lewis M. "Edmund Wilson and *The Sixties.*" Introduction. *The Sixties: The Last Journal, 1960–1972.* By Edmund Wilson. New York: Farrar, 1993. xxi–xlvii.

Finnegan, William. Epilogue. *Crossing the Line: A Year in the Land of Apartheid.* New York: Harper, 1986. 401–09.

Pamphlet When a pamphlet contains clear and complete information, it is cited like a book. When information is missing, use these abbreviations: *N.p.* for "No place of publication," *n.p.* for "no publisher," *n.d.* for "no date," and *N. pag.* (with a space between the abbreviations) for "no page."

America's Cup? The Sober Truth about Alcohol and Boating. Alexandria: Boat/U.S., n.d.

Lyme Disease and Related Disorders. Groton: Pfizer, 2000.

Dissertation A citation for an unpublished dissertation begins with the author's name, the dissertation title in quotation marks, the abbreviation *Diss.* (not italicized), the name of the degree-granting school (with *University* abbreviated), and the date.

Lehner, Luis. "Gravitational Radiation from Black Hole Spacetimes." Diss. U of Pittsburgh, 1998.

A published dissertation is a book and should be presented as such. However, include dissertation information between the title and the facts of publication.

Salzman, Lisa. *Anselm Kiefer and Art after Auschwitz.* Diss. Harvard U, 1994. New York: Cambridge UP, 1999.

Sacred writings A citation for a sacred writing follows a pattern similar to that of any other book, with several notable variations. First, titles of sacred writings (the parts or the whole) are neither placed in quotation marks nor italicized; they are capitalized only. Second, full facts of publication are not required for traditional editions. When appropriate, include additional information according to the guidelines for the element.

The Bhagavad Gita. Trans. Juan Mascaró. New York: Penguin, 1962.

(Include translators when appropriate.)

The Holy Bible.

(This citation is for the King James version of the Bible, the traditional edition.)

The New Oxford Annotated Bible. Ed. Herbert G. May and Bruce M. Metzger. Rev. Standard Version. New York: Oxford UP, 1973.

(This citation provides full information, highlighting a version other than the King James and the editorial work that it includes.)

Periodicals

Article in a monthly magazine To cite an article in a monthly magazine, include the author's name, the article's title in quotation marks, the magazine's name (italicized), the month (abbreviated) and year, and the inclusive pages of the article (without page abbreviations).

Furrow, Bryant. "The Uses of Crying and Begging." *Natural History* Oct. 2000: 62–67.

(Note that the period comes before the closing quotation marks of the article's title, that one space [but no punctuation] separates the periodical title and the date, and that a colon separates the date and the pages.)

Article in a weekly magazine A citation for an article in a weekly magazine is identical to that for a monthly magazine, with one exception: the publication date is presented in more detailed form, in day-month-year order (with the month abbreviated).

Gest, Ted. "Fixing Your School." *U.S. News and World Report* 9 Oct. 2000: 65–67.

(Even though magazines often use special typography, as in *U.S. News & World Report*, such material is standardized in citations.)

Article in a journal with continuous paging A journal with continuous paging numbers issues sequentially for the entire year. For this kind of journal, place the volume number after the journal title, identify the year in parentheses, follow it with a colon, and then list page numbers.

> Sherman, Aurora, Brian de Vries, and Jennifer E. Lansford. "Friend-
> ship in Childhood and Adulthood: Lessons Across the Life
> Span." *The International Journal of Aging and Human Develop-
> ment* 51 (2000): 31–51.

Article in a journal with separate paging For a journal that pages each issue separately, follow the volume number with a period and the issue number (without spaces).

> Graves, Dan. "Multiculturalism and the Choral Canon: 1975–2000."
> *Choral Journal* 41.2 (2000): 37–44.

Article in a newspaper A citation for a newspaper resembles that for a magazine: it includes the author's name, article title (in quotation marks), newspaper title (italicized), the date (in day-month-year order, followed by a colon), and inclusive pages.

However, when a newspaper has editions (*morning, evening, national*), they must be identified. After the year, place a comma and describe the edition, abbreviating common words.

When sections of a newspaper are designated by letters, place the section letter with the page number, without a space (*A22, C3, F11*). If sections are indicated by numerals, place a comma after the date or edition (rather than a colon), include the abbreviation *sec.* (not italicized), the section number, a colon, a space, and the page number (*sec. 1: 22, sec. 3: 2, sec. 5: 17*).

> Eckstrom, Kevin. "A Year of Front-Page Faith." *Washington Post* 30
> Dec. 2000: B9.

When an article continues in a later part of the paper, indicate the initial page, use a comma, and then add the subsequent page. If the article appears on more than three separated pages, list the initial page, followed by a plus sign (*22+, A17+, sec. 2: 9+*).

Weekly newspapers are cited just like daily newspapers.

> Zeleny, Jeff. "Election Reform Is Popular, Political—and Pricey."
> *Chicago Tribune* 17 Dec. 2000, *sec.* 2: 1+.

Editorial The citation for an editorial resembles that for a magazine or newspaper article, with one exception: the word *Editorial* (not italicized), with a period, follows the title of the essay.

Herbert, Bob. "Addicted to Guns." Editorial. *New York Times* 1 Jan.
2001, natl. ed.: A17.

Letter to the editor   A letter to the editor follows a very simple format. Include the author's
name, the word *Letter* (not italicized), the name of the publication (magazine, journal, or newspaper), and appropriate facts of publication. Do
not record descriptive, attention-getting titles that publications, not authors, supply.

Hancock, Trevor. Letter. *Harper's* Jan. 2001: 6.

**("Flying Too High" served as the functional title of this letter to the
editor. It is not used in the citation.)**

Review   A citation for a review begins with the author's name and the title of the
review (if one is provided). The abbreviation *Rev.* of (not italicized) follows, with the name of the book, film, recording, performance, product,
or whatever is being reviewed, followed by clarifying information. Publication information ends the citation, incorporating elements required
for different kinds of sources.

Gleiberman, Owen. "The High Drama." Rev. of *Traffic*, dir. Steven
Soderbergh. Perf. Benicio Del Toro, Catherine Zeta-Jones, Don
Cheadle, and Michael Douglas. *Entertainment Weekly* 5 Jan.
2001: 45–46.

Nonprint Sources

Finding documentation information for nonprint sources is usually
easy but sometimes requires ingenuity. Compact disc booklets provide
copyright dates and special information. Printed programs for speeches
or syllabuses for course lectures provide names, titles, locations, and
dates. Information about films or television programs can be obtained
from opening or closing credits or from reference books such as *Facts
on File* or web sites such as *All-Movie Guide* (<http://allmovie.com>).
If you have difficulty finding the information to document nonprint
sources clearly, ask your instructor or a librarian for help.

Lecture or speech   A citation for a formal lecture or speech includes the speaker's name,
the title of the presentation (in quotation marks), the name of the lecture
or speaker series (if applicable), the location of the speech (convention,
meeting, university, library, meeting hall), the city, and the date in day-
month-year order.

Johnson, Neil. "Living on the Edge of Chaos." Christmas Lectures. Royal Inst. London, 29 Dec. 1999.

Mitten, David M. "Greek Art and Architecture in the West: Southern Italy, Sicily, and Campania." Class lecture. Harvard University. Cambridge, 15 May 1989.

(For class lectures, provide as much of this information as possible: speaker, title of lecture in quotation marks, a descriptive title, the school, the city, and the date.)

Nixon, Richard. Resignation Speech. White House. Washington, 8 Aug. 1974.

Work of art   When an artist titles his or her own work, include this information: artist's name; the title (italicized); the museum, gallery, or collection where the work of art is housed; and the city (and country if needed for clarity).

Cézanne, Paul. *Houses along a Road.* The Hermitage, St. Petersburg, Russia.

When an artist has not titled a work, use the title that art historians have given to it (without quotation marks), followed by a brief description of the work. The rest of the citation is the same.

Madonna and Child with Cherubim. Bas-relief in marble. Vatican Library, Vatican City.

Map, graph, table, or chart   A map, graph, table, or chart is treated like a book. If known, include the name of the author, artist, designer, scientist, person, or group responsible for the map, graph, table, or chart. Then include the title (italicized), followed by a separately punctuated descriptive title. Also include any other necessary information.

Pope, C. Arden. *Children's Respiratory Hospital Admissions.* Graph. "The Next Battle over Clean Air." By Hillary J. Johnson. *Rolling Stone* 18 Jan. 2001: 49.

Cartoon   Begin with the cartoonist's name, the title of the cartoon in quotation marks, and the word *Cartoon* (not italicized), followed by a period. Then include the citation information required for the source.

Davis, Jack, and Stan Hart. "Groan with the Wind." Cartoon. *Mad* Jan. 1991: 42–47.

(This cartoon appeared in a monthly magazine.)

Film   To cite a film as a complete work, include the title (italicized), the director (noted by the abbreviation *Dir.,* not italicized), the studio, and the date of release. If you include other people's contributions, do so after the director's name by using brief phrases (*Screenplay by, Original score by*) or abbreviations (*Perf.* for "performed by," *Prod.* for "produced by") to clarify their roles. Indicate a nonfilm format—VHS, DVD, or laserdisc—before the studio name. If a film is released by two studios, include both names, separated by a hyphen.

Fight Club. Dir. David Fincher. Perf. Brad Pitt, Edward Norton, and
   Helena Bonham Carter. Regency-20th Century Fox, 1999.

(Regency and 20th Century Fox co-released the film.)

To emphasize the contribution of an individual (rather than the film as a whole), place the person's name first, followed by a comma and a descriptive title (beginning with a lowercase letter). The rest of the citation follows normal patterns.

Coppola, Francis Ford, dir. *Apocalypse Now.* Perf. Martin Sheen, Mar-
   lon Brando, and Robert Duvall. United Artists, 1979. Suggested
   by Joseph Conrad's *Heart of Darkness.*

"Follow the White Rabbit and Take the Red Pills." *The Matrix.* Dir.
   Andy Wachowski and Larry Wachowski. Perf. Keanu Reeves,
   Carrie-Anne Moss, and Laurence Fishburne. DVD. Warner, 1999.

(This citation is for a special feature on a DVD.)

Television broadcast List a regular program by the title (italicized), the network (CBS, CNN, Fox), the local station (including both the call letters and the city, separated by a comma), and the broadcast date (in day-month-year order).

Include other people's contributions after the program title, using brief phrases (*Written by, Hosted by*) or abbreviations (*Perf.* for "performed by," *Prod.* for "produced by") to clarify their roles.

X-Files. Perf. Gillian Anderson and David Duchovny. Fox. WXIN, Indianapolis. 20 June 1999.

To cite a single episode of an ongoing program, include the name of the episode in quotation marks before the program's title. Other elements are presented in the same order as used for a regular program.

"Coffee and Commitment." *Will and Grace.* Perf. Eric McCormack,
   Debra Messing, Sean Hayes, and Megan Mullally. NBC. WTHR,
   Indianapolis. 4 Jan. 2001.

List special programs by title, followed by traditional descriptive information. If a special program is part of a series (for example, Hallmark Hall of Fame, Great Performances, or American Playhouse), include the series name without quotation marks or italics immediately preceding the name of the network.

The Sleeping Beauty. Composed by Peter Ilich Tchaikovsky. Choreographed by Marius Petipa. Perf. Viviana Durante and Zoltan Solymosi. Great Performances. PBS. WFYI, Indianapolis. 24 Dec. 1995.

Radio broadcast A citation for a radio broadcast follows the same guidelines as those for a television broadcast.

The War of the Worlds. CBS Radio. WCBS, New York. 30 Oct. 1938.

Recording A citation for a recording usually begins with the performer or composer, followed by the title of the recording (italicized except for titles using numerals for musical form, key, or number), the recording company, and the copyright date.

List other contributors after the title, using brief phrases or abbreviations (*Cond.,* the abbreviation for conductor; *Perf.* for "performed by"; *Composed by*) to clarify their roles. Orchestras (abbreviated *orch.*) and other large musical groups are listed without clarifying phrases, usually following the conductor's name.

When appropriate, include recording dates immediately following the title. Compact discs (CDs) are now the standard recording format; indicate other formats—LP (long-playing record) or audiocassette— when necessary, before the record company.

A notation of a multidisc set, similar to the pattern for a multivolume book, appears immediately preceding the record company.

The Beatles. *Live at the BBC.* 2 discs. Capital, 1994.

Mahler, Gustav. Symphony no. 1 in D major. Cond. Georg Solti. Chicago Symphony Orch. LP. London, 1984.

(Since this selection is titled by musical form and key, it is not italicized. As noted after the title, this is a long-playing record, not a CD.)

To cite a single selection from a recording, include the selection title in quotation marks followed by the title of the complete recording. All else remains the same.

Yoakam, Dwight. "Crazy Little Thing Called Love." *Last Chance for a Thousand Years.* Reprise, 1999.

To cite liner notes, the printed material that comes with many recordings, list the name of the writer and the description *Liner notes* (not italicized), followed by a period. The rest of the citation follows normal patterns.

McClintick, David, and William Kennedy. Liner notes. *Frank Sinatra: The Reprise Collection.* 4 discs. Reprise, 1990.

An Interview   A citation for a personally conducted interview includes the name of the person interviewed, the type of interview (personal or telephone), and the interview date.

Otwell, Stephen. Personal interview. 11 Nov. 1998.

A citation for a broadcast or printed interview includes the name of the person interviewed, the descriptive title *Interview* (not italicized), and information necessary to describe the source.

Clinton, Hillary. Interview. *Larry King Live.* CNN. 11 Dec. 2000.

A Transcript   A transcript of a program is presented according to the source of the original broadcast, with clarifying information provided.

Hackney, Sheldon, Alberta Arthurs, and Walter Burns. "National Endowment for the Humanities Faces Cuts." *All Things Considered.* Natl. Public Radio. 2 Mar. 1995. Transcript.

Questionnaire or survey   A citation for a personally conducted questionnaire or survey begins with your name (since you are the author of the questions and compiler of the results) and then includes a descriptive title and the date (which may be inclusive) on which you gathered your information. For additional clarity, you may include information about the location of your work.

Greene, Erika. Survey. Terre Haute: Indiana State U. 30 May 2001.

The Internet and Other Electronic Sources

Businesses, organizations, government agencies, and publishers of all kinds have transferred many of their print-based documents to the World Wide Web and other electronic formats. Because of the variety of Internet and other electronic sources, researchers face a considerable challenge when they try to provide clear documentation.

As you gather citation information for Internet and other electronic sources, you must be both resourceful and patient because the patterns of electronic publication are less consistent than those of traditional print publication. Whereas publishers of print texts usually place information in conventional locations—for example, the publication date on the copyright page—web designers seem less confined by such conventions. A web site, for example, may place the publication or posting date at the top of the web page (near the masthead), at the bottom of the home page, or elsewhere (for example, in the "About This Site" link). Further, because of the lack of standardization—or the creativity with which a site is designed—you may discover that some sources do not provide all the information that you need to complete a full citation. In such cases, include all available information. Your goal should be to gather the most complete set of data possible to describe each electronic source, following the patterns described in this section.

Online scholarly project or information database

To cite an entire online scholarly project or information database, present available information in this order: the title of the project or database, italicized; the editor or compiler, if identified, introduced with the abbreviation *ed.* or *comp.* (not italicized); the version number, if applicable; the date of electronic posting or the date of the most recent update; the name of the sponsoring organization or institution, if identified; the date you accessed the site; and the electronic address (URL), in angle brackets.

ProQuest. 2001. Bell and Howell. 16 Jan. 2002 <http://proquest.umi .com/pqdweb/>.

The Victorian Web. Ed. George P. Landow. 2000. Brown U. 15 Jan. 2002 <http://landow.stg.brown.edu/victorian/victor.html>.

To cite a selected source—article, illustration, map, or other—from an online scholarly project or information database, begin with the name of the author (or artist, compiler, or editor) of the individual source, if appropriate; the title of the source, punctuated appropriately (quotation marks for articles, italics for charts, and so on); and print information if the source reproduces a print version. Continue the citation with the name of the online project or database and other required information. However, use the URL of the specific source, not the general address for the project or database, in angle brackets.

Cody, David. "Queen Victoria." *Victorian Web.* Ed. George P. Landow. 2000. Brown U. 19 Jan. 2002 <http://landow.stg.brown.edu/ victorian/victor6.html>.

Zirkel, Paul A. "The 'N' Word." *Phi Delta Kappan* 80.9 (1999): 713–14. *ProQuest.* 2001. Bell and Howell. 27 Mar. 2002 <http://proquest.umi.com/pqdweb/>.

Professional web site

To cite a professional web site, provide the name of the author, editor, or host, if any; the title of the site, italicized; the date of electronic posting or the date of the most recent update; the name of the organization or institution, if any, affiliated with the site; the date you accessed the site; and the URL, in angle brackets.

ABA Law Student Division. 5 Jan. 2002. American Bar Association. 11 Jan. 2002 <http://www.abanet.org/lsd/home.html>.

UNICEF. 7 Jan. 2002. United Nations. 12 Jan. 2002 <http://www.unicef.org/>.

Online book   Online books exist in two forms: those previously published and now available electronically and those available only in electronic form.

To cite an online book that has a corresponding print version, first prepare a standard citation describing the print version. Then provide additional information required for a scholarly project or information database, if applicable; the date you accessed the site; and the specific URL of the book, not the general project or database, in angle brackets.

Lofting, Hugh. *The Voyages of Doctor Dolittle.* Philadelphia: Lippin- cott, 1922. *Project Gutenberg.* Jan. 1998. U of Illinois. 2 Feb. 2002 <ftp://biblio.org/pub/docs/books/gutenberg/etext98/ vdrdl10.text>.

To cite an online book that is available only in electronic form, pro- vide the name of the author or editor; the title, italicized; the date of electronic posting or the date of the most recent update; the name of the sponsoring organization or institution, if provided; the date you ac- cessed the site; and the URL of the book, not the project or database, in angle brackets.

Buxhoeveden, Sophie. *The Life and Tragedy of Alexandra Feodorvna, Empress of Russia.* 1999. *Russian History Website.* 15 Jan. 2002 <http://www.alexanderpalace.org/alexandra/>.

Article in an online encyclopedia or reference source   To cite an article from an online encyclopedia or reference source, pro- vide the author of the entry, if there is one; the title of the entry exactly as it appears in the source ("Paige, Satchel"); the name of the reference work, italicized; the date of electronic posting or the date of the most re- cent update; the date you accessed the site; and the URL for the specific article, not the general reference, in angle brackets.

Coney, Peter. "Plate Tectonics." *Encarta Online Encyclopedia.* 2000. 2 Feb. 2002 <http://encarta.msn.com/find/concise.asp?mod= 1&ti=761554623>.

Online government document   To cite an online version of a government document—book, report, proceedings, brochure, or other—first provide the information required for the print source. Then continue the citation with the information ap- propriate to the electronic source, whether it is a scholarly project, an in- formation database, or a web site.

United States. Cong. Budget Office. *Budgeting for Naval Forces: Struc-*
   turing Tomorrow's Navy at Today's Funding Level. By Eric J. Labs.
   Washington: GPO, 2000. *Budget Statistics.* Oct. 2000. Cong.
   Budget Office. 6 May 2002 <http://www.cbo.gov/showdoc
   .cfm?index=2603&sequence=0&form=1>.

Article in an online magazine   To cite an article in an online magazine, provide the name of the author, if appropriate; the title of the article, in quotation marks; the name of the magazine, italicized; the date of electronic publication or the date of the most recent update; the date on which you accessed the article; and the URL of the specific article, not the general magazine site, in angle brackets.

O'Neill, Hugh. "You Say You Want a Resolution?" *Men's Health.com* 9
   Jan. 2001. 11 Jan. 2002 <http://www.menshealth.com/health/
   resolution.html>.

Note that a magazine article that is retrieved through a periodical database, rather than directly from an online publication, is cited as a source from an information database.

Article in an online journal   To cite an article in an online journal, provide the name of the author, if appropriate; the title of the article, in quotation marks; the name of the journal, italicized; the volume and issue number; the year of publication, in parentheses; the date on which you accessed the article; and the URL of the specific article, not the general journal site, in angle brackets.

Indick, William, et al. "Gender Differences in Moral Judgment: Is
   Non-Consequential Reasoning a Factor?" *Current Research in So-*
   cial Psychology 5.2 (2000). 11 Nov. 2001 <http://www.uiowa
   .edu/~grpproc/crisp/crisp.5.2.htm>.

Note that a journal article that is retrieved through a periodical database, rather than directly from an online publication, is cited as a source from an information database.

Article in an online newspaper   To cite an article in an online newspaper, provide the name of the author, if appropriate; the title of the article, in quotation marks; the name of the newspaper, italicized; the date of electronic publication or the date of the most recent update; the date on which you accessed the article; and the URL of the specific article, not the general newspaper site, in angle brackets.

Rodriguez, Cindy. "Amid Dispute, Plight of Illegal Workers Revisited."
   Boston Globe 9 Jan. 2001. 10 Jan. 2002
   <http://www .boston.com/dailyglobe2/010/nation/amid_
   dispute_plight_of_illegal_workers_revisited+.shtml>.

Note that a newspaper article that is retrieved through a periodical database, rather than directly from an online publication, is cited as a source from an information database.

Online transcript of a lecture or speech   To cite the transcript of a lecture or speech, first provide the information required for a lecture or speech. Then include the word *Transcript,* not italicized; the date of electronic publication or the date of the most recent update; the date on which you accessed the transcript; and the URL of the specific transcript, not the general site, in angle brackets.

King, Martin Luther, Jr. Nobel Peace Prize Acceptance Speech. Nobel Prize Ceremony. Oslo, 10 Dec. 1964. Transcript. 2001. 31 Jan. 2002 <http://www.stanford.edu/group/king>.

Work of art online   To cite a work of art online, provide the name of the artist, if known; the assigned title of the work of art, italicized, or the common name of the work of art, not italicized; a phrase describing the artistic medium; the museum, gallery, or collection where the work is housed; the city; the date on which you accessed the work of art; and the URL of the specific work of art, not the general site, in angle brackets.

Picasso, Pablo. *Les Demoiselles d'Avignon.* Oil on canvas. Museum of Modern Art. New York. 30 June 2002 <http://www.moma.org/docs/collection/paintsculpt/C40.htm>.

Online map, graph, table, or chart   To cite a map, graph, table, or chart online, first provide the information required for the kind of visual element. Then continue the citation with the information appropriate to the electronic source, whether it is a scholarly project or an information database or a web site.

"New York City Subway Route Map." Map. 5 Mar. 2000. New York City Subway Resources. 9 Jan. 2002 <http://www.nycsubway.org/maps/route/>.

Online cartoon   To cite a cartoon online, provide the name of the cartoonist, if known; the assigned title of the cartoon, in quotation marks; the word *Cartoon,* not italicized; the source, italicized; the date of electronic publication or the date of the most recent update; the date on which you accessed the cartoon; and the URL of the cartoon, not the general site, in angle brackets.

Steiner, Peter. "Don't Anybody Move: This Is a Merger." Cartoon. *Cartoonbank.* 10 Jan. 2001. 13 Jan. 2001 <k.com/cartoon_closeup.asp?/mscssid=2BGLVUGOU7S92MD000GPBQXMNAB6808>.

Online film or filmclip   To cite an online film or filmclip, first provide the information required for a film. Then include the name of your electronic source, italicized; the date of electronic publication or the date of the most recent update;

the date on which you accessed the film or filmclip; and the URL of the film or filmclip, not the general site, in angle brackets.

Reefer Madness. Dir. Louis J. Gasnier. 1938. *The Sync.* 2000. 22 Apr.
    2002 <http://www.thesync.com/ram/reefermadness.ram>.

Online transcript of a television or radio broadcast   To cite an online transcript of a television or radio broadcast, first provide the information required for a television or radio broadcast. Then include the word *Transcript,* not italicized; the date on which you accessed the transcript; and the URL of the transcript, not the general site, in angle brackets.

"High Drama in the High Court." *Nightline.* With Ted Koppel. ABC,
    New York. 1 Dec. 2000. Transcript. 24 Dec. 2000. 11 Jan. 2002
    <http://abcnews.go.com/onair/nightline/transcripts/nl001201
    _trans.html>.

Online recording   To cite an online recording of previously released material, first provide the information required for a traditional recording. Then include the date of electronic publication or the date of the most recent update; the date on which you accessed the recording; and the URL of the recording, not the general site, in angle brackets.

    To cite an online recording that has not been previously released, provide the name of the recording artist; the title of the selection; and performance information such as concert locations and dates, recording studios, locations, or other relevant information. Then provide information about your source for the recording, whether a database or a web site.

Dylan, Bob. "I Am the Man Thomas." Continental Airlines Arena.
    Rutherford, 13 Nov. 1999. *Essential Bob Dylan.* 2000. 27 Jan.
    2002 <http://bobdylan.com/audio/live/bd/thomas_111399>.

CD-ROM sources   Because Internet sites provide researchers with more easily updated materials than do CD-ROMs, most libraries are phasing out CD-ROMs from their collections. However, you may still need to cite a CD-ROM source.

    If a CD-ROM source reproduces material available in print form, begin the citation with full print information: author (or editor), title, and facts of publication. If the material is not available in print form, begin the citation with identifying information: author, if given; title, italicized; and the date of the material, if appropriate. Next, citations for both kinds of materials include the title of the publication, italicized; the description *CD-ROM,* not italicized; the city, if known, and name of the company that produced the CD-ROM; and the date of electronic publication.

The Baseball Encyclopedia: The Complete and Definitive Record of Major League Baseball. CD-ROM. New York: Macmillan, 1996.

Becklake, Sue. *All about Space.* Illus. Sebastian Quigley. CD-ROM. New York: Scholastic Reference, 1998.

Email interview   To cite an email interview, include the name of the person you interviewed; the phrase *Email interview,* not italicized; and the date of the email posting.

Washburne-Freise, Marla. Email interview. 14 May 2001.

Online posting   To cite an online posting to a forum or discussion group, provide the name of the author, if known; the official title of the posting, in quotation marks; or a descriptive title, without quotation marks; the phrase *Online posting,* not italicized; the date of electronic publication or the date of the most recent update; the name of the forum or discussion group; the date on which you accessed the posting; and the URL of the posting, not the general forum or discussion site, in angle brackets.

Hamel, E. "Invasive Species Information Source." Online posting. 13 Nov. 2000. Meadows and Prairies Forum. 13 Feb. 2002 <http:// forums.gardenweb/load/natives/msg112040189632.html?15>.

Whinney, Kathryn. "Disturbing Vision." Discussion of *A Clockwork Orange.* Online posting. 11 Jan. 2001. Book Lovers' Discussion. 15 Jan. 2002 <http://www.whatamigoingtoread.com/book .asp?bookid=6395>.

Thinking ↔ Writing Activity

Compiling a Works-Cited Page

From the following sets of scrambled information on sources related to Toni Morrison's novel *Beloved,* produce correct sample works-cited entries and arrange them alphabetically. *Note:* Some information is included for the sake of clarity only; it will not be incorporated into the citations.

1. Produced by Harpo Productions; released in 1998; the movie *Beloved;* directed by Jonathan Demme; distributed by Touchstone Pictures; starring Oprah Winfrey and Danny Glover.

2. Published by Alfred A. Knopf, Incorporated; written by Toni Morrison; published in 1987; the novel *Beloved;* winner of the Pulitzer Prize for fiction; New York, New York.

3. Published in 1998; written by Missy Dehn Kubitschek; published by Greenwood Press; the book *Toni Morrison: A Critical Companion;* 224

pages long; Westport, Connecticut; part of the Critical Companions to Popular Contemporary Writers Series.

4. Directed by Jonathan Demme; a review written by Richard Corliss; the review "Bewitching *Beloved*"; published in *Time* magazine; a review of the film *Beloved;* with performances by Oprah Winfrey and Danny Glover; appearing on pages 74, 75, 76, and 77; published on October 5, 1998.

5. Written by Dinita Smith; the article "Toni Morrison's Mix of Tragedy, Domesticity, and Folklore"; appearing in section E; published in the *New York Times;* appearing on page 1 and on four more separated pages; published January 8, 1998; appearing in a late edition.

6. A collected set of information titled "Historical Events Affecting Characters in *Beloved*"; appearing in a web site titled *Toni Morrison's Beloved;* posted from the University of Texas; first posted on October 30, 1998; retrieved February 12, 2002; compiled by Ali Lakhia, Glenn Schuetz, Katie Gilette, and Scott Lloyd; available at <http://www.cs .utexas.edu/users/lakhia/morrison/history.html>.

7. Appearing on pages 92–110; in a collection edited by Donna Bassin; published by Yale University Press; written by Marianne Hirsch; a chapter titled "Maternity and Rememory: Toni Morrison's *Beloved*"; part of a book titled *Representations of Motherhood;* published in 1991.

8. Published in 1991; appearing on pages 153–69; published in *Journal of Narrative Technique,* which uses continuous pages throughout a volume; written by Eusebio L. Rodrigues; an article titled "The Telling of *Beloved*"; appearing in volume 21.

9. Published in the journal *Religion and Literature,* which uses separate pages with each issue; appearing on pages 119–29; appearing in issue 1 of volume 27; an article titled "Who Are the Beloved? Old and New Testaments, Old and New Communities of Faith"; written by Danille Taylor-Guthrie; published in 1995.

10. Published by Gale Publishers, Incorporated; the 9th edition; an entry titled "Morrison, Toni"; published in 1999; published in *Who's Who Among African Americans.*

11. Appearing on page 14 and on five additional, separated pages; published December 1987; an article titled "Telling How It Was"; written by Geoffrey C. Ward; published in *American Heritage.*

12. A book titled *Conversations with Toni Morrison;* published in 1991; edited by Danille Taylor-Guthrie; published in Jackson, Mississippi; published by the University Press of Mississippi.

American Psychological Association Style

In fields such as psychology, education, public health, and criminology, researchers follow the guidelines given in the *Publication Manual of the American Psychological Association,* fifth edition (Washington: APA, 2001) to document their work. Like MLA style, APA style encourages brevity in documentation, uses in-text parenthetical citations of sources, and limits the use of numbered notes and appended materials.

The following information is a brief overview of APA style. If your major or minor requires APA style, you should acquire the APA manual and study it thoroughly.

Paper Format

Title page Include a descriptive title, your name, and your affiliation (course or university), with two spaces between elements; center this information left to right and top to bottom. In the upper-right corner, include the first few words of the paper's title, followed by five spaces and the page number (without a page abbreviation). Two lines below, at the left margin, type the words *Running head* (not italicized), a colon, and a brief version of the title (no more than fifty letters and spaces) in all capital letters. The title page is always page 1.

Abstract On a separate page following the title page, type the label *Abstract* (capitalized but not italicized). Two lines below, include an unindented paragraph describing the major ideas in the paper; it should contain no more than 120 words.

Introduction Include a paragraph or series of paragraphs to define the topic, present the hypothesis (or thesis), explain the method of investigation, and state the theoretical implications (or context).

Body Incorporate a series of paragraphs to describe study procedures, results obtained, and interpretations of the findings.

In-text documentation In parentheses, include the author and date for summaries and paraphrases; include the author, date, and page number for quotations and facts.

List of sources Cite sources used in the paper in a listing titled "References."

Appendix Include related materials (charts, graphs, illustrations, and so on) that cannot be incorporated into the body of the paper.

Manuscript Format

Fonts Use any standard font with serifs (cross lines on the ends of individual letters). Sans serif fonts like Helvetica are used only for labeling illustrations, not for text. Use italics to identify titles of complete, separately published works.

Spacing All elements of the paper are double-spaced.

Margins Use one-inch margins at the top and bottom and on the left and right. Indent paragraphs five to seven spaces; indent long quotations five spaces.

Paging Put the first two or three words of the title (no more than fifty letters and spaces) in the upper-right corner; after five spaces, include the page number without a page abbreviation.

Headings Whenever possible, use headings to label divisions and subdivisions of the paper.

Number Style Express numbers one through nine (and zero) in words and all other numbers in numeral form. When numbers are used for comparisons, all must appear in numeral form.

Citation Format

The following samples illustrate a number of basic citation forms. If you are using other kinds of sources, consult the APA style guide.

Reference List Format

Book by one author   Monmonier, M. (1999). *Air apparent: How meteorologists learned to map, predict, and dramatize weather.* Chicago: University of Chicago Press.

(Use initials for the author's first name. After the author's name, place the publication date in parentheses, followed by a period. Capitalize only the first word of the title and of the subtitle and any proper nouns and proper adjectives. Spell out the names of university presses. For other publishers, retain only the words *Books* and *Press*.)

Book by two or more authors   Kegley, C. W., & Raymond, G. A. (1999). *How nations make peace.* New York: St. Martin's.

(Invert the names of all authors. Insert an ampersand [&] before the last author's name.)

Book with an organization as author   American Psychological Association. (2001). *Publication manual of the American Psychological Association* (5th ed.). Washington: Author.

(When the organization is also the publisher, use the word Author [not italicized] in the publisher position.)

Edition other than the first   Terrill, R. J. (1999). *World criminal justice systems: A survey* (4th ed.). Cincinnati: Anderson.

(Insert information about the edition in parentheses, following the title but before the period.)

Work in a collection   McKnight, R. (1998). Spirituality in the workplace. In J. D. Adams (Ed.), *Transforming work* (pp. 160–178). New York: Miles River.

(Do not enclose the title of a short work in quotation marks. *In,* not italicized, introduces its source. Provide the editor's name, the abbreviation *Ed.* [capitalized, not italicized, and placed in parentheses] followed by a comma, the collection title, and inclusive page numbers for the short work [given in parentheses]. Abbreviate *pages.*)

Article in a monthly magazine   Furlow, B. (2000, October). The uses of crying and begging. *Natural History, 109,* 65–67.

(Give the year of publication followed by a comma and the month and day [if any]. When appropriate, follow the magazine title with a comma, one space, the volume number, and another comma [all italicized]. Do not use a page abbreviation.)

Article in a journal with separate paging

Graves, D. (2000). Multiculturalism and the choral canon: 1975–2000. *Choral Journal, 41*(2), 37–44.

(Italicize the name of the journal, the comma that follows it, and the volume number. The issue number [or numbers] in parentheses immediately follows the volume number; no space separates them; the issue number is *not* italicized. No abbreviation for pages accompanies the inclusive page numbers.)

Article in a newspaper

Zeleny, J. (2000, January 17). Election reform is popular, political—and pricey. *The Chicago Tribune*, p. 2:1.

(Invert the date. Do not include information about the edition or section. When sections are indicated by letters, present them along with the page numbers with no intervening space.)

Lecture or speech

Gould, S. J. (1998, November 4). *Interactions of art and science and the largely arbitrary nature of academic boundaries.* Lecture presented for the Stanford Presidential Lectures in Humanities and Arts, Stanford University, Stanford.

(Italicize the title of the speech. Follow the title with the name of the sponsoring organization and the location, separated by commas.)

Nonprint materials

Fincher, D. (Director). (1999). *Fight club* [Film]. United States: Regency-20th Century Fox.

(List entries by the name of the most important contributor [director, producer, speaker, and so on]; note the specific role in full in parentheses following the name. Identify the medium [film, filmstrip, slide show, tape recording] in brackets after the title. The country of origin precedes the name of the production company.)

Electronic Sources

Online scholarly project, information database, or web site

Expenditures for health care plans by employers and employees. (1998, December 7). Washington: Bureau of Labor Statistics. Retrieved November 17, 2001, from http://stats.bls.gov/

(To cite an online scholarly project, information database, or professional web site, include the author, if known, and the date in parentheses; the title of the source without special punctuation [followed by the date if there is no author]; the name of the project, database, or web site; and a retrieval statement.)

Article in an online encyclopedia or reference source

Children in foster care. (2000). [Chart]. *Infoplease almanac.* Retrieved December 13, 2001, from http://www.infoplease.com/

(To cite an article from an online encyclopedia or reference source, provide the author of the entry, if there is one, and the date in parentheses; the title of the entry exactly as it appears in the source, without special punctuation [followed by the date if there is no author]; the name of the reference work, italicized; facts of publication, if the source first existed in print form; and the retrieval statement.)

Article in an online magazine

Wheelright, J. (2001, January). Betting on designer genes. *Smithsonian, 31.* Retrieved October 18, 2001, from http://www.smithsonianmag.sr.edu/smithsonian/issues01/jan01/gene.html

(To cite an article in an online magazine, provide the name of the author, if appropriate; the date in parentheses; the title of the article; the name of the magazine and volume number, italicized; and the retrieval statement.)

Article in an online journal

Indick, W. (2000). Gender differences in moral judgment: Is non-consequential reasoning a factor? *Current Research in Social Psychology, 5*(2). Retrieved November 11, 2001, from http://www.uiowa.edu/~grpproc/crisp/crisp.5.2.htm

(To cite an article in an online journal, provide the name of the author, if appropriate; the date in parentheses; the title of the article; the name of the journal and the volume number, italicized, and the issue number, not italicized; and the retrieval statement.)

Article in an online newspaper

Rodriguez, C. (2001, January 9). Amid dispute, plight of illegal workers revisited. *Boston Globe.* Retrieved November 10, 2001, from http://www.boston.com/dailyglobe2/010/nation/Amid_dispute_plight_of_illegal_workers_revisited+.html

(To cite an article in an online newspaper, provide the name of the author, if appropriate; the date of publication in parentheses; the title of the article; the name of the newspaper, italicized; and the retrieval statement.)

CD-ROM sources

Welmers, W. E. (1994). African languages. *The New Grolier Multimedia Encyclopedia.* Retrieved from Grolier database (Grolier, CD-ROM, 1994 release).

(To cite a CD-ROM source, provide the name of the author, if given; the release date; the title of the selection, without special punctuation; the CD-ROM title, italicized; and a special CD-ROM retrieval statement, which includes the publisher's name, without special punctuation, and,

in parentheses, the name of the database; the description *CD-ROM*, not italicized; the release date; and an item number, if applicable.)

Online posting Whinney, K. (2001, January 11). Discussion of *A clockwork orange.* Message posted to Book Lovers' Discussion, archived at http://www.Whatamigoingtoread.com/book.asp?bookid=6395

(To cite an online posting to a forum or discussion group, provide the name of the author, if known; the official or descriptive title of the posting; the phrase Message posted to, not italicized; the name of the forum or discussion group; the phrase archived at, not italicized; and the URL.)

Text Citation Format

One author Greybowski (1995) noted that. . . .

Or:

In a recent study at USC (Greybowski, 1995), participants were asked to . . . .

Multiple authors: first citation Cadrillo, Thurgood, Johnson, and Lawrence (1967) found in their evaluation . . . .

Multiple authors: subsequent citations Cadrillo et al. (1967) also discovered . . . .

Corporate authors: first citation . . . a close connection between political interests and environmental issues (Council on Environmental Quality [CEQ], 1981).

Corporate authors: subsequent citations . . . in their additional work (CEQ, 1981).

Quotations Within the Text

First option She stated, "The cultural awareness of a student depends, by implication, on the cultural awareness of the parents" (Hermann, 1984, p. 219).

Second option Hermann (1984) added that "enrichment in our schools is costly and has little bearing on the later lives of the students" (pp. 230–231).

Third option "A school's responsibility rests with providing solid educational skills, not with supplementing the cultural education of the uninterested," stated Hermann (1984) in her summary (p. 236).

Credits

Chapter 1: Page 10: from *My American Journey* by Colin Powell with Joseph E. Persico, copyright © 1995 by Colin L. Powell. Used by permission f random House, Inc.; page 17: from *Writing Down the Bones* by Natalie Goldberg, © 1986. Reprinted by arrangement with Shambhala Publications, Inc., Boston. www.Shambhala.com; page 20: "The Marginal World" from *The Edge of the Sea* by Rachel Carson. Copyright © 1955 by Rachel L. Carson, renewed 1983 by Roger Christie. Reprinted by permission of Houghton Mifflin Company. All Rights Reserved.

Chapter 2: Page 36: Reprinted by permission of the author; page 43: Copyright © 1998 by Julia Alvarez. Published in *Something To Declare*, Algonquin Books of Chapel Hill, 1998. Reprinted by permission of Susan Bergholz Literary Services, New York. All rights reserved.

Chapter 3: Page 61: © The New Yorker Collection 1998 Frank Cotham from cartoonbank.com; page 69: Submitted excerpt from *An American Childhood* by Annie Dillard. Copyright © 1987 by Annie Dillard. Reprinted by permission of HarperCollins Publishers Inc.; page 71: "Discover Magazine Selection", from *The Blank Slate* by Steven Pinker, copyright © 2002 by Steven Pinker. Used by permission of Viking Penguin, a division of Penguin Group (USA) Inc.; page 81: "Under Water" by Anne Fadiman. Originally appeared in *The New Yorker*. Copyright © 1999 by Anne Fadiman. Reprinted by permission of Lescher & Lescher, Ltd. All rights reserved.

Chapter 4: Page 104: Copyright © 2003 *The New York Times*. Reprinted with permission.

Chapter 5: Page 138: From The New York Times Upfront Magazine. Copyright © by Scholastic Inc. and The New York Times Company. Reprinted by permission of Scholastic Inc.

Chapter 6: Page 155: from *The Autobiography of Malcolm X* by Malcolm X and Alex Haley, copyright © 1964 by Alex Haley and Malcolm X. Copyright © 1965 by Alex Haley and Betty Shabazz. Used by permission of Random House, Inc.; page 162: Donald Murray, "The Maker's Eye: Revising Your Own Manuscripts". Reprinted by permission of the author; page 167: Edite Cunhã is a writer, educator and artist. She lives in western Massachusetts; page 181: Reprinted by arrangement with the Estate of Martin Luther King Jr., c/o Writers House as agent for the proprietor New York, NY. Copyright 1963 Martin Luther King Jr., copyright renewed 1991 Coretta Scott King; page 191: "Shooting an

625

Elephant" from *Shooting an Elephant and Other Essays,* by George Orwell, copyright 1950 by Harcourt, Inc. and renewed 1979 by Sonia Brownell Orwell, reprinted by permission of Harcourt, Inc.

Chapter 7: Page 215: Lowe's Home Improvement Warehouse, "Dividing a Room" from www.lowes.com; page 218: Copyright © 1986 by Scott Russell Sanders; first appeared in The North American Review; from *The Paradise of Bombs*; reprinted by permission of the author and the author's agents, the Virginia Kidd Agency, Inc.; page 227: "The Learning Curve" as it appeared in *The New Yorker,* January 28, 2002 and published in a slightly different version in *Complications: A Surgeon's Notes on an Imperfect Science* as "Education of a Knife" by Atul Gawande. Copyright 2002 by Atul Gawande. Reprinted by permission of Henry Holt and Company, LLC.

Chapter 8: Page 254: Copyright © 1984 by The New York Times, Co. Reprinted with permission; page 257: "My Papa's Waltz", copyright 1942 by Hearst Magazine, Inc., from *The Collected Poems of Theodore Roethke* by Theodore Roethke. Used by permission of Doubleday, a division of Random House, Inc.; page 259: Copyright © 1992 by Louise Erdrich, reprinted with the permission of The Wylie Agency, Inc.; page 264: © 1983, *The Washington Post,* reprinted with permission; page 267: "Girl" from *At the Bottom of the River* by Jamaica Kincaid. Copyright © 1983 by Jamaica Kincaid. Reprinted by permission of Farrar, Straus and Giroux, LLC.; page 269: Copyright © 1997 by The New York Times, Co. Reprinted with permission; page 277: Ways of Being Religious by Streng et. al, © 1973. Reprinted by permission of Pearson Education, Inc. Upper Saddle River, NJ 07458; page 282: From *The Working Poor: Invisible in America* by David K. Shipler, copyright © 2004 by David K. Shipler. Used by permission of Alfred A. Knopf, a division of Random House, Inc.

Chapter 9: Page 309: Copyright © 1965 by The New York Times Co. Reprinted with permission; page 309: Reprinted by permission from *Life* 3/5/61. © 1965 Times Inc.; page 310; Copyright © 1965. Reprinted by permission of the New York Post; page 310: Paragraph on the assassination of Malcolm X, Associated Press, February 22, 1965. Reprinted by permission of the Associated Press; page 311: Excerpt from the Amsterdam News, February 27, 1965/ Reprinted by permission of the New York Amsterdam News; page 312: Copyright © 2001 by The New York Times Co. Reprinted with permission; page 313: Courtesy of The Hamburger Morgenpost; page 314: © 2001 TIME inc. reprinted by permission; page 314: Copyright © Times Newspapers Limited, London (Wednesday, September 12, 2001); page 316: © 2001, The Washington Post, reprinted with permission; page 317: Copyright © 1989 The New York Times Co. Reprinted with permission.

Chapter 10: Page 366: Reprinted by permission; page 370: Copyright 1999 by Natural Resources Defense Council.

Chapter 11: Page 389: "Brother, Don't Spare a Dime" by L. Christopher Awalt, *Newsweek,* October 21, 1991; page 391: from *Rachel and Her Children* by Jonathan Kozol, copyright © 1988 by Jonathan Kozol. Used by permission of Crown Publishers, a division of Random House, Inc.; page 400: Alan Lightman, "Is the Earth Round or Flat?" Reprinted by permission of the author; page 405: Reprinted with the permission of Simon & Schuster

Index

This method is presented in more detail in Chapter 14.

1. **Authority**
   - ❏ Are the sponsor's identity and purpose clear?
   - ❏ Are the author's identity and qualifications evident?
   - ❏ If the material is copyrighted, who is the copyright holder?
   - ❏ Is there a way to verify the legitimacy of the site's sponsor?
   - ❏ Don't forget that some of the people running sites are trying to confuse you.
   - ❏ Look for clues that indicate a personal home page.
   - ❏ Run unfamiliar topics or author names through a search engine.

2. **Accuracy**
   - ❏ Are sources of factual information clearly listed?
   - ❏ Has the sponsor provided links that can be used to verify the sponsor's claims?
   - ❏ Is statistical data well labeled and easy to read?
   - ❏ Is the information free of grammatical errors, spelling errors, and typos?

3. **Objectivity**
   - ❏ Is it evident why the sponsor is providing each piece of information?
   - ❏ Is the information content separate from advertising or opinion?
   - ❏ Is the sponsor's point of view presented clearly with well-supported arguments?
   - ❏ If the site is not objective, does it account for opposing points of view?

4. **Currency**
   - ❏ Is the material recent enough to be relevant to your project?
   - ❏ Are there any indications that the material is kept up to date?
   - ❏ Do you see statements indicating where data for charts and graphs were gathered?
   - ❏ Is there an indication that the site is complete and not still being developed?